SEVENTH EDITION

THE HUMAN SPECIES

An Introduction to Biological Anthropology

JOHN H. RELETHFORD

State University of New York
College at Oneonta

McGraw-Hill
Higher Education

Boston   Burr Ridge, IL   Dubuque, IA   New York   San Francisco   St. Louis
Bangkok   Bogotá   Caracas   Kuala Lumpur   Lisbon   London   Madrid   Mexico City
Milan   Montreal   New Delhi   Santiago   Seoul   Singapore   Sydney   Taipei   Toronto

McGraw-Hill
Higher Education

Published by McGraw-Hill, an imprint of The McGraw-Hill Companies, Inc., 1221 Avenue of the Americas, New York, NY 10020. Copyright © 2008. All rights reserved. No part of this publication may be reproduced or distributed in any form or by any means, or stored in a database or retrieval system, without the prior written consent of The McGraw-Hill Companies, Inc., including, but not limited to, in any network or other electronic storage or transmission, or broadcast for distance learning.

This book is printed on acid-free paper.

1 2 3 4 5 6 7 8 9 0 CCI/CCI 0 9 8 7

ISBN: 978-0-07-340526-1
MHID: 0-07-340526-4

Editor-in-Chief: *Emily Barrosse*
Publisher: *Frank Mortimer*
Sponsoring Editor: *Gina Boedeker*
Marketing Manager: *Lori DeShazo*
Developmental Editor: *Kate Scheinman*
Production Editor: *David Blatty*
Manuscript Editor: *Thomas L. Briggs*
Design Manager: *Cassandra Chu*
Art Manager: *Robin Mouat*
Illustrations: *Parrot Graphics, Judy and John Waller*
Photo Research: *Brian Pecko*
Production Supervisor: *Rich DeVitto*
Composition: *10.5 x 12.5 Legacy Serif Book by Aptara*
Printing: *Courier, Inc.*

Cover images: *Tribesman from New Guinea, Mennonite girl, Kurdish woman:* © *William Coupon; DNA:* © *Comstock/JupiterImages*

Credits: The credits section for this book begins on page C-1 and is considered an extension of the copyright page.

Library of Congress Cataloging-in-Publication Data
Relethford, John.
   The human species : an introduction to biological anthropology / John H. Relethford.—
7th ed.
      p. cm.
   Includes bibliographical references and index.
   ISBN-13: 978-0-07-340526-1
   ISBN-10: 0-07-340526-4
   1. Physical anthropology.   I. Title.
   GN60.R39 2007
   599.9—dc22   2007018432

The Internet addresses listed in the text were accurate at the time of publication. The inclusion of a Web site does not indicate an endorsement by the authors or McGraw-Hill, and McGraw-Hill does not guarantee the accuracy of the information presented at these sites.

www.mhhe.com

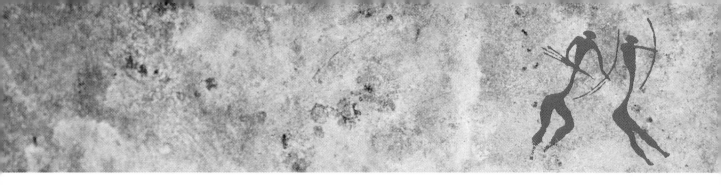

BRIEF CONTENTS

CONTENTS

PREFACE

This text introduces the field of biological anthropology (also known as physical anthropology), the science concerned with human biological evolution and variation. The text addresses the major questions that concern biological anthropologists: What are humans? How are we similar to and different from other animals? Where are our origins? How did we evolve? Are we still evolving? How are we different from one another? and What does the future hold for the human species?

ORGANIZATION

This book is divided into four parts. Part I, "Evolutionary Background," provides the basic background in genetics and evolutionary theory used throughout the remainder of the text. Chapter 1 introduces the science of biological anthropology, the nature of science, and the history of evolutionary thought. Chapter 2 reviews molecular and Mendelian genetics as applied to humans, providing genetic background for later chapters and including a basic review of cell biology for those whose high school biology is a bit rusty. Chapter 3 focuses on evolutionary forces, the mechanisms that produce evolutionary change within and between populations. Chapter 4 looks at evolution over longer periods of time, focusing on the origin of new species, and includes discussion on how species are classified.

Part II, "Our Place in Nature," examines the biology and behavior of the primates, the group of mammals to which humans belong. The focus of this section is on two questions: What are humans? and How are we related to other living creatures? Chapter 5 looks at the basic biology and behavior of mammals in general and primates in particular. Chapter 6 examines the diversity of primate biology and behavior, with particular attention given to our close relatives, the apes. Chapter 7 looks specifically at the human species and includes a comparison of human traits with those of apes.

Part III deals with questions of "Our Origins." Chapter 8 begins with discussion of the methods of paleoanthropology and concludes with a brief history of life on earth prior to the appearance of the first primates. Chapter 9 examines the fossil and genetic evidence for primate evolution from the appearance of the primate-like mammals through the split of ape and human lines by 6 million years ago. Chapter 10 deals with the beginning of human evolution, focusing on the fossil evidence for the first hominins and the evolution of bipedalism. Chapter 11 examines the origin and biological and cultural evolution of the genus *Homo*, including early *Homo*, *Homo erectus*, *Homo heidelbergensis*, and the Neandertals. Chapter 12 looks at the fossil, archaeological, and genetic evidence for the origin of modern humans and includes a discussion of current controversies.

Part IV, "Our Diversity," examines human biological variation in our species today from an evolutionary perspective. Chapter 13 focuses on the measurement and analysis of human variation, and contrasts evolutionary and racial approaches to human diversity. Chapter 14 provides several case studies of how information on genetic variation is used to address questions of population history and individual ancestry. Chapter 15 reviews a number of case studies of natural selection in human populations. Chapter 16 continues examining human variation from the broad perspective of human adaptation, both biological and cultural. Chapter 17 concludes the text by examining recent human evolution (over the past 12,000 years), focusing on the biological impact of culture change, with particular emphasis on changing patterns of disease, mortality, fertility, and population growth.

The organization of this text reflects my own teaching preference in terms of topics and sequence. Not all instructors will use the same sequence of chapters; some may prefer a different arrangement of topics. I have attempted to write chapters in such a way as to accommodate such changes whenever possible. For example, although I prefer to discuss human evolution before human variation, others prefer the reverse, and the chapters have been written and revised so that this alternative organizational structure can be used.

FEATURES

Throughout the text, I have attempted to provide new material relevant to the field and fresh treatments of traditional material. Key features include the following:

- All areas of contemporary biological anthropology are covered. In addition to traditional coverage of areas such as genetics, evolutionary theory, primate behavior, and the fossil record, the text includes material often neglected in introductory texts, including genetics and population history, human growth, epidemiology, and demography.

- The relationship between biology and culture is a major focus. The biocultural framework is introduced in the first chapter and integrated throughout the text.

- Behavior is discussed in an evolutionary context. The evolutionary nature of primate and human behavior is emphasized in a number of chapters, including those on primate biology and behavior (Chapters 5–7) and the fossil record of human evolution (Chapters 10–12).

- Emphasis is on the human species in its context within the primate order. Discussions of mammals and nonhuman primates continually refer to their potential relevance for understanding the human species. In fact, Chapter 7 is devoted *entirely* to treating our species from a comparative perspective.

- Hypothesis testing is emphasized. From the first chapter, in which students are introduced to the scientific method, I emphasize how various hypotheses are tested. Rather than provide a dogmatic approach with all the "right" answers, the text examines evidence in the context of hypothesis testing. With this emphasis, readers can see how new data can lead to changes in basic models and can better understand the "big picture" of biological anthropology.

NEW TO THIS EDITION

The text has been revised in light of new findings in the field and comments from users of the sixth edition and reviewers. Specific changes include the following:

- Several changes have been made in structure and chapter content. The chapters on human variation have been placed together and now appear after the chapters on human evolution, thus forming a more logical sequence of topics in human evolutionary history from past through the present. The discussion of species and classification methods has been moved to the chapter on macroevolution (4).

- The chapter on mammalian and primate biology and behavior (5) has been revised extensively to include material on life history theory, primate reproductive strategies, alloparenting, and dispersal and behavior.

- A new chapter (8) has been added on methods of paleoanthropological research, including dating methods, methods of ecological and behavioral analysis from fossils, and a brief history of evolution before the appearance of the first primates. This chapter also includes new material on how sex and age are determined from fossils, stable isotope analysis, experimental archaeology, and the use of nonhuman primate models for reconstructing behavior.

- The term *hominin* is now used throughout the text to refer to humans and their relatives since the time of divergence from the chimpanzee-bonobo line.

■ The chapters on the fossil record of human evolution have been rewritten extensively to increase clarity and provide data on new discoveries and interpretations, including the virtual reconstruction of *Sahelanthropus,* foraging and the origin of bipedalism, debates over hunting versus scavenging in *Homo erectus,* the expensive tissue hypothesis, discovery of "the Hobbit" (*Homo floresiensis*), the increasing recognition of *Homo heidelbergensis* as a valid fossil species, and the extraction of nuclear DNA from a Neandertal fossil.

■ Additional new topics have been added throughout the remainder of the text, including discussion of uniformitarianism and geologic time, recent developments in the "intelligent design" movement, new research on natural selection in the Duffy blood group and the *CCR5Δ32* allele, and new interpretations on nutrition in hunting-gathering societies, among others.

■ There are four new "Special Topic" boxes, dealing with the issues of "Humans and Apes—What Genes Are Different?" (Chapter 7), "A Perspective on Geologic Time" (Chapter 8), "Our Common Ancestry" (Chapter 14), and "Are Humans Still Experiencing Natural Selection?" (Chapter 15).

STUDY AIDS

To make the text more accessible and interesting, I have included frequent examples and illustrations of basic ideas, as well as abundant maps, to help orient students. I have kept the technical jargon to a minimum, yet every introductory text contains a number of specialized terms that students must learn. At first mention in the text, these terms appear in boldface type, and accompanying short definitions appear in the text margins. A glossary is provided at the end of the book. Each chapter ends with a summary, a list of supplemental readings, and a list of Virtual Explorations, which provide hands-on exercises and activities for real-time applications of text material. Several appendices provide additional reference material, including a primer on mathematical population genetics and figures showing comparative primate anatomy. A list of references appears at the end of the book, providing the complete reference for studies cited in the text.

ANCILLARIES

Visit our Online Learning Center Web site at www.mhhe.com/relethford7 for robust student and instructor resources.

For Students
Student resources include self-quizzes (multiple-choice, true or false, essay), Internet links and exercises, flashcards, and chapter study aids.

For Instructors

The password-protected instructor portion of the Web site includes the instructor's manual, a comprehensive computerized test bank, PowerPoint lecture slides, and a variety of additional instructor resources.

ACKNOWLEDGMENTS

My thanks go to the dedicated and hardworking people at McGraw-Hill, both those whom I have dealt with personally and those behind the scenes. I give special thanks to my sponsoring editor, Monica Eckman for encouragement and support, and for listening to assorted complaints with great patience and understanding. My heartfelt thanks also go to Kate Scheinman, developmental editor, for her guidance in the revision process and patience in answering the same questions repeatedly. Special thanks also go to David Blatty, production editor, for excellence and professionalism. Thanks also Sheri Gilbert, permissions editor; Tom Briggs, manuscript editor; Cassandra Chu, design manager; Robin Mouat, art manager; Brian Pecko, photo researcher; and Rich DeVitto, production supervisor.

I also thank my colleagues who served as reviewers: John A. Alsoszatai-Petheo, Central Washington University, Ellensburg; Alison Bell, Washington and Lee University; Claire Cesareo-Silva, Saddleback College; Patrick F. Clarkin, University of Massachusetts, Boston; Arthur Durband, Texas Tech University; and Gilliane Monnier, University of Minnesota. Having been a reviewer myself, I appreciate the extensive time and effort these individuals have taken.

Last, but not least, I dedicate this as always to my family. To my wonderful sons, David, Benjamin, and Zane—thanks for all the smiles and hugs, which make it all worthwhile. Thanks also for all those questions that really make me think (the ones I couldn't answer as well as those I could). Finally, to my wife, Hollie, love of my life and my best friend—thanks for the love, friendship, and support. I couldn't have done this without you.

WALKTHROUGH

This book is divided into four major units: Part I, "Evolutionary Background," provides the basic background in genetics and evolutionary theory used throughout the remainder of the book. Part II, "Our Place in Nature," examines the biology and behavior of the primates, the group of mammals to which humans belong. The focus of this section are the questions "What are humans?" and "How are we related to other living creatures?" Part III deals with questions of "Our Origins." Part IV, "Our Diversity," examines human biological variation in our species today from an evolutionary perspective. The reorganization of the Seventh Edition provides a more logical sequence of topics in human evolutionary history from the past through the present.

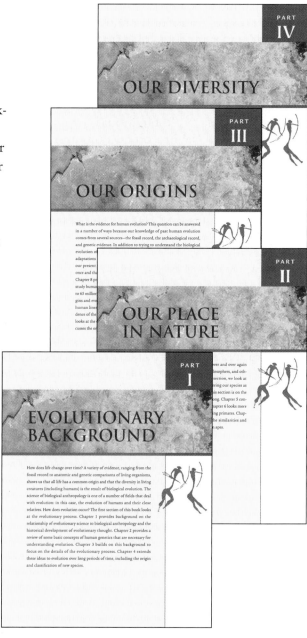

THE BIOCULTURAL FRAMEWORK

The relationship between biology and culture is a major focus of this text. The biocultural framework is introduced in Chapter 1 and integrated throughout the text.

HYPOTHESIS TESTING

Hypothesis testing is emphasized throughout the text, starting with Chapter 1, where students are introduced to the scientific method,. Rather than providing a dogmatic approach with all the "right" answers, the text examines evidence in the context of hypothesis testing. With this emphasis, readers can see how new data can lead to changes in basic models and can better understand the "big picture" of biological anthropology.

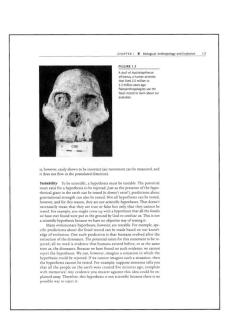

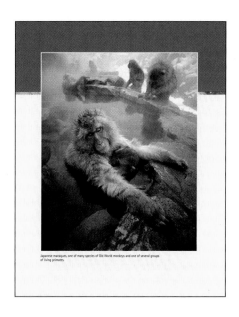

CHAPTER INTRODUCTIONS AND OUTLINES

Spectacular chapter openers provide a general overview of the upcoming content.

RUNNING GLOSSARY

New terms are defined in the text margin when first introduced, and a comprehensive glossary is provided at the end of the book.

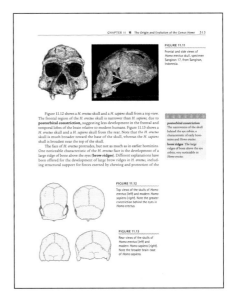

SPECIAL TOPICS BOXES

High-interest, "hot topics" are featured in these boxes. Discussions include "Biological Anthropologists at Work" (Chapter 1), "Humans and Apes—What Genes Are Different?" (Chapter 7), "A Perspective on Geologic Time" (Chapter 8), "Our Common Ancestry" (Chapter 14), and "Are Humans Still Experiencing Natural Selection?" (Chapter 15).

EXTENSIVE VISUAL PROGRAM

To make this text accessible and visually interesting, we have included abundant color illustrations, photographs, and maps.

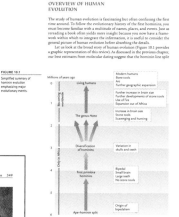

END-OF-CHAPTER AIDS

Each chapter concludes with a summary, a list of supplemental readings, and a list of Virtual Explorations, which provide hands-on exercises and activities for real-time applications of text material.

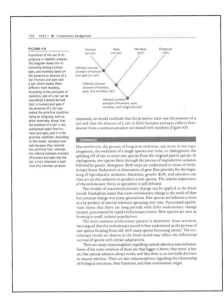

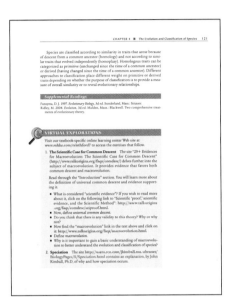

SUPPLEMENTS

Visit our Online Learning Center (www.mhhe.com/relethford7) for student and instructor resources. Student resources include self-quizzes (multiple-choice, true or false, essay), internet links and exercises, flashcards, and chapter study aides. The password-protected instructor portion of the Web site includes the instructorís manual, a comprehensive computerized test bank, PowerPoint lecture slides, and a variety of additional instructor resources.

EVOLUTIONARY BACKGROUND

How does life change over time? A variety of evidence, ranging from the fossil record to anatomic and genetic comparisons of living organisms, shows us that all life has a common origin and that the diversity in living creatures (including humans) is the result of biological evolution. The science of biological anthropology is one of a number of fields that deal with evolution: in this case, the evolution of humans and their close relatives. How does evolution occur? The first section of this book looks at the evolutionary process. Chapter 1 provides background on the relationship of evolutionary science to biological anthropology and the historical development of evolutionary thought. Chapter 2 provides a review of some basic concepts of human genetics that are necessary for understanding evolution. Chapter 3 builds on this background to focus on the details of the evolutionary process. Chapter 4 extends these ideas to evolution over long periods of time, including the origin and classification of new species.

Paleoanthropologist Bill Kimble of the Institute of Human Origins examines a fossil of a human ancestor from Ethiopia. Biological anthropology is the study of the biological evolution and variation of the human species. The fossil record is one source of information on our evolution.

Biological Anthropology and Evolution

W hat is anthropology? To many people, it is the study of the exotic extremes of human nature. To others, it is the study of ancient ruins and lost civilizations. The study of anthropology seems strange to many, and the practitioners of this field, the anthropologists, seem even stranger. The stereotype of an anthropologist is a pith-helmeted, pipe-smoking eccentric, tracking chimpanzees through the forest, digging up the bones of million-year-old ancestors, interviewing lost tribes about their sexual customs, and recording the words of the last speakers of a language. Another popular image presented in the media is Indiana Jones, the intrepid archaeologist of the film *Raiders of the Lost Ark* and other movies. Here is a man who is versed in the customs and languages of many societies past and present, feels at home anywhere in the world, and makes a living teaching, finding lost treasures, rescuing beautiful women in distress, and fighting Nazis (Figure 1.1).

Of course, Indiana Jones is a fictional character and more a treasure hunter than a scientific archaeologist. However, some real-life anthropologists are almost as well known: Jane Goodall, the late Margaret Mead, and the late Louis Leakey. These anthropologists have studied chimpanzees, Samoan culture, and the fossils of human ancestors. Their research conjures up images of anthropology every bit as varied as the imaginary adventures of Indiana Jones. Anthropologists do study all these things and more. The sheer diversity of topics investigated by anthropologists seems almost to defy any sort of logic. The methods of data collection and analysis are almost as diverse. What pulls these different subjects together?

In one obvious sense, they all share an interest in the same subject—human beings. In fact, the traditional textbook definition of anthropology is the "study of humans." Though this definition is easy to remember, it is not terribly useful. After all, scientists in other fields, such as researchers in anatomy and biochemistry, also study humans. And there are many fields within the social sciences whose sole interest is humans. History, geography, political science, economics, sociology, and psychology are all devoted to the study of human beings, and no one would argue that these fields are merely branches of anthropology.

FIGURE 1.1

Indiana Jones, the fictional archaeologist who serves as a model in the popular media for an anthropologist.

WHAT IS ANTHROPOLOGY?

anthropology The science that investigates human biological and cultural variation and evolution.

culture Behavior that is shared, learned, and socially transmitted.

What, then, is a suitable definition of anthropology? **Anthropology** could be described as the science of human cultural and biological variation and evolution. The first part of this definition includes both human culture and biology. **Culture** is shared learned behavior. Culture includes social and economic systems, marriage customs, religion, philosophy, and all other behaviors that are acquired through the process of learning rather than through instinct. The joint emphasis on culture and biology is an important feature of anthropology, and one that sets it apart from many other fields. A biochemist may be interested in specific aspects of human biology and may consider the study of human cultural behaviors to be less important. To a sociologist, cultural behaviors and not human biology are the main focus of attention. Anthropology, however, is characterized by a concern with *both* culture and biology as vital in understanding the human condition.

Biology and Culture

To the anthropologist, humans must be understood in terms of shared learned behavior as well as biology. We rely extensively on learned behaviors in virtually all aspects of our lives. Even the expression of our sexual drives must be understood in light of human cultural systems. Although the actual basis of our sex drive is biological, the ways in which we express it are shaped by behaviors we have learned. The very inventiveness of humans, with our vast technology, is testimony to the powerful effect of learning. However, we are not purely cultural creatures. We are also biological organisms. We need to eat and breathe, and we are affected by our external environment. In addition, our biology sets certain limits on our potential behaviors. For example, all human cultures have some type of social structure that provides for the care of children until they are old enough to fend for themselves. This is not simply kindness to children; our biological position as mammals requires such attentiveness to children for survival. In contrast to some animal species, whose infants need little or no care, human infants are physically incapable of taking care of themselves.

Anthropology is concerned not only with culture and biology but also with their interaction. Just as humans are not solely cultural or solely biological, neither are we simply the sum of these two. Humans are biocultural organisms, which means that our culture and biology influence each other. The **biocultural approach** to studying human beings is a main theme of this book, and you will examine many examples of biocultural interaction. For now, however, consider one—population growth (which will be covered in greater detail in Chapter 17). The growth of a population depends, in part, on how many people are born relative to how many die. If more people are born than die in a given period, then the population will grow. Obviously, population growth is in part caused by biological factors affecting the birth and death rates. A variety of cultural factors, such as economic system and marriage patterns, also affect population growth. Many factors, including technological changes and ideological outlooks, affect the birth rate. Developments in medicine and medical care change the death rate. The entire process of population growth and its biological and cultural implications is considerably more complicated than described here. The basic point, however, should be clear: By studying the process of population growth, we can see how cultural factors affect biological factors, and vice versa.

The biocultural perspective of anthropology points to one of the unique strengths of anthropology as a science: It is **holistic,** meaning that it takes into consideration all aspects of human existence. Population growth again provides an example. Where the sociologist may be concerned with effects of population growth on social structure, and the psychologist with effects of population growth on psychological stress, the anthropologist is interested potentially in *all* aspects of population growth. In a given study, this analysis may include the relationship among diet, fertility, religion, disease, social systems, and political systems, to name but a few factors.

The biocultural nature of anthropology makes it a difficult subject to classify in college catalogs. By now you are aware that different academic departments are grouped under the arts, humanities, natural sciences, mathematics, and social sciences. But where does anthropology, with its interest in both human culture and biology, fit in? Is it a natural science or a social science? Most colleges and universities place departments of anthropology with the social sciences, primarily because historically most anthropologists have been concerned with cultural anthropology. Many schools, however, allow completion of a biological anthropology course to fulfill a natural science requirement. The distinctions drawn between different branches of learning should not prevent you from seeing that anthropology has strong ties with both the natural and social sciences.

biocultural approach Studying humans in terms of the interaction between biology and culture in evolutionary adaptation.

holistic Integrating all aspects of existence in understanding human variation and evolution.

FIGURE 1.2

Biological variation in a group of children. Anthropologists study the differences and similarities among human populations over time.

variation   The differences that exist among individuals or populations.

comparative approach
Comparing human populations to determine common and unique behaviors or biological traits.

evolution   Change in populations of organisms from one generation to the next.

Variation

A key characteristic of anthropology is its concern with **variation.** In a general sense, variation refers to differences among individuals or populations. The anthropologist is interested in differences and similarities among human groups in terms of both biology and culture. Anthropologists use the **comparative approach** to attempt to generalize about those aspects of human behavior and biology that are similar in all populations and those that are unique to specific environments and cultures. *How* do groups of people differ from one another? *Why* do they differ? These are questions about variation, and they apply equally to cultural and biological traits (Figure 1.2). For example, do all human cultures practice the same marriage customs? (They don't.) Are there discernible reasons one group has a certain type of marriage system? An example of a biological trait that raises questions about variation is skin color. Can groups be characterized by a certain skin color, or does skin color vary within groups? Is there any pattern in the distribution of skin color that makes sense in terms of environmental differences?

Evolution

Evolution is change in living organisms over time. Both cultural and biological evolution interest anthropologists. How and why do human culture and biology change? For example, anthropologists may be interested in the origin of marriage systems. When, how, and why did certain marriage systems evolve? For that matter, when did the custom of marriage first originate, and why? As for skin color, an anthropologist would be interested in what skin color the first humans may have had and where, when, how, and why other skin colors may have evolved.

Adaptation

In addition to the concepts of variation and evolution, the anthropologist is interested in the process of **adaptation.** At the broadest level, adaptations are advantageous changes. Any aspect of biology or behavior that confers some advantage on an individual or population can be considered an adaptation. Cultural adaptations include technological devices such as clothing, shelter, and methods of food production. Such technologies can improve the well-being of humans. Cultural adaptations also include social systems and rules for behaviors. For example, the belief in certain societies that sexual relations with a woman must be avoided for some time after she gives birth can be adaptive in the sense that these behaviors influence the rate of population growth.

Cultural adaptations may vary in their effect on different members of a population. What is adaptive for some people may not be adaptive for others. For example, changes in certain tax laws may be advantageous for certain income groups and disadvantageous for others. Beliefs that reduce population growth can be adaptive in certain environments but nonadaptive in others.

Adaptations can also be biological. Some biological adaptations are physiological in nature and involve metabolic changes. For example, when you are too hot, you sweat. Sweating is a short-term physiological response that removes excess heat through the process of evaporation. Within limits, it aids in maintaining a constant body temperature. Likewise, shivering is an adaptive response to cold. The act of shivering increases metabolic rate and provides more heat.

Biological adaptations can also be genetic in nature. Here, changes in genes over many generations produce variation in biological traits. The darker skin color of many humans native to regions near the equator is one example of a long-term genetic adaptation. The darker skin provides protection from the harmful effects of ultraviolet radiation (see Chapter 15 for more information on skin color and variation).

Anthropologists look at patterns of human variation and evolution in order to understand the nature of cultural and biological adaptations. In some cases, explanations are relatively clear, whereas in others, we still seek explanations for the adaptive value of any given behavior or trait. In such a quest, we must always remember two important rules about adaptation. First, adaptations are often specific to a particular environment—what is adaptive in one environment may not be in another. Second, we must keep in mind that not all aspects of behavior or biology are adaptive. For example, some people have earlobes that are attached to the skin of their skulls; others have earlobes that hang free. There is no adaptive significance to either trait.

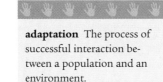

adaptation The process of successful interaction between a population and an environment.

The Subfields of Anthropology

In a general sense, anthropology is concerned with determining what humans are, how they evolved, and how they differ from one another. Where other disciplines focus on specific issues of humanity, anthropology is unique in dealing simultaneously with questions of origins, evolution, variation, and adaptation.

Even though anthropology has a wide scope and appears to encompass anything and everything pertaining to humans, the study of anthropology in North America is often characterized by four separate subfields, each with a specific focus. These four subfields are cultural anthropology, archaeology, linguistic anthropology, and biological anthropology. Some anthropologists add a fifth subfield—applied anthropology, which is concerned with the application of anthropological findings to contemporary matters and issues. Whether one characterizes applied anthropology as a separate subfield or as the practical extension of research in the four subfields, there is growing interest (and employment) in areas in which anthropological ideas and methods can be useful. Some examples include public health, economic policy, agricultural and industrial development, and population control.

cultural anthropology The subfield of anthropology that focuses on variations in cultural behaviors among human populations.

archaeology The subfield of anthropology that focuses on cultural variations in prehistoric (and some historic) populations by analyzing the culture's remains.

linguistic anthropology The subfield of anthropology that focuses on the nature of human language, the relationship of language to culture, and the languages of nonliterate peoples.

Cultural Anthropology   **Cultural anthropology** deals primarily with variations in the cultures of populations in the present or recent past. Its subjects include social, political, economic, and ideological aspects of human cultures. Cultural anthropologists look at all aspects of behavior within a society. Even when they are interested in a specific aspect of a culture, such as marriage systems, they look at how these behaviors relate to all other aspects of culture. Marriage systems, for example, may have an effect on the system of inheritance and may also be closely related to religious views. Comparison of cultures is used to determine common and unique features among different cultures. Information from this subfield will be presented later in the book to aid in the interpretation of the relationship between human culture and biology.

Archaeology   **Archaeology** is the study of cultural behaviors in the historic and prehistoric past. The archaeologist deals with such remains of past societies as tools, shelters, and remains of animals eaten for food. These remains, termed *artifacts,* are used to reconstruct past behavior. To help fill in the gaps, the archaeologist makes use of the findings of cultural anthropologists who have studied similar societies. Archaeological findings are critical in understanding the behavior of early humans and their evolution. Some of these findings for the earliest humans are presented later in this text.

Linguistic Anthropology   **Linguistic anthropology** is the study of language. Spoken language is a behavior that appears to be uniquely human. This subfield of anthropology deals with the analysis of languages, usually in nonliterate societies, and with general trends in the evolution of languages. A major question raised by linguistic anthropology concerns the extent to which language shapes culture. Is language necessary for the transmission of culture? Does a language provide information about the beliefs and practices of a human culture?

Biological anthropology must consider many of the findings of linguistic anthropology in the analysis of human variation and evolution. When comparing humans and apes, we must ask whether language is a unique human characteristic. If it is, then what biological and behavioral differences exist between apes and humans that lead to the fact that one species has language and the other lacks it? Linguistics is also important in considering human evolution. When did language begin, and why?

Biological Anthropology The subject of this book is the subfield of **biological anthropology,** which is concerned with the biological evolution and variation of the human species, past and present. Biological anthropology is often referred to by another name—*physical anthropology.* The course you are currently enrolled in might be known by either name; the two names refer to the same field. Early in the twentieth century, the field was known as physical anthropology, reflecting its then primary interest in the *physical* variation of past and present humans and our primate relatives. Much of the research in the field focused on descriptive studies of physical variations, with little theoretical background. Starting in the 1950s, physical anthropologists became more familiar with the rapidly growing fields of genetics and evolutionary science. As a result, the field of physical anthropology became more concerned with biological processes, particularly genetics. After a while, many in the field began using the term *biological anthropology* to emphasize the new focus on biological processes. In most circles today, the two terms are used more or less interchangeably.

It is useful to consider the field of biological anthropology in terms of three very basic questions that are answered in Parts II, III, and IV in this text. First, *what is our place in nature?* That is, how are we related to other living creatures? How are we unique? The second major question concerns our past. *What are our origins?* Where did we come from? What does the history of our species look like? How were our earlier ancestors similar to us, and how different from us? The third question concerns our diversity. *How are humans around the world like, or unlike, each other?* What causes the patterns of human variation that we see? What is the pattern of recent evolution of our species, and how do we continue to evolve?

There are several traditionally defined areas within biological anthropology, such as primate studies, human evolution, and human variation. Primates are the group of mammals to which we belong, and studies of the anatomy, ecology, and behavior of the nonhuman primates provide us with a comparative perspective from which to view our own evolutionary history. In this way, we learn something about what it is to be human. The study of human evolution necessarily involves analysis of the fossil and archaeological remains of our ancestors in order to determine where, when, how, and why they evolved. The study of human variation deals with how and why humans differ from each other in their biological makeup, including studies of ancestry and population history, recent and ongoing human evolution, and ways in which changes in human culture have affected our biology.

Applied research is an expanding focus in biological anthropology. Forensic anthropologists apply their knowledge of human skeletal variation to the identification of human skeletal remains. These remains (including

biological anthropology The subfield of anthropology that focuses on the biological evolution of humans and human ancestors, the relationship of humans to other organisms, and patterns of biological variation within and among human populations. Also referred to as physical anthropology.

Biological Anthropologists at Work

The research interests of biological anthropologists are quite varied. This photo essay provides some examples.

Dr. Barry Bogin is professor of anthropology in the Department of Behavioral Sciences at the University of Michigan at Dearborn and author of *Patterns of Human Growth* (1999) and *The Growth of Humanity* (2001). His area of specialization is human growth, with particular emphasis on biocultural interactions and the evolution of human physical growth. Much of his recent research has focused on the cultural correlates of differences in physical growth patterns of Ladinos and Mayans in Guatemala and the United States. He is shown here measuring the height of a Mayan woman who has immigrated to the United States.

Dr. Michael Crawford is a professor of anthropology at the University of Kansas. He specializes in anthropological genetics, the study of the forces affecting genetic variation between and within human populations. Dr. Crawford's research focuses on genetic markers from human populations across the globe. His research has taken him to Mexico, Belize, Ireland, Italy, Alaska, and Siberia. He is shown here with the Altai reindeer herders of Siberia as he investigates their genetic relationship to the first inhabitants of the New World and their adaptation to extremely cold climates.

Dr. Dawnie Steadman, an associate professor at Binghamton University in New York, specializes in forensic anthropology, bioarchaeology, paleopathology, and the application of forensics to human rights investigations. Her current research includes the interpretation of skeletal trauma and healing rates, the coevolution of humans and tuberculosis, and the impact of warfare on prehistoric community health. Her edited volume, *Hard Evidence: Case Studies in Forensic Anthropology* (2003), illustrates the interdisciplinary nature of modern forensic anthropology.

Dr. Dean Falk is a professor of anthropology at Florida State University. Her primary research interest is the evolution and comparative anatomy of primate brains, including the human brain. Dr. Falk is an expert in the field of paleoneurology, which involves the reconstruction of brain anatomy from fossil evidence. Her recent research deals with how the brain cools itself, including implications for human evolution and the origin of an enlarged brain in our early ancestors. Her model of brain evolution is described in *Braindance* (2004).

Dawnie Steadman

Barry Bogin

Michael Crawford

Dean Falk

Dr. Lyle Konigsberg, a professor of anthropology at the University of Illinois, is particularly interested in integrating the study of prehistoric human skeletal remains with genetic and demographic theory. Dr. Konigsberg investigates patterns of prehistoric biological variation across space and time. His current work involves an analysis of prehistoric Native American populations, dating between 500 and 6,000 years ago.

Dr. Rachel Caspari is an assistant professor at Central Michigan University. Her primary research interest is the anatomy of recent humans and their evolutionary relationship with earlier humans. Her most recent research has focused on the skeletal morphology of the neck region in central European human fossils. She is also interested in the history of biological anthropology and is coauthor of the book *Race and Human Evolution* (Wolpoff and Caspari 1997).

Dr. Lorena Madrigal, a professor of anthropology at the University of South Florida, studies the biology and microevolution of human populations in Costa Rica, particularly through their demography and genetics. Together with her colleagues from the University of Costa Rica, she is working with the Culís of Limón, Costa Rica, a group descended from East-Indian indentured workers. The project focuses on obesity, high blood pressure, and the population genetics of this group. In addition, Dr. Madrigal has researched the historical demography of Escazú, Costa Rica, by looking at its mortality and fertility cycles.

Dr. Karen Strier is a professor of anthropology at the University of Wisconsin at Madison. Her primary research interests are in comparative primate behavioral ecology and its links to conservation biology. Since 1982, Dr. Strier has studied the endangered muriqui monkeys of Brazil's Atlantic forest. Her research has demonstrated that muriquis differ from most other primates in their nonaggressive, egalitarian societies. More recently, she has expanded her behavioral studies to include investigations into muriqui reproductive and life history strategies.

Lyle Konigsberg

Rachel Caspari

Karen Strier

Lorena Madrigal

11

the teeth) are used to classify individuals by sex, age, stature, and, where possible, likely ancestry. Information about the cause of death and existing pathologies is recorded, and these clues, combined in some cases with identification of DNA from skeletal remains, provide information that is used in legal cases, for identification of missing persons, in analysis of mass grave sites, and for other forensic applications (Steadman 2003).

SCIENCE AND EVOLUTION

Biological anthropology is an evolutionary science. All the major questions just presented may be addressed using modern evolutionary theory. Biological evolution simply refers to change in the genetic makeup of populations over time.

Characteristics of Science

Before we consider how evolution works, it is important to understand exactly what a science is and what the relationship between facts, hypotheses, and theories is.

Facts   At one time or another, you have probably heard someone make the statement that evolution is a theory, not a fact. Or you might have heard that it is a fact, not a theory. Which is it, theory or fact? The truth of the matter is that someone who makes either of these statements does not understand what a theory or a fact is. Evolution is both fact and theory. A fact is simply a verifiable truth. It is a scientific fact that the earth is round. It is a fact that when you drop something, it falls to the ground (assuming you are in the presence of a gravitational field and are not dropping something that floats or flies away!). Evolution is a fact. Living organisms have changed in the past, and they continue to change today. There are forms of life today that did not exist millions of years ago. There are also forms of life that existed in the past but are not around today, such as our ancestors (Figure 1.3). Certain organisms have shown definite changes in their biological makeup. Horses, for example, used to have five toes, then three, and today only one. Human beings have larger brains and smaller teeth today than they did a million years ago. Some changes are even apparent over shorter intervals of time. For example, human teeth are on average smaller today than they were only 10,000 years ago. All of these statements and many others are verifiable truths. They are facts.

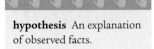

hypothesis An explanation of observed facts.

Hypotheses   What is a hypothesis? A **hypothesis** is simply an explanation of observed facts. For example, consider gravity. Gravity is a fact. It is observable. Many hypotheses could be generated to explain gravity. You could hypothesize that gravity is caused by a giant living in the core of our planet drawing in air, thus causing a pull on all objects on the earth's surface. Bizarre as it sounds, this is a scientific hypothesis because it can be tested. It

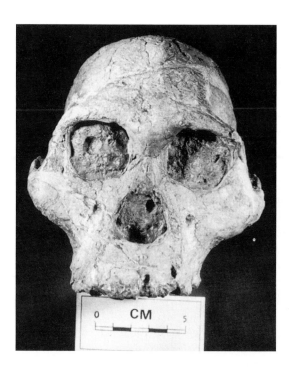

FIGURE 1.3

A skull of *Australopithecus africanus,* a human ancestor that lived 2.5 million to 3.3 million years ago. Paleoanthropologists use the fossil record to learn about our evolution.

is, however, easily shown to be incorrect (air movement can be measured, and it does not flow in the postulated direction).

Testability To be scientific, a hypothesis must be testable. The potential must exist for a hypothesis to be rejected. Just as the presence of the hypothetical giant in the earth can be tested (it doesn't exist!), predictions about gravitational strength can also be tested. Not all hypotheses can be tested, however, and for this reason, they are not scientific hypotheses. That doesn't necessarily mean that they are true or false but only that they cannot be tested. For example, you might come up with a hypothesis that all the fossils we have ever found were put in the ground by God to confuse us. This is not a scientific hypothesis because we have no objective way of testing it.

Many evolutionary hypotheses, however, are testable. For example, specific predictions about the fossil record can be made based on our knowledge of evolution. One such prediction is that humans evolved after the extinction of the dinosaurs. The potential exists for this statement to be rejected; all we need is evidence that humans existed before, or at the same time as, the dinosaurs. Because we have found no such evidence, we cannot reject the hypothesis. We can, however, imagine a situation in which the hypothesis could be rejected. If we cannot imagine such a situation, then the hypothesis cannot be tested. For example, suppose someone tells you that all the people on the earth were created five minutes ago, complete with memories! Any evidence you muster against this idea could be explained away. Therefore, this hypothesis is not scientific because there is no possible way to reject it.

Theories   What is the difference between a theory and a hypothesis? In some disciplines, the two terms are sometimes used to mean the same thing. In the natural and physical sciences, however, theory means something different from hypothesis. A **theory** is a set of hypotheses that have been tested repeatedly and that have not been rejected. Evolution falls into this category.

There seems to be continuing confusion about the difference between "fact" and "theory" in our culture, giving rise, for example, to arguments about whether evolution is a fact *or* a theory. Such arguments show unfamiliarity with the definitions of "fact," "hypothesis," and "theory." Too often, there is a tendency to view a theory as a mere speculation as opposed to the more accurate definition as a set of confirmed hypotheses. The argument about whether evolution is a fact *or* a theory incorrectly suggests that evolution may or may not exist. One only has to use the same debate over atoms and atomic theory to see the problem with such reasoning. When you hear about atomic theory, does that suggest to you that atoms may or may not exist? Of course not. Atoms are real (facts), and atomic theory refers to a set of confirmed hypotheses used to explain these facts. As such, atoms refer to *both* a fact *and* a theory.

Likewise, evolution is *both* a fact *and* a theory. As noted below, we have evidence that evolution has occurred in the past and continues to occur today. Various hypotheses have been suggested in the past to explain *why* and *how* evolution has occurred. Over time, the hypothesis of natural selection, developed by Charles Darwin and explained below, has stood the test of time as a major component (along with other mechanisms discussed in later chapters) of modern evolutionary theory.

The Development of Evolutionary Theory

As with all general theories, modern evolutionary theory is not static. Scientific research is a dynamic process, with new evidence being used to support, clarify, and, most important, reject previous ideas. There will always be continual refinements in specific aspects of the theory and its applications. Because science is a dynamic process, evolutionary theory did not come about overnight. Charles Darwin (1809–1882) is most often credited as the "father of evolutionary thought" (Figure 1.4). It is true that Darwin provided a powerful idea that forms the center of modern evolutionary thought. He did not work in an intellectual vacuum, however, but rather built on the ideas of earlier scholars. Darwin's model was not the first evolutionary theory; it forms, rather, the basis of the one that has stood the test of time.

Pre-Darwinian Thought   To understand Darwin's contribution and evolution in general, it is necessary to take a look at earlier ideas. For many centuries, the concept of change, biological or otherwise, was rather unusual in Western thought. Much of ancient Greek philosophy, for example, posited a static, unchanging view of the world. In later Western thought, the universe, earth, and all living creatures were regarded as having been created by God in

theory A set of hypotheses that have been tested repeatedly and that have not been rejected. This term is sometimes used in a different sense in social science literature.

FIGURE 1.4

Charles Darwin developed the idea of natural selection as a way of explaining how organisms evolve over time by adapting to their environment. Organisms that are more likely to survive and reproduce pass their genetic material on to future generations.

their present form, showing little if any change over many generations. Many biologists (then called natural historians) shared this view, and their science consisted mainly of description and categorization. A good example is Carolus Linnaeus (1707–1778), a Swedish naturalist who compiled one of the first formal classifications of all known living creatures. **Taxonomy** is the science of describing and classifying organisms. Linnaeus's taxonomic research produced a classification of all known living creatures into meaningful groups. For example, humans, dogs, cats, and many other animals are mammals, characterized primarily by the presence of mammary glands to feed offspring. Linnaeus used a variety of traits to place all then-known creatures into various categories. Such a classification helps clarify relationships between different organisms. For example, bats are classified as mammals because they possess mammary glands—and not as birds simply because they have wings.

Linnaeus also gave organisms a name reflecting their genus and species. A **species** is a group of populations whose members can interbreed and produce fertile offspring. A **genus** is a group of similar species, often sharing certain common forms of adaptation. Modern humans, for example, are known by the name *Homo sapiens*. The first word is the genus and the second word is the species (more detail on genus and species is given in Chapter 4).

The reason for the relationships among organisms, however, was not often addressed by early natural historians. The living world was felt to be the product of God's work, and the task of the natural historian was description and classification. This static view of the world began to change in the eighteenth and nineteenth centuries. One important reason for this change was that excavations began to produce many fossils that did not fit neatly into the classification system. For example, imagine that you found the remains of a modern horse. This would pose no problem in interpretation; the bones are those of a dead horse, perhaps belonging to a farmer several years ago. Now suppose you found what at first glance appeared to be a horse but was somewhat smaller and had five toes instead of the single hoof of a modern horse. If you found more and more of these five-toed horses, you would ask what creature the toes belonged to. Because horses do not have five toes today, your only conclusion would be that there once existed horses with five toes and that they do not exist anymore. This conclusion, though hardly startling now, was a thunderbolt to those who believed the world was created as it is today, with no change.

Apart from fossil remains of creatures that were somewhat similar to modern-day forms, excavations also uncovered fossil remnants of truly unusual creatures, such as the dinosaurs. This fossil record led scientists to chip away at the view that the world is as it always had been, and the concept of change began to be incorporated into explanations of the origin of life. Not all scholars, however, came up with the same hypotheses.

One French anatomist, Georges Cuvier (1769–1832), analyzed many of the fossil remains found in quarries. He showed that many of these belonged to animals that no longer existed; that is, they had become extinct. Cuvier used a hypothesis called catastrophism to explain these extinctions. The

taxonomy The science of describing and classifying organisms.

species A group of populations whose members can interbreed naturally and produce fertile offspring.

genus Groups of species with similar adaptations.

hypothesis posited a series of catastrophes in the planet's past during which many living creatures were destroyed. Following these catastrophes, organisms from unaffected areas moved in. The changes over time observed in the fossil record could therefore be explained as a continual process of catastrophes followed by repopulation from other regions (Mayr 1982).

The work of the French scientist Jean-Baptiste Lamarck (1744–1829) more explicitly attempted an explanation of evolution. He believed that the environment would affect the future shape and organization of animals (Mayr 1982). His specific mechanism stressed the use and disuse of body parts. For example, a jungle cat that developed stronger legs through constant running and jumping would pass these changes on to its offspring. Although we now know that Lamarck's ideas are not genetically correct, it is important to note that he was quite astute in noticing the relationship between organisms, their environment, and evolution.

Uniformitarianism and Geologic Time   Central to an explanation of biological evolution is the nature of the passage of time and the age of the earth. In earlier times, it was generally thought that the earth was young, with age estimates based on biblical interpretations. Perhaps the most well known estimate of earth's antiquity is that of Archbishop James Ussher (1581–1656). Based on his analysis of biblical writings and events, Ussher concluded that the earth was less than 6,000 years old, and he assigned a precise date of 4004 B.C. as the year that God created the universe.

Geological research, however, was moving in a different direction with the growing realization that the earth was considerably older than several thousand years. Scottish geologist James Hutton (1726–1797) developed the idea of **uniformitarianism,** which means that the geologic processes we observe in the world today, such as erosion or continental drift, operated in the same way in the past. This important principle means that we can study the world around us in the present and use what we see to make inferences about the past. The principle of uniformitarianism was adopted and extended by another Scottish geologist, Charles Lyell (1797–1875), who provided considerable geologic evidence for a slowly changing earth. Critical to the development of evolutionary thought was the observation that because the earth was shaped slowly over time, it would have therefore taken a considerable amount of time to form the many geologic features present in the world today. Thus, geological research was showing that the earth was *much* older than several thousand years. Indeed, according to current estimates, based on a variety of physical and chemical methods (see Chapter 8), the earth is 4.6 *billion* years old—over 750,000 times as old as estimated by Ussher! The work of Lyell also suggested that small biological processes could add up over time to produce considerable evolutionary change. In fact, Lyell's work greatly influenced the key figure in the history of evolutionary thought— Charles Darwin.

Charles Darwin and Natural Selection   With this background in mind, let us look at Darwin and his accomplishments. Charles Darwin had been

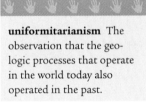

uniformitarianism The observation that the geologic processes that operate in the world today also operated in the past.

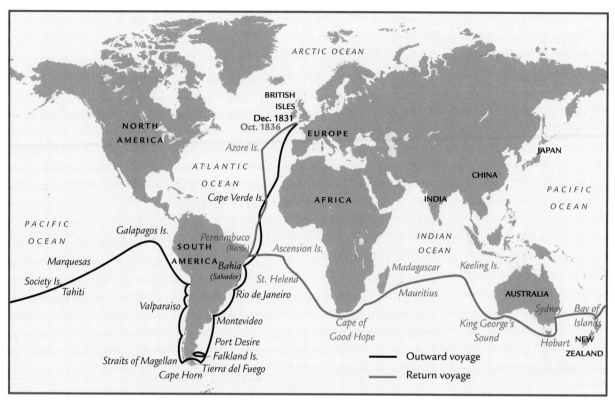

FIGURE 1.5

Darwin's observations of variation in the different regions he visited aboard the HMS *Beagle* shaped his theory of natural selection.

interested in biology and geology since he was a small child. Born to well-to-do parents, Darwin attended college and had planned to enter the ministry, although he was not as enthusiastic about this career as he was about his studies of natural history. Because of his scientific and social connections, Darwin was able to accompany the scientific survey ship *Beagle* as an unpaid naturalist. The *Beagle* conducted a five-year journey around the world collecting plant and animal specimens in South America and the Galapagos Islands (in the Pacific Ocean near Ecuador), among other places (Figure 1.5).

During these travels, Darwin came to several basic conclusions about variation in living organisms. First, he found a tremendous amount of observable variation in most living species. Instead of looking at the world in terms of fixed, rigid categories (as did mainstream biology in his time), Darwin saw that individuals within species varied considerably from place to place. With careful attention, you can see the world in much the same way that Darwin did. You will see, for example, that people around you vary to an incredible degree. Some are tall, some short; some are dark, and some light. Facial features, musculature, hair color, and many other characteristics come in many different forms, even in a single classroom. Remember, too, that what you see are only those visible characteristics. With the right type of equipment, you could look at genetic and biochemical variation within your classroom and find even more evidence of tremendous diversity.

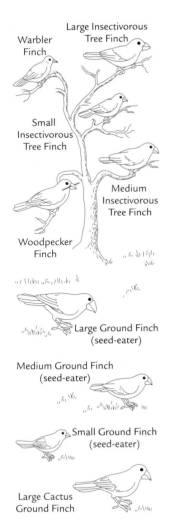

FIGURE 1.6

The sizes, beak shapes, and diets of this sample of Darwin's finches show differences in adaptation among closely related species. (From E. Peter Volpe, *Understanding Evolution*, 5th ed. © 1985 Wm. C. Brown Communications, Inc., Dubuque, Iowa. All rights reserved. Reprinted by permission of the McGraw-Hill Companies.)

Darwin also noted that the variations he saw made sense in terms of the environment (Figure 1.6). Creatures in cold climates often have fur for protection. Birds in areas where insects live deep inside tree trunks or branches have long beaks to enable them to extract these insects and eat them. In other words, organisms appear well adapted to specific environments. Darwin believed that the environment acted to change organisms over time. But how?

To help answer this question, Darwin turned to the writings of the economist Thomas Malthus (1766–1834), who had noted that more individuals are born in most species than can possibly survive. In other words, many organisms die before reaching maturity and reproducing. If it were not for this mortality, populations would grow too large for their environments to support them. Certain fish, for example, can produce as many as 8,000 eggs in a single year. Assume for the moment that half of these eggs are female. Now assume that each of these females then also lays 8,000 eggs in a single year. To make things simple, let us further assume that a female fish breeds only once in her life. If you start with two fish (one male and one female), in the next generation, you have 8,000 fish. Half of these are females, and each produces 8,000 more fish, for a total of 32 million fish. If the fish continue reproducing in this way, there will be roughly 2.1×10^{36} fish (i.e., 2.1 followed by 36 zeroes) after only 10 generations! Suppose these are relatively small fish, each one weighing only 100 grams (a little less than a quarter of a pound). The total weight of all fish after 10 generations would be roughly 2.1×10^{38} grams (or roughly 2.3×10^{32} tons).

To give you an idea of exactly how large these numbers are, consider the fact that the total weight of our sun is 1.99×10^{33} grams (Pasachoff 1979). If the cycle begins with two fish, after 10 generations, the total weight of the fish will be greater than the weight of the sun. Because we are not all currently smothered in fish, something is wrong with this simple model.

Malthus provided the answer. Most of the fish will die before they reproduce. Some eggs will become diseased and die, and others will be eaten by predators. Only a small number of the eggs will actually survive long enough to reproduce. Malthus is best known for extrapolating the principle of population growth into human terms; his lesson is that unless we control our growth, there will soon be too many of us to feed.

To Darwin, the ideas of Malthus provided the needed information to solve the problem of adaptation and evolution. Not all individuals in a species survive and reproduce. Some failure to reproduce may be random, but some is related to specific characteristics of an individual. If there are two birds, one with a short beak and one with a long beak, in an environment that requires reaching inside trees to feed, it stands to reason that the bird with the longer beak is more likely to feed itself, survive, and reproduce. In certain environments, some individuals possess traits that enhance their probability of survival and reproduction. If these traits are due, in part or whole, to inherited characteristics, then they will be passed on to the next generation.

In some ways, Darwin's idea was not new. Animal and plant breeders had applied this principle for centuries. Controlled breeding and artificial selection

FIGURE 1.7

Adaptation in the peppered moth. The dark-colored moth is more visible on light-colored tree trunks and therefore at greater risk of being seen and eaten by a bird (*left*). The light-colored moth is at greater risk of being eaten on dark-colored tree trunks (*right*).

had resulted in many traits in domesticated plants and animals, such as livestock size and milk production in cows. The same principle is used in producing pedigreed dogs and many forms of tropical fish. The difference is that Darwin saw that nature (the environment) could select those individuals that survived and reproduced. Hence, he called his concept **natural selection.** Given the influence of Lyell's thoughts on uniformitarianism, as well as the great antiquity of the earth, Darwin further argued that small changes due to natural selection could add up over long periods to produce the diversity of species we see in the world today.

Although the theory of evolution by natural selection is most often associated with Charles Darwin, another English natural historian, Alfred Russel Wallace (1823–1913), came up with essentially the same idea. In fact, Darwin and Wallace communicated their ideas to each other and first presented the theory of natural selection in a joint paper in 1858. Many scholars feel that Wallace's independent work impelled Darwin finally to put forward the ideas he had developed years earlier but had not published. To ensure timely publication, Darwin condensed his many years of work into a book titled *On the Origin of Species by Means of Natural Selection,* published in 1859.

natural selection A mechanism for evolutionary change favoring the survival and reproduction of some organisms over others because of their biological characteristics.

Examples of Natural Selection One example of how natural selection works involves populations of the peppered moth in England over the past few centuries (Figure 1.7). These moths come in two distinct colors, dark and light. Early observations found that most of these moths were light-colored, thus allowing them to camouflage themselves on tree trunks covered by light-colored lichen. By blending in, they had a better chance of avoiding the birds that tried to eat them. Roughly 1 percent of the moths, however, were dark-colored and thus at an obvious disadvantage. In the century following the beginning of the Industrial Revolution in England, naturalists noted that the frequency of dark-colored moths increased to almost 90 percent

(Grant 1985). The explanation for this change was the massive pollution in the surrounding countryside brought about by industrialization. The pollution killed the lichen, exposing the dark trees. The light moths were at a disadvantage, and the dark moths, now better camouflaged, were better off. Proportionately, more dark moths survived and passed their dark color to the next generation. In evolutionary terminology, the dark moths were *selected for* and the light moths were *selected against.* After antipollution laws were passed and the environment began to recover, the situation was reversed: Once again, light moths survived better and were selected for, whereas dark moths were selected against (Cook et al. 1999).

To illustrate one of the ways that natural selection can be detected, consider the relationship between moth color and survival revealed in a recapture experiment. In such a procedure, moths of different colors are marked and then released into the environment in known proportions of light and dark. Later, moths are recaptured, the relative proportions of light and dark compared, and the ratio of observed to expected used as a measure of survival rate. For example, in one study of a polluted area in Birmingham, England, 158 moths were recaptured, of which 18 were light-colored and 140 were dark-colored. Given the initial proportions, the expected numbers (given a total of 158 recaptured moths) were 36 light-colored moths and 122 dark-colored moths. In other words, fewer light-colored moths and more dark-colored moths survived than was to be expected if there were no survival value of color. In another recapture experiment, conducted in an unpolluted area, the findings were the opposite—more light-colored moths and fewer dark-colored moths survived than expected. This observation also makes sense, as the survival rate of light-colored moths is expected to be higher in an area without industrial pollution (Ridley 2004).

The peppered moth example shows us more than just the workings of natural selection. It also illustrates several important principles of evolution. First, we cannot always state with absolute certainty which traits are "good" and which are "bad." It depends on the specific environment. When the trees were light in color, the light-colored moths were at an advantage, but when the situation changed, the dark-colored moths gained the advantage. Second, evolution does not proceed unopposed in one direction. Under certain situations, biological traits can change in a different direction. In the case of the moths, evolution produced a change from light to dark to light again. Third, evolution does not occur in a vacuum. It is affected by changes in the environment and in other species. In this example, changes in the cultural evolution of humans led to a change in the environment, which further affected the evolution of the moths. Finally, the moth study shows us the critical importance of variation to the evolutionary process. If the original population of moths did not possess the dark-colored variation, they might have been wiped out after the trees turned darker in color. Variation must exist for natural selection to operate effectively.

The peppered moth example also provides a good example of the application of the scientific method. Although the relationship between changing frequency of moth color and bird predation has long been considered a "classic" example of natural selection, there have also been criticisms of the underlying methods of the studies. The point here is that criticism of methods and interpretations is an important part of science; results must be repeatable. In the case of the peppered moth studies, there have been sufficient analyses employing different methods to confirm early observations of differential survival (Cook 2000; Ridley 2004). It is also important to note that such criticism and reanalysis revealed that the geographic distribution of moth colors is a bit more complicated than once thought; apparently, migration, in addition to bird predation, has affected the evolution of the peppered moth (Ridley 2004).

The study of the peppered moth is only one of many examples of evolution through natural selection. Another example is found in P. R. Grant's continuing work on the variation and evolution of Galapagos finches. Grant found that average beak size changed over time in direct response to changes in the environment. In drought years, the average beak is larger. Why? The simplest explanation is that drought conditions make those finches with larger beaks better able to crack the larger seeds that are more common under drought conditions. Grant has observed these changes over several decades. The changes in beak size over time show that the changing environment affects the probability of survival and reproduction (Grant 1991; Weiner 1994).

Modern Evolutionary Thought   Darwin provided part of the answer to the question of how evolution worked, but he did not have all the answers. Many early critics of Darwin's work focused on certain questions that Darwin could not answer. One important question concerns the origins of variation: Given that natural selection operates on *existing* variation, where do those variations come from? Why, at the outset, were some moths light and others dark? Natural selection can act only on preexisting variation; it cannot create new variations. Another question is, How are traits inherited? The theory of natural selection states that certain traits are selected for and passed on to future generations. How are these traits passed on? Darwin knew that traits were inherited, but he did not know the mechanism. Still another question is, How do new forms and structures come into being?

Darwin is to be remembered and praised for his work in providing the critical base from which evolutionary science developed. He did not, however, have all the answers, as no scientist does. Even today, people tend to equate evolutionary science with Darwin, to the exclusion of all work since that time. Some critics of evolutionary theory point to a single aspect of Darwin's work, show it to be in error, and then claim that all of evolutionary thought is suspect. In reality, a scientific theory will continue to change as new evidence is gathered and as further tests are constructed.

Modern evolutionary theory relies not only on the work of Darwin and Wallace but also on developments in genetics, zoology, embryology, physiology, and mathematics, to name but a few fields. The basic concept of natural selection as stated by Darwin has been tested and found to be valid. Refinements have been added, and some aspects of the original idea have been changed. We now have answers to many of Darwin's questions.

Biological evolution consists of changes in the genetic composition of populations. As shown in Chapter 3, the relative frequencies of genes change over time because of four mechanisms, or evolutionary forces. Natural selection is one of these mechanisms. Those individuals with genetic characteristics that improve their survival or reproduction pass their genetic material on to the next generation. In the peppered moth example discussed earlier, the dark moths were more likely to survive in an environment where pollution made the trees darker in color. Thus, the relative frequency of genes for dark moth color increased over time (at least until the environment changed again).

Evolutionary change from one generation to the next, or over many generations, is the product of the joint effect of the four evolutionary forces. Our discussion here simplifies a complex idea, but it does suggest that evolution is more than simply natural selection. Modern evolutionary theory encompasses all four evolutionary forces and will be discussed in greater detail in the next three chapters.

Evidence for Evolution

Because this book is concerned with human variation and evolution, you will be provided with numerous examples of how evolution works in human populations, past and present. It is important to understand from the start that biological evolution is a documented fact and that the modern theory of evolution has stood up under many scientific tests.

The fossil record provides evidence of evolution. The story the fossils tell is one of change: Creatures existed in the past that are no longer with us. Sequential changes are found in many fossils showing the change of certain features over time, as in the case of the horse. Apart from demonstrating that evolution did occur, the fossil record also provides tests of the predictions made from evolutionary theory. For example, the theory predicts that single-celled organisms evolved before multicelled organisms. The fossil record supports this prediction—multicelled organisms found in layers of the earth appeared millions of years after the first single-celled organisms. Note that the possibility always remains that the opposite could be found. If multicelled organisms were indeed found to have evolved before single-celled organisms, then the theory of evolution would be rejected. A good scientific theory always allows for the possibility of rejection. The fact that we have not found such a case in countless examinations of the fossil record strengthens the case for evolutionary theory. Remember, in science, you do not prove a theory; rather, you fail to reject it.

The fossil record is not the only evidence that evolution has occurred. Comparison of living organisms provides further confirmation. For example, the African apes are the closest living relatives of humans. We see this in a number of characteristics. African apes and humans share the same type of dental pattern, have a similar shoulder structure, and have DNA (the genetic code) that is over 98 percent identical. Even though any one of these traits, or others, could be explained as coincidental, why do so many independent traits show the same pattern? One possibility, of course, is that they were designed that way by an ultimate creator. The problem with this idea is that it cannot be tested. It is a matter of faith and not of science. Another problem is that we must then ask ourselves why a creator would use the same basic pattern for so many traits in different creatures. Evolution, on the other hand, offers an explanation: Apes and humans share many characteristics because they evolved from a common ancestor.

Another example of shared characteristics is the python, a large snake. Like many vertebrates, the python has a pelvis, the skeletal structure that connects the lower legs to the upper body (Futuyma 1983). From a structural standpoint, of what possible use is a pelvis to a creature that has no legs? If the python was created, what purpose could there have been to give it a pelvis? We can, of course, argue that no one can understand the motivations of a creator, but that is hardly a scientific explanation. Evolutionary reasoning provides an answer: The python has retained the pelvis from an earlier ancestor that did have legs. In fact, new fossil discoveries dating back 95 million years provide evidence of early snakes that actually had limbs (Tchernov et al. 2000).

Further fascinating evidence of shared characteristics is the discovery of fossils of early whales with reduced hind limbs (Gingerich et al. 1990). Whales are aquatic mammals that have lost hind limbs and pelvic bones since their evolutionary separation from other mammals more than 50 million years ago. The discovery of fossil whales with small, and perhaps somewhat functional, hind limbs provides another example of shared characteristics that can be explained only through evolution. This discovery also provides an excellent illustration of a transitional form—a fossil that links both early and modern forms. Another excellent example of a transitional fossil is the species known as *Tiktaalik roseae,* recently discovered, that provides a link between early lobe-finned fishes and the first vertebrates with limbs (Daeschler et al. 2006; Shubin et al. 2006). Such fossils are exactly what are predicted by evolutionary theory.

Another line of evidence supporting evolution is the laboratory and field studies of living organisms. Ongoing evolutionary change has been documented in many organisms, including humans. Specific predictions of the effect of evolutionary mechanisms have been tested and verified in controlled experiments and observational studies. The study of moth color is but one of many examples of this kind of analysis.

Science and Religion

The subject of evolution has always been controversial, and the implications of evolution have sometimes frightened people. For example, the fact that humans and apes evolved from a common ancestor has always upset some people who feel that their humanity is somehow degraded by having ancestors supposedly less worthy than themselves. Another conflict lies in the implications evolution has for religious views. In the United States, even into the late 1960s, a number of laws prohibited teaching evolution in public schools.

FIGURE 1.8

The Scopes trial. William Jennings Bryan (*right*) represented the state of Tennessee, and Clarence Darrow (*left*) represented John Scopes, who was on trial for violating the law that prohibited teaching evolution in public schools.

Numerous legal battles have been fought over these anti-evolution laws. Perhaps the most famous of these was the "Scopes Monkey Trial" in 1925. John Scopes, a high school teacher in Dayton, Tennessee, was arrested for violating the state law prohibiting the teaching of evolution. The town and trial quickly became the center of national attention, primarily because of the two celebrities in the case—William Jennings Bryan, a former U.S. secretary of state, who represented the state of Tennessee, and Clarence Darrow, one of the most famous American trial lawyers ever, who represented Scopes. The battle between these two eloquent speakers captured the attention of the nation (Figure 1.8). In the end, Scopes was found guilty of violating the law and fined $100. The fine was later suspended on a legal technicality. The story of this trial, which has been dramatized in play and movie versions as *Inherit the Wind,* is a powerful story portraying the fight of those who feel strongly about academic freedom and freedom of speech against ignorance and oppression. In reality, the original arrest of Scopes was planned by several local people to gain publicity for the town (Larson 1997).

Creation Science   In retrospect, the Scopes trial may seem amusing. We laugh at early attempts to control subject matter in classrooms and often feel that we have gone beyond such battles. Nothing could be further from the truth, however. For many people, evolution represents a threat to their beliefs in the sudden creation of all life by a creator. Attempts to legislate the teaching of the biblical view of creation in science classes, however, violate the First Amendment of the Constitution as an establishment of religion. To circumvent this problem, opponents of evolution have devised the strategy of calling their teachings "creation science"—supposedly, the scientific study of special creation. The word *God* does not always appear in definitions of creation science, but the word *creator* often does.

In March 1981, the Arkansas state legislature passed a law (Act 590) requiring that creation science be taught in public schools for equal amounts of time as evolution. The American Civil Liberties Union challenged this law, and it was overturned in a federal district court in 1982. A similar law passed in Louisiana in 1981 was later overturned. The Louisiana case was later appealed and brought to the U.S. Supreme Court, which upheld the ruling of the lower court in 1987. Among other legal problems they raise, both the Arkansas and Louisiana laws have been found to be unconstitutional under the First Amendment.

What is "creation science"? Why shouldn't it be taught in science classes? Shouldn't science be open to new ideas? These questions all center on the issue of whether creation science actually is a science. As typically applied, creation science is not a science; at best, it is a grab bag of ideas spruced up with scientific jargon.

One of the original definitions is found in Act 590 of the Arkansas law, which defines creation science as

> the scientific evidence for creation and inferences from these scientific evidences. Creation-science includes the scientific evidences and related inferences that indicate: (1) Sudden creation of the universe, energy, and life from nothing; (2) The insufficiency of mutation and natural selection in bringing about development of all living kinds from a single organism; (3) Changes only within fixed limits of originally created kinds of plants and animals; (4) Separate ancestry for man and apes; (5) Explanation of the earth's geology by catastrophism, including the occurrence of a worldwide flood; and (6) A relatively recent inception of the earth and living kinds. (Montagu 1984:376–377)

None of these statements is supported by scientific evidence, and creationist writers generally use very little actual evidence to support their views. The main "scientific" work of the creationists consists of attempting to find fault with evolutionary theory. The reasoning is that if evolution can be rejected, then "special creation" must be true. This strategy actually uses an important feature of scientific research by attempting to reject a given hypothesis. The problem is that none of the creationists' attacks on evolution has been supported by scientific evidence. Certainly, some predictions of evolutionary theory have been proven incorrect, but that is to be expected because science is a dynamic process. The basic findings of evolution, however, have been supported time and time again.

On an emotional level, the doctrines of creation science attract many people. Given the concept of free speech, why shouldn't creation science be given equal time? The problem with this plea is that it assumes that both ideas have equal merit. Consider that some people still believe the earth is flat. They are certainly entitled to their opinion, but it would be absurd to mandate "equal time" in geography and geology classes for this

TABLE 1.1	Some Religious Organizations Opposed to Creation Science
American Jewish Congress	
Central Conference of American Rabbis	
General Convention of the Episcopal Church	
Lutheran World Federation	
Roman Catholic Church	
Unitarian Universalist Association	
United Methodist Church	
United Presbyterian Church	

Source: National Center for Science Education, www.ncseweb.org.

idea. Also, the concept of equal time is not really that fair-minded after all. The specific story many creationists refer to is the biblical story of Genesis. Many other cultures have their own creation stories. Shouldn't they receive equal time as well? In one sense, they should, though the proper forum for such discussions is probably a course in comparative religions, not a science class.

Perhaps the biggest problem advocates of creation science have introduced is that they appear to place religion and science at odds with each other. Religion and science both represent ways of looking at the world, and though they work on different levels, they are not contradictory. You can believe in God and still accept the fact of evolution and evolutionary theory. Only if you take the story of Genesis as a literal, historical account does a conflict exist. Most major religions in the world accept the findings of evolution. Many people, including some scientists, look to the evolutionary process as evidence of God's work, an idea known as **theistic evolution.** As such, many religions support the teaching of evolution in science education rather than creation science (Table 1.1). As further evidence that there is no necessary conflict between religion and evolution, Pope John Paul II stated in his October 22, 1996, message to the Pontifical Academy of Sciences that "knowledge has led to the recognition of the theory of evolution as more than a hypothesis" (Gould 1999:81).

Intelligent Design   In recent years, another approach to creationism has become popular in the United States. Known as **intelligent design creationism,** this approach centers on the idea that the biological world was created by an intelligent entity, although "God" is not generally specified directly as the creator, thus trying to divorce intelligent design from objections regarding the establishment of religion under the First Amendment.

The basic concept of intelligent design is that certain characteristics of biological organisms are too complex to be explained through natural

theistic evolution The belief that God operates through the natural process of evolution.

intelligent design creationism The idea that the biological world was created by an intelligent entity and did not arise from natural processes.

processes such as natural selection, and therefore *must* have been created. This idea actually dates back to the "watchmaker analogy" of the eighteenth-century theologian William Paley, who argued that a complex mechanical object such as a watch, with its intricate mechanisms, could not have arisen naturally, and so its existence automatically implies the existence of a watchmaker (Dawkins 1987).

This basic idea has been extended by proponents of intelligent design to the concept of "irreducible complexity," whereby if any part of a system were removed, the entire system would fail (Scott 2004). A classic example of the concept of irreducible complexity is a mousetrap, a simple mechanical device consisting of only several parts. If any of these parts were removed, the mousetrap would fail to operate. Thus, a mousetrap is "irreducibly complex." Extending this concept to biological organisms suggests that biochemical structures that are irreducibly complex could not have arisen piece by piece through natural selection, and that such complex structures or phenomena, such as the animal eye or the mechanism of blood clotting, must therefore have been "designed."

One major problem with the argument of irreducible complexity is that complex biological structures *can* arise through natural selection operating on intermediate forms, often for separate purposes, to produce what appears to us today as irreducibly complex (Dawkins 1987; Pennock 1999; Scott 2004). In addition, the function of different structures can change over time, giving an end result that is quite different from an original function. An example of this is the evolution of the jaw joint in the first mammals. As parts of the jaw joint became superfluous, they were then available to evolve through natural selection to serve a different need. In this case, the bones that had made up part of an ancestral reptilian jaw joint but were no longer necessary for the function of chewing served a new purpose—sound reception—and evolved into the inner ear of mammals (Strickberger 2000).

There is also a logical problem with the idea of irreducible complexity. The basic premise is that if we cannot explain something through natural processes, then it must constitute evidence of design. This has been termed the "argument from ignorance" (Scott 2004), whereby an intelligent designer is the explanation for anything that we do not know. If science does not at present have a natural explanation, does that necessarily imply a creator? A simpler explanation is that we lack sufficient evidence for a natural explanation. As such, intelligent design creationism uses the same either-or dichotomy as biblical creation science. Anything that is not explained by evolutionary theory at present must therefore constitute proof of a creation, even though science never claims to have all the answers at any given point in time.

From a scientific perspective, there are no testable hypotheses regarding the specific actions of a creator, or any way to check on the proposed hypothesis. In short, intelligent design creationism is not science. It is important to note that science deals with testable hypotheses about natural processes.

Supernatural actions or entities do not fall within the realm of science. Science does not *require* a creator or creation, but it does not rule them out; creationism, on the other hand, requires both.

Science and Society   Despite scientific, legal, and theological objections, creationism has not gone away. Various surveys have shown a sizable number of people wanting the teaching of intelligent design as an alternative to evolutionary theory in the public schools. There has even been growth of the intelligent design movement among college students (Brumfiel 2005).

One of the most recent battles over public school curriculum took place in Dover, Pennsylvania, when the local school board passed a resolution in 2004 that "students will be made aware of gaps/problems in Darwin's theory and of other theories of evolution including, but not limited to, intelligent design" (*Kitzmiller et al. v. Dover Area School District*, p. 1). The parents of 11 students filed a civil suit that culminated in a federal district court ordering the school to remove references to intelligent design from the biology curriculum. In this ruling, Judge John Jones stated that intelligent design (ID), with its focus on supernatural explanation, was *not* a science (Mervis 2006). Another key point in his decision was the recognition that the strategy of ID, whereby criticism of evolutionary theory equates to proof of a designer, is invalid. The language of the decision states this clearly and unequivocally:

> ID proponents primarily argue for design through negative arguments against evolution, as illustrated by Professor Behe's argument that "irreducibly complex" systems cannot be produced through Darwinian, or any natural, mechanisms . . . However, we believe that arguments against evolution are not arguments for design. Expert testimony revealed that just because scientists cannot explain today how biological systems evolved does not mean that they cannot, and will not, be able to explain them tomorrow. (*Kitzmiller et al. v. Dover Area School District*, pp. 71–72)

The Dover case is no doubt not the last battle, but it is illustrative of the basic problem of educating the public as to what science is and is not.

Perhaps one of the more noticeable casualties of the debate over teaching evolution has been the erosion in science education. Due to continued and often very vocal opposition to the teaching of evolution, educational standards have sometimes been altered to appease anti-evolution forces or to avoid confrontation. In the most recent analysis of state science standards, Gross and colleagues (2005) assigned a "failing" grade for 13 out of 50 states in their treatment of evolution in the public school science curriculum, with an additional 10 states receiving a "marginal" score. Gross and colleagues note that in one state (Kansas), the state school board went further and redefined the very meaning of science to include both natural and supernatural phenomena!

The arguments about creationism and evolution also play a role in individuals' views on ethics, morality, and social philosophy. Many creationists fear that science has eroded our faith in God and led to a decline in morals and values. They imply that science (and evolution in particular) makes statements about human morality. It does not. Science has nothing to say about right and wrong; that is the function of social ethics, philosophies, and religion. Religion and science are important to many people. To put them at odds with each other does both a disservice. It is no surprise that many ministers, priests, and rabbis have joined in the fight against creationism.

Summary

Anthropology is the study of human biological and cultural variation and evolution. Anthropology asks questions that focus on what humans are and what the origins and evolution of, and variation in, their biology and behaviors are, because humans are both biological and cultural organisms. In the United States, anthropology is characterized by four subfields with specific concerns: cultural anthropology (the study of cultural behavior), anthropological archaeology (the study of past cultures), linguistic anthropology (the study of language as a human characteristic), and biological anthropology (the study of human biological evolution and variation).

As a science, anthropology has certain requirements and characteristics. Hypotheses must be testable and verifiable. The main theoretical base of biological anthropology is the theory of evolution. A major feature of evolutionary theory is Darwin's idea of natural selection. In any environment in which resources are necessarily limited, some organisms are more likely to survive and reproduce than others because of their biological characteristics. Those who survive pass these traits on to the next generation.

A current controversy involves the efforts of people who advocate that creationism be taught in public schools. Examination of this field shows that it is not a science at all. Apart from these debates, it should be noted that today there is little conflict between religion and science in the United States. Each perspective addresses different questions in different ways.

Supplemental Readings

Larson, E. J. 1997. *Summer for the Gods: The Scopes Trial and America's Continuing Debate over Science and Religion.* Cambridge, Mass.: Harvard University Press. Winner of the Pulitzer Prize in History, an excellent book that provides a comprehensive description and analysis of the Scopes trial and creationism in the United States.

Pennock, R. T. 1999. *Tower of Babel: The Evidence against the New Creationism.* Cambridge, Mass.: MIT Press. A detailed description and critique of intelligent design creationism.

Scott, E. C. 2004. *Evolution vs. Creationism: An Introduction.* Westport, Conn.: Greenwood Press. An excellent and comprehensive review of the evolution–creationism debate, including excerpts from scientific and creationist writings.

Weiner, J. 1994. *The Beak of the Finch.* New York: Vintage Books. A highly readable account of the work of Peter and Rosemary Grant on natural selection and evolution among finch populations.

VIRTUAL EXPLORATIONS

Visit our textbook-specific online learning center Web site at
www.mhhe.com/relethford7 to access the exercises that follow.

1. **What Do Anthropologists Do?**   **http://anthro.fullerton.edu/
   anthropologists.htm**. For a list of some of the many different types
   of work done by anthropologists, visit California State University-
   Fullerton's "What Do Anthropologists Do?" Web site and examine
   its list.

   ■ Which of these occupations surprised you?
   ■ Is it easy to match the occupation with a particular subfield in
     anthropology?
   ■ How many of these occupations relate specifically to biological
     anthropology? To cultural anthropology?

2. **Anthropology in the News**   **http://www.tamu.edu/anthropology/
   news.html**. Look at Texas A&M University's "Anthropology in the
   News" and review the articles from the past month.

   ■ Which subfields of anthropology can you identify?
   ■ Do you remember reading or hearing about any of these stories?
   ■ Which story do you find of particular interest, and why?
   ■ What are the title and source of the article?
   ■ How does the story relate to humans? Is it about human culture?
     Human biology? Human history? A combination of these?
   ■ How does anthropology provide unique and vital knowledge or
     information on this subject?

3. **Pre-Darwinian Theories**   **http://anthro.palomar.edu/evolve/
   evolve_1.htm**. Go to the "Pre-Darwinian Theories" page from the
   Anthropology Department at Palomar College. Read the page that
   discusses pre-Darwinian evolutionary theories. Now, select two scientists whose work is unfamiliar to you. Additional information
   about these scientists can be found on a link to the University of
   California Museum of Paleontology site:
   http://www.ucmp. berkeley.edu/history/evothought.html.

   ■ What effect did the intellectual climate have on formulating their
     theories?
   ■ What were their contributions to the theory of evolution as we
     know it today?
   ■ Were you at all surprised by their ideas?
   ■ Do you think their work helped provide a foundation for later
     discoveries in evolution? If so, how?
   ■ What was the end result of their conclusions and explanations
     toward the larger problem of explaining? Were they correct?

- Considering modern scientific theories we now accept as true, do you think anyone will ever disprove them? If so, which theory or theories?

4. **PBS Evolution Web site** http://www.pbs.org/wgbh/evolution/educators/teachstuds/svideos.html. The PBS evolution Web site has 7 short videos about evolution available to watch.

  - What do the various topics tell you about the subject of evolution today? Is there controversy? If so, why? What are some of the issues?
  - Choose the issue that you find the most interesting or that helps expand on an important point from your text. You can watch it with QuickTime or RealPlayer.
  - Can you think of an example of evolutionary forces at work that you see in today's world?

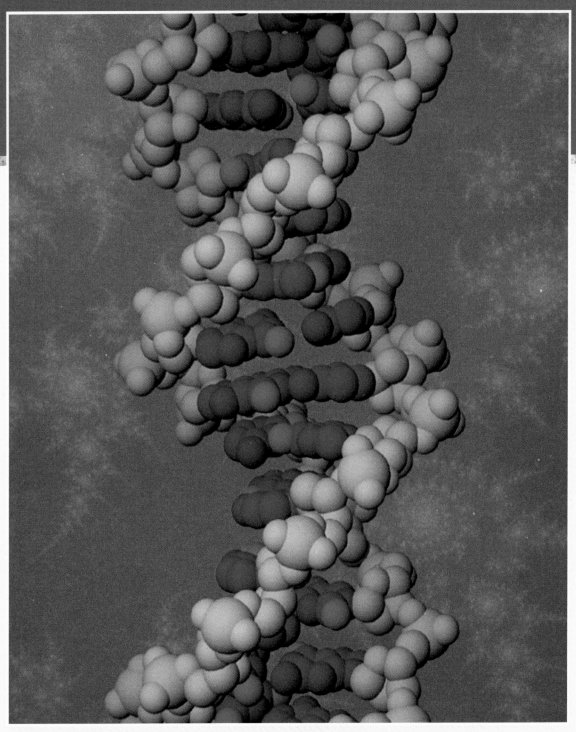

Computer-generated model of DNA, the molecule that provides the genetic code. The study of human genetics includes the biochemical makeup of DNA and the transmission of genes from one generation to the next.

Human Genetics

I n order to understand human biological variation and evolution, we must consider the science of genetics. The study of genetics actually encompasses a number of different areas, depending on the level of analysis. Genetics can be studied on the molecular level, with the focus on what genes are and how they act to produce biological structures.

Genetics also involves the process of inheritance. To what extent are we a reflection of our parents? How are traits inherited? This branch of the field is called **Mendelian genetics,** after the scientist Gregor Mendel (1822–1884), who first worked out many of the principles of inheritance.

Finally, genetics can be studied at the level of a population. Here we are interested in describing the patterns of genetic variation within and among different populations, and their relationship with biological evolution. The changes that take place in the frequency of genes within a population constitute the process of **microevolution.** At the level of the population, we seek the reasons for evolutionary change from one generation to the next. Projection of these findings allows us to better understand the long-term pattern of evolution over thousands and millions of years as well as the origin of new species—**macroevolution.**

MOLECULAR GENETICS

DNA: The Genetic Code

The study of genetics at the molecular level concerns the amazing properties of a molecule known as deoxyribonucleic acid, or **DNA** for short. The DNA molecule provides the codes for biological structures and the means to translate this code. It is perhaps best to think of DNA as a set of instructions for determining the makeup of biological organisms. Quite simply, DNA provides information for building, operating, and repairing organisms. In this context, the process of genetic inheritance is seen as the transmission of this information, or the passing on of the instructions needed for biological structures. Evolution can be viewed in this context as the transfer of information from one generation to the next, along with the possibility that this information will change.

Mendelian genetics The branch of genetics concerned with patterns and processes of inheritance, named after Gregor Mendel, the first scientist to work out these principles.

microevolution Short-term evolutionary change.

macroevolution Long-term evolutionary change.

DNA The molecule that provides the genetic code for biological structures and the means to translate this code.

FIGURE 2.1

Computer representation of the DNA molecule (*left*) and the structure of the DNA molecule (*right*). DNA consists of two strands arranged in a helix joined together by chemical bases.

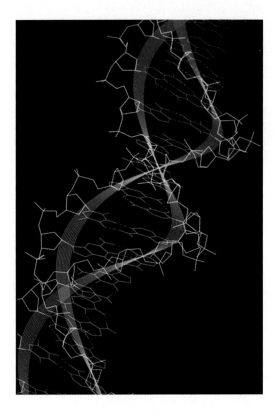

base Chemical units (adenine, thymine, guanine, cytosine) that make up part of the DNA molecule and specify genetic instructions.

An understanding of both the structure and function of DNA is necessary to understand the processes of genetic inheritance and evolution. The exact biochemistry of DNA is beyond the scope of this text, but its basic nature can be discussed in the context of information transfer.

The Structure of DNA In many organisms (including humans), most of the DNA is contained in the nucleus of the cell. However, a small amount of DNA (16,569 base pairs) also exists in the mitochondria, the parts of the cell that produce energy. (See the review of cell biology at the end of this chapter if your high school biology is a bit rusty.) Physically the DNA molecule resembles a ladder that has been twisted into the shape of a helix (Figure 2.1). In biochemical terms, the rungs of the ladder are of major importance. These rungs are made up of chemical units called **bases.** There are four possible types of bases, identified by the first letter of their longer chemical names: A (adenine), T (thymine), G (guanine), and C (cytosine). These bases form the "alphabet" used in specifying and carrying out genetic instructions.

All biological structures, from nerve cells to blood cells to bone cells, are made up predominantly of proteins. Proteins in turn are made up of amino acids, whose chemical properties allow them to bond together to form proteins. Each amino acid is coded for by three of the four chemical bases just discussed. For example, the base sequence CGA provides the code for the amino acid alanine, and the base sequence TTT codes for the

TABLE 2.1   DNA Base Sequences for Amino Acids

First Base	Second Base			
	A	T	C	G
A	AAA Phenylalanine	ATA Tyrosine	ACA Cysteine	AGA Serine
	AAT Leucine	ATT Stop	ACT Stop	AGT Serine
	AAC Leucine	ATC Stop	ACC Tryptophan	AGC Serine
	AAG Phenylalanine	ATG Tyrosine	ACG Cysteine	AGG Serine
T	TAA Isoleucine	TTA Asparagine	TCA Serine	TGA Threonine
	TAT Isoleucine	TTT Lysine	TCT Arginine	TGT Threonine
	TAC Methionine	TTC Lysine	TCC Arginine	TGC Threonine
	TAG Isoleucine	TTG Asparagine	TCG Serine	TGG Threonine
C	CAA Valine	CTA Aspartic acid	CCA Glycine	CGA Alanine
	CAT Valine	CTT Glutamic acid	CCT Glycine	CGT Alanine
	CAC Valine	CTC Glutamic acid	CCC Glycine	CGC Alanine
	CAG Valine	CTG Aspartic acid	CCG Glycine	CGG Alanine
G	GAA Leucine	GTA Histidine	GCA Arginine	GGA Proline
	GAT Leucine	GTT Glutamine	GCT Arginine	GGT Proline
	GAC Leucine	GTC Glutamine	GCC Arginine	GGC Proline
	GAG Leucine	GTG Histidine	GCG Arginine	GGG Proline

Rows refer to the first of the three bases, and columns refer to the second of the three bases. These base sequences are for the DNA molecule. The 64 different combinations code for 20 amino acids and one termination sequence ("Stop"). To convert to messenger RNA, substitute U for A, A for T, G for C, and C for G. To convert to transfer RNA, substitute U for A.

amino acid lysine. There are 64 (4^3) possible codes that can be specified, using some combination of three bases. This might not seem like a lot, but in fact there are only 20 amino acids that need to be specified by the genetic code. The three-base code provides more than enough possibilities to code for these amino acids. In fact, some amino acids have several different codes; alanine, for example, can be specified by the base sequences CGA, CGT, CGC, and CGG. Some of the base sequences, such as ATT, act to form "punctuation" for the genetic instructions; that is, they provide the code to start or stop "messages." A list of the different DNA sequences is shown in Table 2.1.

The ability of four different bases, taken three at a time, to specify all the information needed for the synthesis of proteins is astounding. It boggles the mind that the diverse structure of complex protein molecules can be specified with only a four-letter "alphabet." As an analogy, consider the way in which computers work. All computer operations, from word processing to complex mathematical simulations, ultimately are translated into a set of instructions that use only a simple two-letter alphabet—on or off! These two instructions make up a larger set of codes that provide information on computer operations. These operations are combined to generate computer languages that can be used to write a variety of programs.

The ability of the DNA molecule to use the different amino acid codes derives from a simple property of the chemical bases. The base A bonds with the base T, and the base G bonds with the base C. This chemical property enables the DNA molecule to carry out a number of functions, including making copies of itself and directing the synthesis of proteins.

Functions of DNA   The DNA molecule can make copies of itself. Remember that the DNA molecule is made up of two strands that form the long arms of the ladder. Each rung of the ladder consists of two bases. If one part of the rung contains the base A, then the other part of the rung will contain the base T because A and T bond together.

To understand how DNA can make copies of itself, consider the following sequence of bases on one strand of the DNA molecule—GGTCTC. Because A and T bond together and G and C bond together, the corresponding sequence of bases on the other strand of the DNA molecule is CCAGAG. The DNA molecule can separate into two distinct strands. Once separate, each strand attracts free-floating bases. The strand GGTCTC attracts the bases CCAGAG, and the strand CCAGAG attracts the bases GGTCTC. When the new bases have attached themselves to the original strands, the result is two identical DNA molecules. This process is diagrammed in Figure 2.2. Keep in mind that this description is somewhat oversimplified—in reality, the process is biochemically much more complex.

The ability of the DNA molecule to control protein synthesis also involves the attraction of complementary bases, but with the help of another molecule—ribonucleic acid, or **RNA** for short. In simple terms, RNA serves as the messenger and decoder for the information in the DNA molecule. One major difference between DNA and RNA is that in RNA the base A attracts a base called U (uracil) instead of T.

Consider the DNA base sequence GGT. In protein synthesis, the DNA molecule separates into two strands, and one strand (containing CCA) becomes inactive. The active strand, GGT, attracts free-floating bases to form a strand of **messenger RNA.** Because A bonds with T and G bonds with C, this strand consists of the sequence CCA. The strand then travels to the site of protein synthesis. Once there, the strand of messenger RNA transfers its information via **transfer RNA,** which is a free-floating molecule. The sequence of messenger RNA containing the sequence CCA attracts a transfer RNA molecule with a complementary sequence—GGU. The result is that the amino acid proline (specified by the RNA sequence GGU or the DNA sequence GGT) is included in the chain of amino acids making up a particular protein. To summarize, one strand of the DNA molecule produces the complementary strand of messenger RNA, which attracts a complementary strand of transfer RNA, which carries the specified amino acid. This process is illustrated for the DNA sequence GGT in Figure 2.3.

This simplified discussion shows the basic nature of the structure and functions of the DNA molecule. More advanced discussion can be found in most genetics textbooks. It is interesting to note that the conventional view of the relationship between DNA, RNA, and proteins has increasingly been

RNA The molecule that functions to carry out the instructions for protein synthesis specified by the DNA molecule.

messenger RNA The form of RNA that transports the genetic instructions from the DNA molecule to the site of protein synthesis.

transfer RNA A free-floating molecule that is attracted to a strand of messenger RNA, resulting in the synthesis of a protein chain.

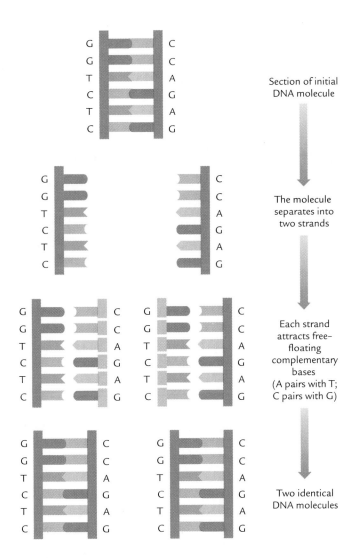

FIGURE 2.2

Replication of the DNA molecule.

Section of initial DNA molecule

The molecule separates into two strands

Each strand attracts free-floating complementary bases (A pairs with T; C pairs with G)

Two identical DNA molecules

shown to be more complex than once thought (Pearson 2006). For our purposes, however, the broad view will suffice. If we consider DNA as a "code," we can then look at the processes of transmission and change of information without actually having to consider the exact biochemical mechanisms.

Chromosomes and Genes

As noted above, most of the DNA is contained in the nucleus—and hence known as **nuclear DNA.** The nuclear DNA sequences are bound together by proteins in long strands, called **chromosomes,** that are found within the nucleus of each cell. With the exception of those in the sex cells (egg and sperm), chromosomes occur in pairs. Most body cells contain both members of these pairs. Different species have different numbers of chromosomes. For example, humans have 23 pairs, chimpanzees have 24, fruit flies have 4, and certain plant species have thousands. There is no relationship

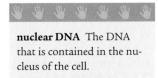

nuclear DNA The DNA that is contained in the nucleus of the cell.

chromosome A long strand of DNA sequences.

1. Section of the initial DNA molecule.

2. The DNA molecule temporarily separates, and one strand becomes active. Free-floating complementary bases (with U replacing T) are attracted to form messenger RNA.

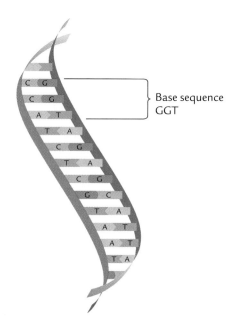

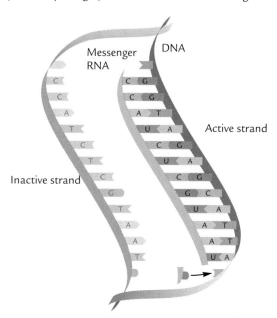

3. Messenger RNA travels to the ribosomes, the site of protein synthesis. As ribosomes move along messenger RNA, transfer RNA picks up amino acids and lines up according to the base complements. Each transfer RNA molecule transfers its amino acid to the next active transfer RNA as it leaves, resulting in a chain of amino acids.

4. This chain of amino acids forms a protein.

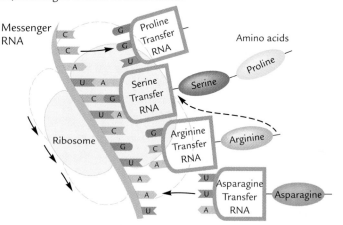

FIGURE 2.3

Protein synthesis.

between the number of chromosome pairs a species has and its intelligence or biological complexity.

With certain exceptions, each cell in the human body contains a complete set of chromosomes and DNA. Nerve cells contain the same DNA as bone cells, for example, and vice versa. Some type of regulation takes place

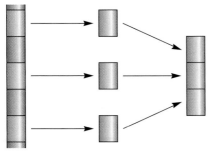

FIGURE 2.4

Diagram of messenger RNA (mRNA) showing regions of coding (exons) and noncoding (introns). The introns are removed from the pre-mRNA, and the exons then splice together to form the mature mRNA.

Pre-mRNA consists of exons (green) and introns (red).

Introns are removed.

Exons are spliced together to form mature mRNA.

within different cells to ensure that only certain genes are expressed in the right places, but the exact nature of this regulation is not known completely at present.

Genes   The term *gene* can have a number of different meanings depending on context. Here, **gene** refers to a DNA sequence that includes the code for a functional polypeptide (a compound containing many amino acids) or RNA product (Strachan and Read 1996); that is, a section of DNA that has an identifiable function, such as the gene that determines a particular blood group. One example, referred to in later chapters, is the **hemoglobin** molecule in your blood (which transports oxygen), which is made up of four protein chains. For each chain, a section of DNA (the gene) contains the genetic code for the proteins in that chain.

Not all DNA contains genes; much of our DNA is made up of noncoding sequences of DNA whose purpose (if any) is not known. Even within genes, not all of the DNA sequence results in a polypeptide product. The DNA sequence of a gene can contain both sections that code for amino acids that make up proteins—called **exons**—and sections that do not code for amino acids that make up proteins—called **introns.** The formation of mature RNA involves removal of the noncoding sections and splicing together of the coding sections (Figure 2.4).

Aside from the manufacture of proteins, another function of genes is the regulation of biological processes. For example, in many humans, the enzyme needed to digest milk sugar stops being produced several years after birth. Or consider the fact that sexual maturation in humans occurs during adolescence and not in infancy. The expression of many biological characteristics is regulated to take effect at particular times. Genes that are responsible for this regulation are known as **regulatory genes,** and they act by turning other genes on or off at the appropriate time.

Regulatory genes may have great evolutionary significance. For example, regulatory genes may help explain the great physical differences between chimpanzees and humans even though more than 98 percent of our structural

gene A DNA sequence that codes for a functional polypeptide or RNA product.

hemoglobin The molecule in blood cells that transports oxygen.

exon A section of DNA that codes for the amino acids that make up proteins. It is contrasted with an intron.

intron A section of DNA that does not code for the amino acids that make up proteins. It is contrasted with an exon.

regulatory gene A gene that codes for the regulation of biological processes such as growth and development.

genes are identical. The major genetic difference between humans and chimpanzees may be caused by regulatory genes, which act on the timing of growth and development and could lead to differences in brain size, facial structures, and other physical features.

A possible example of regulatory genes involves the absence of teeth in birds. Evolutionary analysis has concluded that modern birds evolved from primitive reptiles. One major change in this evolution is that birds have no teeth (other than the egg tooth they use in hatching). In 1980, however, scientists were able to induce the tissue of a hen to grow teeth! Teeth are produced by certain outer embryonic tissues that form the enamel and by other inner tissues that form the dentin underneath. In what appears at first to be a bizarre experiment, Kollar and Fisher (1980) combined the outer tissues of a hen with the inner tissues of a mouse. These grafts produced dentin and teeth. Modern birds lack the necessary type of tissue to form dentin but still have the capacity to form it when we combine their tissue in the laboratory with the appropriate tissue from another animal (the mouse, in this case). This experiment shows that the genetic code for teeth still exists in birds, but it is turned off, most likely by some combination of regulatory genes.

Another example suggesting the action of regulatory genes involves the number of toes in horses. Modern horses have a single toe, although occasionally horses are born with two or three toes (Gould 1983). Apparently, horses still have the genetic code for additional toes, but these instructions are turned off.

During the 1980s, a group of regulatory genes known as **homeobox genes** was discovered. These genes encode a sequence of 60 amino acids that regulate embryonic development. Specifically, they subdivide a developing embryo into different regions from head to tail that then form limbs and other structures. One fascinating aspect of this discovery is that these genes are similar in many organisms, such as insects, mice, and humans. Preliminary research suggests that the process of embryonic development into head, trunk, and tail may have occurred only once in evolution (De Robertis et al. 1990). Another example of homeobox genes was found in a study of the development of wings in insects. Some insects have wings and some do not. One analysis showed that wings developed *once* in the common ancestor of all insects, but in some later forms, homeobox genes repressed their development (Carroll et al. 1995). In other words, even wingless insects may carry the genetic code for wings—it has simply been "switched off."

Mitosis and Meiosis   The DNA molecule provides for the transmission of genetic information. Production of proteins and regulation are only two aspects of information transfer. Because organisms start life as a single cell that subsequently multiplies, it is essential that the genetic information within the initial cell be transferred to all future cells. The ability of DNA to replicate itself is involved in the process of cell replication, known as **mitosis** (Figure 2.5). When a cell divides, each chromosome duplicates and then splits. Each chromosome has replicated itself so that when the cell finishes dividing, the result is two cells with the full set of chromosomes.

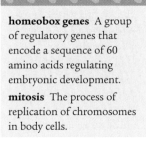

homeobox genes A group of regulatory genes that encode a sequence of 60 amino acids regulating embryonic development.

mitosis The process of replication of chromosomes in body cells.

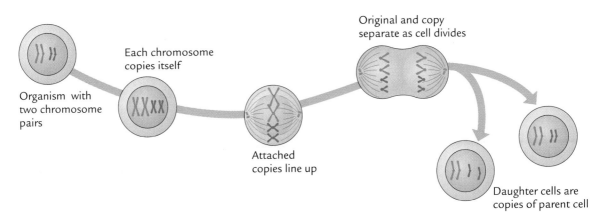

Organism with two chromosome pairs

Each chromosome copies itself

Attached copies line up

Original and copy separate as cell divides

Daughter cells are copies of parent cell

FIGURE 2.5

The process of mitosis, the formation of body cells. Each chromosome copies itself, the attached copies line up in the cell, and the original and copy split when the cell divides. The result is two identical cells. (From *Human Antiquity: An Introduction to Physical Anthropology and Archaeology,* 4th ed., by Kenneth Feder and Michael Park, Fig. 4.4. Copyright © 2001 by Mayfield Publishing Company. Reprinted by permission of The McGraw-Hill Companies.)

The process is different when information is passed on from one generation to the next. The genetic code is passed on from parents to offspring through the sex cells—the sperm in males and the egg in females. The sex cells, however, contain not the full set of chromosomes but only one chromosome from each pair (i.e., only one-half of the set). Whereas your other body cells have a total of 46 chromosomes (2 each for 23 pairs), your sex cells contain only 23 chromosomes (1 from each pair). When you have a child, you contribute 23 chromosomes and your mate contributes 23 chromosomes. Your child then has the normal complement of 46 chromosomes in 23 pairs.

Sex cells are created through the process of **meiosis** (Figure 2.6). In this process, chromosomes first replicate themselves, then the cell divides and then divides again without replicating. For sperm cells, four sex cells are produced from the initial set of 23 pairs of chromosomes. The process is similar in egg cells, except that only one of the four cells is functional.

The process of meiosis is extremely important in understanding genetic inheritance. Because only one of each pair of chromosomes is found in a functional sex cell, this means that a person contributes half of his or her genes to his or her offspring. The other half of their offspring's genes comes from the other parent. Usually, each human child has a full set of 23 chromosome pairs, one of each pair from each parent (Figure 2.7).

The Human Genome Project

The total DNA sequence of an organism is known as its **genome.** In humans, the genome is approximately 3 billion base pairs in length. Here is one way to appreciate the total length of the human genome: If you were to read the sequence aloud (A, T, T, etc.) at the rate of one base per second, it would take you close to 100 years to finish, assuming you never slept or did anything else. Over the past 15 years, the growth of new technologies has enabled researchers to completely sequence the genomes for a number of organisms, one of which is fruit flies.

meiosis The creation of sex cells by replication of chromosomes followed by cell division.

genome The total DNA sequence of an organism.

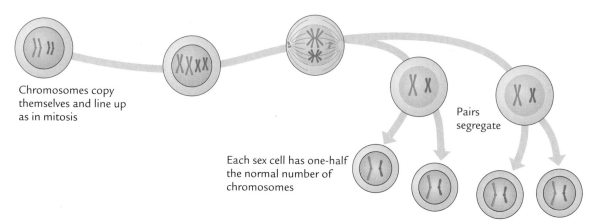

Chromosomes copy themselves and line up as in mitosis

Pairs segregate

Each sex cell has one-half the normal number of chromosomes

FIGURE 2.6

The process of meiosis, the formation of sex cells. Meiosis begins in the same way as mitosis: Each chromosome makes a copy of itself. The pairs of chromosomes then segregate, forming four sex cells, each with one chromosome rather than a pair of chromosomes. (Adapted from *Human Antiquity: An Introduction to Physical Anthropology and Archaeology*, 4th ed., by Kenneth Feder and Michael Park, Fig. 4.4. Copyright © 2001 by Mayfield Publishing Company. Reprinted by permission of The McGraw-Hill Companies.)

The Human Genome Project (HGP) began in 1990 as an international effort to sequence the human genome. By the end of 2000, this sequencing was more than 95 percent complete. Preliminary reports were published in early 2001 by two different groups—the International Human Genome Sequencing Consortium (2001) and another group led by Celera Genomics (Venter et al. 2001). The entire sequence was completed in April 2003, 2 years ahead of schedule and 50 years after the initial description of the molecular structure of DNA by Watson and Crick (Collins et al. 2003). Although this is an incredible achievement, the sequencing of the human genome is just the start of a new era in genetics research. Even though the actual genetic code is sequenced, we are far from understanding how all of it operates or what the relationship of different genes to actual biological structures is.

FIGURE 2.7

All 23 pairs of chromosomes typically found in a human being. This set of chromosomes came from a man—note that the 23rd pair has an X chromosome and a Y chromosome.

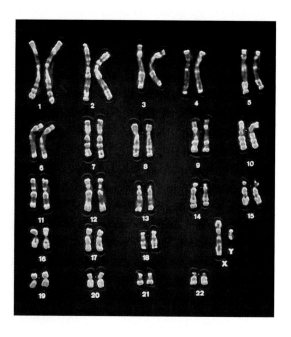

Preliminary analyses of the human genome have yielded some interesting results. Only a small fraction of our genome, roughly 1.1–1.5 percent, actually codes for proteins (Pennisi 2001). The remaining DNA does not contain coding DNA sequences and has often been referred to as "junk DNA." This label may simply be a reflection of our uncertainty, however, as some of this noncoding DNA may serve some purpose, such as the sequences that determine whether certain genes are turned on or off (Vogel 2001; Makalowski 2003).

One of the most unexpected results to date is the estimated number of genes in the human genome. Previous work had suggested a total of roughly 100,000 genes, but the Human Genome Project has yielded estimates of roughly 30,000 genes, which is only twice the number of genes found in worms or flies (International Human Genome Sequencing Consortium 2001). However, human genes are more complex and are able to serve multiple functions. Rather than the older view that a single gene codes for a single protein, it appears that human genes can code for three proteins on average by using different combinations of exons in a given gene (Pennisi 2001).

Another avenue of research in the human genome is the comparison of the human genetic sequence with other organisms. Of particular interest in the study of human evolution is the DNA sequence of our closest living relatives, the African apes (discussed further in Chapters 6 and 7). A significant advance came in 2005 with a draft sequence of the chimpanzee genome (Chimpanzee Sequencing and Analysis Consortium 2005). Work is also under way for sequencing the genome of two other apes—the gorilla and the orangutan (Dennis 2005). Such data can provide us with valuable information regarding the specific genetic differences that have arisen since we and our ape relatives shared a common ancestor, which in turn can give us clues regarding the origin of unique human characteristics (discussed further in Chapter 7).

Although the news media have focused on possible biomedical applications of the findings of the Human Genome Project, such as genetic therapies for disease, keep in mind that we are still far from understanding the complexity of our genetic code. In addition, the genetic sequence tells us only a portion of the story; we also need to understand how genetic information is expressed in different environments. It would be overly simplistic to view genetics, and genetics alone, as determining our biology or behavior. Still, it is likely that continuing work on the human genome will contribute to our understanding of such complex issues and provide us with a clearer understanding of genetics in relationship to morphology, disease, behavior, population history, and other aspects of humanity.

MENDELIAN GENETICS

Many of the facts about genetic inheritance were discovered over a century before the structure of DNA was known. Although people knew where babies came from and noted the close resemblance of parents and children, the

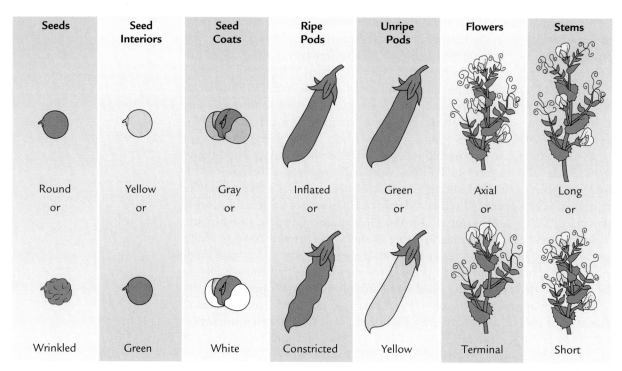

Seeds	Seed Interiors	Seed Coats	Ripe Pods	Unripe Pods	Flowers	Stems
Round or	Yellow or	Gray or	Inflated or	Green or	Axial or	Long or
Wrinkled	Green	White	Constricted	Yellow	Terminal	Short

FIGURE 2.8

The seven phenotypic characteristics investigated by Gregor Mendel in his experiments on breeding in pea plants. Each of the seven traits has two distinct phenotypes.

mechanisms of inheritance were unknown until the nineteenth century. An Austrian priest, Gregor Mendel (1822–1884), carried out an extensive series of experiments in plant breeding. His carefully tabulated results provided the basis of what we know about the mechanisms of genetic inheritance.

Before Mendel's research, it was commonly assumed that inheritance involved the blending together of genetic information in the egg and sperm. The genetic material was thought to mix together in the same way that different color paints mix together. Mendel's experiments showed a different pattern of inheritance—that the genetic information is inherited in discrete units (genes). These genes do not blend together in an offspring.

In one experiment, Mendel crossed pea plants whose seeds were yellow with pea plants whose seeds were green (Figure 2.8). Under the idea of blending, one might expect all offspring to have mustard-colored seeds—a mixture of the yellow and green. In reality, Mendel found that all the offspring plants had yellow seeds. This discovery suggested that somehow one trait (yellow seed color) dominated in its effects.

When Mendel crossed the plants in this new generation, he found that some of their offspring had yellow seeds and some had green seeds. Somehow the genetic information for green seeds had been hidden for a generation and then reappeared. Mendel counted how many there were of each color. The ratio of plants with yellow seeds to those with green seeds was very close to 3:1. This finding suggested to Mendel that a regular process occurred during inheritance that could be explained in terms of simple mathematical principles. With these and other results, Mendel formulated several principles of inheritance. Though Mendel's work remained virtually unknown during his lifetime, his work was rediscovered in 1900. In recognition of his accomplishments, the science of genetic inheritance is called *Mendelian genetics.*

Genotypes and Phenotypes

The specific position of a gene or DNA sequence on a chromosome is called a **locus** (plural loci). The alternative forms of a gene or DNA sequence at a locus are called **alleles.** For example, a number of different genetic systems control the types of molecules present on the surface of red blood cells. One of these blood groups, known as the MN system, determines whether or not you have M molecules, N molecules, or both on the surface of your red blood cells. The MN system has two forms, or alleles—*M* and *N.* Another blood group system, the ABO system, has three alleles—*A, B,* and *O.* Even though three different forms of this gene are found in the human species, each individual has only two genes at the ABO locus. Some genetic loci have only one allele, some have two, and some have three or more.

Mendel's Law of Segregation   The genetic basis of any trait is determined by an allele from each parent. At any given locus there are two alleles, one on each member of the chromosome pair. One allele came from the mother, and one allele came from the father. Within body cells, alleles occur in pairs, and when sex cells are formed, only one of each pair is passed on, according to **Mendel's Law of Segregation.**

   The two alleles at a locus in an individual specify the **genotype,** the genetic endowment of an individual. The two alleles might be the same form or might be different. If the alleles from both parents are the same, the genotype is **homozygous.** If the alleles from the parents are different, the genotype is **heterozygous.**

   The actual observable trait is known as the **phenotype.** The relationship between genotype and phenotype is affected by the relationship between the two alleles present at any locus. If the genotype is homozygous, both alleles contain the same genetic information. But what happens in heterozygotes, where the two alleles are different?

Dominant and Recessive Alleles   In a heterozygote, an allele is **dominant** when it masks the effect of the other allele at a given locus. The opposite of a dominant allele is a **recessive** allele, whose effect may be masked. A simple example helps make these concepts clearer. One genetic trait in human beings is the ability to taste certain substances, including a chemical known as PTC. The ability to taste PTC appears to be controlled by a single locus and is also affected to some extent by environmental factors such as diet. There are two alleles for the PTC-tasting trait: the allele *T,* which is also called the "taster" allele, and the allele *t,* which is also called the "nontaster" allele. Given these two alleles, three combinations of alleles can be present in an individual. A person could have the *T* allele from both parents, which would

locus The specific location of a gene or DNA sequence on a chromosome.

allele The alternative form of a gene or DNA sequence that occurs at a given locus. Some loci have only one allele, some have two, and some have many alternative forms. Alleles occur in pairs, one on each chromosome.

Mendel's Law of Segregation Sex cells contain one of each pair of alleles.

genotype The genetic endowment of an individual from the two alleles present at a given locus.

homozygous When both alleles at a given locus are identical.

heterozygous When the two alleles at a given locus are different.

phenotype The observable appearance of a given genotype in the organism.

dominant allele An allele that masks the effect of the other allele (which is recessive) in a heterozygous genotype.

recessive allele An allele whose effect is masked by the other allele (which is dominant) in a heterozygous genotype.

TABLE 2.2	Genotypes and Phenotypes for PTC Tasting
Genotype	*Phenotype*
TT	Taster
Tt	Taster
tt	Nontaster

Because *T* is dominant, the genotypes *TT* and *Tt* both produce the taster phenotype. This example is somewhat oversimplified because in reality the phenotype can also be affected by diet.

give the genotype *TT*. A person could have a *t* allele from both parents, giving the genotype *tt*. Both *TT* and *tt* are homozygous genotypes because both alleles are the same. The third possible genotype occurs when the allele from one parent is *T* and the allele from the other parent is *t*. This gives the heterozygous genotype of *Tt*. It does not matter which parent provided the *T* allele and which provided the *t* allele; the genotype is the same in both cases.

What phenotype is associated with each genotype? The phenotype is affected both by the relationship of the two alleles and by the environment. For the moment, let us ignore possible environmental effects. Consider the *T* allele as providing instructions that allow tasting and the *t* allele as providing instructions for nontasting. If the genotype is *TT,* then both alleles code for tasting, and the phenotype is obviously "taster." Likewise, if the genotype is *tt,* then both alleles code for nontasting, and the phenotype is "nontaster." What of the heterozygote *Tt*? One allele codes for tasting and one codes for nontasting. Does this mean that both will be expressed and that a person will have the tasting ability, but not to as great a degree as a person with genotype *TT*? Or does it mean that only one of the alleles is expressed? If so, which one?

There is no way you can answer this question using only the data provided so far. You must know if either the *T* or *t* allele is dominant, and this can be determined only through experimentation. For this trait, it turns out that the *T* allele is dominant and the *t* allele is recessive. When both alleles are present in a genotype, the *T* allele masks the effect of the *t* allele. Therefore, a person with the genotype *Tt* has the "taster" phenotype (Table 2.2). The relationship between genotype and phenotype does not take into consideration known environmental effects on PTC tasting. Under certain types of diet, some "tasters" will show less ability to taste weaker concentrations of PTC.

The action of dominant and recessive alleles explains why Mendel's second-generation pea plants all had yellow seeds. The allele for yellow seed color is dominant, and the allele for green seed color is recessive.

Dominance and recessiveness refer only to the effect an allele has in producing a phenotype. These terms say nothing about the frequency or value of an allele. Dominant alleles can be common or rare, harmful or helpful.

TABLE 2.3	Genotypes and Phenotypes of the MN Blood Group System

Genotype	Phenotype
MM	M molecules
MN	M and N molecules
NN	N molecules

The *M* and *N* alleles are codominant, so they are both expressed in the heterozygote.

TABLE 2.4	Genotypes and Phenotypes of the ABO System

The ABO system has three alleles (*A, B, O*) that code for the type of molecule on the surface of the red blood cells (A, B, and O molecules). The *A* and *B* alleles are codominant, and the *O* allele is recessive to both *A* and *B*.

Genotype	Phenotype
AA	A
AO	A
BB	B
BO	B
AB	AB
OO	O

Note: There are also different forms of the *A* allele not shown here (A_1, A_2).

Codominant Alleles   Some alleles are **codominant,** meaning that when two different alleles are present in a genotype, both are expressed. That is, neither allele is dominant or recessive. One example of a codominant genetic system in humans is the MN blood group, mentioned previously. There are two alleles—*M*, which codes for the production of M molecules, and *N*, which codes for the production of N molecules. Therefore, there are three possible genotypes: *MM, MN,* and *NN*.

The phenotypes for the homozygous genotypes are easy to determine. Individuals with the genotype *MM* will have two alleles coding for the production of M molecules and will have the M molecule phenotype. Likewise, individuals with the genotype *NN* will have two *N* alleles and will have the N molecule phenotype. But what of the heterozygote genotype *MN*? Again, there is no way to answer this question without knowing the pattern of dominance. Experimentation has shown that the *M* and *N* alleles are codominant. When both are present (genotype *MN*), both are expressed. Therefore, an individual with genotype *MN* will produce both M and N molecules. Their phenotype is MN, indicating the presence of both molecules (Table 2.3).

In complex genetic systems with more than two alleles, some alleles may be dominant and some may be codominant. A good example of dominance and codominance in the same system is the ABO blood group. The alleles, genotypes, and phenotypes of this system are described in Table 2.4.

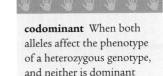

codominant When both alleles affect the phenotype of a heterozygous genotype, and neither is dominant over the other.

Predicting Offspring Distributions

When parents each contribute a sex cell, they are passing on to their offspring only one allele at each locus. The possible genotypes and phenotypes of the offspring reflect a 50 percent chance of transmittal for any given allele

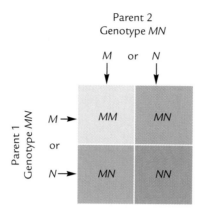

FIGURE 2.9

Inheritance of MN blood group genotypes for two parents, both with MN genotype.

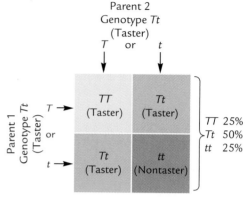

FIGURE 2.10

Inheritance of PTC-tasting genotypes and phenotypes for two parents, both with the *Tt* genotype. Phenotypes are shown in parentheses.

of a parent. This simple statement of probability allows prediction of the likely distribution of genotypes and phenotypes among the offspring.

Figure 2.9 illustrates this method using the MN blood group system for two hypothetical parents, each with the genotype *MN*. Each parent has a 50 percent chance of passing on an *M* allele and a 50 percent chance of passing on an *N* allele. Given these probabilities, we expect one out of four offspring (25 percent) to have genotype *MM*, and therefore phenotype M. In two out of four cases (50 percent), we expect the offspring to have genotype *MN*, and therefore phenotype MN. Finally, in one out of four cases (25 percent), we expect the offspring to have genotype *NN*, and therefore phenotype N. Of course, different parental genotypes will give a different set of offspring probabilities.

Remember that these distributions give the expected probabilities. The exact distributions will not always occur because each offspring is an independent event. If the hypothetical couple first has a child with the genotype *MN*, this will not influence the genotype of their next child. The distributions give the proportions expected for a very large number of offspring.

To help understand the difference between expected and actual distribution, consider coin flipping. If you flip a coin, you expect to get heads 50 percent of the time and tails 50 percent of the time. If you flip 10 coins one after another, you expect to get five heads and five tails. You may, however, get four heads and six tails, or six heads and four tails, and so on.

Analysis of possible offspring shows that recessive alleles can produce an interesting effect: It is possible for children to have a different phenotype from either parent. For example, consider two parents, both with the genotype *Tt* for the PTC-tasting locus. Both parents have the "taster" phenotype. What genotypes and phenotypes will their children be likely to have? The expected genotype distribution is 25 percent *TT*, 50 percent *Tt*, and 25 percent *tt* (Figure 2.10).

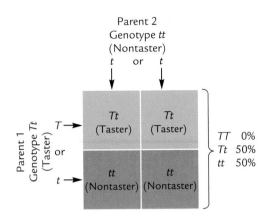

Parent 2
Genotype *tt*
(Nontaster)
t or *t*

Parent 1 Genotype *Tt* (Taster)

T →

or

t →

| *Tt* (Taster) | *Tt* (Taster) |
| *tt* (Nontaster) | *tt* (Nontaster) |

TT 0%
Tt 50%
tt 50%

FIGURE 2.11

Inheritance of PTC-tasting geno-types and phenotypes for two parents, one with the *Tt* genotype and one with the *tt* genotype. Phe-notypes are shown in parentheses.

Given this distribution of genotypes, what is the probable distribution of phenotypes? Genotypes *TT* and *Tt* are both "tasters," and therefore 75 per-cent of the children are expected to also be "tasters." Twenty-five percent of the children, however, are expected to have the genotype *tt*, and therefore will have the "nontaster" phenotype. These children would have a different phenotype from either parent. An additional example, also using the PTC-tasting locus, is shown in Figure 2.11, which looks at the genotype and phenotype offspring distributions in the case where one parent has the *Tt* genotype and the other has the *tt* genotype.

A recessive trait, then, can remain hidden in one generation. This fact has great implications for genetic disease. For example, the disease cystic fibrosis occurs when a person is homozygous for a recessive allele. Therefore, two parents who have the heterozygous genotype do not manifest the dis-ease, but they have a 25 percent chance of giving birth to a child who has the recessive homozygous condition, and therefore the disease.

Chromosomes and Inheritance

Alleles occur in pairs. Mendel showed that when alleles are passed on from parents to offspring, only one of each pair is contributed by each parent. The specific chromosome at any pair that is passed on is random. There is a 50 percent chance of either chromosome being passed on each time a sex cell is created.

Mendel's Law of Independent Assortment Mendel's experiments revealed another aspect of probability in inheritance and the creation of sex cells. **Mendel's Law of Independent Assortment** states that the segregation of any pair of chromosomes does not influence the segregation of any other pair of chromosomes. In other words, chromosomes from separate pairs are inherited independently.

For example, imagine an organism with three chromosome pairs that we will label 1, 2, and 3. To keep the members of each pair straight in our minds, we will also label each chromosome of each pair as A or B. This hypothetical

Mendel's Law of Independent Assortment
The segregation of any pair of chromosomes does not affect the probability of segregation for other pairs of chromosomes.

FIGURE 2.12

Schematic diagram illustrating Mendel's Law of Independent Assortment. This hypothetical organism has three pairs of chromosomes (1, 2, and 3), each of which has two chromosomes indicated by the letters A and B. For example, the chromosomes for chromosome pair 1 are 1A and 1B. During meiosis, only one of each pair is passed on to a sex cell, that is, 1A or 1B, 2A or 2B, and 3A or 3B. The probability of a particular chromosome being passed on from any pair is independent of the other pairs, so there are eight possible combinations.

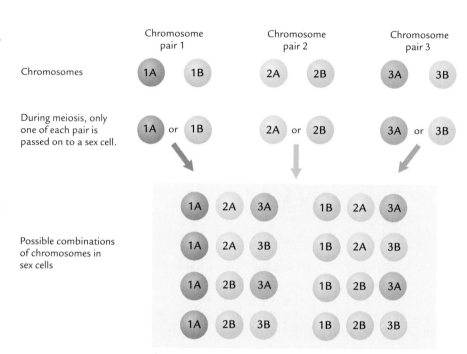

organism has six chromosomes: 1A, 1B, 2A, 2B, 3A, and 3B. During the creation of a sex cell, the 1A chromosome has a 50 percent chance of occurring, and so does the 1B chromosome. This same logic applies to chromosome pairs 2 and 3. According to Mendel's Law of Independent Assortment, the segregation of one pair of chromosomes does not affect the segregation of any other pair of chromosomes. It is just as likely to have a sex cell containing chromosomes 1A, 2A, and 3A as it is to have a sex cell containing chromosomes 1A, 2A, and 3B. There are eight possible and equally likely outcomes for the sex cells: 1A-2A-3A, 1A-2A-3B, 1A-2B-3A, 1A-2B-3B, 1B-2A-3A, 1B-2A-3B, 1B-2B-3A, and 1B-2B-3B (Figure 2.12). Given that any individual could have any one of the eight possible sex cells from *both* parents, the total number of combinations of offspring in this hypothetical organism is $8 \times 8 = 64$.

Independent assortment provides a powerful mechanism for shuffling different combinations of chromosomes, and thus introduces great potential for genetic diversity. In humans, who have 23 chromosome pairs, the numbers are even more impressive. From any given individual, there are $2^{23} = 8,388,608$ possible combinations of chromosomes in sex cells. This means that two parents could produce a maximum of 70,368,744,177,664 genetically unique offspring!

Linkage   A major implication of Mendel's Law of Independent Assortment is that genes are inherited independently. This is true only to the extent that genes are on different chromosomes. Remember, it is the pairs of chromosomes that separate during meiosis, not each individual pair of alleles. When alleles are on the same chromosome, they are inherited together, in a process

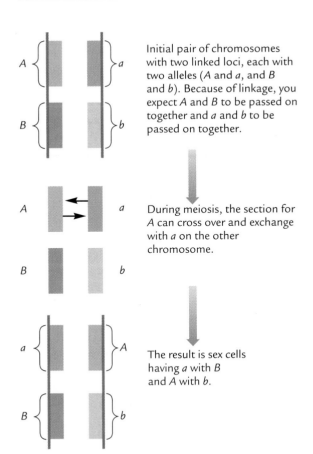

FIGURE 2.13

Crossing over in chromosomes.

Initial pair of chromosomes with two linked loci, each with two alleles (*A* and *a*, and *B* and *b*). Because of linkage, you expect *A* and *B* to be passed on together and *a* and *b* to be passed on together.

During meiosis, the section for *A* can cross over and exchange with *a* on the other chromosome.

The result is sex cells having *a* with *B* and *A* with *b*.

called **linkage.** Linked alleles are not inherited independently because they are, by definition, on the same chromosome.

Recombination   When loci are linked, they will tend to be inherited as a unit. As an example, imagine that two loci, each with two alleles (*A* and *a* for the first locus and *B* and *b* for the second), are located on the same chromosome. Further, imagine that one of the chromosomes contains the *A* allele for the first locus and the *B* allele for the second one, and that the other chromosome contains the alleles *a* and *b* (Figure 2.13). Under linkage, we expect the two loci to be inherited as a unit. That is, your possible sex cells could have *A* and *B* or *a* and *b*. Any offspring inheriting the *A* allele would also inherit the *B* allele, and any offspring inheriting the *a* allele would also inherit the *b* allele.

This does not always happen. During meiosis, chromosome pairs sometimes exchange pieces, a process known as **crossing over.** For example, the segment of DNA containing the *a* allele could switch with the segment of DNA containing the *A* allele on the other chromosome. Therefore, you could have a sex cell with *a* and *B* or a sex cell with *A* and *b* (see Figure 2.13). The result of crossing over is known as **recombination,** the production of new combinations of genes and DNA sequences. (Recombination describes the result, and crossing over describes the process.)

linkage When alleles on the same chromosome are inherited together.

crossing over The exchange of DNA between chromosomes during meiosis.

recombination The production of new combinations of DNA sequences caused by exchanges of DNA during meiosis.

Recombination does not change the genetic material. The alleles are still the same, but they can occur in different combinations. Recombination provides yet another mechanism for increasing genetic variation by providing new combinations of alleles.

Sex Chromosomes and Sex Determination   One of the 23 pairs of human chromosomes is called the sex chromosome pair because these chromosomes contain the genetic information relating to an individual's sex. There are two forms of sex chromosomes, X and Y. Females have two X chromosomes (XX), and males have one X and one Y chromosome (XY).

The Y chromosome is much smaller than the X chromosome. Therefore, almost all genes found on X are not found on Y. This means that males possess only one allele for certain traits because their Y chromosome lacks the corresponding section of DNA. Therefore, males will manifest a trait for which they have only one allele, whereas females require the same allele from both parents to show the trait. An example of this sex difference is hemophilia, a genetic disorder that interferes with the normal process of blood clotting. The allele for hemophilia is recessive and is found on the segment of the X chromosome that has no corresponding portion on the Y chromosome. For females to be hemophiliac, they must inherit two copies of this allele, one from each parent. This is unlikely because the hemophilia allele is rare. Males, however, need to inherit only one copy of the X chromosome from the mother. As a result, hemophilia is more common in males than females.

Inheritance from One Parent   Thus far, patterns of human inheritance have been described in terms of two parents—a mother and a father. Although most of our DNA is inherited from both parents, there are two important exceptions to this general rule. The first concerns **mitochondrial DNA,** the small amount of DNA that exists in the mitochondria of the cell. Unlike the DNA in the nucleus, mitochondrial DNA is inherited *only* through the mother. This happens because in conception the female sex cell (egg) contains mitochondria, whereas the male sex cell (sperm) does not. Your mitochondrial DNA came only from your mother, who inherited it from her mother, who inherited it from her mother, and so on. If you are female and have children, you will pass on your mitochondrial DNA to your children, whereas if you are male, you cannot.

Another form of single-parent inheritance is through the Y chromosome in males. Males (XY) inherit the Y chromosome from their fathers and their X chromosome from their mothers. Because most of the Y chromosome does not recombine with the X chromosome, this means that almost all of the Y chromosome is passed on intact from father to son, with no genetic contribution from the mother.

The Genetics of Complex Physical Traits

The discussion of genetics thus far has focused on simple discrete genetic traits. Traits such as the MN blood group are genetically "simple" because

mitochondrial DNA A small amount of DNA that is located in the mitochondria of cells. Mitochondrial DNA is inherited only through the mother.

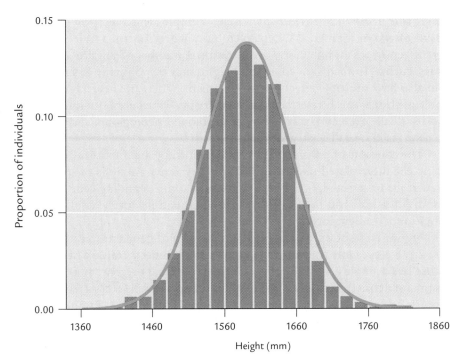

FIGURE 2.14

The distribution of a normally distributed continuous trait. This figure is based on the actual distribution of height (mm) of 1,986 Irish women (author's unpublished data). The height of the curve represents the proportion of women with any given height. Most individuals have a value close to the average for the population (the highest point on the curve, which corresponds to a height of 1,589 mm). The solid line is the fit of the normal distribution.

they result from the action of a single locus with a clear-cut mode of inheritance. These traits are also discrete, meaning that they produce a finite number of phenotypes. For example, you have the M or the N or the MN phenotype for the MN blood group system; you cannot have an intermediate phenotype. Your MN phenotype is also produced entirely from genetic factors. It is not influenced by the environment. Except for a complete blood transfusion, your MN blood group phenotype is the same all of your life.

These simple discrete traits are very useful for demonstrating the basic principles of Mendelian inheritance. It is not wise, however, to think of all biological traits as resulting from a single locus, exhibiting a finite number of phenotypes, or not being affected by the environment. Many of the characteristics of interest in human evolution, such as skin color, body size, brain size, and intelligence, do not fall into this simple category. Such traits have a complex mode of inheritance in that one or more genes may contribute to the phenotype, and they may be affected by the environment. The combined action of genetics and environment produces traits with a continuous distribution. An example is human height. People do not come in 3 different heights (short, medium, and tall), nor 5, nor 20. Height can take on an infinite number of phenotypes. People can be 1,700 mm tall, 1,701 mm tall, and any value in between, such as 1,700.3 mm or 1,700.65 mm.

Complex traits tend to produce more individuals with average values than extreme values. It is not uncommon to find human males between 1,676 and 1,981 mm (5.5 and 6.5 feet) tall. It is much rarer to find someone taller than 2,134 mm (7 feet). A typical distribution of a complex trait, human height, is shown in Figure 2.14.

a. Each gene has a distinct biological effect.

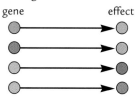

gene   effect

b. Polygenic trait: Many genes contribute to a single effect.

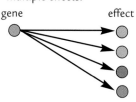

gene   effect

c. Pleiotropy: A gene has multiple effects.

gene   effect

d. Polygenic traits and pleiotropy.

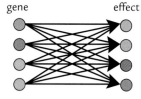

gene   effect

FIGURE 2.15

The relationship between a gene and a biological effect: (a) single gene, single effect; (b) polygenic trait; (c) pleiotropy; (d) a polygenic trait and pleiotropy.

Polygenic Traits and Pleiotropy   Many complex traits are **polygenic,** the result of two or more loci. When several loci act to control a trait, many different genotypes and phenotypes can result. A number of physical characteristics, such as human skin color and height, may be polygenic. A single allele can also have multiple effects on an organism. When an allele has effects on multiple traits, this is referred to as **pleiotropy.** For example, in humans, the sickle cell allele affects the structure of the blood's hemoglobin and also leads to changes in overall body growth and health.

The concepts of polygenic traits and pleiotropy are important in considering the interrelated nature of biological systems. Analysis of simple discrete traits on a gene-by-gene basis is useful in understanding genetics, but it should not lead you to think that any organism is simply a collection of single, independent loci.

Figure 2.15 shows several different models of genetic interaction. Figure 2.15a represents the nature of some simple genetic traits, whereby each cause has a single effect. Figure 2.15b represents a polygenic trait, whereby many loci contribute to a single effect. Pleiotropic effects are shown in Figure 2.15c, whereby a single allele has multiple effects. Figure 2.15d is the most realistic model for many complex traits; each allele has multiple effects, and each effect has multiple causes. In this case, the trait is caused by polygenic and pleiotropic effects. To complicate matters, consider variations of this model in which not all alleles have the same effect, some alleles are dominant and some are not, and environmental factors act to obscure what we actually observe. It is no wonder that the study of the genetics of complex traits is extremely difficult, requiring sophisticated mathematical methods.

Heritability   Complex traits reflect the joint effect of genetics and the environment. A common measure in studies of complex traits is **heritability,** which is the proportion of total variance in a trait that is attributable to genetic variation in a specific population (the value can be different in different populations). Complex traits show variation; for example, some people are taller than others, and some people have longer heads than others. The variation that we see is the total phenotypic variation. Some of this variation is due to genetic factors; some people may have a genetic potential for being taller, for example. The variation caused by genetic factors is called the *genetic variation.* Some of the total variation is also due to differences in environmental factors. For example, some people may have different diets, which would affect their height. We call this the *environmental variation.* Thus, total variation is made up of two components: genetic variation and environmental variation (or, in mathematical terms, total variation = genetic variation + environmental variation). Heritability is simply the *proportion* of total variation that is due to genetic variation. That is,

$$\text{Heritability} = \frac{\text{Genetic variation}}{\text{Total variation}} = \frac{\text{Genetic variation}}{\text{Genetic } + \text{ Environmental}}$$
$$\text{variation} \qquad \text{variation}$$

Heritability is computed with this formula using complex methods of comparing relatives and environmental factors to estimate the genetic and environmental components. Heritability can range from 0 (no genetic variation) to 1 (no environmental variation). A high heritability—say, greater than 0.5—indicates that the majority of variation is caused by genetic variation.

Although useful, the concept of heritability can be misleading. When we hear of a trait that has a high heritability, we are tempted to conclude that the trait is controlled almost exclusively by genetic factors and that environmental factors have little effect. The problem with reading too much into the concept of heritability is that it is a *relative* measure of the degree of genetic variation in a *specific* environment. Consider, for example, an estimate of heritability for human height. If the specific population we are looking at has little variation in diet, disease, and other environmental factors that can affect height, then the environmental variation will be low. As a result, the heritability will be high. If, however, the environmental variation changes, resulting in greater differences within the population in terms of diet and other factors, then the environmental variation increases, and heritability will be lower. Heritability, then, is a relative measure that can vary from one population to the next. It is not a measure of the extent to which genetics controls a trait; it is only a relative measure of variation.

Major Genes   Recently, more attention has been given to **major genes.** In a major gene model, a discernible portion of genetic variation is due to a single locus. The continuous distribution of the trait is the result of environmental effects and can be enhanced by the smaller effect of other loci. In contrast to certain polygenic models whereby all loci contribute equally, a major gene model postulates that a single locus has the greatest effect. A trait controlled by a major gene often shows the same type of distribution as a polygenic trait (see Figure 2.14). Developments in statistical analysis have allowed tests for major genes. Examples of major genes that have been discovered in humans include oxygen saturation of arterial hemoglobin (Beall et al. 1994) and obesity (Comuzzie et al. 1997). In each case, however, there was evidence that phenotypic variation was not due solely to a single gene and that other genes had an additional effect.

MUTATIONS

As shown earlier, the process of genetic inheritance produces genetic variation in offspring. The independent assortment of chromosomes during meiosis and the action of crossing over both act to create new genetic combinations. They do not act to create any new genetic material, however. To explain past evolution, we need a mechanism for introducing new alleles and variation. The origin of new genetic variation was a problem for Darwin, but we now know that new alleles are brought about through the process of mutation.

polygenic A complex genetic trait affected by two or more loci.

pleiotropy A single allele that has multiple effects on an organism.

heritability The proportion of total variation of a trait due to genetic variation.

major genes Genes that have the primary effect on the phenotypic distribution of a complex trait.

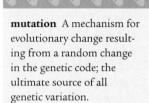

mutation A mechanism for evolutionary change resulting from a random change in the genetic code; the ultimate source of all genetic variation.

Evolutionary Significance of Mutations

A **mutation** is a change in the genetic code. Mutations are the ultimate source of all genetic variation. Mutations are caused by a number of environmental factors such as background radiation, which includes radiation from the earth's crust and from cosmic rays. Such background radiation is all around us, in the air we breathe and the food we eat. Mutations may also be caused by heat and ingested substances such as caffeine.

A growing concern is the effect of environmental changes on mutation rates. Human-made radiation, as from certain industries, not only might be dangerous to exposed individuals but also might affect their future offspring by creating mutational effects in sex cells. Numerous studies of laboratory animals, such as fruit flies, have shown clearly that the mutation rate increases with exposure to radiation. Less is known about the effect of increased radiation on mutations in humans and other mammals. Studies of the children of survivors of the atomic bombs dropped on Japan at the end of World War II have so far failed to show definite evidence of any increase in the rate of mutations in sex cells (although mutations in body cells in the exposed parents were frequent). Given the definite evidence of radiation effects from experimental animals, this failure may reflect an inadequate sample size or other methodological difficulties in the human studies. Another possibility is that mammalian cells have a high capacity for DNA repair.

Mutations can take place in any cell of the body. To have evolutionary importance, however, the mutation must occur in a sex cell. A mutation in a skin cell on the end of your finger has no evolutionary significance because it will not be passed on to your offspring.

Mutations are random. That is, there is no way of predicting when a specific mutation will take place or what, if any, phenotypic effect it will have. All we can do is estimate the probability of a mutation occurring at a given locus over a given amount of time. The randomness of mutations also means that mutations do not appear when they might be needed. Many mosquitoes have adapted to insecticides because a mutation was present in the population that acted to confer some resistance to the insecticide. If that mutation had not been present, the mosquitoes would have died. The mosquitoes' need for a certain genetic variant had no effect on whether the mutation appeared.

Mutations can have different effects depending on the specific type of mutation and the environment. The conventional view of mutations has long been that they are mostly harmful. A classic analogy is the comparison of the genetic code with the engine of an automobile. If an engine part is changed at random, the most likely result is that the car will not operate, or at least not as well as it did before the change.

Some mutations, however, are advantageous. They lead to change that improves the survival and reproduction rates of organisms. In recent decades, we have also discovered that some mutations are neutral; that is, the genetic change has no detectable effect on survival or reproduction. There is continued controversy among geneticists about the relative frequency of neutral mutations. Some claim that many mutations are neutral in their effect. Others note the difficulties in detecting the effects of many mutations.

Whether or not a mutation is neutral, advantageous, or disadvantageous depends in large part on the environment. Genetic variants that are harmful in certain environments might actually be helpful in other environments.

Types of Mutations

We now recognize that there are a variety of ways in which mutations occur. Mutations can involve changes in a single DNA base, in larger sections of DNA, and in entire chromosomes. One example is the substitution of one DNA base for another, such as the widely studied **sickle cell allele.** The red blood cells produced in individuals with two copies of this allele (one from each parent) are misshapen and do not transport oxygen efficiently. The result is a severe form of anemia (sickle cell anemia) that leads to sickness and death. The specific cause of this allele is a mutation in the sixth amino acid (out of 146 amino acids) of the beta chain of hemoglobin. The DNA for the normal beta hemoglobin allele contains instructions for the amino acid, glutamic acid, at this position (CTC). The sickle cell mutation occurs when the base T is changed to an A, which specifies the amino acid valine (CAC). This small change affects the entire structure of the red blood cells and, in turn, the well-being of the individual.

Substitution of one base for another is only one type of mutation. Mutations can also involve the addition or deletion of a base or of large sections of DNA. In these cases, the genetic message is changed. Also, sections of DNA can be duplicated or moved from one place to another, and sections of DNA can be added or lost when crossing over is not equal.

The genetic information contained in the chromosomes can also be altered by the deletion or duplication of part or all of the chromosome. For example, an entire chromosome from a pair can be lost (**monosomy =** one chromosome) or can occur in duplicate, giving three chromosomes (**trisomy**). One result of the latter is Down syndrome, a condition characterized by certain cranial features (Figure 2.16), poor physical growth, and mental retardation (usually mild). Down syndrome is caused by the duplication of one of the 21st chromosome pair. Affected individuals have a total of 47 chromosomes, one more than the normal 46. Down syndrome can also be caused by mutations of the 21st chromosome. In some individuals, the change involves the exchange of parts of the 21st chromosome with other chromosomes.

Several chromosomal mutations involve the sex chromosomes. One, known as Turner syndrome, occurs when an individual has only one X chromosome instead of two. These individuals thus have only 45 chromosomes and develop as females. Those with Turner syndrome are generally short, have undeveloped ovaries, and are sterile. Another condition, known as Klinefelter syndrome, occurs in males with an extra X chromosome. Instead of the normal XY combination, these males have an XXY combination for a total of 47 chromosomes. They are characterized by small testes and reduced fertility.

sickle cell allele An allele of the hemoglobin locus. Individuals homozygous for this allele have sickle cell anemia.

monosomy A condition in which one chromosome rather than a pair is present in body cells.

trisomy A condition in which three chromosomes rather than a pair occur in body cells.

FIGURE 2.16

Facial appearance of a child with Down syndrome. Down syndrome is often caused by the duplication of one chromosome in the 21st chromosome pair.

Rates of Mutations

Specific mutations are relatively rare events, although the *exact* rate of mutations is difficult to determine in many cases. Part of the problem in determining the rate of mutations is the fact that several different base sequences can specify the same amino acid. For example, the amino acid glycine is specified by the sequence CCA. If a mutation occurs in which the third base changes from an A to a G, the net result is the sequence CCG, which also specifies glycine. This hypothetical mutation leads to no biochemical change and is considered neutral. If there is no observable change, then the mutation will usually go unnoticed.

A mutation is also more apparent if it involves a dominant allele, because a heterozygote receiving one copy of the mutant allele will show the mutant phenotype. If a mutant allele is recessive, then phenotypic expression will require two copies of the mutant allele, which is a less common event. Recessive mutant alleles go unnoticed under these circumstances.

Another problem in identifying mutations is that harmful mutations may result in spontaneous abortion (miscarriage) before pregnancy has been detected. Roughly 15 percent of all recognized conceptions result in spontaneous abortion, of which 50 percent can be traced to specific chromosomal mutations (Sutton and Wagner 1985). For such an event to be recorded, however, a woman must be aware that she is pregnant, which she usually doesn't know until a month or more after conception. Some researchers feel that a large number of unrecognized conceptions are expelled spontaneously during the first few weeks after conception. If so, any prediction of mutation rates based on recognized conceptions will be an underestimate.

PCR and Ancient DNA

In the summer of 1994, filmgoers were thrilled by the movie *Jurassic Park,* based on the novel of the same name by Michael Crichton (who studied anthropology as an undergraduate). The plot revolves around the construction of a dinosaur theme park—with live dinosaurs! In *Jurassic Park,* scientists recover amber dating back to the time of the dinosaurs. Trapped in the amber are mosquitoes that, prior to being encased in the tree sap that becomes amber, had drunk the blood of dinosaurs. Using this blood, the fictional scientists reconstruct the DNA of the original dinosaurs and bring a number of extinct species back to life.

A fascinating story, but how accurate is it? Could we reconstruct sufficient DNA sequences of ancient creatures to bring them back to life? At present, we lack the technology to do so. However, we *can* reconstruct some ancient DNA sequences (although not well enough to re-create a dinosaur). Fragments of ancient DNA *have* been reconstructed, including some from amber many millions of years old. We also have been able to obtain DNA fragments from human populations many thousands of years old (Stone and Stoneking 1993; Hagelberg 1994).

The heart of these achievements is a relatively new technique called the *polymerase chain reaction* (PCR). This technique involves the laboratory synthesis of millions of copies of DNA fragments from very small initial amounts (Erlich et al. 1991). The process is essentially cyclical—the DNA strands are separated and form the template for new strands, thus resulting in a doubling of the DNA each time through the cycle (see accompanying figure). This method is very efficient in extracting DNA sequences from very small samples. In fact, it is so efficient that one of the technical problems is that it often picks up DNA from people's cells floating around the lab as dust (Hagelberg 1994). The PCR method is also useful to anthropologists working on living human populations. Samples can be collected and transported easily—such as single plucked hairs.

The PCR method has also proven valuable in the field of forensics. Very small samples can yield sufficient DNA to help identify skeletal remains of murder victims. One notorious case involved the skeletal remains that were attributed to the infamous Nazi doctor Joseph Mengele. Extracts of bone were taken, and the DNA was amplified using PCR and then compared to the known surviving relatives of Mengele. Based on this comparison, the skeletal remains were definitely identified as having been Mengele (Hagelberg 1994). DNA analysis also has been used to look at the genetics of ancient humans dating back many tens of thousands of years. These studies are described in more detail in Chapter 11.

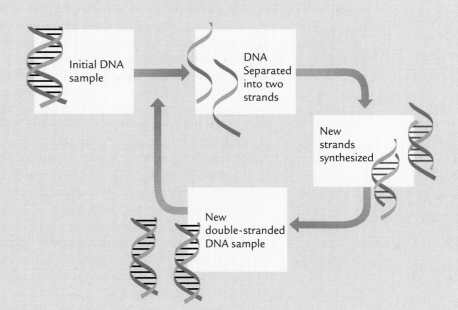

Simplified diagram of the polymerase chain reaction (PCR) used to amplify small amounts of DNA. Each time through the cycle, the amount of DNA doubles.

Initial DNA sample

DNA Separated into two strands

New strands synthesized

New double-stranded DNA sample

Despite these problems, research has provided a range in the rates of mutation. In human populations, the probability of mutation is roughly 0.1–10 mutations per million genes per generation. Certain types of DNA sequences, such as repeated units (described in Chapter 13), have higher rates.

Regardless of the specific mutation rates for a given gene or chromosome, one thing is clear—mutation rates are generally low. Given these low probabilities, it may be tempting to regard mutation as so rare that it has no special evolutionary significance. The problem with this reasoning is that the estimated rates refer to a *single* specific locus. Human chromosomes have many loci. The probability that a specific locus will show a mutation in any individual is low, but the probability of *any* locus showing a mutation is much higher.

Even though mutation is a rare event for any given locus, there is a high probability of at least one new mutation in each individual. When we consider the genetics of an entire population or species, the net result is that mutation is common within a single generation. In fact, many studies estimate that all of us carry at least one lethal recessive mutant allele.

GENETICS AND BEHAVIOR

Perhaps the most controversial topic in genetics is the extent to which behavior is governed by genetic factors. The controversy arises not so much from academic debate but from the social implications, real and imagined, of this question. Problems arise out of a misunderstanding of the basic concepts of genetics or are caused by those seeking any "scientific" fact, regardless of truth, to support and further their own social or political agenda. Much of this controversy revolves around the concept of race, which is discussed in Chapter 13. The present section focuses on basic strategies involved in relating genes and behavior.

Is a behavior trait, such as intelligence or shyness, caused by genes ("nature") or by the physical and cultural environment ("nurture")? The debate over nature versus nurture has a long history in Western civilization. The prevalent view among scientists reflects not only current research but also the social and cultural climate of the times. Scientists are people too, as susceptible to biases and prejudices as everyone else. A major lesson of the history of science is that cultural beliefs influence methodology and the interpretation of scientific results.

At the beginning of the twentieth century, the prevalent view was that nature was the more important determinant of many behaviors, particularly intelligence. This emphasis shifted to nurture during the period from the 1930s to the 1960s, when environmental factors were seen as being the most, if not the only, important factor.

Much of the debate over nature versus nurture is nonsense, however. Any attempt to relegate human behaviors to either genetics *or* environment is fruitless. Genes and environment are both important in their effect on human behaviors. The proper question is not which is more important but rather how they interact.

Evidence of *some* genetic influence has been found for a variety of human behaviors, including intelligence test scores, autism, reading and language disabilities, eating disorders, schizophrenia, and sexual orientation, among others. These studies do not support a view that behavior is *caused* by genes, but rather suggest that genes can *influence* behavior. In a review of genetic studies of human behavior, Plomin et al. (1994) note that these analyses have consistently shown that there is at least as much environmental variation related to phenotypic variation as there is genetic variation. In other words, *both* genetic and environmental variation have been related to behavioral variation. Further, because environmental effects can be different in different populations, the relative influence of genetic and environmental variation will also differ from one population to the next.

What are the implications of the joint interaction between genetics and environment? If a behavior is affected to some extent by genetics, then is there an innate difference between people with different alleles? Not necessarily. Even if genetic differences in a behavior exist, this does not mean that those differences will override environmental factors. Studies of male sexual orientation, for example, have suggested a moderate heritability for homosexual orientation (Pillard and Bailey 1998), and some have suggested that genetic susceptibility to male homosexuality is linked to a gene (or genes) on the X chromosome (Hamer et al. 1993; Hu et al. 1995). These results do not mean that there is a "gay gene," but rather suggest that genetic factors can *influence* male sexual orientation in certain cases. Such studies also show that environmental factors play a large role in sexual orientation. As Pattatucci (1998) notes, sexual orientation is related to many factors, and "it is highly improbable that any single genetic variation or allele will be present in all homosexual individuals and absent from all heterosexual individuals" (p. 368). As is the case with many behavioral traits, the phenotype reflects a complex interaction between genetic and environmental factors.

Another example of interaction between genes, environment, and behavior can be seen in a study of depression conducted in New Zealand. Researchers examined a large group of people who had been studied for more than two decades, including being tested for depression, and found a strong relationship between depression and a gene that affects transmission of serotonin, a chemical that transmits messages between adjacent nerve cells. An imbalance of serotonin levels has been implicated in a number of mental disorders. The gene investigated has two alleles (*l* and *s*). Although there was no difference in the genetic makeup of people who had not reported any depression, those who did report depression were genetically different. People with the *sl* genotype had a greater probability of depression, and people with the *ss* genotype had an even higher probability (Caspi et al. 2003; Holden 2003). Again, genetics does not dictate the final behavior, but it does appear to influence susceptibility.

Summary

The DNA molecule specifies the genetic code or set of instructions needed to produce biological structures. DNA acts along with a related molecule, RNA, to translate these instructions into proteins. The DNA is contained along structures within the cell called chromosomes. Chromosomes come in pairs.

A segment of DNA that codes for a certain product is called a gene. The different forms of genes present at a locus are called alleles. The DNA molecule has the ability to make copies of itself, allowing transmission of genetic information from cell to cell and from generation to generation.

Meiosis is the process of sex cell formation that results in one of each chromosome pair being transmitted from parent to offspring. Each individual receives half of his or her alleles from each parent. The two alleles together specify the genetic constitution of an individual—the genotype. The physical manifestation of the genotype is known as the phenotype. The relationship between genotype and phenotype depends on whether an allele is dominant, recessive, or codominant. In complex physical traits, the phenotype is the result of the combined effect of genetics and environment.

The ultimate source of all genetic variation is mutation—a random change in the genetic code. Some mutations are neutral in effect; others are helpful or harmful. The effect of any mutation often depends on the specific environmental conditions. Mutations for any given allele are relatively rare events, but given the large number of loci in many organisms, it is highly probable that each individual has at least one mutant allele.

Genetic factors have been linked to human behaviors. Such behaviors appear to be influenced by both genetics and environment. Given the biocultural nature of human beings, it should be no surprise that both genes and environment have an effect on both biology and behavior.

Supplemental Readings

Jones, S. 1993. *The Language of Genes: Solving the Mysteries of Our Genetic Past, Present and Future.* New York: Doubleday. A well-written general introduction to human genetics.

Marks, J. 1995. *Human Biodiversity: Genes, Race, and History.* New York: Aldine de Gruyter. A historically oriented review of different approaches to human biological variation, with many discussions of the nature of genes and the mechanisms of human genetics.

Nature 409(6822) (February 15, 2001); *Science* 291(5507) (February 16, 2001). Two specific issues of leading science journals that both contain preliminary analyses of the human genome and include many commentaries regarding the history, current status, and possible use of data obtained from the Human Genome Project.

VIRTUAL EXPLORATIONS

Visit our textbook-specific online learning center Web site at **www.mhhe.com/relethford7** to access the exercises that follow.

1. **Basic Principles of Genetics** **http://anthro.palomar.edu/ mendel/default.htm**. Visit the "Basic Principles of Genetics" page from the Anthropology Department at Palomar College. Read through the sections on "Mendel's Genetics" and "Probability of Inheritance." Additional helpful information about the allele can be

found on an About.com, biology basics link: **http://biology.about .com/library/glossary/ bldefalleles.htm**.

Now click on the link to "Exceptions to Simple Inheritance."

- Read through the topic and familiarize yourself with the diseases mentioned that have a genetic component (diabetes, Huntington's disease, Angelman syndrome, or multiple sclerosis).
- Learn more about the many varieties of genetic disorders on the University of Utah's Genetic Science Learning Center site "Genetic Disorders Library": **http://learn.genetics.utah.edu/units/ disorders/whataregd/**. The site categorizes disorders into three levels: Single Gene Disorders, Chromosome Abnormalities, and Multifactorial Disorders.
- Chose the Klinefelter Syndrome link.
- Go also to the Image File graphic below. (You will need to have Adobe Flash Player to play the link.)

Be sure to read through the entire section on Klinefelter.

- Create a test question based on Klinefelter Syndrome. (Your question might focus on the cause of the disease, symptoms, or treatment.)
- Compose three possible answers, one correct and two incorrect. Make sure the incorrect answers sound plausible, not impossible!
- Go back and explore each of the other levels of genetic disorders and diseases you may not have heard of before.

2. **Genome News**   **http://www.genomenewsnetwork.org/**. Look at the GNN Genome News Network home page. The site provides information on Genomes of the World as well as genome basics and other timely news stories, including bio-terrorism, cloning, and stem cell research.

Go to the NEWS STORIES categories. Select the link for Stem Cells: **http://www.genomenewsnetwork.org/categories/index/stem cells.php?s=0&n=15**.

- Review the articles listed.
- What are some of the major issues concerning stem cells?
- Which are the more controversial ones?
- To learn more about stem cells basics, go to the University of Utah's Genetic Science Learning Center site "Stem Cells in the Spotlight" link: **http://learn.genetics.utah.edu/units/stemcells/**.
- Click on the "Quick Guide to Sequenced Genomes" at **http://www .genomenewsnetwork.org/resources/sequenced_genomes/ genome_guide_p1.shtml**. The site offers detailed information on the more than 180 organisms that have been sequenced since 1995. The organisms are each described, and links are provided to explore the sequencing centers and scientific abstracts concerning research.

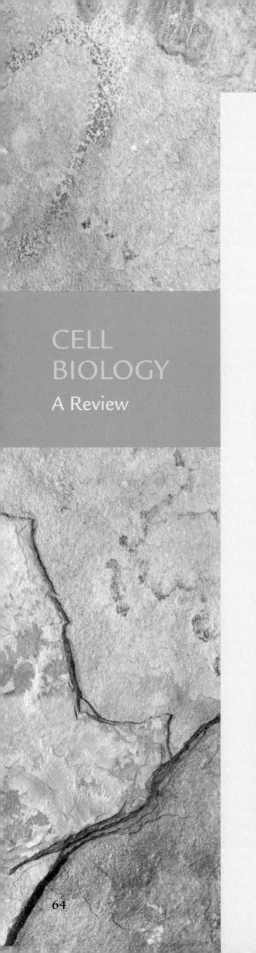

CELL BIOLOGY
A Review

This section, which focuses on the structure of the cell and on the processes of mitosis and meiosis, can be used as a supplement for students wishing to review the basic biology necessary for an understanding of the fundamental principles of Mendelian genetics.

THE CELL

All living creatures are made up of cells. Humans, like many organisms, are multicelled. Figure 2.17 shows some of the components of a typical cell. Two major structures are the *nucleus* and the *cytoplasm;* the latter contains a number of other structures. The entire body of the cell is enclosed by a *cell membrane.*

Within the cytoplasm, *mitochondria* convert some cellular material into energy that is then used for cellular activity. *Ribosomes* are small particles that are frequently attached to a larger structure known as the *endoplasmic reticulum.* Composed of RNA and proteins, ribosomes serve as sites for the manufacture of proteins.

As discussed in Chapter 2, the DNA sequences that make up the genetic code are bound together by proteins in long strands known as *chromosomes.* In body cells, chromosomes come in pairs; humans have 23 pairs of chromosomes. The chromosomes within the nucleus of the cell contain all of the DNA, with the exception of mitochondrial DNA.

MITOSIS

DNA has the ability to make copies of itself. This ability is vital for transmitting genetic information from cell to cell and for transmitting genetic information from generation to generation. The replication of DNA is part of the process of cell replication. We will examine two basic processes: mitosis, the replication of body cells, and meiosis, the replication of sex cells.

Mitosis produces two identical body cells from one original. Between cell divisions, each chromosome produces an exact copy of itself, resulting in two pairs with two chromosomes

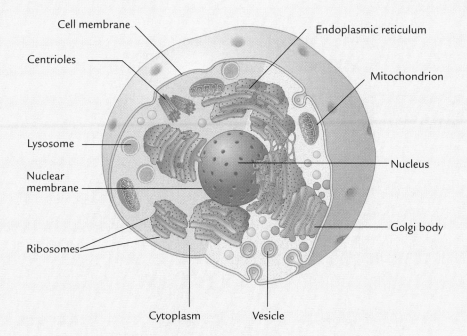

Cell membrane

Centrioles

Lysosome

Nuclear membrane

Ribosomes

Cytoplasm

Vesicle

Endoplasmic reticulum

Mitochondrion

Nucleus

Golgi body

FIGURE 2.17

Schematic diagram of a cell.

each. When a cell divides, each part contains one of each of the pairs of chromosomes. Thus, two identical body cells, each with the full number of chromosome pairs, are produced. As outlined in Figure 2.18, five stages compose the process of mitosis: interphase, prophase, metaphase, anaphase, and telophase. (Some people do not refer to interphase as a stage.)

During *interphase,* the chromosomes that are dispersed throughout the nucleus duplicate. During *prophase,* the chromosomes, each of which is attached to its copy, become tightly coiled and move toward one another in the nucleus. Each of the two copies is called a *chromatid,* and their point of attachment is called the

centromere. Small structures located outside the nuclear membrane, known as *centrioles* (see Figure 2.17), move toward opposite ends of the cell, and *spindle fibers* form between the centrioles. The nuclear membrane then dissolves.

During *metaphase,* the duplicated chromosomes line up along the middle of the cell, and the spindle fibers attach to the centromeres. During *anaphase,* the centromere divides, and the two strands of chromatids (original and duplicate) split and move toward opposite ends of the cell. During *telophase,* new nuclear membranes form around each of the two clusters of chromosomes. Finally, the cell membrane pinches in the middle, creating two identical cells.

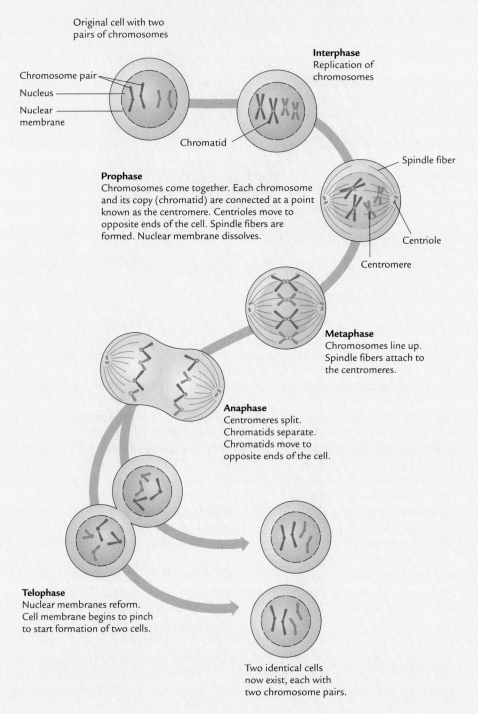

FIGURE 2.18

The five phases of mitosis. In this example, the original body cell contains two pairs of chromosomes. Mitosis produces two identical body cells, each containing two chromosome pairs (a total of four chromosomes each).

Original cell with two pairs of chromosomes

Chromosome pair

Nucleus

Nuclear membrane

Chromatid

Interphase
Replication of chromosomes

Spindle fiber

Prophase
Chromosomes come together. Each chromosome and its copy (chromatid) are connected at a point known as the centromere. Centrioles move to opposite ends of the cell. Spindle fibers are formed. Nuclear membrane dissolves.

Centriole

Centromere

Metaphase
Chromosomes line up. Spindle fibers attach to the centromeres.

Anaphase
Centromeres split. Chromatids separate. Chromatids move to opposite ends of the cell.

Telophase
Nuclear membranes reform. Cell membrane begins to pinch to start formation of two cells.

Two identical cells now exist, each with two chromosome pairs.

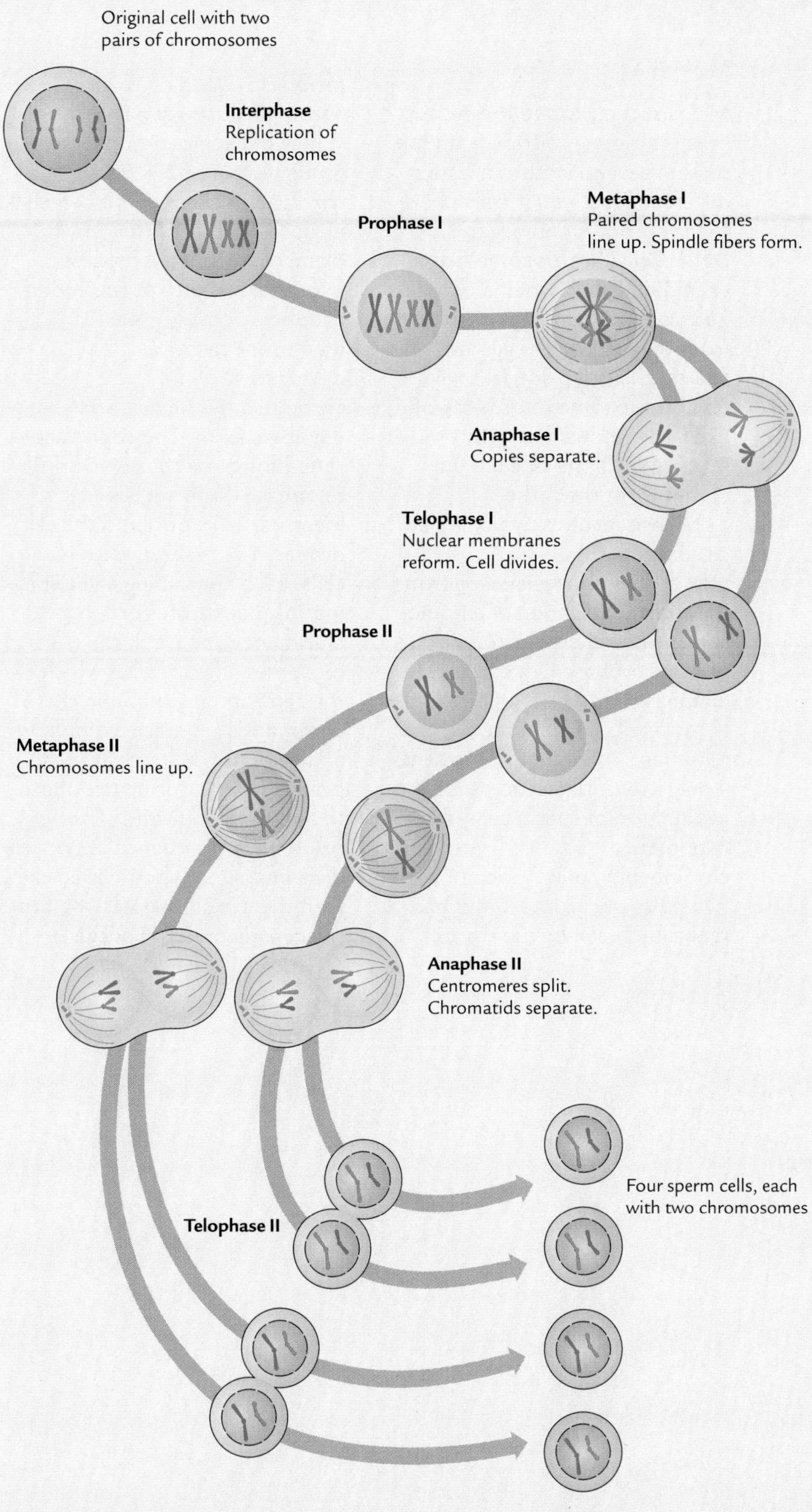

Original cell with two pairs of chromosomes

Interphase
Replication of chromosomes

Prophase I

Metaphase I
Paired chromosomes line up. Spindle fibers form.

Anaphase I
Copies separate.

Telophase I
Nuclear membranes reform. Cell divides.

Prophase II

Metaphase II
Chromosomes line up.

Anaphase II
Centromeres split. Chromatids separate.

Telophase II

Four sperm cells, each with two chromosomes

FIGURE 2.19

The phases of meiosis for a sperm cell. In this example, the original cell contained two chromosome pairs. As a result of meiosis, four sperm cells were produced, each with two chromosomes. The process is similar for egg cells, except that one egg cell and three polar bodies are produced.

MEIOSIS

Meiosis, the production of sex cells (gametes), differs from mitosis in several ways. The main difference is that sex cells contain only half of an organism's DNA—one chromosome from each pair. Thus, when a new zygote, or fertilized egg, is formed from the joining of egg and sperm, the offspring will have 23 chromosome pairs. One of each pair comes from the mother, and one of each pair comes from the father.

Meiosis involves two cycles of cell division (Figure 2.19). The total sequence of events following the initial duplication of chromosomes (interphase) involves eight stages: prophase I, metaphase I, anaphase I, telophase I, prophase II, metaphase II, anaphase II, and telophase II. Figure 2.19 presents a diagram of this process for the production of sperm cells, for a hypothetical organism with two chromosome pairs. Each of the two pairs of chromosomes has replicated itself by the start of

prophase I, leading to eight chromatids: the two chromosomes of each pair duplicate, giving a total of $2 \times 2 \times 2 = 8$ chromatids, each pair of which attaches to one of the centromeres through a process known as *synapsis*. At the end of prophase I, the nuclear membrane dissolves. Then, during metaphase I, the paired chromosomes line up and spindle fibers form. The copies separate during anaphase I. During telophase I, the nuclear membranes reform and the cell divides. The realization of two cells, each containing eight chromatids, constitutes prophase II. During metaphase II, the chromosomes line up, after which the centromeres split and the chromatids separate, completing anaphase II. The nuclear membranes reform during telophase II, and the cell divides. The net result of this sequence of two cell divisions is four sperm cells, each with two chromosomes—half of the genetic material of the father. The process is similar for the production of egg cells from the female, except that the net result is one egg cell and three structures known as *polar bodies* that do not function as sex cells.

Meiosis thus allows half of a parent's genetic material to be passed on to the next generation. When a sperm cell fertilizes an egg cell, the total number of chromosomes is restored. For humans, the resulting zygote contains $23 + 23 = 46$ chromosomes, or 23 chromosome pairs.

Sex cells may also contain genetic combinations not present in the parent. When synapsis occurs during prophase I, and the chromosomes pair with their copies, becoming attached to one another at several places, the potential exists for genetic material to be exchanged, a process known as *crossing over*. The resulting genetic combinations allow for variation in each sex cell from its source.

Independent assortment also enhances genetic variability. As discussed in Chapter 2, according to this principle, the segregation of any pair of chromosomes does not affect the probability of segregation of any other pair of chromosomes. If you had two chromosome pairs, A and B, with two chromosomes each (A1 and A2, and B1 and B2), only one of each pair will be found in any sex cell. However, you might have one sex cell with A1 and B1, and another sex cell with A1 and B2. Whichever member of the first pair of chromosomes is found in any given sex cell has no bearing on whichever member of the second pair is also found in that sex cell. Independent assortment results from processes occurring during metaphase I. When the paired chromosomes line up, they do so at random and are not influenced by whether they originally came from the person's mother or father. This process allows for tremendous genetic variability in potential offspring

Two closely related species, a wolf and a dog. Similarities and differences between species, and between populations within a species, are the focus of evolutionary investigation. Changes over time reflect the action of several evolutionary forces: mutation, natural selection, genetic drift, and gene flow.

Evolutionary Forces

CHAPTER

3

Biological evolution is genetic change over time and can be studied at two different levels. Microevolution consists of changes in the frequency of alleles in a population from one generation to the next. Macroevolution comprises long-term patterns of genetic change over thousands and millions of generations, as well as the process of species formation. This chapter deals with the general principles of microevolution. Macroevolution is discussed in Chapter 4.

POPULATION GENETICS

Microevolution takes into account changes in the frequency of alleles from one generation to the next. The focus is generally not on the specific genotypes or phenotypes of individuals but rather on the total pattern of an entire biological population. We are interested in defining the relative frequencies of different alleles, genotypes, and phenotypes for the entire population being studied. We then seek to determine if any apparent change in these frequencies has occurred over time. If changes have occurred, we try to explain them.

What Is a Population?

The term **breeding population** is used frequently in evolutionary theory. In an abstract sense, a breeding population is a group of organisms that tend to choose mates from within the group. This definition is a bit tricky, however, because it is not clear what proportion of mating within a group defines a breeding population.

For example, suppose you travel to a village in a remote mountain region. You find that 99 percent of the people in the villages are married to others who were born in the same village. In this case, the village would appear to fit our ideal definition. But what if only 80 percent of the people chose their mates from within the village? What if the number were 50 percent? At what point do you stop referring to the population as a "breeding population"? There is no quick and ready answer to this question.

breeding population
A group of organisms that tend to choose mates from within the group.

On a practical level, human populations are initially most often defined on the basis of geographic and political boundaries. A small, isolated island, for example, easily fits the requirements of a defined population. In most cases, the local geographic unit (such as town or village) is used. Because many human populations have distinct geographic boundaries, this solution often provides the best approach. We must take care, however, to ensure that a local geographic unit, such as a town, is not composed of distinct subpopulations, such as groups belonging to different religious sects. A rural Irish village fits this criterion because most of its residents belong to the same religion, social class, and occupational group. New York City, on the other hand, clearly contains a number of subpopulations defined in terms of ethnicity, religion, social class, and other factors. In this case, subpopulations defined on the basis of these factors would serve as our units of analysis.

In many cases, the definition of a population depends on the specific research question asked. For example, if the goal of a study is to look at spatial variation of biological variation, populations defined on the basis of geography are most suitable. If, however, the goal of a study is to look at genetic variation among ethnic groups, then ethnicity should be used to define the populations.

Another potential problem in defining populations is determining the difference between the total census population and the breeding population. Microevolutionary theory specifically concerns those individuals who contribute to the next generation. The *total* population refers to everybody, whether or not they are likely to breed. The *breeding* population is smaller than the total population because of a number of factors. First, some individuals in the total population will be too young or too old to mate. Second, cultural factors and geographic distribution may act to limit an individual's choice of mate, and as a consequence, some individuals will not breed. If, for example, you live in an isolated area, there may not be enough individuals of the opposite sex from which to choose a mate. Such factors must be taken into consideration in defining a breeding population.

Once a population has been defined, the next step in microevolutionary analysis is to determine the frequencies of genotypes and alleles within the population.

Genotype Frequencies and Allele Frequencies

The genotype frequency is a measure of the relative proportions of different genotypes within a population. Likewise, an allele frequency is simply a measure of the relative proportion of alleles within a population. Genotype frequencies are obtained by dividing the number of individuals with each genotype by the total number of individuals. For example, consider a hypothetical population of 200 people for the MN blood group system in which there are 98 people with genotype *MM,* 84 people with genotype *MN,* and 18 people with genotype *NN.* The genotype frequencies are therefore:

Frequency of *MM* = 98/200 = 0.49

Frequency of *MN* = 84/200 = 0.42

Frequency of *NN* = 18/200 = 0.09

Note that the total frequency of all genotypes adds up to 1 (0.49 + 0.42 + 0.09 = 1). These frequencies are *proportions.* If you find it easier to think about the frequencies in terms of *percentages,* then simply multiply the proportions by 100. Thus, we see that 0.49 × 100 = 49 percent of the population has genotype *MM.* Likewise, 42 percent have genotype *MN,* and 9 percent have genotype *NN.*

Allele frequencies are computed by counting the number of each allele and dividing that number by the total number of alleles. In the example here, the total number of alleles is 400 because there are 200 people, each with 2 alleles. To find out the number of *M* alleles for each genotype, count up the number of alleles for each genotype, and multiply that number by the number of people with that genotype. Finally, add up the number for all genotypes. In the example, 98 people have the *MM* genotype, and therefore 98 people have two *M* alleles. The total number of *M* alleles for people with the *MM* genotype is 98 × 2 = 196. For the *MN* genotype, 84 people have one *M* allele, giving a total of 84 × 1 = 84 *M* alleles. For the *NN* genotype, 18 people have no *M* alleles, for a total of 18 × 0 = 0 *M* alleles. Adding the number of *M* alleles for all genotypes gives a total of 196 + 84 + 0 = 280 *M* alleles. The frequency of the *M* allele is therefore 280/400 = 0.7. The frequency of the *N* allele can be computed in the same way, giving an allele frequency of 0.3. Note that the frequencies of all alleles must add up to 1. Another example of allele frequency computation is given in Table 3.1.

The method of counting alleles to determine allele frequencies can be used only when the number of individuals with each genotype can be determined. If one of the alleles is dominant, this will not be possible, and we must use another method. We may also need to use special methods to compute allele frequencies when more than two alleles are present at a given locus.

Hardy-Weinberg Equilibrium

Now that we have computed the allele frequencies for the MN blood group for our hypothetical population, we turn to the next question: What are the *expected* genotype frequencies in the next generation? If the population reproduces, what proportion of the children in the next generation will have genotype *MM*? What proportion will have *MN,* or *NN*?

As shown in Chapter 2, we can easily answer this question for any specific pair of parents. For example, if a man with genotype *MN* mates with a woman with genotype *MN,* we expect that 25 percent of the offspring will have genotype *MM,* 50 percent will have genotype *MN,* and 25 percent will have genotype *NN* (see Figure 2.9). Extending this computation to the

TABLE 3.1   Example of Allele Frequency Computation

Imagine you have just collected information on *MN* blood group genotypes for 250 humans in a given population. Your data are:

Number of *MM* genotype = 40
Number of *MN* genotype = 120
Number of *NN* genotype = 90

The allele frequencies are computed as follows:

Genotype	Number of People	Total Number of Alleles	Number of M Alleles	Number of N Alleles
MM	40	80	80	0
MN	120	240	120	120
NN	90	180	0	180
Total	250	500	200	300

The relative frequency of the *M* allele is computed as the number of *M* alleles divided by the total number of alleles: 200/500 = 0.4.

The relative frequency of the *N* allele is computed as the number of *N* alleles divided by the total number of alleles: 300/500 = 0.6.

As a check, note that the relative frequencies of the alleles must add up to 1.0 (0.4 + 0.6 = 1.0).

entire population means that we would need to consider *all* possible pairings (e.g., *MM* and *MN, MM* and *NN,* and so forth) and the number of each pairing (e.g., how many men with *MN* mate with women with *MN,* and so forth).

Although this might seem to be an overly complex question to answer, two scientists, G. H. Hardy and W. Weinberg, independently arrived at a simple and elegant solution in 1908, known today as **Hardy-Weinberg equilibrium.** This is a mathematical statement that relates the allele frequencies in a population to the expected genotype frequencies in the next generation. It is best explained using a simple model of a single locus with two alleles, such as the MN blood group above. First, we need to know the allele frequencies, which were derived above as 0.7 for the frequency of the *M* allele and 0.3 for the frequency of the *N* allele. By convention, we use the symbols p and q to refer to the allele frequencies, and in this case, p is shorthand for "the frequency of the *M* allele" and q is shorthand for "the frequency of the *N* allele." Using these symbols, we say that $p = 0.7$ and $q = 0.3$.

The Hardy-Weinberg equilibrium model states that, given allele frequencies p and q, the expected genotype frequencies in the next generation are:

Frequency of the *MM* genotype = p^2
Frequency of the *MN* genotype = $2pq$
Frequency of the *NN* genotype = q^2

A mathematical proof of this relationship is given in Appendix 1 for those interested in how this simple relationship was derived. For our hypothetical

Hardy-Weinberg equilibrium A mathematical statement whereby, in the absence of nonrandom mating and evolutionary forces, genotype and allele frequencies will remain the same from one generation to the next.

example (where $p = 0.7$ and $q = 0.3$), we can now predict the genotype frequencies in the next generation using these formulae:

Frequency of the *MM* genotype $= p^2 = (0.7)^2 = 0.49$

Frequency of the *MN* genotype $= 2pq = 2 \times 0.7 \times 0.3 = 0.42$

Frequency of the *NN* genotype $= q^2 = (0.3)^2 = 0.09$

Thus, we expect that in the next generation, 49 percent of the offspring will have genotype *MM,* 42 percent will have genotype *MN,* and 9 percent will have genotype *NN.*

You may have noticed something interesting about the above example. We started with a set of genotype frequencies for one generation, used them to compute the allele frequencies, and then used the allele frequencies to compute the genotype frequencies in the next generation. In this particular case, however, we wound up with the exact same genotype frequencies that we started with: $MM = 0.49$, $MN = 0.42$, $NN = 0.09$. Nothing changed! If we started over and computed the allele frequencies for the next generation, we would still get the same results. This shows an example of a subtle but important application of the Hardy-Weinberg model: *Given certain assumptions, the genotype and allele frequencies will remain the same from one generation to the next.*

This may not appear to make a lot of sense because the model appears to predict *no* evolution! After all, if we define microevolution as a change in allele frequencies over time, and if Hardy-Weinberg predicts *no* change, then what relevance does this have? The relevance becomes clear when we go back and examine that critical phrase—*given certain assumptions.*

When Hardy and Weinberg showed that there was no inherent tendency of allele frequencies to change over time, they used a simple model that had a number of assumptions. Simply put, the model makes a prediction—no change in allele frequency over time. In the real world, however, we have countless examples of allele frequencies changing over time in many species. When observed reality does not match the predictions of the model, this means that one or more of the assumptions of the model is incorrect. By framing the process of evolution in terms of the equilibrium model, population geneticists were able to discover exactly what *does* cause evolutionary changes.

What are the assumptions that Hardy-Weinberg makes? First, the model assumes random mating with respect to the locus of study. That is, every individual has an equal chance of mating with any individual of the opposite sex (both sexes are assumed to have equal allele frequencies). The model also assumes that no new alleles are introduced by mutation, that there is no difference in fertility or survival of the different genotypes (no natural selection), that there are no changes caused by movement into or out of the population (no gene flow), and that there is no variation caused by random sampling (no genetic drift). Given all of these assumptions, there will be no change in the genotype frequencies or allele frequencies over time. If there *is* an observed change, it means that one or more of these assumptions is

FIGURE 3.1

Inbreeding is used with many domesticated animals to produce certain types of characteristics.

evolutionary forces Four mechanisms that can cause changes in allele frequencies from one generation to the next: mutation, natural selection, genetic drift, and gene flow.

nonrandom mating Patterns of mate choice that influence the distributions of genotype and phenotype frequencies.

inbreeding Mating between biologically related individuals.

incorrect. By extending the Hardy-Weinberg model mathematically, population geneticists have determined how these changes could take place and provided us with an understanding of the real world.

A population might not be in Hardy-Weinberg equilibrium for two basic reasons. Observed and expected genotype frequencies may differ because of the effects of evolutionary forces and/or nonrandom mating. **Evolutionary forces** are those mechanisms that can actually lead to a change in allele frequency over time. There are four evolutionary forces: mutation, natural selection, genetic drift, and gene flow (each is described in detail in the following section). These four forces are the only mechanisms that can cause the frequency of an allele to change over time. For example, if you observed a population with an allele frequency of 0.5 and returned a generation later to find an allele frequency of 0.4, then you have observed evolution. This change could be due to mutation, natural selection, genetic drift, and/or gene flow. Given the large amount of change in a single generation, it is unlikely that mutation would be responsible because mutation usually causes much lower amounts of change in a single generation. In that case, you could conclude that the observed change was due to natural selection, genetic drift, and/or gene flow. You would need to examine more information, such as migration rates, population size, and environmental variation, to determine which factors were responsible for the change.

When allele frequencies change, so do genotype frequencies, but genotype frequencies can change without altering the underlying allele frequencies. This happens when there is significant **nonrandom mating,** which refers to the patterns of mate choice within a population and its genetic effects. One form of nonrandom mating is **inbreeding,** which occurs when there is mating between biologically related individuals (Figure 3.1). Another form of nonrandom mating is **assortative mating,** which is mating based on phenotypic similarity or dissimilarity (such as blondes having a preference to mate only with other blondes or tall people preferring to mate only with other tall people). In both inbreeding and assortative mating, there is no change in the actual allele frequency, but there is a change in the genotype frequencies. Thus, nonrandom mating does not *cause* evolution (because the allele frequencies do not change), but it can affect the *rate* of evolutionary change, as discussed later in this chapter.

THE EVOLUTIONARY FORCES

This section discusses the four evolutionary forces in detail. Although they are described here one at a time, keep in mind that in the real world all four operate at the same time.

Mutation

Mutation introduces new alleles into a population. Therefore, the frequency of different alleles will change over time. Consider a genetic locus with a single allele, *A,* for a population of 100 people (and therefore 200 alleles, because each person has two alleles). Everyone in the population will have genotype *AA,* and the frequency of the *A* allele is 1.0 (100 percent). Now, assume that one of the *A* alleles being passed on to the next generation changes into a new form, *a.* Assuming the population stays the same size (to make the mathematics a bit easier), there will be 199 *A* alleles and 1 *a* allele in the next generation. The frequency of *A* will have changed from 1.0 to 0.995 (199/200), and the frequency of *a* will have changed from 0.0 to 0.005 (1/200).

If there is no further evolutionary change, the allele frequencies will remain the same in future generations. If this mutation continues to recur, the frequency of the *a* allele will slowly increase, assuming no other evolutionary forces are operating. For typical mutation rates, such a process would take a very long time.

Mutations can also occur in the reverse direction; that is, an *a* allele could mutate back to the original form *A.* Not much information is available on back mutation rates in human populations, but they do appear to be much rarer than the usual mutation rate.

Although mutations are vital to evolution because they provide new variations, mutation rates are low and do not lead, by themselves, to major changes in allele frequency. The other evolutionary forces increase or decrease the frequencies of mutant alleles. If you visited a population over two generations and noted that the frequency of a given allele had changed from 0.30 to 0.40, it would be extremely unlikely that this magnitude of change would be due solely to mutation. The other evolutionary forces would be responsible for such large changes.

Many discrete genetic traits are **polymorphisms** (many forms). A genetic polymorphism is a locus with two or more alleles having frequencies

assortative mating Mating between phenotypically similar or dissimilar individuals.

polymorphism A discrete genetic trait in which there are at least two alleles at a locus having frequencies greater than 0.01.

too large to be a result of mutation alone. The usual, somewhat arbitrary, cutoff point for these allele frequencies is 0.01. If an allele has a frequency greater than 0.01, we can safely assume that this relatively high frequency is caused by factors other than mutation. For example, a locus with allele frequencies of $A = 1.0$ and $a = 0.0$ would not be polymorphic because only one allele (A) is present in the population. Likewise, a locus with frequencies of $A = 0.999$ and $a = 0.001$ would not be a genetic polymorphism because only one allele has a frequency greater than 0.01. If the allele frequencies were $A = 0.2$ and $a = 0.8$, this would be evidence of genetic polymorphism. Both alleles have frequencies greater than 0.01. Such frequencies are explained by natural selection, genetic drift, and/or gene flow.

Natural Selection

As discussed in Chapter 1, natural selection filters genetic variation. Individuals with certain biological characteristics that allow them to survive to reproduce pass on the alleles for such characteristics to the next generation. Natural selection does not create new genetic variation (only mutation can do that), but it can change the relative frequencies of different alleles.

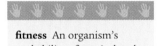

fitness An organism's probability of survival and reproduction.

The analysis of natural selection focuses on **fitness,** the probability of survival and reproduction of an organism. For any locus, fitness is measured as the relative genetic contribution of a genotype to the next generation. Imagine a locus with two alleles, A and a, and the genotypes AA, Aa, and aa. If all individuals with genotypes AA and Aa survive and reproduce but only half of those with genotype aa do so, then the fitness of genotype aa is half that of genotypes AA and Aa. Fitness refers to the proportion of individuals with a given genotype who survive and reproduce.

Depending on the fitness of each genotype, natural selection can have different effects. Some of the more common forms of natural selection are discussed here, along with a few examples from human populations. Additional examples will be presented in Chapter 15.

Selection against Recessive Homozygotes   Even simple genetic traits with only two alleles have a number of different models of natural selection to investigate. The result of natural selection depends on what the initial allele frequencies are, whether one allele is dominant, and what the exact fitness values for each genotype are.

Consider what happens when one allele is dominant and one is recessive. Let A be the dominant allele and a the recessive allele. As you learned in Chapter 2, the genotypes AA and Aa will both give rise to the same phenotype because A is dominant. Because AA and Aa specify the same phenotype, they have the same fitness. For this hypothetical example, let us assume that the fitness of AA and Aa is 100 percent. That is, all individuals with these genotypes survive and reproduce in equal numbers. Let us further assume that the people with the recessive phenotype (those with the genotype aa) have a fitness of 0 percent; that is, no one with this genotype will survive and reproduce. This hypothetical example corresponds to a situation in which a

TABLE 3.2	Example of Natural Selection against a Recessive Homozygote

This example uses an initial population size before selection of 200 people. The locus has two alleles, *A* and *a*. Initially, there are 50 people with genotype *AA*, 100 people with genotype *Aa*, and 50 people with genotype *aa*. The allele frequencies before selection are therefore 0.5 for *A* and 0.5 for *a*. The fitness values have been chosen to illustrate total selection against the recessive homozygote.

	Genotype			
	AA	Aa	aa	*Total*
Number of people before selection	50	100	50	200
Fitness (percentage that survives)	100%	100%	0%	—
Number of people after selection	50	100	0	150

There are 150 people after selection. Using the method of allele frequency computation shown in Table 3.1 and in the text, the allele frequencies after selection are 200/300 = 0.667 for the *A* allele and 100/300 = 0.333 for the *a* allele.

recessive allele (*a*) is fatal for those who have two copies (*aa*). Now, assume a population of 200 people before selection with the following distribution of genotypes: *AA* = 50, *Aa* = 100, *aa* = 50. Using the methods discussed earlier, the allele frequencies can be found: *A* = 0.5, and *a* = 0.5.

Table 3.2 shows the process of natural selection using these hypothetical numbers. After selection, the number of individuals in each genotype is *AA* = 50, *Aa* = 100, *aa* = 0. All individuals with genotypes *AA* and *Aa* survive, and none of those with genotype *aa* survive. After selection, there are 150 individuals, and the allele frequencies are *A* = 0.6667 and *a* = 0.3333.

This example shows the effect of selection against the recessive homozygote. The frequency of the *a* allele drops from 0.5 to 0.3333. Because *a* is a harmful allele, however, you might expect that the *a* allele would be totally eliminated. This does not occur. Because the heterozygote (*Aa*) is not eliminated through selection, these individuals continue to pass the *a* allele on to the next generation. The recessive allele *a* cannot be eliminated in a single generation.

This simple example illustrates another feature of natural selection. Figure 3.2 shows the frequency of the *a* allele for 100 generations of natural selection. The allele frequencies in subsequent generations can be determined by finding out the expected genotype frequencies after selection (using the Hardy-Weinberg equilibrium model) and examining the expected effects of another generation of selection. Note that the frequency of *a* does not decrease at the same rate over time. The amount of reduction in *a* actually slows down over time. As the frequency of *a* slowly approaches zero, an increasingly

FIGURE 3.2

Change over time in the frequency of a recessive allele when there is complete selection against the recessive homozygote and the initial allele frequency is 0.5.

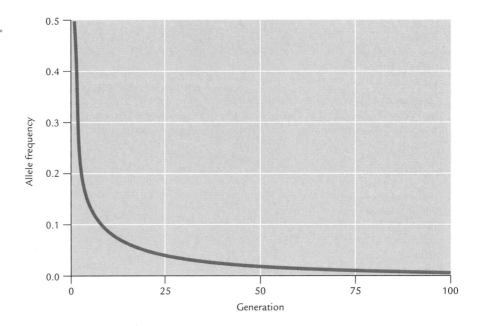

lower percentage of the population will be recessive homozygotes; consequently, fewer will be eliminated every generation. Ultimately, a balance will be reached as the reduction in the *a* allele due to selection is offset by new mutations from *A* to *a*. Because mutation rates are very low, this frequency of the *a* allele will be only slightly greater than zero.

Tay-Sachs disease is one case of selection against recessive homozygotes in humans. This affliction is caused by a metabolic disorder that results in blindness, mental retardation, and destruction of the central nervous system. Children with Tay-Sachs disease generally die within the first few years of life. The disease is caused by a recessive allele and occurs in those individuals who are homozygous. Heterozygotes carry the allele but do not show any major biological impairments.

When deleterious alleles are recessive, such as with Tay-Sachs disease, the frequency is generally not zero because heterozygotes continue to pass the allele on from generation to generation. Nonetheless, the frequency of a harmful recessive allele will still be very low. This low frequency is maintained by mutation but is kept from increasing by natural selection.

Selection against Dominant Homozygotes   What if a dominant allele is selected against? As an example, consider the same starting point as in the previous example: *AA* = 50, *Aa* = 100, and *aa* = 50, giving initial allele frequencies of *A* = 0.5 and *a* = 0.5. In this example, we will consider partial selection against the dominant allele (*A*) of 50 percent for individuals with the *AA* or *Aa* genotype, and let the recessive genotype (*aa*) have a fitness of 100 percent. After selection, there are 25 individuals with genotype *AA*, 25 with genotype *Aa*, and 50 with genotype *aa* (Table 3.3). The allele frequencies after selection are *A* = 0.375 and *a* = 0.625. Because of selection against

TABLE 3.3	Example of Natural Selection against the Dominant Homozygote

This example uses an initial population size before selection of 200 people. The locus has two alleles, *A* and *a*. Initially, there are 50 people with genotype *AA*, 100 people with genotype *Aa*, and 50 people with genotype *aa*. The allele frequencies before selection are therefore 0.5 for *A* and 0.5 for *a*. The fitness values have been chosen to illustrate partial selection against the dominant homozygote and the heterozygote.

| | *Genotype* | | | |
	AA	Aa	aa	*Total*
Number of people before selection	50	100	50	200
Fitness (percentage that survives)	50%	50%	100%	—
Number of people after selection	25	25	50	100

There are 100 people after selection. Using the method of allele frequency computation shown in Table 3.1 and in the text, the allele frequencies after selection are 75/200 = 0.375 for the *A* allele and 125/200 = 0.625 for the *a* allele.

the dominant homozygote, the frequency of the dominant allele (*A*) has gone down and the frequency of the recessive allele (*a*) has gone up.

Achondroplastic dwarfism is an example of a dominant allele in human beings. This type of dwarfism (small body size and abnormal body proportions) is caused by a dominant allele found in very low frequencies in human populations—roughly 0.00005 (Figure 3.3). Because the achondroplastic allele is dominant, individuals with one or two of the alleles will show the disease. Virtually all achondroplastic dwarfs are heterozygotes. The condition is usually caused by a mutation occurring in the sex cells of one parent. We know that a mutation is involved in a majority of these cases because roughly 80 percent of dwarfs have two normal parents. Because the condition is caused by a dominant allele, the only way a child could receive the allele would be from a parent or through mutation. If the parent had the allele, he or she would also be a dwarf. Therefore, when both parents of a dwarf are not dwarfs, we know that the offspring's dwarfism is the result of a mutation. In cases in which two dwarfs mate, the offspring can be homozygous for the disease, and such offspring generally die before, or shortly after, birth.

The low frequency of achondroplastic dwarfs is the result of natural selection acting to remove the harmful allele from the population. Although there is no major risk of mortality for a heterozygous achondroplastic dwarf, selection acts on differential reproduction. Given their physical appearance, these dwarfs have few opportunities to mate. The most likely mating is between two dwarfs. In these cases, there is additional selection because they

FIGURE 3.3

Achondroplastic dwarfism is a genetic disorder caused by a dominant allele. This toddler has very short arms and legs.

have an increased risk of having children with two copies of the achon-droplastic allele; these children generally die early in life. Thus, differences in both mortality and fertility can affect the degree of selection against an allele.

Selection for the Heterozygote   The previous examples discussed selection against recessive and dominant homozygotes, which acts to increase the frequency of one allele and decrease the frequency of another. Selection could also occur *for* recessive or dominant homozygotes, which would act to increase the frequency of an allele. With time, the allele frequencies will approach 0 or 1, depending on which allele is selected against.

These models might lead us to expect patterns of genetic variation whereby most populations have allele frequencies close to either 0 or 1, and few populations have intermediate values. However, studies of human genetic variation have found that for many loci the allele frequencies are intermediate, with values such as 0.3, 0.5, or 0.8. We could argue that selection is not yet complete and that given enough time all allele frequencies would be close to 0 or 1, but the wealth of information regarding allele frequencies in human groups makes this very unlikely. Why, then, do many loci show intermediate frequencies? Is there a way that natural selection can produce such values?

A classic example of an intermediate allele frequency in human populations is the sickle cell allele, discussed briefly in the previous chapter. Because people homozygous for this allele have sickle cell anemia and are likely to die early in life, this appears to be a classic situation of selection against a homozygote. If this were the case, we might expect most human populations to have frequencies of the sickle cell allele close to 0, and, in fact, many do. However, a number of populations in parts of Africa, India, and the Mediterranean show higher frequencies. In some African groups, the frequency of the sickle cell allele is greater than 20 percent (Roychoudhury and Nei 1988). How can a harmful allele exist at such a high frequency?

The answer is a form of selection known as selection for the heterozygote (and therefore against the homozygotes). Consider fitness values of $AA = 70$ percent, $Aa = 100$ percent, and $aa = 20$ percent. Here, only 70 percent of those with genotype AA and 20 percent of those with genotype aa survive for every 100 people with genotype Aa (the heterozygote). Selection is for the heterozygote and against the homozygotes. Let the frequency of both the A and a alleles be 0.5. In a population of 200 people, this means we start with 50 AA people, 100 Aa people, and 50 aa people before selection. Given these fitness values, there will be 35 people with AA, 100 with Aa, and 10 with aa after selection. The allele frequencies after selection are $A = 0.586$ and $a = 0.414$ (Table 3.4).

Why would the frequency of the A allele increase and the frequency of the a allele decrease? In selection for the heterozygote, both alleles are being selected for, because every Aa person can contribute both alleles to the next generation. But both alleles are also being selected against. When AA people die or fail to reproduce, two A alleles are lost from the population. When aa people die or fail to reproduce, two a alleles are lost from the population.

TABLE 3.4	Example of Natural Selection for the Heterozygote

This example uses an initial population size before selection of 200 people. The locus has two alleles, *A* and *a*. Initially, there are 50 people with genotype *AA*, 100 people with genotype *Aa*, and 50 people with genotype *aa*. The allele frequencies before selection are therefore 0.5 for *A* and 0.5 for *a*. The fitness values have been chosen to illustrate selection for the heterozygote and partial selection against both homozygotes. Note that because this is a codominant system, each genotype specifies a different phenotype.

	Genotype			
	AA	Aa	aa	*Total*
Number of people before selection	50	100	50	200
Fitness (percentage that survives)	70%	100%	20%	—
Number of people after selection	35	100	10	145

There are 145 people after selection. Using the method of allele frequency computation shown in Table 3.1 and in the text, the allele frequencies after selection are $170/290 = 0.586$ for the *A* allele and $120/290 = 0.414$ for the *a* allele.

Selection for the heterozygote involves selection for and against both alleles. Because the fitness of *AA* is greater in this example than the fitness of *aa* (70 percent versus 20 percent), proportionately more individuals with genotype *AA* will survive and reproduce. Hence, proportionately more *A* alleles will appear in the next generation.

Figure 3.4 shows the pattern of allele frequency change over 20 generations using the initial values and fitness values in this example. Note that the frequency of *A* continues to increase for the first few generations but soon levels off. There is no change in the allele frequency after approximately eight generations. This is the expected pattern when there is selection for the heterozygote. A balance is reached between selection for and against the two alleles *A* and *a*. The exact value of this balancing point will depend on the fitness values of the homozygous genotypes. Selection for the heterozygote is also called **balancing selection.**

Given this model, the distribution of sickle cell allele frequencies in humans makes sense. In many environments, there is selection against the sickle cell homozygote, and the frequency is low. In environments in which malaria is common, the heterozygotes have an advantage because they are less susceptible to malaria. People homozygous for the sickle cell allele are likely to suffer from sickle cell anemia and die. People homozygous for the normal allele are more likely to suffer from malaria. Thus, there is selection against both homozygotes (although more selection against those with sickle cell anemia) and selection for the heterozygote. A balance of allele frequencies is

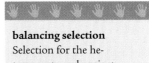

balancing selection
Selection for the heterozygote and against the homozygotes (the heterozygote is most fit).

FIGURE 3.4

Change over time in allele frequencies when there is selection for the heterozygote (*Aa*). The initial allele frequencies are both 0.5. The fitness of each genotype (the relative frequency of survival) is *AA* = 70 percent, *Aa* = 100 percent, and *aa* = 20 percent.

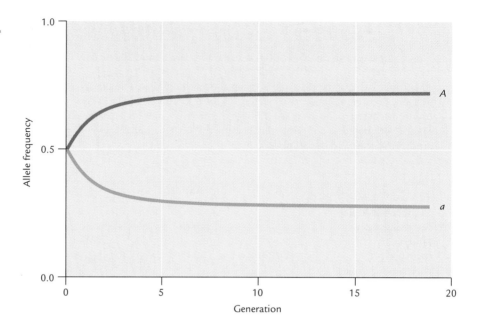

predicted and has been found in many human populations. A more complete discussion of the sickle cell example is given in Chapter 15.

Another possible example of balancing selection in humans concerns cystic fibrosis, a genetic disease caused by a recessive allele. Studies have shown that individuals heterozygous for the cystic fibrosis allele are resistant to other diseases, such as cholera (Rodman and Zamudio 1991) and typhoid fever (Pier et al. 1998). If so, then heterozygotes would have the greatest fitness, and the optimal frequency of the cystic fibrosis allele would be determined by the balance between selection relating to cystic fibrosis and these other diseases.

Selection against the Heterozygote   This final example of a type of natural selection also focuses on the heterozygote, but this time, we discuss what happens if there is selection *against* the heterozygote. For example, consider a hypothetical case of 100 individuals before selection with genotype numbers of *AA* = 64, *Aa* = 32, and *aa* = 4. Using the allele counting method, we see that the allele frequencies are *A* = 0.8 and *a* = 0.2. Now let us simulate selection against the heterozygote with fitness values of *AA* = 100 percent, *Aa* = 75 percent, and *aa* = 100 percent. After selection, there will be 64 individuals with genotype *AA,* 24 with genotype *Aa,* and 4 with genotype *aa.* Completing the calculations in the usual way, we see that the allele frequencies after selection are *A* = 0.826 and *a* = 0.174. We would then conclude that selection against the heterozygote causes an increase in *A* and a decrease in *a.* However, this conclusion turns out to be dependent on the initial starting values. If, for example, we start with allele frequencies of *A* = 0.2 and *a* = 0.8, and use the same fitness values, the allele frequencies after selection would be *A* = 0.174 and *a* = 0.826. In this case, the frequency of *A* decreased and the frequency of *a* increased.

Selection against a heterozygote results in a decrease in the less common allele. If *A* is more common than *a* to start with, then it will increase. On the other hand, if *A* is less common than *a* to start with, then it will decrease. Quite simply, because selection against the heterozygote removes equal numbers of *A* and *a,* then one of these will be removed first. As an analogy, imagine there is a large table in the front of your classroom loaded with 50 apples and 30 oranges. Each student in the class comes up and removes 1 apple and 1 orange (analogous to removal of a heteroyzygote because the two "alleles" are different). After the first student comes up, there will be 49 apples and 29 oranges. After the second student, there will be 48 apples and 28 oranges. This will continue until there are 20 apples and 0 oranges. We ran out of oranges first because there were fewer to begin with.

An example of selection against the heterozygote in humans is the Rhesus (Rh) blood group. Inheritance of the Rh blood group involves three linked loci. The locus described here (D) has two alleles, *D* and *d,* where *D* is dominant and *d* is recessive. Individuals with genotypes *DD* or *Dd* are called *Rh positive,* and those with genotype *dd* are called *Rh negative.* Those with Rh positive blood produce a certain chemical (D), and those with Rh negative blood can produce a corresponding antibody (anti-D). In terms of blood chemistry, anti-D antibodies can destroy red blood cells with D molecules. During some pregnancies, a mother with Rh negative blood carries a fetus with Rh positive blood. In such cases, the child may be at risk and selected against. Each time this happens, the affected child *must* be a heterozygote. Why? Consider that a mother with Rh negative blood has the genotype *dd,* which means that she has passed a *d* allele on to her child. If the child is Rh positive and has one *d* allele, then the other allele, inherited from the father, must be *D.* Therefore, in all cases in which the mother is Rh negative and the fetus is Rh positive, the fetus is heterozygous (*Dd*).

Selection and Complex Traits   The previous examples used simple genetic traits to illustrate basic principles of natural selection. Selection also affects complex traits, however, such as those discussed in Chapter 2. For complex traits, we focus on measures of the average value and on variation around this average. Because complex traits are continuous, we look at the effects of selection on the average value of a trait and on the lower and higher extremes.

There are several forms of selection on complex traits. **Stabilizing selection** refers to selection against both extremes of a trait's range in values. Individuals with extreme high or low values of a trait are less likely to survive and reproduce, while those with values closer to the average are more likely to survive and reproduce. The effect of stabilizing selection is to maintain the population at the same average value over time. Extreme values are selected against in each generation, but the average value in the population does not change.

Human birth weight is a good example of stabilizing selection. The weight of a newborn child is the result of a number of environmental factors, such as mother's age, weight, and history of smoking, among many others. There is also a genetic component to birth weight. Newborns who are very small (less than 2.5 kg) are less likely to survive than are newborns who

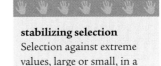

stabilizing selection
Selection against extreme values, large or small, in a continuous trait.

FIGURE 3.5

Stabilizing selection for human birth weight based on data from Karn and Penrose (1951). Babies born smaller or larger than the optimum birth weight have increased mortality. (From E. Peter Volpe, *Understanding Evolution*, 5th ed. Copyright © 1985 Wm. C. Brown Communications, Inc., Dubuque, Iowa. All Rights Reserved. Reprinted by permission of The McGraw-Hill Companies.)

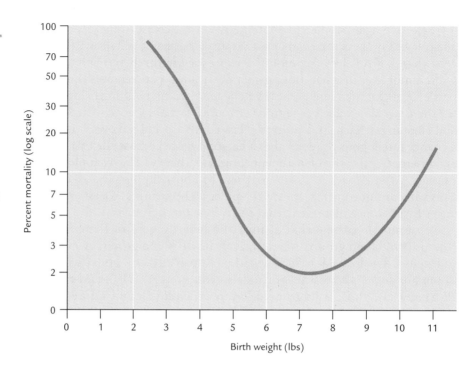

are heavier. Very small babies are more prone to disease and have weaker systems, making their survival more difficult. Newborns who are too large are also likely to be selected against, because a very large child may create complications during childbirth and both mother and child may die. Thus, there is selection against both extremes, small and large.

Stabilizing selection for birth weight has been documented for a number of human populations. These studies show a definite relationship between birth weight and mortality. The results of one study based on 13,730 newborns (Karn and Penrose 1951) are shown in Figure 3.5. Mortality rates are highest for those newborns with low (less than 2.7 kg) and high (greater than 4.5 kg) birth weights.

Another type of selection for complex traits is known as **directional selection,** selection against one extreme and/or for the other extreme. In other words, a direct relationship exists between survival and reproduction on one hand and the value of a trait on the other. The result is a change over time in one direction. The average value for a trait moves in one direction or the other. Perhaps the most dramatic example of directional selection in human evolution has been the threefold increase in brain size over the past 4 million years. Another example is the lighter skin that probably evolved in prehistoric humans as they moved north out of Africa (see Chapter 15).

directional selection Selection against one extreme in a continuous trait and/or selection for the other extreme.

genetic drift A mechanism for evolutionary change resulting from the random fluctuations of gene frequencies from one generation to the next.

Genetic Drift

Genetic drift is the random change in allele frequency from one generation to the next. These random changes are the result of the nature of probability.

TABLE 3.5	Probability of Getting Different Numbers of Heads and Tails from 10 Coin Flips	
Name of Heads	*Number of Tails*	*Probability*
0	10	0.001
1	9	0.010
2	8	0.044
3	7	0.117
4	6	0.205
5	5	0.246
6	4	0.205
7	3	0.117
8	2	0.044
9	1	0.010
10	0	0.001

These probabilities refer only to the case in which a coin is flipped 10 times. Other numbers of coin flips will give different probabilities.

Think for a moment about flipping a coin. What is the probability of its landing with the head facing up? It is 50 percent. The coin has two possible values, heads and tails, and when you flip it you will get one or the other. Suppose you flip a coin 10 times. How many heads and how many tails do you expect to get? Because the probability of getting a head or a tail is 50 percent, you expect to get five heads and five tails. Try this experiment several times. Do you always get five tails and five heads? No. Sometimes you get five heads and five tails, but sometimes you get different numbers. You may get six heads and four tails, or three heads and seven tails, or, much less likely, all heads.

The probability for different combinations of heads and tails from flipping a coin 10 times is shown in Table 3.5. The probability of getting all heads (or all tails) is rather low—0.001. Note, however, that the probability of getting four heads and six tails (or six heads and four tails) is much higher—0.205. Also note that the probability of getting exactly five heads and five tails is 0.246. This means that there is roughly a 75 percent chance of *not* getting exactly five heads and five tails.

The probability of 50 percent heads and 50 percent tails is the expected distribution. If you flip 10 coins enough times, you will find that the number of heads and tails grows closer to a 50:50 ratio. Often we hear about the "law of averages." The idea here is that if you flip a coin and get heads several times in a row, then you are very likely to get a tail the next time. This is wrong, and applying this "law" is an easy way to lose money if you gamble. *Each* flip of the coin is an independent event. Whatever happened the time before cannot affect the next flip. *Each* time you flip the coin, you have a 50 percent chance of getting a head and a 50 percent chance of getting a tail.

What does this have to do with genetics? The reproductive process in this way is like a coin toss. During the process of sex cell replication (meiosis), only one allele out of two at a given locus is used. The probability of either allele being passed on is 50 percent, just like a coin toss. Imagine a locus with two alleles, *A* and *a*. Now imagine a man and a woman, each with genotype *Aa*, who have a child. The man can pass on either an *A* allele or an *a* allele. Likewise, a woman can pass on either an *A* allele or an *a* allele. As we saw in the previous chapter, the probable distribution of genotypes among the children is 25 percent *AA*, 50 percent *Aa*, and 25 percent *aa*. If the couple has four children, you would expect one with *AA*, two with *Aa*, and one with *aa*. Thanks to random chance, however, the couple may get a different distribution of genotypes. You can model such a simple example by flipping a coin to simulate a child receiving an *A* allele or an *a* allele from either parent. Let "heads" represent the *A* allele and "tails" represent the *a* allele.

I performed this experiment four times to simulate four children born to these parents. Two of the children had genotype *AA*, and two had genotype *Aa*. Note that the allele frequencies have changed from the parent's generation to the children's generation. The allele frequencies of the parents were *A* = 0.5 and *a* = 0.5. The four children have a total of eight alleles, of which six are *A* and two are *a*. The frequency of *A* in the children is 6/8 = 0.75, and the frequency of *a* is 2/8 = 0.25. You might want to try this experiment several times to see the range of allele frequencies that can result.

When genetic drift occurs in populations, the same principle applies. Allele frequencies can change because of random chance. Sometimes the allele frequency will increase, and sometimes it will decrease. The direction of allele frequency change caused by genetic drift is random. The only time drift will not produce a change in allele frequency is when only one allele is present at a given locus. For example, if each parent passed on an *A* allele to each of the four children, the frequency of the *A* allele would be 1.0 among the children. The *a* allele would have been lost.

Genetic drift occurs in each generation. Such a process is too complicated to simulate using coins, but computers or random number tables can be used to model the effects of drift over time (see Cavalli-Sforza and Bodmer 1971:389). Figure 3.6 shows the results of three computer simulations of drift. In each case, the initial allele frequency was 0.5, and the population size was equal to 10 individuals (20 alleles) in each generation. The simulation was allowed to continue in each case for 20 generations. The graphs show the changes in allele frequency over time. Note that each of the three simulations shows a different pattern. This is expected because genetic drift is a random process. Each simulation is an independent event.

In each of these three graphs, the allele frequency fluctuates up and down. In Figure 3.6a, the allele frequency after 20 generations is 0.3. In Figure 3.6b, the allele frequency after 20 generations is 0.75. In Figure 3.6c, the allele frequency is equal to 1.0 after 10 generations, and it does not change any further. Given enough time, and assuming no other evolutionary forces affecting allele frequencies, genetic drift will ultimately lead to an allele's

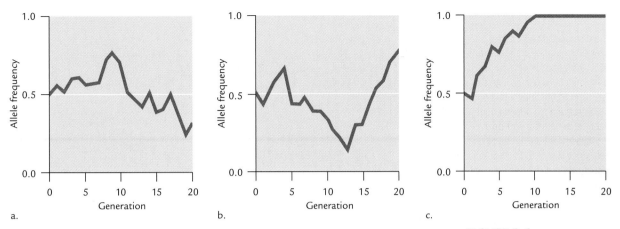

a.   b.   c.

FIGURE 3.6

Three computer simulations of 20 generations of genetic drift for populations of 10 individuals. Each simulation started with an initial allele frequency of 0.5.

becoming fixed at a value of 0.0 or 1.0. Thus, genetic drift leads to the reduction of variation within a population, given enough time.

Population Size and Genetic Drift   The effect of genetic drift depends on the size of the breeding population. The larger the population size, the less change will occur from one generation to the next. Thinking back to the coin toss analogy will show you that this makes sense. If you flip a coin 10 times and get three heads and seven tails, it is not that unusual. If you flip a coin 1 million times, however, you would be much less likely to get the same proportions—300,000 heads and 700,000 tails. This is because of a basic principle of probability: the greater the number of events, the fewer deviations from the expected frequencies (50 percent heads and 50 percent tails).

The effect of population size on genetic drift is shown in Figure 3.7. These graphs show the results of 1,000 simulations of genetic drift for four different values of breeding population size: $N = 10, 50, 100, 1,000$. In each computer run, the initial allele frequency was set to 0.5, and the simulation was allowed to continue for 20 generations. The four graphs show the distribution of allele frequency values after 20 generations of genetic drift. Figure 3.7a shows this distribution for a population size of $N = 10$. Note that the majority of the 1,000 simulations resulted in final allele frequencies of less than 0.1 or greater than 0.9. In small populations, genetic drift more often results in a quick loss of one allele or another. Figure 3.7b shows the distribution of final allele frequencies for a population size of $N = 50$. Here there are fewer extreme values and more values falling between 0.3 and 0.7. Figures 3.7c and 3.7d show the distributions for population sizes of $N = 100$ and $N = 1,000$. As these graphs show, the larger the population size, the fewer deviations in allele frequency caused by genetic drift. The main point here is that genetic drift has the greatest evolutionary effect in relatively small breeding populations.

Examples of Genetic Drift   Genetic drift in human populations is shown in a case study of a group known as the Dunkers, a religious sect that

FIGURE 3.7

Allele frequency distributions for 1,000 computer simulations of 20 generations of genetic drift. The distributions show the number of times a given allele frequency was reached after 20 generations of drift. In all cases, the initial allele frequency was 0.5. Each graph represents a different value of population size: (a) = 10, (b) = 50, (c) = 100, (d) = 1,000.

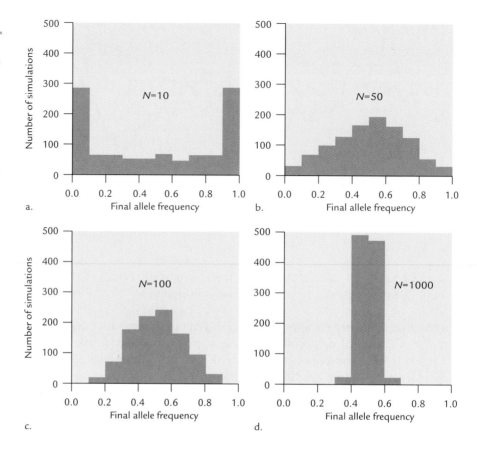

emigrated from Germany to the United States in the early 1700s. Approximately 50 families composed the initial group. Glass (1953) studied the genetic characteristics of the descendants of the original founding group living in Pennsylvania. These populations have never been greater than several hundred people and thus provide a unique opportunity to study genetic drift in a small human group. Glass found that the Dunker population differed in a number of genetic traits from both the modern German and U.S. populations. Further, the allele frequencies of Germany and the United States were almost identical, suggesting that other factors such as natural selection were unlikely. For example, the allele frequencies for the MN blood group were roughly $M = 0.55$ and $N = 0.45$ for both the U.S. and German samples. In the Dunker population, however, the allele frequencies were $M = 0.655$ and $N = 0.345$. Based on these and additional data, Glass concluded that the genetics of the Dunker population was shaped to a large extent by genetic drift over two centuries. Although 200 years seems like a long time to you and me, it is a fraction of an instant in evolutionary time. Genetic drift can clearly produce rapid changes under the proper circumstances.

Genetic drift in human populations has also been found on Tristan da Cunha, a small island in the south Atlantic Ocean. In 1816, the English established a small garrison on the island. When they left, one man and his wife remained, to be joined later by a handful of other settlers. Given such a small number of original settlers, what do you suppose is the probability that the families represented all the genetic variation present in the population they came from? The probability would be very low. Genetic drift is often caused when a small number of founders form a new population; this type of genetic drift is known as **founder effect.** An analogy would be a barrel containing thousands of red and blue beads, mixed in equal proportions. If you reached into the barrel and randomly pulled out a handful of beads, you might not get 50 percent red and 50 percent blue. Because of random chance, founders are not likely to be an exact genetic representation of the original population. The smaller the number of founders, the greater the deviation will be.

Over time, the population of Tristan da Cunha remained small. The population size was further reduced twice because of emigration and disaster. Given its initial small population, combined with two further reductions and a maximum population size less than 300, the island had the opportunity to experience considerable genetic drift. This effect is seen dramatically through analysis of historical records for the island; for example, it was found that two of the original founders contributed genetically to more than 29 percent of the 1961 population (Roberts 1968).

founder effect A type of genetic drift caused by the formation of a new population by a small number of individuals.

gene flow A mechanism for evolutionary change resulting from the movement of genes from one population to another.

Gene Flow

The fourth evolutionary force is **gene flow,** the movement of alleles from one population to another. The term *migration* is often used to mean the same thing as gene flow. From a conservative standpoint, however, this is not completely accurate. Migration refers to the more or less permanent movement of individuals from one place to another. Why the confusion? After all, excepting artificial insemination, your alleles do not move unless you do. You can migrate, though, without passing on any alleles. You can also be involved in gene flow without actually making a permanent move to a new place. In many texts on microevolution, the terms *gene flow* and *migration* are used interchangeably. Keep in mind, however, that there are certain distinctions in the real world.

Genetic Effects of Gene Flow   Gene flow involves the movement of alleles between at least two populations. When gene flow occurs, the two populations mix genetically and tend to become more similar. Under most conditions, the more the two populations mix, the more similar they will become genetically (assuming that the two environments are not different enough to produce different effects of natural selection).

Consider a genetic locus with two alleles, *A* and *a*. Assume two populations, 1 and 2. Now assume that all the alleles in population 1 are *A* and all the alleles in population 2 are *a*. The allele frequencies of these two imaginary populations are:

Population 1	*Population 2*
Frequency of $A = 1.0$	Frequency of $A = 0.0$
Frequency of $a = 0.0$	Frequency of $a = 1.0$

FIGURE 3.8

Effects of gene flow over time. Population 1 started with an allele frequency of 1.0, and population 2 started with an allele frequency of 0.0. The two populations exchange 10 percent of their genes with each generation. Over time, the continued gene flow acts to make the two populations more similar genetically.

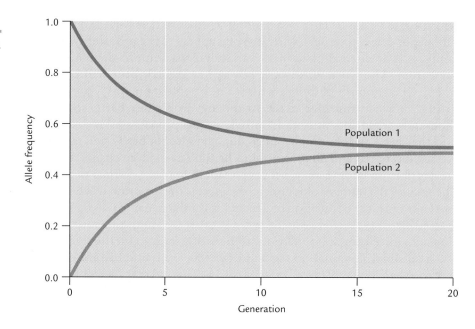

Now imagine a situation in which 10 percent of the people in population 1 move to population 2, and vice versa. This movement constitutes gene flow. What effect will the gene flow have? After gene flow has taken place, population 1 is made up of 90 percent *A* alleles and 10 percent *a* alleles. Population 2 is made up of 10 percent *A* alleles and 90 percent *a* alleles. The allele frequencies of the two populations, though still different, have become more similar as a consequence of gene flow. If the same rate of gene flow (10 percent) continues generation after generation, the two populations will become more and more similar genetically. After 20 generations of gene flow, the two populations will be almost identical. The accumulated effects of gene flow over time for this hypothetical example are shown in Figure 3.8.

Apart from making populations more similar, gene flow can also introduce new variation within a population. In the example, a new allele (*a*) was introduced into population 1 as the result of gene flow. A new mutation arising in one population can be spread throughout the rest of a species by gene flow.

Compared to many other organisms, humans are relatively mobile creatures. Human populations show a great deal of variation in degree of migration. Even today, many humans live and work within a small area and choose mates from nearby. Some people are more mobile than others, the extent of their mobility depending on a number of factors, such as available technology, occupation, and income.

In spite of local and regional differences, humans today all belong to the same species. Even though genetic variation exists among populations, they are in fact characterized more by their similarity. A critical factor in the cohesiveness of the human species, gene flow acts to reduce differences among groups.

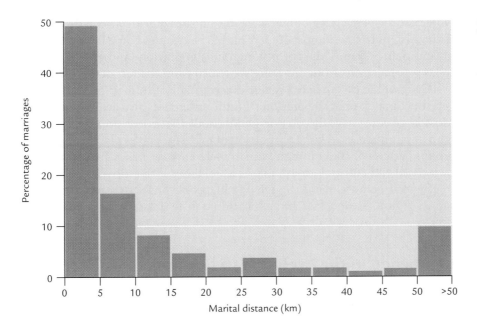

FIGURE 3.9

Percentage of marriages taking place at various marital distances (the distance between the premarital residences of bride and groom) for the town of Leominster, Massachusetts, 1800–1849. (*Source:* author's unpublished data.)

Determinants of Gene Flow The amount of gene flow between human populations depends on a variety of environmental and cultural factors. Geographic distance is a major determinant of migration and gene flow. The farther two populations are apart geographically, the less likely they are to exchange mates. Even in the highly mobile modern world, you are more likely to choose a spouse from nearby than from across the country. Exceptions to the rule do occur, of course, but the influence of geographic distance is still very strong.

Studies of migration and gene flow often look at distance between birthplaces or premarital residences of married couples. If, say, you were born in New York City and your spouse was born in Chicago, the distance between your birthplaces would be approximately 1,300 km (roughly 800 miles). If both you and your spouse came from the same neighborhood in the same city, your marital distance would be close to zero. The relationship between migration and geographic distance is similar in most human populations (Relethford 1992). Most marriages take place within a few kilometers, and the number of marriages quickly decreases as the distance between populations increases. This indicates that the majority of genes flowing into human populations come from a local area, and a small proportion from farther distances.

The relationship between the frequency of marriages and geographic distance is shown in Figure 3.9. This graph presents the results of a historical study of migration into the town of Leominster, Massachusetts, using marriage records for 1800–1849. A total of 1,602 marriages took place in the population over the 50-year period. Of these, almost half (49.2 percent) were between a bride and groom who were both native to Leominster. An additional 16.5 percent of the marriages took place between couples whose premarital residences were between 5 and 10 km (roughly 8–16 miles) apart.

Note that the percentage of marriages diminishes quickly after a distance of 5 km. Also note that almost 10 percent of the couples come from distances greater than 50 km. This type of long-range migration (and gene flow) acts to keep populations from diverging too much from the rest of the species.

Geographic distance is a major determinant of human migration and gene flow, but it is not the only one. Ethnic differences also act to limit them. Most large cities have distinct neighborhoods that correspond to different ethnic communities. A large proportion of marriages takes place within these groups because of the common human preference for marrying within one's own social and cultural group. Likewise, religious differences act as barriers to gene flow because many, though not all, people prefer to marry within the same religion. Social class and educational differences can also limit gene flow.

Interaction of the Evolutionary Forces

It is convenient to discuss each of the four evolutionary forces separately, but in reality they act together to produce allele frequency change. Mutation acts to introduce new genetic variants; natural selection, genetic drift, and gene flow act to change the frequency of the mutant allele. Sometimes the evolutionary forces act together, and sometimes they act in opposition. Their exact interaction depends on a variety of factors, such as the biochemical and physical effects of different alleles, the presence or absence of dominance, population size and distribution, and the environment, to name but a few. Many biological anthropologists attempt to unravel some of these factors in human population studies.

In general, we look at how natural selection, genetic drift, and gene flow act to increase or decrease genetic variation within and between groups. (Mutation gets less attention even though it introduces new genetic variants because the change in allele frequency in one generation is low.) An increase in variation within a population means that individuals within the population will be more genetically different from one another. A decrease in variation within a population means the reverse; individuals will become more similar to one another genetically. An increase in variation among populations means that two or more populations will become more different from one another genetically, and a decrease in variation within populations means the reverse.

Let us first consider the effects of genetic drift, gene flow, and natural selection on allele frequency variation. Genetic drift tends to remove alleles from a population and therefore acts to reduce variation within a population. On the other hand, because genetic drift is a random event and occurs independently in different populations, the pattern of genetic drift will tend to be different on average in different populations. On average, then, genetic drift will act to increase variation between populations. Gene flow acts to introduce new alleles into a population and can have the effect of increasing variation within a population. Gene flow also acts to reduce variation between populations in most cases.

TABLE 3.6	Summary of the Effects of Selection, Drift, and Gene Flow on Variation within and among Populations		

Evolutionary Force	Variation within Populations	Variation between Populations
Selection	Increase or decrease	Increase or decrease
Genetic drift	Decrease	Increase
Gene flow	Increase	Decrease

A decrease in variation within a population makes individuals more similar to one another, whereas an increase in variation within a population makes individuals less similar to one another. A decrease in variation among populations makes the populations more similar to one another, whereas an increase in variation among populations makes the populations less similar to one another. Note that natural selection can either increase or decrease variation; the exact effect depends on the type of selection and on differences in environment (see text).

Natural selection can either increase or decrease variation within a population, depending on the specific type of selection and the initial allele frequencies. Selection against recessive homozygotes, for example, will lead to the gradual decrease of one allele and consequently reduce variation. Selection for an advantageous mutation, however, will result in an increase in the frequency of the mutant and act to increase variation within the population. Selection can also either increase or decrease variation between populations, depending on environmental variation. If two populations have similar environments, then natural selection will take place in the same way in both groups and so will act to reduce genetic differences between them. On the other hand, if the two populations are in different enough environments that natural selection operates in different ways, then variation between the populations may be increased. Table 3.6 summarizes the effects of different evolutionary forces on variation within and among populations.

Different evolutionary forces can produce the same, or opposite, effects. Different forces can also act in opposition to one another. Genetic drift and gene flow, for example, have opposite effects on variation within and between populations. If both of these forces operate at the same time, they can counteract each other.

Several examples will help illustrate the ways in which different evolutionary forces can interact. Consider the forces of mutation and genetic drift. How might these two forces interact? Mutation acts to change allele frequency by the introduction of a new allele, whereas genetic drift causes random fluctuations in allele frequency from one generation to the next. If both operate at the same time, drift may act to increase or decrease the frequency of the new mutation. Consider what happens when everyone in a population has two A alleles and there is then a mutation from A to a in one individual. The person with the mutation can pass on either the A allele or the a allele, each with a 50 percent probability. It is possible that the

TABLE 3.7	Results of Computer Simulation of Mutation and Genetic Drift

A total of 1,000 independent computer simulations were performed using a population size of 10 individuals with a single initial mutation (1 mutant allele out of 20 in the population, giving an initial allele frequency of $1/20 = 0.05$). Following mutation, the computer simulated genetic drift for 20 generations. The following shows the distribution of the frequencies of the mutant allele after 20 generations (see text).

Final Frequency of the Mutant Allele	Number of Cases
0.0	889
0.01–0.09	2
0.10–0.19	22
0.20–0.29	11
0.30–0.39	16
0.40–0.49	15
0.50–0.59	9
0.60–0.69	11
0.70–0.79	9
0.80–0.89	9
0.90–0.99	2
1.0	5

new mutant allele will be lost from the population because of random chance. It is also possible that the frequency of the mutant allele will increase because of random chance. The person with the mutation may pass the mutant form on to all of his or her children, and each of them might continue to pass it on to their children.

To give you an idea of how mutation and genetic drift can interact, I performed a simple computer simulation that allowed for a single mutation followed by genetic drift. In this simulation, a population size of 10 was used in which all individuals initially had the same allele. A single mutation event was then allowed, which meant that the frequency of the mutant allele was $1/20 = 0.05$ (1 mutant allele out of all 20 alleles in the population). Genetic drift was then simulated for 20 generations. This simulation was repeated 1,000 times; the results are shown in Table 3.7.

As expected, genetic drift leads to the loss of the mutant allele most of the time (in this case, 889 out of 1,000 times). In most of the remaining cases, however, the frequency of the mutant allele actually increased. In 45 cases, the frequency of the mutant allele was greater than 0.5 after 20 generations. In 5 cases, the mutant allele had become fixed (a frequency of 100 percent) within the population! Such computer simulations are a bit

Tay-Sachs Disease: Genetic Drift or Natural Selection?

Tay-Sachs disease is an example of a lethal recessive allele—people with two Tay-Sachs alleles generally die very early in life. As expected, the frequency of this disease tends to be rather low around the world, affecting roughly 1 in every 500,000 births. What is unusual about Tay-Sachs disease is the fact that among Jews of Eastern European ancestry (Ashkenazi Jews) the rate is much higher: Tay-Sachs affects roughly 1 in every 2,500 births in these populations (Molnar 1998). The occurrence of Tay-Sachs is also high in some other human populations.

What might be responsible for higher frequencies of a lethal allele in certain populations? Is it something related to their history, their environment, or some complex set of factors? One suggestion is genetic drift. Jewish populations have tended to be rather small and isolated, factors that increase the likelihood of genetic drift. Although selection acts to reduce the frequency of the allele, the random nature of genetic drift might have caused an increase relative to larger populations, which experienced less genetic drift.

Closer examination, however, argues against the genetic drift hypothesis. Tay-Sachs disease is not due to a specific mutant allele but actually can arise from several different mutations. All of these mutant alleles have elevated frequencies in Ashkenazi populations. It seems unlikely that all of these mutant forms would drift to higher frequencies (Marks 1995).

What else could be responsible for the elevated frequency of Tay-Sachs disease? Some evidence suggests that people who carry one Tay-Sachs allele (heterozygotes) have increased resistance to tuberculosis. If so, then the heterozygotes would have greater fitness than either the normal homozygote (who would be more susceptible to tuberculosis) or those homozygous for the Tay-Sachs allele (who have zero fitness). This is a case of balancing selection and, as discussed in the text, would lead to a balance in allele frequencies.

However, why would this type of selection take place only among the Ashkenazi? Cultural and historical data provide a possible answer. Due to discrimination, the Jewish populations of Eastern Europe were frequently isolated into overcrowded ghettos under conditions that would increase the threat of tuberculosis (Marks 1995).

The tuberculosis hypothesis is just that—a possible explanation that remains to be fully tested. If correct, it provides us with yet another example of the compromises that occur during evolution. There is no "perfect" genotype. Everything has a price in terms of fitness, and natural selection often reflects this balance between cost and benefit.

simplistic and somewhat unrealistic, but they do show how two evolutionary forces can interact.

Many other possibilities for interaction also exist. For example, natural selection reduces the frequency of a harmful recessive mutant allele. Gene flow tends to counter the effects of genetic drift on variation among populations. Genetic drift can increase the frequency of a harmful allele even if it is being selected against.

Much of microevolutionary theory deals with the mathematics describing such interactions. Studies of actual populations must take these interactions into account and try to control for them in analysis. There are some basic rules for interpreting genetic variation. If populations are large, then drift is unlikely to have much of an effect. Gene flow can be measured to some extent by looking at migration rates to determine how powerful an effect it would have. Natural selection can be investigated by looking at patterns of fertility and mortality among different classes of genotypes.

Imagine that you have visited a population over two generations. You note that the frequency of a certain allele has changed from 0.4 to 0.5.

Further, assume that the population has been totally isolated during the last generation and that the size of the breeding population has stayed at roughly 50 people. What could have caused the allele frequency change? Because mutation occurs at much lower rates, it could not be responsible. Given that the population was totally isolated, gene flow could not be responsible. Drift may have caused the change in allele frequency, for the size of the breeding population is rather low. Natural selection could also have produced the change. You would have to know more about the specific alleles and genotypes involved, environmental factors, and patterns of mortality and fertility to determine whether selection had an effect. Even given this rather limited information, you can rule out mutation and gene flow and proceed to develop tests to determine the relative influence of drift and selection.

The study of any natural population is much more complex. With laboratory animals, you can control for a variety of factors to help your analysis. In dealing with human populations, however, you must rely on observations as they occur in nature.

Nonrandom Mating

Recall that one of the assumptions of the Hardy-Weinberg equilibrium model is random mating. Populations often show deviations from random mating, such as inbreeding, where mates are closely related. Actually, we are all inbred to some extent, but we generally reserve the term for "close" biological relatedness, such as between first cousins. What is the genetic effect of inbreeding? Closely related individuals are more likely to have similar alleles inherited from a common ancestor. Thus, inbreeding increases the probability of having a homozygous genotype. For example, if two first cousins mate, the probability that their offspring will have a homozygous genotype is 6.25 percent greater than that for a noninbred mating (this number is called the inbreeding coefficient and is discussed further in Appendix 1).

The genetic effects of inbreeding are often harmful. Studies have shown that the incidence of congenital birth defects and mortality during the first year of life is higher among inbred offspring than among the offspring of others (Bittles et al. 1991). Some studies have suggested higher rates of mental retardation among inbred children, but others have not confirmed this. For the most part, overall rates of inbreeding in human populations tend to be low compared to rates among other organisms. These lower rates in part are due to the high mobility of the human species (more gene flow) and in part reflect the fact that most societies have cultural rules discouraging, if not prohibiting, mating with close relatives.

At a broader level, the evolutionary effect of inbreeding is to change *genotype* frequencies but not *allele* frequencies. Inbreeding results in more homozygotes and fewer heterozygotes but does not change the frequency of the alleles (only their distribution into genotypes). As such, inbreeding does not change allele frequencies over time. Inbreeding can, however, affect the *rate* of allele frequency change. If, for example, there is selection against a homozygote, then inbreeding will produce more homozygotes to be selected against, and the rate of selection will change.

Assortative mating is another form of nonrandom mating. With this type of mating, individuals choose mates who are biologically similar to themselves. Humans typically choose mates similar to themselves on a variety of social and biological traits (Buss 1985). A typical example is assortative mating for skin color; on average, people tend to choose mates with similar skin color. Evolutionarily, the effect is the same as for inbreeding—genotype frequencies are changed, but not allele frequencies.

Summary

The study of microevolution looks at changes in the frequencies of alleles from one generation to the next. Such analyses allow detailed examination of the factors that can alter allele frequencies in the short term and also provide us with inferences about long-term patterns of evolution. Changes in allele frequencies stem from four evolutionary forces: mutation, natural selection, genetic drift, and gene flow.

Mutation is the ultimate source of all genetic variation, but it occurs at low enough rates that additional factors are needed to explain polymorphic frequencies (whereby two or more alleles have frequencies greater than 0.01). The other three evolutionary forces are responsible for increasing or decreasing the frequency of a mutant allele. Natural selection changes allele frequencies through the process of differential survival and reproduction of individuals having certain genotypes. Genetic drift, the random change in allele frequencies from one generation to the next, has the greatest effect in small populations. Gene flow, the movement of alleles between populations, acts to reduce genetic differences between different groups.

The rate of allele frequency change is affected by nonrandom mating patterns such as inbreeding and assortative mating. The allele frequencies do not change, but the genotype frequencies are affected. More homozygotes occur than expected from random mating, which can result in more rapid change in allele frequencies because of natural selection.

Supplemental Readings

Gillespie, J. H. 2004. *Population Genetics: A Concise Guide,* 2d ed. Baltimore: Johns Hopkins University Press.

Hartl, D. L. 2000. *A Primer of Population Genetics,* 3d ed. Sunderland, Mass.: Sinauer. Two good short introductions to population genetics with a minimum of mathematical background needed (basic algebra).

Hartl, D. L., and A. G. Clark. 1997. *Principles of Population Genetics,* 3d ed. Sunderland, Mass.: Sinauer.

Hedrick, P. W. 2005. *Genetics of Populations,* 3d ed. Sudbury, Mass.: Jones and Bartlett. Two more comprehensive and advanced treatments of population genetics.

VIRTUAL EXPLORATIONS

Visit our textbook-specific online learning center Web site at **www.mhhe.com/relethford7** to access the exercises that follow.

1. **The Hardy-Weinberg Equilibrium Model** **http://anthro .palomar. edu/synthetic/synth_2.htm**. "The Hardy-Weinberg Equilibrium Model" part of the larger "Synthetic Theory of Evolution" (Dr. Dennis O'Neil's Web site Behavioral Sciences Department, Palomar College) provides an excellent introduction and foundation in explaining both the theory of evolution in general and the Hardy-Weinberg model specifically.

   Read through the text. Click on the "Sample Problem" link **http://anthro.palomar.edu/synthetic/sample.htm**, which covers "Albinism."

   - Were you able to follow the formula through the various steps?
   - Has this helped clarify the theory for you?
   - Why are there more carriers of this trait than albinos?
   - Return to the earlier link and re-read the description of Hardy-Weinberg if not.

2. **Natural Selection: Modes of Selection** **http://www.evotutor.org/ Selection/Sl5A.html**. Visit the EvoTutor simulation Web site, "Natural Selection: Modes of Selection." If you do not see a diagram on the right-hand side, click the apple in the upper right corner to open an applet window.

   Read through the three general modes of selection in a population. Check "Frequency" at the top of the diagram. Check "Directional selection" at the bottom of the diagram. Now run the simulator for mean color in a population.

   - What happens to the color frequencies in the population?
   - Now run the simulator for both "Stabilizing selection" and "Disruptive selection."
   - How do these results differ from each other? How are they different from the results of "Directional selection"?
   - Which selection mode plays the greatest role in speciation?

   Check "Histogram" at the top of the diagram and run each simulation again to see a different way of visualizing natural selection operating on a population.

3. **The Micro Evolution Program: Allele Frequency Exercise**   This exercise requires the Micro Evolution Program by John Relethford. You will find the link on the home page for your book

(http://highered.mcgraw-hill.com/sites/0072963816/student
_view0/micro_evolution_program.html) under Course-wide Content. Download the program (1.4 megabytes).

Plot the natural selection curve for a population using the Natural
Selection function button. Assume your initial allele frequency is 0.5
(50/50 ratio of recessive to dominant alleles). Plot for q, which is the
frequency of a, the recessive allele. Assume that natural selection is
operating against the recessive homozygote (aa). This means that the
fitness values are $AA = 100$, $Aa = 100$, $aa = 0$.

- What pattern does the recessive allele frequency (q) show after
  100 generations? Why? What disease is an example of this selective force?
- Now assume that natural selection is operating against the dominant allele (A). Also assume that partial selection is at work, so
  that the fitness values are $AA = 50$, $Aa = 50$, $aa = 100$.
- What pattern does the recessive allele frequency (q) show after 100
  generations? Why? Now plot for the dominant allele frequency (p).
  What pattern does the dominant allele frequency show after 100
  generations? Why? What disease is an example of this selective
  force?

4. **The Micro Evolution Program: Genetic Drift-Multiple Groups
   Exercise**   This exploration uses the Micro Evolution Program by John
   Relethford (see above). Experiment with the Genetic Drift-Multiple
   Groups plotting function.

Plot the allele frequency over time (p), using a small population size,
such as 2 or 5 individuals. Try it several times, using a different number of populations (2–6). What happens to the allele frequency?
Now plot the allele frequency with a large population size, such as 100
or 200. Try it several times, using a different number of populations.

- What happens to the allele frequency?
- Is genetic drift operating equally on small and large populations?
  Is the allele ever lost completely?
- Come up with a scenario where an allele might be lost from an ac-
  tual population. Under what circumstances could this take place?

The fossil remains of *Confuciusornis sanctus,* the earliest known bird, found in China and dating to 130 million years ago. The study of long-term evolution, or macroevolution, is centered on the origin and evolution of new species.

The Evolution and Classification of Species

W hen so-called creation scientists dispute evolution, they generally mean macroevolution. Few doubt the existence of short-term, microevolutionary changes; we can see such changes in our daily lives, from changing patterns of disease to the kinds of alterations brought about by animal and plant breeding. The long-term pattern of evolution, including the origin and evolution of species, is generally more difficult to grasp. Creationism argues that we cannot directly observe changes over millions of years and therefore cannot make scientific tests. It is true that we cannot undertake laboratory tests lasting for millions of years, but we can still make scientific predictions. Many sciences, including geology and astronomy, are historical in nature. That is, we rely on some record (geologic strata or stellar configurations, for example) to note what has happened. We can establish the facts of change. The same is true of macroevolution. The fossil record provides us with information about *what* has happened. We must then utilize other information available to us to determine *why* such change has occurred. Geology makes use of the fact that geologic processes occur in a regular manner and so occurred in the same way in ancient times; that is, available information about current geologic processes helps explain patterns of change in the past. In much the same way, evolutionary science takes what we know about microevolution and extends it to explain the long-term pattern of macroevolution.

This chapter deals with three related aspects of the central focus of macroevolution—the origin and evolution of species. In addition to outlining the nature of species and the process by which species change over time (including the birth and death of species), we examine several common misconceptions about how macroevolution works, and discuss the relationship between macroevolutionary change and the classification of living organisms.

THE BIRTH AND DEATH OF SPECIES

The origin of new species has been observed in historical times and in the present. Some new species have been brought about by human intervention and controlled breeding; examples include many species of tropical fish. New species have also arisen naturally in the recent past, such as certain types of fruit flies. In addition, we have information on populations in the process of forming new species, such as certain groups of snails. We also have seen (and contributed to) many examples of extinction—the death of a species.

How do new species come into being? Why do some species die out? Even though the title of Darwin's book is *On the Origin of Species,* ironically, Darwin did not focus much on this question. Instead, he sought to explain the basic nature of evolutionary change, believing that extension of these principles could explain the formation of new species.

What Is a Species?

biological species concept
A definition of species that focuses on reproductive capabilities, whereby organisms from different populations are considered to be in the same species if they naturally interbreed and produce fertile offspring.

The term *species* is used in a number of different ways in evolutionary biology (Ereshefsky 1992). In this chapter, the emphasis is on the **biological species concept,** which defines species in terms of reproductive capability. If organisms from two populations are capable of breeding naturally and can produce fertile offspring, then they are classified in the same species. Note that this definition has several parts. First, organisms from different populations must be capable of interbreeding. Second, these matings must occur in nature. Organisms that breed together in zoos, such as lions and tigers, are still considered separate species because they do not breed together *in nature.* In understanding evolutionary history, we are interested in breeding that takes place naturally. Third, the offspring must be *fertile,* that is, capable of producing further offspring.

Perhaps the best-known example of an application of the biological species concept is the mule. Mules are farm animals produced as the offspring of a horse bred with a donkey. The horse and donkey interbreed naturally, which satisfies the first and second parts of the species definition. However, the offspring (mules) are sterile and cannot produce further offspring. The only way to get a mule is to mate a horse and a donkey. Because the offspring are not fertile, the horse and the donkey are considered separate species (Figure 4.1). All human populations around the world belong to the same species (*Homo sapiens*) because members can interbreed and produce fertile offspring.

The biological species concept assumes that two organisms either belong or do not belong to the same species. It does not allow for any kind of intermediate state. Why should this be a problem? Consider two modern species that had a common ancestor at some point in the past. We usually draw an evolutionary "tree," showing the point at which a new "branch," or species, comes into being. If some populations of species A evolved into species B, at what point did those populations stop being species A and start being species B? The species concept suggests that this change was instantaneous, because a creature belongs to either one species or the other. Any system of classification tends to ignore variation within groups. In the real world, however, evolution and variation work to break down rigid systems of classification. Organisms become difficult to classify when they are constantly changing.

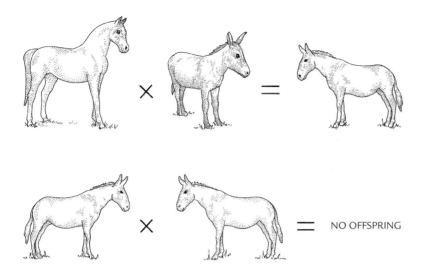

FIGURE 4.1

The horse and donkey can mate and produce offspring (a mule), but two mules cannot produce offspring. Therefore, the horse and donkey belong to two separate species although they are closely related.

NO OFFSPRING

One suggested solution to such situations is the concept of a **semispecies,** whereby the two (or more) populations are partially, but not completely, reproductively isolated from each other (Futuyma 1986; Price 1996). Such situations are likely when the process of reproductive isolation is not yet complete. In such cases, geographically separate semispecies are still capable of interbreeding with each other along a "hybrid zone."

semispecies Two or more populations that are partially reproductively isolated but are not yet completely separate species.

Species Change

As outlined above, the biological species concept is useful in comparing two or more populations in the world today. How does the concept of species work when we consider changes in populations over time? There are two different ways of looking at species over time. First, a single species can change over time such that enough differences accumulate that we would choose to give it a different species name. According to this mode of evolutionary change, a single species exists at any given point in time but evolves over a period of time. This mode of species change is known as **anagenesis,** or straight-line evolution. It is illustrated as a straight line, as shown in Figure 4.2, where form A evolves into form B and then into form C. Although this mode of evolutionary change is fairly straightforward, complications arise when naming species. Should form A be called a different species from form B? The problem is that the traditional biological species concept doesn't really apply. Form A and form B are, by necessity, isolated from each other reproductively because they lived at different times. There is no way they could interbreed any more than you could mate with a human who lived 2 million years ago (we'll leave out science fiction and time machines here).

Many researchers modify the species concept to deal with this situation. Different physical forms along a single lineage (an evolutionary line such as

anagenesis The transformation of a single species over time.

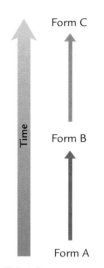

FIGURE 4.2

Anagenesis, the linear evolution of a species over time. Form A changes over time into form B and then further changes into form C.

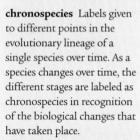

chronospecies Labels given to different points in the evolutionary lineage of a single species over time. As a species changes over time, the different stages are labeled as chronospecies in recognition of the biological changes that have taken place.

cladogenesis The formation of one or more new species from another over time.

that shown in Figure 4.2) are given different species names out of convenience and as a label to represent the types of physical change shown over time. Such forms are referred to as **chronospecies** and are used as labels for different stages of biological change over time, even though only one species exists at any point in time. As such, the different physical forms illustrated in Figure 4.2 would be labeled as chronospecies A, chronospecies B, and chronospecies C. The important point here is that there is only *one* species at any point in time. As an analogy, consider the different labels given to humans as they grow: "infant," "child," "teenager," and "adult." These labels indicate the different stages of a person's life, but they all refer to the same individual. In evolution, chronospecies are different stages in the evolution of a single evolutionary lineage.

Anagenesis is not the only mode of species change. If you think about it, anagenesis is not completely sufficient as an explanation of macroevolution. Where do new species come from? The other mode of species change is **cladogenesis,** or branching evolution. Cladogenesis involves the formation of new species (speciation) whereby one or more new species branch off from an original species. In Figure 4.3, a portion of species A first branches off to produce species B (living at the same time), then a portion of species B branches off to produce species C. This example starts with one species and ends up with three. The factors responsible for speciation will be discussed later in this chapter.

The problem of species naming is complicated by the fact that evolutionary relationships among fossil forms are not always clear. Some of these problems will be addressed later. For now, keep in mind that species names often mean different things to different people. The naming of species might adhere to an evolutionary model or might serve only as convenient labels of physical variation.

FIGURE 4.3

Cladogenesis, the origin of new species. Species A splits and forms a new species B, which later splits to form species C. The process begins with a single species (A) and ends with three species (A, B, C).

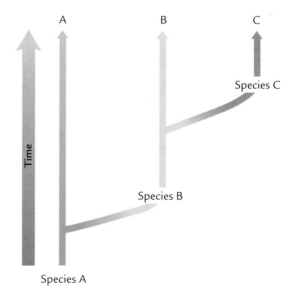

Speciation

The fossil record shows many examples of new species arising through cladogenesis. How does this come about? You know that genetic differences between populations come about as a result of evolutionary forces. For a population to become a new species, these genetic differences must be great enough to prevent successful interbreeding with the original parent species. For this to occur, the population must become reproductively isolated from the original parent species.

Reproductive Isolation **Reproductive isolation** is genetic change that can lead to an inability to produce fertile offspring. How does this happen? Evolutionary forces can produce such a situation. The first step in **speciation**—the formation of a new species from a parent species—is the elimination or reduction of gene flow between populations. Because gene flow acts to reduce differences between populations, its continued action tends to keep all populations in the same species. Gene flow does not need to be eliminated altogether, but it must be reduced sufficiently to allow other evolutionary forces to make the populations genetically different. Populations must become genetically isolated from one another for speciation to occur.

The most common form of isolation in animal species is geographic isolation. When two populations are separated by a physical barrier, such as a river or mountain range, or by great distances, gene flow is cut off between the populations. As long as the populations remain isolated, genetic changes occurring in one group will not spread to other groups. As we saw in Chapter 3, geographic distance limits gene flow even in our own highly mobile species. The effects of geographic distance in causing reproductive isolation are even more dramatic in other species.

Geographic separation is the most common means of producing reproductive isolation among animal populations, but other mechanisms may also cause isolation. Some of these can operate within a single geographic region. Populations may be isolated by behavioral differences such as feeding habits. Some groups may eat during the day, and others at dusk. Because the groups are not in frequent contact with one another, there is opportunity for isolation to develop.

Genetic Divergence Isolation is the first step in the speciation process. By itself, this isolation does not guarantee speciation. Elimination of gene flow merely provides the *opportunity* for speciation. Other evolutionary forces must then act upon this isolation to produce a situation in which the isolated groups have changed sufficiently to make fertile interbreeding no longer possible. Isolation, however, does not always lead to speciation.

How can evolutionary forces lead to speciation? Mutation might act to increase variation among populations because it occurs independently in the genetic composition of separate groups. Without gene flow to spread them, individual mutations will accumulate in each group, making isolated populations genetically divergent. Genetic drift also contributes to differences in

reproductive isolation The genetic isolation of populations that may render them incapable of producing fertile offspring.

speciation The origin of a new species.

allele frequencies among small populations. In addition, if the two populations are in separate environments, then natural selection will lead to genetic differences. Once gene flow has been eliminated, the other evolutionary forces will act to make the populations genetically divergent. When this process continues to the point where the two populations can no longer interbreed and produce fertile offspring, they have become separate species.

There is continued debate over the role of the various evolutionary forces in producing genetic divergence. For many years, speciation was believed to be solely the by-product of natural selection. That is, as two populations came to occupy separate environments, the action of natural selection would cause these groups to become different. Speciation has been viewed as a consequence of this differential adaptation. In recent years, however, more attention has been given to the contributions to speciation of mutation and genetic drift in small populations. In the former view, the old species gradually formed two or more species, with natural selection operating on large populations. The more recent view is that new species often form from small populations and, as such, are affected extensively by mutation and genetic drift.

Adaptive Radiation

The process of speciation minimally results in two species: the original parent species and the new offspring species. Under certain circumstances, many new species can come into being in a short period of time. This rapid diversification of species is associated with changing environmental conditions. When new environments open up, or when new adaptations to a specific environment develop, many new species can form—a process known as **adaptive radiation.** An example of adaptive radiation is the Darwin finches mentioned in Chapter 1. All of the finch species that Charles Darwin observed descended from a single original finch species. The availability of new environmental niches led to the rapid speciation of finches in the Galapagos Islands.

adaptive radiation The formation of many new species following the availability of new environments or the development of a new adaptation.

gradualism A model of macroevolutionary change whereby changes occur at a slow, steady rate over time.

The Tempo and Mode of Macroevolution

What are the tempo and mode (mechanism) of macroevolutionary change? That is, how quickly do new species form? Does speciation occur in large or small populations? What are the effects of natural selection and the other evolutionary forces in producing new species? These are all questions about the tempo and mode of macroevolution.

Gradualism   Charles Darwin saw speciation as a slow and gradual process, taking thousands or millions of years. To Darwin, natural selection acted on populations ultimately to produce new species. The view that macroevolution is a slow and gradual process is called **gradualism.** According to this view, small changes in each generation over time result in major biological changes.

According to gradualism, then, speciation is a slow, lengthy process in which new species form from large portions of an original species. In such

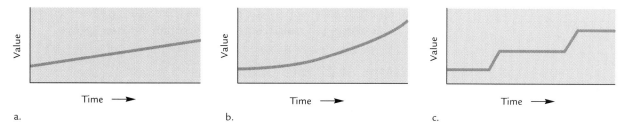

a.   b.   c.

FIGURE 4.4

The tempo of macroevolution: gradualism and punctuated equilibrium. Each portion of this figure has a line showing the change in value of a physical trait over time.
(a) Gradualism: The change over time is linear and constant.
(b) A geometric, gradual pattern: The rate of change increases with time, but the curve is still smooth; there are no discontinuities.
(c) Punctuated equilibrium: There are periods of no change (stasis) punctuated by periods of rapid change; the net result is a "staircase" pattern.

large populations, genetic drift and mutation have little impact in each generation. Natural selection, slowly operating on some initial mutation(s), is primarily responsible for speciation.

The gradualistic model predicts that, given a suitable fossil record, we will see a smooth and gradual transition from one species into another. Although there are examples of such change in the fossil record, it is not always apparent. In some cases, we lack transitional forms. Does this lack of evidence indicate problems in the fossil record or with the theory of gradualism itself?

Punctuated Equilibrium   An alternative hypothesis has been suggested by Niles Eldredge and Stephen Jay Gould in the form of a model known as **punctuated equilibrium** (Eldredge and Gould 1972; Gould and Eldredge 1977). This hypothesis suggests that the pattern of macroevolution consists of long periods when little evolutionary change occurs (stasis) and short periods when rapid evolutionary change occurs. According to Eldredge and Gould, the tempo of macroevolution is not gradual; rather, it is static at times and rapid at other times. Long periods of stasis are punctuated by short periods of rapid evolutionary change. Examples of gradualism and punctuated equilibrium are given in Figure 4.4.

Eldredge and Gould also view speciation as a rapid event occurring within small, isolated populations on the periphery of a species range. Mutations can spread quickly in small populations as a consequence of inbreeding and genetic drift. If such genetic changes are adaptive, and if the newly formed species gains access to the parental species' range, it may then spread throughout an area, replacing the original parent species. According to this model, most biological change occurs during speciation. Once a species has been established, it changes little throughout time. Eldredge and Gould argue that stabilizing selection and other factors act to keep a species the same over time. This view contrasts with the gradualistic model, which sees biological change occurring at a slow rate, ultimately leading to separate species.

Punctuated equilibrium makes a prediction about how the fossil record should look. Given stasis, we should see long periods when little evolutionary change takes place. Certain organisms, such as the cockroach and coelacanth, seem to follow this pattern—they have not changed much over many millions of years. The punctuated equilibrium model also predicts that new species will appear rather quickly, often without any evidence of a transitional state. Because the model predicts that speciation occurs within small,

punctuated equilibrium A model of macroevolutionary change in which long periods of little evolutionary change (stasis) are followed by relatively short periods of rapid evolutionary change.

isolated populations, there is little chance that we will have fossil evidence actually documenting the initial stages of the origin of a new species.

Extinctions and Mass Extinctions

In considering macroevolutionary trends, we must not forget the most common pattern of all—extinction. It is estimated that more than 99 percent of all species that ever existed have become extinct (Futuyma 1986). In historical times, humans have witnessed (and helped cause) the extinction of a number of organisms, including the passenger pigeon.

What causes extinction? When a species is no longer adapted to a changed environment, it may die. The exact causes of a species' death vary from situation to situation. Rapid ecological change may render an environment hostile to a species. For example, temperatures may change and a species may not be able to adapt. Food resources may be affected by environmental changes, which will then cause problems for a species requiring these resources. Other species may become better adapted to an environment, resulting in competition and, ultimately, the death of a species.

Extinction seems, in fact, to be the ultimate fate of all species. Natural selection is a remarkable mechanism for providing a species with the ability to adapt to change, but it does not always work. When the environment changes too rapidly or when the appropriate genetic variations do not exist, a species can become extinct.

The fossil record shows that extinction has occurred throughout the history of the planet. Recent analysis has also revealed that on some occasions a large number of species became extinct at the same time—a **mass extinction.** One of the best-known examples of mass extinction occurred 65 million years ago with the demise of dinosaurs and many other forms of life. Perhaps the most severe mass extinction occurred roughly 250 million years ago when more than 90 percent of marine species, about 70 percent of terrestrial vertebrates, and most land plants became extinct (Becker et al. 2001). Mass extinctions can be caused by a relatively rapid change in the environment, compounded by the close interrelationship of many species. If, for example, something were to happen to destroy much of the plankton in the oceans, then the oxygen content of our planet would drop, affecting even organisms not living in the oceans. Such a change would probably lead to a mass extinction.

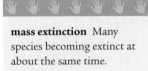

mass extinction Many species becoming extinct at about the same time.

MISCONCEPTIONS ABOUT EVOLUTION

Evolution is a frequently misunderstood subject. Many of our basic ideas regarding evolution are misconceptions that have become part of the general culture. The often-used phrase "survival of the fittest" conjures up images that are sometimes at odds with the actual findings of evolutionary science. It is common for such misconceptions to continue even after initial exposure to evolutionary theory.

The Nature of Selection

Many people have a basic understanding of the general principles of natural selection. The problem lies in their misinterpretation of the nature of selection.

Misconception: Bigger Is Better   A common misconception is that natural selection will *always* lead to larger structures. According to this idea, the bigger the brain and the bigger the body, the better. At first, this idea seems reasonable. After all, larger individuals may be more likely to survive because they can compete more successfully for food and mates. Therefore, larger individuals are more likely to survive and pass their genes on to the next generation. Natural selection is expected to lead to an increase in the size of the body, brain, and other structures. However, this isn't always true. There are numerous examples of species in which *smaller* body size or structures were more adaptive and selected for. Keep in mind that in evolution nothing is free. A larger body may be more adaptive because of sheer size, but a larger body also has greater energy needs. Any advantage gained by a larger body may be offset by the disadvantage of needing more food. What we have to focus on is a *balance* between the adaptive and nonadaptive aspects of any biological characteristic. By walking upright, humans have their hands free, which is rather advantageous. However, we pay the price with varicose veins, back pain, fallen arches, and other nonadaptive consequences of walking on two legs. Again, we need to focus on the relative costs and benefits of any evolutionary change. Of course, this balance will vary in different environments.

Misconception: Newer Is Better   There is a tendency to believe that traits more recent in origin are superior because they are newer. Humans walk on two legs, a trait that appeared close to 6 million years ago. We also have five digits (fingers and toes) that date back many hundreds of millions of years. Is upright walking better because it is newer? Of course not. Both features are essential to our toolmaking way of life. The age of a structure has no bearing on its usefulness.

Misconception: Natural Selection Always Works   The idea that natural selection will always provide an opportunity for some members of a species to survive is not accurate. Occasionally, I hear statements such as "we will evolve to tolerate air pollution." Such statements are absurdities. Natural selection operates only on variations that are present. If no genetic variation occurs to aid in breathing polluted air, natural selection will not help us. Even in cases in which genetic variation is present, the environment may change too quickly for us to respond through natural selection. All we have to do is examine the fossil record to see how inaccurate this misconception is—that 99 percent of all past species are extinct shows us that natural selection obviously doesn't always work!

Misconception: There Is an Inevitable Direction in Evolution   An idea popular in the nineteenth century was **orthogenesis,** the notion that evolution

orthogenesis A discredited idea that evolution would continue in a given direction because of some vaguely defined "force."

FIGURE 4.5

The idea of orthogenesis predicts continued change in a given direction. Illustrated here is the popular but incorrect notion that humans in the future will have progressively larger brains.

would continue in a given direction because of a vaguely defined nonphysical "force" (Mayr 1982). As an alternative to the theory of natural selection, orthogenesis suggested that evolutionary change would continue in the same direction until either a perfect structure was attained or a species became extinct. Apart from the problems of dealing with metaphysical "forces," orthogenesis has long been rejected on the basis of analysis of the fossil record and the triumph of natural selection as an explanatory mechanism for evolutionary change. Some of its basic notions, however, are still perpetuated. A common belief is that humans will evolve larger and larger brains, as a continuation of earlier trends (Figure 4.5). The view of orthogenesis is tied in with notions of "progress" and with the misconception that bigger is better. There are many examples from the fossil record of nonlinear change and many examples of reversals in sizes of structures. In the case of human evolution, brains actually stopped getting larger 50,000 years ago. In fact, the average brain size of humans since that time has decreased slightly as a consequence of a general decrease in skeletal size and ruggedness (Henneberg 1988).

Is it possible for a trend to continue in a given direction under the right circumstances? Of course, but change comes through the action of natural selection, not through some mysterious internal force. Continuation of any trend depends on the environment, present genetic variation, and basic biological limits. (A 50-foot spider can't exist because it wouldn't be able to absorb enough oxygen for its volume.) Such change also depends on the relative costs and benefits of change. Suppose an increase in human brain size was combined somehow with an increase in pelvic size (assuming genetic variation was present for both features). A larger pelvis would make walking difficult or even impossible. Evolution works on the entire organism, not one trait at a time. Any change can have both positive and negative effects, but it is the net balance that is critical to the operation of natural selection.

Structure, Function, and Evolution

A number of misconceptions about evolution focus on the relationship between biological structures and their adaptive (or nonadaptive) functions.

Misconception: Natural Selection Always Produces Perfect Structures   There is a tendency to view nature as the product of perfect natural engineering. Granted, there are many wondrous phenomena in the natural world, but a closer examination shows that biological structures are often far from perfect. Consider human beings. Is the human body perfect? Hardly. Just to note one aspect, consider your skeleton when you stand upright. What is holding in your internal organs? Skin and muscles. Your rib cage provides little support for lower internal organs because it reflects ancestry from a four-legged form. When humans stood up (adaptive), the rib cage offered less support. The result? A variety of complaints and complications, such as hernias. The human skeleton is not perfect but rather is the result of natural selection operating on the variation that was present.

Science Fiction and Orthogenesis

Evolution, especially human evolution, is a common theme in science fiction. Although a good many science fiction stories have a strong scientific base, others—most likely due to plot needs—do not. Even these latter stories, though, are valuable in terms of what they tell us about misconceptions about evolution, one of the themes of this chapter.

A personal favorite is an episode of the 1960s science fiction television show *The Outer Limits*. The episode, titled "The Sixth Finger," is an entertaining treatment of a popular science fiction question: What will humans evolve into? The episode, aired in 1963, begins with a young coal miner, Gwyllm Griffiths, who yearns for something more than a life of manual labor. Through his girlfriend, Cathy, he meets a local scientist, Professor Mathers, who had once worked on an atomic bomb project. Because of guilt, the scientist is seeking an end to violence and war—through evolution. Reasoning that humans will someday evolve beyond the need for violence, and tormented by the "slow pace of evolution," Mathers invents a machine that will move an organism into its own predestined evolutionary future.

Gwyllm volunteers as a human subject, and the results are predictable. With each exposure to the machine, his head and brain increase in size, as does his intelligence. Additionally, he "evolves" a sixth finger (for "increased dexterity") and assorted mental powers (the sixth finger is particularly interesting because some people today are born with a sixth finger, and there does not appear to be any evolutionary advantage). Gwyllm also develops a dislike for the people around him and eventually decides to destroy them. On his way to demolish the town with his mental powers, he suddenly "evolves beyond the need for violence." He returns to the professor's laboratory and enlists the help of Cathy to operate the machinery while he evolves into "the man of the future." Once Gwyllm is in the machine's chamber, Cathy cannot bear to lose him forever and pushes the machine's lever to "Backward" rather than "Forward." For a brief moment, she pushes too far and the viewer sees Gwyllm devolve to some sort of subhuman ape, but she quickly corrects the lever, and they live happily ever after (in one alternate ending, the script called for Gwyllm to continue evolving back to protoplasm) (Schow and Frentzen 1986).

This episode is quite entertaining and also provides some good examples of evolutionary misconceptions. For example, the doctrine of orthogenesis, the notion that evolution follows a particular path, is central to the entire plot. This message is not subtle—at one point, Gwyllm speaks about "the goal of evolution." The professor's machine embodies the idea of orthogenesis, with its lever marked "Forward" and "Backward," implying that all of life evolves along a fixed path from past to present. Orthogenesis is also apparent in the continued expansion of the brain and mental powers as Gwyllm evolves "forward," enabling him to read massive volumes at a glance and become a concert pianist overnight.

Despite the scientific inaccuracies, "The Sixth Finger" remains a captivating story. It was also somewhat controversial in that it dealt, on television, with evolution, a theme that had drawn criticism from the network's censor.

Misconception: All Structures Are Adaptive Natural selection is such a powerful model that it is tempting to apply it to all biological structures. Indeed, many anthropologists and biologists have done so. They examined a structure and explained its function in terms of natural selection. But are all structures adaptive? Many structures simply reflect a by-product of other biological changes and have no adaptive value of their own (Gould and Lewontin 1979). Other structures, such as the human appendix, may have served a function in the past but appear to have no present function.

An example deals with an old question: Why do human men have nipples? Earlier explanations suggesting that in ancient times men could assist women in breast feeding are ludicrous. The true explanation is simple. Both males and females develop from the same basic body plan during the embryonic stage of prenatal life. Under the influence of sex hormones, various structures develop in different ways (just as the same structure develops into a penis in men and a clitoris in women). The basic body plan for nipples is present in both sexes; for women, these structures develop into breasts capable of lactation. In men, nipples serve no functional purpose. Thus, male nipples are a by-product of the fact that males and females share a similar developmental path and are not the result of some adaptive value (Gould 1991).

Misconception: Current Structures Always Reflect Initial Adaptations   The idea here is that any given structure, with an associated function, originally evolved specifically for that function. Human beings, for example, walk on two legs; this allows us to hold tools and other objects that are constructed with the aid of an enlarged brain. Although it is tempting to say that both upright walking and a larger brain evolved at the same time because of the adaptive value of having both structures, this is not what happened. Upright walking evolved millions of years before the use of stone tools and the expansion of the brain (Chapter 10).

As another example, consider your fingers. You have five of these digits on each hand, which enable you to perform a variety of manipulative tasks. We use our hands to manipulate both natural and human-made objects. Manipulative digits are essential to our nature as tool-using creatures. We might therefore suggest that our grasping hands *first* evolved to meet this need, but this is not the case. Grasping hands *first* developed in early primate ancestors to meet the needs of living in trees (Chapter 9). Even though we don't live in trees, we have retained this trait and use it *for a different purpose.* Natural selection operates on the variation that is present. Structures are frequently modified for different uses.

CLASSIFICATION OF SPECIES

In Chapter 1, you read about Linnaeus's system of classification for all living creatures. Instead of simply making a list of all known organisms, Linnaeus developed a scheme by which creatures could be grouped according to certain shared characteristics. Even though we now make use of Linnaeus's scheme to describe patterns of evolution, Linnaeus himself did not have this objective in mind. Rather, he sought to understand the nature of God's design in living organisms.

We use systems of classification every day, often without being aware that we do so. We all have the tendency to label objects and people according to certain characteristics. We often use terms such as "liberal" and "conservative" to describe people's political views and terms such as "white" and "black" to describe people's skin color. Movies are classified into different groups by a rating, such as G, PG, PG-13, and R.

If you think about it, a great deal of your daily life revolves around your use and understanding of different systems of classification. In biology, we are interested in a system of classification that shows relationships between different groups of organisms. This may sound simple but can actually be rather difficult. For example, consider the following list of organisms: flounder, bat, shark, canary, lizard, horse, and whale. How would you classify these creatures? One way might be to put certain animals together according to size: the flounder, bat, canary, and lizard in a "small" category; the shark and horse in a "medium" category; and the whale in a "large" category. Another method would be to put the animals in groups according to where they live: the flounder, shark, and whale in the water; the bat and canary in the air; and the lizard and horse on the land. Still another method would be to put the shark in a separate category from all the others because the shark's skeleton is made of cartilage instead of bone.

The problem with this example is that none of these three ways of classification agrees with the other two. There is no consistency. Biologists actually classify these animals into the following groups: fish (flounder and shark), reptiles (lizard), birds (canary), and mammals (bat, horse, whale). These groups reflect certain common characteristics, such as mammary glands for the mammals. What makes this system of classification any better than those based on size or habitat or skeletal form? For our purposes, we require classifications that reflect evolutionary patterns. As you will see, organisms can have similar traits because they inherited these traits from a common ancestor. Thus, the presence of mammary glands in the bat, horse, and whale represents a trait that has been inherited from a common ancestral species.

Classifications are useful in trying to understand evolutionary relationships. In order to reflect the evolutionary process, the classifications must reflect evolutionary changes. The groups of mammals, birds, reptiles, and fish are based on characteristics that reflect evolutionary relationships. The bat and the whale are placed in the same group because they have a more recent common ancestor than either does with the lizard, as reflected by certain shared characteristics such as mammary glands. Biological classification should reflect evolutionary processes, but only careful analysis of both living and extinct life forms allows us to discover what characteristics reflect evolutionary relationships.

Taxonomic Categories

The Linnaean system is a hierarchical classification. That is, each category contains a number of subcategories, which contain further subcategories, and so on. Biological classification uses a number of categories. The more commonly used categories are kingdom, phylum (plural *phyla*), class, order, family, genus (plural *genera*), and species. In addition, we often add prefixes to distinguish further breakdowns within a particular category, such as subphylum or infraorder. The scientific name given to an organism consists of the genus and species names in Latin or Latinized form. The scientific name for the common house mouse, for example, is *Mus musculus*. Modern human beings are known as *Homo sapiens*, translated roughly as "wise humans."

Any given genus may contain a number of different species. The genus *Homo*, for example, contains modern humans—***Homo sapiens***—as well as

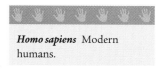

Homo sapiens Modern humans.

extinct human species (*Homo erectus,* among others). These species are placed in the same genus because of certain common characteristics, such as large brain size. Another level of classification that is sometimes used is **subspecies,** which are groups within a species that are physically distinct from one another but still capable of interbreeding. Subspecies labels are indicated by a third name attached to that of the genus and species. Gorillas, for example, are often classified into different subspecies (such as *Gorilla gorilla beringei,* the mountain gorilla) because different groups are geographically, physically, and genetically distinct.

The categories of classification are often vaguely defined. Genus, for example, refers to a group of species that shares similar environments, patterns of adaptation, and physical structures. An example is the horse and the zebra, different species that are placed in the genus *Equus* (there are several species of zebra). These species are four-legged, hoofed grazers. The basis for assigning a given species to one genus or another is often unclear. This uncertainty is even more problematic when fossil remains are assigned to different categories. The only category with a precise meaning is the species, and even that has certain problems in application.

Methods of Classification

Classification involves making statements regarding the similarity of traits between species. The process can be somewhat confusing because biological similarity can arise for different reasons.

Homology and Homoplasy   Two species may have the same trait for two different reasons. They may have inherited this trait from a common ancestor, or they may have evolved the same trait independently.

Homology refers to similarity due to descent from a common ancestor. Humans and apes, for example, share certain features of their shoulder anatomy that enables them to hang by their arms. In this case, the similarity is because both humans and apes inherited this anatomy from a common ancestor. Homology is often apparent by comparing the actual structure of different species. For example, Figure 4.6 shows the forelimb anatomy of three different animals—a human, a whale, and a bird. In each case, the basic anatomical structure is similar; all three have a limb made up of a single upper limb bone (humerus) and two lower limb bones (radius and ulna). Further, note that the "hand" of each has five digits made up of carpal and metacarpal bones. These three animals use their limbs for different purposes, but the basic structure is the same; they are the same bones, but they differ in size, shape, and function. The reason for this similarity is descent from a common ancestor (an ancient vertebrate).

Homoplasy refers to similarity due to the independent evolution of the same trait(s) in both species. Birds and flies are both capable of flight, but this similarity is due to independent evolution of an anatomy capable of flight and not to descent from a common ancestor. This is apparent when

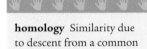

subspecies Groupings within a species that are quite physically distinct from one another but capable of fertile interbreeding. When used, subspecies are often listed as a third name in a taxonomic classification, such as *Homo sapiens sapiens,* the subspecies to which all living humans belong.

homology Similarity due to descent from a common ancestor.

homoplasy Similarity due to independent evolution.

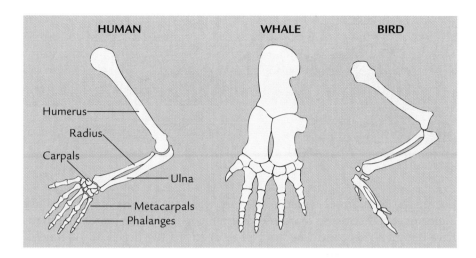

HUMAN   WHALE   BIRD

Humerus
Radius
Carpals
Ulna
Metacarpals
Phalanges

FIGURE 4.6

An example of homology: the forelimbs of a human, whale, and bird. Note that the same bones are found in all three vertebrates. Even though the limbs are used differently by all three organisms, the bones show a structural correspondence, reflecting common ancestry. (Adapted with permission from T. Dobzhansky, F. J. Ayala, G. L. Stebbins, and U. W. Valentine, *Evolution*, 1977, page 264. Copyright © 1977 by W. H. Freeman and Company.)

considering their anatomy (Figure 4.7); both creatures can fly, but their anatomy is quite different and reflects independent origins.

There are two different types of homoplasy. **Parallel evolution** is the independent evolution of similar traits in closely related species, such as the increase in dental size among a number of early human ancestors (see Chapter 10). **Convergent evolution** is the independent evolution of similar traits in more distantly related species, such as the evolution of flight in both birds and flies.

If we want our classification system to reflect evolutionary relationships, we need to focus on traits that exhibit homology. We would not want to include traits that reflect homoplasy because those reflect independent evolutionary origins. For this reason, we classify birds and flies into different taxonomic categories—their similarity does not tell us anything about evolutionary relationships.

As an example, consider three of the organisms mentioned earlier in this chapter—a horse, a shark, and a whale. Which two are more similar to each other than to the third? Looking at overall similarity (including body shape, presence of fins rather than limbs, and habitat), you might conclude that the shark and the whale are more similar to each other than either is to the horse. The problem here is that these similarities all reflect homoplasy—specifically, the independent evolution in the shark and the whale of characteristics related to living in the water. Focusing on homologous structures, such as the limb structure described previously, we see that the horse and the whale are actually more closely related, and for that reason, we classify them both as mammals, whereas the shark is classified as a fish.

Primitive and Derived Traits Homologous biological traits can also be characterized as primitive or derived. When a trait has been inherited from an earlier form, we refer to that trait as **primitive.** Traits that have changed from an ancestral state are referred to as **derived.** As an example, consider the number of digits in humans and horses. Both humans and horses are

parallel evolution Independent evolution of traits in closely related species.

convergent evolution Independent evolution of similar traits in rather distinct evolutionary lines.

primitive trait A trait that has not changed from an ancestral state. The five digits of the human hand and foot are primitive traits inherited from earlier vertebrate ancestors.

derived trait A trait that has changed from an ancestral state.

FIGURE 4.7

The wings of a bird and a fly. Even though both structures provide the same function (flight), they are structurally different, reflecting independent evolutionary origin. (Adapted with permission from T. Dobzhansky, F. J. Ayala, G. L. Stebbins, and U. W. Valentine, *Evolution*, 1977, page 264. Copyright © 1977 by W. H. Freeman and Company.)

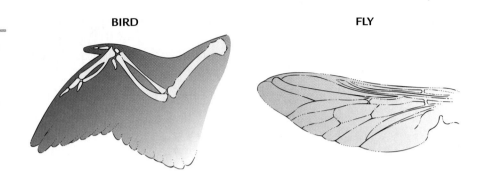

BIRD   **FLY**

mammals. From fossil evidence, we know that the first mammals had five digits on each hand and foot (as did other early land vertebrates). Humans have retained this condition, and we refer to the five digits of the human hand and foot as primitive traits. The horse's single digit (a toe), however, is a derived trait relative to the first mammals.

The concept of primitive and derived traits is relative. What is considered primitive at one level of comparison might be considered derived at another level. For example, neither modern apes nor modern humans have a tail. If apes are compared to humans, the absence of a tail is a primitive characteristic—they share this absence because they inherited this characteristic from a common ancestor. Monkeys, however, do have tails. If modern monkeys are compared to modern apes, the lack of a tail in the modern apes is a derived condition—it has changed since the common ancestor of monkeys and apes. The relative nature of primitive and derived traits must always be kept in mind.

To make any comparison, we must have information on modern and fossil forms so that we can determine whether a trait is primitive or derived. We cannot assume that any given organism will be primitive or derived for a given trait without knowing something about the ancestral condition. In other words, we cannot equate the terms *primitive* and *derived* with biased notions of "higher" or "lower" forms. In the past, there was a tendency to regard all traits of modern humans as derived relative to the apes. For some traits, such as increased brain size and upright walking, this holds true. For other traits, such as certain features of the teeth, the opposite is true.

When we compare the distribution of derived traits between two or more species, we are also interested in whether these traits are *shared* or *unique*. For example, when comparing humans and apes, the absence of a tail is a *shared derived* trait, as both apes and humans lack a tail. On the other hand, upright walking in humans is a *unique derived* trait because it is not found in any other primates. Different methods of taxonomic classification consider the use of primitive traits, shared derived traits, and unique derived traits in different ways.

Approaches to Classification

The problem of biological classification may be approached in many different ways, but there are two major schools of classification: evolutionary systematics and cladistics. Although they both rely on the analysis of homologous traits, they are different in how they treat primitive and derived homologous traits.

Evolutionary Systematics   The traditional method of classification is based on **evolutionary systematics,** a school of thought that considers *all* homologous traits, whether primitive or derived, when classifying organisms into taxonomic groups. Species that share the largest number of homologous traits are placed into the same group even if all of these traits do not reflect an ancestor–descendant relationship. As a result, species that do not necessarily share a common ancestor may be placed in the same taxonomic group. Consider, for example, crocodiles, lizards, and birds. The evolutionary systematics approach would place crocodiles and lizards in the same taxonomic class—Reptilia (reptiles)—and birds in a different class—Aves—because crocodiles and lizards share more homologous traits. Although this classification fits traditional views on overall similarity, it does not show the actual evolutionary relationship between these organisms. When derived traits are considered, birds and crocodiles are found to be more closely related to each other than either is to lizards (Harvey and Pagel 1991).

Cladistics   An alternative approach is **cladistics,** which looks only at shared derived homologous traits and classifies organisms based solely on their evolutionary relationship. A cladist would place birds and crocodiles in the same taxonomic group, and lizards in another. The guiding principle of cladistics is that *only* shared derived traits should be used to construct classifications; primitive traits and unique derived traits are not considered. The fact that humans, apes, and monkeys all have five digits would not be used to judge their relationship to each other because comparative data and the fossil record show us that having five digits is a *primitive* trait. Because all of these organisms share the same trait, that trait cannot help us determine which two groups are more closely related to each other than the third group.

The large brain of humans would not be used to separate humans from monkeys or apes because the large brain is a *unique* derived trait. As such, it cannot tell us whether we are more closely related to the apes or the monkeys. Cladistics uses only homologous traits that are shared and derived. For example, both humans and apes share certain features of their shoulder anatomy (see Chapter 7) that are not shared with monkeys or other primates. Humans and apes have these traits in common because they inherited them from a common ancestor that had changed from an ancestral state.

How do we tell if a given trait is primitive or derived? A commonly used method is to compare the groups of interest with an **outgroup,** a group that is more distantly related to the species being classified. For example, consider the presence or absence of a tail in three different but related groups— humans, apes, and monkeys. Humans and apes do not have tails, but monkeys do. According to the cladistic method, we would place humans and apes in the same group if the absence of a tail were a shared derived trait— that is, one that was present in the common ancestor of humans and apes but not in the common ancestor of humans, apes, and monkeys. How do we know whether the common ancestor of all three groups had a tail or not? An appropriate outgroup for this example might be more distantly related primates or other mammals. Because a tail is found in most of these

evolutionary systematics A school of thought that stresses the overall similarity of all (primitive and derived) homologous traits in classification.

cladistics A school of thought that stresses evolutionary relationships between organisms based on derived homologous traits.

outgroup A group used for comparison in cladistic analyses to determine whether the ancestral state of a trait is primitive or derived.

FIGURE 4.8

Illustration of the use of an outgroup in cladistic analysis. This diagram shows the relationship among humans, apes, and monkeys based on the presence or absence of a tail. Humans and apes lack a tail, which makes them different from monkeys. According to the principles of cladistics, lack of a tail can be considered a shared derived trait in humans and apes if the presence of a tail was indeed the primitive condition. Using an outgroup, such as other mammals, shows that the presence of a tail is very widespread apart from humans and apes, and it is the primitive condition. According to this model, monkeys have tails because they retained this primitive trait, whereas the inferred common ancestor of humans and apes lost the tail, a trait inherited in both from this common ancestor.

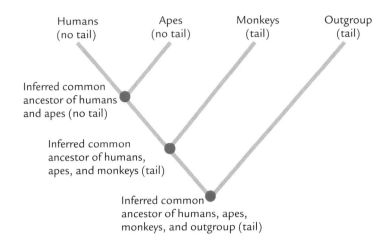

mammals, we would conclude that the primitive state was the presence of a tail and that the absence of a tail in both humans and apes reflects their descent from a common ancestor not shared with monkeys (Figure 4.8).

Summary

Macroevolution, the process of long-term evolution, can occur in two ways: anagenesis, the evolution of a single species over time, or cladogenesis, the splitting off of one or more new species from the original parent species. In cladogenesis, new species form through the process of reproductive isolation followed by genetic divergence. Both steps are understood in terms of evolutionary forces. Reduction or elimination of gene flow provides for the beginning of reproductive isolation. Mutation, genetic drift, and selection can then act on this isolation to produce a new species. The relative importance of the evolutionary forces in speciation is still debated.

Two models of macroevolutionary change can be applied to the fossil record. Gradualism states that most evolutionary change is the result of slow but constant change over many generations. New species are believed to form as a by-product of natural selection operating over time. Punctuated equilibrium states that there are long periods with little evolutionary change (stasis), punctuated by rapid evolutionary events. New species are seen as forming in small, isolated populations.

The most common evolutionary pattern is extinction. Some scientists have argued that the evolutionary record is best understood as the process of new species forming from old, with many species becoming extinct. The evolutionary trends we observe in the fossil record may reflect the differential survival of species with certain adaptations.

There are many misconceptions regarding natural selection and evolution. Some of the more common of these are that bigger is better, that newer is better, that natural selection always works, and that there is an inevitable direction to natural selection. There are also misconceptions regarding the relationship of biological structures, their functions, and their evolutionary origin.

Species are classified according to similarity in traits that arose because of descent from a common ancestor (homology) and not according to similar traits that evolved independently (homoplasy). Homologous traits can be categorized as primitive (unchanged since the time of a common ancestor) or derived (having changed since the time of a common ancestor). Different approaches to classification place different weight on primitive or derived traits depending on whether the purpose of classification is to provide a measure of overall similarity or to reveal evolutionary relationships.

Supplemental Readings

Futuyma, D. J. 1997. *Evolutionary Biology*, 3d ed. Sunderland, Mass.: Sinauer.
Ridley, M. 2004. *Evolution*, 3d ed. Malden, Mass.: Blackwell. Two comprehensive treatments of evolutionary theory.

VIRTUAL EXPLORATIONS

Visit our textbook-specific online learning center Web site at **www.mhhe.com/relethford7** to access the exercises that follow.

1. **The Scientific Case for Common Descent**   The site "29+ Evidences for Macroevolution: The Scientific Case for Common Descent" (**http://www.talkorigins.org/faqs/comdesc/**) delves further into the subject of macroevolution. It provides evidence that favors both common descent and macroevolution.

   Read through the "Introduction" section. You will learn more about the definition of universal common descent and evidence supporting it.

   - What is considered "scientific evidence"? If you wish to read more about it, click on the following link to "Scientific 'proof,' scientific evidence, and the Scientific Method": **http://www.talkorigins .org/faqs/comdesc/sciproof.html**.
   - Now, define *universal common descent*.
   - Do you think that there is any validity to this theory? Why or why not?
   - Now find the "macroevolution" link in the text above and click on it: **http://www.talkorigins.org/faqs/macroevolution.html**.
   - Define *macroevolution*.
   - Why is it important to gain a basic understanding of macroevolution to better understand the evolution and classification of species?

2. **Speciation**   The site **http://users.rcn.com/jkimball.ma. ultranet/ BiologyPages/S/Speciation.html** contains an explanation, by John Kimball, Ph.D, of why and how speciation occurs.

Read through the explanation of how speciation occurs.

- Name three factors that contribute to speciation.
- Name three mechanisms by which speciation occurs. Come up with an existing example for each type (for example, Darwin's finches demonstrate adaptive radiation).
- What evolutionary process do the house mice of Madeira demonstrate? How did the island's original house mouse population evolve into six separate "races" or species?

3. **What Killed the Dinosaurs?** http://www.pbs.org/wgbh/evolution/extinction/dinosaurs/index.html. Visit the PBS Web site on evolution and extinction. Follow the animated program "What Killed the Dinosaurs?" You will arrive at a table of Hypotheses and Evidence about the demise of the dinosaurs.

Click on the various hypotheses and watch the animations that explain them. You also can click on the bodies of evidence to examine them.

- Which hypothesis seems most probable to you? Why?
- Which hypothesis has the most convincing evidence to support it?

Now click on the "Conclusion" link and read it. Does this conclusion agree with your own? This mystery is open-ended, so the PBS conclusion is not necessarily the only possibility.

- Do you have an alternative interpretation of the evidence?

OUR PLACE IN NATURE

What are humans? This question has been asked over and over again throughout human history by scientists, artists, philosophers, and others. Where do we fit into the animal world? In this section, we look at human beings in a comparative framework, considering our species as part of the total diversity of life. The emphasis in this section is on the primates, a group of mammals to which humans belong. Chapter 5 considers the basic nature of mammals and primates. Chapter 6 looks more closely at variation in the biology and behavior of living primates. Chapter 7 focuses on the human species, emphasizing the similarities and differences with our closest living relatives, the African apes.

A slow loris (*Nycticebus coucang*), one of the species of prosimian. The prosimians, along with monkeys, apes, and humans, make up the order Primates, a group of mammals possessing grasping hands and depth perception.

The Primates

To understand the place of humans in nature, it is first necessary to understand the group of mammals to which humans belong—the **primates.** Humans are primates, as are other creatures such as the apes, the monkeys, and the primitive primates known as prosimians. The basic nature of primate biology and behavior is discussed in this chapter. However, because primates belong to a group known as mammals, who in turn belong to a larger group known as vertebrates, it is first necessary to understand the basic characteristics of these larger taxonomic groups. We begin, therefore, by discussing first vertebrates and then mammals, and then go on to discuss the special characteristics of primates.

As with all living creatures, human beings can be classified according to the different levels of Linnaean taxonomy—kingdom, phylum, class, and so on. A traditional taxonomic description of modern humans is given in Table 5.1. Kingdom is the most inclusive taxonomic category. All living organisms can be placed into one of five kingdoms: plants, animals, fungi, nucleated single-celled organisms, and bacteria. Major differences among these kingdoms are their source of food and their mobility. Whereas plants produce their own food through photosynthesis, animals must ingest food. Humans belong to the animal kingdom. Given that animals must ingest food, it is no surprise that most animals have well-developed nervous, sensory, and movement systems to enable them to sense and acquire food.

Humans belong to the phylum **Chordata** (the chordates, animals with a spinal cord). Perhaps the most important characteristic of chordates is that they possess at some point in their life a **notochord,** a flexible internal rod that runs along the back of the animal. This rod acts to strengthen and support the body. In humans, it is present early in gestation and is later reabsorbed.

Humans belong to the subphylum **Vertebrata** (the vertebrates, animals with backbones). One characteristic of vertebrates is that they have **bilateral symmetry,** which means that the left and right sides of their bodies are approximately mirror images. Imagine a line running down a human being from the top of the head to a spot between the feet. This line divides the body into two mirror images. This pattern contrasts with other phyla of animals such as starfish.

primates The order of mammals that has a complex of characteristics related to an initial adaptation to life in the trees.

Chordata A vertebrate phylum consisting of organisms that possess a notochord at some period during their life.

notochord A flexible internal rod that runs along the back of an animal.

Vertebrata A subphylum of the phylum Chordata, defined by the presence of an internal, segmented spinal column and bilateral symmetry.

bilateral symmetry Symmetry in which the right and left sides of the body are approximately mirror images.

TABLE 5.1   Classification of Humans

Taxonomic Category	Taxonomic Name	Common Name
Kingdom	Animalia	Animals
Phylum	Chordata	Chordates
Subphylum	Vertebrata	Vertebrates
Class	Mammalia	Mammals
Subclass	Eutheria	Placental mammals
Order	Primates	Primates
Suborder	Anthropoidea	Anthropoids
Infraorder	Catarrhini	Old World anthropoids
Superfamily	Hominoidea	Hominoids
Family	Hominidae	Hominids
Subfamily	Homininae	Hominines
Tribe	Hominini	Hominins
Genus/species	*Homo sapiens*	Modern humans

Note: Alternative classifications are discussed in Chapter 6.

Another characteristic of vertebrates is an internal spinal cord covered by a series of bones known as vertebrae. The nerve tissue is surrounded by these bones and has an enlarged area of nerve tissue at the front end of the cord—the brain.

The general biological structure of human beings can be found in many other vertebrates. Most vertebrates have the same basic skeletal pattern: a single upper bone and two lower bones in each limb, and five digits. Some vertebrates have changed considerably from this basic pattern. For example, a modern horse has one digit (a toe) on the end of each limb. Humans may seem to be rather specialized and sophisticated creatures, but they actually have retained much of the earliest basic vertebrate skeletal structure.

The subphylum of vertebrates also includes several classes of fish along with the amphibians, reptiles, birds, and mammals. Humans belong to the class of mammals, and much of our biology and behavior can be understood in terms of what it is to be a mammal.

CHARACTERISTICS OF MAMMALS

The first primitive mammals evolved from early reptiles approximately 200 million years ago. The distinctive features of modern mammals and modern reptiles are the result of that long period of separate evolution in the two classes. It is important to realize that the further back in time we look, the more difficult it is to tell one form from another. Keep in mind that the definition and characteristics of any modern form reflect continued evolution from an earlier ancestor.

Because mammals and reptiles are related through evolution, it is logical and useful to compare these two classes to determine the unique features of each. Modern mammals differ from modern reptiles in reproduction, temperature regulation, diet, skeletal structure, and behavior. As we look at each of these factors separately, do not forget that they are interrelated.

Reproduction

Mammals are often identified as animals that give birth to live offspring, whereas other vertebrates lay eggs. This is not completely accurate. Some fish, such as guppies, give birth to live infants. Also, some mammals, such as the platypus, lay eggs. Others, such as kangaroos, give birth to an extremely immature fetus that completes development inside a pouch in the mother. The most common mammal found today belongs to the subclass of placental mammals, characterized by the development of the fetus inside of the mother's body. Humans are placental mammals.

Placental Mammals The **placenta** is an organ that develops inside the female during pregnancy. It functions as a link between the circulatory systems of the mother and fetus, acting to transport food, oxygen, and antibodies, as well as to filter out waste products. The efficiency of the placenta means that the developing offspring of placental mammals have a much greater chance of survival than does a reptile developing in an egg or in a nonplacental mammal (both egg layers and marsupials, Figures 5.1 and 5.2). Development inside the mother provides warmth and protection along with proper nutrition. Although placental mammals appear at first glance to be superior to egg-laying reptiles, the presence of a placenta has a cost as well as a benefit. Pregnant mammals consume a great deal of energy,

placenta An organ that develops inside a pregnant placental mammal that provides the fetus with oxygen and food and helps filter out harmful substances.

FIGURE 5.1

The spiny anteater, an egg-laying mammal.

FIGURE 5.2

The wallaby, a marsupial mammal.

making ample food resources vital to successful birth. Also, the demand on energy sets a limit on the number of offspring any female mammal can have at one time.

A main feature of mammals is the female mammary glands, which provide food for the newborn infant. Important immunities are also provided in mother's milk. The ready availability of food increases the child's chance of survival. Although advantageous, nursing also has a price; energy is expended by the mother during this process, and only a limited number of offspring can be taken care of at one time.

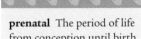

prenatal The period of life from conception until birth.

postnatal The period of life from birth until death.

Parental Care   The **prenatal** (before birth) and **postnatal** (after birth) patterns of parental care in mammals contrast with those of reptiles, which expend less energy during reproduction and care of offspring. Pregnancy and the raising of offspring take energy; the more offspring an organism has, the less care a parent can give each of them. Consequently, some animals have many offspring but provide little care to them, whereas other animals have few offspring and provide much more care to each.

Species vary in terms of the balance between number of offspring and degree of parental care. One extreme example is the oyster, which produces roughly half a billion eggs a year and provides no parental care. Fish can produce 8,000 eggs a year and provide a slight amount of parental care. Frogs can lay 200 eggs a year and provide slightly more parental care.

Compared to other animals, mammals have relatively few offspring but provide much more parental care. The development of the placenta and the mammary glands are biological features that maximize the amount of care given to an offspring. A female lion, for example, has only two offspring per year and provides a great deal of care to them. An extreme example among mammals is the orangutan, an ape that has roughly one offspring every eight years (Galdikas and Wood 1990).

From an evolutionary viewpoint, which strategy is better: having many offspring but providing little care, or having fewer offspring and providing greater care? Each strategy has its advantages and disadvantages. In general, those species that have many offspring tend to be at an advantage in rapidly changing environments, whereas those that provide greater care are at an advantage in more stable environments (Pianka 1983).

Temperature Regulation

Modern mammals are **homeotherms;** they are able to maintain a constant body temperature under most circumstances. Modern reptiles are cold-blooded and cannot keep their body temperature constant; they need to use the heat of the sun's rays to keep themselves warm and their metabolism active. Mammals maintain a constant body temperature in several ways. They are covered with fur or hair that insulates the body, preventing heat loss in cold weather and reducing overheating in hot weather. Temporary changes in the size of blood vessels also aid in temperature regulation. When blood vessels contract, blood flow is reduced, and less heat is lost from the mammal's extremities. When blood vessels dilate, blood flow is increased to the extremities, thus allowing greater heat loss.

Mammals also maintain a constant body temperature by ingesting large quantities of food and converting the food to energy in the form of heat. When you feel hot, your body is not losing the produced heat quickly enough. When you feel cold, you are losing heat too quickly. The ability to convert food energy to heat enables mammals to live comfortably in many environments where reptiles would slow down or even die.

Mammals are thus able to exploit a large number of environments. However, heat production and temperature regulation, though obviously useful adaptations in certain environments, are not without a price. To obtain energy, mammals need to consume far greater quantities of food than do reptiles. In environments where food resources are limited, mammals may be worse off than reptiles. Again, the evolutionary benefit of any trait must be looked at in terms of its cost.

Humans, of course, have gone beyond the basic temperature-regulating abilities of other mammals. We have developed a variety of technologies that help keep us warm or cool. Fire and clothes were the earliest inventions of this sort. Today we have all sorts of heating and cooling devices that enable us to live in virtually any environment on the earth, as well as in outer space. Our culture has allowed us to go beyond our biological limits.

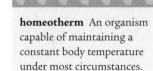

homeotherm An organism capable of maintaining a constant body temperature under most circumstances.

Teeth

The saying "You are what you eat" is not usually made literally, but in fact, it embodies an important truth of ecology and evolution. The nutritional requirements of organisms dictate, in part, their environmental needs. Also, diet is reflected in the physical structure of organisms, particularly the teeth and jaws. Because mammals maintain a constant body temperature by converting food energy to heat, they require a considerable amount of food. The physical features of mammalian teeth reflect this need.

The teeth of modern reptiles are all the same, that is, **homodontic;** they all have sharp sides and are continually replaced throughout life. A major function of reptilian teeth is to hold and kill prey. The food is then most often eaten whole. Mammals, on the other hand, have different types of teeth; that is, they are **heterodontic.** Mammals usually have two sets of teeth during their lives: a set of deciduous ("baby") teeth and a set of permanent teeth. As a mammal grows and matures, the baby teeth fall out and are replaced with the adult teeth. In modern humans, this replacement normally starts around age 6 and takes the first 18–20 years of life to complete.

Types of Teeth   Most mammals have four types of teeth: **incisors, canines, premolars,** and **molars.** These teeth in a chimpanzee and a human are shown in Figure 5.3. The incisor teeth are chisel- or spatula-shaped and located in the front of the jaw. Both the human and the chimpanzee (and other higher primates) have a total of four incisors in each jaw. These teeth are used for cutting and slicing food. You use your incisors when you eat an apple or corn on the cob. Behind the incisors are the canine teeth, which are often long and sharp, resembling fangs or tusks. Apes and humans have two canine teeth in each jaw. In many mammals, the canine teeth are used as weapons or for killing prey. Although the canine teeth of most mammals are rather large and project beyond the level of the rest of the teeth, human canines are usually small and nonprojecting.

The premolar and molar teeth are also known collectively as the back teeth or cheek teeth. Both of these types of teeth are often large in surface

homodontic All teeth are the same.

heterodontic Having different types of teeth.

incisor The chisel-shaped front teeth used for cutting, slicing, and gnawing food.

canine The teeth located in the front of the jaw behind the incisors, which are normally used by mammals for puncturing and defense.

premolar One of the types of back teeth, used for crushing and grinding food.

molar The teeth farthest back in the jaw used for crushing and grinding food.

FIGURE 5.3

The lower jaws and teeth of a chimpanzee and a modern human.

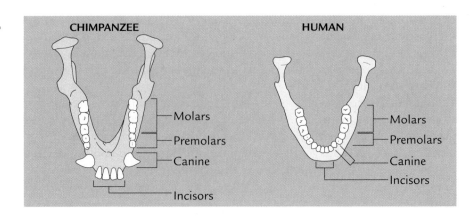

area and are used for grinding and chewing food. When you chew food between your back teeth, you do not simply move your lower jaw up and down. Instead, your upper and lower back teeth grind together in a circular motion as your jaw moves up and down and sideways as well. The structures of the premolar and molar teeth are different, and in some mammals, these teeth have different functions as well.

Dental Formulae   Mammals can be characterized by the number of each type of tooth they have. The usual method of counting teeth is to consider the number of each type of tooth in one-half of one jaw, upper or lower. Only one-half of the jaw is considered because both the right and left sides of the jaw contain the same number of teeth. These numbers are expressed using a **dental formula,** which lists the number of incisors, canines, premolars, and molars in one-half of a jaw. A dental formula looks like this: I-C-PM-M. Here I = number of incisors, C = number of canines, PM = number of premolars, and M = number of molars. For example, the typical dental formula of humans (as well as apes and some monkeys) is 2-1-2-3. This means that in one-half of either jaw there are two incisors, one canine, two premolars, and three molars. Each half of each jaw therefore contains $2 + 1 + 2 + 3 = 8$ teeth. The typical number of teeth in humans is therefore $8 \times 4 = 32$ (two sides of each of two jaws). Some mammals have different numbers of teeth in the top and bottom jaws. In these cases, we use two dental formulae. For example, a dental formula of 2-1-2-3/2-1-2-2 would indicate fewer molars in the lower jaw.

Diet and Teeth   The basic description of the types of teeth is somewhat simplistic. Many mammals have evolved specialized uses of one or more of these tooth types. As noted earlier, human canines are rather different in form and function from those of many other mammals. The general description is useful, however, in showing the importance of differentiated teeth in mammals. By having different types of teeth capable of slicing, cutting, and grinding, mammals are able to eat a wide variety of different foods in an efficient way. In addition, the ability to chew food rather than swallow it whole allows greater efficiency in eating. By chewing, mammals break down the food into smaller pieces that can be digested more easily and efficiently. Also, saliva released in the mouth during chewing begins the process of digestion.

The nature of mammalian diet and teeth relates to their warm-bloodedness. Mammals need more food than reptiles, and their teeth allow them to utilize a wider range of food and to process it more productively. The benefits of differentiated teeth lie in these abilities. The cost is the fact that the teeth tend to wear out over time. When a mammal's adult teeth are worn down, it may not be able to eat or may develop serious dental problems, which could lead to death. As far as recent humans are concerned, we can circumvent these potential problems to a certain extent with dental technology, personal hygiene, and processed foods. Even so, dental problems continue to pose a serious threat to human health.

dental formula A short-hand method of describing the number of each type of tooth in one half of one jaw on a mammal.

Skeletal Structure

Both mammals and reptiles share the basic skeletal structure of all vertebrates, but there are some differences, especially in movement. In reptiles, the four limbs come out from the side of the body for support and movement (Figure 5.4). In four-legged mammals, the limbs slope downward from the shoulders and hips. Having the limbs tucked in under the body allows more efficient and quicker movement. The weight of the body is supported better. Humans differ from the pattern of many mammals in using only two limbs for movement. Even so, the configuration of the legs follows the basic pattern; the legs slope inward from the hips and are not splayed out to the sides.

Behavior

The brains of all vertebrates have similar structures but differ in size, relative proportions, and functions. All vertebrates have a hindbrain, a midbrain, and a forebrain. In most vertebrates, the hindbrain is associated with hearing, balance, reflexive behaviors, and control of the autonomic functions of the body, such as breathing. The midbrain is associated with vision, and the forebrain is associated with chemical sensing, such as smelling ability. Compared to fish, reptiles have a relatively larger midbrain and hindbrain because they rely more extensively on vision and hearing. The midbrain of a reptile is

FIGURE 5.4

The orientation of the limbs to the body in reptiles and in mammals.

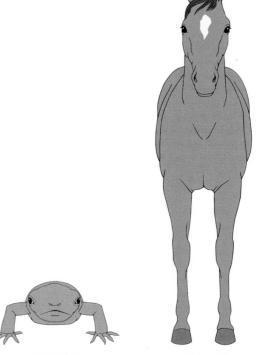

REPTILE   MAMMAL

particularly enlarged because it functions to coordinate sensory information and body movements.

The brain of a mammal reveals several important shifts in structure and function. The mammalian brain has a greatly enlarged forebrain that is responsible for the processing of sensory information and for coordination. In particular, the forebrain contains the **cerebrum,** the outermost layer of brain cells, which is associated with learning, memory, and intelligence. The cerebrum becomes increasingly convoluted, which allows huge numbers of interconnections between brain cells. It accounts for the largest proportion of the mammalian brain.

The overall functions of a brain include basic body maintenance and the ability to process information and respond accordingly. Mammals rely more on learning and flexible responses than do reptiles. Behaviors are less instinctual and rigid. Previous experiences (learning) become more important in responding to stimuli. As a consequence, mammals are more capable of developing new responses to different situations and are capable of learning from past mistakes. New behaviors are more likely to develop and can be passed on to offspring through the process of learning. Humans have taken this process even further; our very existence depends on flexible behaviors that must be learned. Although our behavior is to a large extent cultural, our ability to transfer information through learning relies on a biological trait: the mammalian brain.

The behavioral flexibility of mammals ties in with their pattern of reproduction. In general, the more a species relies on parental care, the more intelligent it is, and the more it relies on learning rather than instinct. Extensive parental care requires increased intelligence and the ability to learn new behaviors in order to provide maximum care for infants. The increased emphasis on learning requires, in turn, an extended period of growth during which the information needed for adult life is absorbed. Furthermore, the extension of childhood requires more extensive child care so that offspring are protected during the time they are completing their growth and learning.

The major characteristics of mammals are all interrelated. Reproductive behaviors are associated with learning, intelligence, and social behaviors. The ability to maintain body temperature is related to diet and teeth; warm-bloodedness requires vast amounts of energy that in turn is made available from differentiated teeth and a wide dietary base. Also, the reproductive pattern of placental mammals requires great amounts of energy, which in turn relates to diet. In fact, the major characteristics of any group of animals are not merely a list of independent traits; they represent an integrated complex of traits.

PRIMATE CHARACTERISTICS

There are many different forms of mammals—they are as diverse as mice, whales, giraffes, cats, dogs, and apes. Patterns of biology and behavior vary considerably, although all mammals share to some extent the basic characteristics outlined in the previous section.

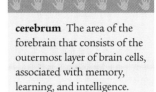

cerebrum The area of the forebrain that consists of the outermost layer of brain cells, associated with memory, learning, and intelligence.

Recall that the mammalian class is broken down into a number of orders. Humans, as noted, are primates, as are the apes, such as the chimpanzee, bonobo, and gorilla, which are our closest living relatives. Monkeys are also primates, as are more biologically primitive forms known as prosimians. The basic characteristics of primates are discussed in this section. The next chapter describes variation in the biology and behavior of primates, including a discussion of different types of primates.

No single characteristic identifies primates; rather, they share a set of features. Many of these features relate to living in the trees. Though humans, as well as a few other modern primates, clearly do not live in the trees, they still retain certain features inherited from ancestors who did.

An **arboreal** (tree-living) environment presents different challenges than a **terrestrial** (ground-living) environment. Living in the trees requires an orientation to a three-dimensional environment. Animals that live on the ground generally contend with only two dimensions: length and width. Arboreal animals must also deal with the third dimension, height. Perception of distance and depth is vital to a tree-living form, which moves quickly from one branch to the next and from one level of the forest to another. Agility is also important, as is the ability to anchor oneself in space.

Many forms of animals, such as squirrels and birds, have adapted to living in the trees. Primates, too, are capable of extensive rapid movement through the trees and are able to move to all areas of a tree, including small terminal branches. A squirrel can climb up and down the trunk of a tree and traverse larger branches, but primates are even better equipped to move out to feed on the smallest branches. The two major characteristics of primates that account for their success in the trees are the ability to use hands and feet to grasp branches (rather than digging in with claws) and the ability to perceive distance and depth.

Although primate characteristics relate to living in the trees, there has been debate over *why* these characteristics first evolved. Some researchers favor a model whereby both grasping hands and depth perception evolved as arboreal adaptations at the same time; others have suggested that grasping hands evolved first, perhaps as an adaptation for eating food at the ends of branches, and that depth perception evolved later (Sargis 2002). This section describes these adaptations as they exist in living primates. The evolutionary hypotheses regarding their origin are discussed in Chapter 9.

Not all modern primates have kept the original adaptations of the first primates. For example, humans can still use their hands to grasp objects but cannot do so with their feet. We do not normally use our hands to grasp and hang onto branches. We have taken our inherited ability to grasp and put it to work in another arena: We hold tools, weapons, food, and children. The grasping hands of a human and a tree-living monkey are homologous—that is, they are similar structures because of common descent. The different functions of the hands of humans and tree-living monkeys reflect adaptive changes from the original primate ancestors. Even though humans do things differently, we are still primates and have the basic set of primate characteristics.

arboreal Living in trees.
terrestrial Living on the ground.

The Skeleton

First let us consider some general characteristics in the primate skeletal structure.

Grasping Hands   A characteristic of the earliest known mammals (and reptiles) is five digits on each hand or foot. Certain mammals, such as the horse, have changed from this ancestral condition and have only a single toe on each limb. Other mammals, such as the primates, have kept the ancestral condition.

In the case of primates, the retention of the primitive characteristics of five digits on the hands and feet turned out to be an important adaptation. The hands and feet of primates are **prehensile,** that is, capable of being used to grasp objects. The ability to grasp involves the movement of the fingers to the palm, thus allowing the fingers to wrap around an object. In many primates, the toes can also wrap around an object. This grasping ability is a remarkable adaptation to living in the trees. Primates can grab onto branches to move about, to provide support while eating, and in general to allow for a high degree of flexibility in moving about their environment. More specialized structures, such as the horse's single hoof, would be useless in the trees because there would be no way to grasp branches.

Another feature of primate hands and feet is their expanded tactile pads (such as the ball of your thumb) and nails instead of claws. Nails serve to protect the sensitive skin at the ends of the fingers and the toes. The numerous nerve endings in the tips of fingers and toes of primates provide an enhanced sense of touch that is useful in manipulating objects.

As mentioned earlier, the characteristics possessed by primates are not the only possible solution to the challenge of living in the trees. Squirrels, for example, use their claws to dig into the bark of limbs and branches when they climb in the trees. The grasping ability of primate hands, however, provides much greater flexibility. They can reach food at the end of small branches by grasping surrounding branches for support, using a free arm to reach out and grab the food, and then bringing it to the mouth. A small branch might not provide enough surface area for a squirrel to dig its claws into, but a primate can use its grasping hands and feet to hold onto it.

Variations on these themes occur even within primates. Humans differ from the general primate conditions. We have lost the ability to use our feet for grasping as a result of anatomical changes relating to our ability to walk on two legs.

Generalized Structure   Biological structures are often classified as specialized or generalized. **Specialized structures** are used in a highly specific way, whereas **generalized structures** can be used in a variety of ways. The hooves of a horse, for example, are a specialization that allows rapid running over land surfaces. The basic skeletal structure of primates is generalized because it allows movement flexibility in a wide variety of circumstances.

The arm and leg bones of primates follow the basic pattern of many vertebrates: Each limb consists of an upper bone and two lower bones (refer

prehensile Capable of grasping.

specialized structure A biological structure adapted to a narrow range of conditions and used in very specific ways.

generalized structure A biological structure adapted to a wide range of conditions and used in very general ways.

back to Figure 4.6). This structure allows limbs to bend at the elbows or knees. In climbing or jumping in a tree, you must have this flexibility, or you would not be able to move about (imagine trying to jump from one branch to another with your arms and legs made up of one long bone). That the lower part of the limb is made up of two bones provides even greater flexibility. Hold your arm out straight in front of you with your palm down. Now turn your hand so that the palm side is up. This is easy to do, but only because you have two lower arm bones. When turning the hand over, one lower arm bone crosses over the other. Imagine trying to climb in a tree without the ability to move your hand into different positions. This flexibility is obtained by the retention of a generalized skeletal structure.

Vision

The three-dimensional nature of arboreal life requires keen eyesight, particularly depth perception. This feature has evolved from the need to judge distances successfully. (Jumping through the air from branch to branch demands the ability to judge distances. After all, it is not very adaptive to fall short of your target and plunge to the ground!)

Depth perception involves **binocular stereoscopic vision.** *Binocular* refers to overlapping fields of vision. The eyes of many animals are located at the sides of the skull so that each eye receives a different image with no overlap. The eyes of primates are located in the front of the skull so that the fields of vision overlap (Figure 5.5). Primates see objects in front of them with both eyes. The *stereoscopic* nature of primate vision refers to the way in which the brain processes visual signals. In nonstereoscopic animals, the information from one eye is received in only one hemisphere of the brain. In primates, the visual signals from both eyes are received in both hemispheres of the

binocular stereoscopic vision Overlapping fields of vision, with both sides of the brain receiving images from both eyes, thereby providing depth perception.

FIGURE 5.5

Binocular stereoscopic vision in primates. The fields of vision for each eye overlap, and the optic nerve from each eye is connected to both hemispheres of the brain. (From *Human Antiquity: An Introduction to Physical Anthropology and Archaeology,* 4th ed., by Kenneth Feder and Michael Park. Fig. 5.1. Copyright © 2001 by Mayfield Publishing Company. Reprinted by permission of The McGraw-Hill Companies.)

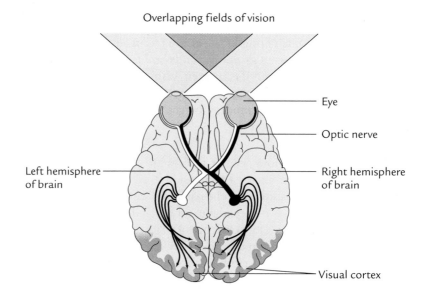

Overlapping fields of vision

Eye

Optic nerve

Left hemisphere of brain

Right hemisphere of brain

Visual cortex

brain. The result is an image that has depth. Moving quickly and safely in three dimensions requires depth perception.

Many primates also have the ability to perceive colors. Color vision is extremely useful in detecting objects in moderate-contrast environments. In fact, color vision is found in other animals for this reason, including whales, fish, bumblebees, and certain birds. Color vision is also important in primate species that use color as a visual signal of various emotional states, such as anger or receptivity to sexual relations.

Primates are vision oriented. On average, their sense of smell is less keen. As a result, the areas of the face devoted to smelling are reduced in primates. Compared to other mammals, primates have short snouts.

The Brain and Behavior

Primates have expanded on the basic pattern of mammalian brains. Their brains are even larger relative to body size. Primate brains have larger visual areas and smaller areas for smelling, corresponding to their increased emphasis on vision over smell as the main sense. Also, primate brains are even more complex than those of most other mammals. Primates have larger proportions of the brain associated with learning and intelligence. Areas of the brain associated with body control and coordination are also proportionately larger, as expected given the demands of arboreal life. Hand–eye coordination, for example, is crucial for moving about in trees.

Learning   The greater size and complexity of primate brains are reflected in their behaviors. Many primates rely extensively on learned behaviors. As a result, it is often difficult to assign specific behaviors to a given species of primate because the increased emphasis on learning allows a great deal of flexibility in behavior patterns.

The increased emphasis on learning means that primates spend a greater proportion of their lives growing up, both biologically and socially, than do other animals. The more an animal needs to learn, the longer the time needed for learning. An increase in the amount of time spent learning as an infant or child also means that greater amounts of attention and care are required from parents. Again, we see the intimate relationship among reproduction, care of offspring, learning, and intelligence.

The basic pattern of primate learning provides a means by which new behaviors can be passed on from one generation to the next. If we define culture simply as learned behavior, all primates can be said to have culture. Most of the time, however, the distinctive characteristic of human culture is identified as its reliance on language for transmission. Within this framework, the cultural behaviors and social organization of nonhuman primates are often referred to as *protoculture*. No matter what terms we use, however, or how we define human and nonhuman culture, the fact remains that social learning provides a means by which behaviors are passed on from one generation to the next in all primates (and, indeed, in many other mammals).

FIGURE 5.6

A macaque washing food in water.

An Example of Learned Behavior in Primates   Primate studies have provided many good examples of the introduction of new behaviors to a group by one or more individuals that are then learned by other individuals. Studies of the Japanese macaque monkeys on the island of Koshima during the 1950s revealed a number of cases of cultural transmission of new behaviors. The Koshima troop has been provisioned (provided with food) since the early 1950s to keep all the monkeys out in the open for observation purposes.

In 1953, a young female macaque named Imo began washing sweet potatoes in a stream before eating them (Figure 5.6). Within three years, this behavior had been learned by almost half of the troop. Of the 19 younger monkeys, 15 had adopted this behavior, however, and thereafter, almost all newborns acquired it by observing their mothers (Bramblett 1976).

Another food-related behavior developed among the troop in 1956 when scientists began feeding the monkeys grains of wheat. The wheat was scattered on a sandy beach to slow down the monkeys' eating so that researchers would have more time to study them. Imo developed a new method of eating the grains of wheat. She took handfuls of sand and wheat down to the water and threw them in. The sand sank while the wheat floated, thus letting her skim the grains off the surface of the water. This new behavior provided a much quicker way of getting the wheat than picking out grains from the sand. The young female's method of wheat washing spread quickly through most of the rest of the troop (Bramblett 1976).

The studies of cultural transmission among the Japanese macaques show the importance of learning in primate societies. Washing sweet potatoes and separating wheat from sand are not innate behaviors in Japanese macaques. These behaviors are transmitted through learning, not genetic inheritance. The studies also show the importance of individual behavior: In both cases, the same monkey introduced the behaviors. If that monkey were not present in that troop, these behaviors might not have developed.

PRIMATE BEHAVIOR

In terms of both biology and behavior, primates are an extremely variable group of mammals. Examples of this diversity are explored in the next chapter, which reviews the different subgroups of nonhuman primates. For now, however, it is useful to consider some general characteristics of primate behavior in an evolutionary context.

Primate Behavioral Ecology

Studies of primate behavior have often used ecological approaches to explain variation in primate behavior, both between different species and within a single species. Early ecological studies of primates focused on habitat—specifically, the contrast between species that live in the trees and species that live on the ground (DeVore 1963). This arboreal-terrestrial contrast suggested some basic relationships between habitat and social organization, territoriality, group size, and **home range** (the size of the geographic area normally occupied in a group). Additional studies showed that this simple contrast in habitats did not fully explain variation in primate behavior. Crook and Gartlan (1965) and Jolly (1972) later expanded on this idea by breaking down primate species into groups defined by habitat and diet. Other researchers began focusing on other ecological principles, such as food density, mating strategies, and predation, to help explain differences in primate behavior and social organization (for example, Denham 1971).

By the mid-1980s, the study of primate behavior had shifted toward the field of **behavioral ecology,** the study of behavior from an ecological and evolutionary perspective. The primary concern of primate behavioral ecology is the evolutionary analysis of behaviors as strategies for adapting to specific conditions, with a focus on feeding, social, and reproductive strategies (Fedigan and Strum 1999; Strier 2003). This focus relates primate behavior to the basic problems of adaptation from an evolutionary perspective: finding food, reproducing, and getting along with others. Analysis of primate behavior needs to take into account multiple costs and benefits for various behaviors.

Consider, for example, something as basic as the nature of the social group. Why live in groups? Some advantages of group living include more successful defense against predators and cooperative defense of valuable food resources (Wrangham 1987a; Fedigan and Strum 1999). Large groups, however, may be *disadvantageous* if food resources are limited. To what extent are

home range The size of the geographic area that is normally occupied and used by a social group.

behavioral ecology The study of behavior that focuses on the adaptive value of behavior from an ecological and evolutionary perspective.

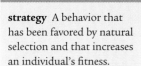

strategy A behavior that has been favored by natural selection and that increases an individual's fitness.

life history theory The study of how characteristics of an organism's life cycle affects reproduction, focusing on tradeoffs between energy expended for numbers and fitness of offspring.

parental investment Parental behaviors that increase the probability that offspring will survive.

group size and structure (or any social behavior, for that matter) a trade-off between the costs and benefits of different behavioral strategies? As used here, the term *strategy* does not imply a conscious decision. Instead, **strategy** has a very specific meaning in behavioral ecology, referring to any behavior that has been selected for because it increases an individual's overall fitness (in terms of reproduction and survival) (Strier 2003).

Reproductive Strategies

Reproduction is central to evolution. In terms of behavior, it is useful to examine the costs and benefits associated with different reproductive strategies. **Life history theory** deals with characteristics of an organism's life cycle and their effects on the quantity and quality of reproduction. These characteristics include age at maturity, age at reproduction, gestation length, the interval between births, and overall life span, among others. A central concept of life history theory is the allocation of energy. Energy is used by organisms for growth, maintenance, and reproduction, and energy expended for one function cannot be used for something else. Life history theory focuses on the trade-off between energy needs, and one of the most important trade-offs is between the number of offspring and their fitness (Hill 1993; Leigh and Blomquist 2007).

Some animal species can be described as having "fast" life histories, whereby individuals reach maturity early and have a large number of offspring during their reproductive life. Other species have "slow" life histories, whereby maturation is delayed until later in the life span, and the total number of offspring is lower (Strier 2003). In general, primates have "slow" life histories characterized by a small number of offspring and a great deal of parental care. Primates tend to mature more slowly, live longer, have larger brains, and have fewer offspring. Almost all primates have a reproductive pattern of having one offspring at a time. The next offspring is generally not born until the previous one is mature enough, biologically and socially, to survive on its own. In some primates, such as the apes, the interval between offspring may be five years or more. Humans are an exception to this rule because we have overlapping births without sacrificing the quality of parental care.

The Mother–Infant Bond   Evolutionary explanations of behavior often focus on maximizing fitness. This refers to behaviors that increase the probability that an individual's DNA will be passed on to the next generation. If such behaviors are affected even partially by genetic factors, then natural selection will cause those behaviors to increase in frequency. A related concept is the idea of **parental investment,** which refers to parental behaviors that increase the probability that the offspring will survive. Mammalian (and especially primate) females invest a great deal of time and energy in care of offspring. Even though this investment reduces the number of offspring a female can have, the benefits outweigh the costs.

Thus, primates have a strong and long-lasting bond between mother and infant. Unlike some mammals, infant primates are entirely helpless. They

FIGURE 5.7

Female chimpanzee and her offspring. The greater amount of care and attention given by the mother can be interpreted as maximizing reproductive success by increasing parental investment.

depend on their mothers for food, warmth, protection, affection, and knowledge, and they remain dependent for a long time (Figure 5.7). Of all the different types of social bonds in primate societies, the mother–infant bond is the strongest. In many primate species, this bond continues well past infancy. Chimpanzees, for example, regularly associate with their mothers throughout their adult lives (Goodall 1986).

The biological importance of the mother–infant bond is easy to see: The infants are dependent on mother's milk for nourishment. Is that all there is to it? In the early twentieth century, some researchers suggested that the entire basis of "mother love" seen in primate infants arose from the infant's need for food. Laboratory experiments and field observations soon showed that this is not the case; the social aspects of the mother–infant bond are also crucial for survival.

One of the most famous of these experiments was performed by psychologist Harry Harlow, who isolated infant rhesus monkeys from their mothers. He raised them in cages in which he placed two "surrogate mothers," the first a wire framework in the approximate shape of an adult monkey and the second the same structure covered with terry cloth. He then attached a bottle of milk to the "wire mother" (Figure 5.8). Harlow reasoned that if the need for food were stronger than the need for warmth and comfort, the infant monkeys would spend most or all of their time clinging to the "wire mother." If the need for warmth and comfort were more important, the infant would

FIGURE 5.8

Harlow's maternal deprivation experiment on infant rhesus monkeys. These monkeys preferred to spend almost all of their time clinging to the cloth surrogate mother (*right*), which provided warmth, rather than to the wire surrogate mother (*left*), which provided food. Even when hungry, the infants would often remain partially attached to the cloth mother.

spend most or all of the time clinging to the "cloth mother." The monkeys invariably preferred the warmth and security of the "cloth mothers" to the food provided by the "wire mothers." Even when the infants needed to eat, they often kept part of their body in contact with the "cloth mother." Additional experiments showed that under the stimulus of stress or fear, the monkeys would go to the "cloth mothers" for security (Harlow 1959).

These experiments showed that motherhood was not merely important in terms of nutrition; warmth and comfort were also necessary in an infant's development. But do these experiments mean that natural mothers can be replaced by a bottle and a blanket? Definitely not. As Harlow's monkeys grew up, they showed a wide range of abnormal behaviors. They were often incapable of sexual reproduction, they could not interact normally with other monkeys, and they often were extremely aggressive. The motherless females who later had children did not know how to take care of them and frequently rejected or mistreated them.

These findings have powerful implications. We often speak of "maternal instincts," suggesting that the behaviors associated with successful mothering are somehow innate. Although the basic mother–infant bond is part of the biological basis of mammals, and maternal feelings are to some extent innate, the specific behaviors that are part of this bond are learned. Mammals, and especially primates, rely extensively on learned behaviors. As a result, variation in behavior is often great and can be influenced by a variety of other factors. Observations of the behavior of primates in their natural environments confirm the fact that maternal behaviors are to a large extent learned. Studies of chimpanzee mothers have shown that young females tend to model their own later parental behaviors after those of their mothers. Similar patterns are seen in humans. For example, the children of abusive parents often tend to be abusive parents themselves. Such research shows us that the study of animal behavior, especially that of other primates, is not an esoteric subject but rather helps us to understand ourselves.

Primates in Danger

By the late 1990s, roughly 270 primate species had been identified in the world (Eudey 1999), with additional species being discovered in recent years (Jones et al. 2005). Counting subspecies as well as species, a report issued in 2005 by Russell Mittermeier and colleagues identified 625 distinct types of primates. Many, however, live a precarious existence. As of 2005, 26 percent of these taxa had been classified as "Endangered" or "Critically Endangered" by conservation experts, with an additional 11 percent classified as "Vulnerable" (Mittermeier et al. 2005). We have also seen the recent extinction of the red colobus monkey subspecies *Procolobus badius waldroni* (Chapman and Peres 2001).

What has caused this danger to living primates? One major factor is the destruction of native habitats. More than 90 percent of all primate species live in tropical rain forests, which are disappearing at an alarming rate as forest is cleared for human use (Wright 1992; Chapman and Peres 2001). Other primates, such as the mountain gorilla, have had their habitats reduced through farming to meet the demands for food of growing human populations (Mittermeier and Sterling 1992).

Hunting by humans is another threat to primate survival (Strier 2003, 2007). The demand for bushmeat (the meat of wild animals) has increased in parts of the world even when it is illegal. In addition to being a food resource, primates are hunted in many parts of the world for use as bait for other animals, for sale of their body parts for ornaments, or because they are considered agricultural pests. Another threat is the capture of live animals for sale, although international efforts have reduced this demand to some extent. Live capture is a particular problem when infants are sought because their mothers are frequently shot during capture of the infant. Logging is another human activity that has endangered many primate species, as the loss of habitat contributes significantly to the endangered status of many primates (Chapman and Peres 2001). The Ebola virus has been spreading among great ape populations in western Africa, causing as much mortality as hunting in some cases (Walsh et al. 2003).

What can be done? There is no single solution; a series of conservation efforts must be applied at the international level to have the greatest impact. Strier (2003) lists several general strategies, including developing economic incentives for conservation, raising public awareness of the potential problems, and increasing the role of nongovernmental organizations (NGOs) in providing an opportunity for interaction and information exchange among conservationists, primate researchers, and policy makers. Attention is also needed to reduce the impact of diseases such as that caused by the Ebola virus in African apes. Other approaches to primate conservation include developing protected parks and preserves, implementing less harmful agricultural practices, and breeding endangered primate species in captivity (Mittermeier and Sterling 1992; Wright 1992). Chapman and Peres (2001) emphasize the role that scientists can play in such conservation efforts. All of these efforts, and more, are needed if we are to save these remarkable relatives of ours.

Adult Males and Infant Care Maternal care is found throughout the primate order. The mother–infant bond is the strongest tie within primate groups. What role do males play in the care of infants in primate societies? Such care is variable among primate societies, in terms of both its presence and intensity. A number of **monogamous** primate species (characterized by a more or less permanent bond forming between a single male and female) show the most intensive levels of infant care by males (Whitten 1987). From a genetic perspective, this makes sense if we assume that the male is the father, because taking care of his offspring increases his reproductive fitness. If so, then infant care may be less likely in **polygamous** species, in which a number of males could potentially be the father.

The situation is more complex, however, than a simple dichotomy of monogamous versus polygamous species. For one thing, adult females in monogamous societies have been observed to have sexual relationships

monogamy An exclusive sexual bond between an adult male and an adult female for a long period of time.

polygamy A sexual bond between an adult male and an adult female in which either individual may have more than one mate at the same time.

outside of their pair-group (Strier 2003). In addition, adult males in some monogamous species engage in very little infant care, whereas some males in polygamous species do provide such care. Infant care by adult males may be a function of females choosing mates, as a number of studies have shown that females in polygamous species are more likely to mate with males that actively care for infants (van Schaik and Paul 1996). In such cases, it would be adaptive for males to engage in infant care because it increases their chances of mating, and therefore their chances for reproductive success.

alloparent An individual that cares for an infant but is not a biological parent.

infanticide The killing of an infant.

Alloparenting   An **alloparent** is an individual who takes care of an infant but is *not* his or her biological parent. An alloparent can be another adult or a sibling. As a rule, primate females who have not given birth are more likely to engage in this behavior than females who have given birth (MacKinnon 2007). There is variation in the extent to which mothers allow others to touch and interact with their infants. Alloparent care can be potentially adaptive for both the infant and the alloparent. In cases in which a mother dies (and assuming that the infant has already been weaned), an alloparent can take care of the orphan. In cases in which the mother is present, alloparents can gain valuable experience in helping to take care of infants. In addition, as discussed above, if adult males help take care of infants, they may increase their chances of mating with the mother.

Infanticide   The killing of an infant—**infanticide**—by an adult male has been observed in several nonhuman primate species, spurring a debate as to whether this is deviant behavior or is instead adaptive for the killer. The classic study of infanticide was conducted by Sarah Hrdy (1977) on a group of monkeys, known as langurs, that live in societies with a single adult male (see the section "Social Groups" for more information on the structure of primate societies). Because there is only one adult male in the social group, he frequently faces challenges from other adult males attempting to displace him. When a new male successfully takes over the group, he often attempts to kill all the infants fathered by the previous male (Figure 5.9). At first, such behavior seems abnormal and contrary to the survival of the group. An alternative explanation, however, is that the new male is increasing his own fitness. First, killing the infants sired by other males can increase the proportion of his own offspring in the next generation. The competition has been eliminated. Second, females who are still nursing infants are not yet able to become pregnant by the new male (as nursing tends to inhibit resumption of the normal cycle of ovulation), and he has to wait. By killing the infants, the new male ensures that the females are more quickly able to have offspring with him.

This explanation of infanticide has been challenged, and alternative hypotheses, such as overcrowding and deforestation leading to social pathology, have been proposed. One critical difference between explanations for infanticide is the genetic relationship between the killer and the killed infant. If we assume infanticide increases the new male's reproductive success, then we would expect this behavior to be directed *only* at offspring of other males.

FIGURE 5.9

Adult female langurs attempting to rescue an infant from an adult male langur.

On the other hand, if the social pathology hypothesis is correct, we might expect that a deviant male would kill his own as well as other males' infants. Borries and colleagues (1999) tested this hypothesis by examining the DNA of langur infants and attackers from fecal samples for 16 infant attacks. In all cases, the DNA analysis showed that the attacking male was *not* the infant's father. Although the sample size is relatively small, this study does suggest that infanticide is related to male reproductive success in langur monkeys.

Growing Up

The importance of the extended period of infant and juvenile growth in primates cannot be overstated. The long period of growth is necessary for learning motor skills and social behaviors. The close bond between mother and infant provides the first important means by which an infant primate learns. It is not the only important social contact for a growing primate, however. The process of socialization in most primates depends to a large extent on close contact with peers. Interaction with other individuals of the same age provides the opportunity to learn specific types of social behaviors, as well as how to interact socially in general.

Experiments by Harlow clearly demonstrate the importance of social contact with peers. Monkeys raised by their mothers but kept apart from other infants often grew up showing a range of abnormal behaviors. They would stare at their cages for long periods, were often self-destructive, and did not show normal patterns of sexual behavior (Harlow and Harlow 1962). Although some primate species are basically solitary apart from the mother–infant bond, most belong to larger social groups and require contact with peers during their growth.

Growing up and learning as a primate also requires that infants and juveniles play a great deal of the time. Play behaviors have often been ignored in studies of human and nonhuman behavior because they are regarded as nonproductive. In truth, play behaviors are essential to the proper biological and social development of primates.

Play behavior can serve several functions. First, physical play allows an infant to develop and practice necessary motor skills. Second, social play provides the opportunity to learn how to behave with others. Needed social skills are learned through play (Dohlinow 1999). The importance of play becomes very obvious when we consider what happened to the monkeys that Harlow had separated from their peers. Without normal contact and the opportunity to develop socially, these monkeys became sociopathic.

Social Groups

Primates are essentially social creatures, but they show an amazing amount of variation in the size and structure of their primary social groups. The main social group can range in size and can vary in terms of the number of males, females, young, and old. A social group is generally defined as a group within which there is frequent communication or interaction among members. The size and structure of a social group can vary within a species and even within a group over time. Some primates are relatively solitary, and the primary social group consists of a mother and her dependent offspring; adult males and adult females have infrequent contact, mostly for mating.

Most primate species, however, are more social and live in larger and more complex groups. The traditional labels used to describe primate social groups reflect the relative number of adult males and adult females in the social group (Fuentes 1999). The **one-male/one-female group** consists of a single adult male and single adult female in a monogamous relationship and their offspring. Although this social group corresponds to a typical Western notion of a "family," it is not that common among nonhuman primates. It should be noted that genetic evidence shows that reproduction is not strictly monogamous in these groups.

Two types of primate social groups consist of a single adult of one sex and more than one adult of the opposite sex: the **one-male/multifemale group** and, less commonly, the **one-female/multimale group.** The most common type of social group in primates is the **multimale/multifemale group,** which consists of more than one adult of each sex and their offspring. Given multiple adult males and adult females, these complex social groups are often quite large, and members may be promiscuous. There is considerable variation in this type of social structure in terms of size, composition, and distribution. These categories are, of course, rough labels that may not always apply easily to any particular primate species at all times, as there are many examples of variation *within* a species.

Social Behaviors

As social animals who rely on learning, we should not be surprised at the range of social behaviors (interactions with others) found among primates.

one-male/one-female group A social structure in which the primary social group consists of a single adult male, a single adult female, and their immature offspring.

one-male/multifemale group A social structure in which the primary social group consists of a single adult male, several adult females, and their immature offspring.

one-female/multimale group A social structure in which the primary social group consists of a single adult female, several adult males, and their immature offspring.

multimale/multifemale group The most common type of social group in nonhuman primates, consisting of several adult males, several adult females, and their immature offspring.

FIGURE 5.10

Chimpanzees grooming.

We see variations both within and between different species. This section focuses on a few examples of social behaviors in primates.

Affiliative and Agonistic Behaviors   Social interactions between individuals can be friendly or unfriendly. As a rule, primatologists classify relationships as **affiliative,** which indicates strong and friendly bonds, or **agonistic,** which indicates unfriendly and often aggressive interactions. Affiliative bonds and behaviors are particularly important in maintaining large social groups (Ray 1999a).

One common means of developing and maintaining strong affiliative bonds that is practiced by all nonhuman primates is **grooming,** the practice of handling and cleaning another individual's fur (Figure 5.10). Although grooming has hygienic utility (the removal of dirt and parasites), it is first and foremost a social activity. For example, McKenna (1978) observed 1,907 cases of grooming in langur monkeys and found that 96 percent involved reciprocal social grooming; only 4 percent involved a monkey grooming itself. Grooming can function to reduce tension and conflict as well as maintain affiliative bonds.

Altruism   When social relationships are analyzed from an evolutionary perspective, the bottom line is the individual's evolutionary fitness. Behaviors

affiliative Friendly behaviors that promote social bonds.

agonistic Unfriendly social relationships.

grooming The handling and cleaning of another individual's fur. In primates, grooming serves as a form of communication and provides reassurance.

that increase chances of survival or reproduction will be favored by natural selection, whereas behaviors that are not conducive to survival or reproduction will be weeded out. How, then, do we explain examples of altruistic behavior that have been observed among primates? For example, Strier (2003) observed a young male baboon (an African monkey) being chased by a hyena when an adult female who was not his mother attempted to intercede at risk to herself. Why would she put herself in danger?

More generally, how do we explain altruism from an evolutionary perspective? Is there an evolutionary benefit to sacrificing oneself or risking sacrifice? One evolutionary explanation involves the concept of **kin selection.** Here, altruistic behaviors may be selected for when they are directed toward biological relatives. If you die saving your own child, this act will have two genetic consequences. First, because you die, you will no longer pass alleles on to the next generation. Second, your child will live and have the opportunity to pass on his or her DNA, of which 50 percent came from you. Thus, by saving your child, you actually contribute to the survival of some of your own DNA. If your altruistic action was at least partially affected by genetic factors, this behavior will also be passed on through the survival of your child. A number of case studies have shown examples of kin selection in nonhuman primates, but there remain a number of questions regarding its operation in primate societies, including determining *how* primates recognize their kin (Strier 2003).

What about altruistic acts that are directed toward individuals who are *not* kin, such as the baboon defense cited above? Here, the concept of **reciprocal altruism** comes into play—an extension of the adage that "one hand washes another." The basic idea is that any altruistic action directed toward nonkin can be selected for if it increases the possibility that the action will someday be rewarded. It may be useful to help others because you will in turn be more likely to receive help from them at some future time (assuming, of course, you do not die in the attempt). Coalitions of unrelated individuals form in a number of primate societies and provide evidence of reciprocal altruism.

Dispersal and Social Behavior   Dispersal occurs when an individual leaves the birth group and moves to another social group (or, in some cases, lives alone). Such dispersal can be voluntary or involuntary, as when an individual is kicked out of a group. In many primate species, males typically leave and move to another group. In some primate species, however, females are more typically the dispersing sex, and in some cases, both sexes disperse (Pusey and Packer 1987). Genetically, dispersal is important because it reduces inbreeding and introduces new genetic material. There are also important behavioral effects of dispersal, including a reduction in the competition of males for mates.

One of the most important effects of dispersal is that it changes social relationships based on kinship. If you move to a new group, you must develop new relationships with nonkin. There are both costs and benefits associated with having social relationships based on kinship. Staying in one's

kin selection   The concept that altruistic behavior can be selected for if it increases the probability of survival of close relatives.

reciprocal altruism   The concept that altruistic behaviors will be directed toward nonkin if they increase the probability that the recipient will reciprocate at some future time.

FIGURE 5.11

Two adult male baboons engaged in a dominance dispute. Though physical violence does occur in such encounters, much of the display is bluff.

birth group increases the chances of developing long-term relationships and coalitions, and by extension increases the probability of kin selection. Likewise, those who disperse are less likely to develop such long-term relationships. Because dispersal in most primate species is sex-based (that is, either males or females are more likely to disperse), the act of dispersal affects the social relationships of the sexes in different ways.

Social Organization and Dominance Nonhuman primate societies rank individuals in terms of their relative dominance in the group. A **dominance hierarchy** is the ranking system within the society and reflects which individuals are most and least dominant (Figure 5.11). Dominance hierarchies are found in most nonhuman primate societies, but they vary widely in their overall importance in everyday life. The dominance hierarchy provides stability in social life. All individuals know their place within the society, eliminating to some extent uncertainty about what to do or whom to follow.

The dominance hierarchy in nonhuman primates is usually ruled by those individuals with the greatest access to food or sex or those that control social behaviors to the greatest extent. Societies with strong male dominance hierarchies are likely to show a moderate to large difference in the sizes of adult males and adult females. The **sexual dimorphism** in body size has

dominance hierarchy The ranking system within a society that indicates which individuals are dominant in social behaviors.

sexual dimorphism The average difference in body size between adult males and adult females.

often been considered the result of competition among males for breeding females. The males that are larger and stronger are considered more likely to gain access to females and hence pass on their genetic potential for larger size and greater strength.

There has often been controversy over the extent to which a male's position in the dominance hierarchy is related to his reproductive success (Fedigan 1983). Altmann and colleagues (1996) used DNA analysis to determine paternity of a group of baboon offspring during a four-year period. They found that the top-ranking male baboon fathered 81 percent of the surviving offspring. When they examined other periods when this baboon was not the highest-ranking male, they found that he fathered fewer offspring. Although there is a strong relationship between a male's rank and his short-term reproductive success, the fact that the ranking of adult male baboons changes so much over a short time means that the long-term relationship is weaker.

Studies of primate behavior have demonstrated a number of factors that affect dominance rank (Ray 1999b; Strier 2003). These include an individual's size, strength, age, and ability to form coalitions, among others. In some species, such as Japanese macaque monkeys, studies have found that the rank of one's mother has an influence on her son's dominance rank (Eaton 1976). Males born to high-ranking mothers have a greater chance of achieving high dominance themselves, all other factors being equal.

In a number of primate societies, the dominance hierarchy of females is more stable over time than that of the males. Whereas the position of most dominant males can change quickly, the hierarchy among females remains more constant. Even in cases in which all males are dominant over females, the female dominance hierarchy exerts an effect on social behaviors within the group, as in the case in which mother's rank affects the rank of male offspring.

Summary

Humans are animals, chordates, and vertebrates. We share certain characteristics, such as a more developed nervous system, with other creatures in these categories.

Humans are mammals, which means we rely a great deal on a reproductive strategy of few births and extensive parental care. This reproductive pattern is associated with higher intelligence and a greater capacity for learned behaviors. Other adaptations of mammals include differentiated teeth, a skeletal structure capable of swift movement, and the ability to maintain a constant body temperature.

Humans belong to a specific order of mammals known as primates. The primates have certain characteristics, such as skeletal flexibility, grasping hands, and keen eyesight, that evolved in order to meet the demands of life in the trees. Though many primate species no longer live in the trees, they have retained these basic characteristics and use them in new ways to adapt to the environment. Most humans no longer use their grasping hands to move about in trees, but use them instead for tool manufacture and use.

Primate behavior is best studied from the perspective of behavioral ecology, which looks at the ecology and evolution of traits by focusing on their adaptive value, and by placing behaviors in the context of trade-offs between costs and benefits. Although there is considerable variation in specific behaviors within and between primate species, some generalities apply to all primates. Primates are highly social and have strong mother–infant bonds. All primates strengthen social bonds through grooming. Primate societies have dominance hierarchies, although their influence on social interactions is variable. Some individuals in all primate societies disperse to other groups (or to live alone), with males being more likely to disperse in some groups, and females in others. Dispersal affects social relationships that develop between kin.

Supplemental Readings

Campbell, C. J., A. Fuentes, K. C. MacKinnon, M. Panger, and S. K. Bearder, eds. 2007. *Primates in Perspective*. New York: Oxford University Press.

Dohlinow, P., and A. Fuentes, eds. 1999. *The Nonhuman Primates*. Mountain View, Calif.: Mayfield. Two excellent textbooks on primates. Both books have individual chapters on different primate species, as well as general discussion of primate behavior and ecology.

Strier, K. B. 2003. *Primate Behavioral Ecology*, 2d ed. Boston: Allyn and Bacon. A comprehensive review of basic principles of primate behavioral ecology.

VIRTUAL EXPLORATIONS

Visit our textbook-specific online learning center Web site at **www.mhhe.com/relethford7** to access the exercises that follow.

1. **Primate Taxonomy**   **http://www.umanitoba.ca/anthropology/ courses /121/primatology/taxonomy.html**

Primate taxonomy is best understood graphically. Go to Professor Brian Schwimmer's Web link above.

- Look across the top of the chart on the main page. How many different taxonomic levels are listed?
- What order do humans belong in? Suborder?
- What other suborder shares our classification?

Now, click on the link for "Primates": **http://www.umanitoba.ca/ anthropology/courses/121/primatology/index.html**.

- List some of the general primate behavioral characteristics.
- Are there any surprises here? If so, list one or two.
- The "general primate anatomical features" lists hand and eye features common to all primates.
- See if you can remember what the significance of these features is from the material in Chapter 5.

2. **Primate Info Net**   The Wisconsin National Primate Research Center at the University of Wisconsin–Madison continues its work on primates in the tradition of Dr. Harry Harlow (discussed in Chapter 5). The site **http://pin.primate.wisc.edu** provides a wealth of helpful information concerning issues as contemporary as "Primates in Pop Culture and the Movies" and issues involving biomedical research and recent news articles about primates

Primate Factsheets provides a quick way to locate particular primates geographically or taxonomically: **http://pin.primate.wisc.edu/factsheets**. Select the link that allows you to view by *common name:* **http://pin.primate.wisc.edu/factsheets/index/taxon/common/all**. Choose the first link listed for "Allen's swamp monkey."

- Is this an Old World or New World monkey?
- What does the photo tell you?
- What other information is there?
- Now click on the "African Mammals Databank" link.
- What additional information does the link provide?
- Why are teeth and dental patterns so important in classification?

Follow the "Alternative Classification" link to see an older version of how scientists classified primates.

3. **Comparative Primate Behavior**   **http://pin.primate.wisc.edu/aboutp/behavior/index.html**. Primate InfoNet contains resources on primate behavior and ecology.

Select the essay "A Comparison of Some Similar Chimpanzee and Human Behaviors" by James Q. Jacobs in the Comparative section: **http://www. jqjacobs.net/anthro/paleo/primates.html**.

- What are some of the behavioral traits of chimps and humans that are discussed in the article? What are some differences?
- Sex and aggression have been subjects of interest since the time of Freud. In what ways do we approach these subjects?
- Do sex and aggression have a similar form of expression in chimps and humans?

- What is the state of knowledge about the particular group of primates you have chosen? Do scientists know much about this particular type of behavior in this species? Does this research build on what scientists know about primates, or does it investigate a new area of behavior?
- Do different authors have similar views of primates, or do their views on the capabilities of primates differ?

4. **What's New on PIN**   http://pin.primate.wisc.edu/whatsnew.html. Review the many past and recent articles concerning primates.

- What are some of the main topics covered?
- Do many of the articles focus on great apes?
- What about monkeys?

Japanese macaques, one of many species of Old World monkeys and one of several groups of living primates.

Primate Diversity

T his chapter looks more closely at the diversity of the biology and
behavior of the living primates, with particular attention to the apes,
our closest living relatives.

PRIMATE SUBORDERS

The two major subgroups of the living primates are the suborder **Prosimii**
and the suborder **Anthropoidea.** These are the official scientific names (in
Latin) for the two suborders, although here we will use the more common
terms *prosimians* and *anthropoids*. Each of these suborders is broken down into
smaller taxonomic units, such as infraorders, superfamilies, families, and so
on. Figure 6.1 shows the traditional primate taxonomy used throughout
most of this chapter.

Prosimians

The word *prosimian* means literally "before simians" (monkeys and apes). In
biological terms, prosimians are more primitive, or more like early primate
ancestors, than are monkeys and apes.

Prosimian Characteristics   The prosimians often lack one or more of the
general characteristics of primates. For example, some prosimians lack color
vision, and some have a single claw on each hand or foot.

Another primitive characteristic of prosimians is that they rely to a much
greater extent on the sense of smell than do the anthropoids. Prosimian
brains are also generally smaller relative to body size than are the brains of
anthropoids. Prosimians are usually small in size and tend to be solitary, and
many are **nocturnal** (active at night). These characteristics and others point
to the basic primitive nature of most prosimians. Many prosimians are vertical clingers and leapers. That is, they cling to tree trunks until they are ready
to move, and then they propel themselves through the air.

Prosimii (prosimians) The
suborder of primates that
are biologically primitive
compared to anthropoids.
**Anthropoidea (anthro-
poids)** The suborder of
primates consisting of monkeys, apes, and humans.
nocturnal Active during
the night.

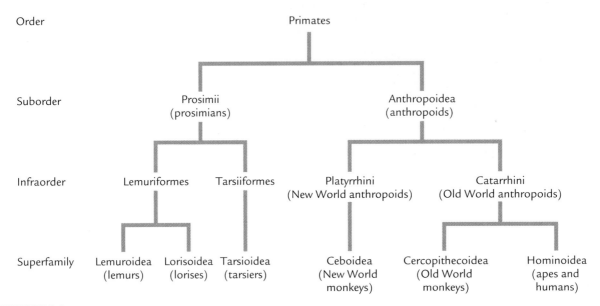

Order — Primates

Suborder — Prosimii (prosimians) / Anthropoidea (anthropoids)

Infraorder — Lemuriformes, Tarsiiformes / Platyrrhini (New World anthropoids), Catarrhini (Old World anthropoids)

Superfamily — Lemuroidea (lemurs), Lorisoidea (lorises), Tarsioidea (tarsiers) / Ceboidea (New World monkeys), Cercopithecoidea (Old World monkeys), Hominoidea (apes and humans)

FIGURE 6.1

Summary of traditional primate classification. Names within parentheses are common names.

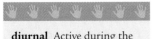

diurnal Active during the day.

loris A nocturnal prosimian found today in Asia and Africa.

tarsier A nocturnal prosimian found today in Indonesia.

lemur A prosimian found today on the island of Madagascar.

Prosimians themselves show considerable variation. Some prosimians have larger body sizes, some have larger social groups, and some are **diurnal** (active in daylight). This variation makes classification difficult, but it does show us both the general trends of the prosimians and specific differences among them.

Types of Prosimians   There are three different groups of prosimians in the world today, each with a number of different species. One group, the **lorises,** are small, solitary, nocturnal prosimians found in Asia and Africa (Figure 6.2). Another group, the **tarsiers,** also small, solitary, and nocturnal, are found in Indonesia. The nocturnal nature of tarsiers is evidenced by their large eyes, the size of which serves to gather available light (Figure 6.3). Tarsiers eat only insects, spiders, and other invertebrate animals, as well as some vertebrates, an unusual pattern among nocturnal prosimians, which typically eat leaves and fruit. Tarsiers also lack the moist nose of other prosimians, and some classification schemes (see below) view them as more closely related to anthropoids that also lack a moist nose.

The most biologically diverse group of prosimians is the **lemurs,** which are found only on the island of Madagascar off the southeast coast of Africa (Figure 6.4). Some species of lemurs are nocturnal and some are diurnal. The lemurs depart from the typical pattern of prosimians as nocturnal, solitary primates. Their wide range of biological and behavioral characteristics probably reflects their isolation on Madagascar. Because the island has no competing monkey or ape species and not many other mammals either, the lemurs have expanded into a variety of ecological niches. Apart from these variations, the lemurs are still definitely prosimians—having, among other primitive features, the characteristic reliance on smell.

FIGURE 6.2

A loris, a prosimian from Southeast Asia.

FIGURE 6.3

A tarsier, a prosimian from Southeast Asia. Unlike other prosimians, the tarsier does not have a moist nose.

FIGURE 6.4

Ring-tailed lemur from the island of Madagascar.

Lemurs have some interesting aspects of social structure and behavior compared with other primates. Although some lemur species have the multimale/multifemale social structure, a large proportion (more than 25 percent) live in monogamous groups with one adult male and one adult female, a number much higher than other primates or mammals in general. This high proportion might reflect an adaptation to dietary sources that exist in small patches that are regularly distributed in the environment; in such cases, small groups might be more efficient (Wright 1999).

Another peculiar lemur trait is the prevalence of female dominance in lemur species. Among other prosimians, males tend to be dominant. Many lemur species, with clear female dominance, are an exception to this general pattern. Female lemurs typically win aggressive encounters with males and have priority in eating—males generally wait to feed until the females are done. Female dominance in lemurs may reflect a dietary adaptation such that females have priority access to a limited food supply in order to have sufficient food for raising offspring (Wright 1999).

Anthropoids

The anthropoids are the higher primates and consist of monkeys and hominoids (apes and humans). Anthropoids are generally larger in overall body size, have larger and more complex brains, rely more on visual abilities, and show more complex social structures than do other primates. Except for one monkey species, all anthropoids are diurnal. The anthropoids include both arboreal and terrestrial species.

All living prosimians are found in the Old World, but anthropoids are found in both the New World and the Old World. (A reminder: The Old World consists of the continents of Africa, Asia, and Europe; the New World is the Americas.) New World anthropoids are found today in Central and South America. Old World anthropoids are found today in Africa and Asia (and one monkey species in Europe). The only native New World anthropoids are monkeys, whereas native Old World anthropoids include monkeys, apes, and humans.

Alternative Classification

The traditional division of primates into prosimians and anthropoids is being challenged by a number of scientists. The problem with the traditional classification is that tarsiers, usually classified as prosimians, show several biological characteristics of anthropoids. Lorises and lemurs have moist noses, a trait related to their keen sense of smell. Tarsiers, like anthropoids, lack the moist nose. In addition, some genetic investigations have supported the idea that tarsiers are more like anthropoids than prosimians.

Many researchers now advocate placing the lemurs and lorises in one suborder, **Strepsirhini,** characterized by moist noses, and the tarsiers and anthropoids in another suborder, **Haplorhini,** which lacks the moist nose.

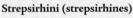

Strepsirhini (strepsirhines)
One of two suborders of primates suggested to replace the prosimian/anthropoid suborders (the other is the haplorhines). Strepsirhines are primates that have a moist nose (lemurs and lorises).

Haplorhini (haplorhines)
One of two suborders of primates suggested to replace the prosimian/anthropoid suborders (the other is the strepsirhines). Haplorhines are primates without a moist nose (tarsiers, monkeys, apes, and humans).

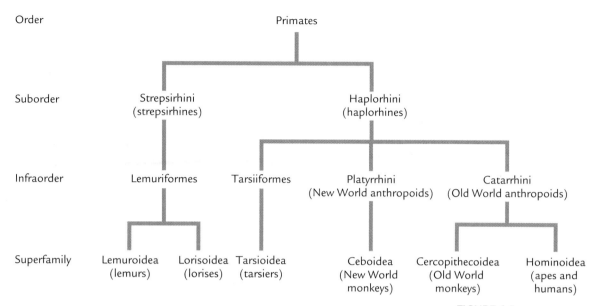

Order — Primates

Suborder — Strepsirhini (strepsirhines) / Haplorhini (haplorhines)

Infraorder — Lemuriformes / Tarsiiformes / Platyrrhini (New World anthropoids) / Catarrhini (Old World anthropoids)

Superfamily — Lemuroidea (lemurs) / Lorisoidea (lorises) / Tarsioidea (tarsiers) / Ceboidea (New World monkeys) / Cercopithecoidea (Old World monkeys) / Hominoidea (apes and humans)

FIGURE 6.5

An alternative primate classification using the suborders Strepsirhini and Haplorhini. Compare this to Figure 6.1, which uses the traditional breakdown into the suborders Prosimii and Anthropoidea. The difference is that the present chart groups tarsiers with monkeys and hominoids in the suborder Haplorhini rather than with lemurs and lorises. According to this view, tarsiers are more closely related to monkeys and hominoids because they lack the moist nose (associated with greater ability to smell) found in lemurs and lorises. There is debate over which approach is more appropriate.

In this text, I will continue to use the traditional division between prosimians and anthropoids because it provides a useful contrast when discussing primate evolution. However, as the alternative classification suggests, there is considerable debate regarding the taxonomic placement of the tarsiers. The suborders Strepsirhini and Haplorhini are shown in the alternative primate taxonomy in Figure 6.5 and can be contrasted with the traditional scheme of Figure 6.10. The major difference is the placement of the tarsiers. Are they more similar evolutionarily to lemurs and lorises or to monkeys and apes?

What is the relevance of alternative classifications? Once again, this controversy demonstrates the difficulty of taxonomic classification. It is not always possible to place living creatures unambiguously in certain categories. Such problems actually provide us with strong evidence of the evolutionary process. The tarsiers, for example, suggest what a transitional form between prosimians and anthropoids might have looked like.

THE MONKEYS

Anthropoids include monkeys and hominoids (apes and humans). Monkeys and apes are often confused in the popular imagination. In reality, they are easy to tell apart. Most monkeys have tails, whereas apes and humans do not. In general, monkeys also have smaller brains relative to body size than do apes or humans. The typical pattern of monkey movement is on all fours—**quadrupedal**—and their arms and legs are generally of similar length so that their spines are parallel to the ground. By contrast, apes have longer arms than legs and humans have longer legs than arms.

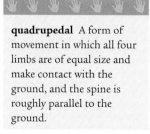

quadrupedal A form of movement in which all four limbs are of equal size and make contact with the ground, and the spine is roughly parallel to the ground.

FIGURE 6.6

A spider monkey, capable of
using its tail as a "fifth limb."

New World Monkeys

The only form of anthropoids found native to the New World is the New
World monkeys (there are no New World apes). Although they share many
similarities with Old World monkeys, several important differences reflect
separate lines of evolution over the past 30 million years or so.

Characteristics   Some of the differences between the New World and Old
World monkeys are useful in reconstructing evolutionary relationships. For
example, New World monkeys have four more premolar teeth than Old World
monkeys. The dental formulae for many New World monkeys is 2-1-3-3,
compared to the 2-1-2-3 dental formula of all Old World monkeys. Other
differences relate to the way in which the monkeys live; for example, some
New World monkeys have prehensile tails.

Because the tail of some New World monkeys is capable of grasping, it
is highly useful in moving about and feeding in the trees (Figure 6.6).
Typically, the monkey uses this "fifth limb" to anchor itself while feeding
on the ends of small branches. Old World monkeys have tails, but none of
them have prehensile tails. Those New World monkeys with prehensile tails
are thus more proficient in terms of acrobatic agility. This difference probably relates to the fact that all New World monkeys are arboreal, whereas
some Old World monkeys are terrestrial. The prehensile tail of many New
World monkeys is a derived trait that did not develop in the Old World
monkeys.

FIGURE 6.7

A Bolivian red howler monkey, one of the New World monkeys with a prehensile tail.

Case Study: Howler Monkeys One interesting group of New World monkeys is the howler monkeys, consisting of nine species in the genus *Alouatta* (Di Fiore and Campbell 2007). Howler monkeys are found in Mexico and in South America (Figure 6.7). Their name reflects their most unusual characteristic—an enlarged hyoid bone (the bone in the throat), which creates a large resonating chamber capable of making sounds that can be heard at a considerable distance. Howlers have prehensile tails and are quite at home in the trees, where they eat primarily fruit and leaves. Adult howlers weigh between 6 and 8 kilograms (13–18 pounds), with males larger than females. Males are capable of making deeper and louder howls (Bramblett 1994). Howler monkeys typically live in small groups ranging from 10 to 15 individuals, and consisting of between one and three adult males (Di Fiore and Campbell 2007).

The loud howling of howler monkeys serves many purposes, including warning and defense. These howls often serve to warn away competitors for food and space, and it has been suggested that these vocalizations are a substitute for active fighting (Carpenter 1965; Crockett and Eisenberg 1987). Because groups are widely separated, fighting may be avoided, and thus the spacing may be a group defense. This spacing has also often been interpreted as evidence that howlers have specific territories, which they defend. A strict definition of **territory** is a home range that is actively

territory A home range that is actively defended.

FIGURE 6.8

Japanese macaques are the most northerly living non-human primates. They adapted to their climate with thick winter coats and lighter summer coats. Males and females compete with each other for sexual partners.

defended and does not overlap with another group's home range. Actually, few primates are territorial in this sense. Carpenter (1965) noted that howlers do not defend specific and constant boundaries but rather defend wherever they are at a given time. Crockett and Eisenberg (1987) suggest that howlers cannot actually be considered territorial because the overlap in home ranges is often quite large, but they also note that others interpret the data as showing some territoriality. (Perhaps the most telling observation is the variation that howlers [and many primates] show from study to study.)

FIGURE 6.9

A mandrill, an Old World monkey. Mandrills are terrestrial monkeys that live in West Africa. Adult males are known for their vividly colored faces.

Old World Monkeys

Old World monkeys are biochemically and physically more similar to humans than are New World monkeys.

Characteristics   Old World monkeys inhabit a wide range of environments. Many species live in tropical rain forests, but other species have adapted to the **savanna,** open grasslands. One species has even learned to survive in the snowy environment of the Japanese mountains (Figure 6.8).

The Old World monkeys, like the New World monkeys, are quadrupedal, running on the ground and on tree branches on all fours. Though Old World monkeys are agile in the trees, many species have adapted to spending more time on the ground in search of food. Most Old World species eat a mixed diet of fruits and leaves (Figure 6.9), although some show dental and digestive specializations for leaf eating. Some Old World species occasionally supplement their primarily vegetarian diet with insects or small animals that they hunt.

Social structure is highly variable among Old World monkeys. Most known species have been characterized as having either multimale/multifemale or one-male/multifemale social groups. However, a large proportion of Old World monkey species has been observed with more than one social structure, depending on the specific group, once again showing behavioral

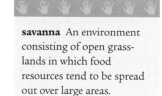

savanna An environment consisting of open grasslands in which food resources tend to be spread out over large areas.

FIGURE 6.10

Variation in social structure among Old World monkeys. Numbers represent the percentage of species that have a particular social structure (species for which this information is not known have been excluded). Note that 17 percent of Old World monkey species have been observed with more than one type of social structure. (Data from Jolly 1985:129, Table 6.5a.)

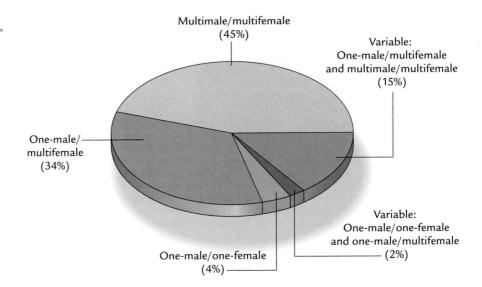

variation (Figure 6.10). One contributing factor to this variation is the availability of food. In species that have less available food, the uni-male structure is more common, perhaps because additional males would consume food without adding much to group survival.

Case Study: Baboons   Baboons are one of the most widely studied and interesting of the Old World monkeys (technically, several different monkeys are given the general label of "baboon"; here we refer to the "savanna baboon"). Baboons live in relatively large (20–200) multimale/multifemale groups on the African savanna (Figure 6.11). The savanna is composed primarily of open grasslands, in which food resources tend to be spread out over large areas. Clusters of trees in the savanna provide additional opportunities for food, as well as for protection. Even though baboons are essentially terrestrial, they still have the basic primate adaptations that allow them to climb effectively, which proves useful in hiding from predators and in obtaining shelter when sleeping. Because food resources are spread out over large areas of the savanna, baboons tend to have rather large home ranges, and they cover this area by foraging as a group. The baboon diet is quite diverse, including grass, leaves, fruit, and occasionally meat that has been obtained from hunting small mammals and birds. In analyzing baboon behavior, keep in mind that even among the "savanna baboons" there are groups that live in other environments, such as deserts (Jolly 2007).

Much of the focus in baboon studies has been on social organization. Adult males are dominant over adult females, and there is a constant shift in the relative position of the most dominant males. Aggressive actions play a role in this continual struggle (Figure 6.12). Adult males are considerably larger than adult females, and the largest and strongest males often have a greater chance of being the most dominant.

FIGURE 6.11

Baboons on the savanna.

FIGURE 6.12

An adult male baboon "yawning"—an expression that is interpreted by others as an aggressive display and a warning. Such threat gestures are used in disputes over dominance.

Size and strength are not, however, the only factors affecting male dominance in baboon society. Coalitions of two or more lower-ranking males have often been observed to displace a more dominant male who was actually larger and stronger than any of the lower-ranking males. The ability to aid others is an important determinant of dominance rank.

Environmental factors also affect patterns of dominance within baboon society. For example, Rowell (1966) found that forest-living baboons have less rigid dominance hierarchies than did groups living on the savanna. In addition, the daily life of the forest baboons was more relaxed, as the level of aggression was lower. In forest environments, food is generally more available and predators are less of a threat. Quite simply, a rigid social organization is not needed in this environment.

In the initial years of baboon research, most of the attention was on the dominance hierarchies of the adult males, and less attention was given to the behaviors of adult females. We now realize that the continuity of baboon society revolves around the females and that adult males frequently move from one social group to another. The dominance hierarchy of the adult females is generally more stable over time. The importance of female continuity in baboon society must be acknowledged because females are responsible for the care of infants and provide the needed socialization prior to maturity.

THE HOMINOIDS

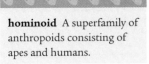

hominoid A superfamily of anthropoids consisting of apes and humans.

In addition to the monkeys, the other major group of living anthropoids is the **hominoids,** composed of apes and humans. The similarity of apes and humans (hence their placement in the same superfamily) has long been a source of fascination. One of our most memorable images of this relatedness comes from the classic 1933 movie *King Kong* (and subsequent remakes). The giant gorilla discovered on "Skull Island" is captured and brought to New York City for display as the eighth wonder of the world. Ignoring the fantastic nature of some of the plot elements (gorillas could not be that large and still walk), the film draws close comparisons between Kong's behavior and that of the humans in the film. Kong shows love, curiosity, and anger, among other emotions and behaviors. Kong is a mirror for the humans, and the humans are a mirror for Kong. We see ourselves in the beast and the beast in ourselves.

Hominoid Characteristics

Whether we choose to look at apes as humanlike, or humans as apelike, the fact remains that of all living creatures the apes are the most similar to humans in both biology and behavior. Before considering the biology and behavior of living apes (in the remainder of this chapter) and humans (in the next chapter), let us examine some of the general characteristics of all living hominoids.

Unlike monkeys, hominoids do not have tails. Another hominoid characteristic is size: In general, most hominoid species are larger than monkeys. Hominoid brains as a rule are larger than monkey brains, both in terms of absolute size and in relation to body size. Their brains are also more complex, which correlates with the hominoid characteristics of greater intelligence and learning abilities. Hominoids also invest the most time and effort in raising their young.

Hominoids share with Old World monkeys the 2-1-2-3 dental formula (two incisors, one canine, two premolars, and three molars in each half of the upper and lower jaws). The structure of the molar teeth, however, is different in monkeys and hominoids. The most noticeable difference is that the lower molar teeth of hominoids tend to have five **cusps** (raised areas) as compared to the four cusps in the lower molars of monkeys. The deeper grooves between these five cusps form the shape of the letter Y. As such, this characteristic shape is called the "Y-5" pattern (Figure 6.13). This difference may seem trivial, but it helps us in identifying fossils because we can often tell whether a form is a monkey or a hominoid on the basis of the molar teeth.

Perhaps one of the most important characteristics of hominoids is their upper body and shoulder anatomy. Hominoids can raise their arms above their heads with little trouble, whereas a monkey would find this difficult. This ability of hominoids to raise their arms above their heads is based on three basic anatomical features. First, hominoids have a larger and stronger collarbone than monkeys. Second, the hominoid shoulder joint is very flexible and capable of a wide angle of movement. Third, hominoid shoulder blades are located more toward the back. By contrast, monkeys' shoulder blades are located more toward the sides of the chest (Figure 6.14). Hominoid shoulder joints face outward, compared to the shoulder joints of monkeys, which are downward-facing.

Most hominoids have longer front limbs than back limbs. Modern humans are an exception to this rule, with longer legs than arms. This trait facilitates upright walking (discussed later). In apes, the longer front limbs represent an adaptation to hanging from tree limbs. In addition, hominoids generally have long fingers that help them hang suspended from branches. The wrist joint of hominoids contains a disc of cartilage (called a *meniscus*) between the lower arm bones and the wrist bones. This disc cuts down on contact between bones. As a result, the wrist joints of hominoids are more flexible than those of monkeys, allowing greater hanging ability.

Hominoid anatomy allows them a different type of movement from that of monkeys. Hominoids are adept at climbing and hanging from branches; they are **suspensory climbers.** As hominoids, humans have retained this ability, although we seldom use it in our daily lives. One exception is children playing on so-called monkey bars at playgrounds (which should more properly be called "hominoid bars"). The ability to suspend by the arms and then swing from one rung of the bars to the next is a basic hominoid trait.

Living hominoids all share this basic ability but vary quite a bit in terms of their normal patterns of movement. Some apes, for example, are proficient arm swingers, whereas others are expert climbers. Humans have evolved a totally different pattern in which the arms are not used for movement; this allows us to carry things while walking on two legs. These differences in locomotion are discussed later in the chapter. In spite of these differences in function, the close relationship between apes and humans is seen in their shared characteristics of the upper body and shoulder.

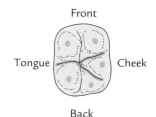

FIGURE 6.13

The Y-5 lower molar pattern of hominoids. Circles represent cusps. The heavier line resembles the letter Y on its side.

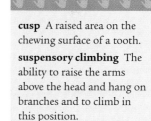

cusp A raised area on the chewing surface of a tooth.

suspensory climbing The ability to raise the arms above the head and hang on branches and to climb in this position.

FIGURE 6.14

Top view of the shoulder complex of a monkey (*top*) and a human (*bottom*) drawn to the same scale top to bottom. In hominoids (apes and humans), the clavicle is larger and the scapula is located more toward the rear of the body.

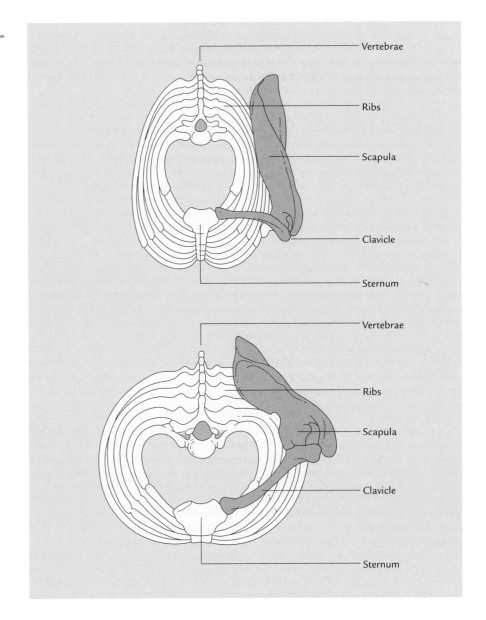

Classification of the Hominoids

Between 20 million and 8 million years ago, there were many different types of hominoids. Today we have only the representatives of a few surviving species from this once diverse, widespread group. Living hominoids are divided into three categories: the lesser apes, the great apes, and humans. The lesser apes are the gibbons (12 species) and are the least related to humans. The great apes are the Asian orangutan and the African gorilla, chimpanzee, and bonobo. A list of the scientific and common names of all living hominoids is given in Table 6.1.

TABLE 6.1   Species of Living Hominoids

	Genus	*Species*	*Common Name*
Lesser Apes	Hoolock	hillock	Hillock gibbon
	Hylobates	agilis	Agile gibbon
	Hylobates	klossii	Kloss's gibbon
	Hylobates	lar	White-handed gibbon
	Hylobates	moloch	Silvery gibbon
	Hylobates	muelleri	Mueller's gibbon
	Hylobates	pileatus	Pileated gibbon
	Nomascus	concolor	Western black-crested gibbon
	Nomascus	nasutus	Eastern black-crested gibbon
	Nomascus	gabriellae	Yellow-cheeked crested gibbon
	Nomascus	leucogenys	White-cheeked crested gibbon
	Symphalangus	syndactylus	Siamang
Great Apes	Pongo	pygmaeus	Orangutan
	Gorilla	gorilla	Gorilla
	Pan	troglodytes	Chimpanzee
	Pan	paniscus	Bonobo
Humans	Homo	sapiens	Modern human

Source: Bartlett (2007) for lesser apes, Falk (2000) for all others.

That all of these species have certain shared characteristics allows us to classify them as hominoids and to infer that they are related through evolution. The specific evolutionary relationship of the different hominoids is more difficult to establish. To uncover our own origins, we are interested in determining which ape species is the most similar to us. In this way, we are able to compare the anatomy of living and fossil hominoids to determine what changed in our line, what changed in the ape line, and what stayed the same.

Two different approaches are used to ascertain evolutionary relationships between different living species. One approach is to focus on the physical anatomy—the **morphology**—of living forms. The other approach is to examine the biochemistry and genetics of living species. Similarities and differences between species are revealed by a number of methods that compare proteins and even the genetic code. Constructing taxonomies from biochemical and genetic data has a definite advantage. If we focus on proteins or sections of DNA not affected by natural selection (or at least those we assume not to be affected), then any degree of similarity should reflect relative evolutionary relationships.

Genetic analyses of living hominoids show a clear and consistent pattern. The African apes and humans form a closely related group, with orangutans more distant from this group, and gibbons more distant still. Early genetic studies (e.g., King and Wilson 1975) found that humans and chimpanzees were genetically very similar to each other, sharing more than 98 percent of their DNA and indicating a close evolutionary relationship. This basic finding has since been extended to the other African apes—the gorilla and the bonobo—as well. Some aspects of physical anatomy, such as soft tissue anatomy, show a similar pattern (Gibbs et al. 2000).

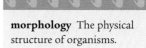

morphology The physical structure of organisms.

FIGURE 6.15

An evolutionary "tree" showing the relationships among the living great apes and humans. Note that humans and the African apes are more closely related to each other than any are to the orangutan.

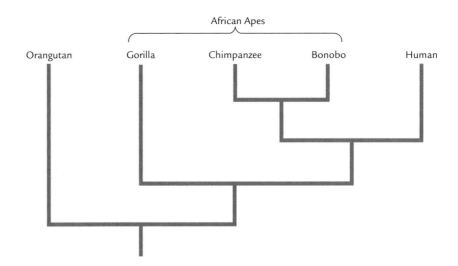

It is now clear that humans and African apes are more closely related to each other than either is to the Asian great ape, the orangutan. There is also an indication that chimpanzees and bonobos are even more closely related to humans than either is to gorillas (e.g., Horai et al. 1995; Gagneux et al. 1999). If so, then we can reconstruct a family tree of the relationships of the great apes and humans. As shown in Figure 6.15, this tree suggests that the orangutan split off from the common ancestor of African apes and humans. The next split was between the line leading to the gorilla and the line leading to the common ancestor of humans and chimpanzees and bonobos, the latter two of which diverged later in time.

What, then, is the best way to classify the living hominoids? A traditional classification, shown in Figure 6.16, is based on an evolutionary systematics approach that considers overall physical similarity, grouping the great apes together in one family (Pongidae) and placing humans in their own family (Hominidae, or hominids). This classification is problematic. Although separation of the great apes from humans is useful in some discussions of anatomy and behavior, it clearly does not reflect evolutionary relationships. We know from a number of analyses of genetics and anatomy that some of the great apes are more closely related to humans than they are to the other great apes. If our focus in classification is cladistic, then the classification must place humans and African apes in the same group to the exclusion of the orangutan.

A solution to this problem that has been accepted increasingly in recent years is to place humans and the African apes in the same taxonomic group, thus mirroring the genetic and evolutionary relationships shown in Figure 6.15. One common approach, used throughout this book and shown in Figure 6.17, is based on genetic and evolutionary relationships. Hominoids are broken down into two families: hylobatids (the gibbons) and **hominids** (great apes and humans). The hominid family is further broken down into three separate subfamilies—one for orangutans, one for gorillas, and one (called *hominines*) that includes humans and their closest living relatives—the chimpanzee and bonobo.

hominid A family (Hominidae) within the hominoids. In recent years, this family has been defined as including humans and the great apes (orangutan, gorilla, chimpanzee, and bonobo). Some scientists still use a more traditional definition that refers only to humans and their humanlike ancestors.

hominin Humans and their ancestors since the time of divergence from the common ancestor of humans, chimpanzees, and bonobos.

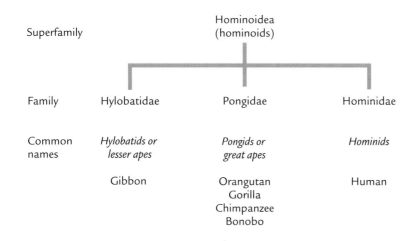

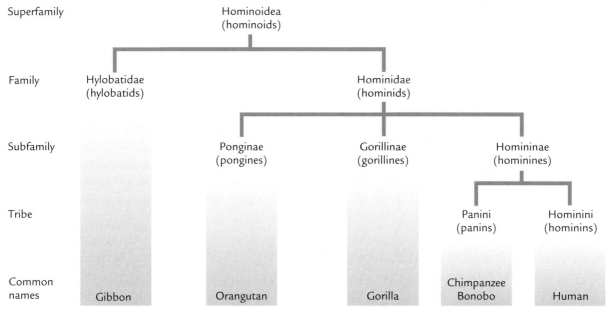

FIGURE 6.16

Traditional taxonomic classification of hominoids. Names
in italics refer to common
names. To emphasize certain
aspects of behavior and
physical characteristics,
the orangutan, gorilla,
chimpanzee, and bonobo are
all placed in a separate
category from humans.
Although useful for some
purposes, this classification
does not reflect the fact that
humans and the African apes
are more genetically similar to
each other than any are to the
orangutan. Compare this
classification with Figure 6.17.

FIGURE 6.17

Revised taxonomic class-
ification of hominoids
to emphasize genetic and
evolutionary relationships
(see Figure 6.15). Humans,
chimpanzees, and bonobos
form a group separate from
the gorilla and orangutan.
(Wood and Richmond 2000.)

According to this revised taxonomy, humans are classified as a tribe within the subfamily of hominines. This tribe, termed **hominins,** refers to humans and our ancestors since the time of divergence from the common ancestor of humans, chimpanzees, and bonobos (Figure 6.18). The revised taxonomy is useful in that it shows clearly the exact genetic and evolutionary relationship of humans and the great apes. Although it is certainly true that living humans look much different from apes, those changes in physical appearance reflect the many changes that have occurred during hominin evolution, a topic covered in detail in later chapters.

FIGURE 6.18

The evolutionary relationships between humans and their closest living relatives—the chimpanzee and bonobo. Humans and all their ancestors since the time of the divergence from the common ancestor (represented by the large dot) are called *hominins*.

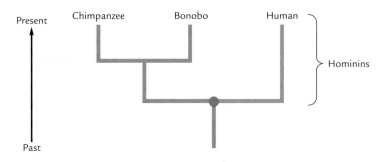

As noted in Chapter 4, there are different schools of thought when it comes to classification schemes, and the relationship between humans and the great apes is no exception. The scheme used in this book is based on a cladistic approach that emphasizes evolutionary relationships. The more traditional scheme places humans in their own family. Consequently, keep in mind that you might come across material in lectures or in other readings that uses the term *hominid* to refer to humans and their immediate ancestors rather than to humans and the great apes. Thus, in some readings, *hominid* means the same thing as *hominin* does in this text. It sounds confusing, but it is generally easy to tell how the different taxonomic labels are being used from their context.

THE LIVING APES

To provide a better comparison of the biology and behavior of apes and humans, let us consider briefly the physical characteristics, distribution, environment, and social structure of all the hominoids. Although the living hominoids all share a number of features, they also show a great deal of biological and behavioral variation.

Gibbons

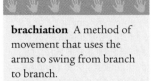

brachiation A method of movement that uses the arms to swing from branch to branch.

Physical Characteristics   Gibbons are classified into four genera based on differences in chromosome number, and these genera include 12 species as listed in Table 6.1 (Bartlett 2007). The gibbon is the smallest of the living apes.

The physical characteristics of gibbons reflect adaptation to life in the trees. The climbing and hanging adaptations of hominoids have evolved in the gibbon to allow highly agile movement through trees. The gibbon's usual form of movement, known as **brachiation,** consists of hand-over-hand swinging from branch to branch. Many primates are portrayed as arm swingers, but only the gibbon can perform this movement quickly and efficiently (Figure 6.19).

A number of anatomical adaptations allow gibbons efficient arm swinging. Body size ranges from about 5.5 kg (12 lb) to 13.5 kg (30 lb) (Richard 1985; Falk 2000). Their arms are extremely long relative to their trunks and

FIGURE 6.19

Gibbons brachiating. Gibbons are the most acrobatic of the apes and can swing by their arms easily.

legs. Gibbon fingers are elongated and their thumbs are relatively short. The long fingers enable gibbons to form a hook with their hands while swinging from branch to branch. The thumb is short enough to prevent its getting in the way while swinging but still long enough to allow manipulation.

On the ground, gibbons walk on two legs, though their arms are so long that they look awkward to us. Gibbons use these long arms for balance. They also walk on two legs when they move along a branch, often using their arms to grab onto overhead branches for support.

Gibbons show almost no sexual dimorphism in body size. Males and females are the same body size, and both have large canine teeth, with male canines slightly larger on average than females'.

Distribution and Environment   Gibbons are found in the tropical rain forests of Southeast Asia—specifically, Thailand, Vietnam, Burma, and the Malay Peninsula. The rain forest environment is characterized by heavy rainfall that is relatively constant throughout the year. Rain forests have incredibly rich and diverse vegetation. The gibbons' diet consists primarily of fruits supplemented by leaves.

Social Structure   Gibbons have long been characterized as having a monogamous family structure—an adult male, an adult female, and their offspring—with the adult male and female forming a mating pair for long periods. Fuentes (2000) suggests that this is not always the case, and gibbon groups do not necessarily form nuclear family units. Instead, he argues that gibbons (like most other primates) originally had a multimale/multifemale social structure but now have a more variable system. Often, the small social groups result in a typical family structure, but not always. Once again, continued research has shown us the variable nature of primate social behavior.

FIGURE 6.20

Mother and infant orangutans.

Gibbons actively defend territories. They do this by making loud, complex sounds or songs and putting on aggressive displays to warn off other groups (Bartlett 2007). When groups come into contact in overlapping areas, the males often fight to drive the other group away.

Though it may be interesting to speculate on the nature of gibbon aggression and territorial behavior as it relates to primate behavior, in reality, territorial behavior is rather rare among primates, including the hominoids. Territorial behavior is most often a function of the environment. In tropical rain forests, food is abundant and spread throughout the region. Because food resources are not clumped together, neither are the animal populations. Food is spread out over a large area, so family groups come into frequent contact with one another, necessitating territorial boundaries to establish

FIGURE 6.21

A young orangutan foraging.

group boundaries (Denham 1971). In environments where food resources are clustered, social groups tend to cluster as well and are spaced apart from one another at the outset.

Orangutans

The orangutan is a large ape found only in certain areas of Southeast Asia. The word *orangutan* translates from Malay as "man of the forest."

Physical Characteristics One of the orangutan's most obvious physical features is its reddish brown hair (Figure 6.20). Males are roughly twice the size of females; an average adult male weighs between 80 and 90 kg (roughly 175–200 lb), and an average adult female weighs between 33 and 45 kg (roughly 73–99 lb) (Markham and Groves 1990). Males also have large pads of fat on their faces. The high degree of sexual dimorphism in orangutans has often been thought surprising because this trait occurs most often in terrestrial species. More recent evidence, however, suggests that orangutans spend more time on the ground than once thought. The orangutan is responsible, with the gorilla and chimpanzee, for many reports by early explorers of "wild men," "monsters," and "subhumans."

Orangutans are agile climbers and hangers. In the trees, they use both arms and legs to climb in a slow, cautious manner. They will use one or more limbs to anchor themselves to branches while using the other limbs to feed (Figure 6.21). Younger orangutans occasionally brachiate, but the larger adults generally move through the trees in a different manner. A large orangutan will not swing from one tree to the next; rather, it will rock the tree it is on slowly in the direction of the next tree and then move over when the two trees are close together. The orangutan's great agility in climbing is due, in part, to its basic hominoid shoulder structure.

Orangutans are largely arboreal. Males, however, frequently come to the ground and travel along the forest floor for long distances. On the ground, orangutans walk on all fours but with their fists partially closed. Unlike monkeys, who rest their weight on their palms, orangutans rest on their fists, a form of movement often called *fist walking*.

Data suggest that orangutans produce offspring more slowly than do the other great apes (Galdikas and Wood 1990). The average birth interval (the time between successive births) for orangutans is 7.7 years, compared to birth intervals of 3.8 years for gorillas and 5.6 years for chimpanzees.

Distribution and Environment   The orangutan is found today only in Sumatra and Borneo in Southeast Asia. Although orangutans in Borneo and Sumatra have often been classified as different subspecies based on physical and genetic differences, there have been recent suggestions that they should be placed into different species (Knott and Kahlenberg 2007). As noted in previous chapters, classification of different species is not always that clear. Orangutans are vegetarians, with the bulk of their diet consisting of fruit (Knott 1999). As does the gibbon, the orangutan lives in tropical rain forests.

The natural range of the orangutan was probably greater in the past, given the fact that fossil apes similar to orangutans have been found in Asia dating from 12 million years ago (see Chapter 9). Some of the reduced distribution is the result of climatic change in the past. The limited range of orangutans—and of the other apes—today is also due in part to human intervention. As its natural habitats continue to be destroyed, the orangutan is an endangered species and faces extinction.

Social Structure   Adult orangutans tend to be solitary, and the primary social group consists of a mother and infant. Males are not needed for protection because there is little danger from predators. Adult males generally live by themselves, interacting only during times of mating. Orangutans are polygamous; they do not form long-term bonds with any one partner. The small group size of orangutans may be related to the nature of the environment; when food resources are widely scattered, there is not enough food in any one place for large groups (Knott 1999).

Among nonhuman primates, a distinctive behavior of orangutans is the forced copulation of adult females by adult males, characterized by active resistance of the females. This behavior may be related to mate choice. Orangutan males have an interesting pattern of physical development whereby they first become sexually mature and capable of reproduction, and only later become socially mature and develop secondary sexual characteristics, such as cheek pads and longer fur. Females tend to resist sexual encounters with the less mature males because they prefer mating with the more socially mature males, although the reason for this mate choice is not yet clear (Knott and Kahlenberg 2007).

FIGURE 6.22

An adult male gorilla knuckle walking. Note the angle of the spine relative to the ground because of the longer front limbs.

Gorillas

Gorillas, the largest living primates, are found only in equatorial Africa. Gorillas have typically been classified into three subspecies within a single species, but some researchers have suggested recently that gorillas should be classified into two species, each containing two subspecies (Robbins 2007).

Physical Characteristics An adult male gorilla weighs 160 kg (roughly 350 lb) on average. Adult females weigh less but are still very large for primates (70 kg/155 lb) (Leutenegger 1982). Besides a much larger body size, the adult males also have larger canine teeth and often large crests of bone on top of their skulls for anchoring their large jaw muscles. Gorillas usually have blackish hair; fully mature adult males have silvery gray hair on their backs. These adult males are called *silverbacks*.

Their large size makes gorillas predominantly terrestrial. Their typical means of movement is called **knuckle walking:** They move about on all fours, resting their weight on the knuckles of their front limbs. This form of movement is different from the fist walking of orangutans. Gorilla hands have well-developed muscles and strengthened joints to handle the stress of resting on their knuckles. Because their arms are longer than their legs, gorilla spines are at an angle to the ground (Figure 6.22). In contrast, the spine of a typical quadrupedal animal, such as a monkey, is roughly parallel to the ground when walking.

knuckle walking A form of movement used by chimpanzees and gorillas that is characterized by all four limbs touching the ground, with the weight of the arms resting on the knuckles of the hands.

FIGURE 6.23

A gorilla social group.

Distribution and Environment   Gorillas are found in only three forested areas in Africa. Their range is disappearing rapidly, primarily as the result of replacement of forests by farmland and human poaching (Fossey 1983). Three recognized subspecies of gorilla live in different regions in western Africa: the western lowland gorilla, the eastern lowland gorilla, and the mountain gorilla.

Many myths have circulated regarding the gorilla's lust for human and nonhuman flesh, but the fact is that gorillas eat a diet almost entirely made up of leaves and fruit. Diet varies by location; the lowland gorillas eat more fruit than the mountain gorillas. Differences in diet may affect social organization in the different gorilla subspecies, but it is not yet clear exactly how (Doran and McNeilage 1998).

Social Structure   Gorillas live in small social groups of typically 8–10 individuals (Robbins 2007). The social group consists of an adult male (the silverback), several adult females, and their immature offspring (Figure 6.23). Occasionally, one or more younger adult males are part of the group, but they tend not to mate with the females. Though dominance rank varies among the females and subadult males, the adult silverback male is the most dominant individual in the group and is the leader. The silverback sets the

SPECIAL TOPIC

Social Structure and Testes Size in Primates

Bizarre as it may sound at first, scientists have collected information on the size of the testes, the male reproductive organ that produces sperm, in different primate species and have made some interesting observations. For example, the size of the testes ranges from roughly 1.2 grams (0.04 oz) in one New World monkey species to 119 grams (over 4 oz, or 1/4 lb) in chimpanzees. However, not all hominoids have such large testes. The average testes size is roughly 30 grams (1 oz) in gorillas, 35 grams (1.25 oz) in orangutans, and 41 grams (1.4 oz) in humans.

A quick look at the testes size of all primate species for which we have data shows that part of the reason for so much variation is differences in body size. In general, the larger the body, the larger the testes. The graph shows the overall relationship between average body size and average testes size for 33 primate species, including prosimians, monkeys, apes, and humans. For technical reasons, we plot the logarithms of both body weight and testes weight. The straight line shows the best fit between the logarithm of body weight and the logarithm of testes weight, and clearly shows that the larger the body, the larger the testes. (The relationship is actually curved somewhat, which is why we use logarithms. This means that the increase is not linear.)

Nevertheless, when we look at the actual data points on the curve, we can see that although there is an average relationship between body weight and testes weight, it is not perfect. Some species are above the line, meaning they have larger testes than expected, and some species are below the line, meaning they have smaller testes than expected. For example, humans have testes that are about two-thirds the size expected on the basis of our body weight. Chimpanzees, however, have testes that are 2.5 times that expected! Both orangutans and gorillas have smaller testes than expected on the basis of body weight.

Are these deviations random, or do they reflect that some factor other than body weight may be responsible for testes size? Harcourt and colleagues (1981) investigated this question and came to the conclusion that an important factor was the type of social structure associated with each primate species. The graph shows their results. Species that have a single adult male are indicated by the filled-in squares. There is a definite tendency for those species to fall below the predicted line—that is, to have smaller testes than expected. Species with a multimale social structure, indicated by filled-in circles, tend to fall above the predicted line, showing that they have larger testes than expected. The bottom line is that once we control for body size, males in multimale societies have larger testes.

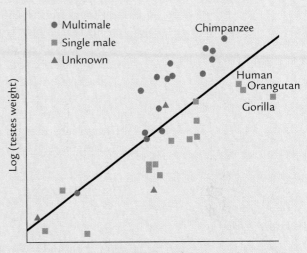

Relationship between body weight (logarithm) and testes weight (logarithm) in 33 primate species. The solid line is the predicted relationship between body weight and testes weight. Individual points correspond to the different species. Species with a single-male society are indicated by a filled-in square. Species with multimale societies are indicated by a filled-in circle. Species with an unknown social structure are indicated by a filled-in triangle.

What is the reason for differences according to social structure? Harcourt and colleagues suggest that larger testes are needed in primate societies in which mating is frequent and in which many males mate with a female during estrus. Chimpanzees are a good example of this. Natural selection may have favored males with larger testes, and hence a greater amount of sperm, so they could compete genetically with other males. In primate societies with less frequent mating and in which females generally mate with only one male, larger testes would not be selected for. Examples here include orangutans and gorillas.

Of course, testes size is not only a function of body size and social structure. Harcourt and colleagues note other potential influences, such as seasonality of mating. However, the strong relationship observed in their study suggests that there is often a link between biology and behavior that is best interpreted in an evolutionary context.

Source: Data from Harcourt et al. 1981.

pace for the rest of the group, determining when and how far to move in search of food.

A typical day for a gorilla group consists of eating and resting. Given their large body size and the limited nutritional value of leaves, it is no wonder that gorillas spend most of their day eating. Because of their size, gorillas have few problems with predators (except for humans with weapons). The life of a gorilla is for the most part peaceful, a dramatic contrast to their stereotypical image as aggressive creatures.

Because gorillas are rather peaceful and slow-moving, we have a tendency to think they are "slow" in a mental sense as well. This is another myth of gorilla behavior. Laboratory and field studies of gorillas have shown them to be extremely intelligent creatures. As discussed later, they have even learned sign language.

Chimpanzees

The chimpanzee is perhaps the best known of all the nonhuman primates. Most of our experience with chimpanzees, however, is with captive or trained animals. We like to watch chimpanzees perform "just like humans" and delight in a chimpanzee's smile (which actually signals tension, not pleasure).

From a scientific perspective, chimpanzees are equally fascinating. Genetic studies during the past several decades have shown that humans and chimpanzees are even more similar than they were previously thought to be. Laboratory and field studies have shown that chimpanzees are capable of behaviors we once thought of as unique to humans, such as toolmaking and language acquisition. Any examination of the human condition must take these remarkable creatures' accomplishments into account.

Physical Characteristics   Chimpanzees are found in Africa. They are smaller than gorillas and show only slight sexual dimorphism. Adult males weigh about 45 kg (99 lb) on average, and adult females about 37 kg (82 lb) on average (Leutenegger 1982). Chimpanzees have extremely powerful shoulders and arms. Like humans, chimpanzees show great variation in facial features and overall physical appearance (Figure 6.24).

Chimpanzees, like gorillas, are knuckle walkers, with longer arms than legs. Chimpanzees, however, are more active and agile than gorillas. They are both terrestrial and arboreal. They spend considerable time in the trees, either sleeping or looking for food, and often hanging by their arms. On the ground, they sometimes stand on two legs to carry food or sticks.

Distribution and Environment   Most chimpanzees are found in the African rain forests, although some groups are also found in the mixed forest–savanna environments on the fringe of the rain forests. The chimpanzee diet consists mainly of fruit (almost 70 percent), although they also eat leaves, seeds, nuts, insects, and meat. Chimpanzees have been

FIGURE 6.24

Variation in chimpanzee faces.

observed hunting small animals, such as monkeys, and sharing the meat. Though some of the hunting occurs spontaneously when chimpanzees encounter small animals, other hunting behavior appears to be planned and coordinated.

Social Structure   Chimpanzees live in large communities of 50 or more individuals. Their social structure constantly changes, with individuals and groups fragmenting and later rejoining the main group. This type of social structure is a **fission-fusion** society, which can occur when food resources fluctuate. When food in the local area is more limited, the population breaks into smaller groups for feeding (fission) and then later comes back together. All chimpanzees recognize and interact with others in the group. Chimpanzee groups are less rigid than other multimale primate societies, such as baboons. Although all members of the group interact to some extent, it is common for smaller subgroups to form much of the time. The actual composition of these subgroups also changes frequently.

Most social behaviors revolve around the bond between mother and infant (Figure 6.25). Chimpanzees tend to associate with their mothers and other siblings throughout their lives, even after they are fully grown. As with other primates, young females watch and observe their own mothers taking care of children and learn mothering behaviors. There is

fission-fusion A primate society in which the population splits into smaller subgroups at times (fission) and then later reunites (fusion). The process is affected by the distribution of food resources.

Mother and infant chimpanzees. The mother–infant bond, which provides an infant chimpanzee with protection and socialization, often continues throughout life.

no close bond between adult males and infants except for associations through the mother. Overall, chimpanzee society can be seen as a collection of smaller groups, defined in terms of mothers and siblings, forming a larger community. Other associations are also common, such as temporary all-male groups. Some chimpanzees are even solitary for periods of time.

Adult males are generally dominant over adult females, although there is much more overlap than is found in baboon societies. Some females, for example, are dominant over the lower-ranking males. As with other primates, dominance is influenced by a variety of factors, such as size, strength, and the ability to form alliances. Individual intelligence also appears to affect dominance, as was revealed in Jane Goodall's study of chimpanzees in the Gombe Stream National Park near Lake Tanganyika. In 1964, the community studied by Goodall had 14 adult males. The lowest-ranking male (Mike) replaced the most dominant male (Goliath) after displaying a particularly innovative form of dominance. There were a number of empty kerosene cans lying around Goodall's camp that the chimpanzees generally ignored. Mike would charge other males while hitting the cans in front of him, creating an unusual, noisy display. This behavior was so intimidating to other males that Mike rose from the lowest to the highest rank (Goodall 1986). This study shows not only the changing nature of dominance hierarchy but also the role of individual intelligence and initiative; all the males had access to the cans, but only Mike used them.

Although adult males are generally dominant over adult females, dominance rank among the females also has an influence on the group. Because female dominance is less noticeable, some have suggested that it is of little importance. However, Anne Pusey, Jennifer Williams, and Jane Goodall

(1997) found that female dominance rank correlated with reproductive success. Using data from 35 years of observation, they found that the higher-ranking adult female chimpanzees tended to have more offspring. In addition, they found that infants born to the higher-ranking females tended to have higher rates of survival through infancy.

Studies of the Gombe Stream chimpanzee community have revealed a number of other interesting features of chimpanzee social behavior and intelligence. The chimpanzees have been observed making and using tools (discussed at length in Chapter 7), hunting in cooperative groups, and sometimes engaging in widespread aggression against other groups. We examine some of these findings when we consider what behaviors may be considered uniquely human.

Bonobos

The bonobo is the third and least well known of the African apes. The bonobo is closely related to the chimpanzee and is commonly considered a separate species of chimpanzee known as the "pygmy chimpanzee" (compared to what is often termed the "common chimpanzee"). The close similarity of chimpanzees and bonobos is reflected in their assignment to the same genus—*Pan* (the scientific names are *Pan troglodytes* for the chimpanzee and *Pan paniscus* for the bonobo).

Physical Characteristics   At first glance, bonobos seem quite similar to chimpanzees (Figure 6.26). On closer examination, however, we see that the bonobo has relatively longer legs, a higher center of gravity, and a narrower chest. It also tends to have a higher forehead and differently shaped face (Savage-Rumbaugh and Lewin 1994). Like gorillas and chimpanzees, bonobos are frequent knuckle walkers. Of particular interest is the fact that bonobos can walk upright more easily than other apes (Figure 6.27). This observation, combined with other evidence, suggests that the first hominids may have been quite similar in many ways to bonobos. There is some sexual dimorphism—adult males average 43 kg (95 lb) compared to adult females, which average 33 kg (73 lb) (de Waal 1995).

Distribution and Environment   Bonobos are found only in a restricted rain forest region in Zaire in central Africa. It is estimated that there are fewer than 10,000 bonobos alive today. Their diet consists primarily of fruit, supplemented with plants. Unlike chimpanzees, bonobos consume little animal protein and do not hunt monkeys (de Waal 1995).

Social Structure   As with chimpanzees, bonobos live in multimale/multifemale groups. However, there are important differences in the social organization of these two species. In chimpanzee society, males are dominant over females, and some of the strongest bonds in the social order are between adult males. In bonobo society, things are quite different. Here, the strongest

FIGURE 6.26

A bonobo mother and infant.

social bonds are between adult females (White 1996), and even though they are physically smaller, the females are sometimes the most dominant (Fruth et al. 1999). In addition, the dominance status of a male depends in large part on the dominance status of his mother (de Waal 1995).

Some of the most interesting observations of bonobo behavior have to do with the function of sexual activity in their social interactions. In addition to sexual intercourse, bonobos engage in a variety of sex play, including rubbing of genitals and oral sex. Continued observation of bonobo groups

FIGURE 6.27

A bonobo.

has revealed that such sex play is frequently used to reduce tension and avoid conflict. Researchers have shown repeatedly that bonobos will engage in a brief period of sex play in a tense social situation. In bonobo society, sexual play is a method of peacemaking (de Waal 1995).

Summary

There is a great deal of biological and behavioral variation among the living primates. The order Primates is composed of the more biologically primitive prosimians and the anthropoids, which consist of monkeys (New World and Old World), apes, and humans. Monkeys are quadrupedal (four-footed) and have a tail. Although New World monkeys are exclusively arboreal, some species of Old World monkeys are arboreal and others are terrestrial.

The hominoids (apes and humans) are a group of anthropoids that share certain characteristics, such as the lack of a tail, similar dental features, larger brains, and a shoulder complex suitable for climbing and hanging. Hominoids consist of the "lesser apes" (gibbons) and the "great apes." The great apes consist of an Asian species (orangutan) and three African species (gorilla, chimpanzee, bonobo). The African apes are the most similar to humans, although it is not clear which of these three is the *most* similar.

The living apes show a great deal of environmental and anatomical variation. Some are arm swingers (gibbon), others are knuckle walkers (gorilla, chimpanzee, bonobo), and one is primarily a climber (orangutan). Although the great apes are all similar genetically and have a fairly recent common ancestor (roughly 20 million years ago), they show a great deal of social variation.

Supplemental Readings

In addition to the primate texts listed in Chapter 5, some other useful sources include:

Ciochon, R. L., and R. A. Nisbett, eds. 1998. *The Primate Anthology: Essays on Primate Behavior, Ecology, and Conservation from Natural History.* A collection of 33 short articles on primate behavior that originally appeared in the magazine *Natural History.*

Fossey, D. 1983. *Gorillas in the Mist.* Boston: Houghton Mifflin. A popular and well-written account of the late Dian Fossey's research on the behavior of the mountain gorilla. The book deals specifically with the problem of human intervention and the likely extinction of the mountain gorilla.

Goodall, J. 1986. *The Chimpanzees of Gombe: Patterns of Behavior.* Cambridge, Mass.: Harvard University Press. A comprehensive review of Jane Goodall's early research on chimpanzee behavior.

VIRTUAL EXPLORATIONS

Visit our textbook-specific online learning center Web site at **www.mhhe.com/relethford7** to access the exercises that follow.

1. **World of Primates**   At the beginning of this chapter, we were introduced to the two major primate suborders, Prosimii and Anthropoidea. A good way to review primate diversity is to familiarize yourself with images representing these two suborders. Go first to Michigan State University's Prosimii site: **http://www .msu.edu/%7Eheckaaro/prosimii.html.** Read over the introductory paragraph. It provides a brief overview of this suborder.

   Below the introduction are links for the infraorders of the Prosimii:
   Lemuriforms: **http://www.msu.edu/%7Eheckaaro/lemur.html**
   Lorisiforms: **http://www.msu.edu/%7Eheckaaro/loris.html**
   Tarsiiforms: **http://www.msu.edu/%7Eheckaaro/tarsier.html**

   The site allows you to navigate back and forth between the three links.

   ■ Are any of these primates unfamiliar to you?
   ■ What about their habitats?
   ■ What types of specializations does each have?
   ■ What other information about them is new to you?

   Now visit the Anthropoidea site: **http://www.msu.edu/%7 Eheckaaro/anthropoidea.html.** The introductory paragraph about the anthropoid suborder discusses size and dietary difference and other physical features that distinguish them from other primates. Recall what your learned about in the earlier chapters in your book about advantages and disadvantages of evolutionary change. The two Anthropoid infraorders, Platyrrhini (New World monkeys) and Catarrhini (Old World monkeys), each have separate links:

Platyrrhini: **http://www.msu.edu/%7Eheckaaro/plats.html**
Catarrhini: **http://www.msu.edu/%7Eheckaaro/cats.html**

Explore *each* of the two links.

- What are some of the features that distinguish the two infraorders?
- What about differences *within* each infraorder?
- What do you recall from your reading in Chapter 6?
- What features make the Catarrhini more similar to humans?
- What features distinguish the Platyrrhini?

2. **The Callicam: Compare and Contrast Marmoset Behavior** **http://pin.primate.wisc.edu/callicam**. The Wisconsin Regional Primate Research Center Callicam makes it possible to remotely control the site's Web cam and observe live marmoset behavior in two-minute intervals. Click on the "Open the Callicam" link. You are now able to view the marmoset enclosure and move the camera with horizontal and vertical slide buttons around the viewing frame. Make five 2-minute observations. (If the marmosets are inactive, you may wish to come back to the site later.)

- How many different types of behavior (i.e., grooming, aggression, play, feeding) were you able to observe?
- Were you able to determine which individuals were dominant and which were submissive?
- Would you consider marmosets to be solitary or social?
- Which behaviors did you find most interesting?

3. **Understanding Bonobos**   **http://songweaver.com/info/bonobos.html**. Bonobos were classified as a species following their discovery in a Belgian colonial museum in 1929. This article discusses the many aspects of bonobo social life and their connections to humans.

Read *Bonobo Sex and Society* by Frans de Waal, 1995.

- Bonobos are unique in some ways among primates. How are they different from other chimpanzees? How are they similar to humans?
- What is unique about bonobo social structure? How does the bonobo estrus cycle differ from the estrus cycle of other primates?
- How do observations of bonobo behavior help us understand our own evolutionary history?

4. **Chimpanzee Central**   **http://www.janegoodall.org/chimp_central/default. asp**. Visit the Jane Goodall Institute Web site.

Explore the links under "About Chimpanzees" on the left-side menu.

- Do chimpanzees engage in cooperative behavior? If so, in what contexts?
- Do chimpanzees make and use tools? If so, is this considered culture?
- In what ways are chimps similar to humans? Are they different in any significant ways?

Read the biography of the F family of chimpanzees from Gombe.

- How have these specific individuals helped us to understand chimpanzees in general?
- What do you think of the written description of this family? Is it the writer making them seem extremely human, or is it the chimpanzees' behavior?

Koko the gorilla using sign language to communicate. The ability of apes to learn sign language is one of several findings during the late twentieth century that caused us to reassess our own place in nature. To what extent are humans unique?

The Human Species

What are humans? This question has been a focus of science, art, and literature. Many different fields, from theology to psychology, have addressed its ultimate significance. Our perspective on ourselves is not abstract; the way we define what we are affects the way we treat others and the rest of the world.

One of the earliest written definitions of humanity is found in Psalm 8:4–6 of the Bible, where the question is put to God:

> What is man, that thou art mindful of him? and the son of man, that thou visitest him? For thou hath made him a little lower than the angels, and hast crowned him with glory and honor. Thou hast madest him to have dominion over the works of thy hands; thou hast put all things under his feet.

This brief statement reflects a long-standing belief of Western civilization that humans are inherently superior to all other life forms on the planet, ranking far above animals yet "lower than the angels." The view that humans are the supreme creatures in the natural world is also apparent in the works of many ancient Greek philosophers. Aristotle, for example, constructed an arrangement of all things with inanimate matter at the "bottom" and humans at the "top" (Kennedy 1976).

What is the scientific definition of humans? Many sciences attempt to answer this question—zoology, biochemistry, and even computer science among them. In addition, a wide range of disciplines, such as history, geography, economics, political science, sociology, psychology, and anthropology, deal almost exclusively with human beings and their behaviors. From a scientific standpoint, we are interested in a definition of humans that incorporates differences and similarities with respect to other living creatures. This is not always as simple as it sounds. For example, are humans the same as fish? Of course not, but can you explain why? Suppose you say that humans walk on two legs. Certainly, that definition separates fish and humans, but it does not separate humans and kangaroos, which also move about on two legs (albeit quite differently).

This chapter examines modern humans from the same perspective as the previous two chapters, focusing on the biological and behavioral uniqueness assigned to human beings. The final part of the chapter examines the question of how unique we are by comparing certain human behaviors (tool use, culture, language) with similar behaviors seen in some living apes.

CHARACTERISTICS OF LIVING HUMANS

This section focuses on certain key features of modern humans, particularly our brains, upright walking, teeth, reproductive patterns, and social structure.

Distribution and Environment

Humans are the most widely distributed living primate species. As later chapters will outline, humans originally evolved in a tropical environment. In fact, much of our present-day biology reflects the fact that we are tropical mammals. During the course of human evolution, however, we have expanded into many different environments. Biological adaptations have aided humans in new environments, such as cold weather and high altitude. The cultural adaptations of humans have allowed even greater expansion. Today there is no place on the planet where we cannot live, given the appropriate technology. Humans can live in the frozen wastes of Antarctica, deep beneath the sea, and in the vacuum of space. Our cultural adaptations have enabled us to range far beyond our biological limitations. These adaptations have also permitted incredible population growth. In the past, the planet supported no more than a few million people at a hunting-and-gathering level of existence (Weiss 1984). Today the population of the world is more than 6.5 billion and counting. It is easily argued that the quality of life is still low for much of the world's human population, but there is no doubting that our ability to learn and to develop technology has led to immense potential for population expansion.

Brain Size and Structure

One very obvious biological characteristic of the human species is the large brain. Our bulging and rounded skulls and flat faces contrast with these features in other animals, including the rest of the hominoids. Whereas an ape's skull is characterized by a relatively small brain and large face, modern humans have relatively large brains and small faces.

Figure 7.1 shows the brain size (in cubic centimeters) for a number of primate species. There is a clear relationship between taxonomic status and brain size: Monkeys have the smallest brains, followed by the lesser apes, great apes, and humans. Absolute brain size is not as useful a measure of intellectual ability because larger animals tend to have larger brains. Elephants and whales, for example, have brains that are four to five times the size of the average human brain.

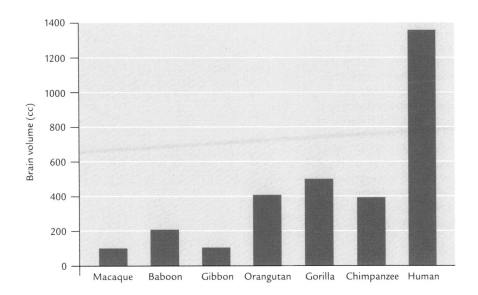

FIGURE 7.1

Average brain volume (cubic centimeters) of selected living primates. (Data from Campbell 1985 for macaques and baboons, and Tobias 1971 for all other species.)

An alternative way of looking at brain size is to express the weight of the brain as a ratio of body weight. The larger this ratio, the larger the brain is relative to body size. For humans, this ratio is $1/49 = 0.020$. However, this ratio is not very useful; many other primates have larger ratios, but we tend not to think of them as more intelligent (e.g., the ratio for the squirrel monkey is $1/31 = 0.032$) (Passingham 1982).

Among mammals, however, the relationship of brain and body weight is not linear. That is, as body size increases, brain size increases—but not at the same rate. Differences in relative size because of disparate growth rates among various parts of the body are common. The study of this phenomenon is known as **allometry.** Parts of the body grow at different rates. Brain size increases at a nonlinear rate with body size. For example, consider two species of primates, such that one species has twice the body weight of the other. If the ratio of brain size to body size were linear, we would expect the brain size of the species with the larger body size to be twice that of the smaller species. Actually, the brain size of the larger-bodied species is on average only 1.6 times as large. Because of this relationship, larger species appear to have smaller brain/body size ratios.

This allometric relationship between brain size and body size is quite regular among almost all primates. The most notable exception is humans. We have brains that are three times the size we would expect for a primate of our body size (Figure 7.2). Human brains are not simply allometrically larger nonhuman primate brains. Human brains also show a number of specializations not found in other primates. In particular, the human brain has a higher proportion of neocortex (part of the cerebral cortex), involved in conscious thought and language (Rilling 2006).

Brain size differences are readily apparent when comparing different species. This raises the question of the significance, if any, of brain size

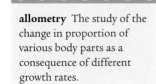

allometry The study of the change in proportion of various body parts as a consequence of different growth rates.

FIGURE 7.2

Relationship between body weight and brain weight in primates. The line indicates the average relationship among various primate species excluding humans. The two dots show expected and observed brain weight for humans. Our brains are three times the weight expected if we followed the typical primate curve. (Data from Harvey et al. 1987.)

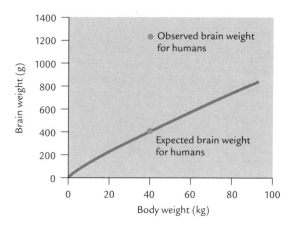

variation *within* a species. Are people with larger brains (relative to body size) more intelligent? Most texts state that there is no relationship between relative brain size and intelligence within the human species, although only a few studies are without methodological flaws. It is problematic, however, whether the fossil record of human evolution shows an increase in absolute and relative brain size that corresponds to an increase in mental abilities. Could there be a relationship between relative brain size and intelligence between species, but not within species? A study by Willerman and colleagues (1991) helps resolve some of the conflict. They measured the brain size of 40 adults using magnetic resonance imaging (MRI) and compared these values, adjusted for body size, with IQ test scores. Adjusting their results to the general population, they found a correlation of 0.35 between relative brain size and IQ scores (a positive correlation can take on a value from 0 to 1; the higher the value, the closer the correspondence). Several other studies have shown similar results, with an average correlation between relative brain size and IQ of roughly 0.4. Schoenemann and colleagues (2000) note that the MRI studies are potentially confounded by environmental differences between families. That is, the correlation between brain size and IQ might be affected by environmental factors that vary from one family to the next. To get around this difficulty, they analyzed correlations *within* families and found that the correlation between general IQ and brain size is close to zero. They acknowledge the possibility that correlations between brain size and cognitive tests could be very small and still have an evolutionary impact over long periods of time. But these correlations cannot be used to make any predictions regarding IQ in living humans. That is, differences in brain size between people today are not related to differences in IQ scores. The lack of correlation might be due to a constraint on further increases in brain size because pelvic size limits the size of a newborn's brain. Larger brains in infants would be dangerous during childbirth, and this might halt any further directional selection for larger brains (Holden 2006). Or there might have been a strong relationship between relative brain size and intelligence in early human evolution that is no longer in effect.

Studies have also looked at the relationship among brain size, body size, and metabolism. Larger mammals have larger brains and produce greater amounts of metabolic energy. Mammals show a great deal of variation, however, in the amount of energy used by the brain. The brains of many mammals, such as dogs and cats, use from 4 percent to 6 percent of their body metabolism. Primate brains use a considerably greater proportion of energy; the Old World macaque uses 9 percent and modern humans use 20 percent (Armstrong 1983).

What does all this mean? The human brain is not merely large; it also has a different structure than the brains of other primates. This difference in structure is also probably related to the higher proportion of metabolic energy used by the human brain. The bottom line is that brain size does not tell the whole story. Thus, the human brain is not only larger than the brain of a chimpanzee; it is also structurally different. The increased convolution of the human cerebral cortex (the folding of brain tissue) means that the brain of a human child with the same volume of that of a chimpanzee has more cerebral cortex.

Discussion of brain size and its relationship to intellectual prowess has historically been part of debates about relative differences in the mental abilities of male and female humans. When *absolute* brain size is used to assess these differences, male brains tend *on average* to be larger. This finding has been used in the past to support ill-conceived claims about the mental superiority of males. However, as pointed out by Gould (1981), researchers did not take into account the fact that body size is on average larger in human males and that absolute brain size is closely related to body size. That is, men often have larger brains because they tend to be larger overall. This fact, combined with an understanding of some of the methodological problems of earlier studies, led Gould to conclude that there is no gender difference in relative brain size or overall intellectual ability.

Certain studies, however, do indicate that average gender differences may influence *specific* mental abilities. Falk (2004) reviewed evidence that females tend on average to score higher on tests of verbal ability and males to score higher on tests of spatial and mathematical abilities. Falk suggests that these findings may be due to gender differences in patterns of brain lateralization. Of course, these tests and measures must be replicated cross culturally to ensure that various forms of bias are not responsible for such observed differences (e.g., the fact that females in many cultures are actively discouraged from mathematics). Also, we must never forget that these results focus on *average* test scores and not on total distribution. Both male and female test score distributions overlap each other. For example, some males score higher in verbal skills than some females. As with many comparisons of biology and behavior between the sexes, we do not find exclusively separate distributions, but instead a great deal of overlap.

Bipedalism

Another striking difference between humans and apes is that humans walk on two legs. We are **bipedal** (literally, "two-footed"). This does not mean that

bipedal Moving about on two legs. Unlike the movement of other bipedal animals such as kangaroos, human bipedalism is further characterized by a striding motion.

FIGURE 7.3

The skeletal structure of the feet of a chimpanzee (*left*) and a modern human (*right*). Note how the big toe of the human lies parallel to the other toes.

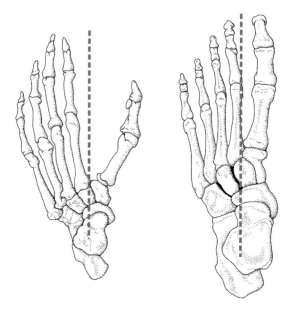

apes cannot walk on two legs. They can, but not as well and not as often. The physical structure of human beings shows adaptations for upright walking as the normal mode of movement.

Humans are not the only animal that is routinely bipedal. The kangaroo also moves about on two legs, but in a totally different manner from humans. Consider walking in slow motion. What happens? First, you stand balanced on two legs. Then you move one leg forward. You shift your body weight so that your weight is transferred to the moving leg. As that leg touches the ground on its heel, all of your body weight has been shifted. Your other leg is then free to swing forward. As it does so, you push off with your other foot.

Human walking is more graceful than a slow-motion description sounds. The act of walking consists of legs alternately swinging free and standing still. We balance on one leg while the other leg moves forward to continue our striding motion. We tend to take these acts for granted, but they are actually quite complicated, requiring both balance and coordination. For example, when you pick up one leg to move it forward, what keeps your body from falling over?

Human bipedalism is made possible by anatomical changes involving the toes, legs, spine, pelvis, and various muscles. In terms of actual anatomy, these changes are not major: after all, no bones are added or deleted; the same bones can be found in humans and in apes. The changes involve shape, positioning, and function. The net effect of these changes, however, is dramatic. Humans can move about effectively on two legs, allowing the other limbs to be free for other activities.

The feet of human beings reflect adaptation to bipedalism. The feet of a human and a chimp are shown in Figure 7.3. The big toe of the chimp sticks

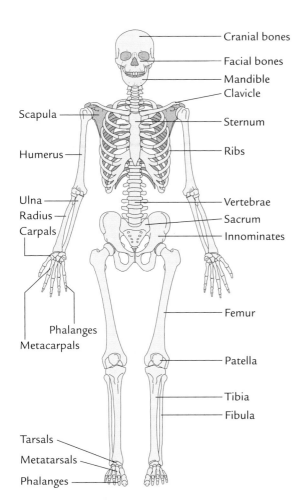

Cranial bones
Facial bones
Mandible
Clavicle
Scapula
Sternum
Humerus
Ribs
Ulna
Radius
Carpals
Vertebrae
Sacrum
Innominates
Phalanges
Metacarpals
Femur
Patella
Tibia
Fibula
Tarsals
Metatarsals
Phalanges

FIGURE 7.4

The modern human skeleton from a frontal view.

out in the same way that the thumb of all hominoids sticks out from the other fingers. The divergent big toe allows chimps to grasp with their feet. The big toe of the human is tucked in next to the other toes. When we walk, we use the nondivergent big toe to push off during our strides.

Our balance while we stand and walk is partly the result of changes in our legs. Figure 7.4 shows a human skeleton from the frontal view. Note that the width of the body at the knees is less than the width of the body at the hips. Humans are literally "knock-kneed." Our upper leg bones (the femurs) slope inward from the hips. When we stand on one leg, the angle of the femur transmits our weight directly underneath us. The result is that we continue to be balanced while one leg is moving. In contrast, the angle of an ape femur is very slight. The legs of an ape are almost parallel from hips to feet. When an ape stands on two legs and moves one of them, the ape is off balance and tends to fall toward one side (more so than humans, because we compensate more quickly). When an ape walks on two legs, it must shift its whole body weight over the supporting leg to stay on balance. This shifting explains their characteristic waddling when apes walk on two legs.

FIGURE 7.5

Side view of the skeletons of a chimpanzee (*left*) and a modern human (*right*), illustrating the shape and orientation of the spine. (Adapted with permission from Bernard Campbell, *Human Evolution,* 3d ed. New York: Aldine de Gruyter. Copyright © 1985 Bernard Campbell.)

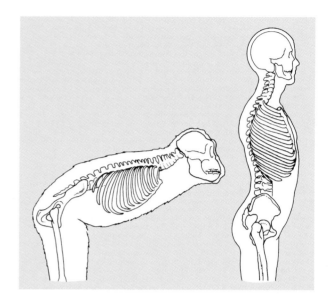

The human spine also promotes balance when we walk upright (Figure 7.5). The spinal column of humans is vertical, allowing weight to be transmitted down through the center of the body. In knuckle-walking apes, the spine is bent in an arc so that when the apes stand on two legs, the center of gravity is shifted to the front of the body. The ape is off balance and must compensate greatly to stay upright. What is difficult for apes is easy for humans. The human spine is vertical but not straight. It curves in several places, allowing it to absorb the shocks we incur while we walk.

The human pelvis is shaped differently from an ape pelvis (Figure 7.6). It is shorter top to bottom and wider side to side. The sides of the pelvis are broader and flair out more to the sides, providing changes in muscle attachment that permit striding bipedalism. The shortness of the human pelvis allows greater stability when we stand upright.

The changes in the human pelvis also involve changes in the positioning of various muscles. For example, certain leg muscles attach more on the sides of the pelvis. This change allows humans to maintain their balance while standing without having to bend their knees. The gluteus minimus and gluteus medius muscles have also shifted position relative to apes, allowing the pelvis to remain stable when one leg is lifted during walking.

Canine Teeth

Human canine teeth are different from the canines in many other mammals. Human canines are small and do not project beyond the level of the other teeth. Human canine teeth serve much the same function as the incisor teeth.

That we have small, nonprojecting canines has led to much speculation concerning causes and effects of human evolution. Given that canine teeth serve as weapons in many primate species, the lack of large canine teeth in

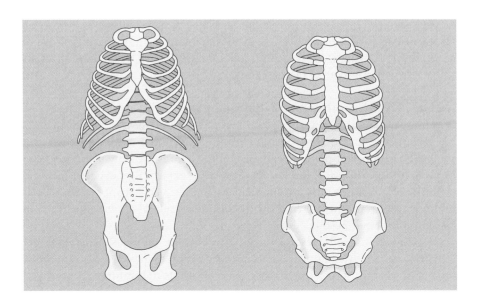

FIGURE 7.6

The trunk skeletons of a chimpanzee (*left*) and a modern human (*right*) drawn to the same size. Note the proportionately shorter and wider pelvis of the human being, reflecting adaptations to upright walking. (Adapted with permission from Bernard Campbell, *Human Evolution*, 3rd ed. New York: Aldine de Gruyter. Copyright © 1985 Bernard Campbell.)

humans seems to imply that we do not need them for weapons anymore. One scenario is that when human ancestors began using tools, they no longer required large canines. As you will see in later chapters, the uniqueness of human canine teeth is a more complex topic than we once thought.

Sex and Reproduction

We humans consider ourselves the sexiest primates. That is, we are more concerned with sex than is any other primate. The fact that humans do not have the **estrus** cycle has often been cited as a unique aspect of human sexuality. For the most part, temperate-zone domestic animals breed only during certain seasons and mate around the time of ovulation. Human females, in contrast, cycle throughout the year and often mate at any time during the cycle. However, this distinction between humans and other primates may not be as clear as often suggested. Orangutans, for example, also lack an estrus cycle. Bonobos do have an estrus cycle but have been observed to mate outside of it to some extent.

Much has been made of the fact that humans have sexual relations while facing each other (the so-called missionary position), whereas other primates typically engage in sex with the male behind the female. One explanation is that there is some social benefit to facing each other during sexual intercourse; it is said to increase emotional bonds between male and female. A problem with this suggestion is that most studies of human sexual behavior have found that humans engage in a wide variety of sexual positions. Though the missionary has been cited as the most common sexual position for certain societies at certain times, it is not the most common everywhere. Human bipedal anatomy may influence the fact that humans use the missionary position, whereas other primates rarely use it. The changes in the human

estrus A time during the month when females are sexually receptive.

pelvis have shifted the position of the vagina so that the missionary position is easier to attain. Apes rarely have sex in this manner simply because it is not comfortable for them. An exception is the bonobo, which has been observed to have sexual intercourse face to face.

Human Sexual Anatomy and Physiology   Several unique features of human sexual anatomy and physiology have been suggested. Some authors have claimed that female orgasm is unique among primates and have constructed a number of possible explanations. There is growing evidence, however, that nonhuman primate females also experience orgasm. Several evolutionary explanations for female orgasm have been proposed that focus on how orgasm might increase the likelihood of sexual activity and/or conception (Campbell 2007).

Human females have relatively large breasts, whereas other primate females do not. One hypothesis is that large breasts developed to resemble buttocks. Assuming that face-to-face sex is desirable in reinforcing emotional bonds and that males prefer the buttocks (both questionable assumptions), large breasts would serve to attract human males to the female's front. Another suggestion is that large breasts in human females are a by-product of the evolution of fat in human females. Fat reserves are important for females in hunting-and-gathering societies because fat is stored energy that can be used in times of food shortages. It has been hypothesized that hormonal changes accompanying increased fat reserves led to increased breast size in human females (Mascia-Lees et al. 1986). Pawlowski (1999) has also suggested that permanent breast enlargement in humans was a by-product of increased selection for subcutaneous fat, but for a different reason. According to Pawlowski, increased amounts of subcutaneous fat served as insulation against the cool nights that occurred even in tropical Africa. This hypothesis views the increased subcutaneous fat as a replacement for dense hair that has disappeared over the course of human evolution. Although reasonable, these hypotheses still need to be tested.

Another unique feature of human sexual anatomy is the large relative size of the penis in males. Both penis and testes size varies among apes and humans, with chimpanzees having the largest testes of any hominoid species, as expected given their polygamous mating patterns. Humans have the longest erect penises of all hominoids (Diamond 1992b), but no satisfactory evolutionary reason has been proposed. Some have argued that the long penis serves some sort of display function when threatening other males or marks status, but there is no supporting evidence for this.

Human Childbirth   The human pattern of reproduction is basically the same as that of most other primates: single births. Unlike apes, however, humans have additional infants before previous offspring have matured socially or physically. Because of cultural adaptations and an extended childhood, humans have increased reproduction without sacrificing parental care.

Childbirth in humans is more difficult and more complicated than in apes, due to our enlarged brains and the changes in pelvic anatomy that accompanied bipedalism. The pelvic anatomy of living humans means that a new baby has to rotate through a narrow and twisting birth canal. The baby is also born facing backward relative to the mother, making it difficult for the mother to guide the infant from the birth canal without assistance. Rosenberg and Trevathan (2001) suggest that these problems explain why childbirth is assisted in virtually all human cultures and may be an ancient adaptive behavior of human beings.

Social Structure

Human social structure is a topic of almost infinite complexity. One observation is obvious—there is extensive variation. Because variation in social structure is great even among monkeys and apes, it should come as no surprise that humans also show considerable variation.

A common Western assumption is that the "normal" social structure of human beings is the nuclear monogamous family group: mother, father, and children. Actually, the majority of human societies studied have a stated preference for **polygyny**—a pattern in which one husband has several wives (Harris 1987)—and a few cultures practice **polyandry,** in which one woman has several husbands. Because of this, anthropologists have often argued that the basic human pattern is polygyny. However, it must be noted that although many societies state a *preference* for polygyny, it is still much more common for men to have a single wife. In many cases, only the most wealthy or powerful have multiple wives. Fisher (1992) concluded that for all practical purposes monogamy is the predominant *marriage* pattern for humans (although with considerable infidelity in many societies). Clearly, it is necessary to consider the difference between stated cultural ideals and actual practices.

Humans show a great deal of variation in other aspects of their culture as well, such as economic systems, political systems, and legal systems. The dramatic changes in such institutions over the past 12,000 years—since the origin of agriculture—show exactly how variable our species' behavior can be. During this time, humans developed state-level societies, social stratification, formal legal codes, and many other aspects of culture that we take for granted today. Biological needs, such as for food and sex, place some limits on our behavior. One such limitation is the need for a family of some sort to care for dependent children. All humans live in families, although the actual structure can vary considerably depending on circumstances and tradition, including nuclear families, extended families, monogamous and polygamous marriage, single-parent families, and same-sex families.

polygyny A form of marriage in which a husband has several wives.

polyandry A form of marriage in which a wife has several husbands.

THE HUMAN LIFE CYCLE

The major stages of growth and development are prenatal (before birth) and postnatal (after birth). The general nature of these two stages is reviewed briefly, followed by consideration of what is unique about human growth.

FIGURE 7.7

A 2-month-old embryo. The fingers have developed and the eye is oval in shape. The total body length at this stage is 3.18 cm (1.25 in.).

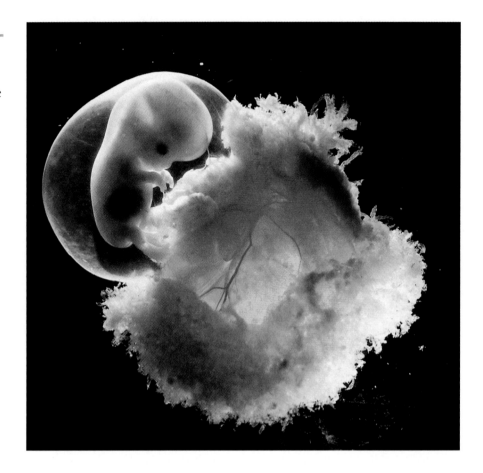

Prenatal Growth

zygote A fertilized egg.

embryo The stage of human prenatal life lasting from roughly two to eight weeks following conception; characterized by structural development.

fetus The stage of human prenatal growth from roughly eight weeks following conception until birth; characterized by further development and rapid growth.

Prenatal life is the period from fertilization through childbirth. After fertilization, the fertilized egg, or **zygote,** develops into a cluster of identical cells deriving from the initial fertilized egg. During the first week, the fertilized egg multiplies as it travels into the uterus. By this time, there are roughly 150 cells arranged in a hollow ball that implants itself into the wall of the uterus. Cell differentiation begins. During the second week, the outer layer of this ball forms the beginning of the placenta. Some early differentiation of cells can be seen in the remainder of the ball.

The embryonic stage stretches from roughly two to eight weeks after conception. The **embryo** is very small during this time, reaching an average length of 25 mm (1 in.) by the eighth week. During this time, the basic body structure is completed and many of the different organ systems develop; the embryo has a recognizably human appearance, although it is still not complete (Figure 7.7). The fetal stage lasts from this point until birth. Development of body parts and organ systems continues, along with a tremendous amount of body growth and changes in proportions. During the second trimester of pregnancy, the **fetus** shows rapid growth in overall length.

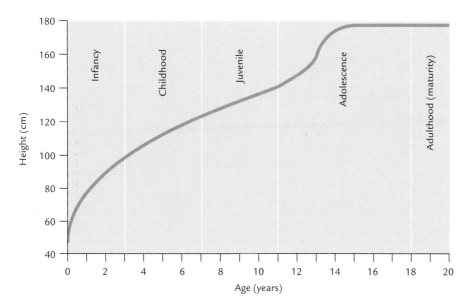

FIGURE 7.8

Typical distance curve for human height. (Adapted from *Growth and Development* by Robert M. Malina, © 1975, publisher Burgess Publishing Company. Used by permission.)

During the third trimester, the fetus shows rapid growth in body weight, head size, and brain size.

The Pattern of Human Postnatal Growth

We can identify five basic stages in growth from birth until adulthood (Bogin 1999, 2001). The first stage, *infancy,* refers to the time from birth until weaning (typically up to 3 years in nonindustrialized societies) and is characterized by rapid growth. The second stage, *childhood,* refers to the time from weaning until the end of growth in brain weight, which takes place at about 7 years (Cabana et al. 1993). The *juvenile* stage is from this point until the beginning of the fourth stage, *adolescence,* which is the time of sexual maturation and a spurt in body growth. Adolescence begins at about age 10 in females and age 12 in males, although there is considerable variation across people and populations. The fifth stage is labeled *adulthood.*

Human growth is usually studied by looking at growth curves. One type of growth curve, the **distance curve,** is a measure of size over time—it shows how big someone is at any given age. Figure 7.8 is a typical distance curve for human height. As we all know, until you reach adulthood, the older you get, the taller you get. However, note that this is not a straight line—you do not grow the same amount each year. This shows that the *rate* of body growth is not the same from year to year. Changes in the rate of growth are best illustrated by a **velocity curve,** which plots the rate of change over time. The difference between a distance curve and a velocity curve can be illustrated by a simple analogy—driving a car. Imagine driving a car on a highway between two cities. How *far* you have come is your distance, and how *fast* you are going is your velocity.

distance curve A measure of size over time—for example, a person's height at different ages.

velocity curve A measure of the rates of change in growth over time.

FIGURE 7.9

Typical velocity curve for human height. (Adapted from *Growth and Development* by Robert M. Malina, © 1975, publisher Burgess Publishing Company. Used by permission.)

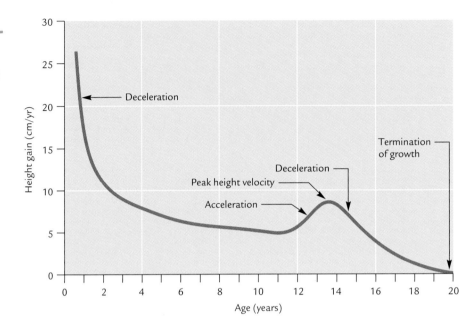

A typical velocity curve for human height is shown in Figure 7.9. The rate of growth is greatest immediately after birth, followed by a rapid deceleration during infancy. Even though the rate of growth decreases, we still continue to grow. Referring again to the car analogy, if you decelerate from 50 miles per hour to 30 miles per hour, you are still going forward, just not as fast. During childhood and the juvenile stage, height velocity decreases slightly, but then it increases rapidly for a short time during adolescence. At adulthood, the rate of growth again decreases until there is no further significant growth.

Comparing distance and velocity curves for human body size with other organisms has revealed two basic differences: Humans have an extended childhood and an adolescent period (Bogin 1995, 2001). In most mammals, the rate of growth decreases from childbirth, and adulthood occurs without any intervening stages. In other mammals, there is a stage of juvenile growth. Only in humans, however, do we see childhood, adolescence, and a long postreproductive period.

The discussion thus far has centered on body size. To understand the unique aspects of the human growth pattern, it is also necessary to look at changes in growth for other parts of the body, such as the head and brain tissue. Quite simply, not everything grows at the same rate. Figure 7.10 compares human distance curves for body size, brain size, and the reproductive system. All three are drawn to illustrate the percentage of total adult size attained at any given age. Note the differences in these curves—our brains and reproductive systems obviously do not grow at the same rate as our bodies. In particular, our brain grows most rapidly at first, reaching adult weight during childhood (Cabana et al. 1993). The reproductive system grows most slowly, showing hardly any growth until adolescence.

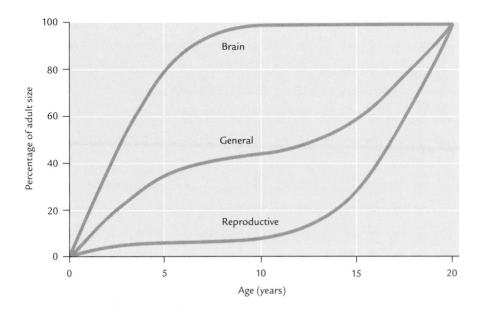

FIGURE 7.10

Distance curves for different body tissues, showing the percentage of total adult size reached at different ages. The general curve represents overall body size (height or weight). The brain curve represents brain weight. The reproductive curve represents the weight of sex organs and tissues. (From Bogin [1995], based on Scammon [1930] and updated to include more recent data on brain growth [Cabana et al. 1993].) (Barry Bogin)

The Evolution of Human Growth

If you think about it for a moment, these differences in timing of growth make sense. Because humans are dependent on learning as a means of survival, it makes sense to have a large brain in place as soon as possible. The physical limits to the rate of brain growth while in the womb mean that the best time for extended brain growth to occur is during the first few years of life. Likewise, it makes sense to have sexual maturity postponed until later in life so that we have time to develop physically and socially enough to provide adequately for offspring.

The evolutionary advantage to delayed maturation and an extended childhood is clear—a longer childhood allows more time for brain development and learning. In addition, a shorter infancy and subsequent childhood is adaptive for the human mother. As the mother does not have to nurse the older child, she is free to have another baby earlier. Over the past 6 million years, this reproductive advantage is one reason for the tremendous growth of the human species (Bogin 2001).

Why do humans have an adolescent growth spurt? Traditional explanations see it as a means of "catching up." If our childhood has been extended, then we have proportionately less time in our lives as reproductive adults. Rapid growth during adolescence allows us to reach sexual maturity and adult body size more quickly, thus allowing us to have our extended childhood and an adequate reproductive period. Without this growth spurt, we would reach adulthood later and possibly not have enough time to adequately care for offspring.

Bogin (2001) has questioned this traditional explanation, suggesting that an adolescent stage of growth offers advantages in terms of learning social skills before reproduction. Noting that males and females experience their growth spurt at different times relative to their sexual and social maturity, he concludes that "girls best learn their adult social roles while they are infertile but perceived by adults as mature; whereas boys best learn their adult social roles while they are sexually mature but not yet perceived as such by adults" (p. 140). The evolution of human adolescence is thus seen as having both biological and social dimensions.

Menopause

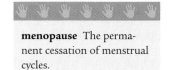

menopause The permanent cessation of menstrual cycles.

Menopause is the permanent cessation of menstrual cycles that occurs before the aging of other body systems and before the end of the average life span. Other mammals show a decline in reproductive function with age, but this is not usually considered menopause because it occurs near the end of life or is associated with the decline in other body functions. As defined here, menopause has been found only in humans and in one species of toothed whales (Pavelka and Fedigan 1991; Peccei 2001). Menopause is universal among human societies and generally occurs at about 50 years of age (Fedigan and Pavelka 2007).

A continuing question concerns the origin of menopause in humans. Is it adaptive (i.e., shaped by natural selection) or a by-product of other biological processes? Adaptive explanations generally focus on the presumed benefits of a mother living past her reproductive years. One model, known as the "mother hypothesis," suggests that rather than having additional children, it makes more sense for a woman to invest time and energy in her existing children for the remainder of her life, thus increasing their probability of survival. After a certain point in life, the odds are against a mother living long enough to raise her children. One variant of this model extends the adaptive benefit of menopause to the next generation. This explanation, known as the "grandmother hypothesis," suggests that menopause evolved to provide a period for females to help take care of their slow-growing and big-brained grandchildren. Although some studies of living humans have shown increased fitness associated with helpful grandmothers, others have not, leaving the status of the grandmother hypothesis unclear (Fedigan and Pavelka 2007).

Peccei (2001) argues that the mother hypothesis is more likely to be true than the grandmother hypothesis but notes that the evidence is inconclusive, and testing difficult. Other researchers have argued that menopause is not the result of natural selection but instead represents a by-product of the aging process. Leidy (1998), for example, has suggested that menopause is simply the result of humans living beyond their egg supply.

IS HUMAN BEHAVIOR UNIQUE?

Humans and apes show a great many similarities, as well as a great many differences. When we ask whether humans are unique, we do not suggest that we cannot tell an ape and a human apart. Rather, we ask what the extent of

Humans and Apes—What Genes Are Different?

Biochemical and genetic studies have shown that humans and the African apes are close relatives. As noted earlier in the text, humans and chimpanzees share over 98 percent of their DNA sequences (referring to the amino acid sequences). It is also clear from the material reviewed in this chapter that humans and chimpanzees have a number of anatomical differences, such as in brain size and structure, locomotion, size of the canine teeth, and characteristics of growth and development. Given the close genetic relationship of humans and chimpanzees, these significant differences must reside in the remaining 2 percent or less of our genomes. Given approximately 3 billion base pairs in both species, a 2 percent difference translates to 60 million potentially different base pairs, implying a large number of different genes. However, what genes could be different, and why? These differences could provide additional clues about *why* humans evolved certain characteristics.

One example is the *FOXP2* gene, located on human chromosome 7. A rare mutant allele of this gene is associated with language impairment, and two copies of the nonmutant functional form of *FOXP2* are needed for normal language acquisition. The gene is the same in chimpanzees, gorillas, and rhesus monkeys, all of which differ from humans by two amino acid substitutions, a pattern that suggests that these two changes occurred after the hominin line split from the common ancestor with African apes. Statistical analysis of genetic differences suggests that this gene has been selected for during the course of human evolution within the past 200,000 years (Enard et al. 2002). Although these analyses suggest that *FOXP2* might be involved somehow in the evolution of human language acquisition, we still need to determine exactly how (and if) the normal functioning *FOXP2* genes in humans and apes relate to differences in speech and/or language acquisition.

Another example concerns the difference between ape and human jaws. Apes have large jaws and powerful jaw muscles for chewing. By contrast, living humans have rather small, less powerful jaws. The fossil record of hominin evolution (see Chapters 10–12) shows that early hominins also had large jaws and chewing muscles, but this pattern changed over the past 2 million years with the origin of the genus *Homo*. Since then, jaws have become smaller as brain size increased. Genetic comparison of humans and other primates shows a difference in the gene for myosin (a protein in muscles). The human form of this gene that controls one of the proteins, *MYH16*, is characterized by a mutation that inactivates it, resulting in smaller jaw muscles. What is particularly interesting about these preliminary results is that the estimated date of the human mutation is 2.4 million years ago, corresponding roughly to the appearance of the genus *Homo* (with smaller jaws) in the fossil record (Stedman et al. 2004). Recent comparison of human and chimpanzee genomes suggests that many genetic differences between African apes and humans are the result of genetic inactivation of functional genes (Wang et al. 2006).

A third example is the comparative genetic analysis of the gene that codes for the protein prodynorphin (*PDYN*), the chemical precursor of endorphins, which are involved in behavior, social bonds, learning, memory, and experience of pain. Rockman et al. (2005) examined the 68 base-pair regulatory section of *PDYN* DNA in humans, apes, and Old World monkeys. They found that humans possess five mutations that have arisen since humans and African apes shared a common ancestor. Five differences is a large number for this small a section of DNA, suggesting natural selection for the human form of the gene over time. The behavioral significance of these genetic changes for human evolution is still not known.

these differences is. Are the behaviors of apes and humans completely different, or are differences present only in the expression of specific behaviors? Can we say, for example, that humans make tools and apes do not? Or should we say instead that there are differences in the ways in which these two groups make and use tools?

According to the view that apes and humans show distinct and major differences, humans possess culture and apes do not. Any cultural behaviors found in apes are labeled as fundamentally different from human cultural behaviors. According to the view that ape–human differences are variations on something that is fundamentally similar, both humans and apes possess culture—the only difference being that humans rely more on culture or that humans have a more developed culture. This debate is semantic to a large extent. A more worthwhile approach is to examine some of the suggested differences between apes and humans in an effort to determine what is truly different.

Tool Use and Manufacture

Tool use has often been cited as a unique human behavior. As defined here, a tool is an object that is not part of the animal. Human tools include pencils, clothes, eating utensils, books, and houses. These are all objects that are not part of the biological organism (humans) but are used for a specific purpose. Tool use, however, does not seem to be even a unique primate characteristic. Birds use sticks for nests, and beavers use dirt in their dams. Both sticks and dirt can be considered tools by this definition.

A more common definition of modern humans focuses on humans as toolmakers (this definition is complicated by the fact that the earliest hominins may not have made tools—see Chapter 10). The key element of this definition is that some object is taken from the environment and modified to meet a new function. Humans take trees to make lumber to build houses. It can be argued that birds modify sticks and beavers modify dirt, but tool manufacture implies something different. Birds, for example, use sticks for building nests, but they do not use these sticks for defensive or offensive weapons. Humans, however, can take sticks and use them to make shelters, defend themselves, hunt, dig up roots, and draw pictures in the sand. When we discuss tool manufacture, we mean the new and different ways to modify an object for a task. Humans can apply the same raw materials to a variety of tasks.

In this sense, tool manufacture has long been considered a unique human activity. But research on apes, particularly Jane Goodall's work on chimpanzees, has since shown that this is not true. Apes make and use tools. Though their tools are extremely simple by modern human standards, the difference between apes and humans cannot be reduced to humans making tools and apes not making tools. Differences exist in the method and use of manufactured tools, but not in the fact of toolmaking itself.

Chimpanzee Termite Fishing   In the early 1960s, Goodall reported a remarkable finding—chimpanzees were making and using tools! Though chimpanzees are predominantly fruit eaters, they also enjoy a variety of other foods, including termites. One group of chimpanzees demonstrated a method for capturing termites. They took a grass stem or a stick, went up to a termite mound, and uncovered one of the entrance holes left by the termites. They inserted the stick into the hole, twirled the stick a bit to attract termites down in the mound, and then withdrew the stick. Termites had attached themselves to the stick, and the chimpanzees ate them directly off the stick (Figure 7.11).

FIGURE 7.11

Chimpanzees using simple tools to fish for termites.

Close analysis of this "termite fishing" behavior shows it to be both true tool manufacture and rather complex tool use. Chimpanzees often spent a great deal of time selecting the appropriate stick. When a suitable stick was not available, they pulled a branch out of the ground or off a bush and stripped away the leaves. This is deliberate manipulation of an object in the environment—toolmaking. The act also reflects a conscious decision-making process.

Termite fishing is not easy. One anthropologist who tried found that it was a difficult process that required a great deal of skill and practice. Even finding the right kind of stick is tricky. If a stick is too flexible or too rigid, it cannot be inserted into the termite tunnel. Taking the stick out without knocking the termites off also calls for careful handling.

Termite fishing is not an innate chimpanzee behavior. It is passed on to others in the group by means of learning. Young chimpanzees watch their elders and imitate them, thus learning the methods and also developing practice. As Goodall has documented, termite fishing has become part of the local group's culture.

Other Examples of Toolmaking Termite fishing is only one of many types of tool manufacture reported among chimpanzees. Sticks are also used to hunt for ants. A chimpanzee will dig up an underground nest with its hands and then insert a long stick into the nest. The ants begin swarming up the stick, and the chimpanzee withdraws it to eat the ants. Sticks have also been used to probe holes in dead wood and to break into bee nests (Goodall 1986).

In addition, chimpanzees have been observed making sponges out of leaves. After a rainfall, chimpanzees will drink out of pools of water that collect in the holes of tree branches. Often the holes are too small for the chimps to fit their head into, so they create a tool to soak up the water: they take a leaf, put it into their mouth, and chew it slightly. (Chewing increases the ability of the leaf to absorb water.) They insert this "sponge" into the hole in the branch to soak up the water.

Other examples of chimpanzee toolmaking and tool use include using leaves as napkins and toilet paper, using sticks as weapons, using branches and rocks to crack open nuts, and using a bone pick to dig out marrow from a bone, among others (Goodall 1986; McGrew 1992). Excavations in the African rain forest have provided archaeological evidence of chimpanzee tool use. Stones were transported to places where they were used to process food, suggesting some antiquity of chimpanzee tool use (Mercader et al. 2002). Although most observations of tool use in the wild have been made on chimpanzees, there are reports of occasional tool use by bonobos, gorillas, and orangutans (Breuer et al. 2005).

Human and Chimpanzee Toolmaking   It is obvious that chimpanzees make and use tools in a systematic manner. It is also clear that they use genuine problem-solving abilities in their toolmaking. They see a problem (e.g., termites in the mound) and create a tool to solve the problem. The implication of these studies is that we can no longer define humans as the only toolmakers.

One of the hallmarks of human behavior is the ability to plan ahead. In terms of tools use, humans typically save tools for later use, whereas we have generally thought apes incapable of such foresight. A recent set of experiments involving captive bonobos and orangutans suggest that apes *do* possess some ability to plan ahead (Mulcahy and Call 2006). As with tool use in general, future planning may be a human behavior that is built upon capabilities already present in a common ancestor, not a behavior that emerged completely and uniquely in the human line.

Do Apes Have Culture?

Observations of ape toolmaking have narrowed the perceived gap between humans and apes. Our understanding of the ways in which these behaviors develop and are passed on from one generation to the next through learning (recall the young chimpanzee watching the adults fish for termites) has led to an interesting question: Is this cultural behavior?

A growing body of evidence suggests that a number of nonhuman species exhibit cultural behavior. That is, certain behaviors are shared among a group and are transmitted from one generation to the next through learning rather than genetically. Certain species of whales and birds, for example, have characteristic songs that are transmitted culturally (e.g., Noad et al. 2000). In addition, as noted in Chapter 5, one group of Japanese macaques developed the sweet potato–washing behavior. It has been argued, however, that these cases are not conclusive demonstrations of culture because they concern only a single behavior, whereas human culture is characterized by a combination of behavior patterns (de Waal 1999).

In 1999, Andrew Whiten and colleagues published a landmark review of cultural behavior in chimpanzees based on observations of seven chimpanzee communities. They examined 65 different behaviors in an effort to find behaviors that were specific to some, but not all, communities. Their goal was to identify a set of behaviors in some communities that were not seen species-wide. Of the 65 behaviors, 26 were excluded because they were rare in all communities, could be explained by local ecological conditions (e.g., no termites to fish), or were present in all communities, suggesting species-wide behaviors best explained by genetic rather than cultural transmission. The remaining 39 behaviors were found in high frequencies in some, but not all, communities and were therefore likely to be examples of local culture. For example, ant-fishing using a probe was found in four communities but was absent in the other three. Picking marrow out of bones was found in one community but not in the other six.

This study confirmed earlier work (e.g., McGrew 1992) showing that many chimpanzee behaviors are *not* species-wide but are confined to specific communities and passed on to each generation culturally. Further, some behaviors were found to be unique to a single community, whereas others were found in two or more communities. In addition, the cultural profiles of each community were distinct from others, a pattern typical of human cultures and unlike that found in other species. Similar results have since been reported in a comparative study of orangutan behavior (van Schaik et al. 2003), providing additional support for cultural ability in apes.

The answer to the question of whether apes have culture now appears to be yes. As noted by primatologist Frans de Waal (1999) in a commentary on the Whiten et al. paper, "The 'culture' label befits any species, such as the chimpanzee, in which one community can readily be distinguished from another by its unique suite of behavioral characteristics. Biologically speaking, humans have never been alone—now the same can be said of culture" (p. 636). Although there are differences between human and ape culture, such as the use of language in the former, this is a difference of degree and not a difference in kind (McGrew 1998). Of course, these conclusions depend on the definition of culture being used. Some anthropologists prefer to use a more specific definition that could exclude apes.

Language Capabilities

Language has long been considered a unique human property. Language is not merely communication but also a symbolic form of communication. The nonhuman primates communicate basic emotions in a variety of ways.

FIGURE 7.12

A chimpanzee hooting.

Chimpanzees, for example, use a large number of vocalizations to convey emotional states such as anger, fear, or stress (Figure 7.12). Many primates also use their sense of touch to communicate some emotions by grooming. Humans, however, rely on language, which is more complex than simple communication.

What Is Language?   Primate communication through vocalizations, grooming, or other methods does not constitute language. Language, as a symbolic form of communication, has certain characteristics that distinguish it from simple communication. Language is an *open system;* that is, new ideas can be expressed that have never been expressed before. Chimpanzee vocalizations, on the other hand, form a closed system capable of conveying only a few basic concepts or emotions. Human language can use a finite number of sounds and create an infinite number of words, sentences, and ideas from these sounds.

Another important characteristic of language is *displacement.* Language allows discussion of objects and events that are displaced—that is, not present—in time and/or space. For example, you can say, "Tomorrow I am going to another country." This sentence conveys an idea that is displaced in both time (tomorrow) and space (another country). We can discuss the past, the future, and faraway places. Displacement is very important to our ability to plan future events—imagine the difficulty in planning a hunt several days from now without the ability to speak of future events!

Language is also arbitrary. The actual sounds we use in our languages need not bear any relationship to reality. Our word for "book" could just as easily be "gurmf" or some other sound. The important point is that we understand the relationship of sounds to objects and ideas. This in turn shows yet another important feature of language—it is learned.

FIGURE 7.13

A chimpanzee using American Sign Language.

Apes and American Sign Language Early efforts to teach English to apes were failures. One classic experiment was conducted on a young female chimpanzee named Vicki. After years of extensive work, Vicki could speak only four words: "Mama," "Papa," "up," and "cup." Later, researchers noted that the failure of this experiment might mean only that apes cannot *speak* English; it said nothing about their ability to *understand*. Looking back at this study, it is no surprise that Vicki could not speak very well because the vocal anatomy of chimpanzees makes speaking a human language next to impossible.

In the 1960s, two scientists, Allen and Beatrice Gardner, began teaching American Sign Language to a young female chimpanzee named Washoe. Devised for the deaf, American Sign Language (ASL) is a true symbolic language that does not require vocalization but instead uses hand and finger gestures. Because chimpanzees are capable of making such signs, ASL was considered the most suitable medium to determine whether they were capable of using language (Figure 7.13). Washoe quickly learned many signs and soon developed an extensive vocabulary.

Washoe also demonstrated the ability to generalize—to take a concept learned in one context and apply it to another. For example, she would use the sign meaning *open* to refer to boxes as well as doors. This suggests that Washoe truly understood the general concept of *open* and not just the use of the sign in one specific context. Washoe also invented new signs and "talked" to herself while playing alone, an act human children perform when learning language. Washoe was even observed to swear!

One of the most intriguing findings of the Gardners' research was that Washoe would form simple two- and three-word sentences (e.g., "You tickle me"). Early observations suggested that Washoe was capable not only of symbolism but also of grammar and sentence construction.

Washoe was the first ape taught ASL. Since then there have been many experiments into the nature of the language capabilities of apes. Gorillas, as well as chimpanzees, have been taught ASL. Other languages were also invented, including one based on plastic tiles and another using a computer keyboard. Experiments were devised that required two chimpanzees to interact with each other using language. These experiments confirmed their ability to generalize signs and to create new ones. For example, one chimpanzee named Lucy combined the signs *drink* and *fruit* to refer to a watermelon for which she had not been taught a sign. She also invented the phrase "cry hurt food" to refer to radishes, which presumably she found bitter.

As Washoe grew older, it became natural to wonder whether she would some day have an infant who would then learn ASL from her, thus showing cultural transmission of language. During the 1970s, Washoe's adopted infant, Loulis, began using ASL, learning two dozen signs within 18 months. Because care was taken to ensure that Loulis was not exposed to *humans* signing, the results of the study suggest strongly that chimpanzees can learn ASL from each other (Fouts and Mills 1997).

Human and Ape Language Abilities   The purpose of the original research with Washoe was to determine what was unique about the way in which a human child learns language. It was suggested that a comparison of human and chimpanzee language acquisition would reveal at what point human abilities surpassed those of the ape. Washoe's abilities exceeded early expectations, and soon the research focus shifted to the language capabilities of the apes themselves. The ability of Washoe and other apes to learn a symbolic language suggested that language acquisition could no longer be regarded as a uniquely human feature.

There is considerable debate about the meaning of these studies. Some claim that many of the positive results are the result of unconscious cues given to the apes by humans. Also, there is the problem of interpreting the data and seeing what one wants to see. For example, Washoe signed "water bird" the first time she saw a swan. Some researchers have interpreted this as a true invention. Others have suggested that Washoe simply saw the water and then the bird and responded with the two signs in sequence. Obviously, much of this research is fraught with the danger of speculation and excessive interpretations for the simple reason that we cannot get inside the chimpanzee's mind.

In any event, there is little doubt that apes can learn and understand the meaning of many signs. Chimpanzees, gorillas, and orangutans have all mastered a certain number. Some chimps have learned more than 150 signs by the time they were 7 years old (Snowden 1990). Carefully controlled experiments have shown that the basic vocabulary of apes is not a reflection of unconscious cues given by the scientists. The behavior of signing correctly while playing alone strongly suggests that the apes actually do understand, *in some manner,* the meaning of signs.

Much of the controversy over language acquisition in apes revolves around two different training approaches. Many studies, including the Washoe project, attempted to teach language in an environment similar to that in which human children develop linguistic skills, one offering continued exposure in an unstructured environment with many opportunities for creativity and expression. Other ape studies used controlled, less flexible environments. The controlled experiments were of course designed to minimize cues from humans and to provide more definitive measurements. The problem is that this type of sterile approach is not the most conducive to learning language.

One of the most interesting observations came about by accident during a study conducted by Savage-Rumbaugh, in which researchers were attempting to teach a female bonobo a keyboard-based language. At the time, the bonobo was caring for an infant, Kanzi, who frequently interrupted his mother. Later, when the mother was returned to the breeding colony, Kanzi began to use the keyboard to make requests. Over time, he performed well on a variety of measures (Savage-Rumbaugh and Lewin 1994). Significantly, he learned language by observation, and not through direct training. (After all, the experiment was not designed to teach him; he was simply there to be nursed.) In other words, Kanzi learned elements of language in the same way that human children do.

The suggested ability of apes to understand grammar and to construct sentences is also controversial. Though apes do create correct two- and three-word sentences, the few longer sentences they create are often grammatically incorrect. There has also been evidence that the apes respond to unconscious cues in constructing sentences (as opposed to simple vocabulary identification). Though some see definite evidence of grammar (e.g., Linden 1981), others do not (e.g., Terrace 1979). The debate continues.

Regardless of the outcome, it is clear that the difference between human and ape is not as great as we once thought. We can no longer define modern humans in terms of the capability to learn certain aspects of symbolic language. Apes are certainly capable of symbolic behavior. Both humans and apes can learn symbols, though humans are clearly better at it. Perhaps one of the major differences is the fact that humans rely on language and apes do not. In their natural habitat, apes do not use sign language. The fact that they are capable of learning language to a certain extent should not detract from the point that they do not use language in their natural environment. As with tool manufacture, we see evidence of capabilities in the apes for behaviors that are optional for them but mandatory for modern humans.

The question of human uniqueness becomes more complicated when we consider possible behaviors of our fossil ancestors. Given a common ancestry with the African apes, at what point did our own patterns of toolmaking and language acquisition begin? Studies of modern apes help answer such questions because we can see the *potential* for such behaviors in the modern apes. Using these potentials as a guide to the behavior of the common ancestor of African apes and humans, we can attempt to determine what changes were necessary to arrive at the modern human condition.

Summary

Humans share many features with the other hominoids but also exhibit a number of differences. The main biological characteristics of humans are a large and complex brain, three times its expected value; bipedalism; and small canine teeth. In addition, humans have a growth pattern that differs from other primates in its extended childhood and adolescent growth spurt. Behaviorally, humans are quite variable.

Past behavioral definitions of humans have often focused on humans as toolmakers. However, studies of apes in their native habitat show that they also make and use simple tools. Accumulated data on chimpanzee behavior in the wild show that chimpanzees, like humans, possess culture. Another oft-cited human characteristic is the use of symbolic language. Although apes are unable physically to speak a human language, studies of American Sign Language and other symbolic, visually oriented languages show that apes have some language acquisition capabilities. Studies of toolmaking and language acquisition show that the difference between apes and humans may be more a matter of degree than kind. Modern humans remain unique in the specific ways they use tools and language and in their reliance on these behaviors for survival. What is mandatory for humans is optional for apes. Still, the capabilities shown by apes provide us with possible clues regarding human origins.

Supplemental Readings

Bogin, B. 2001. *The Growth of Humanity.* New York: John Wiley & Sons. Includes a detailed review of the human life cycle with particular attention to the evolution of human growth.

Fisher, H. 1992. *Anatomy of Love: A Natural History of Mating, Marriage, and Why We Stray.* New York: Ballantine. A well-written and fascinating account of evolutionary explanations of human marriage and mating.

Fouts, R., and S. T. Mills. 1997. *Next of Kin: What Chimpanzees Have Taught Me About Who We Are.* New York: William Morrow.

Savage-Rumbaugh, S., and R. Lewin. 1994. *Kanzi: The Ape at the Brink of the Human Mind.* New York: John Wiley. Two excellent popular accounts of the studies of ape language acquisition.

VIRTUAL EXPLORATIONS

Visit our textbook-specific online learning center.Web site at **www. mhhe.com/relethford7** to access the exercises that follow.

1. **The Physical Characteristics of Humans**   http://www.wsu.edu/ **gened/learn-modules/top_longfor/phychar/culture-humans 1one.html**. Visit the Washington State University General Education's Web site, "The Physical Characteristics of Humans." The site covers topics including brain size, erect posture and bipedalism, other topics related to human anatomy, sexual dimorphism, and several maladies.

Click on the link for "brain size" and read the entire section.

- Has the evolution of brain size in humans impacted other physical changes?
- Apart from some apparent advantages of increased brain size, what are the negatives?
- What role does culture play in mediating the effect of these changes?

Now go to the NewScientist.com Web site: **http://www.newscientist .com/article.ns?id=dn7974**. Read the article "Human Brains Enjoy Ongoing Evolution." Although brain size has remained relatively the same in humans for the past 200,000 years, other less subtle changes have occurred. Two active genes regulating brain size are of particular interest, Microcephalin and ASPM. Mutations of each suggest change.

- What is the effect of the Microcephalin mutation? Where has the incidence of this mutation occurred most often?
- What is the impact of the ASPM mutation on the human brain?

2. **Walking Tall: PBS Evolution Library** **http://www.pbs.org/ wgbh/evolution/library/07/1/l_071_02.html**. Watch the Walking Tall video (56 seconds)from the PBS Evolution Library and read the "Backgrounder."

- What are the three main differences between chimpanzee and human anatomy that affect locomotion as shown in the video?
- Name two additional anatomical differences between humans and chimpanzees that affect our means of walking.
- What physical drawbacks have we inherited with this bipedal adaptation?
- Now think like an engineer! In your opinion, are we perfectly adapted to walking upright? If not, what structural improvements can you suggest? (Think about features such as height, posture, and bone density.)

3. **Adolescence Came Late in Human Evolution** **http://news .nationalgeographic.com/news/2001/12/1205_humanteeth.html**. Read "Adolescence Came Late in Human Evolution" from *National Geographic News* and "Evolution's Youth Movement" from *Science News* about evidence for adolescence in human ancestors.

- When in human history did adolescence evolve as a developmental stage?
- Did members of the species *Homo erectus* go through a prolonged growth period to reach adulthood? How about Neandertals?
- How does this maturation period provide an evolutionary advantage?

■ Why might it be easier to determine growth rates in more recent ancestors (such as early *H. sapiens* or *H. antecessor*) than in those from long ago (*H. habilis* and *H. erectus*)?

4. **For Monkeys, a Millipede a Day Keeps Mosquitoes Away** http://www.emory.edu/living_links/capuchins/NYT_millipede _article.htm. Read the article "For Monkeys, a Millipede a Day Keeps Mosquitoes Away" from the *New York Times*.

■ What kind of primate does the article discuss? Are these animals closely or distantly related to humans?
■ How do the monkeys use millipedes for medicinal purposes? Why is this significant?
■ What kind of social aspects are involved in this behavior? Is it a solitary endeavor?
■ Would this qualify as a cultural behavior? Can you foresee a behavior, such as the use of certain organic materials as medicines, being transmitted from monkeys to humans?

OUR ORIGINS

What is the evidence for human evolution? This question can be answered in a number of ways because our knowledge of past human evolution comes from several sources—the fossil record, the archaeological record, and genetic evidence. In addition to trying to understand the biological evolution of human beings, we need to understand how our cultural adaptations have changed over time. It is important to keep in mind that our present state, biologically and culturally, did not come about all at once and that different human characteristics evolved at different times. Chapter 8 provides some background on the methods of research used to study human evolution, as well as on the history of life on our planet up to 65 million years ago. Chapter 9 reviews the fossil record of primate origins and evolution from their initial appearance to the split of ape and human lines roughly 6 million years ago. Chapter 10 examines the evidence of the first hominins and the evolution of bipedalism. Chapter 11 looks at the origin and evolution of the genus *Homo,* and Chapter 12 discusses the origin of anatomically modern humans.

Robert Pleyer is excavating the skeleton of a 4,500-year-old man from a tomb near Altdorf in southern Germany.

Paleoanthropology

CHAPTER
8

W e can discover our past from clues that have accumulated over time. The *fossil* record provides us with bits and pieces of a small proportion of living organisms that have lived and died in the past, those whose remains became fossilized and remained intact. These fossil remains yield information on what past ancestors looked like, which in turn can tell us about their relationships to other ancient ancestors, as well as to ourselves. The *archaeological* record gives us clues about what tools our ancestors used and how they lived and fed themselves.

Not all information on human evolution comes from what can be dug out of the ground. Studies of the genetics of living humans and living nonhuman primates can help us create "family trees" showing the patterns of relationship and estimates of the dates of the origin of new evolutionary lines. Studies of the behavior of living humans and of living nonhuman primates give us clues about possible patterns of behavior of our ancestors.

All of these avenues of research, and others, make up the field of **paleoanthropology,** the study of primate and human evolution in the broadest possible sense. Although the focus is anthropology, the field of paleoanthropology necessarily involves contributions from other disciplines, including geology, chemistry, and physics. This multidisciplinary approach, using information from *all* relevant fields, is critical for current research on human evolution. No one person can possibly become expert in all of the areas and methods used to extract information about our past. The study of human evolution requires a team approach, tapping the strengths of different fields, all focused on the question of our origins. This chapter provides some basic background on methods of paleoanthropological research and on the history of vertebrate evolution up until the origin of the primates, setting the stage for discussion of primate and human evolution in Chapters 9–12.

DATING THE PAST

Evolution is a process that occurs over time. Therefore, if we are analyzing information from either the fossil or the archaeological records, we need to know *when* a particular organism lived or *when* a particular tool was used. We

CHAPTER OUTLINE
- Dating the Past
- Reconstructing the Past
- Life before the Primates
- SPECIAL TOPIC: A Perspective on Geologic Time

paleoanthropology The study of primate and human evolution.

221

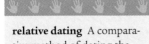

relative dating A comparative method of dating the older of two or more fossils or sites, rather than providing a specific date.

chronometric dating The method of estimating the specific date of fossils or sites.

B.P. Before Present (1950), the internationally accepted form of designating past dates.

stratigraphy A relative dating method based on the fact that older remains are found deeper in the earth because of cumulative buildup of the earth's surface over time.

fluorine dating A relative dating method, based on the accumulation of fluorine in a bone, that tells if two bones from a site are of the same age.

need a way to determine the time sequence of fossil and archaeological remains in order to make sense of what changed over time, and how.

Two basic classes of methods are used to date fossil and archaeological sites and specimens. **Relative dating** determines the *sequence* in time by showing which specimen is older, but not its exact date. **Chronometric dating** determines an "exact" date for a specimen, subject to statistical fluctuation.

Different nomenclature has been used to refer to geological and historical dates. The abbreviation **B.P.,** meaning "Before Present," is often used. (The "Present" has been set arbitrarily as the year 1950.) Some people have used the term B.C., meaning "Before Christ," but because not all peoples share a belief in Christ, the term B.P. is preferable and has been agreed upon internationally. A date of 800,000 years B.P. would therefore mean 800,000 years before the year 1950. The term "years ago" is sometimes used instead of "Before Present." Two abbreviations are commonly used in paleontology and throughout this book: ka (thousands of years ago) and Ma (millions of years ago).

Relative Dating Methods

If we have two sites containing fossil or archaeological material, relative dating methods can tell us which is older, but not by how much. It is preferable to have exact dates, but this is not possible for all sites. Relative dating methods can tell us the basic time sequence of fossil and archaeological sites.

Stratigraphy   **Stratigraphy** makes use of the geological process of superposition, which refers to the cumulative buildup over time of the earth's surface. When an organism dies or a tool is discarded on the ground, it will ultimately be buried by dirt, sand, mud, and other materials. Winds move sand over the site, and water can deposit mud on it. In most cases, the older a site is, the deeper it is. That is, if you find one fossil 3 feet deep and another 6 feet deep, the principle of stratification allows you to infer that the latter fossil is older. You still do not know the age of the fossils or the exact amount of time between the two, but you have established which is older in geologic time.

In some situations, stratigraphy is more difficult to use. Where the earth's crust has folded and broken through the surface of the ground, the usual stratigraphic order is disturbed. This does not invalidate the method, however, for careful geological analysis can reconstruct the patterns of disturbance and allow relative dates to be determined.

Other Relative Dating Methods   A number of other methods can provide relative dates. One example is a form of chemical analysis known as **fluorine dating,** which measures the accumulation of fluorine levels in bone. When an organism dies, its bones absorb fluorine from water. The more time that has passed since the organism died, the more fluorine has accumulated. Unfortunately, the rate of this process varies from site to site, so we cannot tell exactly how old a bone is by using this method. The method does allow us, however, to determine if two bones found at the same site are the same age by comparing their fluorine levels, which should be the same if the fossils are the same age. Sometimes bones from different ages can be found at the same location because of geological factors affecting deposition, and fluorine dating can help in such cases to determine if the bones are from the same time. As noted in Chapter 10, fluorine dating has also been useful in uncovering situations in which bones were planted at a site to perpetuate a hoax.

Other relative dating methods can provide, with comparative data, an approximate age of a site. One example is **biostratigraphy,** which involves comparison of animal remains found at different sites to determine similarity in time levels. Imagine that you have discovered a site that contains a fossil of a certain species of fossil pig. Suppose you know from previous studies that this species of pig has always been found between 2.0 million and 1.5 million years ago wherever it has been found (using chronometric dating methods discussed below). Logically, this suggests that your newly discovered site is also between 2.0 million and 1.5 million years old. Plant pollens can sometimes be used in a similar manner.

Another relative dating method involves **paleomagnetic reversals.** At present, a compass will point toward the North Pole, but there have been times in earth's history when this was reversed. The magnetic field of the earth runs between the North and South Poles, and the polarity of this field changes at irregular intervals over long periods of time. The last time a reversal occurred was approximately 780,000 years ago, known as the Brunhes-Matuyama Reversal, which separated the current period of normal polarity (Brunhes) from the previous time of reversed polarity (Matuyama). Sedimentary rocks preserve a record of these past changes. By calibrating against known ages derived from other methods (discussed in the next section), we can assign dates to past records of paleomagnetic reversal (Figure 8.1). When a new site is discovered that preserves a good stratigraphic section recording past reversals, we can compare it with a known sequence to obtain an approximate date (Figure 8.1).

biostratigraphy A relative dating method in which sites can be assigned an approximate age based on the similarity of animal remains to those from other dated sites.

paleomagnetic reversal A method of dating sites based on the fact that the earth's magnetic field has shifted back and forth from the north to the south in the past at irregular intervals.

Chronometric Dating Methods

Chronometric dating methods provide an "exact" date, subject to statistical variation. Chronometric dating relies on physical and chemical processes in the universe that remain constant. Many of these methods utilize the fact that the average rate of radioactive decay is constant for a given radioactive atom no matter what chemical reaction it might be involved in. If we know that a certain element decays into another at a constant rate, and if we can measure the relative proportions of the original and new elements in some object, then we can mathematically determine the age of the object. Radioactive decay is a probabilistic phenomenon, meaning that we know the average time for decay over many atoms. Such processes allow us to specify an average date within the limits of statistical certainty.

Carbon-14 Dating Living organisms take in the element carbon (C) throughout their lives. Ordinary carbon, carbon-12 (^{12}C), is absorbed by

FIGURE 8.1

The paleomagnetic record for the past 6 million years. The different colors correspond to periods of normal polarity (magnetic north) and reversed polarity. The four polarity epochs (Brunhes, Matuyama, Gauss, and Gilbert) refer to periods when the polarity is primarily normal or reversed. Note that these epochs include intervals (polarity events) when the polarity is reversed for a short time.

(Data from Conroy 2005.)

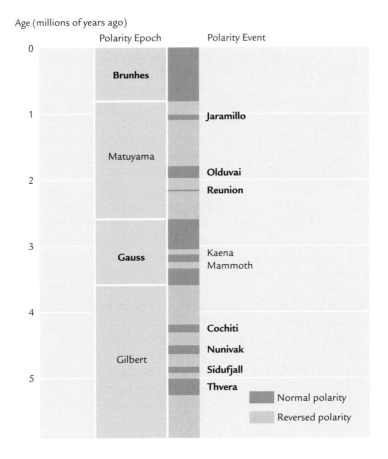

half-life The average length of time it takes for half of a radioactive substance to decay into another form.

carbon-14 dating A chronometric dating method based on the half-life of carbon-14 that can be applied to organic remains, such as charcoal, dating back over the past 50,000 years.

plants, which take in carbon dioxide gas from the air, and by animals, which eat the plants (or animals that eat the animals that eat the plants). Because of cosmic radiation, some of the carbon in the atmosphere is a radioactive isotope known as carbon-14 (^{14}C). An organism takes in both ^{14}C and ^{12}C, and the proportion of ^{12}C to ^{14}C is constant during the organism's life because the proportion is constant in the atmosphere. When an organism dies, no additional ^{14}C is ingested, and the accumulated ^{14}C begins to decay. The rate at which ^{14}C decays is constant; it takes 5,730 years for one-half of the ^{14}C to decay into ^{14}N (nitrogen-14). Carbon-14 is therefore said to have a **half-life** of 5,730 years (Figure 8.2). The half-life is the time it takes for half of a radioactive substance to decay.

Carbon-14 dating uses this constant rate of decay to determine the age of materials containing carbon. The process of the decay of ^{14}C results in the emission of radioactive particles that can be measured. We look at the rate of radioactive emissions for a sample and compare it to the rate of emissions expected in a living organism (a rate of 15 particles per minute per gram of carbon). For example, suppose a sample is analyzed and is found to emit 3.75 particles per minute per gram of carbon. Compared to a living organism, two half-lives have elapsed (one half-life results in 7.5 particles, and a second

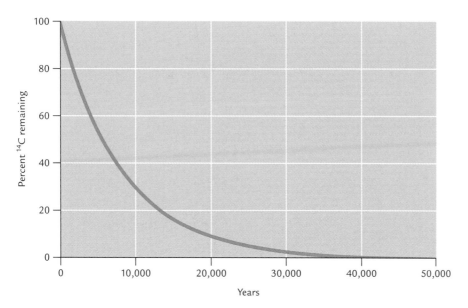

FIGURE 8.2

The process of radioactive decay. The half-life of ^{14}C (carbon-14) is 5,730 years, which is the time it takes for *half* of ^{14}C to decay into ^{14}N (nitrogen-14). After 5,730 years, 50 percent of the ^{14}C remains. It then takes another 5,730 years for half of the remaining ^{14}C to decay, such that after two half-lives, 75 percent of the ^{14}C has decayed into ^{14}N, leaving 25 percent ^{14}C.

half-life results in half of this number, or 3.75 particles). Because the half-life of ^{14}C is 5,730 years, the age of our sample is $5{,}730 \times 2 = 11{,}460$ years old. If the sample were analyzed in 2008, its date would be 11,402 years ago (or 11.402 ka in abbreviated form). Because 58 years have passed since the reference year of 1950 (the "Present"), the date is $11{,}460 - 58 = 11{,}402$.

In theory, any sample containing carbon can be used. In practice, however, bone tends not to be reliable in all cases because of chemical changes during fossilization, in which carbon is replaced. In most circumstances, charcoal is the best material to use. If we find that a fire occurred at a certain site, either naturally or human-made, we can use the charcoal for carbon-14 dating. But careful attention must be given to possible contaminants at any given site. Another problem is that there has been a certain amount of variability in the proportions of atmospheric carbon over the past few centuries due to industrial pollution. Techniques exist for partial control of this factor.

Carbon-14 dating is useful only for sites dating back over the past 50,000 years at most. Any older samples would contain too little ^{14}C to be detected. Though carbon-14 dating is extremely valuable in studies of recent hominin evolution, it is not useful for dating most of earth's geological history.

Argon Dating   Two related chronometric dating methods make use of radioactive decay of isotopes into argon gas using samples of volcanic rock. One method, known as **potassium-argon dating** (abbreviated as $^{40}K/^{40}Ar$ dating), makes use of the decay of an isotope of potassium (^{40}K) into argon gas (^{40}Ar) with a half-life of roughly 1.25 billion years. This slow rate of radioactive decay means that this method works best on samples older than 100,000 years.

Potassium-argon dating requires rocks that did not possess any argon gas to begin with. The best material for this method is volcanic rock, because

potassium-argon dating
A chronometric dating method based on the half-life of radioactive potassium that can be used to date volcanic rock older than 100,000 years.

FIGURE 8.3

Hypothetical example of the use of potassium-argon dating. Hominin remains are found between two layers of volcanic ash, one dating to 3.8 million years ago and the other dating to 3.2 million years ago. The hominin can therefore be dated at between 3.8 million and 3.2 million years ago. (From *Human Antiquity: An Introduction to Physical Anthropology and Archaeology*, 2d ed., by Kenneth Feder and Michael Park, Fig. 7.7. © 1993 by Mayfield Publishing Company. Reprinted by permission of The McGraw-Hill Companies.)

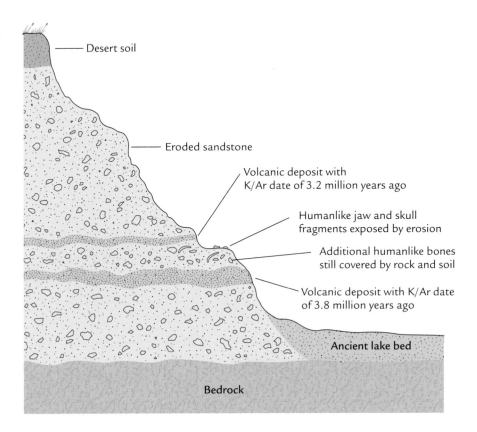

— Desert soil

— Eroded sandstone

Volcanic deposit with K/Ar date of 3.2 million years ago

Humanlike jaw and skull fragments exposed by erosion

Additional humanlike bones still covered by rock and soil

Volcanic deposit with K/Ar date of 3.8 million years ago

Ancient lake bed

Bedrock

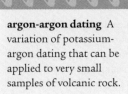

argon-argon dating A variation of potassium-argon dating that can be applied to very small samples of volcanic rock.

the heat generated by volcanic eruptions removes any initial argon gas. Thus, we can be sure that any argon gas we find in a sample of volcanic rock is the result of radioactive decay. By looking at the proportions of ^{40}K and ^{40}Ar, we can determine the number of elapsed half-lives and therefore the age of the volcanic rock.

Though we cannot date a fossil directly with this method, we can assign a date based on the relationship of a fossil find to different levels of volcanic ash (Figure 8.3). If we find a fossil halfway between two layers of volcanic rock with dates of 4.6 million and 4.5 million years ago, we can then assign the fossil an age of roughly 4.55 million years ago. Potassium-argon dating is best applied in areas with frequent volcanic eruptions. Fortunately, much of hominin evolution in East Africa took place under such conditions, allowing us to date many fossil sites.

Potassium-argon dating has largely now been replaced with a more accurate and useful variant, known as **argon-argon dating** ($^{39}Ar/^{40}Ar$ dating). Here, the sample is first irradiated to convert the ^{39}K isotope of potassium into the ^{39}Ar isotope of argon. Because the amount of the ^{39}Ar isotope is a function of potassium content, the method allows estimation of the ratio of potassium and argon. The argon-argon method is more accurate because the final estimates can be calculated from a single extraction of argon gas, whereas the potassium-argon dating method requires two separate samples

FIGURE 8.4

Tree rings can be dated by the method of dendrochronology.

for assessing potassium and argon. The argon-argon method, however, can be accurately applied to small samples—even a single crystal (Brown 2000).

Other Chronometric Dating Methods Many other types of chronometric dating methods can be used in certain circumstances. Some utilize radioactive decay and some use other constant effects for determining age. Archaeologists working on the relatively recent past (within the last 10,000 years) often use a method known as **dendrochronology,** or tree ring counting (Figure 8.4). We know that a tree will accumulate a new ring for every period of growth. The width of each ring depends on available moisture and other factors during that specific period. In dry areas, there is usually only one growth period in a year. By looking at the width of tree rings, archaeologists have constructed a master chart of tree ring changes. Any new sample, such as a log from a prehistoric dwelling, can be compared to this chart to determine its age.

In addition to radioactive decay, other physical constants allow an estimate of age to be assigned to a sample. **Fission-track dating** relies on the fact that when uranium decays into lead in volcanic glass (obsidian) and other igneous rocks, it leaves small "tracks" across the surface of the glass. We can count the number of tracks and determine the age of the obsidian from the fact that these tracks occur at a constant rate. Fission-track dating is useful for dates from several hundred thousand years to billions of years ago (Schwarcz 2000).

Thermoluminescence is a dating method that relies on the fact that certain heated objects accumulate trapped electrons over time, thus allowing us to determine, in some cases, when the object was initially heated. This method has been applied to pottery, bronze, and burned flints. Thermoluminescence can be used to date objects as far back as 1 million years.

Electron spin resonance (ESR) is a method that provides an estimate of dating from observation of radioactive atoms trapped in the calcite

dendrochronology
A chronometric dating method based on the fact that trees in dry climates tend to accumulate one growth ring per year.

fission-track dating
A chronometric dating method based on the number of tracks made across volcanic rock as uranium decays into lead.

thermoluminescence
A chronometric dating method that uses the fact that certain heated objects accumulate trapped electrons over time, which allows the date when the object was initially heated to be determined.

electron spin resonance (ESR) A chronometric dating method that estimates dates from observation of radioactive atoms trapped in the calcite crystals present in a number of materials, such as bones and shells.

crystals present in a number of materials, such as bones and shells. Although this method can be used for sites over a million years old, it works best for dates under 300,000 years (Grün 1993).

RECONSTRUCTING THE PAST

In addition to dating fossil and archaeological sites, paleoanthropologists use a variety of methods to reconstruct the past and provide a more complete picture of human evolution.

Interpreting Fossils

Imagine that you have uncovered the fossil remains of some hominin ancestors. What can you tell from these fossil remains? To what species do they belong? What is the level of variation within the species?

Identifying Species   As was described in Chapter 4, the biological species concept provides a test to determine if individuals from two populations belong to the same species—they must be capable of reproducing naturally and giving rise to fertile offspring. Application of the biological species concept to the fossil record is particularly problematic because we will never have any direct evidence on interbreeding. Instead, we must make our species assignments for fossils based on inferences from the physical appearance, or morphology, of the fossils. Here, we compare the physical structure of the fossils with other fossils and living organisms, keeping in mind the ranges of variation. When we find two specimens that exceed the normal range of variation of similar organisms, we can make a stronger case for assigning the two specimens into different species. We also look for unique characteristics not found in other recognized species.

paleospecies Species identified from fossil remains based on their physical similarities and differences relative to other species.

Because direct evidence of interbreeding is not possible, we often refer to species identified from the fossil record as **paleospecies** and note that the relationship of a paleospecies to the biological species can be subjective. In this sense, some scientists treat paleospecies as convenient labels of physical characteristics and recognize that the question of interbreeding is complex and not easily resolved from fossil evidence alone (we will return to this question in Chapter 11 in the discussion of the evolutionary status of a group of humans known as Neandertals).

Species identification is also complicated by philosophical differences among scientists regarding the nature of species and speciation. Some feel that the range of variation within species is often rather large and suggest that it therefore makes more sense to assign fossils to species already known and described than to create new categories. Scientists with this view are often called "lumpers" because of the preference for lumping new fossils into a small number of preexisting categories. Lumpers view much of evolutionary change as taking place within lineages (anagenesis). Others take a different approach, seeing the fossil record as evidence of frequent speciation

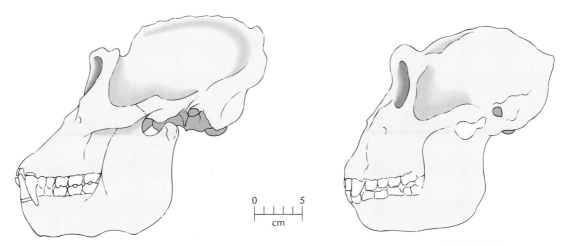

0   5

cm

FIGURE 8.5

Sexual dimorphism in gorilla skulls. The skull of a male gorilla (*left*) is larger than that of the female gorilla (*right*) and also shows heavy crests of bones on top of the skull for muscle attachment. Such sexual differences must be taken into account in analyzing fossil remains and assigning such remains to different species.

(cladogenesis). In this case, they anticipate numerous species at any point in time and tend to call any new fossil that is somewhat different a new species. Scientists with this view are often referred to as "splitters."

Variation within Species   Any description of the characteristics of a species should provide lists of traits that are common to all members in that species but are different from other species. This is easy enough when dealing with very different types of organisms, such as grasshoppers and elephants, but is more difficult when comparing closely related species. In such cases, we must be aware of the amount of variation that exists *within* a species and make sure that we do not confuse differences arising within a species with differences *between* species.

One source of variation within a species is the difference between males and females. As noted in Chapters 5 and 6, some primate species show a great deal of sexual dimorphism. Consider, for example, the skulls of male and female gorillas as shown in Figure 8.5. Adult male and female gorillas are quite different in size and other features. If we were to encounter such specimens in the fossil record without knowing beforehand that they represented male and female from the same species, we might be tempted to place them in different species based on size differences. Thus, if we find fossils that differ in overall size or in the size of certain features, we must consider what we know about levels of sexual dimorphism before drawing any conclusions about species status.

How do we know whether a particular specimen is male or female? A number of methods exist to identify sex from the skeletal remains of humans and other primates. These methods are often very accurate, depending on what part of the body we have for analysis. Sometimes we can estimate sex from skulls. Overall skull size and the size of certain features of the skull, such as the ridge of bone above the eyes (supraorbital torus) or the large bump of bone behind the ear (mastoid process), can be used to separate males and females. The best source of skeletal information on sex (for adult specimens) comes from the pelvis because of anatomical differences related

FIGURE 8.6

Comparison of the pelvic anatomy of modern human males and females. (From *Human Antiquity: An Introduction to Physical Anthropology and Archaeology*, 2d ed., by Kenneth Feder and Michael Park, Fig. 7.17. Copyright © 1993 by Mayfield Publishing Company. Reprinted by permission of The McGraw-Hill Companies.)

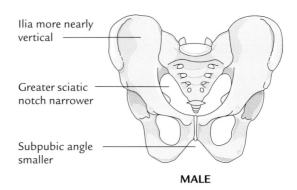

Ilia more nearly vertical

Greater sciatic notch narrower

Subpubic angle smaller

MALE

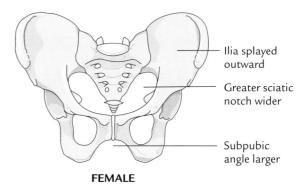

Ilia splayed outward

Greater sciatic notch wider

Subpubic angle larger

FEMALE

to females' being capable of childbearing. As Figure 8.6 shows, in adult females, the subpubic angle is greater in females and the greater sciatic notch is wider. In addition, the side blades of the pelvis (the ilia) are not as vertical as in adult males. These and other differences provide a means of sexing pelvic remains with high accuracy.

Another factor that must be considered when looking at anatomical variation is age. Given that adults are larger than infants and children and have different body proportions, age can be determined from a variety of skeletal measures. For example, the bones of the skull join at lines called *sutures*, which eventually close. Some sutures close at an early age, such as the two pieces of the frontal bone of the skull, which fuse completely early in childhood. Other cranial sutures fuse later, into middle age. Examining which sutures have closed and which have not can provide an estimate of an individual's age. Arm and leg bones, as well as those of the hands and feet, provide another way of estimating age. These bones grow as cartilage fuses between the two ends of the bones (known as *epiphyses*). This fusion is complete at different ages for different bones, and for the different ends of the bone. Examination of which parts of which bones have fused can give an estimate of age (see Figure 8.7). Age-related changes in the appearance of different bones can also be used to estimate age into the elderly years (Bass 1995).

Teeth also provide an excellent source of information on the age of a fossil at least from childhood through early adulthood. The deciduous teeth ("baby

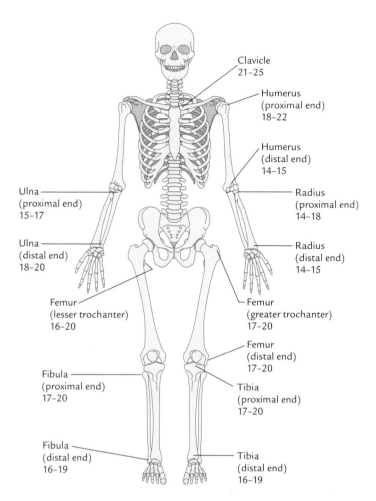

FIGURE 8.7

Average age (in years) of the fusion of some epiphyses in long bones based on a European sample (males and females pooled). Different standards may apply to males and females and to different populations. (Data from Schwartz 1995.)

teeth") are replaced by the permanent ("adult") teeth at different times during an individual's life (Figure 8.8). For example, the third permanent molar tooth (the "wisdom tooth") in living humans typically erupts in the late teens or early 20s. Therefore, if we find a fossil with a third permanent molar that has just erupted, we can estimate that the individual was 18 or so when he or she died. Keep in mind that this is an *estimate* of biological age and might not correspond directly to chronological age because of variations in individual dental development (the same thing is true of skeletal estimates). Also keep in mind that the estimated ages are based on a human pattern of growth, and if we are looking at a very early hominin ancestor, it might be more appropriate to use an ape model for dental development. Either way, we could at least make a case for judging the individual to be an adult rather than a child.

Interpreting Behavior

In addition to interpreting the fossil remains of our ancestors, we are interested in their behavior and the environment they lived in. Paleoanthropology employs a number of methods that allow inferences of behavior to be made.

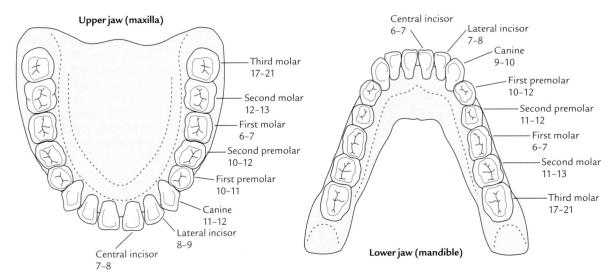

FIGURE 8.8

Average age (in years) of dental eruption for adult human teeth. (Data from Ash and Nelson 2003.)

taphonomy The study of what happens to plants and animals after they die.

Taphonomy   When describing the behavior of early hominins or other organisms, we rely on a wide variety of data to reconstruct their environment and to provide information on population size, diet, presence or absence of predators, and other ecological aspects. Often, we rely on what is found at a given site other than the fossil. For example, the presence of animal bones, particularly those that are fractured, might indicate hunting. The distribution of animal bones might also give us clues regarding behavior. The types of animal bones found at human hunting sites are different from those found at carnivore sites. A major problem is figuring out how animal bones and other objects got there and what happened to them. Imagine finding the leg bone of a fossil antelope and the leg bone of a fossil hominin at the same site. How did these bones wind up in the same place? Did the hominin hunt and kill the antelope? Did a predator hunt and kill both the antelope and the hominin? Did both bones wash down a river and land at the same place even though they might have originally been separate in time and space?

Some of these questions can be answered by methods developed within the field of **taphonomy,** the study of what happens to plants and animals after they die. This field provides us with valuable information about which bones are more likely to fossilize, which bones are more likely to wash away, the distribution of bones left by a predator, the likely route of pollen dispersal in the air, and many other similar topics. Taphonomic studies also provide us with ways of finding out whether objects or fossils have been disturbed or whether they have stayed where they were first deposited. Such studies can also help us distinguish between human and natural actions. A fractured leg bone of a deer might result from normal wear and tear on a fossil or might reflect the action of a prehistoric hunter. By understanding what happens to fossils in general, we are in a better position to infer what happened to *specific* fossils.

Paleoecology   When reconstructing the past, we need to know more than just what early organisms looked like. We also need to know about the environment in which they lived. What did they eat? Were they predators or prey? What types of vegetation were available? Where were water sources? These questions, and many others, involve **paleoecology,** the study of ancient environments.

One example of the many methods used in reconstructing ancient environments is **palynology,** the study of fossil pollen. By looking at the types of pollen found at a given site, experts can identify the specific types of plants that existed at that time. They can then make inferences about yearly and seasonal changes in temperature and rainfall based on the relative proportion of plant species. Further information on vegetation can be extracted from analysis of fossil teeth. Microscopic analysis of scratch patterns on teeth can tell us whether an organism relied more heavily on leaves, fruits, or meat.

Diet can also be inferred using **stable isotope analysis** of fossil remains. Stable isotopes are nonradioactive isotopes and so remain stable over time and are preserved in fossil remains. Ratios of different isotopes can provide information on diet. In carbon isotope analysis, for example, the ratio of ^{13}C to ^{12}C in animal bones is different depending on the type of plant predominantly eaten, such as grasses versus trees and other plants. If the animal eats other animals, then this analysis could tell us about the diet of the animal being eaten and, by extension, the type of animal. Other stable isotope ratios make use of nitrogen, hydrogen, oxygen, and strontium (Schoeninger 1995; Conroy 2005). Each type of analysis can add to the picture of ancient diets and environments.

Experimental Archaeology   Humans are toolmakers and tool users. Given that many ape species, particularly the chimpanzee, are also capable of toolmaking and tool use, it seems reasonable to assume that the ability to make and use tools was also present in the last common ancestor of humans and African apes, and therefore present throughout hominin evolution. When reconstructing the past, however, we are limited to what kinds of material remain intact over thousands and millions of years. A hominin from 4 million years ago might have used a stick to dig termites out of a mound or some other task, but we will not find that stick 4 million years later. Instead, our record of early toolmaking and tool use is necessarily limited to stone tools, which can remain intact over time.

There is therefore a justifiable interest in the remains of stone tools used by our ancestors and discovered by archaeologists. The function of such tools is less clear. Were they used to butcher animals? Were they used to break open bone? There is also the question of how they were made. **Experimental archaeology** involves learning how to make and use tools in the present in order to shed some light on toolmaking and tool use in ancient times. For example, by attempting to re-create a stone tool, the experimental archaeologist can learn about the kinds of materials that work best, possible methods of manufacture, and potential uses. Likewise, if a question comes up regarding the efficiency of a small stone blade for butchering, the experimental archaeologist can test the idea by trying to butcher an animal with such a

paleoecology The study of ancient environments.

palynology The study of fossil pollen.

stable isotope analysis Analysis of the ratio of stable (nonradioactive) isotopes of elements such as carbon that provides information about ancient diet.

experimental archaeology A field of archaeology that involves the study of the manufacture and use of tools in order to learn how they were made and used by people in the past.

tool to see if it can be done, and how. Experimental archaeology can provide insight into other aspects of behavior as well. For example, Schick and Toth (1993) found that the pattern of flaking of a stone tool core was different in right-handed and left-handed people, an observation that was then extended to past remains to discover similar proportions of right- and left-handed people in the past.

Nonhuman Primate Models for Behavior   What can we say about the social behavior of our distant ancestors? Can we make any inferences about mating patterns or social structure or dispersal patterns, among other behaviors? Paleoanthropology relies on insights into behavior during human evolution by using comparative data from studies on nonhuman primates. As was shown in Chapters 5 and 6, primate behavior is quite variable, and that leaves us with the question of *which* primate species, if any, should be used to provide insights into early hominin evolution.

There have been several approaches to this question. Some early studies of baboons focused on aspects of baboon society and behavior, such as large multimale/multifemale societies with strong male dominance hierarchies, as potential models for early hominin behavior. The reason for the baboon analogy was environmental; many baboon groups live in the savannas of Africa, the same type of environment thought to have been inhabited by the earliest hominins. If certain behaviors represented adaptations to the savanna-particular environment, then we might expect that our earliest ancestors also shared such behaviors. The recognition that baboon societies, environments, and behaviors were more variable than first thought led to the baboon's falling out of favor as a possible model for hominin behavior, in light of the difficulty of making generalizations even within a species, let alone predictions about ancestors (Strum and Mitchell 1987).

Many paleoanthropologists now argue that a better choice of model would be one of the African apes because they are most closely related to us. Chimpanzees have long served as possible models for early hominin behavior, but some scholars have also argued for using the bonobo. However, the choice of chimpanzee or bonobo is problematic because these species split from each other *after* the hominin line diverged. As such, they are equally related to us. Which one should serve as the common ancestor for a given behavior? In some cases, we would get different answers—for example, when looking at patterns of dominance, given that bonobos tend to show strong patterns of female dominance, whereas chimpanzees do not.

Primatologist Richard Wrangham (1987b) has suggested an alternative approach—comparing human behaviors to those of the three African apes (gorillas, chimpanzees, and bonobos). He argues that since all four species share a common ancestor, any behaviors that are shared at present in all four species likely have been inherited from that common ancestor. Using this logic, he has suggested that the common ancestor lived in societies in which males mated with more than one female. Males also engaged in hostile relationships between social groups, and some males lived alone outside of a social group. Females dispersed from their birth group and tended not to form alliances (Wrangham 1987b; Lewin and Foley 2004).

LIFE BEFORE THE PRIMATES

The next four chapters outline the fossil record for primate and human evolution. Before moving on, it is important to understand two points about primate and human evolution. First, *all* of the events covered in the next four chapters took place within a relatively short time, geologically speaking. The first primates appeared about 50 million years ago, and the first hominins about 6 million years ago. These dates seem incredibly remote, but when we compare them to the 4.6-*billion*-year history of the planet, they are recent events (see the Special Topic box). The second point is that primates and humans did not appear out of nowhere, but instead evolved from earlier mammals. Therefore, in order to place primates and humans in evolutionary perspective, we need to review some basic features of mammalian evolution, which in turn requires that we look more generally at vertebrate evolution, and so forth back into the past. Although the focus of the next four chapters is on primate and human evolution, it is useful to review briefly some of the major events that preceded these events.

The Origin of Life

Geologists and paleontologists divide the history of the earth into four **eons,** which are further broken down into **eras,** which are still further broken down into **periods.** Each of these units of time is defined by geologic and/or biological events observed in the fossil record and dated with long-range dating methods.

Almost 90 percent of the earth's 4.6-billion-year history is often referred to as the **Precambrian,** a period that includes the first three of four eons. The **Hadean eon** (4,600–3,800 Ma) covers the time from the origin of the earth prior to any fossil evidence for life. The **Archean eon** (3,800–2,500 Ma) is characterized by fossil evidence for the first forms of life, which were simple single-celled organisms. In the **Proterozoic eon** (2,500–542 Ma), there was a transition to an oxygen atmosphere, and the first simple multicelled organisms appeared.

Although the fossil record preserves some of the earliest life in the Archean and Proterozoic eons, we lack direct evidence for the initial origin of life, generally thought to be a period of prebiological chemical evolution. We must rely instead on knowledge of the early conditions of the planet and combine these observations with laboratory evidence suggesting possible origins of life (Schopf 1999).

Vertebrate Evolution

The fourth geologic eon is the **Phanerozoic eon,** which covers the last 542 million years of earth's history and is characterized by the rapid origin and continued evolution of more complex life forms. In the beginning of this eon, the first vertebrates appeared, which eventually evolved into the five classes of vertebrates that live today—fish, amphibians, reptiles, birds, and mammals. The Phanerozoic eon is broken down into three geologic eras: Paleozoic, Mesozoic, and Cenozoic. Table 8.1 lists the eras and periods of the Phanerozoic eon and the major evolutionary events that occurred during each.

eon A major subdivision of geologic time.

era A subdivision of a geologic eon.

period A subdivision of a geologic era.

Precambrian A term that is used informally to refer to earth's history before the Cambrian period of the Paleozoic era. Precambrian time includes the Hadean, Archean, and Proterozoic eons, and lasted from 4,600 million to 542 million years ago.

Hadean eon The first geologic eon, dating from 4,600 to 3,800 Ma, which occurred before the oldest fossil evidence of life.

Archean eon The second geologic eon, dating from 3,800 to 2,500 Ma, characterized by the appearance of the first single-celled organisms.

Proterozoic eon The third geologic eon, dating from 2,500 to 542 Ma, characterized by the appearance of the first simple multicelled organisms.

Phanerozoic eon The fourth geologic eon, covering the past 542 million years.

A Perspective on Geologic Time

We lose sight of the immense age of the universe (roughly 14 billion years) and the earth (4.6 billion years) because we are not used to dealing with such large numbers. To many of us, the difference between a million and a billion years is hard to fathom because both numbers are so extremely large relative to our own much shorter life span. The immensity of geologic time is very apparent when considering the relative length of human evolution. Anatomically modern humans have been around for 200,000 years, and the earliest hominins (essentially bipedal apes—see Chapter 10) date back about 6 million years. Both numbers seem very large when we consider that humans live a maximum of 120 years. As a consequence, it becomes difficult for us to grasp intuitively the relative ages of different evolutionary events.

The late astronomer Carl Sagan (1977) used an analogy he called the "Cosmic Calendar" to help put these dates into perspective by relating the age of the universe to a single year. A similar approach is used in the accompanying figure by equating the age of the earth (4.6 billion years) to the length of a football field—100 yards. Imagine standing on a football field where one end represents the origin of the earth and the other end, 100 yards away, represents today. On this scale, you have to travel almost 25 yards to get to the origin of the first single-celled organisms, and almost 87 yards to get to the first forms of simple multi-celled life! The first vertebrates, which in real time appeared about 500 million years ago, are over 89 yards away.

The inset on the figure shows a close-up of the last 10 yards of the football field. Mammals do not appear until almost 96 yards, and the dinosaurs become extinct at over 98.5 yards. In terms of human evolution, the first hominins appear at about 99 yards, 2 feet, 7 inches. Other significant and ancient events are not shown in the figure because they would all be crowded together in the last few inches of the field. The first stone tools are found at 99 yards, 2 feet, 10 inches. The first modern humans appear at 99 yards, 2 feet, 11.9 inches. The origin of agriculture, which in real time began 12,000 years ago and which most of us consider quite "ancient," would occur at 99 yards, 2 feet, 11.99 inches. The first civilizations appear at 99 yards, 2 feet, 11.995 inches. Thus, all of recorded history took place within the last five-thousandths of an inch, which is slightly more than the average thickness of human hair! This simple computational exercise shows exactly how recent human history and evolution has been. It also shows how long it took for the initial steps in the origin and evolution of life on earth.

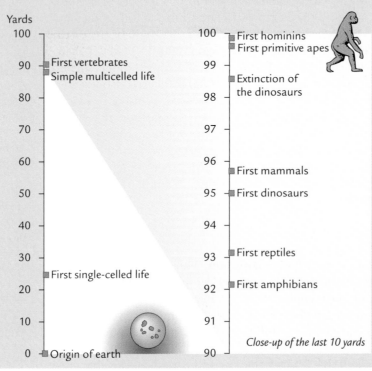

Yards

100 —
90 — ■ First vertebrates
     ■ Simple multicelled life
80 —
70 —
60 —
50 —
40 —
30 —
20 — ■ First single-celled life
10 —
0 — ■ Origin of earth

100 — ■ First hominins
     ■ First primitive apes
99 —
     ■ Extinction of the dinosaurs
98 —
97 —
96 — ■ First mammals
95 — ■ First dinosaurs
94 —
93 — ■ First reptiles
92 — ■ First amphibians
91 —
90 —

Close-up of the last 10 yards

TABLE 8.1	Geologic Eras and Periods of the Phanerozoic Eon		
Era	*Period*	*Millions of Years Ago*	*Major Evolutionary Events*
Cenozoic	Neogene	23.0–today	Origin and evolution of hominoids and hominins
	Paleogene	65.5–23.0	Origin and evolution of many mammals, including first prosimians and anthropoids
Mesozoic	Cretaceous	145.5–65.5	Extinction of dinosaurs; first birds and placental mammals
	Jurassic	199.6–145.5	Dinosaurs dominate; first bird-like reptiles
	Triassic	251.0–199.6	First dinosaurs; first egg-laying mammals
Paleozoic	Permian	299.0–251.0	Radiation of reptiles; first mammal-like reptiles
	Carboniferous	359.2–299.0	Radiation of amphibians; first reptiles and insects
	Devonian	416.0–359.2	Many fish; first amphibians; first forests
	Silurian	443.7–416.0	First fish with jaws; first land plants
	Ordovician	488.3–443.7	Early vertebrates, including jawless fish; trilobites and many other invertebrates
	Cambrian	542.0–488.3	"Explosion" of life; marine invertebrates

Source: Dates from Gradstein et al. (2004).

The Paleozoic Era The **Paleozoic era** is the term given for the time period between 542 million and 251 million years ago. At the Cambrian period at the beginning of the Paleozoic era, there was a rapid diversification of many complex multicelled organisms, sometimes referred to as the "Cambrian explosion." As we have fossil evidence of life before this time, the "explosion" marks a time of rapid evolution and not a sudden origin (Ridley 2004). Of particular interest is the origin of the first vertebrates, the primitive jawless fish. Over time, some of these early vertebrates adapted to living partially on land—the first primitive amphibians. The recently discovered fossil vertebrate *Tiktaalik* documents the transition from early fish to tetrapods (vertebrates with limbs) (Daeschler et al. 2006). Later in the Paleozoic era, complete adaptation to living on land occurred in the first primitive reptiles.

Mammals and birds eventually evolved from reptiles. The first primitive reptiles split into two major evolutionary lines. One line ultimately led to modern-day reptiles, as well as dinosaurs and birds. The other group was the **therapsids,** often referred to as the "mammal-like reptiles." The therapsids had many anatomical features that were reptilian. They also possessed certain characteristics that are mammalian, such as different types of teeth and greater emphasis on chewing food. The therapsids are accordingly labeled as "mammal-like" reptiles, and they represent the beginning of transitions that eventually led to later mammals. Therapsids underwent an adaptive radiation in the Permian period of the Paleozoic era, exhibiting a wide variety of shapes and sizes. Dental adaptations made the therapsids well suited to life on land, allowing them to forage and hunt. Although this group was highly successful for a time, they ultimately declined following the adaptive radiation of dinosaurs in the Mesozoic era.

Paleozoic era The first era of the Phanerozoic eon, dating from 542 to 251 Ma, when the first vertebrates appeared.

therapsids An early group of mammal-like reptiles, ancestors of later mammals.

FIGURE 8.9

Two well-known dinosaurs: *Triceratops* (*top*) and *Tyrannosaurus* (*bottom*). Dinosaurs were the dominant form of life on land during the Mesozoic era. The extinction of the dinosaurs (and other life forms) 65 million years ago created new opportunities for the evolution of mammals.

Mesozoic era The second geologic era of the Phanerozoic eon, dating from 251 to 65.5 Ma, when the dinosaurs were dominant and when mammals and birds appeared.

The Mesozoic Era   The **Mesozoic era,** lasting from 251 million to 65.5 million years ago, is often called the "Age of Dinosaurs" because it was a time when dinosaurs were the dominant form of life on land (Figure 8.9). The major characteristic of the dinosaurs was the modification of the leg and pelvic structures. Many dinosaurs were bipedal, and some appear to have been extremely quick movers and efficient walkers and runners (Wilford 1985). As the dinosaurs became more dominant, the therapsids declined and eventually became extinct. Before they died out, however, some therapsids evolved to become the first "true mammals," by roughly 200 million years ago.

During the Triassic period, the monotremes, or egg-laying mammals, evolved. Some, such as the platypus of Australia, have survived until the present day. The first placental mammals evolved during the Jurassic period, which was the heyday of the dinosaurs. Bird-like reptiles also evolved during this time. The end of the Cretaceous period is marked by a mass extinction, when the dinosaurs and many other organisms became extinct.

What caused this mass extinction? The most accepted hypothesis is that an asteroid or comet hit the earth with tremendous force, kicking up vast clouds of dust and blocking the sun. Temperatures dropped, and many plant forms became extinct. As plants died, so did the plant eaters and those who ate the plant eaters. As such, the entire ecology of the planet shifted following this mass extinction. There is considerable geologic evidence to support the hypothesis of an extraterrestrial impact (e.g., Sheehan et al. 1991).

The Cenozoic Era When the dinosaurs died out, a variety of opportunities opened up for the mammals, which underwent a series of adaptive radiations that filled vacant environmental niches. The last 65.5 million years of earth's history is known as the **Cenozoic era,** often called the "Age of Mammals" because of the rise of mammals in the wake of the extinction of the dinosaurs. During this time, all modern groups of mammals evolved, including the primates. The earliest primates appeared by 50 million years ago, the early primitive apes by 20 million years ago, and the first hominins by around 6 million years ago. The history of primate and hominin evolution is covered in the next three chapters.

Cenozoic era The third and most recent geologic era of the Phanerozoic eon, dating to the last 65.5 Ma. Primate and human evolution occurs during the Cenozoic era.

Summary

Paleoanthropology is a multidisciplinary approach to the analysis of primate and human evolution, relying primarily on information from the fossil record (and the archaeological record for human evolution). Dating methods provide the means by which to place fossils and other ancient data in sequence over time. Relative dating methods provide information on which samples are older or younger, but not the exact age. A commonly used relative dating method is stratigraphy, which makes inferences about age from a specimen's position in geologic strata—the deeper the specimen, the older it is. Chronometric dating methods make use of radioactive decay and other physical phenomena to provide an estimate of the actual age of a specimen. Commonly used methods of chronometric dating include carbon-14 dating for relatively "recent" specimens (less than 50,000 years old) and argon dating for very ancient specimens.

The fossil record provides a direct view on what our ancestors looked like and how they adapted. Analysis of fossil remains involves considering the relationships of a given specimen to known species in order to classify it into a known species or to designate a new species. Anatomical variation within species, such as due to sex and age, is important in distinguishing between fossil remains. Reconstruction of our ancestor's behavior makes use of information we can obtain from ancient environments including diet. Analysis of the archaeological record helps us understand human evolution over the past 2.5 million years, following the origin of stone tool technology. Our understanding of the creation and function of stone tools is enhanced through experimental archaeology. Attempts to reconstruct behavior can also benefit by inferences made from the behavior of living primates, particularly our closest living relatives, the African apes.

The earth is 4.6 billion years old. Roughly half a billion years ago, the first vertebrates appeared, followed by the first amphibians, and then the first reptiles. The therapsids, or mammal-like reptiles, were one of the first groups of reptiles. The therapsids eventually died out under competition from the dinosaurs, but some evolved into primitive mammals. When the dinosaurs and other organisms died in a mass extinction over 65 million years ago, the mammals had the opportunity to expand, and they underwent a series of adaptive radiations. One group of mammals, the primates, appeared about 50 million years ago.

Supplemental Readings

Conroy, G. C. 2005. *Reconstructing Human Origins*, 2d ed. New York: W. W. Norton.

McKee, J. K., F. E. Poirier, and W. S. McGraw. 2005. *Understanding Human Evolution*, 5th ed. Upper Saddle River, NJ: Pearson Prentice Hall. Two comprehensive, up-to-date books on the fossil record for human evolution, each including several chapters on methods of paleoanthropological research.

Schick, K. D., and N. Toth. 1993. *Making Silent Stones Speak: Human Evolution and the Dawn of Technology*. New York: Simon and Schuster. A very readable discussion of life during the Stone Age that includes many examples of experimental archaeology.

VIRTUAL EXPLORATIONS

Visit our textbook-specific online learning center Web site at **www.mhhe.com/relethford7** to access the exercises that follow.

1. **Chronological Methods**   http://id-archserve.ucsb.edu/Anth3/Courseware/Chronology/01_Contents.html. On their Anthropology 3 Courseware site, Professors George H. Michaels and Brian M. Fagan (University of California) offer an excellent introduction to archaeological methods.

   Note: To view the videos within the exercises, you will need to have Quick Time version 4.0 or later. You can install this program free at the Quick Time Web site: http://www.apple.com/quicktime/download/win.html. Be sure to select the QuickTime only version.

   Look over the drop down menu and select "Chronological Methods 2 — Introduction": **http://id-archserve.ucsb.edu/Anth3/Courseware/Chronology/02_Introduction.html**. This exercise will help to familiarize you with fundamental methods in archaeology: relative dating and absolute dating.

   - Use the "next" button to navigate through this section.
   - Read each section in order and view the brief videos accompanying each section. The graphics will help reinforce your understanding of how paleoanthropologists are able to establish time sequence for archaeological remains and fossils.
   - First select Superposition, Stratigraphy, Cross-Dating, and Artifacts of Known Age.
   - Move on to Dendrochronology, Radiocarbon Dating, Potassium-Argon Dating, Obsidian Hydration Dating, Paleomagnetic and Archaeomagnetic Dating, Luminescence Dating, and Other Isotopic Dating Methods.

2. **Electron Spin Resonance**   http://physicsweb.org/articles/world/13/5/10. This Physicsweb May 2000 article discusses how other sciences (in this case, physics) assist paleoanthropologists in dating objects and in the discovery of new archaeological sites.

Read the section on radiocarbon dating and how this technology was successfully used in 1989 to determine the real age of the Turin Shroud.

■ How effective would radiocarbon dating be in determining the age of most fossil hominin remains? What are its limitations?
■ The "Luminescence, Spin and Magnetism" section discussed some other practical applications of observing radioactive atoms in different materials: crystal structure and tooth enamel.
■ What other practical applications of this technique offer a means of reconstructing hominin origins?
■ Ground-penetrating radar, used to produce a 3-D model of an archaeological site (and used in a scene in the Hollywood movie *Jurassic Park*), is also discussed.
■ At what type of archaeological site might this technique prove most helpful?

3. **Taphonomy & Preservation**   http://paleo.cortland.edu/tutorial/ **Taphonomy&Pres/taphonomy.htm**. This SUNY (State University of New York) Cortland Web site provides an excellent tutorial on taphonomy and preservation. Taphonomy examines what happens to an organism after its death and fossilization, until it is discovered. The site explores the process of decomposition, postmortem transport, burial, compaction, and other forces and their effect on an organism.

Paleoanthropologists can better understand and reconstruct paleoenvironments through the use of taphonomy. In doing so, they are able to describe the behavior of early hominins and gain insights on their living habits, population, and other organisms that may have lived around them.

■ What are three taphonic features that can affect a fossil?
■ What causes fragmentation?
■ What types of degradation are involved in bioerosion?
■ How might an untrained field worker misinterpret orientation?

Now click on the **"Forms of Preservation"** link: http://paleo .cortland.edu/tutorial/Taphonomy&Pres/preservation.htm. This page describes the various ways in which fossils (hominin and nonhominin) are preserved: unaltered, molds and casts, replacement and recrystallization, carbonization, and permineralization. Figure 2 on the site provides a helpful graphic illustrating the various forms.

■ Which form(s) do you imagine most often preserve hominin remains?
■ How does a specific paleoenvironment affect the type of preservation of a fossil?

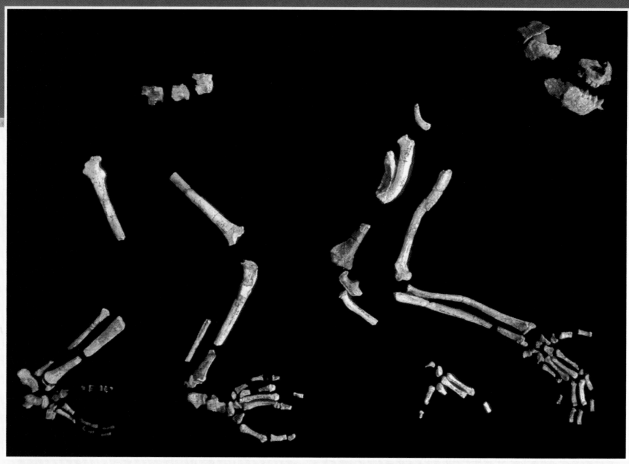

The fossil remains of *Proconsul,* one of the earliest known apes, which lived in Africa 20 million years ago. *Proconsul* had a mixture of apelike and monkey-like traits, perhaps reflecting the origin of the first apes.

Primate Origins and Evolution

As noted at the end of the previous chapter, the dinosaurs became extinct at the end of the Mesozoic era, roughly 65 million years ago. Their demise opened up numerous opportunities for other animals—notably, mammals—to expand into new environments. This adaptive radiation of mammals included the ancestors of modern-day primates. This chapter provides an overview of the major patterns of primate evolution from initial origins to the branching of African apes and the first hominins.

Modern primates did not appear instantaneously 65 million years ago. There were no monkeys, apes, or humans at that time. Rather, a group of mammals began adapting to life in the trees. These changes provided a base for further evolution, leading ultimately to modern-day primates. It is important to realize that the characteristics of modern primates discussed in Chapters 5 and 6 do not always apply to early fossil forms. Any classification based on *modern* characteristics reflects many millions of years of evolution. The further back in time we go, the harder it is to distinguish between different forms of primates. In addition, primate and primate-like species in the past exhibited an amazing diversity. The accumulating fossil record for primate evolution shows us that it not a simple matter to draw a family tree connecting ancient and modern forms of primates. We now know there were many species of prosimians, monkeys, and apes that have no living counterpart.

EARLY PRIMATE EVOLUTION

Primates evolved during the Cenozoic era, which is the past 65.5 million years. (The **epochs** of this era are listed in Table 9.1.) Primate evolution should not be thought of as a simple evolutionary "tree" with a few branches. A better analogy would be a series of "bushes" with many different branches at each stage of primate evolution. One or more adaptive radiations of primate forms occurred during each epoch. Many of the new forms became extinct, some evolved to become present-day representatives, and some moved into the next phase of primate evolution.

CHAPTER OUTLINE

- Early Primate Evolution

- Evolution of the Miocene Hominoids

- SPECIAL TOPIC: The Giant Ape

---

epoch A subdivision of a geologic period.

243

Epoch	Millions of Years Ago	Major Events in Primate Evolution
TABLE 9.1 **Epochs of the Cenozoic Era**		
Holocene	0.01–present	Humans develop agriculture and civilization; recorded history
Pleistocene	1.8–0.01	Evolution and dispersal of genus *Homo;* origin of modern humans
Pliocene	5.3–1.8	Adaptive radiation of hominins; origin of genus *Homo*
Miocene	23.0–5.3	Adaptive radiation of first hominoids; hominin origins
Oligocene	33.9–23.0	Adaptive radiation of first anthropoids
Eocene	55.8–33.9	Adaptive radiation of first true primates (primitive prosimians); first anthropoids
Paleocene	65.5–55.8	Adaptive radiation of primate-like mammals

Source: Dates from Gradstein et al. (2004).

Overview of Early Primate Evolution

Before getting into the details of primate origins and evolution, it is useful to summarize some of the major events that took place. An adaptive radiation of primate-like mammals led to the origin of what we would call "true primates." The primate-like mammals showed evidence of an initial adaptation to life in the trees. Most of these species died out, but some evolved into primitive prosimians, which were fully adapted to living in the trees. These early prosimians then underwent another adaptive radiation. Although many of these early prosimian species became extinct, some species survived to ultimately evolve into the different lines of modern prosimians. Some of the early prosimians evolved into early anthropoids. A subsequent adaptive radiation led to separate groups of New World monkeys, Old World monkeys, and the first primitive apes.

Primate Origins

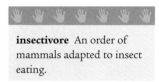

insectivore An order of mammals adapted to insect eating.

At the end of the Mesozoic era, there existed a number of mammals called **insectivores** that were arboreal and nocturnal and that ate insects. A modern-day representative of this group is the tree shrew (Figure 9.1), which illustrates the probable morphology of the ancestor of primates. Of all living mammals, the insectivores are most similar to the primates, suggesting that they are ancestral to primates. Paleoanthropologists look at the variation in this early group to try to identify forms that show the transition to the order Primates.

Continental Drift and Primate Evolution   Most of the fossil evidence on primate origins comes from deposits over 55 million years ago in North America and Europe of a group of insectivores known as the primate-like mammals. This widespread distribution may seem strange given the fact that North

FIGURE 9.1

A tree shrew, an insectivore similar in certain respects to primates.

America and Europe are now separated by the Atlantic Ocean. This was not, however, the configuration at that time. The continents continually move about on large crusted plates on top of a partially molten layer of the earth's mantle—a process known as **continental drift.** This process continues today: North America is slowly drifting away from Europe and toward Asia. The expansion of the South Atlantic has even been measured from satellites. The placement of the different continents at various times in the past is shown in Figure 9.2.

An understanding of past continental drift is crucial in interpreting the fossil evidence for primate evolution. As continents move, their environments change. When continents separate, populations become isolated; when continents join, there is an opportunity for large-scale migrations of populations. Roughly 230 million years ago, all the continents were joined together as one large land mass. By 180 million years ago, this large mass had split in two: one containing North America, Europe, and Asia, and the other containing South America, Africa, Australia, and Antarctica. By the time of the primate-like mammals, South America had split off from Africa, but North America and Europe were still joined. Thus, it is no surprise to find fossils of primate-like mammals on both continents—they represent part of the group's range on a single land mass.

The Primate-like Mammals During the **Paleocene epoch** (66–56 million years ago), we find evidence of what are referred to as "primate-like mammals" (technically known as *plesiadapiforms*), which were small creatures, usually no larger than a cat and often smaller. They were quadrupedal (four-footed) mammals whose arms and legs were well adapted for climbing. Within this general group there was considerable diversity. Fleagle (1999) lists 70 species in 25 different genera. Most of this extensive variation was in body size and dental specializations. Some of the primate-like mammals had large incisors for heavy gnawing, others had teeth better adapted for slicing, and still others had teeth adapted for eating nectar and insects. Such variation is expected from an adaptive radiation. These small insectivores had some ability to climb and thus were able to exploit many different types of food.

continental drift The movement of continental land masses on top of a partially molten layer of the earth's mantle that has altered the relative location of the continents over time.

Paleocene epoch The first epoch of the Cenozoic era, dating between 65.5 million and 55.8 million years ago. The primate-like mammals appeared during the Paleocene.

More than 200 million years ago

180 million years ago

65 million years ago

Present

FIGURE 9.2

Continental drift. More than 200 million years ago, all of the continents formed a single land mass (called Pangea). By 180 million years ago, two major land masses had formed (Laurasia and Gondwana). By 65 million years ago (the beginning of primate evolution), South America had split from Africa, but North America and Europe were still joined. (From *Human Antiquity: An Introduction to Physical Anthropology and Archaeology*, 4th ed., by Kenneth Feder and Michael Park, Fig. 3.6. Copyright © 2001 by Mayfield Publishing Company. Reprinted by permission of The McGraw-Hill Companies.)

postorbital bar The bony ring that separates the eye orbit from the back of the skull in primates.

In spite of their arboreal adaptations, these creatures are not considered true primates. A picture of the skull of one of these creatures (Figure 9.3) shows why. The front teeth are far apart from the rest of the teeth, a feature not found in primates. The eyes are located more toward the sides of the skull, unlike the forward-facing eyes of primates. In addition, the primate-like mammals lack a **postorbital bar,** a bony ring separating the orbit of the eye from the back of the skull. Primates have a postorbital bar. Despite these differences, there are some similarities of this group to modern primates, including certain dental traits and some grasping ability (Gingerich 1986; Bloch and Boyer 2002).

The First Primates   The first "true" primates appeared roughly 50–55 million years ago at the beginning of the **Eocene epoch** (56–34 million years ago). The climate during this time was warm and humid, and the predominant land environment was tropical and subtropical. Initially, the continents of Europe and North America were still joined, resulting in migration and similarity among the fossils we find in this region. Many orders of modern-day mammals first appeared during this time, including aquatic mammals (whales, porpoises, and dolphins), rodents, and horses.

Fossil primates from the Eocene epoch have been found both in North America and in Europe. During the Eocene, there was an adaptive radiation of the first true primates—the early prosimians. This adaptive radiation was part of the general increase in the diversity of mammals associated with the warming of the climate and related environmental changes, and almost 200 different primate species have been discovered (Fleagle 1999).

The Eocene forms possessed stereoscopic vision, grasping hands, and other anatomical features characteristic of primates. A picture of the skull of an Eocene primate (Figure 9.4) shows many of these changes. Compared to the Paleocene primate-like mammals, the snout is reduced and the teeth are closer together. These forms possessed a postorbital bar and had larger brain cases and features of cerebral blood supply similar to that of modern primates. The large size of the eyes of some of the Eocene primates suggests that they were still nocturnal.

These early primitive primates were similar, in a *general* sense, to living prosimians. In a rough sense, there were two basic groups of early Eocene primates. One group, primarily diurnal leaf and fruit eaters, is broadly similar to modern lemurs and lorises. The other group, primarily smaller nocturnal fruit and insect eaters, is broadly similar to modern tarsiers.

What became of these early primates? Many different species ultimately became extinct, leaving no descendants. Others evolved into the present-day prosimians. We lack sufficient data, however, to identify individual species as the ancestors of present-day prosimians. Only in a general sense can we link these two groups of early primates to living prosimians.

Models of Primate Origins   A number of models have been proposed to explain the origin of the first true primates, focusing primarily on the evolution of grasping hands and feet and stereoscopic vision. Some models propose that grasping and stereoscopic vision evolved simultaneously; others propose that grasping came first, and stereoscopic vision later.

One hypothesis of primate origins is that the transition to true primates occurred because of adaptation to an arboreal lifestyle that involved leaping and grasping. According to this view, natural selection favored grasping ability, stereoscopic vision, and increased hand–eye coordination to successfully move about in the trees (Szalay and Dagosto 1988). A second model, proposed by Cartmill (1974), is the visual predation model, whereby grasping hands and stereoscopic vision first evolved as adaptations to hunting insects. Other animals besides primates have stereoscopic vision; it is also found in cats, owls, and hawks, among others. These animals are all active hunters, an

Eocene epoch The second epoch of the Cenozoic era, dating between 55.8 million and 33.9 million years ago. The first true primates, primitive prosimians, appeared during the Eocene.

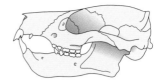

FIGURE 9.3

Side view of a skull of a Paleocene primate-like mammal. (Redrawn from John Fleagle, *Primate Adaptation and Evolution*, 1988, Academic Press, Inc., with permission from Elsevier. Stephen D. Nash, Illustrator.)

FIGURE 9.4

Side view of the skull of an Eocene primate. (Redrawn from John Fleagle, *Primate Adaptation and Evolution*, 1988, Academic Press, Inc., with permission from Elsevier. Stephen D. Nash, Illustrator.)

FIGURE 9.5

Reconstruction of *Carpolestes*, a fruit-eating, primate-like mammal that possessed a grasping foot. (Courtesy of Doug Boyer.)

Carpolestes simpsoni A species of primate-like mammal that had some derived primate traits, such as a grasping foot and an opposable big toe. This species is intermediate in many respects between primitive primate-like mammals and true primates.

activity for which the ability to gauge distance is invaluable. In addition, the ability to grasp branches would allow more successful hunting of insects on slender branches. A third model proposes that grasping hands developed for successful feeding on fruits and flowers at the ends of branches, an activity that would require the ability to anchor oneself on small branches (Susmann 1991). Although other mammals, such as squirrels, take food back to the main trunk of a tree to eat it safely, grasping hands would have allowed early primates to eat more food in less time and to do it more safely.

One way of testing these models is to examine their prediction for the sequence of evolution of grasping hands and stereoscopic vision. Both the grasping/leaping and visual predation models predict that *both* grasping and stereoscopic vision evolved at the same time, whereas the terminal branch feeding model predicts that grasping evolved first, and independently of stereoscopic vision (Sargis 2002, but see Kirk et al. 2003 for a different interpretation of the visual predation hypothesis).

Evidence on primate origins was provided by the discovery of a skeleton belonging to the species **Carpolestes simpsoni,** a primate-like mammal that lived in Wyoming between 56 million and 55 million years ago (Bloch and Boyer 2002). This species was a small, arboreal fruit eater. Although it lacked certain derived primate traits such as stereoscopic vision, it had a foot adapted for grasping and an opposable big toe, as well as a nail rather than a claw on its big toe. Thus, it is intermediate in morphology between primitive primate-like mammals and true primates (Figure 9.5).

The *Carpolestes* specimen sheds light on primate origins. Its grasping ability combined with an opposable big toe, but without forward-facing eye orbits, means that primate grasping evolved *before* stereoscopic vision. This fact, combined with the lack of specialization for leaping in the ankle, leads us to reject the grasping/leaping model of primate origins. The lack of simultaneous evolution of grasping and stereoscopic vision, combined with dental evidence pointing to *Carpolestes* having been a fruit eater, argues against the visual predation model, although this has not yet been settled entirely (Bloch and Boyer 2003; Kirk et al. 2003). In sum, the evidence supports best the hypothesis that primate grasping first evolved as an adaptation for feeding at terminal branches. It remains to be explained why leaping and stereoscopic vision later evolved in the true primates (Bloch and Boyer 2002; Sargis 2002).

Anthropoid Origins

What of the anthropoids? Although living anthropoids are more similar to tarsiers than to lemurs or lorises, identification of the first anthropoids, and their relationship to other fossil primates, is not as clear. Recent fossil discoveries have suggested that anthropoids first evolved during the Eocene epoch, perhaps as much as 50 million years ago or earlier. Debate continues over whether anthropoids first appeared in Africa or Asia (Beard 2004; Miller et al. 2005).

It is possible that anthropoids developed not from the lemur–loris group or the tarsier group but from a third, independent line in early primate evolution. It is too soon to determine which of these ideas (if any) is correct. The main lesson we have learned from recent fossil discoveries is that past diversity was much greater than we once thought, and even given our recent accumulation of data, we are unlikely to have sampled more than a fraction of early primate diversity.

Old World Anthropoids We have evidence of anthropoid fossils from the start of the **Oligocene epoch** (34–23 million years ago) at several locations in the Old World and the New World. The climate cooled during this time, and there was an expansion of grasslands and a reduction in forests. This change in climate seems to have resulted in the southward movement of primate populations, and we find little evidence of further evolution in North America or Europe. Most of the fossil evidence for anthropoid evolution is found in southern climates in Africa and South America and in parts of eastern Asia (Fleagle 1995; Covert 1997).

The Oligocene primates show the continued radiation of anthropoid forms in both the Old World and the New World. The Oligocene anthropoids show continued reduction of the snout and nasal area, indicating greater reliance on vision than on smell. In addition to the postorbital bar shared with all primates, the Oligocene anthropoids have a fully enclosed eye socket, characteristic of modern anthropoids. All of the Oligocene anthropoids were small and arboreal and were generalized quadrupeds; none show signs of specialized locomotion. Their diet appears to have consisted primarily of fruit supplemented with insects and leaves.

Oligocene epoch The third epoch of the Cenozoic era, dating between 33.9 million and 23.0 million years ago. Anthropoids underwent an adaptive radiation during the Oligocene.

FIGURE 9.6

Three-quarters view of the Oligocene anthropoid *Aegyptopithecus,* which lived about 33 million years ago. The smaller eye orbit, relative to the size of the skull, shows that this form was diurnal (nocturnal creatures have bigger eyes). *Aegyptopithecus* was once considered a possible early ape but is now recognized as an anthropoid that lived prior to the split of the Old World monkey and ape lines.

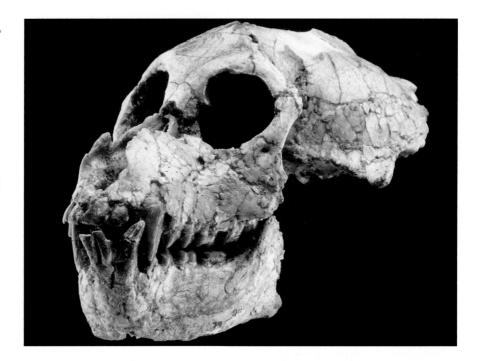

The smaller eye orbits of many early anthropoids suggests that these forms were diurnal (Figure 9.6). The transition from a nocturnal lifestyle to a diurnal lifestyle was extremely important in the later evolution of the anthropoids. Given variation in the daily schedule of living creatures, we can imagine a situation in which some ancestral primates began feeding during daylight hours. As this new environmental niche was exploited, natural selection would act to favor individuals that possessed the abilities needed for such a way of life, such as improved vision. Daylight living also offers increased opportunities for social interactions because animals can see one another at greater distances. As a result, we would expect the development of larger social groups and an increase in social behaviors.

Evolution of the New World Monkeys   What about the New World monkeys? The earliest fossil record of New World monkeys dates back roughly 30 million years (Fleagle 1999). Most of this evidence consists of fragmentary dental remains. Many of these fossils resemble living New World monkeys. Other forms have unusual features, such as narrow jaws and protruding incisors, and do not appear to have any living counterparts.

Where did the New World monkeys come from? Decades ago, it was thought that New and Old World monkeys represented a good example of parallel evolution from prosimians. However, current evidence points to enough similarities between the two groups of monkeys to make it more reasonable to assume a single origin for anthropoids somewhere in the Old World. How did the New World monkeys get to the New World? By this time, continental drift had resulted in the separation of the Old and New Worlds.

One explanation is that anthropoids reached South America by "rafting." No, this does not mean that these early primates built rafts and sailed to South America! Ocean storms often rip up clumps of land near the shore, which are then pulled out into the ocean. Sometimes these "floating islands" contain helpless animals. Often they drown, but occasionally, they will be washed up on an island or continent. Based on what we know of Atlantic Ocean currents and winds, Houle (1999) has calculated that small populations of monkeys could have survived long enough on these floating islands to complete a trans-Atlantic trip.

Present geological evidence supports this rafting hypothesis, with some researchers advocating that the monkeys rafted from North America to South America and others suggesting that they rafted from Africa to South America. At present, the evidence supports an African origin for three reasons. First, no suitable early anthropoid ancestors have been discovered in North America. Second, there is evidence of other animals (rats) rafting from Africa (Fleagle 1995). Third, New World fossil evidence points to a close similarity to African anthropoids (Flynn et al. 1995).

EVOLUTION OF THE MIOCENE HOMINOIDS

Continued evolution of the Old World anthropoids led to two major branches, one line leading to the modern Old World monkeys, and the other to the modern hominoids (apes and humans). The oldest evidence for fossil hominoids is based primarily on dental remains and comes from Old World sites dating to the **Miocene epoch** (23.0 million to 5.3 million years ago). Most Miocene mammals are fairly modern in form, and roughly half of all modern mammals were present during this time. South America and Australia were isolated due to continental drift. The land mass of **Eurasia** (a term given to the combined land masses of Europe and Asia) and Africa joined during part of the Miocene, roughly 16 million to 17 million years ago.

The Early and Middle Miocene (before 16 million years ago) was a time of heavy tropical forests, particularly in Africa. Subsequently, the climate became cooler and drier, and there was an increase in open grasslands and mixed environments consisting of open woodlands, bushlands, and savannas.

The Diversity of Miocene Hominoids

Looking at modern primates, it is apparent that there are more genera and species of monkeys than there are of apes. Monkeys are more diverse than apes. During the Miocene epoch, however, just the reverse was true—apes were incredibly diverse until the past 5 million to 10 million years. Since that time, the number of ape species has been declining. This decline is evident when we consider the diversity of fossil Miocene hominoids now known. Dozens of species are known from Africa, Asia, and Europe (Table 9.2). Compare this to the few apes alive today (see Chapter 6). In addition, remember

Miocene epoch The fourth epoch of the Cenozoic era, dating between 23.0 million and 5.3 million years ago. Several adaptive radiations of hominoids occurred during the Miocene, and the oldest known possible hominins appeared during the Late Miocene.

Eurasia The combined land masses of Europe and Asia.

TABLE 9.2   Genera of Miocene Hominoids

Region	Genus	Early Miocene	Middle Miocene	Late Miocene
Africa	*Dendropithecus*	x		
	Kalepithecus	x		
	Limnopithecus	x		
	Micropithecus	x		
	Morotopithecus	x		
	Proconsul	x		
	Rangwapithecus	x		
	Turkanapithecus	x		
	Nacholapithecus	x		
	Afropithecus	x?	x	
	Nyanzapithecus	x	x	
	Simiolus	x	x	
	Equatorius		x	
	Mabokopithecus		x	
	Kenyapithecus		x	x
	Ardipithecus			x
	Orrorin			x
	Otavipithecus			x
	Sahelanthropus			x
	Samburupithecus			x
Asia	*Dionysopithecus*	x?		
	Platydontopithecus	x?		
	Griphopithecus		x	
	Pliopithecus		x	x
	Ankarapithecus			x
	Gigantopithecus			x
	Laccopithecus			x
	Lufengpithecus			x
	Sivapithecus			x
Europe	*Anapithecus*		x	
	Griphopithecus		x	
	Plesiopliopithecus		x	
	Pierolapithecus		x	
	Dryopithecus		x	x
	Pliopithecus		x	x
	Graecopithecus			x
	Oreopithecus			x
	Ouranopithecus			x
	Sivapithecus			x

Note: Some genera are represented in both Asia and Europe. This list includes three genera (*Ardipithecus, Orrorin,* and *Sahelanthropus*) now known from the Late Miocene that have been suggested to be early hominins (see Chapter 10).

Source: Fleagle (1999), with additions from Ward et al. (1999), Haile-Selassie (2001), Senut et al. (2001), Brunet et al. (2002), Nakatsukaga et al. (2003), and Moyà-Solà et al. (2005).

that the list in Table 9.2 could be incomplete—we find new fossils, and often new genera and species, all the time. In fact, this list could be out of date by the time you look at it!

Why have the number of apes declined and the number of monkeys flourished since the Miocene? One possibility is the slow reproduction rate of modern apes. If Miocene apes were as nurturing of their offspring as modern apes are, then they may have reproduced too slowly and died out. This problem would have been exacerbated by environmental changes over time.

For the purpose of reconstructing the evolution of the apes, this past diversity creates a problem. Given that there were more species in the past than are alive today, this means that many fossil species have no living descendants. Decades ago, when the fossil record was less complete, it was tempting to identify any newly discovered fossil ape as the Miocene ancestor of one of the living apes, such as the chimpanzee or gorilla (Fleagle 1995). Today we have evidence of greater diversity in the past, but we now realize that evolution often produces initial diversity followed by later extinction of many branches. It therefore becomes more difficult to find the ancestors of modern apes. We can certainly recognize fossil apes in a general sense and see general evolutionary trends, but it is much more difficult to arrange the known fossils into a definitive evolutionary tree.

The Fossil Evidence

In general, the identification of the Miocene forms listed in Table 9.2 as *hominoid* is based on dental and cranial features. In most cases, much less is known about the **postcranial** skeleton (the skeleton below the skull), and such evidence that does exist shows characteristics different from those of modern apes. Overall, it appears that the postcranial structure of Miocene hominoids was often more generalized than that of modern apes, whose particular adaptations (e.g., knuckle walking) may be more recent. In light of the great diversity of Miocene hominoids, only a few selected forms are discussed here. Keep in mind that many other forms existed.

Proconsul   One early Miocene hominoid that appears to have evolutionary significance is the genus *Proconsul,* which lived in Africa between 21 million and 14 million years ago (Walker and Shipman 2005). Specimens placed in this genus show considerable variation, particularly in overall size, making assignment to specific species somewhat difficult. The skeletal structure of *Proconsul* shows a mixture of monkey and ape features (Figure 9.7). Like modern apes and humans, *Proconsul* did not have a tail (Ward et al. 1991). The limb proportions, however, are more like that of a monkey than an ape, with limbs of roughly the same size. In a modern ape, the front limbs are generally longer than the rear limbs, reflecting knuckle walking. The arms and hands of *Proconsul* are monkey-like, but the shoulders and elbows are more like those of apes. Analyses of the limb structure suggest that *Proconsul* was an unspecialized quadruped that lived in the trees and ate fruit (Pilbeam 1984; Walker and Teaford 1989).

postcranial Referring to that part of the skeleton below the skull.

Proconsul A genus of fossil hominoid that lived in Africa between 21 million and 14 million years ago and that shows a number of monkey characteristics.

FIGURE 9.7

Reconstructed skeleton of *Proconsul.* (Redrawn from John Fleagle, *Primate Adaptation and Evolution*, 1988, Academic Press, Inc., with permission from Elsevier. Stephen D. Nash, Illustrator.)

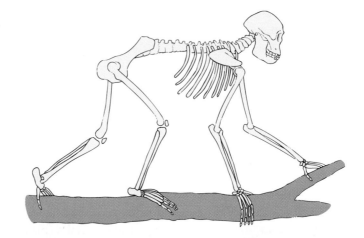

FIGURE 9.8

Side view of the skull of *Proconsul heseloni,* the smallest of several species of *Proconsul.*

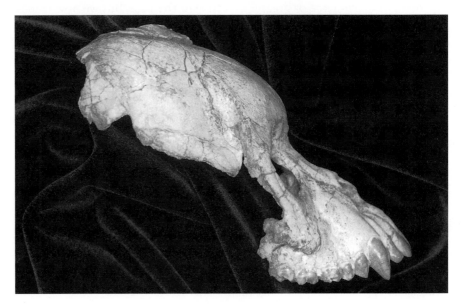

diastema A gap next to the canine tooth that allows space for the canine on the opposing jaw.

The skull of a typical *Proconsul* specimen (Figure 9.8) is more like that of an ape in that it is large relative to overall body size. The teeth also demonstrate that these forms were hominoid (Figure 9.9). The shape of the lower premolar is like that of modern apes, with a single dominant cusp rather than two more or less equal-sized cusps, as found in humans. In apes, the single large cusp rubs against, and sharpens, the upper canine tooth. Ape jaws also have a noticeable gap, called a **diastema,** next to the canine teeth, which allows the jaws to close. Imagine the problem you would have if your canines were long and protruding and you did not have a gap between the teeth in the opposite jaw for them to fit into. You would not be able to close your mouth or chew!

Overall, the teeth and jaws of *Proconsul* are similar enough to those of modern African apes that they were once thought to be direct ancestors of the chimpanzee and gorilla. Today we realize that the situation is more

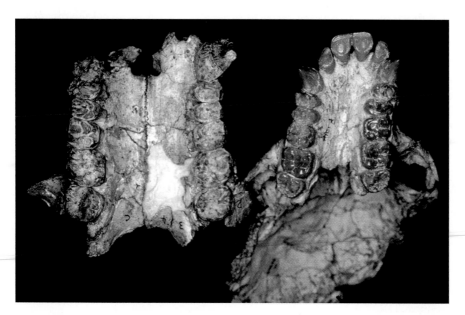

FIGURE 9.9

Two upper jaws of *Proconsul* specimens. Note the size and shape of the canine teeth.

complex than this. Environmental reconstructions show that *Proconsul* lived in the Miocene forests and ate primarily fruits. The mixture of monkey and ape traits points to them as typical of a transition form from early generalized anthropoid to what we think of as an ape. Though definitely not identical to a modern ape, their overall structure is more like that of an ape than a monkey; hence, we refer to them as an early form of hominoid.

Proconsul was adapted to forest living and was a successful group for millions of years. As the climate cooled and became drier in certain regions during the Miocene, their habitat shrank. As competition for dwindling resources increased, other hominoids developed that were more successful in dealing with the new environments.

Although *Proconsul* has long been accepted as representative of the first apes, this position has been challenged based on the discovery of a fossil ape known as **Morotopithecus,** which lived in Africa roughly 20 million years ago. The anatomy of *Morotopithecus* suggests that it moved around more like modern apes than did *Proconsul,* including climbing and arm hanging (MacLatchy 2004). The possibility exists that *Morotopithecus* was the ancestor of later apes.

Morotopithecus A genus of fossil ape that lived in Africa 20 million years ago and whose postcranial anatomy was similar in a number of ways to that of living apes.

Other Miocene Hominoids   As discussed earlier, the sheer diversity of known Miocene hominoids makes constructing specific evolutionary trees difficult. It now appears that most of the Miocene hominoid species discovered to date are not related to the living apes (Larson 1998). Among the Miocene hominoids, some species seem to be too derived to serve as ancestors of any modern-day ape and are therefore representative of extinct side branches. A good example is the genus *Gigantopithecus,* discussed in this chapter's Special Topic box.

Some Miocene hominoids show general similarity to living hominoids, but the diversity of the Miocene forms makes it difficult to determine

The Giant Ape

One of the most interesting Miocene apes found so far is *Gigantopithecus*, which literally means "giant ape." The remains of *Gigantopithecus* have been found in Asia—China, India, and Vietnam—dating back as far as 9 million years ago (Ciochon et al. 1990). The Chinese specimens may be as recent as 500,000 years ago, meaning that this ape lived at the same time as the genus *Homo*.

Although it sounds strange, *Gigantopithecus* was first found in a drugstore! Throughout much of Asia, fossil teeth and bones are ground into powder and used in various potions that are said to have healing properties. The teeth are often called "dragon's teeth" and are sold in apothecary shops. In 1935, the anthropologist Ralph von Koenigswald discovered huge teeth in one such store and later named the fossil remains *Gigantopithecus*. Since then, additional teeth and jaws have been recovered from fossil sites.

The major characteristic of *Gigantopithecus* is that it had huge molar and premolar teeth set in a massive jaw. Another interesting feature is that although the canine teeth are large, they are not that large relative to the rest of the teeth. The *relatively* smaller canines and the thick enamel on the molar teeth suggested to some that *Gigantopithecus* might be related to humans, who have the same characteristics. We now realize that Miocene ape evolution is a lot more complicated than we once thought. *Gigantopithecus* is in some ways similar to *Sivapithecus* and probably represents a side branch in Asian ape evolution.

The large teeth and jaws have always captured people's imagination. Based on the size of the teeth, some have suggested that *Gigantopithecus* might have stood over 9 feet tall! However, there are wide differences among species in the relationship between tooth size and body size, and it is more likely that *Gigantopithecus* was around 6 feet tall (which is still fairly big!). Until we find more of the body, we will not know for sure.

The large molars, thick molar enamel, small canines, and large jaws all suggest an ape that was well adapted for a diet consisting of items that were very hard to chew. In fact, the tips of the canines are worn down in a manner consistent with heavy chewing.

Some have suggested that *Gigantopithecus* is somehow related to the mythical "Abominable Snowman," presumably because of its geographic location and possible size. There is no support for this idea (nor for the existence of the Snowman). What *Gigantopithecus* really shows us is yet another example of the diversity of Miocene apes.

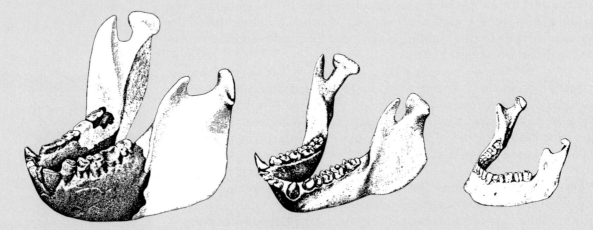

Comparison of the lower jaws of *Gigantopithecus* (*left*), a modern gorilla (*middle*), and a modern human (*right*). *Gigantopithecus* has the largest overall size but relatively small canines compared to the gorilla. (Illustrations by Tom Prentiss from *Gigantopithecus*, by E. L. Simons and P. C. Ettel, *Scientific American*, January 1970. Copyright © 1970 by Scientific American, Inc. Used with permission of Nelson H. Prentiss.)

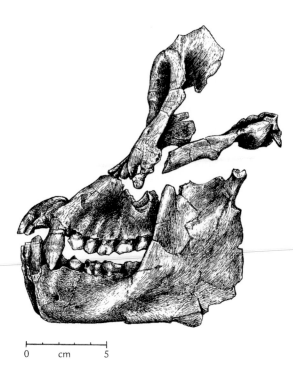

FIGURE 9.10

Side view of a *Sivapithecus* specimen from Pakistan. (From Clark Spencer Larsen, Robert M. Matter, and Daniel L. Gebo, *Human Origins: The Fossil Record*, 3d ed. Copyright © 1998 by Waveland Press, Inc., Long Grove, IL. All rights reserved. Reprinted with permission from the publisher.)

0   cm   5

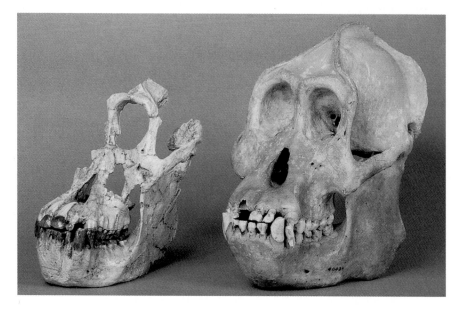

FIGURE 9.11

Comparison of the *Sivapithecus* specimen GSP 15000 (*left*) with a modern orangutan (*right*).

whether they are direct ancestors or closely related side branches. An example is the genus **Sivapithecus** (Figure 9.10), which lived in Asia between 14 million and 7 million years ago. The skull and teeth of *Sivapithecus* are very similar to modern-day orangutans (Pilbeam 1982). The overall shape of the skull, particularly when viewed from the side, is different from that of African apes but similar to the orangutan (Figure 9.11). The eye orbit of *Sivapithecus* has an

Sivapithecus A genus of fossil ape that lived in Asia between 14 million and 7 million years ago, possibly an ancestor to modern orangutans.

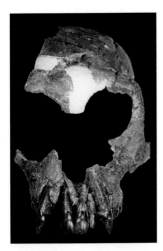

FIGURE 9.12

Frontal view of a *Dryopithecus* specimen RUD 200 from Rudabánya, Hungary. (Copyright David Begun 2003.)

Dryopithecus A genus of fossil ape that lived in Europe during the Middle and Late Miocene. This form and the related form *Ouranopithecus* have cranial traits that suggest one may have been an ancestor of African apes and humans.

molecular dating The application of methods of genetic analysis to estimate the sequence and timing of divergent evolutionary lines.

oval shape, and the two eyes are close together, both features found in the orangutan. Arm bones of *Sivapithecus,* however, are different from those of living orangutans (Pilbeam et al. 1990). Overall, the fossil evidence suggests that *Sivapithecus* was closely related to, but possibly not a direct ancestor of, the orangutan. A related form, *Lufengpithecus chiangmuanensis,* is another possible orangutan ancestor (Chaimanee et al. 2003).

It has been more difficult to determine which fossil apes are likely ancestral to later African apes and hominins. Two possible candidates are the closely related genera **Dryopithecus** and *Ouranopithecus,* both of which lived in Europe. *Dryopithecus* lived in the Middle and Late Miocene and shares a number of cranial features with living African apes and early hominins, including a long and low brain case and a lower face that tilts downward (Figure 9.12) (Kordos and Begun 2002; Begun 2003). It is interesting that *Dryopithecus* (and the similar genus *Ouranopithecus*) has been found in Europe but not Africa, suggesting a scenario whereby early apes arose in Africa, followed by dispersion of some (e.g., *Dryopithecus*) into Europe, followed by a southern movement back into Africa toward the end of the Miocene epoch due to climate change (Begun 2003).

The Genetic Evidence

In addition to fossil evidence, our interpretations of Miocene evolution must also take genetic evidence from the living hominoids into account. Since the 1960s, a comparison of the genetics of living organisms using a set of methods known as **molecular dating** has shed new light on hominoid evolution.

As noted in earlier chapters, comparison of genetic data between different species can give us a picture of the evolutionary relationships between them. If certain assumptions are made, these methods can also be used to provide an estimate of the date at which two species split from a common ancestor. When two species separate, mutations occur, and neutral mutations accumulate in each line independently. If the rate of accumulation is constant in both lines, then a comparison of molecular differences in living forms will provide us with a relative idea of how long the two species have been separated.

Imagine three species—A, B, and C—for which molecular evidence indicates that A and B are more closely related to each other than either is to C. We would hypothesize that initially species C split off from a common ancestor of all three, followed by a split of species A and B later on. Suppose we then determine through genetic comparisons that the difference between species A and B is one-third of the difference between either A or B and species C. This evidence suggests that the date of divergence of A and B was one-third that of the date of divergence between their common ancestor and species C. Now suppose that we know from fossil evidence that species C split off 12 million years ago. We can then infer that species A and B split from a common ancestor 4 million years ago because 4 million years is one-third of 12 million years. Here we have taken the molecular differences

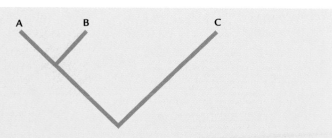

The diagram shows the genetic relationship between three hypothetical species (A, B, and C). Let us assume that the genetic distances between these species have been measured and are:

Distance between species A and species B = 2
Distance between species A and species C = 6
Distance between species B and species C = 6

Based on these data:

The distance between A and B is one-third the distance between A and C (2/6 = 1/3)
The distance between A and B is one-third the distance between B and C (2/6 = 1/3)

Therefore, the date that species A and B diverged is one-third the date that species C diverged from the common ancestor of A and B. If we know from fossil evidence that species C diverged 12 million years ago, then species A and B diverged from a common ancestor 4 million years ago (12 × 1/3 = 4).

FIGURE 9.13

Hypothetical example of molecular dating.

between species and used them as a "molecular clock," with our clock calibrated using the fossil record (Figure 9.13).

Molecular dating rests on two main assumptions. First, we assume that our calibration date is correct. As more fossil evidence accumulates, we might have to change our estimate of the date at which species C first split off. The second, more critical assumption is that neutral mutations do accumulate at the same rate in different lines. There are methods for testing this assumption, and it does appear to hold true for some molecular estimates.

Constancy in rates of mutation might seem inconceivable, given that mutations occur at random. But remember basic probability. If you flip a coin 10 times, you will not expect to get five heads and five tails. If you flip the coin 10 million times, however, you expect to get results closer to the expected 50:50 ratio. Given millions of generations, the random nature of mutations also seems constant.

The first use of molecular dating was by Sarich and Wilson (1967), who looked at differences in albumin protein and found that the difference between humans and the African apes was one-sixth that found between either and the Old World monkeys. Using the then-established estimate of 30 million years for the separation of Old World monkeys, they computed that humans and the African apes shared a common ancestor 5 million years ago. At that time, most

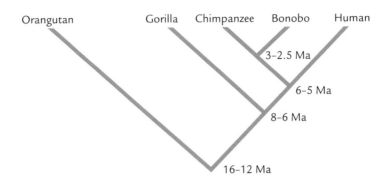

paleoanthropologists thought a date of 15 million to 20 million years ago was more likely and so disagreed strongly with Sarich and Wilson's estimate.

Since that time, a great deal of research has been done on molecular dating and its assumptions. Some researchers disputed the idea of constancy in mutation fixation rates and proposed nonlinear models in their place. Other proteins have been analyzed. Additional fossil material has been found, and new interpretations of older data made. Most paleoanthropologists now accept a much more recent split of humans and apes than was the consensus several decades ago.

Different data and different methods lead to some variation in estimates from molecular dating. Still, in general the results are consistent. Figure 9.14 shows these results superimposed on the picture of evolutionary relationships of humans and great apes that was discussed in Chapter 6. The first split was the line leading to orangutans, roughly 16 million to 12 million years ago. The other line consisted of the African hominoids (as shown in the next chapter, the first hominins arose in Africa). The gorilla line split off next, at roughly 8 million to 6 million years ago, followed by the split between the hominin and chimpanzee–bonobo lines at roughly 6 million to 5 million years ago. The chimpanzee and bonobo lines then split roughly 2.5 million years ago.

One of the more recent analyses of the ape–hominin split found a range of dates for different genetic sequences, and the authors have suggested that the actual pattern of the speciation event that led to separate hominin and chimpanzee–bonobo lines was more complex than we once thought (Patterson et al. 2006). According to their analysis, there was a partial speciation event producing different semispecies at some point before 6.3 million years ago, followed by hybridization, followed by a complete speciation. Thus, the ancestors of hominins and chimpanzees could have exchanged some genes before the final, complete evolutionary split.

Conclusions

By the early 1960s, anthropologists thought that they had reconstructed the evolutionary tree of the living hominoids and had suitable fossil species identified as the ancestors of modern species. The preliminary dental evidence suggested a small number of fossil apes dating back 20 million to 15 million years that resembled, in a general sense, presumed ancestors of gorillas, chimpanzees, and humans. We now realize that these conclusions were premature. The Miocene hominoids were much more diverse than once thought. The postcranial remains of the early forms (e.g., *Proconsul*) showed us that the earliest Miocene hominoids were quite primitive in some features and had only recently branched off from the Old World monkeys. This evidence, combined with insights from genetics and molecular dating, led to our current observation of a much later divergence of modern hominoids. Instead of an ape–human split some 20 million to 15 million years ago, we now suggest a more recent date of 8 million to 5 million years ago, with gorillas branching off earlier than the line leading to chimpanzees and bonobos.

Because there were many more hominoids in the past than live today, the obvious conclusion is that many of the fossils we find belong to species that became extinct side branches. We are able to see, in a general sense, the broad outline of Miocene evolution, but we are not able to draw a detailed and complete "family tree." During the Early Miocene, the first hominoids were primitive in many ways, and they represent a link between monkeys and apes. During the rest of the Miocene, several adaptive radiations of Miocene hominoids led to many species in Africa, Europe, and Asia. By 6 million years ago or so, the line leading to later hominins, our own ancestors, had diverged. As will be discussed in detail in the next chapter, different hominin species evolved by the end of the Miocene.

Summary

Following the extinction of the dinosaurs 65.5 million years ago, early mammal forms dispersed to new environments. Some early insectivores began to adapt more and more to life in the trees, developing grasping hands and binocular stereoscopic vision. These changes may have begun in response to the needs of insect predation and later been used to exploit additional food resources in a three-dimensional environment. The origins of primates can be traced to the primate-like mammals of the Paleocene epoch and the ancient prosimians of the Eocene. Primitive anthropoids evolved from a group of Eocene primates. The early Oligocene anthropoids ultimately gave rise to the separate lines of Old World monkeys and hominoids.

The Miocene epoch is characterized by two major adaptive radiations. In the Early Miocene, primitive hominoid forms appeared in Africa. These forms, placed in the genus *Proconsul,* were similar in some ways to later apes but were also monkey-like in a number of features. They had jaws and teeth like those of later apes and lacked a tail. Their postcranial skeleton was generalized and primitive in a number of features.

During the Middle Miocene, several new genera of hominoids evolved. These hominoids include the ancestors of present-day great apes and humans, although the specific evolutionary relationships between Miocene species and modern species are not clear at present.

We are not able to identify precisely the common ancestor of the African apes and humans. Evidence from molecular dating supports a fairly recent split, roughly 6 million to 5 million years ago. Although several genera of fossil apes could be a common ancestor (or related to a common ancestor), we cannot be definitive at this time. What is clear, however, is that there was extensive diversity in hominoids during the Miocene.

Supplemental Readings

Beard, C. 2004. *The Hunt for the Dawn Monkey: Unearthing the Origins of Monkeys, Apes, and Humans.* Berkeley: University of California Press.

Walker, A., and P. Shipman. 2005. *The Ape in the Tree: An Intellectual and Natural History of Proconsul.* Cambridge, MA: Belknap Press. Two well-written accounts of primate evolution.

VIRTUAL EXPLORATIONS

Visit our textbook-specific online learning center Web site at **www.mhhe.com/relethford7**. to access the exercises that follow.

1. **Our Primate Origins: An Introduction** **http://www.mnh.si.edu/ anthro/humanorigins/ha/primate.html**. The Smithsonian Institution's National Museum of Natural History "Human Origins Program: In Search of What Makes Us Human" Web site offers a rich assortment of valuable and informative links. Click on the "Our Primate Origins: An Introduction" link and read the title page information.

   Now follow the links:
   Eocene **http://www.mnh.si.edu/anthro/ humanorigins/faq/gt/ cenozoic/eocene.htm**
   Oligocene **http://www.mnh.si.edu/anthro/humanorigins/faq/gt/ cenozoic/ oligocene.htm**
   Miocene **http://www.mnh.si.edu/ anthro/ humanorigins/faq/gt/ cenozoic/miocene.htm**
   Pliocene **http://www.mnh.si.edu/anthro/humanorigins/faq/gt/ cenozoic/ pliocene.htm**

   Make a brief timeline to show the general dates for these four epochs. Now mark the following events on your timeline:

   - Appearance of the first primates with modern primate characteristics (grasping hands and feet, nails, reliance on vision)
   - Arrival of primates in South America
   - Appearance of ancestors of Old World monkeys and apes
   - Evolutionary split between Old World monkeys and apes
   - Diversification of apes
   - Appearance of common ancestor of chimps and humans
   - Appearance of bipedal apes

2. **Becoming Human the Documentary** http:// www.becoming human.org/news_features/item_view_fs.php?typeID=3&ID=79. Watch the video *Becoming Human: The Documentary* from The Institute of Human Origins at Arizona State University. This executable program requires that you install it on your computer. Go to the above Web site. In the upper left-hand corner of the screen, select the Mac or PC version, then download and install it. The program contains a prologue by Don Johanson, a paleoanthropologist at Arizona State University.

- There are five sections to the program: Prologue, Evidence, Anatomy, Lineages, and Culture. Each has a documentary.
- Select the Evidence segment and play the documentary section.
- Now select the "Explore a Dig" link related to work at the Hadar site.
- Place your cursor on the "virtual forward" and "virtual backward" buttons within the frame for a virtual exploration of the Hadar site.
- What are some of the different types of physical and social scientists working at the site? What types of instruments and equipment do they use?
- Set your cursor in the "Related Exhibits" section at the bottom and navigate left and right to view other interesting materials.

3. **Did Humans Evolve?** http://www.pbs.org/wgbh/evolution/ library/11/2/e_s_5.html. Watch the video *Did Humans Evolve?* (5 minutes 33 seconds) from the PBS Evolution Web site.

- How are humans related to chimps? Are humans descended from chimps, gorillas, or orangutans, or none of these?
- How long ago did apes and humans share a common ancestor? Might this chronology change in the future, or is this an established fact?
- What kind of evidence best helps us understand the relationship between humans and other apes, fossil evidence or molecular evidence? Which seems more convincing to you? Are they complementary?

4. **Our Early Kin Lived in Trees and Ancestral Handful** Read "Fossil Implies Our Early Kin Lived in Trees" from *National Geographic News* (2002): http://news.nationalgeographic.com/news/2002/11/1121 _021121_PrimateOrigins.html.

- How long ago did *Carpolestes simpsoni* live?
- Is it classified as a primate, a nonprimate mammal, or a transitional animal in primate evolution? Where has it been placed on the human evolutionary tree?

Fossil footprints at the site of Laetoli, Tanzania. These footprints, dating over 3.7 million years old, were most likely made by the species *Australopithecus afarensis*, an early hominin. The inset shows a reconstruction of what this species might have looked like.

The Beginnings of Human Evolution

How old are humans? Anthropologists are frequently asked this question, and it seems simple enough. But in fact we have no simple answer. The answer depends on how we define human beings. If we limit our question to humans who are more or less anatomically the same as living humans, the answer is roughly 200,000 years. If we include all large-brained humans, even those with a somewhat different skull shape, the answer would be several hundred thousand years. If we focus on all members of the genus *Homo,* with some significant cranial expansion and a dependence on stone tools, the answer is more than 2 million years. If we include all bipedal hominins, the answer is roughly 6 million years.

Past human evolution was not a one-step process. Humans did not emerge instantaneously from an apelike ancestor. What we are, biologically and culturally, is the product of many different evolutionary changes occurring at different times. The fossil record of human evolution is complete enough to see that the characteristics of *living* humans have evolved over time in a mosaic fashion. Fossil evidence now suggests that bipedalism first arose close to 6 million years ago, around the time of the divergence of hominins and African apes as estimated from genetic data. A number of dental changes took place over the next few million years. The first major increase in brain size, and the first use of stone tool technology, took place between 2.5 million and 2 million years ago. Brain size roughly equivalent to that of living humans appeared within the past few hundred thousand years, and modern cranial shape within the past 200,000 or so years. Many of our current cultural patterns appeared even more recently. It was only 12,000 years ago that humans began relying on agriculture and only 6,000 years ago that the first civilizations and complex state-level societies appeared. Many of the things we take for granted in our own lives today, such as automobiles, nuclear energy, and computer technology, are even more recent, many developing only in the last generation or two.

This chapter examines the beginning of the story of human evolution, focusing on the earliest hominins prior to the appearance of the genus *Homo.* The fossil species discussed in this chapter all lived in Africa between 6 million and 1 million years ago.

OVERVIEW OF HUMAN EVOLUTION

The study of human evolution is fascinating but often confusing the first time around. To follow the evolutionary history of the first hominins, you must become familiar with a multitude of names, places, and events. Just as rereading a book often yields more insight because you now have a framework within which to integrate the information, it is useful to consider the general picture of human evolution before absorbing the details.

Let us look at the broad story of human evolution (Figure 10.1 provides a graphic representation of this review). As discussed in the previous chapter, our best estimates from molecular dating suggest that the hominin line split

FIGURE 10.1

Simplified summary of hominin evolution emphasizing major evolutionary events.

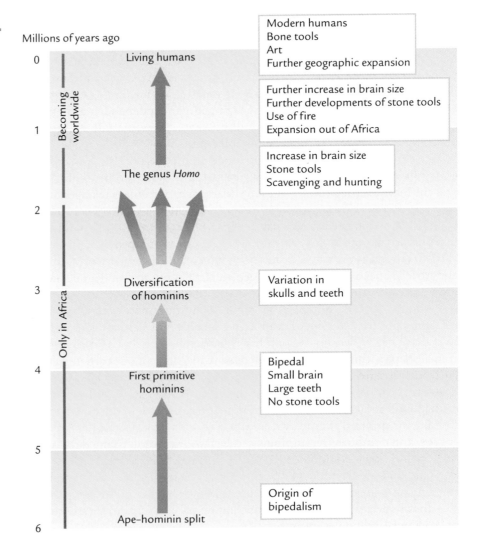

from the African apes about 6 million years ago. At present, there is fossil evidence of several possible candidates for the earliest known hominin, all dating to about 6 million years ago. One or more species of primitive hominins lived in Africa over the next few million years, most classified in the genus *Australopithecus,* and they retained their apelike features in some teeth and had ape-sized brains. These early hominins were bipedal, but they may have spent time climbing in the trees as well as walking on the ground. They foraged for food, primarily fruit, in the woodlands and savanna. By 3 million years ago, a rapid diversification led to at least two distinct lines of hominin evolution. One line led to several species known as the "robusts," so named for their large back teeth and powerful chewing muscles. The robusts were well adapted to a diet that was hard to chew, such as seeds, nuts, and hard-skinned fruits. They became extinct by 1 million years ago. The other line of hominins began to rely more and more on learned behavior and perhaps began using the first stone tools.

One species of *Australopithecus* evolved into the first members of the genus *Homo* sometime between 2.5 million and 2 million years ago. The species known as *Homo erectus* appeared in Africa by 2 million years ago, having an essentially modern skeleton, full bipedal adaptations, and a brain much larger than earlier hominins (roughly 70 percent the size of a modern human, on average). *Homo erectus* was the first hominin to expand out of Africa, moving into parts of Asia and Europe. *Homo erectus* hunted, used fire, and invented a new form of general-purpose stone tool known as the hand axe.

Brain size increased rapidly by about 700,000 years ago, and by 250,000 years ago was roughly the same as ours today. These humans still had a rather large face and a less well-rounded skull compared with modern humans, however. Anthropologists are still debating whether these "archaic" humans are an earlier stage of our own species or represent a different species. The relationship between these archaic humans and the first more "anatomically modern" humans, which appeared in Africa 200,000 years ago, is still quite controversial (and is discussed in detail in Chapter 12).

Modern humans dispersed even farther geographically, reaching Australia by 60,000 years ago and the New World 15,000–20,000 years ago. Starting 12,000 years ago, human populations in several different places developed agriculture, and the human species began to increase rapidly in number. Cities and state-level societies began about 6,000 years ago. Subsequent cultural developments took place at an ever-increasing pace. The Industrial Revolution began only 250 years ago. The use of electricity as a power source became common only during the twentieth century. Finally, it has been only about 50 years since the exploration of outer space began, another step in the geographic expansion of human beings.

This brief review shows one thing very clearly—what we are today as modern humans came about not all at the same time but at different times over millions of years. Thus, we should speak not of a single origin but rather of multiple origins.

THE FOSSIL EVIDENCE OF EARLY HOMININ EVOLUTION

In 1924, anatomist Raymond Dart discovered an early form of hominin that had humanlike teeth and walked upright but still had an ape-sized brain. Dart (1925) named this new species *Australopithecus africanus*. This find marked the beginning of a series of discoveries of fossil hominin species. During the remainder of the twentieth century and into the twenty-first century, numerous fossil discoveries have expanded on Dart's initial discovery. Many of these fossil species have been placed in the genus *Australopithecus*, and others in different genera. Regardless of genus, all of the early hominins discussed in this chapter are often referred to by the more informal name "australopiths."

At present, we have evidence for perhaps as many as 12 different species of early hominin that lived in Africa between 6 million and roughly 1.5 million years ago. This evidence has shown us that early hominin evolution was not a simple family "tree" with one species evolving into the next, but rather was a "bush" with many branches. Although there is only one hominin species alive today (us), the situation was different in the past. One of our challenges is to figure out how these different species were related to each other and to us. Which ones were our direct ancestors, and which ones represent side branches?

Despite the diversity in species of early hominins, we do see some general characteristics that are shared by all of the early hominins discussed in this chapter. All are classified as hominin because they show evidence, direct or indirect, of being bipedal (although, as noted below, some of this evidence for the earliest possible hominins is being debated). The first hominins had small,

TABLE 10.1   Cranial Capacities in Cubic Centimeters for Some Early Hominin Species Compared with Chimpanzees and Humans

Species	Cranial Capacity (cc)	Reference
Sahelanthropus tchadensis[1]	320–380?	6
Australopithecus afarensis	433	2
Australopithecus aethiopicus[2]	410	5
Australopithecus robustus[2]	476	5
Australopithecus boisei	465	3, 5
Australopithecus africanus	451	5
Australopithecus garhi[2]	450	4
Chimpanzees	385	1
Homo sapiens	1,350	1

[1]Range of the preliminary estimates for a single specimen.
[2]Based on a single specimen.

References: 1. Tobias (1971); 2. Aiello and Dunbar (1993); 3. Suwa et al. (1997); 4. Asfaw et al. (1999); 5. Falk et al. (2000); 6. Brunet et al. (2002).

TABLE 10.2 Estimates of Body Weight for Several Early Hominin Species Compared with Chimpanzees

Species	Males		Females	
	Kilograms	Pounds	Kilograms	Pounds
Australopithecus afarensis	45	99	29	64
Australopithecus robustus	40	88	32	71
Australopithecus boisei	49	108	34	75
Australopithecus africanus	41	90	30	66
Chimpanzees	45	99	37	82

Source: Data from McHenry (1992) for early hominins (weights for early hominins estimated from the size of leg joints) and Leutenegger (1982) for chimpanzees.

TABLE 10.3 Estimate of Height for Several Early Hominin Species Compared with Living Humans

Species	Males		Females	
	Centimeters	Feet/Inches	Centimeters	Feet/Inches
Australopithecus afarensis	151	4'11"	105	3'5"
Australopithecus robustus	132	4'4"	110	3'7"
Australopithecus boisei	137	4'6"	124	4'1"
Australopithecus africanus	138	4'6"	115	3'9"
Homo sapiens	175	5'9"	161	5'4"

Source: Data from McHenry (1992) (heights for early hominins estimated from the length of leg bones).

cranial capacities A measurement of the interior volume of the brain case measured in cubic centimeters (cc) and used as an approximate estimate of brain size.

Pliocene epoch The fifth epoch of the Cenozoic era, dating from 5.3 million to 1.8 million years ago. Numerous species of hominins evolved during the Pliocene, including the first members of the genus Homo by the end of the epoch.

ape-sized **cranial capacities,** a measure of the interior volume of the brain case measured in cubic centimeters (cc). Cranial capacities tend to average about 400–500 cc for most early hominin species, which is, on average, only slightly larger than a chimpanzee (Table 10.1). The average estimated body weight tends to be less than 100 pounds for most species (Table 10.2), and the average adult height tends to range from about 3.5 to 5 feet (Table 10.3). Some early hominin species also showed ape characteristics in the teeth.

The time span of the early hominins covered in this chapter ranges from possibly more than 6 million years ago to roughly 1.5 million years ago. This period includes portions of the Miocene epoch, the **Pliocene epoch** (5.3–1.8 Ma),

FIGURE 10.2

Location of some of the major sites in Africa where early hominin specimens have been found.

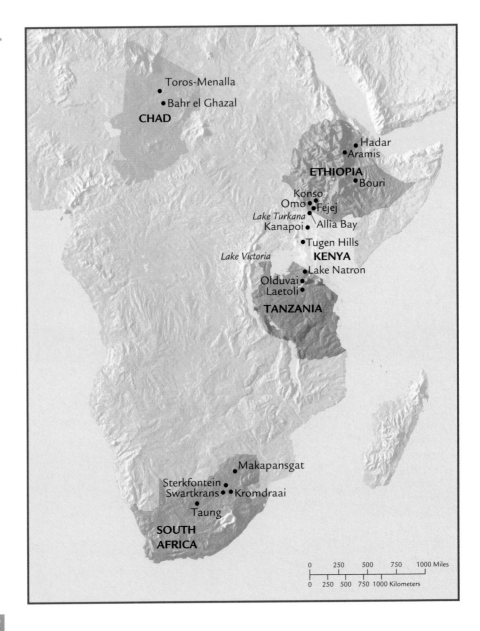

Pleistocene epoch The sixth epoch of the Cenozoic era, dating from 1.8 million to 10,000 years ago. Several species of the genus *Homo* evolved during the Pleistocene, including the first modern humans, *Homo sapiens.*

and the **Pleistocene epoch** (1.8–0.01 Ma). All of the early hominins described in this chapter have been found only in Africa, which supports Darwin's idea that Africa was the birthplace of human evolution and is consistent with the fact that our closest living relatives are the African apes. It also means that early hominins were limited to a specific environment—woodlands and tropical grasslands for the most part. Not until later in hominin evolution do we see evidence for movement out of Africa, as discussed in the next chapter.

Figure 10.2 shows the location of some of the major sites of hominins discussed in this chapter, and Table 10.4 gives details on some of these sites. Most of the early hominin species have been found at sites in South Africa

TABLE 10.4   Major Fossil Sites for Early Hominins

Species	Country	Site	Age (Ma)[1]	Reference for Age	Figure(s) in Text
Sahelanthropus tchadensis[2]	Chad	Toros-Menalla	7–6 (?)[3]	15	10.3
Orrorin tugenensis[2]	Kenya	Tugen Hills	6.0	14	
Ardipithecus kadabba[2]	Ethiopia	Middle Awash	5.8–5.2	16	
Ardipithecus ramidus[2]	Ethiopia	Aramis	4.4	3	10.4
Australopithecus anamensis	Kenya	Kanapoi	4.2–4.1	4, 7	10.5, 10.6
		Allia Bay	3.9	4	
	Ethiopia	Middle Awash	4.2–4.1	19	
Australopithecus afarensis	Kenya	West Turkana	3.4–3.3	12	
	Tanzania	Laetoli	3.7–3.5	18	10.8
	Ethiopia	Fejej	3.6	2	
		Hadar	3.4–3.0	18	10.7, 10.9, 10.10
		Maka	3.4	11	
	Chad[4]	Bahr el Ghazal	3.5	17	
Kenyanthropus platyops	Kenya	Lomekwi	3.5–3.2	13	10.11
Australopithecus aethiopicus[5]	Kenya	West Turkana	2.5	1	10.17
Australopithecus robustus[5]	Republic of	Swartkrans	2.0–1.4?	17	10.13, 10.15
	South Africa	Kromdraii	2.0?	17	
Australopithecus boisei[5]	Ethiopia	Omo	2.4	17	
		Konso	1.4	5	
	Kenya	Lake Baringo	1.4	17	
		East Turkana	1.9–1.6	17	10.14
		West Turkana	1.8	10	
	Tanzania	Olduvai Gorge	1.8	17	
		Lake Natron	1.5	6	10.12
Australopithecus africanus	Republic of	Sterkfontein	3.3–2.5?	9, 17	1.3, 10.18, 10.19
	South Africa	Makapansgat	3.2–2.9?	17	
		Taung	2.5?	10	
Australopithecus garhi	Ethiopia	Bouri	2.5	8	10.20, 10.21

[1]Question marks indicate a range in likely dates for the site/specimen.

[2]Debate continues about the hominin status of this species.

[3]Biostratigraphy shows a date between 7 and 6 Ma.

[4]It has been suggested that these specimens comprise another species, *Australopithecus bahrelghazali,* but most authors consider them as *Australopithecus afarensis.*

[5]Some anthropologists consider the robust australopiths in a separate genus, *Paranthropus,* where they are given the species names *P. aethiopicus, P. robustus,* and *P. boisei.*

References: 1. Walker et al. (1986); 2. Fleagle et al. (1991); 3. White et al. (1994); 4. Leakey et al. (1995); 5. Suwa et al. (1997); 6. Larsen et al. (1998); 7. Leakey et al. (1998); 8. Asfaw et al. (1999); 9. Clarke (1999); 10. Falk et al. (2000); 11. White et al. (2000); 12. Brown et al. (2001); 13. Leakey et al. (2001); 14. Senut et al. (2001); 15. Brunet et al. (2002); 16. Haile-Selassie et al. (2004); 17. McKee et al. (2005); 18. Kimbel et al. (2006); 19. White et al. (2006).

and East Africa. Chronometric dating has been difficult at many of the South African sites, and for many years, we were not sure of exactly how old the early South African sites were. Sites in East Africa are better dated; extensive volcanic activity in East Africa millions of years ago allows us to use argon dating at these sites.

Given the large number of species of early hominins, this section is divided into three parts, each covering a particular span of time characterized by an evolutionary stage, with discussion of individual species variation within each stage. The first part focuses on the first hominins, a number of fossil species that lived from 6+ million years ago to 4.4 million years ago. The fossil remains of these recently discovered species (all have been found since 1994) are fragmentary and not yet fully studied, but they give us evidence of the first appearance of bipedalism, the most definitive trait of hominins. The second part focuses on the "primitive hominins" that lived between 4.2 million and roughly 3 million years ago. These were small-brained bipeds that still retained primitive ape characteristics in their teeth, although over time the teeth became less primitive. The third part deals with the fossil record from approximately 3 million to 1.4 million years ago, a time characterized by a high level of diversity in hominins, with a number of species that lived at the same time. Although all of these species had human-like teeth, the teeth and jaws were much larger than in later *Homo* species. This was also a time when there was a major split in the hominins, with some species evolving massive back teeth and powerful chewing muscles as an adaptation to diet before ultimately becoming extinct, and with other, less robust species setting the stage for the later evolution of the genus *Homo*.

The First Hominins

The oldest fossil evidence of hominins dates back to roughly 6 million years ago or more in Africa. Three different forms have been proposed as early hominins—*Sahelanthropus*, *Orrorin*, and *Ardipithecus*. All three genera have been discovered since the mid-1990s, and the remains found to date are fragmentary. The most distinguishing hominin characteristic is bipedalism, and fossil evidence for bipedalism has been suggested (and debated) for all three of these early forms. All have small brains and some ape characteristics in their teeth.

Sahelanthropus At present, the oldest species thought to be hominin is *Sahelanthropus tchadensis,* discovered in Chad in Central Africa. Comparison of associated fossil animal remains with other firmly dated sites using biostratigraphy indicates that *Sahelanthropus* lived between 7 million and 6 million years ago (Brunet et al. 2002). More recent finds suggest that the older date is more appropriate (Brunet et al. 2005), although chronometric dating is needed for confirmation. The fossil remains consist of a number of jaws and teeth, but the major specimen discovered to date is a distorted partial cranium (Figure 10.3). The back of this specimen resembles an ape, and it had a small, ape-sized brain, but the face does not protrude and as such is more typical in appearance to later hominins. The teeth also show a number of hominin traits, including a small canine.

No postcranial bones have yet been found, but the structure of the base of the skull suggests bipedalism, including the position of the **foramen magnum,** the large hole in the base of the skull where the spinal cord enters. The foramen magnum in quadrupeds is located more toward the rear of the skull,

Sahelanthropus tchadensis An early possible hominin species from Africa, dating between 6 million and 7 million years ago, that has a number of hominin dental traits and may have been bipedal.

foramen magnum The large opening at the base of the skull where the spinal cord enters. This opening is located more toward the center of the skull in hominins, who are bipeds, so that the skull sits atop the spine.

5 cm

FIGURE 10.3

Views of cranial specimen
TM 266-01-060-1
(*Sahelanthropus tchadensis*):
(a) frontal view, (b) side view,
(c) top view, (d) bottom view.

whereas in bipeds it is located more toward the center. This position of the foramen magnum in *Sahelanthropus* has been debated, with resolution difficult given the distorted nature of the specimen (Wolpoff et al. 2002, but see Brunet 2002). In 2005, advanced medical-imaging and computer technology was used to create a "virtual" reconstruction of the cranium to account for deformation after death. The reconstruction shows that the angle between the front part of the face and the base of the cranium is more like that in humans than in apes, and therefore likely to have been a biped (Zollikofer et al. 2005). The significance of this angle and its effectiveness in identifying bipedalism has been debated, and some argue that *Sahelanthropus* is actually a fossil ape (Wolpoff et al. 2006). Postcranial remains will be needed to resolve the hominin status of *Sahelanthropus*.

Orrorin   The species ***Orrorin tugenensis*** is known from fragmentary remains of several individuals found in the Tugen Hills of Kenya in East Africa, dating to 6 million years ago. The fossils include a number of dental remains and some leg and arm bone fragments. According to the discoverers, the leg bone indicates that this species was a bipedal hominin, although the arm bone suggests that it still spent a fair amount of time in the trees (Senut et al. 2001). Computerized tomography scans performed on one of the leg bones suggest that the compact outer layer of the neck of the bone was thicker on the bottom, a pattern that is consistent with bipedalism because of the stress of having weight directly above (Galik et al. 2004, but see White 2006 for a critique of the method). The *Orrorin* femur also shows a groove for muscle attachment that is consistent with bipedalism.

Ardipithecus   The genus *Ardipithecus* is known from fragmentary remains found at sites at the Middle Awash in Ethiopia (Figure 10.4). Two species have been identified: ***Ardipithecus ramidus,*** dating back 4.4 million years ago, and the more primitive species ***Ardipithecus kadabba,*** dating back 5.8 million to 5.2 million years ago (White et al. 1994; Haile-Selassie et al. 2004). The major difference between the two *Ardipithecus* species is in the teeth—the earlier species has even more primitive, apelike canines.

Orrorin tugenensis An early, primitive hominin species from Africa, dating to the Late Miocene (6 Ma).

Ardipithecus ramidus An early primitive hominin species from Africa, dating between 5.8 million and 4.4 million years ago.

Ardipithecus kadabba An early primitive hominin from Africa with very apelike teeth, dating between 5.8 million and 5.2 million years ago.

FIGURE 10.4

Fragmentary remains of *Ardipithecus ramidus,* an early hominid species (dating back 4.4 Ma). Although fragmentary, the remains of *Ardipithecus* suggest a species with bipedalism but very apelike teeth.

Many of the remains are dental, and they show a number of ape features, such as large canines and thin molar enamel. Some features of the teeth are slightly more hominin in nature. Cranial remains, though very fragmentary, are apelike, with a small brain, but the position of the foramen magnum suggests that it was a biped. There are also preliminary unpublished reports of postcranial remains that support the conclusion that *Ardipithecus* was a biped (Gibbons 2006).

Evolutionary Relationships All three forms described so far have been suggested to be early hominins. All date to around 6 million years ago, which is roughly consistent with genetic estimates for the divergence of the African ape and hominin lines (although if *Sahelanthropus* is indeed as much as 7 million years old, the fit of genetic and fossil dates is not as clear). All have a number of primitive ape characteristics but also some derived dental and facial traits, though in different combinations. Some evidence suggests that all of these early forms were bipedal, although confirmation awaits further evidence, particularly more postcranial remains. The issue of the evolutionary relationships of these early forms is still up in the air. If, as current evidence suggests, they might all be hominin, then which, if any, is ancestral to the later hominins that were our ancestors? More data are needed to answer these questions.

Primitive Hominins

We have definitive evidence of at least two (and possibly three) species of primitive hominin dating between 4.2 million and 3 million years ago. The first definite hominins were bipeds that had small brains. They are often labeled "primitive" because of the retention of some apelike characteristics in their teeth and some aspects of their postcranial skeleton.

As noted in Tables 10.1–10.4, many early species of hominin have been classified into the genus ***Australopithecus,*** which literally translates as "southern ape," so named because the first species discovered in this genus was found in *South* Africa (Dart 1925). This may sound confusing given that many of the species of *Australopithecus* have been found only in *East* Africa. The reason for this confusion is that scientists have agreed to an international system of naming organisms in which the first name given takes precedence even if the name is no longer the most descriptive. Thus, after Dart named *Australopithecus* for specimens discovered in South Africa, other species were found in East Africa with the same basic characteristics (bipedal, small brain, large teeth) and were thus placed into the genus *Australopithecus*. Although confusing at times, this system is better than having everyone rename things all the time.

Australopithecus anamensis The species ***Australopithecus anamensis*** has been found at sites in Kenya and Ethiopia in East Africa dating back 4.2 million to 3.9 million years ago (Leakey et al. 1995, 1998; White et al. 2006). The first discoveries were made on the western shores of Lake Turkana in Kenya. The species name is based on the word for lake (*anam*) among the local people, the Turkana. The fossil evidence consists mostly of dental remains, as well

Australopithecus A genus of fossil hominin that lived between 4.2 million and 1 million years ago and is characterized by bipedal locomotion, small brain size, large face, and large teeth.

Australopithecus anamensis A hominin species that lived in East Africa between 4.2 million and 3.9 million years ago. It was a biped but had many primitive apelike features of the skull and teeth.

FIGURE 10.5

Evidence of bipedalism in *Australopithecus anamensis*. (*top*) Specimen KNM-KP 29285, the bottom portion of the right tibia. As shown, the joint surface at the bottom of the tibia is oriented horizontally, and the shaft of the tibia is close to perpendicular. (*bottom*) The same specimen is shown in comparison with human and chimpanzee tibias. The *A. anamensis* tibia shows the same angle of the shaft as the modern human and not like that of the chimpanzee. (Modified from Ward et al. 1999, 2001. Courtesy of Carol Ward.)

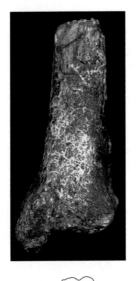

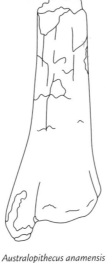
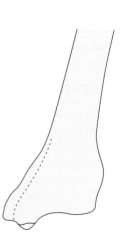

Human   *Australopithecus anamensis*   Chimpanzee

as some pieces of arm and leg bones. Though fragmentary, the remains of *A. anamensis* ("*A.*" is an abbreviation for *Australopithecus*) clearly show biped with evidence of primitive traits, particularly in the teeth.

The evidence for bipedalism is clear from the lower portion of the tibia (the larger of the two lower leg bones—see Appendix 2). The lower portion of the tibia fits together with anklebones and has a different appearance in humans and in apes. As shown in Figure 10.5, if you orient the tibia so that the bottom surface is parallel with the ground, the inclination of the shaft of the bone in a human is close to perpendicular. In an ape, however, there is a definite angle. Note from Figure 10.5 that the tibia of *A. anamensis* shows essentially the same angle as in a human being, providing definite evidence (along with evidence from other arm and leg bone remains) that this species was bipedal (Ward et al. 1999).

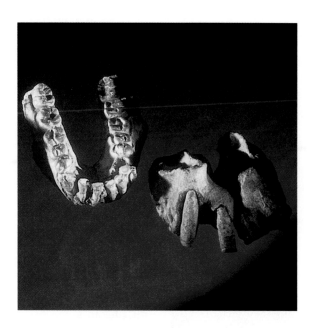

FIGURE 10.6

Some fossil specimens of *Australopithecus anamensis:* lower jaw (*left*) and upper jaw (*right*). *Australopithecus anamensis* was a biped but still had very apelike features in the jaws and teeth.

A. anamensis shows a number of primitive, apelike characteristics in the teeth (Figure 10.6). The canines tend to be fairly large, and the back teeth are in parallel rows, a feature typical of apes and unlike the more parabolic jaw shape of humans (see Figure 10.10 for comparative pictures). Overall, the mixture of primitive and derived traits in *A. anamensis,* along with its date, makes it an excellent transition between *Ardipithecus* and later hominin species (White et al. 2006). This transition is particularly clear when we look at the teeth, which become less apelike over time.

Australopithecus afarensis The best-known primitive hominin is the species ***Australopithecus afarensis,*** which lived in East Africa between 3.7 million and 3.0 million years ago. *A. afarensis* was first discovered by Donald Johanson in the 1970s at the site of Hadar in Ethiopia. The fossils collected by Johanson and colleagues date between about 3.4 million and 3.0 million years old. Additional fossils collected by Mary Leakey at the site of Laetoli in Tanzania (see Figure 10.2) date to 3.7 million years ago (Kimbel et al. 2006). Johanson and colleagues (1978) noted the close similarity between the Hadar and Laetoli finds and placed them together in their newly proposed species *Australopithecus afarensis.* The species name *afarensis* derives from the Afar region in Ethiopia where the Hadar site is located. Additional fossils of *A. afarensis* have been discovered at a number of other sites, mostly in Ethiopia. The abundance of data on this species gives us a detailed picture of its anatomy.

A. afarensis is less primitive than earlier hominins but still more primitive than later hominins, an observation that makes perfect sense in terms of evolutionary changes over time. It is more apelike in certain characteristics than later hominin species. The skull, for example, has a small brain and a face that juts out (see Figure 10.7), as well as a number of primitive features on its back and bottom (Kimbel et al. 1994). Overall, the skull looks like that of a small ape.

Australopithecus afarensis A primitive hominin found in East Africa, dating between 3.7 million and 3.0 million years ago.

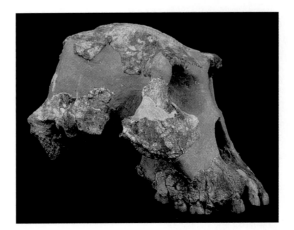

FIGURE 10.7

Side view of a cranium of *Australopithecus afarensis*.

FIGURE 10.8

Fossil footprints at the Laetoli site. These footprints date to 3.7 million years ago and represent at least two individuals, perhaps members of the species *Australopithecus afarensis*.

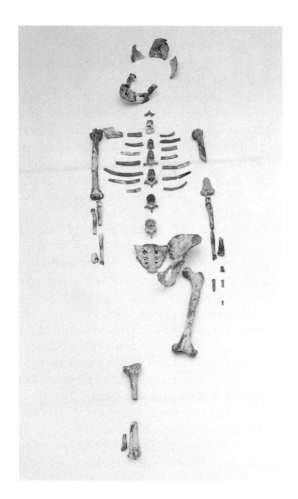

FIGURE 10.9

The skeletal remains of "Lucy," a 40 percent complete specimen of *Australopithecus afarensis.*

There is considerable evidence that *A. afarensis* was a biped, including a knee joint and fossil footprints found at Laetoli and dating back almost 3.7 million years ago (Figure 10.8). Perhaps the clearest evidence of bipedalism, and the most famous fossil of *A. afarensis,* is the partial skeleton nicknamed "Lucy," a rather complete skeleton of an adult female (Figure 10.9). As described in Chapter 8, sex and age can be determined by looking at various anatomical clues. The pelvic anatomy shows that Lucy was a female. The completeness of the arm and leg bones allows Lucy's height and weight to be estimated; she was only a bit taller than a meter (3 ft 3 in.) and weighed about 27 kg (60 lb) (McHenry 1992). Although it might be tempting to attribute Lucy's small size to childhood status, the fact that her third molar teeth (wisdom teeth) had erupted shows clearly that she was an adult when she died. And the anatomy of the pelvis and leg bones show clearly that she was bipedal.

All of the evidence indicates that *A. afarensis* was bipedal, but there is debate over *how* bipedal it was. Some have noted certain apelike tendencies in the postcranial bones, such as relatively long arms and curved finger and toe bones. Analysis of a young child specimen of *A. afarensis* has shown apelike traits in shoulder anatomy (Alemseged et al. 2006). These apelike traits have been interpreted in two ways. First, they might simply be retentions from a recent apelike origin—that is, evolutionary "leftovers" reflecting ape ancestry but having no functional significance. Second, they might indicate that despite its bipedalism *A. afarensis* did not walk exactly the way we do, had considerable climbing ability, and may have spent a fair amount of time in the trees (Stern and Susman 1993). If so, then *A. afarensis* (and perhaps other early hominin species) climbed in the trees at times but walked bipedally when on the ground. If true, then these early hominins were different from later humans, such as us, who are *obligate* bipeds. Other than an occasional acrobatic stunt, bipedalism is our *only* form of locomotion.

The teeth of *A. afarensis* are less primitive than those found in *A. anamensis*, but they are still more primitive than those of the genus *Homo*. The teeth of *A. afarensis* show a number of characteristics that are intermediate in appearance between apes and humans. As noted in earlier chapters, the teeth of modern apes and modern humans can be easily distinguished (Figure 10.10). The canines of apes are generally large and protrude past the surface of the other teeth, whereas modern humans have small, nonprojecting, rather puny canines. The canines of *A. afarensis,* however, are intermediate in appearance; they are larger and more projecting than those of modern humans, but smaller than those of most modern apes. An ape's upper jaw has a diastema (gap) between the canine and the adjacent incisor. This space is needed for the large lower canine to fit into when the ape closes its jaw. Modern humans do not have a diastema. In fact, we are often lucky to be able to get a piece of dental floss between our front teeth! The jaws of *A. afarensis* show an intermediate condition. They have a diastema, but it is smaller than that of modern apes.

Another dental difference between humans and apes is the anatomy of the lower premolar behind the canine. In apes, this lower premolar is pointed and has one cusp, which serves to sharpen the upper canine when the ape's jaw is closed. Modern humans do not have this feature (because we do not have large canines); instead, we have two cusps of the same size (which is why

FIGURE 10.10

Comparison of the teeth and upper jaws of a modern chimpanzee, *Australopithecus afarensis,* and a modern human. In most features, the teeth and jaws of *Australopithecus afarensis* are intermediate between those of modern apes and modern humans. (From *Lucy: The Beginnings of Humankind* by Donald C. Johanson and Maitland A. Edney. Drawings © 1981 Luba Dmytryk Gudz/Brill Atlanta.)

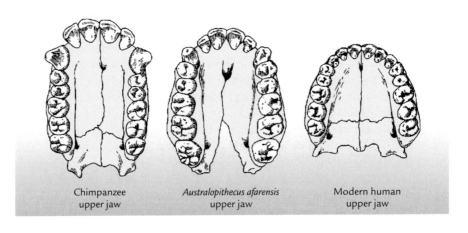

Chimpanzee
upper jaw

Australopithecus afarensis
upper jaw

Modern human
upper jaw

your dentist calls the premolar teeth "bicuspids"). In *A. afarensis,* this lower molar shows an intermediate state with two cusps, but one cusp is more developed, representing a transition from the ape condition to the human condition. Overall, most dental features of *A. afarensis* show a state that is transitional between apelike teeth and humanlike teeth. As such, *A. afarensis* is a good link between earlier and later hominins.

What can we tell about the behavior of *A. afarensis*? No evidence has been found for stone tool manufacture in most early hominin species (the species *Australopithecus garhi,* described later, is an exception). The lack of *stone* tools does not mean that early hominins did not make tools. Instead, they might have made tools from perishable materials, such as wooden digging sticks. The observation that living apes are capable of some toolmaking suggests the possibility that *A. afarensis* and other early hominins must have been at least this creative.

There is now sufficient data to suggest that *A. afarensis* was a species with considerable differences in body size between adult males and adult females (but see Reno et al. 2003 for an opposing view). If our observations based on living primates (see Chapters 5 and 6) can be applied to past species, the presence of substantial sexual dimorphism suggests that *A. afarensis* was polygynous, with one or more adult males living with several adult females, plus offspring. As noted in Chapter 8, this is expected from extrapolation of the behavior of African apes, according to Wrangham's (1987b) model of the behavior of early hominins.

Kenyanthropus platyops   For many years, the fossil evidence suggested that *A. afarensis* was the only hominin species about 4 million to 3 million years ago, forming a single link between some earlier hominin species and those that came later. In 2001, Meave Leakey and colleagues challenged this view with the discovery of fossil hominin remains that they proposed be placed in a new species, ***Kenyanthropus platyops*** (which translates as "the flat-faced man from Kenya"). Remains of *Kenyanthropus* were discovered west of Lake Turkana in Kenya in deposits dating between 3.5 million and 3.2 million years ago.

Like *A. afarensis,* these fossils show a mixture of primitive and derived features, although not the same set as found in *A. afarensis* or other early hominin species. Primitive traits include a small brain, a jutting lower face, and a small ear hole (a trait found in *A. anamensis* as well). *Kenyanthropus* also has a number of derived traits, including small molar teeth, a flat face, and a tall cheek region (Figure 10.11) (Leakey et al. 2001). The designation of *K. platyops* as a new species has been challenged in part because of problems in interpreting the very fragmented and distorted skull (White 2003). Further cranial specimens are needed to resolve this debate.

Kenyanthropus platyops A species of early hominin in East Africa, dating from 3.5 million to 3.2 million years ago. This species combines a number of primitive features (small brain, jutting face) and derived features (small molars, flat face). Its evolutionary status is unclear.

Hominin Diversity

Beginning about 3 million to 2.5 million years ago, there was an adaptive radiation of early hominins followed by additional diversity within the genus

FIGURE 10.11

Three-quarter view of the skull of *Kenyanthropus platyops,* specimen number KNM-WT 40000.

Australopithecus. The apelike characteristics of the teeth disappeared, although teeth were still larger than in modern humans. Some of these hominins evolved into forms with immense back teeth whereas others were less specialized. Clearly, the ancestors of the genus *Homo* were one of the less specialized species.

Robust Australopiths   Three species of *Australopithecus* are often referred to collectively as the **robust australopiths.** The term *robust* means "strongly constructed," in this case referring to the very large and robust back teeth, jaws, and faces relative to other hominins. Despite the name "robust," these species were not that large in terms of body size (see Tables 10.2 and 10.3). These robust species lived in Africa between 2.5 million and 1.4 million years ago, after which time they became extinct. They are not our ancestors but rather our close relatives. As with other early hominins, the robust australopiths were bipedal and had small brains. Although many anthropologists consider the robust australopiths to be part of the genus *Australopithecus,* others have suggested that they be given their own genus, *Paranthropus.*

One of the key characteristics of the robust australopiths is their large back teeth and relatively small front teeth. Apart from size, the overall structure of the teeth is quite human: The canines are nonprojecting, there is no diastema, and the lower premolar has two cusps. In terms of size, however, the robust australopith teeth are quite different from those of modern humans. The front teeth are small, both in absolute size and in relationship to the rest of the teeth. The back teeth (premolars and molars) are huge, more than four times the size of modern human back teeth in some cases (Figures 10.12 and 10.13). Note how massive the jaws are and how large the back teeth are, especially compared to the front teeth. Also note that the premolars are larger side to side than front to back. All of these features indicate heavy chewing.

robust australopiths
Species of *Australopithecus* that had very large back teeth, cheekbones, and faces, among other anatomical adaptations to heavy chewing. They lived in Africa between 2.5 million and 1.4 million years ago. Three species are generally recognized: *A. aethiopicus, A. robustus,* and *A. boisei.* Some anthropologists suggest that they be given their own genus name—*Paranthropus.*

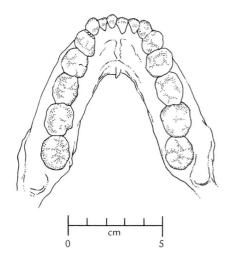

FIGURE 10.12

Lower jaw of a robust australopith (*Australopithecus boisei*) from the Lake Natron site in Tanzania. Note the small front teeth (incisors and canines) and the massive back teeth (premolars and molars). (From Clark Spencer Larsen, Robert M. Matter, and Daniel L. Gebo, *Human Origins: The Fossil Record*, 3d ed., p. 72. Copyright © 1998 Waveland Press, Inc., Long Grove, IL. All rights reserved. Reprinted with permission from the publisher.)

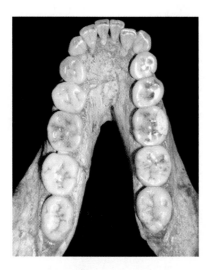

FIGURE 10.13

Lower jaw of a robust australopith (*Australopithecus robustus*), specimen SK 23, Swartkrans, Republic of South Africa. Because of distortion, the rows of the jaw are closer than they should be. Note the small front teeth and the large back teeth.

The skulls of robust australopiths also reflect heavy chewing (Figures 10.14 and 10.15). These skulls show massive dished-in faces, large flaring cheekbones, and a bony crest running down the top. All of these anatomical features are related to large jaws and back teeth and powerful chewing muscles. As shown in Figure 10.16, two muscles are responsible for closing the mouth during chewing. One, the masseter muscle, runs from the back portion of the jaw to the forward portion of the **zygomatic arch** (the cheekbone, which connects the zygomatic and temporal bones). The zygomatic arch and facial skeleton anchor the masseter muscle. In hominins with large jaws and large masseter muscles, the face and zygomatic arch must be massive to withstand the force generated by chewing. The other muscle, the temporalis, runs from the jaw up under the zygomatic arch and attaches to the sides and top of the skull. The larger the temporal muscle is, the more the zygomatic arch must flare out from the side of the skull. To anchor the temporalis muscle on the sides and top of the skull, a ridge of bone sometimes

zygomatic arch The cheekbone, formed by the connection of the zygomatic and temporal bones on the side of the skull.

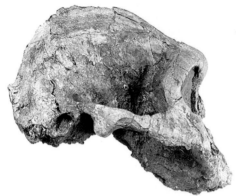

FIGURE 10.14

Side, frontal, and top views of a robust australopith (*Australopithecus boisei*) skull, specimen KNM-ER 406, from Lake Turkana, Kenya.

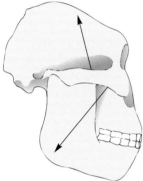

FIGURE 10.16

Skull of a robust australopith, with arrows indicating the action of chewing muscles: (*top*) temporalis, (*bottom*) masseter.

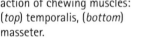

sagittal crest A ridge of bone running down the center of the top of the skull that serves to anchor chewing muscles.

Australopithecus aethiopicus The oldest robust australopith, dating to 2.5 million years ago in East Africa. It combines derived features seen in other robust australopiths with primitive features seen in *A. afarensis*.

FIGURE 10.15

Skull of a robust australopith (*Australopithecus robustus*), specimen SK 48, Swartkrans, Republic of South Africa.

develops down the center of the skull, called a **sagittal crest.** All these cranial and facial features indicate powerful chewing activity.

As noted previously, three species of robust australopiths are generally recognized. The oldest, from 2.5 million years ago, is ***Australopithecus aethiopicus*** (named after Ethiopia). *A. aethiopicus* is very robust but also shows a number of primitive cranial traits, such as the anatomy of the base of the cranium, that

FIGURE 10.17

Specimen KNM-WT 17000 from Lake Turkana, Kenya, also known as the "Black Skull" because of the color of the mineral staining. This skull dates to 2.5 million years ago. It is a robust australopith classified as *Australopithecus aethiopicus* by some and as an early example of *Australopithecus boisei* by others. It shows a mixture of specialized robust features (e.g., the sagittal crest) and primitive features (e.g., the forward jutting of the jaw).

link it to *A. afarensis* (Figure 10.17). The later two species, **Australopithecus robustus** and **Australopithecus boisei,** differ in terms of geography and size. *A. robustus* (named after its robust nature) was found in South Africa, and *A. boisei* (named after Charles Boise, who provided funding for excavation) was found in East Africa. Of the two, *A. boisei* was the more robust.

What does the morphology of the robust australopiths tell us about how they lived? The massive jaws and back teeth point to powerful chewing ability. Evidence from dental anatomy, including microscopic wear patterns on the teeth, show that all early hominins had a diverse diet that often included food that was difficult to chew, such as seeds, nuts, and hard fruits. The robust australopiths appear to have relied more regularly on such hard-to-chew food (Teaford and Ungar 2000), which is best exploited with large back teeth and massive chewing muscles.

There is no direct association of stone tools with the robust australopths. Although stone tools have been found at sites where robust forms were found, fossils of early *Homo* were found at the same sites, and most researchers suggest that *Homo*, not the robust australopiths, was the toolmaker. There is some evidence that the robust forms in South Africa could have made tools. Susman (1988) examined the hand bones of *A. robustus* and concluded that their manual dexterity meant that they *could* have made tools. The most direct evidence for tool use comes from the Swartkrans site in South Africa, where animal bones have been found with scratch patterns indicating their use as digging tools. Based on comparisons with experimentally scratched animal bones, Backwell and d'Errico (2001) concluded that these early hominins were digging for termites.

Australopithecus africanus Although debate continues regarding the specific evolutionary relationships of the robust australopiths to each other and to earlier hominins, there is general agreement that they represent a side branch in human evolution that became extinct 1.4 million

Australopithecus robustus A species of robust australopith, dating between roughly 2 million and 1.4 million years ago and found in South Africa.

Australopithecus boisei A very robust species of robust australopith, dating between 2.4 million and 1.4 million years ago and found in East Africa.

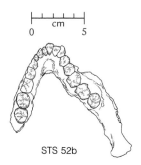

STS 52b

FIGURE 10.19

Lower jaw of *Australopithecus africanus,* specimen STS 52b, Sterkfontein, Republic of South Africa. The teeth are larger than in modern humans, but the relative proportions of front and back teeth are more similar to those of modern humans than are those of the robust australopiths. (From Clark Spencer Larsen, Robert M. Matter, and Daniel L. Gebo, *Human Origins: The Fossil Record,* 3d ed., p. 64. Copyright © 1998 Waveland Press, Inc., Long Grove, IL. All rights reserved. Reprinted with permission from the publisher.)

Australopithecus africanus A species of early hominin, dating between 3.3 million and 2.5 million years ago and found in South Africa. It is not as massive as the robust forms and may be an ancestor of the genus *Homo.*

Australopithecus garhi An early hominin, dating to 2.5 million years ago in East Africa. It differs from other australopiths in having large front and back teeth, although the back teeth are not specialized to the same extent as found in the robust australopiths.

FIGURE 10.18

Skull of *Australopithecus africanus,* specimen STS 5, Sterkfontein, Republic of South Africa.

years ago. Who, then, was our ancestor from the 3-million to 2-million-year period separating the earlier primitive hominins from species in the genus *Homo*? There are two main candidates: *Australopithecus africanus* and *Australopithecus garhi*.

A number of specimens from South Africa have been placed in the species ***Australopithecus africanus*** (named after Africa). Because of the geology of the region, South African hominin sites have always been difficult to date. Most estimates suggest that *A. africanus* lived between 3.3 million and 2.5 million years ago, although some have suggested that some specimens might date back further in time (Partridge et al. 2003). A skull of *A. africanus* is shown in Figure 10.18. Like other early hominins, it had a small brain and a large face. The face is not as massive as the robust forms, however, and there is no sagittal crest. A lower jaw of *A. africanus* is shown in Figure 10.19. Compared to the robust forms, the front teeth are not as small relative to the back teeth, but the back teeth are still larger than those of modern humans. *A. africanus* is generally considered a descendant of *A. afarensis* and may represent an ancestor of the genus *Homo,* although some anthropologists consider it another extinct side branch in hominin evolution.

Australopithecus garhi   Anthropologists agree that the robust australopiths are not our ancestors. Many have proposed *A. africanus* as the ancestor of *Homo.* Others, however, have suggested that *A. africanus* was too specialized to be our ancestor and that the genus *Homo* evolved from *A. afarensis* (Johanson and White 1979). The problem with this hypothesis, however, was that there was a gap between the last known occurrence of *A. afarensis* and the first evidence of *Homo.* If their hypothesis was correct, a suitable transitional species was needed to fill this gap.

There now appears to be a possible transition. Fossils from Ethiopia dating to 2.5 million years ago have been classified as a new species, ***Australopithecus garhi*** (the word *garhi* means "surprise" in the local Afar language) (Asfaw et al. 1999). The main specimen consists of a partial cranium

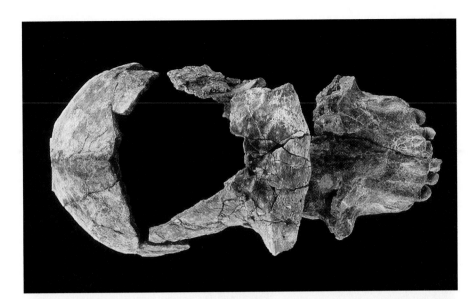

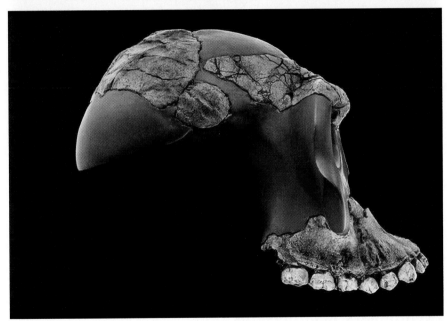

FIGURE 10.20

Top and side views of *Australopithecus garhi* skull, specimen BOU-VP-12/130.

with an upper jaw. Overall, many of its features are similar to *A. afarensis*. The skull (Figure 10.20) has a small brain size and does not have a robust anatomy. Both the front and back teeth of *A. garhi* are large (Figure 10.21), but they do not show the anatomical specializations of the robust australopiths.

It is possible that *A. garhi,* and not *A. africanus,* was the ancestor of the genus *Homo.* Because the fossil record shows the earliest evidence of *Homo* in East Africa about 2.5 million years ago, *A. garhi* is therefore "in the right place, at the right time, to be the ancestor of early *Homo*" (Asfaw et al. 1999:634). Its anatomy, compared with other hominins, fits this hypothesis.

FIGURE 10.21

Upper jaw of *Australopithecus garhi*, specimen BOU-VP-12/130. The teeth are large but do not resemble those of robust australopiths in structure. (© 1999 Luba Dmytryk Gudz/Brill Atlanta.)

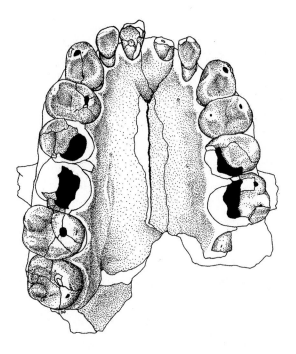

The discovery of *A. garhi* is even more significant when we consider the fact that butchered animal bones showing stone tool cut marks have been found nearby (de Heinzelin et al. 1999). This evidence suggests that *A. garhi* may have been the toolmaker. In any case, the evidence of butchering shows that by 2.5 million years ago, hominins had begun to add animal protein to their diet, a pattern continued in the evolution of the genus *Homo* (covered in the next chapter).

EVOLUTIONARY TRENDS

Given the diversity in early hominins, what conclusions can we reach regarding evolutionary trends and relationships? How were these species related? What were the major evolutionary trends, and what caused them?

Evolutionary Relationships

One of our goals is to use the available information to reconstruct the general patterns of early hominin evolution. The hominins described in this chapter thus far provide a history of evolutionary events that took place from the initial origins of the hominins and the development of bipedalism up to the origin of the genus *Homo*. We are interested, where possible, in trying to link species over time to produce a "family tree."

Historical Overview   The study of the historical development of any scientific discipline is important for a number of reasons. Because science is an ongoing, cumulative process, its current state will partially reflect past ideas and

The Piltdown Hoax

One of the main points made in this chapter is that characteristics of modern humans did not all appear at the same time. In particular, we know that bipedalism started 3.5 million years before we see any significant increase in brain size or the origin of stone tools. This finding is based on the fossil and archaeological records.

Early thinking about human origins suggested just the reverse—that brain size evolved first. Because there were few fossils to show otherwise at that time, this popular hypothesis could not then be rejected. The model predicted that the fossil record would ultimately show that, of all modern human characteristics, large brain size would be the oldest. Of course, today we have sufficient information to reject this hypothesis altogether. At the beginning of the twentieth century, however, we did not.

In fact, fossil evidence *was* found to support the antiquity of the large human brain. Between 1911 and 1915, hominin fossils were discovered at Piltdown, England, alongside stone tools and the fossils of prehistoric animals such as mastodons. A primary specimen ("Piltdown Man") consisted of a large skull and an apelike jaw. The teeth, however, were worn flat, more closely resembling the condition of human teeth. The specimen showed a mixture of ape and human traits and had a modern human brain size. It offered clear proof that large brains came first in human evolution.

Because of Piltdown, any fossils that had human characteristics but did not have the large brain were rejected, for a time, as possible human ancestors. Indeed, this helps explain the reluctance of scientists to accept *Australopithecus* as a hominin. The first australopith specimen was discovered by Raymond Dart in 1924. The specimen consisted of the face, teeth, and cranial fragments (including a cast of the brain case) of a young child. Dart named the specimen *Australopithecus africanus*. Based on cranial evidence relating to the angle at which the spinal cord entered the skull, he claimed that it was an upright walker. The brain size was apelike, as was the protruding face. The teeth, however, were more like those of humans, particularly the small canines. Here was another specimen that had a mixture of ape and human traits, but one suggesting that the large brain evolved *after* bipedalism and humanlike teeth. At the time, more people tended to support Piltdown (in fairness, some of their criticisms of *Australopithecus*, including the difficulty in interpreting the remains of children, were valid).

Some scientists, however, were more skeptical about Piltdown Man. And, eventually, continuing investigation showed that the find was a fake. In 1953, a fluorine analysis (see Chapter 8) confirmed that the jaw bones and skull bones did not come from the same time period. Closer inspection showed that the skull was that of a modern human and the jaw that of an orangutan. The teeth had been filed down, and all of the bones had been chemically treated to simulate age.

Who was responsible for the Piltdown hoax? Over the years, many different suspects have been suggested. One analysis suggests that the guilty party may have been Martin Hinton, then curator of zoology at the London Natural History Museum (Gee 1996), although this is not definite (Feder 2002). The story of Piltdown Man is often offered up as evidence that anthropologists (and other scientists) do not know what they are talking about. After all, look how easily they were fooled. This criticism misses the point altogether. Science and scientists make mistakes, and sometimes they commit outright fraud. It would be foolish to expect otherwise. Science does not represent truth per se but rather a means of arriving at the truth. When Piltdown was discovered, scientific investigation did not stop. Instead, scientists kept looking at the evidence, questioning it and various assumptions, and devising new ways of testing. As a result, the hoax was uncovered. This is how science is supposed to work.

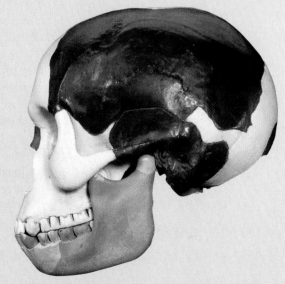

Side view of Piltdown Man. The dark-colored areas and the back part of the lower jaw were found; the rest was reconstructed. This find, which confirmed the then-popular notion that early humans had large brains and apelike jaws, was a hoax; the remains of a modern human and an orangutan were placed together at the Piltdown site.

hypotheses. Even after hypotheses have been rejected, they may continue to influence thinking in a field. Scientists do not work in a vacuum but are part of a larger culture, and current intellectual philosophies and trends can have an impact on the formulation of hypotheses and the interpretation of data.

It is also important to remember that our current knowledge is incomplete and not necessarily the final answer. It is not uncommon to read newspaper headlines such as "Fossil Discovery Overturns Previous Ideas about Human Origins" or "Fossil Discovery Uproots Human Family Tree." The impression some people get from such headlines is that anthropologists must not know much about their subject or else they would not have gotten things wrong. This impression ties in with a common belief that science produces ultimate truth and that mistakes in interpretation are indicative of serious trouble within a discipline. However, this is not how science works. Ideas are not simply accepted on faith but are tested. If shown to be wrong, they are rejected, and alternative hypotheses are constructed. Questioning and skeptical debate form the essence of scientific research.

Many hypotheses in the study of human evolution have been tested and rejected. Others have stood the test of time, some in modified form. Some examples from the study of human evolution show how ideas have been tested as new evidence accumulated and new analyses were conducted. For example, when the first species of early hominin was announced in 1925 (*A. africanus*), it went against then-current thinking that the first stage in human evolution was the origin of a larger brain, followed by the origin of bipedalism. *A. africanus,* and all the other hominins described in this chapter, shows just the reverse—bipedalism arose millions of years before there was a significant increase in the size of the brain. Although it took time, ultimately, the entire scientific community agreed that the "brains first" hypothesis was incorrect.

By the middle of the twentieth century, little was known about early hominin variation. One early debate focused on whether only a single hominin species or two or more hominin species were living at the same time. The single-species hypothesis postulated that only one hominin species was living at any one time and that the pattern of human evolution was essentially a straight line, from earliest hominin to the genus *Homo.* As more species were discovered, this view became harder and harder to maintain. There was simply too much variation at any time to lump all specimens under a single species. Eventually, the single-species hypothesis was rejected. Today, anthropologists debate exactly *how many* species lived at any one time, but they are in complete agreement that at certain times there were two or more. As time went on and new discoveries were made, we realized that the fossil record of early hominins was even more diverse. With seven new species announced since 1994, it seems likely that additional species will be found in the near future.

Family Trees   How might all these early hominins be related? Our first step in trying to answer this question is to reexamine what we know about the dates for these species. Figure 10.22 provides a picture of the dates for each of the 12 species discussed in this chapter and for the genus *Homo.* Keep in mind that these are the dates *as we currently know them.* It is entirely possible

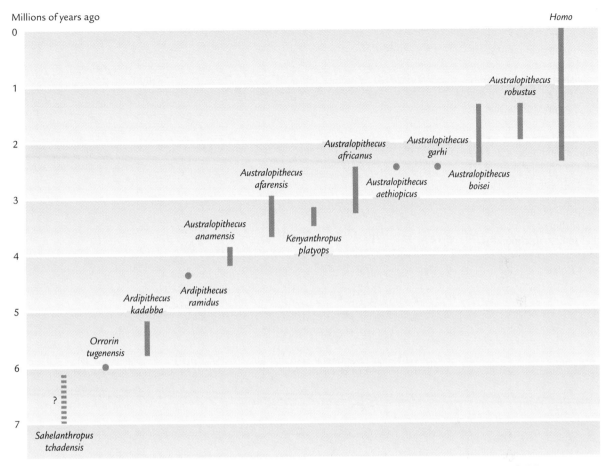

FIGURE 10.22

Known dates for hominin species. All species in the genus *Homo* have been combined for illustrative purposes. Keep in mind that this figure represents the currently known dates and that the true range in dates likely is larger for some species.

that the actual distribution of each species is greater than what we currently know. The diversity of fossil hominins, particularly between 4 million and 2 million years ago, is quite apparent in this figure.

How can these forms be linked? We look for physical similarity and, in particular, for forms that share derived characteristics not found in other species. Formal cladistic analysis has been done on many of these species, but the results are not always consistent across different traits (e.g., McHenry 1996; Strait et al. 1997). Part of the problem is the frequency of homoplasy—similarity that reflects independent evolution. For some traits, such as dental size, homoplasy seems more common than we once thought. For example, some argue that the robust australopiths are all related, but others suggest that the robust anatomy might have developed independently in different species.

Some evolutionary relationships are more definite than others. For example, the robust species *A. aethiopicus* is likely a link between *A. afarensis* and *A. boisei*. A strong argument has been made for evolutionary continuity (anagenesis) between the two *Ardipithecus* species and *A. anamensis* (White et al. 2003), and between *A. anamensis* and *A. afarensis* (Kimbel et al. 2006; White et al. 2006). Other relationships are less clear. As noted previously, two species,

FIGURE 10.23

A family tree of early hominin evolution indicating possible relationships that are better established (solid lines) and those that are subject to more debate at present (dashed lines and question marks). There are three major areas of continuing debate: (1) the evolutionary relationships of the earliest hominins (*Sahelanthropus, Orrorin,* and *Ardipithecus*), (2) the relationship of *A. robustus* to other robust australopiths, and (3) the ancestor of the genus *Homo.*

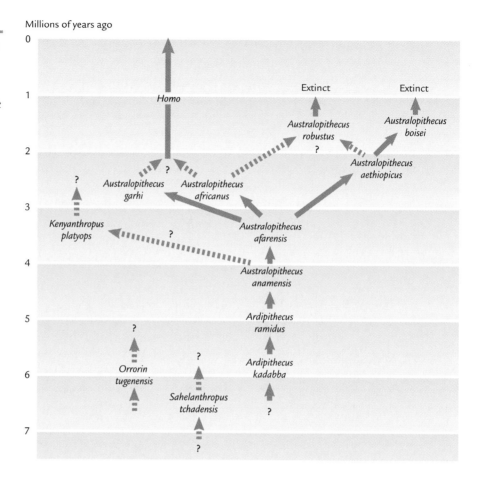

Millions of years ago

A. africanus and *A. garhi,* are possible links of early hominins with the genus *Homo.* The evolutionary relationships of newly discovered species, such as *K. platyops,* are even less clear.

Figure 10.23 represents an attempt to portray some of the current ideas regarding evolutionary relationships, as well as possible alternatives. This family tree should be taken as a summary of hypotheses, not as the final word. Regardless of which specific connections are ultimately shown to be correct, the tree depicts the basic nature of early hominin evolution—several stages of diversification starting with the earliest primitive hominins, leading to a number of diverse species by 3 million to 2 million years ago, followed by the ultimate extinction of all lines except that leading to the genus *Homo.* Some of the unresolved questions are these:

1. What are the evolutionary relationships of the earliest hominins (*Sahelanthropus, Orrorin,* and *Ardipithecus*) to each other and to later hominins? Indeed, are all of these actually hominins, or, as some anthropologists have argued, are some actually apes?

2. Did all of the robust species have a common ancestor (*A. aethiopicus*), or did some evolve independently (e.g., *A. robustus* from *A. africanus* in South Africa)?

3. Which early hominin(s) gave rise to the genus *Homo*? Indeed, did all members of early *Homo* come from the same ancestor, or was an increase in brain size an independent change?

Although the debate over the hominin family tree is fascinating (as well as confusing), it is important not to get bogged down with the specific arguments regarding who is related to whom and thereby miss the general picture and the important points. From a broad perspective, the *general* history of early human evolution is fairly clear (see Figure 10.1). The first hominins walked upright but still had a number of apelike traits. By 3 million to 2 million years ago, there were a number of different species of early hominin resulting from adaptive radiations of these bipedal organisms. From this radiation came hominins with a larger brain and a stone tool culture—the first members of the genus *Homo*. Their story will continue in Chapter 11. For the moment, we need to stop and consider the most important question about the first hominins: Why did they become bipedal?

The Origin of Bipedalism

Of all the unique traits used to define hominins, bipedalism is the oldest. Therefore, any model of hominin origins must consider the origin of bipedalism. We are talking here about the specific anatomical changes, outlined in Chapter 7, that define human bipedalism. Chimpanzees can walk upright, and bonobos frequently do so. What makes us different is that we do it all the time, and our anatomy reflects changes that make bipedalism more efficient.

Locomotion in the Hominin–African Ape Ancestor   The origin of bipedalism raises an interesting question: How did the common ancestor of African apes and hominins move about on the ground? Because we have not yet precisely identified this common ancestor, we must use reconstruction based on two basic facts. First, among living primates, the African apes are the most closely related to humans. Second, humans are bipedal, and the African apes are all knuckle walkers. (Although the African apes frequently move in other ways, their anatomy shows that knuckle walking is their main means of movement on the ground.) These two observations suggest three possibilities for the common ancestor:

1. The common ancestor was bipedal. Hominins retained bipedalism, and knuckle walking evolved in the African ape lineage.
2. The common ancestor had a different pattern of locomotion, perhaps a generalized form capable of suspensory climbing and hanging, and *both* lineages changed, with the African apes evolving knuckle walking and the hominins evolving bipedalism.
3. The common ancestor was a knuckle walker. The African apes retained this ability, and the hominin line changed, evolving bipedalism.

The first suggestion has generally not been accepted. Anatomists agree that a change from bipedalism to knuckle walking is unlikely. Of the remaining two suggestions, the second has been favored historically more often than

FIGURE 10.24

Possible evolutionary changes in locomotion based on the evidence that humans are more closely related to chimpanzees and bonobos than to gorillas. Locomotion: KW = knuckle walking, B = bipedalism, C = generalized suspensory climber. Two models are shown, one in which the common ancestor of African apes and humans was a generalized climber (C) and the other in which the common ancestor was a knuckle walker (KW). Note that if the common ancestor was a climber, then knuckle walking would have evolved twice.

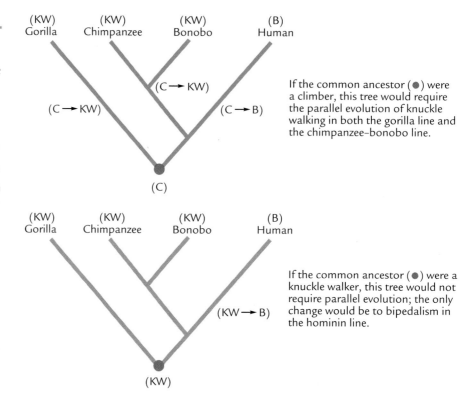

If the common ancestor (●) were a climber, this tree would require the parallel evolution of knuckle walking in both the gorilla line and the chimpanzee–bonobo line.

If the common ancestor (●) were a knuckle walker, this tree would not require parallel evolution; the only change would be to bipedalism in the hominin line.

the third. Here, the common ancestor was a hominoid that was a generalized suspensory climber in the trees and evolved in two directions once it moved to the ground, knuckle walking in the African ape line and bipedalism in the hominin line.

One problem with the idea of a climbing common ancestor is that it conflicts somewhat with evidence that chimpanzees and bonobos are genetically more similar to humans than are gorillas, and therefore diverged later than gorillas. If the common ancestor of the African apes and hominins was a climber, then knuckle walking would have to evolve twice, once in the line leading to the gorillas and again in the chimpanzee–bonobo line (Figure 10.24).

The third idea, that the common ancestor was a knuckle walker, has often been rejected on the ground that there is no indication of a knuckle-walking ancestry in early hominins or modern humans (Johanson and Edey 1981). Although others had argued that a knuckle-walking ancestry *was* compatible with hominin origins, the most convincing evidence to date comes from a comparative analysis of the wrist joint by Brian Richmond and David Strait (2000). They examined four measurements of the wrist bone associated with knuckle walking in African apes and compared living hominoids with data from four fossil hominin species. They found that two early hominins, *A. anamensis* and *A. afarensis*, were very similar to the African apes, whereas the two later hominins, *A. africanus* and *A. robustus*, were more similar to living humans. Their results show that the wrist bones of early hominins retained characteristics indicative of a knuckle-walking ancestry, which then were lost in hominin evolution. Because African apes are knuckle walkers and because the earliest hominins showed some knuckle-walking ancestry, it is reasonable to assume that the common ancestor of African apes and hominins was also a knuckle walker. If true, there are no discrepancies between the genetic and anatomic evidence.

The Environmental Context   To evaluate hypotheses regarding the origin of bipedalism, it is necessary to consider the environmental context within which bipedalism arose. The earth had been changing during the Late Miocene, resulting in a cooler, drier climate in Africa. Over time, the large forests began to shrink, leading to smaller patches of forest and woodlands surrounded by increasing grassland (savanna).

Traditional explanations for the origin of bipedalism have considered the savanna environment critical in understanding hominin origins. For many years, the oldest known fossil hominins were found in environments that were grasslands or a mix of grasslands and woodlands. Given this association, many explanations for the origin of bipedalism focused on the particular stresses imposed by a savanna existence, including greater difficulty finding food, the need to travel long distances, hotter temperatures, and greater vulnerability to predators, among others. These explanations are now being questioned based on new evidence for the environment of the *earliest* hominins (*Sahelanthropus, Orrorin,* and *Ardipithecus*). Before 4.4 million years ago, hominins did not occupy the open grasslands but lived in relatively wet forests and woodlands (Pickford and Senut 2001; Wolde-Gabriel et al. 2001).

Why Bipedalism?   The early hominins were bipedal. Although there is some anatomical evidence suggesting that they were also active climbers, it is clear from their anatomy that they walked upright on the ground. The critical question is *why* they did so. Ever since Darwin's time, hypotheses have been proposed to account for the origin of bipedalism.

Darwin offered one of the first hypotheses, focusing on the link between bipedalism and tool use. By standing up, early hominins had their hands free to carry tools. This basic model was later expanded by a number of anthropologists (e.g., Washburn 1960) to consider the evolution of a number of human characteristics. The model proposed that as tool use increased and became more important, natural selection led to larger brains and enhanced learning abilities. As larger brains evolved along with longer periods of infant and child dependency, tools became even more important for survival. Thus, tool use affected brain size, which in turn affected tool use. Tool use would benefit from walking upright, such that the model predicted a simultaneous evolution of bipedalism, larger brains, and tool use. Although popular for many years, the tool use model has been rejected because fossil evidence from the past several decades has shown that bipedalism evolved *before* significant increases in brain size and emergence of a stone tool technology. Indeed, the fossil record shows evidence of bipedalism around 6 million years ago, a full 3.5 million years *before* the earliest evidence of stone tool technology and brain expansion.

Although the idea of a simultaneous evolution of hominin traits has been rejected, the basic idea that bipedalism offers an evolutionary advantage by freeing the hands to carry things may still have some merit. Wooden tools, such as digging sticks, could be carried. As the early hominins were at least as smart as chimpanzees, which make and use simple tools, it is possible that environmental changes prompted an increase in simple tool use that led to a selective advantage for bipedalism.

Tools are not the only items that can be carried effectively if the hands are free. A hominin could also have carried food and infants, which, under the right conditions, could promote increased survival and reproduction. Owen Lovejoy (1981) has suggested that bipedalism evolved as a strategy to increase the survival of infants and other dependent offspring by having some group members forage for food and then *carry* it back to the group. Consequently, more infants could be cared for, allowing an increase in reproduction and potential population growth. According to Lovejoy, bipedalism is the way in which hominins got around the basic problem faced by apes—a long period of infant dependency, resulting in slow rates of population growth. Bipedalism might have altered the situation and allowed more infants to be cared for at the same time.

The specifics of Lovejoy's model have been rather controversial, as he proposed that the social structure that evolved along with bipedalism was of monogamous family groups, whereby the male foraged for food and the female stayed with the dependent offspring. The fossil evidence to date shows considerable sexual dimorphism in *A. afarensis,* which in turn suggests a polygynous social structure and not monogamy. It is possible, however, that a group of adult females could have shared the care and feeding of offspring, thus producing the same result—selection for bipedalism.

Another suggested advantage of bipedalism is predator avoidance. On the savanna, hominins would be in increased danger of being hunted by large carnivores. By standing on two legs, hominins would be able to see farther, particularly above tall grass, giving them the opportunity to spot potential danger. Day (1986) has suggested that this ability, combined with the retention of tree-climbing ability, would be advantageous. Although predator avoidance would be facilitated by bipedalism *on the savanna,* we now know that the earliest hominins were more likely confined to a woodland and forest environment. Thus, predator avoidance may not explain why bipedalism *first* evolved.

The same criticism is true of another hypothesis that links bipedalism with increased ability to tolerate heat stress (Wheeler 1991). Overheating and water loss are considerable threats to organisms exposed to sunlight on the savanna. Based on laboratory experiments, Wheeler found that standing upright reduces the amount of direct solar radiation that strikes the body (less exposed surface area). Further, the greater air movement and lower temperature felt by an animal standing more upright would increase the rate

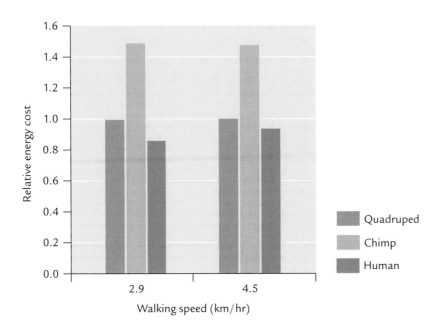

FIGURE 10.25

The relative energy cost of movement for chimpanzees and humans compared with a quadruped of similar size (set equal to 1.0 in this graph). The knuckle-walking chimpanzee uses more energy for movement (values > 1), and the bipedal human uses less (< 1). These comparisons have been made at two speeds: 2.9 km per hour (the normal speed of a chimpanzee) and 4.5 km per hour (the normal speed of a human). These results show that bipedalism is more energy-efficient at normal walking speeds. (Data from Rodman and McHenry 1980.)

of heat dissipation and effective evaporation of sweat. Bipedalism would have been very useful in venturing out onto the savanna, but the evidence suggests that bipedalism had evolved *before* hominins moved into a savanna environment. Therefore, this hypothesis also fails to explain the initial origin of bipedalism.

Bipedalism has also been linked to food acquisition and energy efficiency. Energy efficiency refers to the amount of energy expended relative to the task being performed. Bipedalism is more energy-efficient in traveling long distances in search of food. Increased energy efficiency means using less energy to move about looking for and gathering food.

Though human bipedalism is less efficient than ape locomotion in terms of running, the opposite is true at normal walking speeds. Rodman and McHenry (1980) looked at the energy efficiency of bipedal humans and knuckle-walking chimpanzees at normal walking speeds. The results, shown in Figure 10.25, indicate that bipedalism is more energy-efficient at speeds of both 2.9 km per hour (the normal walking speed of a chimpanzee) and 4.5 km per hour (the normal walking speed of a human). Leonard and Robertson (1995) confirmed these observations and compared the expected daily energy costs for an early hominin (*A. afarensis*) with a knuckle walker of similar size, finding that bipedalism could save more than 50 percent of the expected daily expenditure of calories.

The energy efficiency model is usually discussed in terms of early hominin adaptation to the savanna, which would have necessitated long-distance movement, for which increased energy efficiency would have been a major advantage. The recent evidence that the earliest hominins lived in the woodlands and forests rather than on the savanna would seem to argue against this model. It may not be that simple, however, because climatic data do show that the forests and woodlands were shrinking. Although the earliest hominins may have spent most of their time in the forests and woodlands, they may have needed to travel *between* shrinking clusters to find enough food. As the forests and woodlands continued to shrink, the advantage of bipedalism may have continued to increase, ultimately leaving a form very well adapted for the savanna.

Clues for the *initial* origin of bipedalism also come from observations of chimpanzees practicing bipedalism in the wild. One way that chimps are bipedal is when they stand upright to forage for fruits from lower branches. Another way is when chimps in trees stand upright on branches to reach food (Hunt 1996; Stanford 2006). Bipedalism may have *first* evolved as a feeding posture and *secondarily* as a way of moving around on the ground in the forests and woodlands. The foraging model fits nicely with the fossil evidence for bipedalism of the early hominins, which suggests a life spent partially on the ground and partially in the trees.

Once bipedalism began to be adopted more for locomotion, other advantages, such as energy efficiency, came into play. Later, when hominins ventured out into the savanna, bipedalism offered further advantages in terms of predator avoidance and resistance to heat stress. The use of the foraging model to explain the initial development of bipedalism, combined with other models to explain the further evolution of bipedalism, shows us that there is often not a single simple answer to the evolution of a given trait. Different factors appear to have operated on bipedalism at different times. Indeed, the evolution of bipedalism did not end with the origin of the first hominins, but continued with the genus *Homo,* as shown in the next chapter.

Summary

The origin of the hominins takes place in Africa. The earliest presumed hominins (*Sahelanthropus, Orrorin,* and *Ardipithecus*) date back 6 million years or more, coinciding with the suggested time for hominin divergence based on genetic studies. These earliest hominins were very primitive, and debate continues as to whether all of them are actually hominins. Between roughly 4 million and 3 million years ago, two additional species of primitive hominin (*Australopithecus anamensis* and *Australopithecus afarensis*) appeared that were definitely bipeds but still retained some apelike anatomy, particularly in certain dental features. The evolutionary significance of a newly discovered early hominid, *Kenyanthropus platyops,* is not clear at this time. Starting about 3 million years ago, several lines of hominins, including three species of robust australopiths, emerged, characterized by large back teeth and huge chewing muscles adapted for a hard-to-chew diet. Two other hominins, *Australopithecus africanus* and *Australopithecus garhi,* were less robust, and one of them may represent the ancestor of *Homo.* Preliminary analysis suggests that *A. garhi* made stone tools for scavenging animal flesh and bone marrow. All of these early hominins had small brains but were bipedal.

The origin of bipedalism is a major event in hominin evolution for which a number of hypotheses have been proposed. New evidence on ancient environments shows that the first hominids lived in woodlands and forests. Bipedal posture may have evolved first as a feeding adaptation in the trees and on the ground, and later been selected for as a form of locomotion on the ground. Once bipedalism evolved, hominins were able to adapt to the open grasslands of Africa.

Supplemental Readings

Conroy, G. C. 2005. *Reconstructing Human Origins*, 2d ed. New York: W. W. Norton. A comprehensive text on paleoanthropology with three detailed chapters on the early hominins.

Gibbons, A. 2006. *The First Human: The Race to Discover Our Earliest Ancestors*. New York: Doubleday. A fascinating, easy-to-read account of the discovery of the first hominins and their evolutionary significance.

Stanford, C. 2003. *Upright: The Evolutionary Key to Becoming Human*. Boston: Houghton Mifflin. An easy-to-read discussion of the different models that have been proposed for the origin and evolution of human bipedalism.

VIRTUAL EXPLORATIONS

Visit our textbook-specific online learning center Web site at **www.mhhe.com/relethford7** to access the exercises, that follow.

1. **Family Trees**   Go to the Museum of Science, Boston "Human Evolution: Interpreting Evidence" Web site. Click on the "Family Trees" link: **http://www.mos.org/evolution/overlays/**. This site points out that interpretation of the fossil record can differ greatly, depending on which scientist you talk to. Three scientists (Meave Leakey, Ian Tattersall, and Tim White) are represented. Their respective timelines of hominin evolution are represented graphically.

   ■ Click on each by selecting the box alongside the scientist's name. Notice that all are available as a single, downloadable .PDF file. (The individual scientists are not identified on the .PDF version, so make sure that you label each by comparing them from the Web version.)

   Now compare each timeline side by side.

   ■ What are the most striking differences between them? Are there any similarities?
   ■ What do you think are some of the criteria each scientist used to develop their own schemes of hominin evolution?

2. **Human Evolution**   New Zealand's University of Waikato School of Science and Engineering Web site provides a brief, informative, and understandable overview of human evolution on a single page: **http://sci.waikato.ac.nz/evolution/HumanEvolution.shtml #The earliesthominids**. Read each of the sections: Miocene Apes, The Earliest Hominids, The Australopithecines, Homo Species Trends in Human Evolution, Human Cultural Evolution, and Mitochondrial DNA.

   ■ Do the names for the fossils correspond with those in your textbook?
   ■ Which, if any, are different?
   ■ Why do some of the fossils have more than one name?

   Look down the page and locate the "Taung baby" link. Click on it: **http://www.d.umn.edu/cla/faculty/troufs/anth1602/pctaung.html**. The site includes a photo of Raymond Dart holding the Taung (*Australopithecus africanus*) skull and a separate photo of the skull itself. A small African map identifies australopith sites.

   ■ How many sites are identified?
   ■ Where are most of the sites concentrated?

   Now click on the Taung fossil site link: **http://home.insight.rr .com/jkmckee/taung.htm**.

   ■ What are some things about the Taung site that make it unique?
   ■ What is unusual about the process of deposition?
   ■ What can we infer about the other faunal materials found at the site?

3. **Origins of Humankind**   **http://www.pbs.org/wgbh/evolution/ humans/humankind/index.html**. Watch the interactive "Origins of Humankind" Web activity from the PBS Evolution Web site. Complete the activity and see the Species Gallery for some of the most well-known specimens representing each species.

   ■ Why is the hominin family tree so tentative and unclear? How does it compare to the trees presented in your textbook?
   ■ Will it ever be possible to gather enough evidence to clarify the evolutionary relationships among these species?
   ■ If you could conjure up any fossil or molecular evidence you needed, what evidence would you like to find to answer these unresolved questions?

4. **Palaeoanthropology: Hominin Revelations from Chad**   Go to the journal *Nature* Web site and read the article on *Sahelanthropus:* **http://www.nature.com/nature/journal/v418/n6894/full/418133a .html**. This July 2002 article discusses the find: a cranium, jaw

fragment, and some teeth. The fossil is compared for its significance to Raymond Dart's 1924 discover of the "Taung child."

- What makes this particular find so significant?
- Why was it so difficult to excavate this particular locale?
- Absolute dating methods were not used at this site. Why?
- What method was used instead?
- Two hypotheses concerning hominin evolution are discussed: the linear, or "tidy," model and the "bushy," or "untidy," model. What is the difference between these models, and what are the evolutionary implications of each?

The site of Olduvai Gorge in Tanzania. This site, worked on for many decades by the famous Leakey family, has proven to be a gold mine for hominin fossil studies. The early excavations at Olduvai uncovered many species, including *Homo erectus*, the first hominin species to move outside of Africa.

The Origin and Evolution of the Genus *Homo*

CHAPTER

11

T he history of the first hominins, discussed in the previous chapter, provides us with some insight into the *beginning* of human evolution and the origin of one of the unique characteristics of humankind—bipedalism. Although bipedalism may be 6 million or more years old, it is not until about 2.5 million to 2 million years ago that we begin to see the origin of other human characteristics, such as an increase in brain size and the development of stone tool technology. The genus ***Homo*** is usually defined in terms of an increased brain size, a reduction in the size of the face and teeth, and increased reliance on cultural adaptations. This chapter reviews the fossil and archaeological evidence for the origin of *Homo* in Africa, and its evolution up to the origin of modern humans (which is covered in Chapter 12). Keep in mind that the origin of the genus *Homo* does not correspond to the origin of modern humans. The evolutionary changes leading to modern humans did not occur all at once, but took place over almost 2 million years.

Hominin fossils are assigned to the genus *Homo* partly, but not exclusively, based on brain size. The range of brain size overlaps slightly between *Australopithecus* and *Homo*. The cranial capacity of *Australopithecus* fossils ranges from 390 cubic centimeters (cc) to 545 cc, whereas the cranial capacity of *Homo* fossils, regardless of species, ranges from 509 cc to 1,880 cc (see Figure 11.1 for references). The point here is that although brain size is an important defining characteristic, it is not the only one. Other characteristics of cranial shape, facial shape, dental size, and postcranial anatomy are also important in assigning fossils to different species within the genus *Homo*.

The genus *Homo* also shows an increase in brain size over the past 2 million years. Figure 11.1 plots the cranial capacity of a number of *Australopithecus* and *Homo* crania dating from roughly 10,000 years ago to more than 3 million years ago. This figure shows clearly that brain size in *Homo* has increased over time. Whereas the australopiths show no major increase in brain size over time, the genus *Homo* shows rapid increase over time, particularly after about 700,000 years ago.

Another key characteristic of the genus *Homo* is reliance on cultural behaviors, including increasing sophistication in stone tool technology. Sometime during the course of human evolution, our ancestors became completely

Homo A genus of hominins characterized by large brain size and dependence on culture as a means of adaptation.

FIGURE 11.1

Evolution of hominin brain size. This figure is a plot of cranial capacity over time for fossil specimens of *Australopithecus* and *Homo* from 3.1 million years ago to 10,000 years ago. (Source: Data for *Australopithecus* from Aiello and Dunbar 1993, Suwa et al. 1997, Asfaw et al. 1999, Falk et al. 2000; for early *Homo*, from Aiello and Dunbar 1993; for later *Homo*, from Ruff et al. 1997 with updates and additions from Gabunia et al. 2000, Vekua et al. 2002, White et al. 2003, and Rightmire 2004. Date for the Omo site updated from McDougall et al. 2005.)

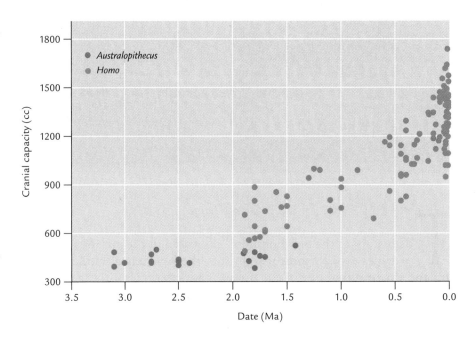

dependent on toolmaking. Keep in mind, however, that the cultural evolution of the genus *Homo* was not simply confined to technological invention and development. As shown in this and the next chapter, different species in the genus *Homo* also used fire, developed hunting and gathering strategies, expanded into new and diverse environments, and developed various types of symbolic expression, including intentional burial and art.

The evolution of the genus *Homo* gets confusing at times, in part because of biological and cultural variation over time and space but also because of the different views on how to explain this diversity. A major controversy involves the number and nature of species within *Homo*. How many were there? Who is related to whom? Because we have only one human species today, what happened to the others (assuming there was more than one to begin with)?

THE ORIGIN OF THE GENUS *HOMO*

The earliest fossil evidence for the genus *Homo* comes from several sites in Africa dating to more than 2 million years ago. As discussed in the previous chapter, early *Homo* most likely evolved from *Australopithecus garhi* or *Australopithecus africanus*. Many anthropologists recognize two species of early *Homo*—*Homo habilis* and *Homo rudolfensis*.

Homo Habilis

The species ***Homo habilis*** refers to a number of African hominin fossils that date between 2 million and 1.6 million years ago (Conroy 2005), and possibly some remains dating back as far as 2.3 million years ago (Kimbel et al. 1996). The first discovered specimens of *Homo habilis* were found at Olduvai Gorge

Homo habilis A species of early *Homo* from Africa that lived between 2 million (or earlier) and 1.6 million years ago, with a brain size roughly half that of modern humans and a primitive postcranial skeleton.

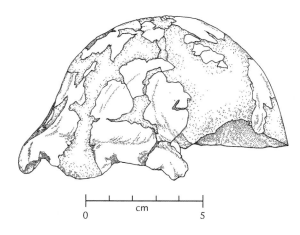

FIGURE 11.2

Skull of *Homo habilis*, specimen OH 16, Olduvai Gorge, Tanzania. Although this skull is small compared to that of a modern human, its cranial capacity (638 cc) marks it as much larger than an australopith skull. (From *Atlas of Human Evolution*, 2d ed. by C. L. Brace, H. Nelson, N. Korn, and M. Brace. Holt, Rinehart and Winston, 1979. Reprinted by permission of the publisher.)

in Tanzania in East Africa. Starting in the 1930s, Louis and Mary Leakey conducted fieldwork at this site. Among their early finds were the remains of the then oldest stone tools. For many years, the Leakeys searched Olduvai Gorge for the makers of these tools. In 1960, they found a jaw, two cranial fragments, and several postcranial bones dating to 1.75 million years ago. This specimen represented a hominin with a larger brain and smaller teeth than that of any australopith (Figures 11.2 and 11.3). Continued work led to the discovery of several more specimens, and in 1964, Louis Leakey and colleagues proposed a new species based on this material: *Homo habilis* (Leakey et al. 1964). The species, whose name translates as "able man" or "handy man," was found in association with stone tools. Since that time, additional specimens have been found elsewhere in East Africa.

Physical Characteristics The most noticeable difference between *H. habilis* and earlier hominins is the larger brain size of *H. habilis*. The average cranial capacity of *H. habilis* is 612 cc (Aiello and Dunbar 1993), which is over 35 percent larger than the average cranial capacity of *A. africanus*. The brain size of *H. habilis* is still small relative to later members of the genus *Homo;* for example, the average brain size of *H. habilis* is roughly half that of the average for living humans. The teeth of *H. habilis* are generally smaller than most australopiths but larger than modern human teeth. The postcranial skeleton is particularly interesting. For many years, little was known about the postcranial skeleton of *H. habilis,* given the discovery of only a few isolated parts. In 1986, a partial adult skeleton of *H. habilis* was discovered at Olduvai Gorge (Johanson et al. 1987). The skeleton is similar to that of earlier hominins, being relatively small (a bit less than 4 feet tall—McHenry 1991) and having relatively long arms. *H. habilis* may have retained climbing ability (Wood 1996). The primitive nature of the postcranial skeleton has led some anthropologists to propose reclassifying *H. habilis* into the genus *Australopithecus* (Wood and Collard 1999).

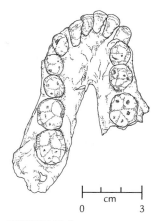

FIGURE 11.3

Lower jaw of *Homo habilis* specimen OH 7, Olduvai Gorge, Tanzania. (From *Atlas of Human Evolution*, 2d ed. by C. L. Brace, H. Nelson, N. Korn, and M. Brace. Holt, Rinehart and Winston, 1979. Reprinted by permission of the publisher.)

FIGURE 11.4

Oldowan tools. (From *The Old Stone Age* by F. Bordes, 1968, Weidenfeld and Nicolson, Ltd. Reprinted by permission of The McGraw-Hill Companies.)

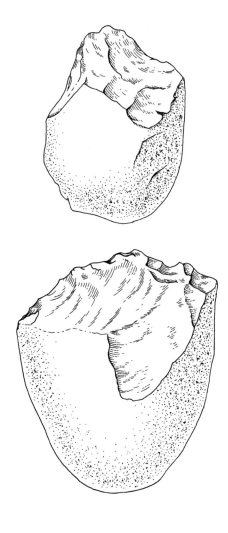

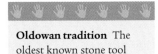

Oldowan tradition The oldest known stone tool culture.

Cultural Behavior   Simple stone tools have been found in association with *H. habilis*. These tools, referred to as the **Oldowan tradition,** are relatively simple chopping tools made by striking several flakes off a rounded stone to give it a rough cutting edge (Figure 11.4). These tools were normally made from materials such as flint, obsidian, or quartz. The stone core was held steady and was then struck with another stone at a certain angle to remove a flake of stone. Several such strikes would produce a rough edge capable of cutting through animal flesh. Proper tool manufacture requires skill in finding the right materials and using the right amount of force.

These tools could have been used for a variety of purposes. For many years, the emphasis in archaeological investigation was on the stone cores produced by flaking. The small flakes, often found in great abundance, were considered garbage—waste material left over from making the stone tool. Analysis of wear on these flakes, however, has shown that they were often used for a variety of tasks, such as cutting meat, scraping wood, and cutting grass stems (Ambrose 2001).

Stone tools are often associated with butchered animal bones that show clear evidence of cut marks. There is also evidence that stone tools were used to crack open animal bones for the marrow inside. Stone tools were thus important in expanding the dietary base of early hominins. It is less clear, however, to what extent *H. habilis* relied on hunting, and it has been argued that *H. habilis* relied instead on scavenging the remains of carnivore kills. More than half the cut marks left by stone tools are found on bones with little meat, such as the lower legs. This suggests that *H. habilis* was taking what was left over from carnivores. In addition, there is no evidence of complete carcasses of larger animals brought to the Olduvai sites, only portions—and these are most often the bones left by carnivores (Potts 1984).

Homo Rudolfensis

For many years, the tendency was to lump any specimen of early *Homo* into the species *H. habilis*. This became a problem after fossils were discovered with larger cranial capacities and different measurements of the face and teeth. Several analyses support the idea of two separate species (e.g., Kramer et al. 1995 and Wood 1996; but see Miller 2000 and Blumenschine et al. 2003 for a differing view). This second species of early *Homo,* dating to 2.4 million to 1.6 million years ago (Conroy 2005), has been named ***Homo rudolfensis*** after the site of Lake Turkana in Kenya, which had, at one time, been named Lake Rudolf (as mentioned in the previous chapter, the history behind species names is often quite confusing).

The cranial capacity of *H. rudolfensis* is somewhat larger than *H. habilis.* Figure 11.5 shows the most famous *H. rudolfensis* fossil—a cranium with a cranial capacity of 752 cc. Falk (1983) investigated an **endocast**—a cast of the interior brain case—of this specimen and found fissures in the frontal lobe similar to those of modern humans but different from those in australopiths. In some dental and facial measures, however, *H. rudolfensis* is more similar to australopiths. The back teeth of *H. rudolfensis* are larger than in *H. habilis,* and the midface is broader (Wood 1996).

How are *H. habilis* and *H. rudolfensis* related to each other and to earlier hominins? Which species of early *Homo* is the ancestor of later humans? These questions do not have easy answers because each species has certain features in common with earlier hominins and others in common with later humans. *H. habilis,* for example, has a primitive postcranial skeleton. Although *H. rudolfensis* has a somewhat larger brain, it also has a number of primitive dental and cranial characteristics (and, in some ways, is similar facially to *Kenyanthropus platyops,* making analysis even more complex). At present, the evolutionary relationships between species of early *Homo* are ambiguous. Even so, sometime prior to 2 million years ago, hominins clearly were evolving larger brains, relying on stone tools, and increasing the amount of meat in their diet. These changes set the stage for the origin and evolution of the species known as ***Homo erectus,*** the ancestor of later humans (including us).

Homo rudolfensis A species of early *Homo* from Africa that lived between 2.4 million and 1.6 million years ago, with a brain size somewhat larger than *H. habilis* but with larger back teeth and a broader face.

endocast A cast of the interior of the brain case used in analyzing brain size and structure.

Homo erectus A species of the genus *Homo* that arose 1.8 million years ago in Africa and then spread to parts of Asia and Europe.

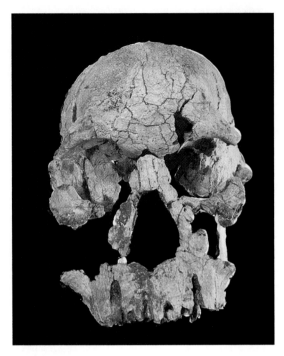

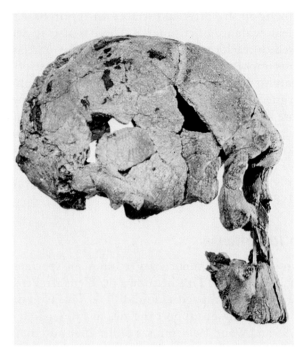

FIGURE 11.5

Frontal and side views of *Homo rudolfensis,* specimen KNM–ER 1470, Lake Turkana, Kenya.

HOMO ERECTUS

The species name *Homo erectus* literally means "upright walking human." This may seem odd given the fact that earlier hominin species also walked upright. When the first specimens of *H. erectus* were found in the late nineteenth century, they were the oldest evidence of bipedalism at that point. Originally, the species was named *Pithecanthropus erectus* (meaning "upright walking ape-man"). Later, the genus name *Homo* was assigned because of the large brain size and reliance on culture. This section reviews the biological and behavioral evidence for *Homo erectus.*

Distribution in Time and Space

The distribution of some key *H. erectus* sites is shown in Figure 11.6, and details about some major sites are given in Table 11.1. The oldest known specimens of *H. erectus* have been found in East Africa, dating back almost 1.8 million years (with some fossils possibly a bit older). What is perhaps most significant about *H. erectus* is that it was the first hominin species to move out of Africa, and current dating suggests that some *H. erectus* populations migrated out of Africa very quickly after their initial African origin. Fossils of *H. erectus* have been found in Indonesia in Southeast Asia dating back as far as 1.8 million to 1.6 million years ago (Swisher et al. 1994). The movement of *H. erectus* into Indonesia might seem puzzling given the fact that today the islands that make up Indonesia are separated from the Asian mainland. In

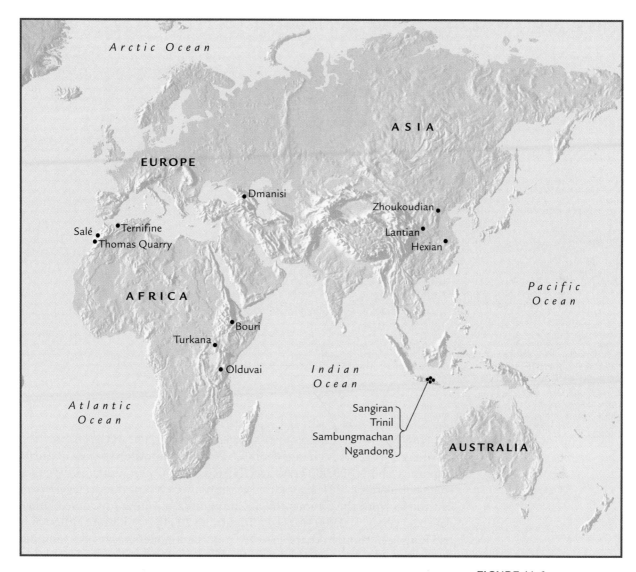

FIGURE 11.6

Location of major *Homo erectus* sites.

the past, however, the sea level was lower during glacial times, and there was a direct land connection between mainland Asia and Indonesia. This happened because water was trapped in ice during glacial times and did not return to the sea, which resulted in a lowering of the sea level. Thus, *H. erectus* could have walked to Indonesia directly from the southeastern coast of Asia.

Further evidence for the early dispersal of *H. erectus* comes from the easternmost fringes of Europe. Several *H. erectus* crania were discovered at Dmanisi in the Republic of Georgia dating to 1.75 million years ago (Gabunia et al. 2000; Vekua et al. 2002). There has not been definitive evidence for the expansion of *H. erectus* further west into Europe. A skull from Ceprano, Italy, dates back 850,000 years and was originally classified as *H. erectus*, but further analysis suggests that it may belong to a later species (Manzi 2004).

TABLE 11.1   Major Fossil Sites for *Homo erectus*

Geographic Region	Country	Site/Specimen	Age (Ma)[1]	Reference for Age	Figure in Text
East Africa[2]	Kenya	East Turkana	1.8–1.6	1	11.9
		West Turkana	1.5	1	11.15
	Tanzania	Olduvai Gorge	1.3–0.7	1	
	Ethiopia	Bouri	1.0	1	
South Africa	Republic of South Africa	Swartkrans	1.8–1.5	2	
North Africa	Algeria	Ternifine	0.6?	2	11.14
	Morocco	Sale	0.4	1	
Eastern Europe	Republic of Georgia	Dmanisi	1.7	1	
Southeast Asia	Indonesia	Sangiran	1.6–1.1	1	11.11
		Trinil	1.0?	2	
		Sambungmachan	?	1	
		Ngandong	0.04	1	
East Asia	China	Lantian	0.8	2	
		Zhoukoudian	0.55–0.45	1	11.10
		Hexian	0.4	1	

[1]Question marks indicate a range in likely dates for the site/specimen.
[2]Some anthropologists classify the East African specimens as a separate species—*Homo ergaster*.
References: 1. Rightmire (2004); 2. Conroy (2005).

How long was *H. erectus* in existence? As shown later in the chapter, the fossil record shows a change from *H. erectus* to another species of *Homo* beginning about 800,000 years ago. There is evidence in Asia, however, that some populations of *H. erectus* lived on until more recent times. *Homo erectus* specimens from the famous site at Zhoukoudian, China (discussed later), date back about 500,000 years ago (Rightmire 2004). In addition, although it had long been thought that *H. erectus* from the Indonesian site of Ngandong lived about 200,000 years ago, redating of this site in the 1990s suggested that some populations of *H. erectus* might have survived until sometime between 53,000 and 27,000 years ago (Swisher et al. 1996).

Physical Characteristics

The following section focuses on the physical characteristics of *Homo erectus*—specifically, those of the skull, teeth, and postcranial skeleton. Following this general review, variation within the species, and the question of whether what we have traditionally called *Homo erectus* is actually two species, will be considered.

Brain Size   The most obvious characteristic of *H. erectus* compared to earlier hominins is its larger brain size (Figure 11.7). The average cranial capacity of *H. erectus* is 970 cc, which is approximately 72 percent of the average of living

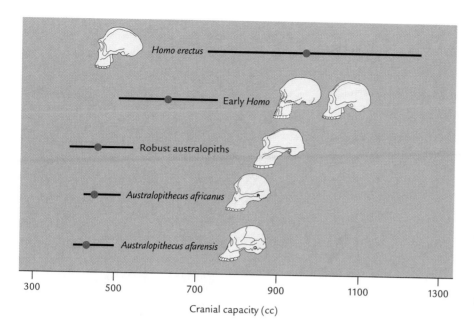

FIGURE 11.7

Comparison of the cranial capacity of *Australopithecus*, early *Homo* (*H. habilis* and *H. rudolfensis* combined), and *Homo erectus*. The dots indicate the average cranial capacity (in cubic centimeters) for each group. The lines indicate the range from minimum to maximum. (Data for *A. afarensis* and early *Homo* from Aiello and Dunbar 1993; for *A. africanus*, from Falk et al. 2000; for robust australopiths, from Suwa et al. 1997 and Falk et al. 2000; and for *Homo erectus*, from Rightmire 2004, excluding the Ceprano specimen.)

humans. On average, the brain size of *H. erectus* is more than 50 percent larger than that of early *Homo* (*H. habilis* and *H. rudolfensis*), and there was a slight increase in the cranial capacity of *H. erectus* over time (Figure 11.8).

Cranial and Dental Characteristics   One of the earliest *H. erectus* skulls, from Lake Turkana in Kenya, is shown in Figure 11.9. Examples of Asian

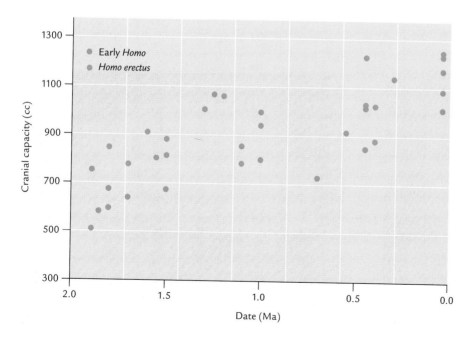

FIGURE 11.8

Plot of cranial capacity over time for fossil specimens of early *Homo* (*H. habilis* and *H. rudolfensis* combined) and *Homo erectus*. Note that there is a slight increase in the cranial capacity of *H. erectus* over time. (Sources of data listed in Figure 11.7.)

FIGURE 11.9

Homo erectus skull, specimen KNM-ER 3733, Lake Turkana, Kenya. Dated at 1.8 million years ago, this is one of the oldest known specimens of *Homo erectus* (some anthropologists consider this specimen a different species, *Homo ergaster*).

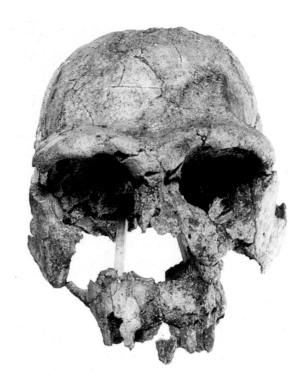

FIGURE 11.10

Frontal and side views of *Homo erectus* from the site of Zhoukoudian, China. The specimens from this site are sometimes referred to as "Peking Man" in older literature.

H. erectus are shown in Figure 11.10 (China) and Figure 11.11 (Indonesia). Overall, the brain case of *H. erectus* is larger than that of earlier hominins, but it is still smaller than that of modern *H. sapiens*. The skull of *H. erectus* is lower, and the face still protrudes more than in modern humans. Neck muscles are attached to a ridge of bone along the back side of the skull. The development of this bony ridge shows that *H. erectus* had powerful neck muscles.

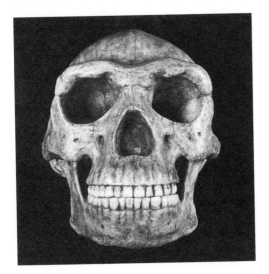

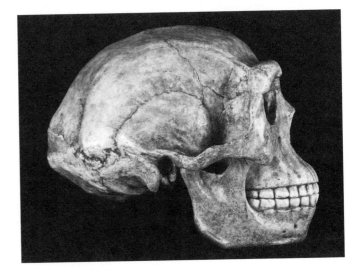

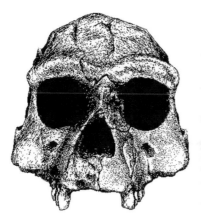

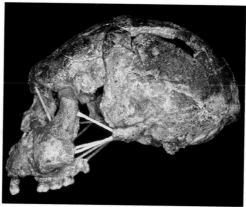

Frontal and side views of *Homo erectus* skull, specimen Sangiran 17, from Sangiran, Indonesia.

Figure 11.12 shows a *H. erectus* skull and a *H. sapiens* skull from a top view. The frontal region of the *H. erectus* skull is narrower than *H. sapiens,* due to **postorbital constriction,** suggesting less development in the frontal and temporal lobes of the brain relative to modern humans. Figure 11.13 shows a *H. erectus* skull and a *H. sapiens* skull from the rear. Note that the *H. erectus* skull is much broader toward the base of the skull, whereas the *H. sapiens* skull is broadest near the top of the skull.

The face of *H. erectus* protrudes, but not as much as in earlier hominins. One noticeable characteristic of the *H. erectus* face is the development of a large ridge of bone above the eyes (**brow ridges**). Different explanations have been offered for the development of large brow ridges in *H. erectus,* including structural support for forces exerted by chewing and protection of the

postorbital constriction The narrowness of the skull behind the eye orbits, a characteristic of early hominins and *Homo erectus.*

brow ridges The large ridges of bone above the eye orbits, very noticeable in *Homo erectus.*

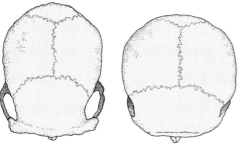

FIGURE 11.12

Top views of the skulls of *Homo erectus* (*left*) and modern *Homo sapiens* (*right*). Note the greater constriction behind the eyes in *Homo erectus.*

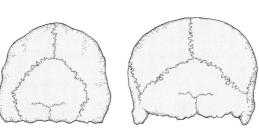

FIGURE 11.13

Rear views of the skulls of *Homo erectus* (*left*) and modern *Homo sapiens* (*right*). Note the broader brain case of *Homo sapiens.*

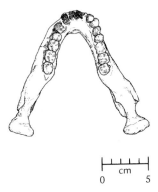

FIGURE 11.14

Lower jaw of *Homo erectus* specimen Ternifine 3, Ternifine, Algeria. (From Clark Spencer Larsen, Robert M. Matter, and Daniel L. Gebo, *Human Origins: The Fossil Record,* 3d ed., p. 101. Copyright © 1998 by Waveland Press, Inc., Long Grove, IL. All rights reserved. Reprinted with permission from the publisher.)

eyes and face (Wolpoff 1999; Boaz and Ciochon 2004). The jaws and teeth of *H. erectus* are still large compared to those of modern humans but smaller than those of earlier hominins, particularly the back teeth (Figure 11.14). Microscopic analysis of the teeth shows wear patterns characteristic of extensive meat eating.

The Postcranial Skeleton   The first specimen of *H. erectus* was discovered by physician Eugene Dubois in Java in 1891. This find consisted of the upper portion of a skull and a femur (upper leg bone). Although the skullcap was smaller than that of a modern human, the femur was virtually the same as that of a modern human. Because the two bones were found together, Dubois reasoned that upright walking had developed before achievement of the modern human brain size, a view we now know is correct.

For many years, however, the postcranial evidence for *H. erectus* was rather limited—a femur here, a pelvic bone there. In 1984, this situation changed with the discovery of a nearly complete *H. erectus* skeleton at Lake Turkana, dating to 1.6 million years ago (Brown et al. 1985) (Figure 11.15). This skeleton is that of a young male. The pattern of dental eruption suggests that he was about 12 years old at the time of his death. This age estimate depends, of course, on the extent to which his growth pattern was similar to that of living humans; some have suggested that his actual age was somewhat less. One of the most striking features of this extremely complete skeleton is that he was tall. Had he lived to adulthood, he might have been 6 feet tall, well above the average for many populations even today. In any case, the skeleton of the "Turkana Boy" (as he is sometimes called) shows that *H. erectus* was likely taller than early *Homo* and the australopiths.

The Turkana Boy shows body proportions that are very similar to those of modern humans, and unlike the australopiths and *H. habilis,* who had longer arms. The modern limb proportions of *H. erectus* reflect that its bipedalism was modern in form, including improvements allowing more efficient long-distance walking. Close examination of the postcranial skeleton of *H. erectus* also suggests that it was capable of endurance running, just like modern humans. We are not very good at sprinting, but we can run at slower speeds for long distances because of certain features of our skeletal and muscular anatomy, such as springlike tendons in our legs, a well-developed arch in the foot, a long stride length, and anatomical specializations that allow stabilization of the neck and trunk while running. Based on the fossil evidence, *H. erectus* could do the same, an ability that could have been very helpful in scavenging and hunting (Bramble and Lieberman 2004).

Portions of the pelvis of the Turkana Boy are narrow relative to modern humans. Noting that little sexual dimorphism occurs in *some* pelvic dimensions, Brown et al. (1985) have argued that some measurements taken on this specimen can apply to both males and females, leading them to conclude that *H. erectus* females could not have given birth to very large-brained babies. To reach the relatively large brain size shown by *H. erectus,* rapid brain growth must have continued *after* birth. Had *H. erectus* shown

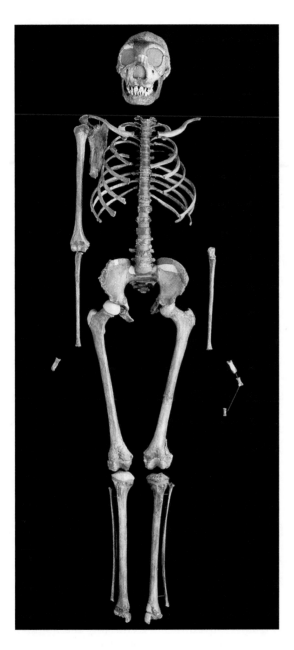

FIGURE 11.15

Homo erectus skeleton, specimen KNM-WT 15000, Lake Turkana, Kenya. This skeleton of a 12-year-old boy, dating to 1.6 million years ago, is the most complete specimen of *Homo erectus* yet found.

the typical primate pattern, with brain size simply doubling after birth, their brains would not have been as large as they were. It seems that the modern human pattern of extensive postnatal brain growth had begun.

The modern body proportions shown by the Turkana Boy also have implications for diet and brain growth. As noted in Chapter 7, the human brain is metabolically expensive. The same is true for other organ systems, including the digestive system. We humans tend to have larger brains and smaller guts than expected for a primate our size, observations that Aiello and

Wheeler (1995) have argued are related in their "expensive tissue hypothesis." They propose that during human evolution an increase in brain size would need a corresponding reduction in the gut size, since both are metabolically expensive. The reduction in gut size would allow more energy for brain metabolism. Smaller gut size would have been possible with the addition of high-quality, easy-to-digest food, such as meat and other animal products, to the diet. Thus, a change in diet would have allowed further brain growth. Aiello and Wheeler suggest that this change occurred in *H. erectus,* because the shape of the thoracic region and the width of the pelvis of the Turkana Boy are more like those of modern humans, marking a change from earlier hominins and reflecting a reduction in gut size.

More Than One Species?   As with most species, *Homo erectus* shows geographic variation. The Asian specimens, for example, tend to have somewhat thicker cranial bones and a slightly different appearance in some features of cranial anatomy. Some anthropologists have suggested that the African and Asian specimens should be classified as different species (e.g., Tattersall 1997). Under this scheme, the early African specimens (such as the Turkana Boy) should be classified as ***Homo ergaster,*** which means "working human." Under this classification scheme, the species name *Homo erectus* would refer primarily to the Asian specimens. Proponents of this view further suggest that it was *H. ergaster* that evolved into later humans (and eventually us), and that *H. erectus* was an extinct side branch. Other anthropologists (e.g., Rightmire 1992) disagree, arguing that because *H. erectus* was a geographically widespread species, regional differences are to be expected and are not sufficient to warrant placing the early African specimens in a separate species. This book supports the latter view.

Cultural Behavior

The behavior of *Homo erectus* is more complex than once thought. The archaeological and fossil evidence shows us that *H. erectus* developed an advanced stone tool technology and had significant amounts of meat in their diet. What is less clear, however, is how they obtained this meat and to what extent they used fire.

Stone Tool Technology   Major changes in stone tool technology did not take place immediately with the origin of *Homo erectus.* Early *H. erectus* in Africa made tools similar to, but somewhat more sophisticated than, Oldowan tools (often called "evolved Oldowan"). Starting 1.5 million years ago, however, *H. erectus* developed a new type of stone tool technology referred to as the **Acheulian tradition.** A key feature of this stone tool culture was a new way of manufacture known as the **soft hammer technique.** Here, flakes are removed from the stone core by using a piece of bone, antler, or wood. Softer materials absorb much of the shock in flake removal, allowing greater precision and control, and the ability to remove smaller flakes (Figure 11.16). The Acheulian tool kit includes **bifaces,** which are stone tools that have been

Homo ergaster A species suggested by some anthropologists consisting of the early African specimens of *Homo erectus.*

Acheulian tradition The stone tool culture that appeared first with *Homo erectus* and was characterized by the development of hand axes and other bifacial tools.

soft hammer technique A method of removing flakes from a stone core by striking it with a softer material, such as bone, antler, or wood.

biface A stone tool with both sides worked, producing greater symmetry and efficiency.

FIGURE 11.16

Making an Acheulian tool. Nicholas Toth uses a piece of antler to remove small flakes from both sides of the flint, producing a symmetric hand axe (*left*). Shown are flint hand axes and a cleaver (*right*).

worked on both sides, producing a symmetric tool. These tools are flatter and have straighter, sharper sides than Oldowan tools.

The basic Acheulian tool is the hand axe (Figures 11.16 and 11.17a), which could be used for a variety of purposes, including meat preparation. Other tools were made for different purposes, such as scrapers and cleavers (Figure 11.17). The use of different tools for different purposes marked an important step in the cultural evolution of humans. Increased specialization allowed for more efficient tool use and required greater mental sophistication in design and manufacture.

There is some geographic variation in the technology of *H. erectus*. Whereas Acheulian hand axes are found in Africa and Europe, they are absent in Asia, where a large number of less sophisticated chopping tools have been found (see Figure 11.17d and 11.17e). Stone tools that show Acheulian-like technology have been found in China, dating to the time of *H. erectus* (Hou et al. 2000), but no hand axes. One explanation for this difference is that there were cultural or perhaps biological differences between *H. erectus* populations. Another is that it might reflect differences in available natural resources. For example, Pope (1989) suggested that Asian *H. erectus* might have been using bamboo for making sharp implements, something that would not preserve in the archaeological record.

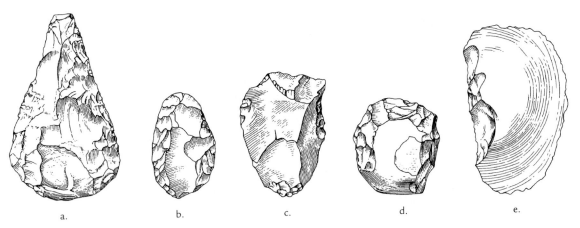

a.   b.   c.   d.   e.

FIGURE 11.17

Examples of tools made by *Homo erectus:* (a) hand axe, (b) side scraper, (c) small chopping tool, (d) chopper, (e) cleaverlike tool. (From *The Old Stone Age* by F. Bordes, 1968, Weidenfeld and Nicolson, Ltd. Reprinted by permission of The McGraw-Hill Companies.)

Hunters or Scavengers? *Homo erectus* ate meat; this is clear from butchered animal bones with stone tool cut marks. The change in the body shape of *H. erectus* discussed previously is also evidence that the diet of *H. erectus* included a substantial amount of meat. An important question is, Where did this meat come from? There are two possibilities—hunting and scavenging. Early investigations of *H. erectus* produced evidence that was consistent with a hunting and gathering lifestyle. *H. erectus* was found with stone tools, butchered animal bones, and artifacts indicating the control and use of fire. Together, this evidence seemed to point to an easy explanation—*H. erectus* hunted animals and then butchered and cooked them. As such, the culture of *H. erectus* was interpreted as equivalent to that of later (and living) hunter-gatherers. With *H. erectus,* the emphasis on hunting rather than gathering is in part a consequence of the archaeological record, as bones and stones preserve better than do plants or wooden containers. Another factor behind the emphasis on hunting was male bias. Modern hunting and gathering societies show a clear division of labor by sex—men are generally the hunters, and women the gatherers. And early (mostly male) anthropologists focused on what males were doing.

Although all agree that *H. erectus* butchered animals, the assumption that they hunted has been questioned. An alternative explanation is that *H. erectus* was a scavenger, using stone tools to obtain meat from animals that had already been killed by predators. Electron microscopes have been used to look at animal bones from *H. erectus* sites. A number of these bones have both the characteristic marks left by stone tools and bite marks from other animals. In some cases, the stone tool cut marks overlaid the bite marks, showing that the stone tools were used *after* a predator had eaten part of the animal's flesh, which in turn suggests that *H. erectus* was likely a scavenger (Boaz and Ciochon 2004). Although such studies have challenged the older view of *H. erectus* as a big-game hunter, it is still possible that *H. erectus* hunted small game.

Fire The use of fire as a source of energy is a significant human activity. Fire provides heat and light and is used for cooking, keeping warm, scaring off animals, and seeing at night. The control of fire marked an important step in the evolution of human culture, and so it is of interest to know when and where fire was first used. *Homo erectus* has long been associated with the first use of fire in human evolution. Documenting the earliest evidence of controlled fire is problematic, however, because it is difficult to distinguish between naturally occurring fire and controlled fire. There are some possible cases of controlled fire dating back 1.5 million years, but these are not conclusive (McKee et al. 2005). The earliest conclusive evidence of fire use is 790,000 years ago (Goren-Inbar et al. 2004).

The best evidence for the use of fire by *H. erectus* comes from the cave sites at Zhoukoudian, in China. Some of this evidence has been questioned, such as the presence of ash that had initially been interpreted as resulting from accumulations of campfires over time. More recent studies have shown that the ash was deposited by water flowing into the cave (Weiner et al. 1998). There is evidence, however, of both fire-cracked stones and burned animal bones at Zhoukoudian that support the use of fire by *H. erectus* (Boaz and Ciochon 2004). Of course, the fact that *H. erectus* used fire does not mean that they knew how to *make* fire. We have no evidence of such ability, and it may be that *H. erectus* had to rely instead on finding naturally occurring fire and keeping it smoldering for long periods of time.

A Dwarf Species of *Homo erectus*?

In 2003, a skull and parts of a skeleton of an adult hominin were discovered at the Liang Bua cave site on the island of Flores in Indonesia (Brown et al. 2004). This find was quite startling because of the specimen's size. Even though it was an adult, it was only 106 cm (about 3.5 ft) tall and had a cranial capacity of only 417 cc (Falk et al. 2005) (Figure 11.18). The specimen's small size has led to it being nicknamed "The Hobbit," after the diminutive characters in J. R. R. Tolkien's book of the same name and his *Lord of the Rings* trilogy. The combination of small height and cranial capacity resembled that of the australopiths, but cranial and dental features were more similar to the genus *Homo,* so it was classified into a new species, ***Homo floresiensis*** (Brown et al. 2004). The species initially was found in association with stone tools and animal bones (Morwood et al. 2004), and additional postcranial bones have since been discovered (Morwood et al. 2005). All of the finds of *H. floresiensis* date to between 95,000–74,000 and 12,000 years ago. These dates are fascinating because modern humans also lived in that region at the same time, although we have no idea of how these species might have interacted.

One explanation of this find is that it represents a dwarf species of *Homo erectus*. A process known as **island dwarfism** has been observed for a number of animal species. When a population of large animals is trapped on an island with limited resources, natural selection favors smaller body size, ultimately leading to dwarfed species that are much smaller than their ancestors were.

Homo floresiensis The species name given to a very small hominin that lived in Indonesia in recent times, and thought by some to be a dwarf species of *Homo erectus*.

island dwarfism The process by which natural selection favors smaller body size on an island with limited resources, leading to dwarfed species.

FIGURE 11.18

The LB1 skull (*left*) and a modern human skull (*right*). The LB1 specimen has been classified in the species *Homo floresiensis*, which some consider a dwarf species of *Homo erectus*.

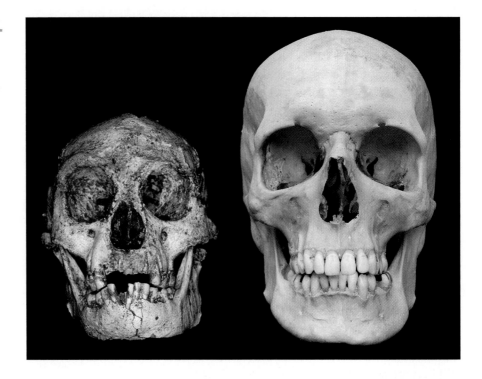

This process has been documented for a variety of animals, including some creatures that were related to elephants that lived on Flores. Brown and colleagues (2004) have suggested that a small population of *H. erectus* wound up isolated on Flores and over time evolved into the dwarf species *H. floresiensis*. Stone tools have been found on Flores dating back 840,000 years ago (O'Sullivan et al. 2001) that may have been made by earlier groups of *H. erectus*. The question of origins is further complicated by the fact that the island of Flores is separated from the rest of Indonesia by a very deep ocean trench. Even during times when sea levels dropped, it would not have been possible to walk to Flores, perhaps implying the use of some sort of raft.

Not everyone accepts the island dwarfism hypothesis or even the conclusion that the Flores finds represent a new species (Wong 2005). Some have argued that the skull is that of a microcephalic (small-headed) modern human. To address this possibility, Dean Falk and colleagues (2005) constructed a virtual endocast of *H. floresiensis* using three-dimensional computer tomography. They found that it did not resemble that of a microcephalic but was most similar to *H. erectus,* although with a brain–body size ratio like that of australopiths. The suggestion that the original specimen was pathological also seems less likely now that other small-sized individuals have been found, even though another skull has not yet been found. Although a number of anthropologists agree that this is a new species, its origin is less clear because of the combination of *Homo* characteristics with australopith body proportions and a small brain. *H. floresiensis* may be the descendant of *H. erectus* or another small hominin (Lieberman 2005; Morwood et al. 2005). Fossil evidence from earlier in Flore's prehistory is needed to address this question.

MIDDLE PLEISTOCENE HOMININS

Although some populations of *Homo erectus* possibly survived until very recently in Southeast Asia, evolutionary changes were taking place elsewhere close to a million years ago in parts of the Old World, ultimately leading to our own species' origins. For many years, the fossil record of the **Middle Pleistocene,** a stage of the Pleistocene epoch that lasted from about 780,000 to 130,000 years ago, has been interpreted as a transition from *H. erectus* to modern *Homo sapiens*. Many hominin fossils dating to this time show differences from both *H. erectus* and modern humans. In particular, their brain size is larger than *H. erectus*, and their face and teeth smaller than *H. erectus* but still larger than *H. sapiens*. Some have simply referred to these fossils as "archaic humans." Others have been more specific, classifying them as "archaic *Homo sapiens*," a label meant to show simultaneously their similarity to *H. sapiens* in terms of brain size and their difference in terms of craniofacial anatomy. Increasingly, a number of anthropologists are arguing that this designation is confusing and does not adequately convey the complexity of the fossil record, and they suggest that these fossils be classified as the species ***Homo heidelbergensis*** (Rightmire 1998). The species name comes from the city of Heidelberg in Germany, near the location of a fossil site. This species name will be used here as a general label for this group of Middle Pleistocene hominins. Following a review of their distribution, anatomy, and cultural behaviors, the question of classification will be considered.

Middle Pleistocene A geological stage of the Pleistocene epoch that lasted from 781,000 to 126,000 years ago.

Homo heidelbergensis A species of archaic human with brain size close to that of modern humans but a larger, less modern face that lived in Africa, Europe, and Asia between 800,000 and 200,000 years ago.

Distribution in Time and Space

Homo heidelbergensis has been found at a number of sites in Europe, Africa, and Asia, dating between 800,000 and 200,000 years ago. The distribution of some *H. heidelbergensis* sites is shown in Figure 11.19, and details about some major sites are given in Table 11.2. Some of the earliest assigned specimens come from the Gran Dolina cave site in the Atapuerca hills of Spain, dating to 800,000 years ago, and the Bodo D'Ar site in Ethiopia, dating to 600,000 years ago. A cranial remain from Ceprano, Italy, dating to 850,000 years ago, may be an early example of *H. heidelbergensis* or a transitional form between *H. erectus* and *H. heidelbergensis* (Manzi 2004).

In terms of geographic distribution of *H. heidelbergensis* (and later hominins), some populations were living in northern parts of Europe and Asia. The Pleistocene is characterized by frequent ice ages—periods of below-average global temperatures and the spread of glaciers over large continental areas. Brief interglacial periods of warmer temperatures occur between the glacial periods. Over the past 700,000 years, glacial conditions have been occurring roughly at 100,000-year intervals (Stringer and Andrews 2005). Thus, we need to remember that our ancestors during the Pleistocene had to cope in some places with colder temperatures than are found today and with a pattern of changing climate over many millennia.

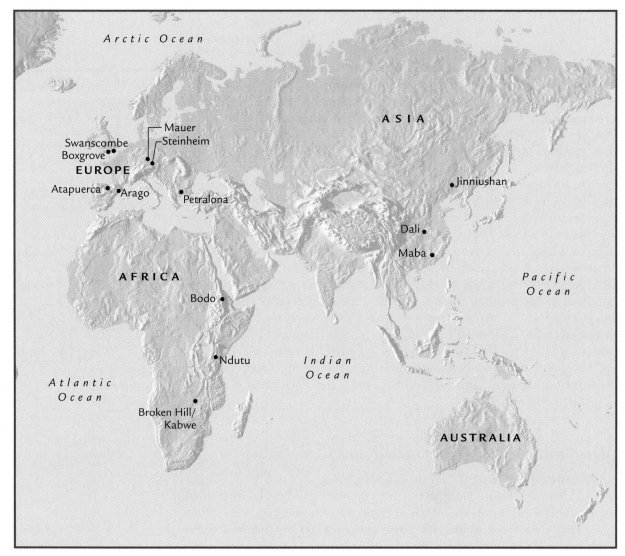

FIGURE 11.19

Location of major *Homo heidelbergensis* sites.

Physical Characteristics

The average brain size of *Homo heidelbergensis* is larger than that of *H. erectus* and almost as large as in modern humans (Figure 11.20). The average cranial capacity of *H. heidelbergensis* is 1,206 cc with a range of 1,100 to 1,390 cc, which is almost 25 percent larger than *H. erectus* and only about 10 percent less than living humans on average. In addition, the skull of *H. heidelbergensis* is higher and more well-rounded than in *H. erectus,* and the face does not protrude as much. Brow ridges remain large, but the brows are more separated with thinner sides, unlike the brow ridges of *H. erectus,* which tend to be more continuous. Compared with *H. sapiens,* the skull of *H. heidelbergensis* is lower and is less well-rounded in the back. The face of *H. heidelbergensis* is still large

TABLE 11.2 Major Fossil Sites for *Homo heidelbergensis*

Geographic Region	Country	Site/Specimen	Age (ka)[1]	Reference for Age	Figure in Text
Africa	Zambia	Kabwe	700–400?	1	11.21
	Ethiopia	Bodo	600	1	
	Tanzania	Ndutu	400–250?	1	
Europe	Spain	Atapuerca (Gran Dolina)[2]	800	2	
		Atapuerca (Sima de los Huesos)	400	1	
	Germany	Mauer	500	2	
		Steinheim	400–300	1	
	France	Arago	450	1	
	England	Boxgrove	500	2	
		Swanscombe	400	2	
	Greece	Petralona	400–250?	1	11.22
East Asia	China	Jinniushan	280	1	
		Dali	200	1	11.23
		Maba	169–129?	2	

[1]Question marks indicate a range in likely dates for the site/specimen.
[2]Some anthropologists classify the Gran Dolina hominins as a separate species—*Homo antecessor*.
References: 1. Rightmire (2004); 2. Conroy (2005).

relative to *H. sapiens*. In addition, *H. heidelbergensis* lacks a chin, something found in modern *H. sapiens*. Overall, the anatomy of the skull shows a form intermediate in many ways between *H. erectus* and *H. sapiens* but with larger brain size. Postcranial remains suggest that *H. heidelbergensis* was often tall and powerfully built (Stringer and Andrews 2005).

An example of *H. heidelbergensis* is shown in Figure 11.21. This skull was found in Zambia, Africa, and dates to between 700,000 and 400,000 years ago. This skull has a large cranial capacity (1,280 cc). The face is rather large,

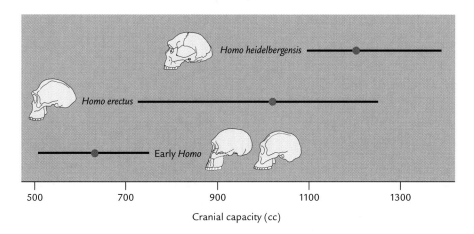

FIGURE 11.20

Comparison of the cranial capacity of early *Homo* (*H. habilis* and *H. rudolfensis* combined), *Homo erectus*, and *Homo heidelbergensis*. The dots indicate the average cranial capacity (in cubic centimeters) for each group. The lines indicate the range from minimum to maximum. (Sources of data listed in Figure 11.7 and, for *H. heidelbergensis*, data from Rightmire 2004.)

FIGURE 11.21

The Broken Hill skull, Kabwe, Zambia. An example of *Homo heidelbergensis* from Africa.

FIGURE 11.22

The Petralona skull, Greece. An example of *Homo heidelbergensis* from Europe. (From Clark Spencer Larsen, Robert M. Matter, and Daniel L. Gebo, *Human Origins: The Fossil Record*, 3d ed., p. 117. Copyright © 1998 by Waveland Press, Inc., Long Grove, IL. All rights reserved. Reprinted with permission from the publisher.)

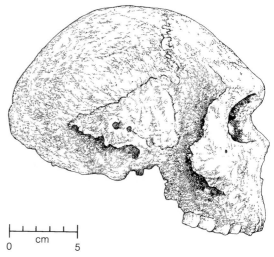

FIGURE 11.23

The Dali skull, Dali County, People's Republic of China. An example of *Homo heidelbergensis* from Asia. (From Clark Spencer Larsen, Robert M. Matter, and Daniel L. Gebo, *Human Origins: The Fossil Record*, 3d ed., p. 128. Copyright © 1998 by Waveland Press, Inc., Long Grove, IL. All rights reserved. Reprinted with permission from the publisher.)

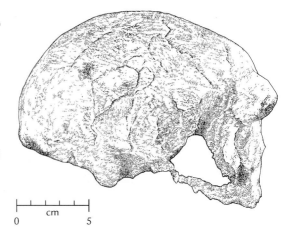

as are the brow ridges, and the skull is higher than in *H. erectus* but lower than in *H. sapiens*. Figure 11.22 shows an example of *H. heidelbergensis* from Europe; this skull, from Petralona in Greece, dates to between 400,000 and 250,000 years ago. Its cranial capacity is about average for *H. heidelbergensis* (1,230 cc). Another example of *H. heidelbergensis,* shown in Figure 11.23, is the skull from Dali, China, which dates to 200,000 year ago and has a cranial capacity of 1,120 cc. All three of these examples show the high cranial capacity of *H. heidelbergensis* relative to *H. erectus* but with a cranial shape different from modern *H. sapiens*.

Cultural Behavior

The archaeological record of *Homo heidelbergensis* shows that they used the same sort of tools as earlier hominins but also developed a new method of stone tool manufacture. The evidence also shows that *H. heidelbergensis* was actively involved in hunting.

Stone Tool Technology   Many *H. heidelbergensis* sites show that they continued to use the same sorts of stone tools (chopping tools and Acheulian tools) as earlier hominins. New stone tool technologies do not emerge in step with the origin of new species. Just as *H. erectus* continued using Oldowan tools prior to the invention of Acheulian tools, *H. heidelbergensis* continued using earlier tools as well. Then, about 300,000 years ago, the situation changed in some populations, and we see the origin of stone tools using a new method of manufacture—the **Levallois technique,** named after a site in France and also known as the prepared-core method (Stringer and Andrews 2005). As shown in Figure 11.24, a flint nodule is first chipped around the edges, shaping the core into the desired shape. Small flakes are then removed from the top surface of the core. In the final step, the core is struck precisely at one end, and the final finished tool is removed.

The Levallois technique produces very sharp and efficient tools. It is also a way of maximizing the utilization of stone cores. Once a finished flake is removed, the core can be prepared again and another tool, identical to the first, can be produced. More tools can be prepared out of a single core, which saves time and effort spent looking for and transporting raw material. The use of the Levallois technique also shows us how skilled these archaic humans were. Their precise toolmaking implies an excellent knowledge of flaking methods and the structural characteristics of stone. It also shows how they were able to visualize the final desired product in their minds while making the tool.

Hunting   As noted previously, there is some debate over the extent to which *H. erectus* was a hunter as well as a scavenger. The evidence that *H. heidelbergensis* was a hunter is more definitive. A number of sites suggest or show evidence of hunting. Many butchered animal bones have been found at the Gran Dolina cave site in Spain. The representation of skeletal parts shows that entire carcasses were brought into the cave for butchering, which indicates that

Levallois technique A method of making stone tools in which a stone core is prepared in such a way that finished tools can be removed from it by a final blow. Also known as the prepared-core method.

FIGURE 11.24

Manufacture of a stone tool, using the Levallois technique or prepared-core method. First, the core is shaped by removing small flakes from the sides and top (a–d). Then the finished tool is removed from the core (e). (From *Archaeology: Discovering Our Past,* 2d ed., by Robert Sharer and Wendy Ashmore, Fig. 10.3. Copyright © 1993 by Mayfield Publishing Company. Reprinted by permission of The McGraw-Hill Companies.)

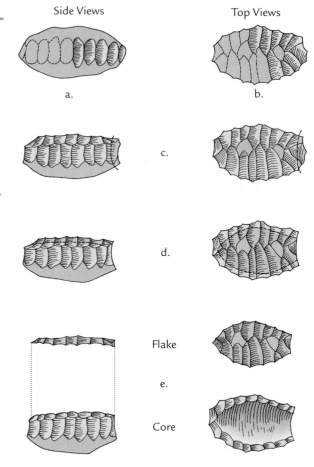

Side Views   Top Views

a.   b.

c.   d.

Flake

e.

Core

humans had the first access to meat. In addition, in those cases where stone tool cut marks and carnivore bite marks overlapped, the pattern shows that humans had first access (Díez et al. 1999). Although it is possible that these archaic humans were scavenging complete carcasses, hunting seems more likely. An interesting side note is that some human bones were found with cut marks indicating removal of flesh, although it is not clear whether this would have been for ritualistic or cannibalistic reasons.

Additional evidence of hunting by *H. heidelbergensis* comes from the Boxgrove site in England. Analysis of animal bones shows that here too humans had access to complete carcasses. Although it is possible that complete carcasses came from animals that were already dead, which would indicate that *H. heidelbergensis* scavenged them, the presence of several butchered rhino adults is more consistent with hunting. To be scavenged, the rhinos would have had to die of natural causes or to be killed but then abandoned by a predator. These rhinos were adults in good health, and it is doubtful that they had any natural predators. Although not conclusive, this evidence argues strongly that the rhinos were hunted (Stringer et al. 1998).

Strong evidence for hunting also appears in wooden spears found at an archaeological site in Schöningen, Germany, dating to 400,000 years ago (Thieme 2000). Although wood generally decomposes, occasionally, when conditions are just right, wooden objects can be preserved over many thousands of years. Several wooden spears have been recovered from the Schöningen site. One was made of spruce and was relatively short—78 cm (roughly 31 in.)—and had both ends sharpened. Others were longer, ranging in length from 1.8 to 2.5 m (roughly 6–8 ft). The spear ends had been sharpened, and the overall appearance and weight balance was very similar to a modern-day javelin. The site also contains numerous butchered animal bones, and the spears were found among the butchered remains of as many as 19 horses. The inference from these remains is that hominins hunted an entire herd at one time. Although no hominin remains were found, the location and date of the site are most consistent with *H. heidelbergensis* being the hunter, as *H. erectus* has not been found in this part of Europe at this late date.

Classification and Evolutionary Relationships

As noted previously, debate continues regarding the appropriate classification of the Middle Pleistocene hominins. This text uses the species name *Homo heidelbergensis* as a label for a paleospecies that may or may not correspond to the biological species concept. Part of the debate is over whether evolution within the genus *Homo* was through anagenesis (evolution within a lineage over time) or cladogenesis (speciation and separation of species at one point in time). Some use the species name *H. heidelbergensis* to represent a stage in the evolution from *H. erectus* to modern *H. sapiens*. As such, the species names represent different chronospecies in a single line, and the boundaries between them are viewed as arbitrary. Others would use the label "archaic *H. sapiens*" or "early *H. sapiens*" to represent the Middle Pleistocene stage (Bräuer 2001). Still others view the transition in the Middle Pleistocene as a true speciation and *H. heidelbergensis* as a reproductively isolated species (Rightmire 1992). There are also advocates of a more complex system, placing some of what are referred to here as *H. heidelbergensis* into different species. For example, some have suggested that the Gran Dolina hominins should be placed into their own species—*Homo antecessor* (Bermúdez de Castro et al. 2004).

Regardless of the name used for the Middle Pleistocene hominins, clearly they are descended from *H. erectus* (although some would argue this is true only of the African forms of *H. erectus*). It is also widely thought that some population(s) of *H. heidelbergensis* evolved into modern humans, a topic covered in the next chapter. It turns out as well that later populations of *H. heidelbergensis* in Europe show a number of physical similarities to a later group of European hominins that lived at the same time as modern humans, the Neandertals.

THE NEANDERTALS

Neandertals A population of humans that lived in Europe and the Middle East between about 130,000 and 28,000 years ago. Debate continues about whether they are a subspecies of *Homo sapiens* or a separate species and to what extent they contributed to the ancestry of modern humans.

The **Neandertals** are a group of large-brained hominins with particular physical characteristics that lived in Europe and the Middle East. Named after the site of the first discovery (see the Special Topic box on page 333), the Neandertals have always been a subject of intense interest because of their similarities to and differences from us, and the question of whether they are part of our ancestry.

Distribution in Time and Space

The distribution of major Neandertal sites is shown in Figure 11.25, and details about the major sites are given in Table 11.3. Neandertals appeared in Europe around 130,000 years ago (McKee et al. 2005), although some Neandertal traits can be seen in earlier (*Homo heidelbergensis*) populations at Atapuerca in Spain 400,000 years ago. Some Neandertal populations survived in Europe until at least 28,000 years ago (Smith et al. 1999) and perhaps several thousand years later (Finlayson et al. 2006). Thus, many of the Neandertals lived in Europe during glacial times. Neandertals also lived in the Middle East at different times in the past; these populations apparently represent the dispersal of Neandertals southward during times of intense cold and diminished resources (Bar-Yosef 1994).

TABLE 11.3   Major Fossil Sites for Neandertals

Geographic Region	Country	Site/Specimen	Age (ka)[1]	Reference for Age	Figure in Text
Europe	Croatia	Krapina	130	3	
		Vindija	28	2	
	Italy	Saccopastore	129–122?	3	
	France	La Ferrassie	75–60	3	11.25
		La Chapelle	56 or 47	3	11.26
		La Quina	55–40?	1	
		Le Moustier	40	3	
		St. Césaire	36	3	
	Gibraltar	Forbe's Quarry	70–45?	1	
	Germany	Neandertal (Feldhofer)	40	4	
		Mt. Circeo	60–50	3	
Middle East	Iraq	Shanidar	46	1	11.28
	Israel	Tabun	103–80?	3	11.27
		Kebara	60	3	
		Amud	55–47	3	

[1]Question marks indicate a range in likely dates for the site/specimen.
References: 1. Larsen et al. (1998); 2. Smith et al. (2004); 3. Wolpoff (1999); 4. Schmitz et al. (2002).

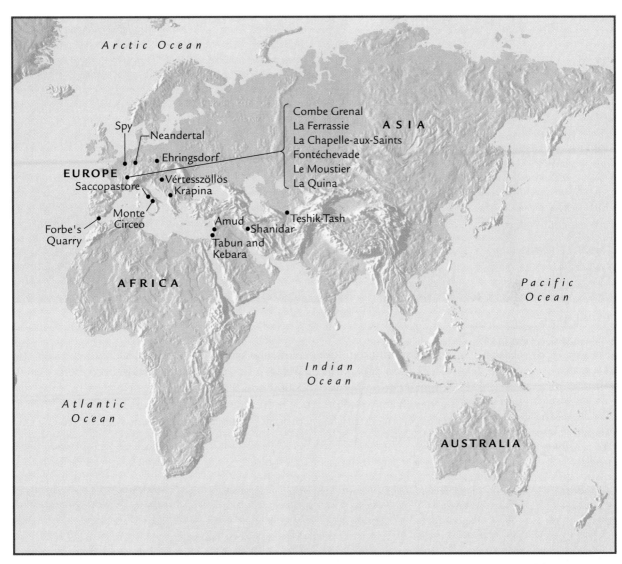

FIGURE 11.25

Location of major Neandertal sites.

Physical Characteristics

The Neandertals had very large brains, averaging about 1,450 cc. Although Neandertals on average had larger brains than living humans do, they also had large body mass. Relative to body size, Neandertal cranial capacity is slightly lower than that of living humans (Ruff et al. 1997). According to Holloway (1985), the structural organization of Neandertal brains, as assessed from endocasts, is no different from that of modern humans.

Cranial Features Neandertals shared many characteristics with earlier hominins, such as a low skull, sloping forehead, lack of chin, and large brow ridges. Neandertals also possessed a number of features that were unique to

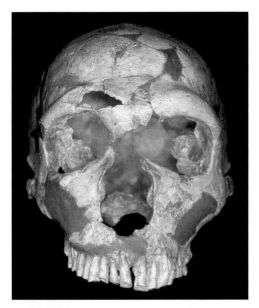

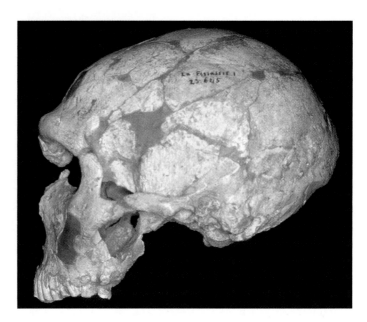

FIGURE 11.26

Frontal and side views of La Ferrassie skull, a Neandertal from France.

FIGURE 11.27

Two side views of La Chapelle skull, a Neandertal from France.

them, or found in lower frequencies in other populations. Figures 11.26 and 11.27 show two skulls of Western European Neandertals, both from sites in France dating between 75,000 and 50,000 years ago. Neandertal faces are generally long and protrude more than in modern humans. The nasal region is large, suggesting large, protruding noses, and the sinus cavities to the side of the nose expand outward. As such, the entire midfacial region protrudes

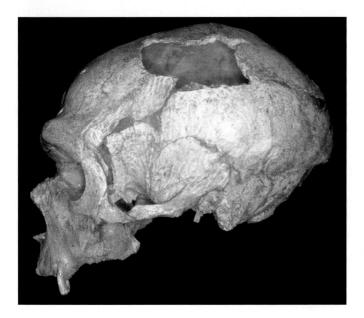

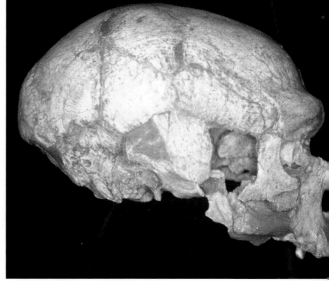

Neandertals: Names and Images

The name "Neandertal" comes from the site in the Neander Valley in Germany where Neandertals were first found. In German, *tal* means "valley." Hence, Neandertal means "Neander Valley." You may be more familiar with an alternative spelling, Neanderthal, and an alternative pronunciation (emphasizing the "THAL" sound). However, the *h* is silent in German so that "thal" is actually pronounced "tal." Because of this characteristic of German pronunciation, many (although not all) anthropologists simply drop the *h* in the spelling as well. Note, however, that the *h* is retained in the original spelling in the species (or subspecies) name *neanderthalensis*, because even though the *h* is silent, the word for valley was spelled "thal" in the nineteenth century, the time when the taxonomic name *neanderthalensis* was established. According to the rules of biological nomenclature, the original spelling must be retained even though modern German no longer uses the *h* in spelling.

The very mention of Neandertals usually invokes a number of images and preconceptions. You may, for example, conjure up one of many images of the Neandertals as crude and simple subhumans with limited intelligence that walked bent over. These images have become such a part of our popular culture that a typical dictionary definition includes "Neandertal" as an adjective meaning "suggesting primitive man in appearance or behavior (Neandertal ferocity)" and "extremely old-fashioned or out-of-date," as well as a noun meaning "a rugged or uncouth person" (*Webster's Third International Dictionary*). It is no wonder that many people use "Neandertal" as an insult.

Why do Neandertals have such a bad reputation? Regardless of whether we view Neandertals as a separate species or as a subspecies of *Homo sapiens,* we know that Neandertals had large brains, walked upright, and possessed a sophisticated culture, including stone tools, hunting, use of fire, and cave burial. Part of the image problem comes from an inaccurate reconstruction of a Neandertal skeleton in the early 1900s. Because of certain physical features, such as curved thigh bones, scientists of the time believed that Neandertals did not walk completely upright, but instead moved about bent over. It was discovered later that the curved bones and other features were simply a reflection of the poor health, including severe arthritis, of that particular Neandertal. Other features once taken to indicate mental inferiority, such as large brow ridges, are now recognized as biomechanical in nature. Even though the scientific interpretation has changed, the popular images of Neandertals unfortunately remain to this day, and the term "Neandertal" is still used as an insult. More information on the history of Neandertals, including further discussion of their image, can be found in Trinkaus and Shipman (1992) and Stringer and Gamble (1993).

from the skull. The large nasal and midfacial areas on Neandertals have often been interpreted as some type of adaptation to a cold climate (see the discussion on nasal size and shape in relation to climate in Chapter 16). Rak (1986), however, interpreted the large faces of Neandertals in terms of the biomechanics of the skull. He suggested that the Neandertal face acted to withstand stresses brought about by the use of relatively large front teeth. The front teeth of Neandertals are large relative to their back teeth and often show considerable wear, suggesting that they were used as tools. Neandertals tend to have large brow ridges that form double arches over the eyes. The cheekbones of Neandertals tend to be swept back, and the back of the skull is rather puffed out, a feature called an **occipital bun.** Cranial differences between Neandertals and modern humans appear to develop early in life (Ponce de León and Zollikofer 2001).

occipital bun The protruding rear region of the skull, a feature commonly found in Neandertals.

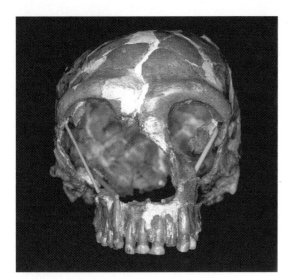

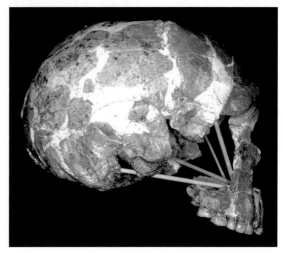

FIGURE 11.28

Frontal and side views of a Neandertal skull from Tabun, Israel.

There is also regional variation within Neandertals. Figures 11.28 and 11.29 show the skulls of two Middle Eastern Neandertals. Though they possess the general characteristics of Neandertals, they are not as morphologically extreme. The skulls are a bit more well-rounded than most Western European Neandertals.

The Postcranial Skeleton   Neandertal postcranial remains show that Neandertals were relatively short and stocky. The limb bones farthest from the body (the lower arm and lower leg) are relatively short, most likely reflecting cold adaptation (Trinkaus 1981). The limb and shoulder bones are more rugged

FIGURE 11.29

Shanidar I skull, Iraq. (From Clark Spencer Larsen, Robert M. Matter, and Daniel L. Gebo, *Human Origins: The Fossil Record*, 3d ed., p. 136. Copyright © 1998 by Waveland Press, Inc., Long Grove, IL. All rights reserved. Reprinted with permission from the publisher.)

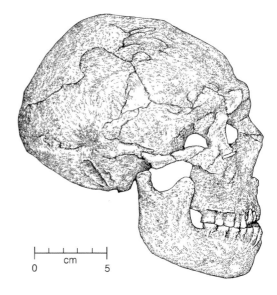

cm
0   5

than those of modern humans, and the areas of muscle attachment show that the Neandertals were very strong. The pelvic bones are also rather robust compared with those of modern humans, with the exception of the upper portion of the pubis (at the front of the pelvis), which is actually thinner and longer than in modern humans. The uniqueness of the Neandertal pelvis may reflect some biomechanical function of posture and locomotion (Rak and Arensberg 1987).

Neandertal DNA

In the summer of 1997, an article in the journal *Cell* announced to the world an amazing technological breakthrough—the extraction of a DNA sequence from a Neandertal fossil at the Feldhofer site in Germany (Krings et al. 1997). This marked the first time human DNA had been successfully extracted from such an old specimen; the site is now dated to about 40,000 years ago (Schmitz et al. 2002). The extracted sequence consisted of 378 mitochondrial DNA bases. Mitochondrial DNA (discussed in Chapter 2) preserves better than nuclear DNA and is commonly used in studies of ancient DNA. Since that time, mitochondrial DNA has been extracted from nine additional Neandertal specimens from Germany, Croatia, Spain, Belgium, and the northern Caucasus, dating from 100,000 to 29,000 years ago (Krings et al. 2000; Ovchinnikov et al. 2000; Schmitz et al. 2002; Serre et al. 2004; Lalueza-Fox et al. 2005; Orlando et al. 2006).

These DNA sequences are quite different from those of living humans. For example, in the first analysis comparing 378 DNA bases, there were 27 differences between Neandertal mitochondrial DNA and living human DNA, compared to an average of 8 differences between pairs of living humans. The other Neandertal specimens also show this high genetic difference relative to living humans. Overall, the Neandertal DNA analyses have been taken by many as evidence that the Neandertals were not among our ancestors and were likely a separate species that became extinct in Europe 28,000 years ago.

The situation may not be that simple. Neandertal mitochondrial DNA *is* different from that of living humans. The question is whether it is different enough for Neandertals to be considered a separate species. Comparative DNA analysis of living primates offers some clues. The difference between Neandertals and living humans is actually less than that found in two out of three comparisons of chimpanzee subspecies (Krings et al. 1999). This suggests that Neandertals might be a different subspecies but still be among our ancestors (Relethford 2001). A second observation is that we do not find any mitochondrial DNA as divergent as Neandertal DNA among living humans. One possible reason they left no mitochondrial DNA is that they were a separate species that became extinct. Another possibility is that their mitochondrial DNA was lost due to genetic drift.

Ultimately, there is only so much information that can be obtained from mitochondrial DNA. Using new technologies, preliminary analyses of the nuclear DNA have been conducted (Green et al. 2006; Noonan et al.

2006). One study extracted over 65,000 base pairs of nuclear DNA and another study extracted one million base pairs. The preliminary results suggest that the Neandertal line split off from a common ancestor with modern humans about half a million years ago, which is consistent with the hypothesis that the Neandertals were a separate species. However, genetic evidence suggests that some genetic mixture with modern humans may have taken place. Further sequencing and analysis will be needed to explore the degree of genetic relationship between Neandertals and modern humans. At present, an ambitious program is underway to sequence the entire Neandertal genome (Dalton 2006), a project that could answer many questions regarding Neandertal evolution.

Cultural Behavior

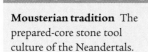

Mousterian tradition The prepared-core stone tool culture of the Neandertals.

As with late *Homo heidelbergensis,* the Neandertals made tools using the Levallois technique. The specific stone tool culture of the Neandertals is known as the **Mousterian tradition.** The Mousterian culture, named after the site of Le Moustier in France, produced a wide variety of different types of tools, including a preponderance of scrapers (Figure 11.30). Wooden spears used for hunting have also been found at Neandertal sites, including one found in an elephant skeleton (Stringer and Andrews 2005).

Archaeological evidence suggests that Neandertals may have been capable of symbolic thought, perhaps even holding beliefs in the supernatural. Neandertals buried their dead deliberately, as did early modern humans (Stringer and Andrews 2005). Evidence of burial comes from a number of European and Middle Eastern sites, where dead persons' bones have been arranged carefully in graves. This intentional burial of the dead has suggested a ritualistic purpose to some researchers. At the Shanidar Cave site in Iraq, flowers had been placed all over the bodies, an event that was reconstructed based on the presence of fossil pollen in the graves, although some have suggested that the pollen was introduced by rodents burrowing into the grave after burial. In any case, deliberate burial sug-

FIGURE 11.30

Examples of Mousterian tools: (a) scraper, (b) point, (c) scraper, (d) point, (e) hand axe. (From *The Old Stone Age* by F. Bordes, 1968, Weidenfeld and Nicolson, Ltd. Reprinted by permission of The McGraw-Hill Companies.)

a.   b.   c.   d.   e.

gests the evolution of symbolic expressions and the possibility of supernatural beliefs.

The physical condition of fossil remains offers another window on the Neandertal behavior. By looking at bone fractures, the condition of teeth, and other features, we can get a good idea of the age and health status of early humans. Many Neandertal remains are of elderly individuals with numerous medical problems. Some of the elderly had lost all of their teeth, many had arthritis, and one had lost part of his arm. By looking for signs of healing or infection, we can tell that many of these elderly individuals did not die from these afflictions. How then did they survive, particularly if they had lost all of their teeth? Survival of many of the elderly and impaired Neandertals suggests that others cared for them. This implies not only compassion as a social value but also the existence of a social system that allowed for the sharing of food and resources. This perspective may be based more on our interpretive biases, however, than on reality. Dettwyler (1991) has questioned the traditional view of the elderly and disabled as nonproductive members of a group. Drawing on cross-cultural studies, she notes that physically disabled individuals in many societies still frequently make important contributions.

Did the Neandertals have language? This question has long been asked, along with the more general question of how we can infer language abilities from skeletal remains. Lieberman and Crelin (1971), who reconstructed the vocal anatomy of Neandertals, concluded that they were incapable of vocalizing certain vowel sounds. The implication was that Neandertals did not possess as wide a range of sounds as modern humans and perhaps had limited language abilities. This hypothesis was criticized, however, because of differences of opinion on vocal anatomy reconstruction. The lack of direct fossil evidence at the heart of the debate was ultimately resolved with the discovery of the first Neandertal hyoid bone, a bone lying in the neck that can be used to provide information on the structure of the respiratory tract. That this specimen is almost identical in size and shape to the hyoid bone of modern humans suggests that there were *no* differences in vocal ability between Neandertals and modern humans (Arensberg et al. 1990). In addition, no evidence exists from brain anatomy to show that Neandertals lacked speech centers (Holloway 1985). Additional data on Neandertal language are considered in the next chapter.

Classification and Evolutionary Relationships

Available fossil evidence shows strong similarities among Middle Pleistocene populations in Europe, which likely represent a large part of Neandertal ancestry. What is less clear, and is a long-term controversy, is the relationship of the Neandertals to modern humans. In the nineteenth century, anatomist William King (1864) assigned the first-known Neandertal remains to a separate species, *Homo neanderthalensis,* because of the physical differences from modern humans. By the middle of the twentieth century, many anthropologists had begun to focus more on the similarities, such as the large brain, than the differences, and to consider Neandertals as a separate subspecies known as *Homo sapiens neanderthalensis,* set apart from living humans, who are classified in the subspecies *Homo sapiens sapiens.* As more data on anatomical differences has accumulated since the last part of the twentieth century, and the ancient mitochondrial DNA has revealed a large difference between Neandertals and modern humans, an increasing number of anthropologists have advocated returning to the practice of placing Neandertals in a separate species. The debate continues over whether to consider Neandertals a species, a subspecies, or even a semi-species.

Underlying discussion of what to call Neandertals is the more significant question of their evolutionary relationship to us. Were they a part of our ancestry, or did they contribute nothing to the current gene pool of our species? The fossil evidence shows that Neandertals as a group were last seen about 28,000 years ago. Toward the end of their existence, anatomically modern humans also lived in Europe, but it appears that they moved there from elsewhere (see the next chapter). Although the amount of time that Neandertals and modern humans may have coexisted in Europe is still being debated, it is clear that after 28,000 years ago, the only fossil hominins in Europe are modern humans. Where did the Neandertals go? Did they become extinct as a species, and if so, why? Or were their genes absorbed into the gene pool of modern humans? In order to begin to answer these questions, we must deal with the fact that while Neandertals were living in Europe, evolutionary changes were taking place elsewhere in the Old World, and anatomically modern *Homo sapiens* had appeared. The key question is, What happened to the Neandertals when modern humans migrated to Europe? Some propose that Neandertals were a separate species. Here, some populations of *H. heidelbergensis* evolved into a new species, *H. neanderthalensis,* in Europe, while other populations of *H. heidelbergensis* evolved into modern humans in Africa. Over time, the modern humans spread into Europe, and the Neandertals, for reasons that are not clear, died out as a species. In this view, there was no genetic mixing of Neandertals and modern humans (e.g., Stringer 2002). Others have argued that there was some genetic mixing and that part of the ancestry of living humans came from Neandertal populations. In this view, Neandertal genes were swamped, and the Neandertals disappeared as a group over several thousand years as they were assimilated into a larger modern population (Smith et al. 2004). This discussion continues with the more general issue of modern human origins in the next chapter.

Summary

The earliest fossil evidence for the genus *Homo* dates back almost 2.5 million years. Two species of early *Homo* have been found in Africa—*H. habilis* and *H. rudolfensis.* It is not clear which of these species may be ancestral to later *Homo.* The species *Homo erectus* appeared in Africa by 1.8 million years ago and rapidly spread to parts of Southeast Asia and Eastern Europe between 1.8 million and 1.6 million years ago. *H. erectus* showed signs of cranial expansion (the average brain size was roughly 72 percent that of modern humans) and human body proportions. The cultural adaptations of *H. erectus* included development of more sophisticated tools (the Acheulian tradition), use of fire, and the addition of significant amounts of meat to the diet, although it is not clear how much of the meat came from hunting rather than scavenging. Some *H. erectus* populations may have lived as recently as about 40,000 years ago. A small-bodied hominin with a very small cranial capacity on the island of Flores in Indonesia has been classified as the species *H. floresiensis;* some propose that this is a dwarf species of *H. erectus,* while others suggest it is a pathological specimen.

Close to 800,000 years ago, at the beginning of the Middle Pleistocene, hominins had evolved a larger brain, close in size to that of modern humans, but still retained a fairly large face and brow ridges and a less well-rounded skull. These hominins, sometimes classified as *H. heidelbergensis* and sometimes as "archaic *H. sapiens,*" lived in Africa, Europe, and Asia until about 200,000 years ago. These Middle Pleistocene hominins were definitely hunters and, by 300,000 years ago, had invented the Levallois technique of making stone tools, a process by which a core is shaped and a finished tool is removed with a single blow.

Two groups of hominins appear to have descended from the Middle Pleistocene hominins. One group was anatomically modern *H. sapiens,* whose origins are discussed in detail in the next chapter. The other group was the Neandertals, large-brained humans with large noses and midfaces, as well as other anatomical differences. Neandertals lived in Europe and the Middle East. Physical differences and the recovery of ancient DNA have convinced a number of anthropologists that the Neandertals were a separate species that became extinct by 28,000 years ago. Other anthropologists argue that Neandertals mixed genetically with modern humans but made little contribution to our gene pool over time, perhaps because of their small numbers. In any event, the Neandertals were skilled toolmakers and hunter-gatherers who buried their dead.

Supplemental Readings

Boaz, N. T., and R. L. Ciochon. 2004. *Dragon Bone Hill: An Ice-Age Saga of* Homo erectus. New York: Oxford University Press. A highly readable account of the history of discoveries at Zhoukoudian, China, and the anatomy and culture of *Homo erectus.*

Stringer, C., and P. Andrews. 2005. *The Complete World of Human Evolution.* New York: Thames and Hudson. A well-illustrated review of human evolution, with many sections on the evolution of *Homo* species.

Stringer, C., and C. Gamble. 1993. *In Search of the Neanderthals: Solving the Puzzle of Human Origins.* New York: Thames and Hudson. An excellent review of Neandertal (and other human) biology and culture.

VIRTUAL EXPLORATIONS

Visit our textbook-specific online learning center Web site at
www.mhhe.com/relethford7 to access the exercises that follow.

1. **Teenagers Special: The Original Rebels**   Read the article "Teenagers
   Special: The Original Rebels " from the March 2005 *New Science* article:
   http://www.newscientist.com/channel/being-human/teenagers/
   mg18524891.100. The article considers the possibility that the
   Turkana Boy found in Kenya at Lake Turkana in 1984 may represent
   evidence of an "adolescent phase" in the hominin record.

   - What has been the predominant argument for the delay in physi-
     cal growth in hominins?
   - Why does the Turkana Boy fossil discovery cause some scientists
     to reconsider this explanation?
   - What unique information do fossilized children provide?
   - Why are there difficulties in assessing the age of a skeleton based
     on "development markers"?
   - What alternate arguments are offered by Susan Anton (New York
     University) and Steven Leigh (University of Illinois) concerning
     the interpretation of Turkana Boy?
   - Do you feel that Turkana Boy offers new insights into our under-
     standing of hominin development? Why or why not?

2. **Homo heidelbergensis: Simply a Chronospecies?**   Archaeology
   Info.com is a project born of the work of Patrick Johnson, Jon Kurpis,
   and other researchers working in northern Kenya. Before you visit
   the ArchaeologyInfo.com site, make sure you are familiar with the
   term "chronospecies." Then go to the *Homo heidelbergensis* link:
   http://www.archaeologyinfo.com/homoheidelbergensis.htm.

   - What was the first evidence of *Homo heidelbergensis* that was dis-
     covered? Why was it first designated *Homo heidelbergensis*?
   - Why do many researchers argue that *heidelbergensis* is not a valid
     designation?
   - The article lists a number of "diagnostic features" that differenti-
     ate it from *H. erectus* and *H. neanderthalensis*. What are three of
     these features?
   - It is possible that several other discoveries in other parts of the
     world can be attributed to *Homo heidelbergensis*. What other sites
     contain hominins attributed to *Homo heidelbergensis*?
   - Do you agree with the assessment that *heidelbergensis* may simply
     be a "chronospecies"? Why or why not?

3. **Code of the Caveman** Read the article "Code of the Caveman" from the July 2006 issue of *Wired* magazine: **http://www.wired.com/ wired/archive/14.07/caveman.html**. In it, writer Annalee Newitz discusses the work of geneticist Eddy Rubin in sequencing and reading Neandertal DNA.

- How was Rubin able to successfully persuade two museums to provide him with small amounts of Neandertal bone fragments?
- The process for extracting Neandertal DNA that Newitz describes refers to "metagenomics." What is another, more familiar application of metagenomics?
- What was Rubin's conclusion concerning the probable divergence date of humans and Neandertals into recognizably separate groups?
- How was Rubin able to determine this?
- What other major evidence did Rubin extract from the data concerning Neandertal DNA and modern humans?

The Origin of Modern Humans

Anatomically modern humans (*Homo sapiens*) first appeared about 200,000 years ago, evolving from an earlier population (or populations) of Middle Pleistocene hominins. Many anthropologists see modern humans as evolving from *Homo heidelbergensis*. We use the term "anatomically modern" to refer to fossils that are the same as we are today, possessing certain physical characteristics such as a well-rounded skull and a noticeable chin. The origin of modern humans is an area of considerable debate among anthropologists today.

At the heart of this debate is a series of basic questions: What is the nature of this change? When and where did it occur? Did the change occur in only one place, or was it widespread? Why did it occur? What cultural changes took place, and how are they related to the biological changes? In short, our questions concern the recent history of the human species.

ANATOMICALLY MODERN HUMANS

Human evolution did not end with *Homo heidelbergensis* or the Neandertals. All fossil humans since 28,000 years ago are anatomically modern in form. Though it is clear that earlier humans evolved into anatomically modern humans, the exact nature of this evolution is less certain. This section deals with the biological and cultural characteristics of anatomically modern humans, followed by consideration of the nature of their evolution.

Distribution in Time and Space

Anatomically modern humans are found in many sites across both the Old World and the New World. Some of these sites are shown in Figure 12.1. Apart from ourselves (and the possible exception of *Homo floresiensis*),

◀ A prehistoric cave painting of two bison from the Altamira Caves in Spain. Cave art is one of several behaviors that either originated with or became much more common with the advent of modern humans.

anatomically modern *Homo sapiens* The modern form of the human species, which dates back 130,000 years.

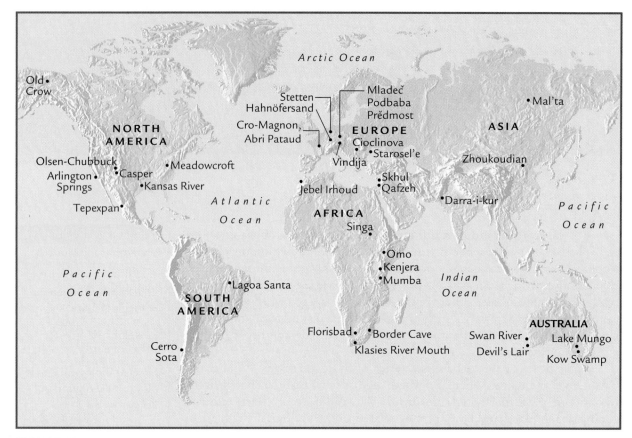

FIGURE 12.1

Location of some anatomically modern *Homo sapiens* sites.

FIGURE 12.2

The Omo 1 skull from Omo, Ethiopia. This skull shows modern human characteristics such as a high, well-rounded cranium and a chin. The Omo site dates to 195,000 years ago, making this specimen the earliest example of anatomically modern *Homo sapiens*.

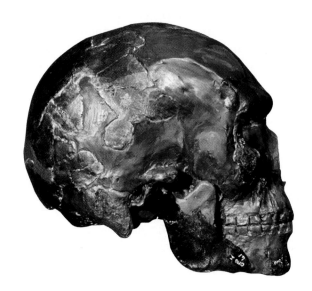

no other hominin species has lived during the last 20,000 years or so. The last Neandertal lived about 28,000 years ago, though some may have survived a few thousand years more (Finlayson et al. 2006). *Homo erectus* may have survived as late as 27,000 years ago in parts of Southeast Asia, although there is still debate over this date. In any event, anatomically modern *Homo sapiens* is the only hominin species that has lived to the present day.

As noted in the previous chapter, modern *H. sapiens* likely evolved from the archaic humans in the Middle Pleistocene—*Homo heidelbergensis* (which some call "archaic *Homo sapiens*"). The fossil evidence shows the earliest appearance of anatomically modern humans in Africa almost 200,000 years ago. At present, the oldest known modern human fossils come from the Omo site in Ethiopia, which dates to 195,000 years ago (McDougall et al. 2005). Though fragmentary, the Omo 1 skull shows a number of modern traits, such as a well-rounded rear of the skull, a high skull, and the presence of a chin (Figure 12.2). Several crania from the Middle Awash area of Ethiopia, dating to almost 160,000 years ago, show a number of modern human traits, including a high, well-rounded cranium (White et al. 2003) (Figure 12.3). And cranial remains from the Border Cave site in southeastern Africa are

FIGURE 12.3

Views of specimen BOU-VP-16/1, an early *Homo sapiens* cranium from the Middle Awash area of Ethiopia. Views clockwise from top left: side, frontal, top, bottom, rear, and three-quarter.

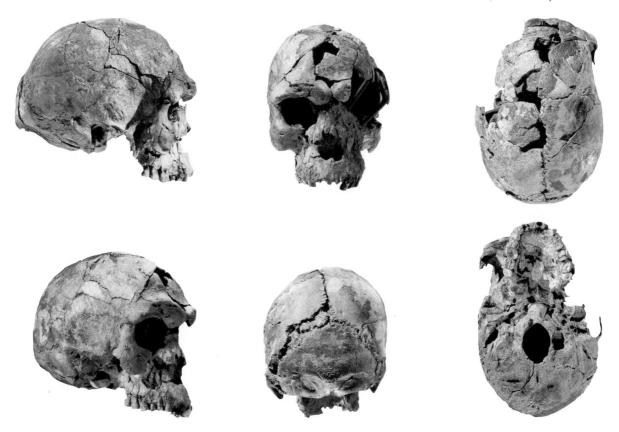

FIGURE 12.4

The Border Cave skull, South Africa. The fragmentary remains are clearly those of anatomically modern *Homo sapiens* (note the vertical forehead). Dating is not precise, but current estimates suggest an age of more than 100,000 years ago.

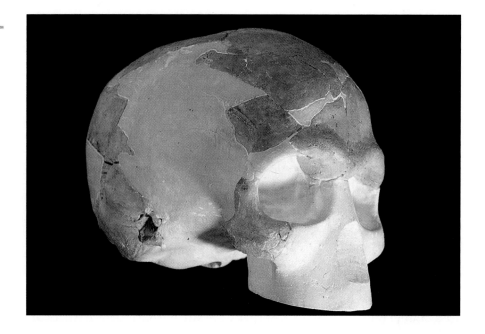

fragmentary but show typically modern features (Figure 12.4). The dating for this site is not definite but ranges from 115,000 to 90,000 years ago. In addition, modern humans may have occupied Klasies River Mouth in South Africa as early as 90,000 years ago (Grün et al. 1990). All of these data show a clear presence of anatomically modern humans in Africa between 100,000 and 200,000 years ago.

Modern humans are not found outside of Africa until later in time. The next appearance of modern humans is in the Middle East at the Qafzeh and Skhul sites in Israel, dating to 92,000 years ago (Grün et al. 1991). Modern humans first appeared in Australia sometime between 60,000 and 46,000 years ago. The fossil record from East Asia is less clear but suggests a date of perhaps 60,000 years ago (Stringer and McKie 1996). Modern humans are relative newcomers in Europe. Although it has long been believed that modern humans reached different parts of Europe between 40,000 and 30,000 years ago, estimates (including recalibration to account for fluctuations in atmospheric carbon-14) now suggest that modern humans may have dispersed across Europe between 46,000 and 41,000 years ago (Mellars 2006).

Physical Characteristics

Figure 12.5 shows a skull from one of the more famous anatomically modern sites—Cro-Magnon, France, dating between 27,000 and 23,000 years ago. This skull shows many of the characteristics of anatomically modern *Homo sapiens*. It is high and well rounded. There is no occipital bun; the back of the skull is rounded instead. The forehead rises vertically above the eye orbits and does not slope, as in archaic humans. The brow ridges are small, the face does not protrude very much, and a strong chin is evident.

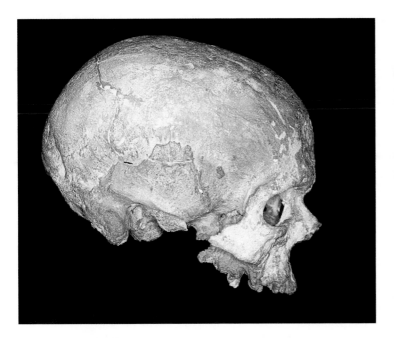

Another example of anatomically modern *H. sapiens* is shown in Figure 12.6, a skull from the Skhul site at Mount Carmel, Israel. This skull also has a high, well-rounded shape without an occipital bun and with a small chin. Compared to the Cro-Magnon skull, the brow ridges are larger and the face protrudes slightly. The differences between the Skhul and the Cro-Magnon

FIGURE 12.5

Side and frontal views of the Cro-Magnon skull, France. This specimen is one of the best-known examples of anatomically modern *Homo sapiens*.

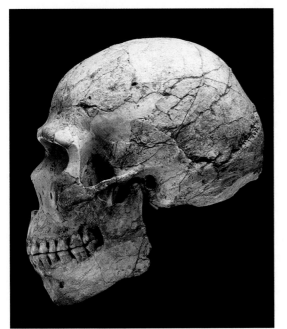

FIGURE 12.6

An early anatomically modern *Homo sapiens* skull from Skhul, Israel.

FIGURE 12.7

The Combe Capelle skull, anatomically modern *Homo sapiens,* France. (From Clark Spencer Larsen, Robert M. Matter, and Daniel L. Gebo, *Human Origins: The Fossil Record,* 3d ed., p. 169. Copyright © 1998 by Waveland Press, Inc., Long Grove, IL. All rights reserved. Reprinted with permission from the publisher.)

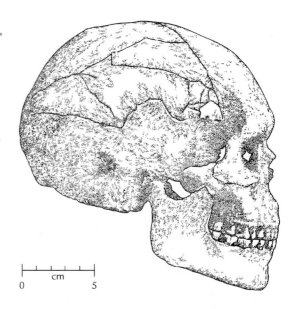

skulls are typical of variation within a species, particularly when we consider that they existed at different times in separate places. Other specimens also show similarities and differences when compared to one another. The skull in Figure 12.7 is from Combe Capelle, France, and dates back 35,000 to 30,000 years ago. It is high and well rounded, but the face protrudes slightly, and the chin is rather weak. There is clearly variation within both archaic and anatomically modern forms of *H. sapiens.* This variation makes evolutionary relationships difficult to assess at times.

Cultural Behavior

Discussing the cultural adaptations of anatomically modern *Homo sapiens* is difficult because they include both prehistoric technologies and more recent developments, such as agriculture, generation of electricity, the internal combustion engine, and nuclear energy. So that we may provide a comparison with the culture of the archaic forms, this section is limited to prehistory before the development of agriculture (roughly 12,000 years ago).

Tool Technologies   There is so much variation in the stone tool technologies of anatomically modern *H. sapiens* that it is impossible to define a single tradition. Earlier populations of anatomically modern *H. sapiens* are found with earlier types of tools, but by about 90,000 years ago, newer technologies appeared. For the sake of discussion, these types of new stone tool industries are often lumped together under the term **Upper Paleolithic** (which means "Upper Old Stone Age"). **Lower Paleolithic** consists of the stone tool traditions of *H. habilis/H. rudolfensis* and *H. erectus,* and **Middle Paleolithic** includes the stone tool traditions of *Homo heidelbergensis* and the Neandertals. Even though we use a single label to describe common features of Upper

Upper Paleolithic A general term used to collectively refer to the stone tool technologies of anatomically modern *Homo sapiens.*

Lower Paleolithic A general term used to collectively refer to the stone tool technologies of *Homo habilis/Homo rudolfensis* and *Homo erectus.*

Middle Paleolithic A general term used to refer collectively to the stone tool technologies of *Homo heidelbergensis* and the Neandertals.

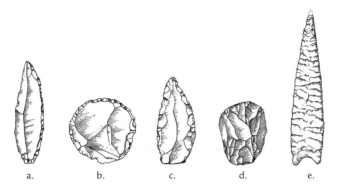

a.   b.   c.   d.   e.

FIGURE 12.8

Examples of Upper Paleolithic stone tools: (a) knife, (b) scraper, (c) point, (d) scraper, (e) point. Tools a, b, and c are from the Perigordian culture; tool d is from the Aurignacian culture; tool e is from the Solutrean culture. (From *The Old Stone Age* by F. Bordes, 1968, Weidenfeld and Nicolson, Ltd. Reprinted by permission of The McGraw-Hill Companies.)

Paleolithic tool industries, do not be misled into thinking that all traditions were the same. Variation, both within and among sites, is even greater in the Upper Paleolithic than in earlier cultures. This variation demonstrates the increasing sophistication and specialization of stone tools.

Figure 12.8 shows some examples of Upper Paleolithic stone tools. These tools are much more precisely made than the stone tools of earlier hominins and are also quite a bit more diverse in function and styles. One notable characteristic of the Upper Paleolithic is the development of **blades,** stone tools defined as being at least twice as long as they are wide (Figure 12.9). Blade tools are made by removing long, narrow flakes off a prepared core. The core is struck by a piece of antler or bone, which in turn is struck by a stone.

blade A stone tool characteristic of the Upper Paleolithic, defined as being at least twice as long as it is wide.

FIGURE 12.9

Example of a flint blade tool. (From *Human Antiquity: An Introduction to Physical Anthropology and Archaeology,* 4th ed., by Kenneth Feder and Michael Park, Fig. 13.3. Copyright © 2001 by Mayfield Publishing Company. Reprinted with permission of The McGraw-Hill Companies.)

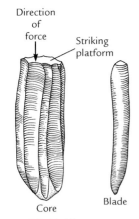

FIGURE 12.10

Method of blade tool manufacture. A striking platform is formed, and a blade tool can then be made by flaking off a long vertical piece from the side. (From *Discovering Anthropology* by Daniel R. Gross, Fig. 7.10. Copyright © 1993 by Mayfield Publishing Company. Reprinted by permission of The McGraw-Hill Companies.)

burin A stone tool with a sharp edge that is used to cut and engrave bone.

That is, the core is not hit directly by the hammerstone; rather, the force of the blow is applied through the antler. This method allows very thin and sharp blade tools to be made (Figure 12.10).

Upper Paleolithic tools were also used to make tools out of other resources, such as bone. A small stone tool called a **burin** has an extremely sharp edge that is used to cut, whittle, and engrave bone. Bone was used to make needles, awls, points, knives, and harpoons, as well as art objects. Bone tools and elaborate art objects first appeared with modern *H. sapiens;* they are not found in the culture of earlier hominins (although there are suggestions of art objects associated with earlier humans, these finds are controversial). For years, it appeared that bone tools were fairly recent, dating back roughly 40,000 years. Research in Zaire, however, has produced a much earlier age of 90,000 years (Brooks et al. 1995; Yellen et al. 1995).

Shelter   Like archaic *H. sapiens,* modern *H. sapiens* lived in caves and rock shelters where available. The archaeological evidence also shows definite evidence of manufactured shelter—huts made of wood, animal bone, and animal hides. Although much of this material decomposes, we can still find evidence of support structures. One example of hut building comes from the 18,000-year-old site of Mal'ta in south-central Russia (Figure 12.11). This hut is particularly interesting because people used mammoth ribs and leg bones for structural support. Other sites, such as the 15,000-year-old site of Mezhirich in the Ukraine, contain evidence of shelters built almost entirely from mammoth bones.

Art   Another form of symbolic behavior is artistic expression, including cave art, sculptures, and engravings. Although some archaeologists consider art to be unique to modern humans, beginning 50,000 to 40,000 years ago, others have suggested that art began earlier in Africa and gradually increased in frequency in later modern humans. Engravings have been found in Africa

FIGURE 12.11

Reconstruction of a hut at the Mal'ta site in Russia. This site dates to 18,000 years ago. (From *Human Antiquity: An Introduction to Physical Anthropology and Archaeology,* 4th ed., by Kenneth Feder and Michael Park, Fig. 13.5. Copyright © 2001 by Mayfield Publishing Company. Reprinted by permission of The McGraw-Hill Companies.)

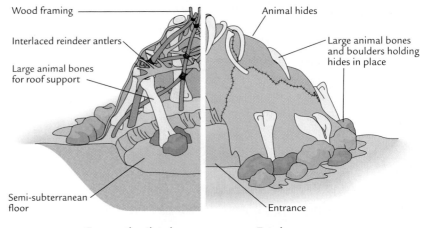

Wood framing

Interlaced reindeer antlers

Large animal bones for roof support

Animal hides

Large animal bones and boulders holding hides in place

Semi-subterranean floor

Entrance

Cross section / interior   Exterior

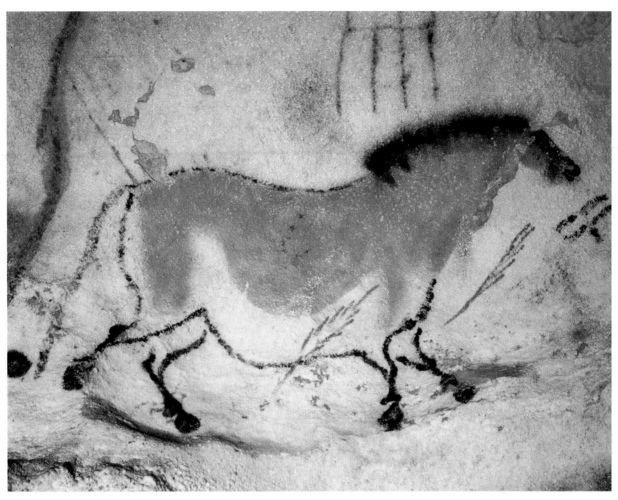

FIGURE 12.12

Cave painting of a running horse from Lascaux Cave, France.

dating to 77,000 years ago, which supports the latter view (Henshilwood et al. 2002). In either case, artistic expression became more pronounced in modern humans.

Perhaps the best example of prehistoric art is cave art, which dates back more than 30,000 years in Europe, Africa, and Australia. Some of the best-known cave art, primarily paintings of large game animals and hunting, comes from sites in Europe (Figures 12.12 and 12.13). These paintings are anatomically correct and are well executed. Painting is a human activity that is spiritually rewarding but has no apparent function in day-to-day existence. Why, then, did early humans paint images on the walls of caves? Several interpretations have been offered, including sympathetic magic (capturing the image of an animal to improve hunters' chances of actually killing it). Other interpretations focus on cultural symbolism or a means of communicating ideas and images. We will never know exactly *why* early humans made these paintings. What is clear, however, is that they did

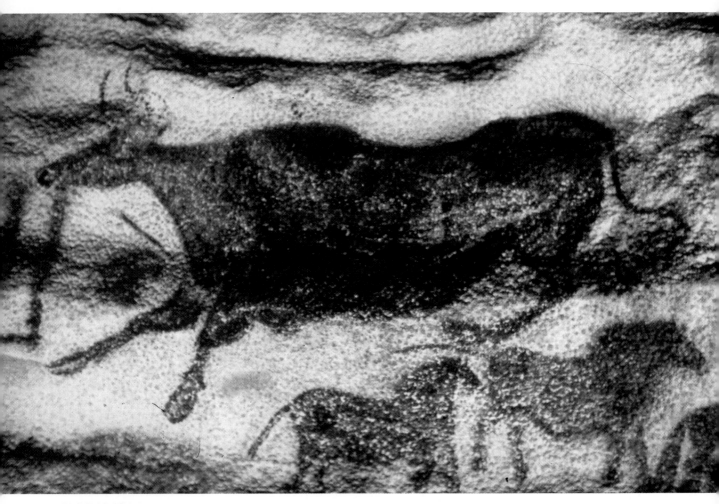

FIGURE 12.13

Cave painting of a cow from Lascaux Cave, France.

something that serves a symbolic purpose. Although we cannot know the reason for these behaviors, the art shows us that humans by this time had developed a need to express themselves symbolically. To these early moderns, life was not just eating and surviving—something else was important to them as well.

Cave paintings are not the only form of art associated with early modern *H. sapiens*. We also find evidence of engravings, beads and pendants, and ceramic sculpture. One of the best-known examples is the "Venus" figurines found throughout parts of Europe. These figures are pregnant females with exaggerated breasts and buttocks (Figure 12.14). Although these figurines are often interpreted as fertility symbols (fertility would have been critical to survival), we are not sure of their exact meaning or function. However, as with cave paintings, the Venus figurines show us that symbolism was fully a part of the life of early modern *H. sapiens*.

FIGURE 12.14

A Venus figurine.

Geographic Expansion The archaeological evidence shows that humans became more and more successful over time in adapting to their environment, and consequently populations grew and expanded into new areas. Although *H. erectus* and archaic humans lived in parts of Africa, Asia, and Europe, it is only with the appearance of modern humans that we see expansion into Australia and the New World.

Australia was first occupied by modern humans at least 46,000 years ago (Bowler et al. 2003) and perhaps as early as 60,000 years ago (Thorne et al. 1999). As mentioned in the previous chapter, during times of glaciation, sea levels drop, extending the land mass of continents, which meant that humans could have reached Southeast Asia. However, Australia was not connected to the mainland, and the only way modern humans could have reached that continent was by crossing many kilometers of sea using some sort of raft or boat. Modern humans probably reached the New World between 20,000 and 15,000 years ago, either by crossing the Bering Land Bridge or by boat, or both (see Chapter 14).

***First Appearance of the Culture of Early Modern* Homo Sapiens**   There is debate over the speed of the emergence of the culture of early modern humans, with some favoring a model of rapid development and others a more gradual accumulation of these behaviors over time. For many years, the archaeological record of early modern humans was interpreted as supporting a rapid "creative explosion" of new technologies and behaviors that first appeared about 40,000 to 50,000 years ago. This interpretation was based in part on the first appearance of modern behaviors in the European archaeological record and did not take into account changes happening elsewhere. In recent decades, archaeological research from Africa has suggested that many of these behaviors actually appeared tens of thousands of years earlier, and the emergence of modern human culture did not take place all at once but instead cumulatively over time in Africa (McBrearty and Brooks 2000; Henshilwood et al. 2002).

THE MODERN HUMAN ORIGINS DEBATE

Where, when, how, and why did anatomically modern humans evolve? The general trend in the fossil record shows that modern humans evolved from the "archaic humans" who lived in the Middle Pleistocene, called *Homo heidelbergensis* by some and "archaic *Homo sapiens*" by others. Details of this evolutionary transition are the focus of the debate over modern human origins.

   The debate over the origin of modern human origins revolves around two key issues: the location of the transition and the nature of the transition (Relethford 2001). In terms of location, where (and when) did modern humans first appear? Did the initial transition take place in one part of the Old World, or did the transition involve the entire Old World? In terms of the nature of the transition, were modern humans a new species, or did they arise through anagenesis from an earlier species?

Location of the Transition to Modern Humans

By the Middle Pleistocene, archaic humans (referred to here as *Homo heidelbergensis*) were spread out over parts of Africa, Europe, and Asia. Some have argued that this was a worldwide transition; others have argued that modern humans arose in Africa. According to the **multiregional evolution model,** human evolution over the past 1.8 million years took place within a single

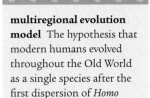

multiregional evolution model The hypothesis that modern humans evolved throughout the Old World as a single species after the first dispersal of *Homo erectus* out of Africa.

evolving lineage from *H. erectus* to *H. heidelbergensis* to *H. sapiens*. According to the general form of this model, our species began 1.8 million years ago in Africa with early humans (*H. erectus*). The species continued to evolve over time, with further increases in brain size and changes in cranial shape, ultimately leading to modern humans. As such, "early," "archaic," and "modern" are merely convenient labels for different stages of human evolution. Proponents of multiregional evolution have often argued that modern human anatomy did not appear in any single place. Instead, they suggest a process whereby the transition from archaic to modern humans took place piecemeal across the Old World, with some changes occurring in different places and at different times. According to this view, modern humans arose through the mixing of these changes through gene flow (Wolpoff et al. 1994; Relethford 2001).

The alternative to a worldwide transition to modern humans is the hypothesis of an African origin. In this model, modern human anatomy appeared first in Africa and then spread throughout the remainder of the Old World. In contrast, in the multiregional model the boundary between archaic and modern humans is less clear, and there is no single point of origin for modern humans.

At this point, the fossil evidence more clearly supports an African origin of modern humans. As noted previously, the most recent dating shows that anatomically modern humans lived in Africa close to 200,000 years ago, with the next-oldest sites dating to about 90,000 years ago in the Middle East, and the younger still in other parts of the Old World. The transition from archaic to modern is not piecemeal, but is instead African in origin. The debate continues, however, over the relative role that Africa and other geographic regions played in terms of the ancestry of modern humans. Were our ancestors only from Africa, or did populations in other parts of the world also contribute to our ancestry?

Replacement or Assimilation?

Although the fossil evidence strongly favors the initial origin of anatomically modern humans in Africa, it is less clear whether the nature of this transition was the origin of a new species (cladogenesis) or evolution within an evolving lineage (anagenesis). Different models have been proposed to explain what happened after the initial African origin of modern humans.

African Origin Models   There are two commonly held models of how modern humans spread following their initial origin in Africa. According to the **African replacement model,** modern humans emerged as a new species in Africa, splitting off from *H. heidelbergensis* roughly 200,000 years ago. Some populations began leaving Africa by 100,000 years ago and spread throughout the Old World, replacing preexisting human populations outside of Africa (Cann et al. 1987; Stringer and Andrews 1988). In this model, any

African replacement model The hypothesis that modern humans evolved as a new species in Africa 200,000 years ago and then spread throughout the Old World, replacing preexisting human populations.

FIGURE 12.15

The African replacement model. Modern humans (*Homo sapiens*) arose as a new species in Africa about 200,000 years ago. This species then spread out across the Old World, replacing humans in other species, such as *Homo heidelbergensis* and *Homo erectus,* outside of Africa.

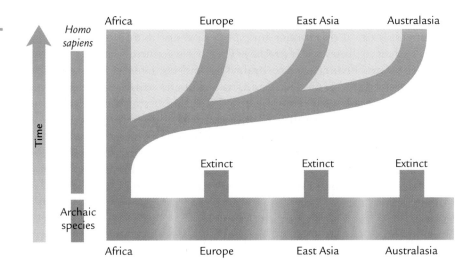

assimilation model The hypothesis that modern human anatomy arose first in Africa as a change within a species and then spread through gene flow to populations outside of Africa. The gene pool of the non-African populations was thus assimilated into an expanding population of modern humans out of Africa.

regional continuity The appearance of similar traits within a geographic region that remain over a long period of time.

humans outside of Africa (such as the Neandertals in Europe) became extinct and are not part of the ancestry of living humans (Figure 12.15).

An alternative view is the **assimilation model,** a variant of the multi-regional model proposing that the initial change to modern humans took place in Africa, as proposed by the African replacement model, but that these changes then spread to other populations outside of Africa through gene flow (Eswaran 2002; Smith 2002). The genes of the non-African populations were assimilated into the gene pool of the expanding modern human population rather than being replaced. The assimilation model shares with the multiregional model the view of the importance of gene flow to the spread of modern humans, but argues for a single point of initial origin in Africa (Smith et al. 2005). The assimilation model stresses anagenesis, so that the transition from archaic (*H. heidelbergensis*) to modern (*H. sapiens*) humans is within a single evolutionary lineage.

Another way of looking at the difference between the African replacement model and the assimilation model is to consider the two models in terms of the ancestry of living humans (Relethford 2003). Where did our ancestors live 200,000 years ago? In the African replacement model, they *all* lived in Africa. In the assimilation model, many lived in Africa, but not all. What is the evidence for these two models?

The Fossil Evidence The assimilation model predicts some ancestry from populations outside of Africa, which would lead to a pattern of **regional continuity** in the fossil record—the appearance of similar traits within the same geographic region over time. For example, some humans, past and present, have a particular dental trait known as shovel-shaped incisors, which have a ridge on the outer margins of the incisor teeth. Although this trait is found across the world today, it is found most frequently in both living *and* ancient populations in East Asia. The fact that this trait is most common throughout time in the same geographic region suggests some genetic contribution over time; that is, earlier hominin populations contributed some of their genes to living Asian populations. Another example is the high angle of the nose, a trait found frequently in both European Neandertals and living Europeans. Even though gene flow will reduce the frequency of regional differences, such that some regional traits will be lost through time, others will persist because of genetic drift and selection (Wolpoff and Caspari 1997; Relethford 2001).

The regional continuity of traits is perhaps best explained by the genetic continuity over time predicted by the assimilation model. The presence of regional continuity is difficult to explain under the African replacement model because it would require traits to reappear independently. There is debate over which traits, if any, show continuity and in which regions. Many anthropologists have argued that the evidence for continuity is strong in the fossil records of East Asia and Australasia (e.g., Kramer 1991; Thorne and Wolpoff 1992; Hawks et al. 2000; Wolpoff et al. 2001). Others (e.g., Lahr 1996) find little evidence of regional continuity and argue further that the few indications of continuity can be explained by common evolutionary trends.

The issue of continuity is more complicated in Europe, where the coexistence of Neandertal and modern human populations for perhaps several thousand years, followed by the disappearance of the Neandertals, is often considered evidence of replacement. This pattern, combined with the distinct morphology of the Neandertals and the findings of divergent ancient DNA, has led a number of anthropologists to support the idea that Neandertals were a separate species that became extinct.

Not everyone agrees, and there is fossil evidence for regional continuity in Europe. One example is the skeleton of a 4-year-old child from 25,000 years ago that was found at the Lagar Velho site in Portugal. Although the child is considered an anatomically modern human, the cranium shows a mix of modern and Neandertal characteristics, and the postcranial skeleton shows Neandertal features (Duarte et al. 1999). This find may represent an example of Neandertal ancestry in modern humans that came about when the two populations encountered each other in Western Europe (Trinkaus and Zilhão 2002). Others disagree, arguing that this find is an example of a rather stocky modern human child (Tattersall and Schwartz 1999).

Another clue comes from looking at changes in the frequency of Neandertal features in Europe over time. Wolpoff (1999) looked at 18 anatomical traits considered unique to Neandertals and examined their frequency in the earliest post-Neandertal European moderns and in living Europeans. In a strict replacement model, these traits should be absent in the early modern populations, but instead there is a pattern of reduction over time. For example, one unique Neandertal dental trait is found in 53 percent of all Neandertals, 18 percent of post-Neandertal early moderns, and 1 percent of living Europeans. Instead of the pattern of complete elimination predicted from replacement, this trait shows a decline over time consistent with Neandertals experiencing gene flow from outside Europe. If verified, this means that Neandertals disappeared due to the cumulative effects of gene flow—they were absorbed into a larger gene pool. Thus, the Neandertals may have become extinct through assimilation, and not replacement (Smith et al. 2005).

The Genetic Evidence   In addition to the fossil evidence, the question of modern human origins can be addressed by looking at patterns of genetic variation in *living* populations. We can observe patterns of genetic variation in the present day and work backward in time, asking what models of evolutionary change could have produced the observed patterns. Whereas with fossils we work from the past to the present, genetic studies start with the present in an effort to reconstruct the past.

One way of reconstructing the past is to compare DNA sequences from pairs of living people and use them to build a "tree" that shows the evolutionary history of a particular gene. Gene tree analysis seeks to determine where and when the most recent common ancestor of a group of people lived, which in turn provides clues about our species' history. Many gene tree analyses have been performed using mitochondrial DNA from living people around the world. As noted in Chapter 2, mitochondrial DNA is useful for this type of genealogical reconstruction because it is inherited solely from the mother and does not recombine. Studies of mitochondrial DNA show that the human species today forms two clusters. One cluster consists of people with African ancestry, and the other contains people of different ancestries, both African and non-African. Because both clusters have people with African ancestry, this pattern shows that the most recent common female ancestor of all living humans lived in Africa. By considering mutation rate in a gene tree analysis, the date when the most recent common ancestor lived researchers can estimate. For mitochondrial DNA analyses, this date is usually around 200,000 years ago (Cann et al. 1987; Vigilant et al. 1991; Penny et al. 1995). This date for the most recent mitochondrial DNA ancestor matches the appearance of anatomically modern humans from the fossil record, thus supporting the African replacement model.

Gene tree analysis has also been applied to a number of different genes and DNA sequences including those from Y chromosome DNA and nuclear DNA. Although many of these show the same pattern as mitochondrial DNA, others show more ancient "roots" (e.g., Harris and Hey 1999), and still others show non-African origins (e.g., Harding et al. 1997).

The problem with gene tree analysis is that each gene or DNA sequence may have a different evolutionary history, and the only way we can actually get at the history of the populations carrying these genes is to look at a number of them. One of the most comprehensive analyses of gene trees was performed by Alan Templeton (2005), who compared gene trees based on 15 DNA regions that showed evidence of an expansion out of Africa. He found evidence of three different expansions; the first took place approximately 1.9 million years ago, the second approximately 650,000 years ago, and the third approximately 130,000 years ago. These expansions correspond (within the margin of error of such estimates) to the initial origin and dispersal of *H. erectus, H. heidelbergensis,* and *H. sapiens,* respectively. Although these multiple expansions are expected under both the replacement and assimilation models, Templeton found statistical evidence from the geographic distributions of DNA regions that each expansion was accompanied by *mixture,* thus supporting the assimilation model.

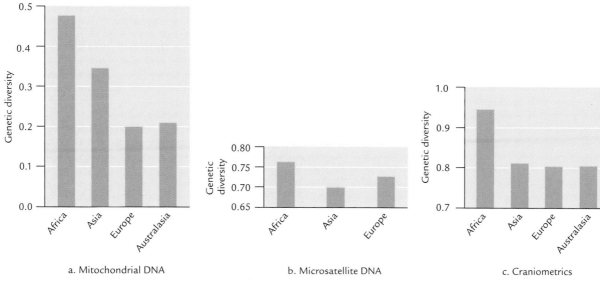

a. Mitochondrial DNA

b. Microsatellite DNA

c. Craniometrics

FIGURE 12.16

Comparison of genetic diversity among different geographic regions of living humans based on (a) mito-chondrial DNA variation, (b) microsatellite DNA varia-tion, and (c) craniometric variation. In each case, different measures of "diversity" are used so that the scales (vertical axes) cannot be compared directly. Instead, simply note that in each case Africa is the most diverse region genetically. (Data from Cann et al. 1987; Relethford and Harpending 1994; Jorde et al. 1997.)

Another avenue of research is to compare patterns of genetic diversity in living humans. Here, we use a variety of data from human populations, including DNA sequences, blood types and other genetic markers, and measures of the face and skull. One way to look at genetic diversity is to compare the level of genetic variation within different populations. Studies using a variety of traits have shown that Africa tends to be more genetically diverse than other geographic regions, such as Europe or Asia (Figure 12.16). The greater diversity of African populations has been used to argue for the African replacement model, based on the assumption that the oldest popu-lation will accumulate the most mutations over time, and therefore be more genetically diverse. If modern humans arose as a new species in Africa and later spread to other regions, the African populations would be the oldest and so would show the highest amount of variation.

This is not the only possible interpretation, because factors other than age can influence a population's genetic diversity. One such factor is popula-tion size. Recall from Chapter 3 the relationship between genetic drift and population size. Smaller populations lose more alleles because of genetic drift than do larger populations and so show lower levels of diversity. Larger populations experience less genetic drift and so show higher levels of diversity. The finding of higher African diversity may simply reflect a larger African population in our species' past. Using mathematical models relating diversity and population size, Relethford and Harpending (1994) and Relethford and Jorde (1999) found that genetic diversity in living humans is consistent with a model asserting that most of our ancestors several hundred thousand years ago lived in Africa. Today, of course, the majority of the human species lives not in Africa but in Asia. The distribution of humans today is influenced strongly by relatively recent events, particularly those occurring after the origin of agriculture some 12,000 years ago. Throughout most of the past, however, it is quite likely that the majority of human ancestors lived in Africa because it has the largest usable land mass and the best ecological conditions for large populations (Wolpoff and Caspari 1997).

Consensus—Mostly Out of Africa?   Keeping in mind that new data and analyses could conceivably change any current conclusions, what is the bottom line today? Based on the fossil record and the genetic data, there is strong evidence that modern human anatomy emerged first in Africa by 200,000 years ago. Although the African replacement model cannot be rejected, the evidence for regional continuity from the fossils, combined with Templeton's evidence of dispersal with mixture, argues strongly in favor of the assimilation model. We need to consider also the implications of a larger population size in Africa than in other regions throughout much of our species' past. A larger population means that a greater proportion of our ancestry derives from Africa, just not all of it. It may be that our ancestry is *mostly, but not exclusively, out of Africa* (Relethford 2001).

If the assimilation model is correct, this does not mean that the process played out the same way in every part of the world. The fossil and genetic evidence on Neandertals suggests that although they may have contributed somewhat to our ancestry, it might have been a small amount (Serre et al. 2004) and that, for all practical purposes, the Neandertal genetic contribution essentially became extinct within a short time (Smith et al. 2005). Further evidence, such as the planned Neandertal genome project (Dalton 2006), may provide definitive answers to the Neandertal question.

Why Did Modern Humans Evolve?

The alternative models for the origin of modern humans are fascinating to debate, but we don't want to lose track of a basic fact that all agree on: Only modern human fossils have been found dating to the past 28,000 years or so. In addition to explaining the timing and nature of the transition to modern humans, we must also ask ourselves why this transition occurred in the first place. The available evidence suggests that anatomically modern humans had some evolutionary advantage. But what was this advantage?

Modern humans differ from the earlier humans in several features, including a more well-rounded skull, smaller brow ridges, and a prominent chin. Lieberman (1998) suggests that these and other changes are all related to reduction in the length of the sphenoid, a bone in the cranial base. Because the anatomical development of a skull consists of interrelated components, a change in one part can influence changes throughout. His analysis suggests that most of the changes to moderns are related to this relatively simple change. However, a problem remains: What *caused* this change?

Language and Modern Human Origins   It has often been suggested that the development of language capabilities marks the origin of modern *H. sapiens*. Cranial changes are seen as related to changes in language ability, with a claim that modern *H. sapiens* was linguistically superior to the archaics. This view is tempting when evidence for the increased symbolic and technological

The Iceman

Our understanding of ancient times comes from reconstructions based on the fossil and archaeological records, supplemented by evidence from past environments. Although new methods and techniques for analysis have aided our ability to reconstruct the past, we are nevertheless dealing with only bits and pieces of what actually once existed.

Occasionally, though, we come across more detailed evidence. On September 19, 1991, hikers in the glacial mountains between Austria and Italy stumbled upon the body of a man. This is not unusual—bodies are often found in this region, the result of accidents while climbing or hiking in the mountains. Initial investigation, however, showed that this was a naturally occurring mummy (mummification occurs when a corpse is cut off from oxygen). How did the corpse remain so well preserved? The body wound up in a shallow depression in the ground, and the advancing glacier moved over him, preserving him in a mummified state without carrying his body downhill. By 1991, the ice had receded and the body was exposed. Because of his discovery in the glacier, he is known today as "The Iceman."

The body became of greater interest because of several items found with it, including a flint knife and an axe. The axe consisted of a wooden shaft attached to what appeared to be a bronze axe head. The bronze implied that the axe and the body dated to the European Bronze Age, roughly 4,000 years ago. Closer analysis of the axe head showed, however, that it was not bronze (which is a mixture of copper and tin) but almost entirely pure copper. Copper is known to have been used more than 4,000 years ago. The greater age was confirmed by carbon-14 dating of the body, which placed it at 5,250 years ago.

Research continues on the Iceman, but preliminary study has revealed much about his life and death. Marks have been found on the body that might be tattoos. In addition to the knife and the axe, he had a bow, arrows, and a leather quiver. Remains of his clothes show that they were made of fur, and boots have been found as well. He also had two lumps of fungus connected by a leather strap. At first, it was thought that the fungus might have been used as tinder for starting fires. The fungus has now been identified as a species that is known to have antibiotic properties, so we might be seeing some evidence of ancient medicine.

How did the Iceman die? Initial analysis suggested the possibility of exhaustion and dehydration, although this was based on circumstantial evidence. X-rays later showed that the Iceman had an arrowhead embedded in his shoulder, leading to suggestions that he was murdered. However, it is also possible that he lived for some time afterward, as we have evidence from other prehistoric skeletons of people surviving such wounds. Regardless of the actual cause of death, it now appears that the Iceman was not in good health when he died and that he may have been rather sick three times during the last six months of his life (Dickson et al. 2003).

achievements of modern *H. sapiens* is also considered. Can cranial changes and these cultural achievements be related? It is possible—but the basic problem remains that these cultural changes took place well after the initial *biological* changes associated with modern *H. sapiens*. Of course, cave art, bone tools, and other achievements may actually be older than we think, an idea supported to some extent by the new dating of bone tools in Africa. However, basing a model on what has *not* been found is not a good idea. We must always deal with the known fossil and archaeological records, and be willing to make appropriate revisions when we make new discoveries.

Our species' linguistic ability lies in part in our ability to make a wider number of sounds, and to do so faster, than apes. During infancy, two components of our vocal anatomy, the larynx and the hyoid bone, are positioned high in the throat as they are in other mammals. In both apes and humans, the larynx descends in the throat, but in humans alone, the hyoid bone continues to descend, thus forming our unique vocal anatomy (Nishimura et al. 2003). Although these changes lead to a clear-cut anatomical

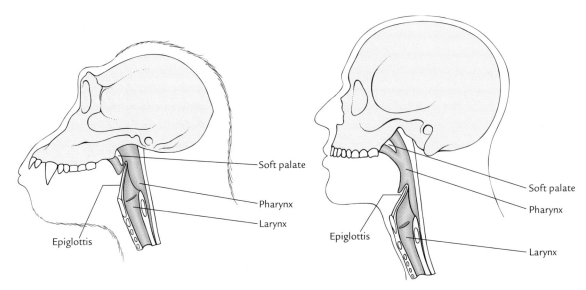

FIGURE 12.17

Side views of the cranium and vocal anatomy of an ape (*left*) and a modern human (*right*). Note that the lower profile of the cranium is fairly straight in apes, whereas it is flexed in modern humans. (From Roger Lewin, *In the Age of Mankind: A Smithsonian Book of Human Evolution,* 1989:181, Smithsonian Institution Press. Used by permission.)

difference between humans and apes, most of the vocal anatomy consists of soft tissue that decomposes, so we cannot detect this anatomy in fossil specimens. However, we can get clues about vocal anatomy by looking at the base of the cranium. In apes, the lower profile of the cranium is fairly straight, whereas it is more flexed in modern humans, reflecting changes in the position of the larynx (Figure 12.17).

What do studies of fossil skulls tell us? Laitman and colleagues (1979) investigated the crania of a number of fossil hominids and concluded that whereas *Australopithecus* had the ape pattern of flexing, the crania of many archaic humans were more similar to modern humans. The Neandertals, however, had a pattern that was between those of a modern subadult and a modern adult human, suggesting that their language abilities might have been somewhat different. Recent studies suggest that the evolution of cranial flexing and its association with speech may be more complicated than once thought. One *Homo erectus* cranium has been found that has a modernlike amount of cranial flexing (Baba et al. 2003). Debate about the fossil evidence for language continues. Although some argue for a relatively recent and sudden evolution of language ability, others suggest that the evolution of complex language was more gradual (e.g., Schepartz 1993).

Another source of information on language origins is the archaeological record. Some argue that complex language is of recent origin, coinciding with a rapid spread of new behaviors roughly 50,000 years ago (e.g., Klein 1999). Others argue that modern human behaviors actually developed over a longer period of time (e.g., Schepartz 1993; McBrearty and Brooks 2000). This latter group believes that by focusing on the more recent cultural innovations, such as bone tools and cave art, we are ignoring significant earlier innovations, such as complex stone tool manufacture and burial of the dead. Could such activities be possible without some language abilities? Although it seems unlikely, the possibility exists that some enhancement of language ability coincided with the origin of modern *H. sapiens*. We have too few data at present to answer these questions.

Technology and Biological Change   If changes in language abilities are not the reason for the origin of modern *H. sapiens,* what else might have been involved? Technological changes have also been suggested as mechanisms for the change from archaic to modern forms. On this view, many of the structural characteristics of *H. heidelbergensis* and the Neandertals were the result of stresses generated by the use of their front teeth as tools. The large size and wear patterns of the incisor teeth (especially in Neandertals) support the notion that these teeth were used for a variety of purposes. The stresses generated by heavy use of the front teeth can also be used to explain the large face, large neck muscles, and other features of archaic skulls. Once technological adaptations had developed sufficiently, these physical adaptations were no longer necessary and would not be selected for. Smaller teeth and faces might then be advantageous because smaller structures require correspondingly less energy for growth and maintenance (Smith et al. 1989). Similar arguments can be advanced to explain the reduction in body size and musculature (e.g., Frayer 1984). Once tools reduced the need for larger teeth, faces, and bones, smaller structures actually became more adaptive.

Calcagno and Gibson (1988) present evidence that larger teeth can be nonadaptive. They cite clinical evidence from contemporary human populations showing that large teeth can have many disadvantages. Larger teeth are more susceptible to dental decay due to crowding of teeth and periodontal disease. In earlier prehistoric times, the advantages of larger teeth as tools may have outweighed the disadvantages. When cultural change led to more efficient tools, however, these advantages diminished, and selection would then have been *against* large teeth.

Once again, evolution is best seen in terms of the overall balance between costs and benefits. Human evolution is particularly interesting because human behaviors frequently affect this balance. In the past, as new technologies and behaviors arose, they changed the balance between cost and benefit. At some point in the past, for example, the less rugged and less muscular modern morphology may have shifted from being a disadvantage to being an advantage. The origin of modern *H. sapiens* may itself reflect this type of process. If so, we would expect the kind of "lag" between cultural and biological change that we see in the fossil record. Biological changes allow further cultural changes, which in turn allow further biological changes. Each change shifts the balance.

RECENT BIOLOGICAL AND CULTURAL EVOLUTION IN *HOMO SAPIENS*

Human evolution did not end with the origin of modern *Homo sapiens*. Biologically, we have continued to change in subtle ways even over the past 10,000–20,000 years or so. Cranial capacity has declined somewhat

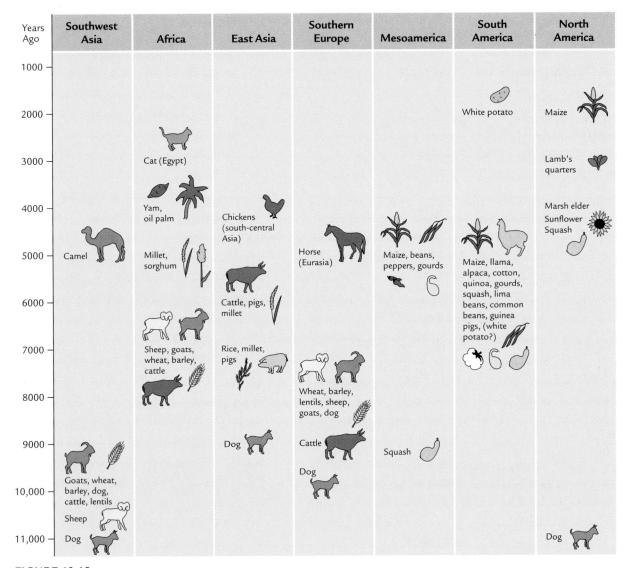

Years Ago	Southwest Asia	Africa	East Asia	Southern Europe	Mesoamerica	South America	North America
1000							
2000						White potato	Maize
3000		Cat (Egypt)					Lamb's quarters
4000		Yam, oil palm	Chickens (south-central Asia)				Marsh elder Sunflower Squash
5000	Camel	Millet, sorghum		Horse (Eurasia)	Maize, beans, peppers, gourds	Maize, llama, alpaca, cotton, quinoa, gourds, squash, lima beans, common beans, guinea pigs, (white potato?)	
6000			Cattle, pigs, millet				
7000		Sheep, goats, wheat, barley, cattle	Rice, millet, pigs				
8000				Wheat, barley, lentils, sheep, goats, dog			
9000			Dog	Cattle	Squash		
10,000	Goats, wheat, barley, dog, cattle, lentils Sheep			Dog			
11,000	Dog						Dog

FIGURE 12.18

Chronological outline of the origins of domestication and agriculture. (From *Human Antiquity: An Introduction to Physical Anthropology and Archaeology*, 3d ed., by Kenneth Feder and Michael Park, Fig. 14.1. Copyright © 1997 by Mayfield Publishing Company. Reprinted by permission of The McGraw-Hill Companies.)

(Henneberg 1988; Ruff et al. 1997), probably a reflection of a general decrease in size and ruggedness. Teeth have also become somewhat smaller (Brace et al. 1987), most likely reflecting the changing costs and benefits of larger teeth.

Within the very recent past (10,000–15,000 years), the major changes in human evolution have been cultural. One major change in human existence—the invention of agriculture—began roughly 12,000 years ago. Up to this point, humans had been exclusively hunters and gatherers. Agriculture changed the entire ecological equation for human beings. Humans began manipulating the environment to increase the availability of food through the domestication of plants and animals. Many explanations are offered as to why agriculture developed, including that it was a solution to the increased population size that had resulted from more efficient hunting and gathering. In any case, the effects of agriculture were and continue to be quite dramatic—the human population grew and continues to do so today (see Chapter 17).

Agriculture did not have a single origin but rather developed independently in many parts of both the Old World and the New World. Over the next several thousand years, the use of agriculture became increasingly dominant around the world (Figure 12.18). Today there are very few hunters and gatherers left. Our current focus on agriculture often blinds us to the reality that we have changed so much culturally in so short a time. Biologically, we are still hunters and gatherers.

Cultural change continued at an even faster rate following the origin of agriculture and rapid population growth. Cities and state-level societies developed. Exploration brought the inhabitants of the Old World and the New World back into contact, and industrialization spread rapidly. Today, only 12,000 years after the time our ancestors survived by hunting and gathering, we are able to explore and live in every environment on earth and beyond (Figure 12.19). However one feels about the rapid cultural

FIGURE 12.19

The space shuttle is one feature of our species' continuing exploration and utilization of new environments.

changes of *H. sapiens,* these changes can be viewed as a continuation of the basic adaptations of culture and learning that have been apparent for at least the past 2.5 million years of human evolution.

Summary

Among other features, anatomically modern *Homo sapiens* is characterized by a higher, more well-rounded skull and a smaller face than most archaics and by the presence of a noticeable chin. Modern *H. sapiens* is best known from fossil records dating over the past 30,000 years. There is considerable evidence, however, that these humans appeared first roughly 200,000 years ago in Africa and by 100,000–90,000 years ago in the Middle East. By 50,000 years ago, the culture of *H. sapiens* had begun to change rapidly; the use of more sophisticated stone tools (especially blade tools) and bone tools spread, burials of the dead became more elaborate, and art appeared. Modern humans had colonized Australia by 60,000 years ago and the New World by at least 15,000 years ago.

There is ongoing debate regarding the origin of modern humans. The African replacement model proposes that modern humans arose as a new species around 200,000 years ago in Africa and then spread across the Old World, replacing preexisting archaic humans. The assimilation model proposes that modern human anatomy did appear first in Africa, but that there was genetic mixing with the expanding African populations and populations outside of Africa. At present, there is some consensus that modern humans did evolve first in Africa, but debate continues as to whether non-African populations were replaced or assimilated. Current fossil and genetic evidence appears to better support the assimilation model, although it is not clear how much mixing occurred.

Human evolution did not end after the initial appearance of modern humans. Although there have been some biological changes during our recent past, most of our species' evolution over the past 10,000 years has been cultural. Perhaps the single most important event was the development of agriculture, which changed our entire way of life. Predicting the specifics of future human evolution is problematic, but our future will no doubt involve more and more cultural change, which occurs at a far greater rate than biological evolution. This does not mean that biological evolution has stopped; rather, our fate is becoming increasingly affected by cultural change.

Supplemental Readings

Relethford, J. H. 2001. *Genetics and the Search for Modern Human Origins.* New York: Wiley-Liss. A review of different models for the origin of modern humans and the genetic evidence that has been used to test them.

Stringer, C., and R. McKie. 1996. *African Exodus: The Origins of Modern Humanity.* New York: Henry Holt.

Wolpoff, M. H., and R. Caspari. 1997. *Race and Human Evolution.* New York: Simon and Schuster.

Two excellent and interesting summaries of the modern human origins debate.

VIRTUAL EXPLORATIONS

Visit our textbook-specific online learning center Web site at **www.mhhe.com/relethford7** to access the exercises that follow.

1. **Human Migration Hypotheses**   **http://www.learner.org/ channel/courses/biology/textbook/humev/humev_5.html**. Go to the Annenberg Media Web site and read the article "Out of Africa?" You will become familiar with the two major competing hypotheses concerning the origins of modern humans, the "out of Africa" (or "replacement") hypothesis and the "multiregional" hypothesis.

   - What is the scientific evidence that supports the "out of Africa" hypothesis?
   - What about the "multiregional" hypothesis?
   - Who is "mitochondrial Eve"?
   - Why is there so much controversy in human evolutionary genetics today?

   Watch this brief "Animation Archive" on the Annenberg Media Web site: **http://www.learner.org/channel/courses/biology/archive/ animations/hires/a_humev4_h.html**.

2. **New Analysis Shows Three Human Migrations Out of Africa** **http://www.sciencedaily.com/releases/2006/02/060209184558.htm** Read the Tony Fitzpatrick article "New Analysis Shows Three Human Migrations Out of Africa" from the *Science Daily* Web site. The article discusses the work of Alan R. Templeton, PhD, of Washington University in St. Louis. Dr. Templeton suggests that three, not two, major waves of human migration came out of Africa. The older theory, the "out of Africa" or "replacement" theory, is challenged by Templeton's work.

   - There are major differences in the two scenarios suggested by these competing theories. How is the story of *Homo sapiens'* exodus out of Africa radically different in these two versions?
   - What might you infer from this concerning hominin behavior?
   - What is GEODIS?
   - What evidence do Templeton and his colleagues offer to refute the "out of Africa" theory?
   - What is a "haplotype tree"?
   - Does this new evidence suggest that we seriously consider genetic interchange between African and Eurasian populations?

3. **Cultural Behavior**   **http://www.nhm.ac.uk/about-us/news_2006/ june/news_8437.html**. Read the article "World's Oldest Piece of Jewelry" on the Natural History Museum of London Web site. At the Skhul site in Israel, tiny marine shell beads were found in association with human remains.

- Re-examination of the beads, first collected from the site in 1931 and 1932, suggests that they may have been used for ornamentation. What is the evidence that suggests this?
- How were the beads dated?
- Why did it take so long for scientists to discover that the beads may have been used for jewelry?
- What does the evidence suggest about human behavior through Africa to the Middle East?

4. **The Venus of Willendorf** http://witcombe.sbc.edu/willendorf/willendorfwomen.html. Christopher L. C. E. Witcombe's article, "Women in the Stone Age," considers the reasons why "Venus" figurines found throughout Europe in modern *H. sapiens* sites had such unusual proportions. A great deal of speculation still surrounds these figurines today.

- What does Witcombe have to say about "stone age" women being fat?
- Why are there so few male figurines found?
- What is the religious explanation for the abundance and similarities in the overall shape and proportions of the Venus figurines?
- Is there a possible explanation for Paleolithic social organization from the Venus of Willendorf?

OUR DIVERSITY

How and why are human beings similar to and different from each other? We all encounter biological variation (diversity) every day of our lives. Some people are taller than others are or have rounder heads or lighter skin color. Additional diversity exists in many genetic traits that are not visible to the naked eye, such as blood groups and DNA sequences. Biological anthropologists are interested in describing and explaining such variation, particularly in terms of the recent evolution of our species. Chapter 13 describes the ways in which biological anthropologists measure variation, looks at global diversity from an evolutionary perspective, and examines the biological concept of race as applied to human populations. Chapter 14 explores the ways in which data on human biological variation can be used to reconstruct the recent history of human populations and patterns of ancestry. Chapter 15 looks at examples of natural selection in human populations, including some examples of recent evolution. Chapter 16 examines biological diversity from the perspective of biocultural adaptations. Chapter 17 concludes with an examination of the biological impact of our species' rapid cultural changes over the past 12,000 years, since the origin of agriculture.

The Saami people of northern Europe during the spring migration of their reindeer herd. The Saami are genetically similar to populations in both Europe and Asia. Human variation and the biological relationship between different groups of humans and their origin have long been a focus of biological anthropology.

The Study of Human Variation

E very day we encounter human biological diversity in physical characteristics such as skin color, hair color, and hair form (Figure 13.1),
but these observable variations are only the tip of the iceberg. Variation also
exists in less easily observed characteristics such as teeth and fingerprints.
Still more variation exists at the molecular level, which is not directly visible
to the naked eye.

One task of biological anthropology is to make sense out of data on
human variation. To do this, we typically ask three questions. First, what is
the pattern of variation *within* a population? That is, what are the different
genotypes and phenotypes? If we are looking at simple genetic traits, we
would be interested in knowing how many alleles are found at a given locus
and the relative frequencies of each. If we are looking at complex traits,
such as height or skin color, we would be interested in knowing the average
value and some measure of variation around this average. For example,
what is the average height in a population? What is the range of heights
from shortest to tallest? The second question is, What is the pattern of variation *between* populations? Is the frequency of an allele different from one
population to the next? Is the average height in one population different
from that of another population? Is there a noticeable pattern in differences
and similarities between populations? For example, are high frequencies of a
given allele found in one part of the world but found at lower frequencies
elsewhere? Is there a geographic pattern to the distribution of a trait? Questions about the patterns of variation within and between populations lead
inevitably to the third question: Why? What is the explanation for the
observed patterns of variation? Specifically, can we explain human biological
variation in terms of what we know about genetics and evolutionary models?
If so, can we test our hypotheses?

Although the study of human variation sounds straightforward, in reality,
debate and discussion concerning diversity can become quite heated, given the
fact that we are studying ourselves. Although biological anthropologists discuss variation in terms of evolutionary forces and biocultural adaptations, we
seldom hear such terms in daily discourse on human variation. More often
than not, discussion focuses on issues of race and ethnicity. Historically, we
have a long tradition of describing human variation in terms of a small number

FIGURE 13.1

Human biological variation in external physical traits. Human beings vary considerably in terms of skin color, hair color, and some craniofacial measures.

of discrete groups (races) and not in more appropriate statistical and evolutionary language. For example, many people would react to the images in Figure 13.1 by automatically trying to place each person in her respective race. The tendency to classify and reduce variation to averages and group stereotypes is difficult to break, but as you will learn, there are more accurate ways to describe and analyze human biological variation.

This chapter provides some background on human variation and has two main goals. The first is to explore different measures of human variation (including some you can see and many that you can't). The second goal is to provide some background on global patterns of human genetic diversity and how we make sense out of observations of human variation. You will learn about the general nature of variation within our species and how this has been approached from racial and evolutionary perspectives. Subsequent chapters provide additional case studies that examine specific populations, traits, and approaches to studying human variation.

MEASURING HUMAN VARIATION

In measuring human variation, exactly *what* are we talking about? Whether we approach human variation from a racial perspective or an evolutionary perspective, we need to know what we mean by "human variation." Variation, of course, refers to the differences that exist among people and populations. We are all aware of biological variation—some people are taller or darker, or have differently shaped skulls. We also know from Chapters 2 and 3 that people frequently have different blood groups or other varying aspects of their biochemical makeup. Is the measure of human variation simply a matter of examining how different people look? Although we frequently do just that in our daily lives, simple observation is not adequate for scientific analysis, for several reasons. First, it is too subjective. Looking at people and rating them as "tall" versus "short" or "dark" versus "light" is too fraught with problems of observer bias to be of much use. Second, our mental categories of variation (e.g., "light" versus "dark") do not acknowledge that traits such as human skin color do not come in three or four groups but are instead continuous. Third, much of the genetic variation that exists is invisible to our eyes—you cannot tell a person's blood group by looking at him or her.

Many different measures and methods have been devised to assess biological variation, and new methods are being developed all the time. A few of these methods are reviewed here.

Red Blood Cell Polymorphisms

Since the early twentieth century, anthropologists and geneticists have collected abundant data on genetic traits that are detectable through analysis of red blood cells. Of particular interest are loci that show variation within and between populations. Red blood cell polymorphisms include blood types and protein and enzyme types. Recall from Chapter 2 that a polymorphism is a genetic trait whereby there are at least two alleles each with frequencies greater than 1 percent.

Blood Type   One of the most common genetic measures used in studies of human variation is a person's blood type, such as the ABO blood type and the MN blood type discussed in Chapter 2. These are only a couple of the blood type systems that have been discovered; others include the Rhesus, Diego, Duffy, and Kell blood group systems, to name only a few. Different blood group systems are identified by the types of molecules present on the surface of the red blood cells. Each blood group system has a particular

TABLE 13.1	Determining a Person's ABO Blood Type		
		Reaction with Antibody	
Blood Type	Antigen(s) Present in Blood	Anti-A	Anti-B
A	A	Yes	No
B	B	No	Yes
AB	A and B	Yes	Yes
O	None	No	No

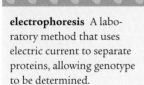

antibody A substance that reacts to other substances invading the body (antigens).

antigen A substance invading the body that stimulates the production of antibodies.

antibody–antigen reaction that can be used to identify the different blood groups. **Antibodies** are substances that react to foreign substances—**antigens**—invading the blood stream. This antibody–antigen reaction (clumping of red blood cells) allows us to classify different blood groups.

As an example, consider the ABO blood group discussed in Chapter 2. Remember that this system has three alleles (*A, B,* and *O*), where *A* and *B* are codominant and *O* is recessive. There are four different phenotypes: type A (genotypes *AA* and *AO*), type B (genotypes *BB* and *BO*), type O (genotype *OO*), and type AB (genotype *AB*). Two antibodies react to specific antigens. One of these, anti-A, reacts to A-type molecules (in people with blood type A or AB). The other, anti-B, reacts to B-type molecules (in people with blood type B or AB). Because each blood type has a different combination of A and B antigens (Table 13.1), these reactions allow us to find out which of the four ABO blood types a person has. For example, people with type A blood have the A antigen but not the B. Suppose we take a sample of a person's blood and find that the blood clumps when exposed to anti-A antibodies but not when exposed to anti-B antibodies. This means the person has A antigens but not B antigens and therefore has type A blood. The same basic method (although sometimes more complex) is used to determine the phenotypes of other blood group systems.

Blood Proteins and Enzymes   In addition to red blood cell groups, genetic analyses have been done on many human populations for red blood cell proteins and enzymes. Different genotypes can be detected using a method known as **electrophoresis.** Here, blood samples are placed at one end of a gel through which an electrical current is passed. Electricity flows from the negative to positive, and the blood samples are placed initially at the negative end. As electricity flows through the gel, proteins from the blood sample will move along the flow of electrons. Different proteins have different rates of electrical mobility and will move at faster or slower rates. The difference in distance traveled through the gel allows us to determine a person's genotype.

As an example, consider the beta hemoglobin gene discussed in Chapter 2. The most common allele is known as hemoglobin *A,* which codes for normal hemoglobin. Another allele is the sickle cell allele, *S,* which will lead to sickle cell anemia if you have two copies. Although there are other alleles in the human species, let us focus only on these two for the moment. If we have

electrophoresis A laboratory method that uses electric current to separate proteins, allowing genotype to be determined.

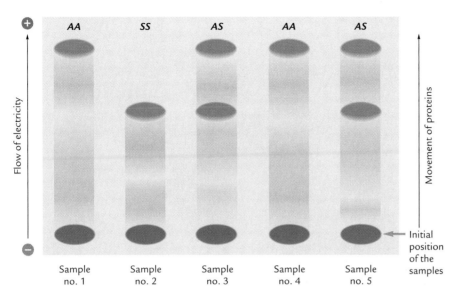

FIGURE 13.2

Example of electrophoresis for detection of hemoglobin genotypes. Five samples are placed in a tray containing a gel through which electricity is flowing from negative to positive. Over time, proteins will move along in the gel. Differences in chemical structure lead to differences in how far proteins move. Samples of genotype *AA* move the farthest, and samples of genotype *SS* the least far. Note that heterozygotes (*AS*) show two bands, corresponding to the *A* and *S* alleles. The final analysis shows that samples 1 and 4 have genotype *AA*, samples 3 and 5 have genotype *AS*, and sample 2 has genotype *SS*.

two alleles, *A* and *S,* there are three possible genotypes: *AA, AS,* and *SS.* As shown in Figure 13.2, each of these genotypes will produce a different pattern of movement through a gel, allowing us to detect a person's genotype.

The HLA System

Genetic variation in the antigens is found on the surface of white blood cells (leukocytes). The **HLA (human leukocyte antigen) system** is controlled by several linked loci on chromosome 6. The HLA system is of medical interest because of its role in the body's autoimmune response. For example, a person's HLA type affects the probability of a successful organ transplant. Different HLA antigens have also been associated with a variety of diseases including arthritis and juvenile diabetes. The HLA system has an amazing amount of diversity; there are hundreds of genes and alleles (Mielke et al. 2006). There are many differences in HLA allele frequencies among human populations, which makes it a useful genetic marker for examining patterns of genetic similarity.

DNA Analysis

Due to advances in genetic technology, many new measures of human variation can now be examined directly through sequences of DNA that can be easily extracted from hair samples (Figure 13.3) or cheek swabs.

Methods of DNA Analysis One method of DNA analysis focuses on **restriction fragment length polymorphisms (RFLPs).** Certain enzymes produced by different species of bacteria (known as *restriction enzymes*) bind to sections of DNA and cut the DNA sequence at a given point. For example, the restriction enzyme known as *Eco*RI will bind to the 6-base-pair DNA sequence GAATTC and then cut the sequence between the G and the first A.

HLA (human leukocyte antigen) system A diverse genetic system consisting of linked loci on chromosome 6 that control autoimmune response.

restriction fragment length polymorphism (RFLP) A genetic trait defined in terms of the length of DNA fragments produced when certain enzymes cut the DNA sequence.

FIGURE 13.3

Dr. Michael Crawford collecting hair samples from the Evenki, a group of reindeer herders in Siberia. DNA can be extracted from hair samples and cheek swabs.

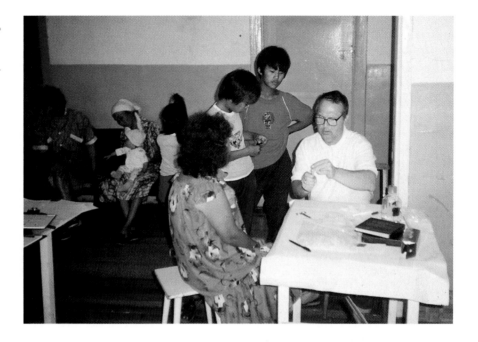

haplotype A combination of genes or DNA sequences that are inherited as a single unit.

microsatellite DNA Repeated short sequences of DNA; the number of repeats is highly variable.

You then wind up with two fragments of DNA, one containing G and the other containing the remaining 5-base-pair sequence AATTC. However, if you have had a mutation of one or more of the base pairs and wind up with a different sequence, such as CAATTC, then the DNA sequence will not be cut. Differences in the lengths of DNA fragments thus give us a useful measure of human variation at the molecular level (White and Lalouel 1988).

RFLPs can provide us with information on haplotype frequencies. A **haplotype** is a combination of genes that are inherited as a single unit, as happens when loci are linked (one example of this is the Rhesus blood group, discussed in Chapter 3; another is the HLA system). RFLP analysis is also expressed in terms of haplotypes by examining whether particular restriction sites are present or absent. If a restriction site is present, the corresponding restriction enzyme will cut the DNA, and if absent, the DNA is not cut. For example, consider three restriction sites, each of which could be present (+) or absent (−) in any given DNA sample. A number of different combinations (haplotypes) is possible, such as + + + (all three sites are present), + + − (the first two are present but not the third), and others, including + + −, − + −, − − −, and so on. These different combinations are RFLP haplotypes.

Another source of genetic information comes from the analysis of noncoding DNA sequences that are repeated. One example is **microsatellite DNA,** which consists of repeated short sections of DNA (2–5 bases). These are also called simple tandem repeats, or STRs. One type of analysis counts the number of repeats. For example, the DNA sequence CACACACACA contains five repeats of the CA sequence, and the DNA sequence CACACA contains three repeats. The number of such repeats is highly variable and of use in detecting population relationships (e.g., Jorde et al. 1997).

Another interesting method of analysis focuses on **_Alu_ insertions,** which are short DNA sequences that have replicated and moved to different locations on different chromosomes. It is estimated that roughly 5 percent of human DNA consists of these repeated elements (Stoneking et al. 1997). Polymorphisms are identified by noting the presence or absence of an _Alu_ insertion at a given chromosome location. This trait has proven useful in analyses of human population history.

Recent investigations in genetics have focused on **single-nucleotide polymorphisms (SNPs),** loci where DNA sequences differ by one base. For example, consider the following two DNA sequences:

Sequence 1: GAACCTTTA

Sequence 2: GAATCTTTA

These two sequences differ in the fourth position, where sequence 1 has a C and sequence 2 has a T. The existence of so many SNPs provides geneticists with the ability to map the genome and look for linkages with a number of traits, including genes that might influence disease susceptibility. The International HapMap Project has so far identified over one million SNPs, with plans to identify an additional 4.6 million in the future (International HapMap Consortium 2005).

Geneticists and anthropologists also compare entire DNA sequences across individuals and populations. One method of analysis consists of examining the "mismatch," the number of differences between sequences. Consider, for example, the following DNA sequences from three different individuals:

Individual 1: GGTGGTGAATCC

Individual 2: GGTCGTGAATCC

Individual 3: GGTGGTGTTTCC

If you look closely at each sequence, you will see that individual 1 and individual 2 differ at one position. Further, individuals 1 and 3 differ by two positions, and individuals 2 and 3 differ by three positions. From such comparisons (performed on _much_ longer sequences), we can make inferences regarding genetic similarity and the evolutionary history of DNA sequences.

Assessing Different Patterns of Inheritance

Assessing Different Patterns of Inheritance   As discussed in Chapter 2, almost all of the DNA a person has is nuclear DNA, which is inherited from both parents and subject to recombination. Mitochondrial DNA, inherited solely from the mother, is not subject to recombination. The same is true of almost all of the DNA on a male's Y chromosome, which is inherited solely from the father, and almost none of which is subject to recombination. The single-parent mode of inheritance of mitochondrial DNA and Y-chromosome DNA makes tracing ancestry simpler than for nuclear DNA. Your nuclear DNA is inherited from two ancestors (your parents) who in turn have each inherited their DNA from two parents (your grandparents), and so on into the past. Each generation back in time, the number of possible ancestors

Alu insertion A sequence of DNA repeated at different locations on different chromosomes.

single-nucleotide polymorphisms (SNPs) Specific positions in a DNA sequence that differ at one base. For example, the DNA sequences CCTGAA and CCCGAA differ in the third position—one sequence has the base T, and the other the base C.

FIGURE 13.4

The author measures his son's height. Height and weight are two of the most common anthropometric measures.

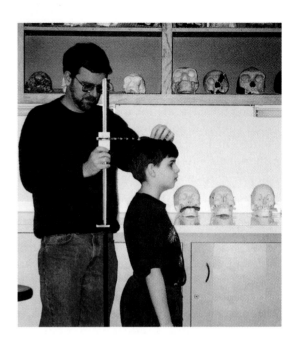

doubles. The situation is different for mitochondrial DNA and Y-chromosome DNA; here, you have only one ancestor in each generation in the past. Your mitochondrial DNA, for example, comes from your mother, who inherited it from her mother, who inherited it from her mother, and so on back into the past. Thus, you have only one mitochondrial DNA ancestor in any given generation in the past, unlike the thousands and thousands of nuclear DNA ancestors. The same is true for Y-chromosome DNA in males.

Complex Traits

Many of the traits of interest in studying human variation are complex traits—those that are frequently affected by growth and the environment and that reflect a much more complicated relationship between genotype and phenotype.

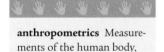

anthropometrics Measurements of the human body, skull, and face.

Anthropometrics   Measurements of the human body, including the head and the face, are known as **anthropometrics.** Two of the most commonly used anthropometric measures are height and weight (Figure 13.4). Other measurements of the body include the length of limbs and limb segments and the width of the body at different places, such as the shoulders and the hips. Skinfold measures—the thickness of a section of skin and fat that have been pinched together—provide a useful means of assessing body fat and nutritional status.

Numerous methods have been developed to measure the human face and skull. These include measures of the length and width of the skull and face at various locations (notably near the eyes, cheekbones, and lower jaw). Other measures are taken of the height and width of the nose (Figure 13.5). These

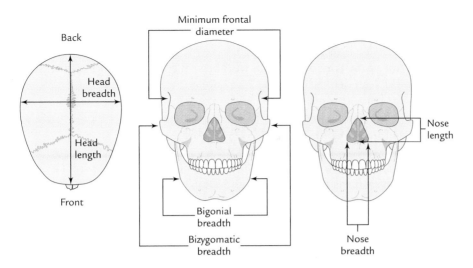

FIGURE 13.5

Common craniofacial measurements include head length and breadth (*left*), various facial breadths (*middle*), and nose length and height (*right*). These measures are shown on the human skull for convenience, but they can also be measured on living humans in much the same way.

craniofacial measures have proven quite useful in reconstructing past history and the relationships between human populations (e.g., Howells 1989; Relethford and Crawford 1995; also see Chapter 14).

Skin Color In the past, skin color was often measured by comparing a person's skin to a set of standardized tiles, a method that was too subjective and inaccurate. The more common method today involves the use of a reflectance spectrophotometer—a device that measures the percentage of light reflected back from a given source at different wavelengths. (Lighter skin reflects more light back.) To minimize the effects of tanning, we measure skin color on the inside of the upper arm, which is generally not as exposed to the sun as other parts of the body. The more light that is bounced back off the skin, the lighter the person is. Instead of trying to shove people into categories such as "light" or "dark," we can measure skin color precisely. Newer devices have been invented specifically for measuring skin color; these devices convert the percentage of reflected light into a melanin index (Shriver and Parra 2000).

Other Measures A number of measures exist for human teeth. **Odontometrics** are measures of the size of human teeth. The length (front to back) and width (side to side) of each tooth is measured using calipers. These measures can be made directly from skeletal material; measurements of teeth in living humans are made from dental casts. In addition to size, a number of other features can be observed in human teeth. One example is shovel-shaped incisors, in which individuals have ridges on the inside margins of their front teeth. This trait is most common in East Asian and Native American populations and occurs less frequently elsewhere. Such traits are useful in examining relationships between populations.

Finger and palm prints (**dermatoglyphics**) are another source of information on human variation. Although each person has a unique set

odontometrics Measurements of the size of teeth.

dermatoglyphics Measurements of finger and palm prints, including type classification and ridge counts.

of fingerprints, certain features and patterns tend to be found in different frequencies among human populations. One measure is the classification of prints into different types, such as loops, whorls, and arches, for each finger. Another measure consists of the number of ridge lines on each finger (counted between defined points).

RACE AND HUMAN VARIATION

We know many ways to measure human variation, but how do we make sense of what we have measured? How can we best describe and explain patterns of biological variation within and among human populations, and do these patterns relate to cultural diversity? A number of case studies are presented in the next three chapters that deal with specific populations and biological traits. The remainder of this chapter provides some background on *global* patterns of human variation—that is, genetic similarities and differences within our entire species, and explanations for them.

Given the background in Chapters 2 and 3, it should be no surprise that biological anthropologists look at differences between human populations by applying genetic and evolutionary principles. The focus here is on the population as the unit of analysis. The goal is to explain population similarities and differences in terms of the evolutionary forces, as well as their interaction with cultural factors and the physical environment.

An evolutionary approach to human variation emerged primarily in the last half of the twentieth century. Before this, the dominant approach had focused on racial classification—attempting to identify the major races of humanity and determine what characteristics could be used to define each. Even though the biological concept of race has been abandoned by many for describing human biological variation, it is important to understand this concept, because it continues to be used as the primary viewpoint on human variation in our daily life outside of science and academia.

What Is Race?

What is race, and why have many biological anthropologists and geneticists abandoned the concept? One of the major problems is that there are many different definitions of the term *race,* and these definitions are not always in agreement (Graves 2001). **Race** has been used to refer to everything from skin color (the "white" race), to nationality (the "Japanese" race), to religion (the "Jewish" race). In everyday terms, there is an unfortunate tendency to use "race" to refer to everything from a biological unit, to an ethnic group, to one's nationality.

Problems arise because the two different approaches to race—cultural and biological—do not always match up or even overlap with each other. In many state and federal government reports, race refers to some aspect of nationality or ethnic identity that may not connect directly to any specific

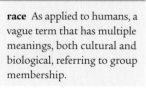

race As applied to humans, a vague term that has multiple meanings, both cultural and biological, referring to group membership.

biological population. For example, "black" refers to someone with African or African American ancestry, which in turn could include individuals who also have some European ancestry (see Chapter 14). "Hispanic" refers to Spanish speakers but actually encompasses a wide variety of people from Mexicans to Bolivians. Such classifications have their use, particularly in defining social groups that have suffered inequities, but they should not be construed as necessarily reflecting biological reality. We must understand the context to know whether someone is talking about a cultural or a biological definition of race. For our purposes, the question is whether the *biological* meaning of race has value in describing human variation.

Biological Race   Historically, there have been a number of different definitions of **biological race** (Feldman et al. 2003). A taxonomic definition equates race with the concept of a subspecies, a division of a species into distinct and distinguishable types. A good example would be the three different subspecies of gorillas. Although these subspecies all belong to the same species, the three groups are physically and geographically distinct. The subspecies approach does not work for humans because there are no clearly distinct types of humanity (Graves 2001). There is generally less genetic variation within the human species relative to species such as gorillas, and virtually all scientists agree that living humans belong to a single subspecies. Unlike subspecies of gorillas, humans are widespread geographically and are constantly moving across population boundaries. Although human variation does exist, it does not fall neatly into biologically discrete groups. Taxonomic race (subspecies) works fine with gorillas but not with humans.

Geography and Biological Race   Another approach to biological race is based on geography—identifying clusters of populations similar to each other that differ from other clusters in terms of allele frequencies and physical characteristics. This approach essentially equates geographic regions, such as sub-Saharan Africa, East Asia, or Polynesia, with different races. The focus here is on distinguishing distinct groups of populations that are genetically similar. A typical definition of biological race is "a division of a species that differs from other divisions by the frequency with which certain hereditary traits appear among its members" (Brues 1977:1). Although scientists agree that the subspecies view of race does not apply to humans, they are more mixed on the utility of geographic races.

Problems with the Biological Race Concept

Debates over the existence of biological races are *not* the same as the debate over the existence of genetic variation or the fact that it is geographically structured (i.e., people in different parts of the world tend to be genetically different from each other). Genetic variation *does* exist and it *is* geographically structured.

biological race A group of populations sharing certain biological traits that distinguish them from other groups of populations. In practice, the biological concept of race has been difficult to apply to human populations.

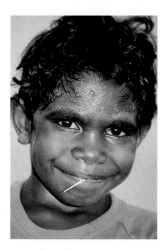

FIGURE 13.6

An Australian aborigine with dark skin and curly hair.

Debate over the biological race concept focuses on the *pattern* of this variation. The race concept has long been associated with the idea of discrete and easily distinguishable groups of human populations; adherents assume that a species can easily be categorized into several discrete races. If so, then how many human races are there?

The Number of Races   It may come as a surprise, but scientists attempting racial classification of humans have never agreed on how many races exist. Some have suggested that there are three human races: Europeans, Africans, and Asians (often referred to by the archaic terms "Caucasoid," "Negroid," and "Mongoloid," which are almost never used in scientific research today). But many populations do not fit neatly into one of these three basic categories. What about native Australians (aborigines)? As shown in Figure 13.6, these are dark-skinned people who frequently have curly or wavy (and, in some cases, blond) hair. On the basis of skin color, we might be tempted to label these people as African, but on the basis of hair shape, they might be considered a different race. Another approach is to place them into their own race—"Australoid."

As we travel around the world, we find more and more populations that do not fit a three- or four-race system. Consequently, some authors added more races to their lists, but over time there has never been any consensus on the number of human races. In 1758, for example, the botanist Linnaeus listed 4 human races, but since that time others have argued for other numbers, including 3, 5, 7, 9, and even more. The fact that there has never been clear consensus illustrates that the race concept does not fit human biological variation very well.

The Nature of Continuous Variation   The failure to agree on the number of races is partly the result of trying to divide a continuum into a number of discrete units; the decision is often arbitrary. For example, consider human height. No one would deny that there is variation in human height; clearly, some people are shorter and some people are taller. The question is how best to describe this variation. If you asked a large number of adults to line up from shortest to tallest, you would see that height has a continuous distribution, ranging from one extreme to the other with virtually every value in between. Could you then divide this range up into a number of distinct groups? Yes, but any such division would be arbitrary. How many groups would you use? Three? Ten? Some other number? The decision would be arbitrary because there are no naturally occurring distinct groups.

Many of the traits that historically have been used to define human races suffer from the same problem of trying to subsume continuous variation into a small number of discrete groups. Human skin color is a good example. Our everyday language describing skin color implies discrete groups: "white," "brown," and "black." In reality, human skin color does *not* come in 3 or 5 or even 10 different shades. Instead, when we consider the full range of humanity, human skin color varies from the darkest to the lightest people without any breaks in the distribution (Figure 13.7).

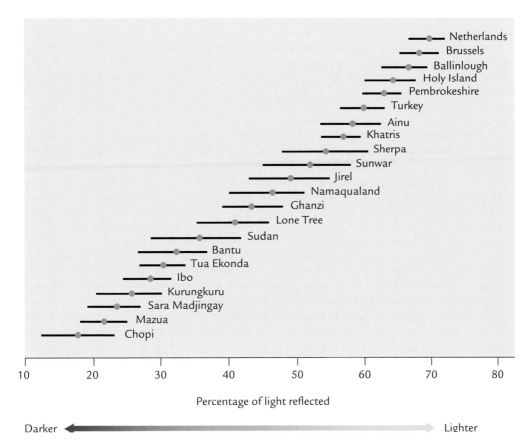

Percentage of light reflected

Darker ◄─────────────────────────────► Lighter

FIGURE 13.7

Variation in skin color in 22 human populations (males). Dots indicate the mean skin reflectance measured at a wavelength of 685 nanometers; lines indicate one standard deviation on each side of the mean, an interval that includes 68 percent of the cases within each sample. Clearly, there is overlap between different populations, and there are no abrupt breaks in the distribution from dark to light. Human skin color does not come in a finite number of shades but varies continuously from darkest to lightest. (All data from published literature. Original references listed in Relethford 1997.)

We could acknowledge this arbitrariness of classification but still come up with some grouping based on geography. For one reason or another, we sometimes find it convenient to represent a range of variation in terms of a small number of discrete groups. Course grades are a good example. Instead of representing a student's course grade as a number between 0 and 100 percent, most schools divide this range into a number of discrete categories, such as "A," "B," "C," and so forth. Other schools use more categories (such as "B+"), but the principle is the same. Likewise, there might be times when it is convenient to refer to someone's height as "short," "medium," or "tall." When we refer to geographic groupings as races, aren't we doing the same thing?

Yes, but there is a vital difference. Because of the historical origin and development of the race concept, there is a tendency to consider races as naturally occurring discrete groups rather than definitional groups. This does not occur with the height example. Although variation in height is real, and you can crudely describe it in terms of height groups (short, medium, tall), you know that human height does not naturally cluster this way and that humans do not come only in three different heights. Again, the debate over the existence of human races is a debate not over the existence of human differences but instead over the best way to describe them—as discrete groups or as part of a range of variation.

Classification and Racial Identification

If the biological concept of race does not apply to humans, how is it that we can accurately identify people's ancestry from different parts of the world based on their genetic or physical makeup? Or, to quote the title of a paper by forensic anthropologist Norman Sauer (1992), "If races don't exist, why are forensic anthropologists so good at identifying them?" Some have argued that even though the concept of subspecies does not fit human variation, the presence of clear geographic differences in many traits means that the geographic race concept, while limited and somewhat arbitrary, does have some utility. In many cases, forensic studies of the human skeleton are able to correctly assign individuals to a given geographic region, such as Europe or Africa, based on a combination of measurements (e.g., Gill 1998). Recent studies of microsatellite DNA and *Alu* insertions have also shown high accuracy in classification by geographic region (Rosenberg et al. 2002; Bamshad et al. 2003). Because we can accurately classify individuals according to different geographic regions, one could argue that these regions must be equivalent to different geographic races.

Does this mean that geographic races are real in the sense of being distinct groups? Although the ability to classify individuals accurately by region is high in some studies, this does not mean that the race concept, with its focus on discrete groupings of humanity, is a logical consequence of these studies. As Sauer (1992) notes, the ability to "identify a person as having ancestors from, say, Northern Europe does not identify a biological race of Northern Europeans" (110). The ability to place an individual within a range of variation does not mean that this variation is best represented by discrete groups. We must consider that the genetic studies are discriminating between people widely separated in space; when populations from geographically intermediate locations are included, the classification accuracy decreases (Bamshad et al. 2003). The question is not whether genetic diversity exists in humanity—it does—but how this variation is distributed. Genetic difference (and classification of individuals) is greatest when comparing human populations widely separated in space. The farther two populations are apart, the more likely it is that they will be genetically different. However, the race concept implies something else—that populational differences can be assigned to discrete and discontinuous races. In reality, genetic differences between human populations are typically gradual and not discontinuous (King and Motulsky 2002).

What Use Is the Race Concept?

Those who argue both for and against the validity of geographic races agree on the geographic pattern of human biological variation. The debate is over whether race is a useful way of describing this variation. In any case, what harm is there in using this concept? Some would argue that the very term *race* has so many meanings and such heavy historical baggage that its use tends to confuse more than to clarify, and that we should perhaps use different terms. In any case, *race* is a purely descriptive term that does not tell us anything about the underlying *causes* of variation. There are better ways to understand and analyze the geographic distribution of human genetic variation than race, as shown in the next section.

GLOBAL PATTERNS OF HUMAN GENETIC VARIATION

Historically, initial attempts at racial classification focused on external physical characteristics such as skin color, hair color, and hair form because physical features were the only human variations that could be observed. Because many of these traits showed large differences in human populations, it was often assumed that *all* genes showed large differences among people around the world (Feldman et al. 2003). This turns out not to be the case.

The Distribution of Human Genetic Variation

Even if we accept a definition of biological race that is synonymous with geographic region, the reality of most human variation is that the level of genetic variation is far greater *within* than *between* human populations. Racial classifications focus on differences between groups. This is apparent in the use of group stereotypes (e.g., "they are short" or "they have broad heads"). Such statements provide information about the *average* in a group but say nothing about variation *within* the group. For example, consider the statement that adult males in the United States tend to be taller than adult females in the United States. No one can argue with this basic fact regarding the average height of adult men and women. However, does it imply that *all* males are taller than *all* females? Of course not. There is variation within both sexes and a great deal of overlap.

Variation between and within Groups   A number of studies have quantified the relative amount of genetic variation within and between different groupings of humanity. We start by acknowledging that genetic variation exists within our species. The question is how this variation is partitioned. Imagine a species consisting of only two populations (Figure 13.8). We wish to examine genetic variation *within* and *between* the two populations. In terms of population genetics, genetic variation within populations refers to the relative numbers of different alleles. If all the alleles are the same within a population, then there is no genetic variation in that population. Genetic variation between populations refers to the differences in allele frequencies. If the two populations have the same allele frequency, there is no genetic variation between the populations.

   If everyone is genetically the same within each population but the two populations are genetically different from each other, then by definition there is no genetic variation *within* populations, and all of the genetic variation in the species exists *between* populations (Case 1 in Figure 13.8). To put

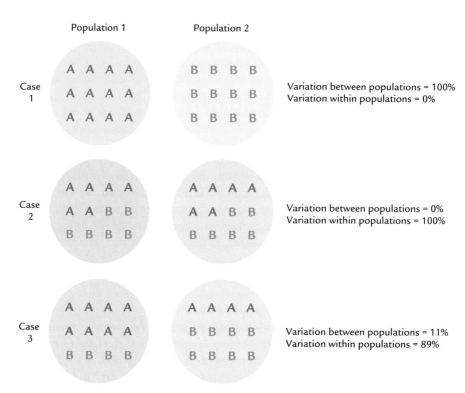

FIGURE 13.8

Three different examples showing how variation is partitioned between and within populations. The circles each enclose a population with a specific number of two alleles, *A* and *B*. In case 1, population 1 consists entirely of *A* alleles and population 2 consists entirely of *B* alleles. There is no variation *within* either population, but the two populations are completely different in terms of the frequencies of the *A* and *B* alleles. As such, 100 percent of the variation is *between* the populations and 0 percent is *within* populations. Case 2 shows the opposite pattern. The genetic composition of both populations is the same—50 percent *A* alleles and 50 percent *B* alleles. There is therefore no variation *between* the populations, and all of the variation occurs *within* populations. Case 3 shows a less extreme condition, where the frequency of the *A* allele is $8/12 = 0.67$ in population 1 and $4/12 = 0.33$ in population 2. There is variation *within* each population, and there is some variation *between* the populations. The actual partitioning of variation (11 percent between populations and 89 percent within populations) is of the magnitude seen among major geographic regions of humans (see text)—most genetic variation exists *within* populations. Both populations have *A* and *B* alleles but differ in their relative frequency. Note that the percentage of variation within and between populations was computed using a measure known as F_{ST}, which relates allele frequencies to the proportion of variation between populations.

this numerically, we would say that the variation within populations is 0 percent and that the variation between populations is 100 percent. This scenario is consistent with the most extreme view of races—"they all look alike" (0 percent variation within populations) and "they look different from others" (100 percent variation between populations).

Now, consider a completely different scenario in which there are genetic differences between individuals within each population, but the allele frequencies are the same in both populations (case 2 in Figure 13.8). Here, there is no difference between the two populations, and all of the genetic variation exists *within* populations. Numerically, this means that the variation within populations is 100 percent and the variation between populations is 0 percent.

Apportionment of Human Genetic Diversity   What does human genetic variation look like? Anthropologists and geneticists have computed these percentages based on data from native populations in various large geographic regions of the world, such as sub-Saharan Africa, Europe, East Asia, and North America. Studies of blood groups and other genetic markers show that roughly 10 percent of the total variation in the human species exists *between* geographic regions, with the remaining 90 percent existing *within* geographic regions (Brown and Armelagos 2001; Relethford 2001). The same pattern has been found for DNA markers (Barbujani et al. 1997) and craniometric traits (Relethford 1994). Further, most of the variation within regions is due to variation within local populations (85 percent) and far less between local populations (5 percent) (Barbujani et al. 1997; Relethford 2002).

Skin color, on the other hand, shows more variation between regions than within regions (Relethford 2002). The large difference in skin color is expected because it has been affected by natural selection in different parts of the world (see Chapter 15). Although skin color has been a primary means of racial classification, its global distribution is atypical; thus, one should not extrapolate from skin color variation to genetic variation on the whole.

Geographic Distance and Human Genetic Variation

To assess patterns of genetic variation between populations, we need a measure of relative similarity that tells us something about the relationship between populations, such as common history or shared genes through gene flow. If we look at a small number of populations and a single trait, this is not that complicated. Imagine, for example, that you have data on the frequency of an allele in three different populations (A, B, C) and that your data look like this:

> Allele frequency in population A = 0.6
>
> Allele frequency in population B = 0.7
>
> Allele frequency in population C = 0.2

Given these data, what can you say about the genetic similarity of these populations? Just looking at the numbers, it is apparent that populations A and B are more similar because their allele frequencies are more similar to each other than to population C.

Genetic Distance   In reality, such analyses are more complicated. For one thing, we would want to sample more than one gene or trait to have a better chance of detecting average genetic similarity between populations. This is the

Genetics, Race, and IQ

Perhaps the most controversial topic in the study of human variation is the relationship between genetics, race, and IQ test scores. What is IQ? It stands for "intelligence quotient" and is a measure derived by dividing a person's "mental age" by her or his chronological age; it is designed so that the average score for a reference population is 100. The IQ test was developed in France by Alfred Binet, who sought a means by which to identify children with learning disabilities. The purpose of the test was not to measure intelligence per se, but rather to identify those children who would most likely require special education. The test was not meant to provide a ranking of intelligence among the rest of the students. There continues to be controversy over the extent to which IQ tests measure innate intelligence.

Are there "racial" differences in IQ scores? If so, what are the causes of these differences? Do they reflect genetics, environment, or both? Over time, as observations were collected that showed group differences in IQ test scores, several researchers argued that this difference is at least partially due to genetic differences between the races. A common line of argument goes as follows:

1. Differences in IQ scores are partly due to genetic differences.
2. The races have different average IQ scores.
3. Therefore, because races are by definition genetically different, the racial differences in IQ scores are due to genetic differences.

It is worthwhile to examine briefly each of these claims.

There is evidence for both genetic (Bouchard et al. 1990) and environmental components for IQ (Gould 1981). The latter include diet, education, social class, and health, among others. The exact heritability of IQ has been widely debated. Some have suggested that 60–80 percent of the variation in IQ scores may be due to genetic variation, while others suggest heritability might be closer to 34–48 percent (Devlin et al. 1997). In any case, we can make a case that the heritability of IQ is moderate to high.

The second claim is that there are racial differences in IQ test scores. In the United States, for example, European Americans tend to score, on average, roughly 15 points higher than African Americans. Asian Americans tend to score, on average, several points higher than European Americans. What exactly is being compared?

Categories such as "European American," "African American," and "Asian American" are broad groupings based on ethnicity and national origin, but they are not by any stretch of the imagination homogeneous populations, in terms of either genetics or environment. People within any of these broad ancestral groupings can come from a wide variety of countries and environments. Group averages therefore obscure much of the variation within groups, which makes comparative analysis difficult.

The next problem is the third claim in the list. We assume that any group differences in a trait that has a genetic basis must themselves be genetic in nature. This is not a valid assumption, however, as group differences could be the result of genetics, environment, or both. As noted in Chapter 2, heritability is a measure of genetic variation *within* groups and not between groups. If we estimate the heritability of IQ as x percent, this does not mean that x percent of the difference between groups in IQ scores is due to genetics.

We have no way of telling beforehand the causes of group differences; this requires testing. In terms of racial comparisons, we know that these groups show average differences in environmental conditions that affect performance on IQ tests, such as education and income. To date, the bulk of the evidence supports an environmental explanation of racial difference in IQ test scores (Loehlin et al. 1975; Gould 1981; Mackintosh 1998). One of the most revealing studies, reviewed by Mackintosh (1998), looked at the IQ scores of German women children fathered by African American soldiers after World War II. The IQ scores of these children, who were raised by their mothers or foster parents, were no different from those of white German children when matched for other characteristics. In this study, the ancestry of the two groups was different, but the environment was the same, as were the IQ scores.

Another test of the hypothesis that group differences in IQ test scores are genetic involves comparing scores by individual ancestry. If IQ differences reflect genetics, then test scores among African Americans should vary proportionately according to the degree of European admixture; those with greater European ancestry should score higher. However, analyses have shown no relationship between amount of European ancestry and IQ score (Flynn 1980; Mackintosh 1998).

same reason you would not want to pick a single person out of a population to get an estimate of average height; by chance, you might get someone much taller or shorter than average. To minimize error in our estimates, we sample as many genes or traits as possible. In addition, we would not want to include genes or traits that have been affected strongly by natural selection because our purpose is to reconstruct relationships based on shared ancestry and gene flow. Traits that have been affected by natural selection could give us an inaccurate estimate. For example, both Central African and Australian native populations have dark skin color. If we used this physical similarity to infer a recent common ancestry or gene flow between the groups, we would be making a mistake. In this case, the two populations are similar in skin color because of adaptation to a similar environment (see Chapter 15).

A variety of methods exist to compute an average measure of genetic similarity, known as a **genetic distance,** but discussion of how this is done is beyond the scope of this book; simply realize that genetic distances represent relative similarity. Genetic distances are computed between pairs of populations. If, for example, we are looking at four populations (A, B, C, D), we would compute the genetic distance between six pairs of populations: A and B, A and C, A and D, B and C, B and D, and C and D. Imagine that we have computed a genetic distance from allele frequencies in the four hypothetical populations and that these distances are as follows:

Distance between A and B = 0.007

Distance between A and C = 0.090

Distance between A and D = 0.079

Distance between B and C = 0.139

Distance between B and D = 0.130

Distance between C and D = 0.010

Don't worry about the units of measure; most genetic distance measures are relative. The key to understanding genetic distances is recognizing that the smaller the number the more *similar* the populations, and the larger the number the more *dissimilar.* In this case, the smallest distances are between populations A and B and between populations C and D. The distances between A and C, A and D, B and C, and B and D are much larger. Therefore, populations A and B form a related group and populations C and D form a related group, but these two groups are more distant from each other.

Even with only four populations, it may take a few minutes looking at the actual genetic distances to see these patterns. As we add more populations to the analysis, it quickly becomes impossible to make sense out of the table of genetic distances. If, for example, we were looking at the genetic distances between 10 populations, we would have to consider 45 different pairs of distances, which is too many to make any sense from. Studies of genetic distance instead use one of several methods to produce a simple picture that captures the pattern of genetic distances. Several of these methods produce a **genetic distance map,** which is simply a two-dimensional plot showing the genetic relationship between the populations. These maps are

genetic distance An average measure of relatedness between populations based on a number of traits. Genetic distances are used to understand the effects of genetic drift and gene flow, which should affect all loci to the same extent.

genetic distance map A picture that shows the genetic relationships between populations, based on genetic distance measures.

FIGURE 13.9

Example of a genetic distance map showing the genetic relationships between four hypothetical populations (A, B, C, D) whose genetic distances are given in the text. This map was produced using a method known as *principal coordinates analysis.* The scales correspond to positions in genetic space and are dependent on the method used to construct the map. The map is easy to interpret—the closer two populations plot to each other on the map, the more genetically similar they are. This map shows clear separation into two major groups, one consisting of populations A and B, and the other consisting of populations C and D.

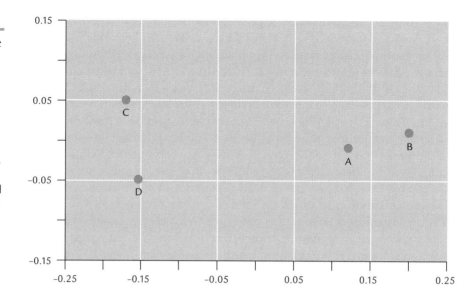

easy to interpret—the closer two populations plot to each other on the genetic distance map, the more genetically similar they are. Just as we use a road map to get a picture of how different places are located relative to each other in geographic space, we use a genetic distance map to show how similar populations are to each other in genetic space. Figure 13.9 shows the genetic distance map for the hypothetical distances between A, B, C, and D. Interpretation is very clear. We see that populations A and B plot next to each other on one side of the map, and populations C and D plot next to each other on the other side of the map. We can easily see that A and B are more genetically similar to (less distant from) each other than either is to C or D, which in turn are more genetically similar to each other than either is to A or B. This map does not explain *why* we find this pattern. It might reflect some barrier to gene flow, such as a large geographic distance or a mountain range separating A and B from C and D. Alternatively, this map might reflect cultural differences that have resulted in low levels of gene flow between the two clusters. In any actual study of genetic distance, we would require more information to be able to explain the observed patterns of genetic distance.

Genetic Distance between Human Populations   A number of studies have examined genetic distance between native populations across the world using a variety of genetic and physical traits. One of the most comprehensive studies conducted to date was performed by geneticist Luigi Cavalli-Sforza and colleagues (1994), who computed the genetic distance between 42 human populations worldwide using data on 120 allele frequencies (mostly red blood cell polymorphisms and HLA markers). A genetic distance map based on their published genetic distances is shown in Figure 13.10, and the overall picture corresponds well to geography and known history. Many of the populations in Europe and Asia plot near the center of the map, with native

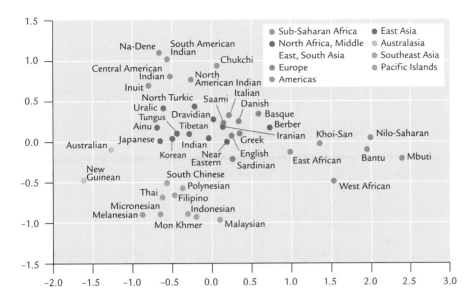

FIGURE 13.10

Genetic distance map showing the genetic relationships among 42 native human populations around the world. The genetic distances are based on 120 allele frequencies. This map was constructed using a method known as *multidimensional scaling.* The scales correspond to positions in genetic space and are dependent on the method used to construct the map. European and many Asian populations plot near the center of the map, with Native American, sub-Saharan African, Southeast Asian, and Pacific Island populations plotting farther away. Overall, this map reproduces the geographic distances between human populations to a large extent. (Data from Cavalli-Sforza et al. 1994.)

populations in sub-Saharan Africa, the Pacific Islands, and the Americas plotting farther away. Native American populations plot closer to populations in Northeast Asia, consistent with their origin there (see Chapter 14). Populations in the Pacific (Melanesia, Micronesia, Polynesia) plot closest to Southeast Asian populations, which is consistent with geography and history.

Isolation by Distance in Human Populations Overall, the picture of genetic relationships in Figure 13.10 shows a strong relationship to the geographic distances between populations. This is expected when looking at genetic relationships that have been averaged over many genes because gene flow has the same effect on all genes. By averaging many genes, we have a better chance of detecting underlying common patterns. The expected relationship between geographic distance and genetic distance is explained by the **isolation by distance** model. Genetic similarity is a function of gene flow; the more gene flow between two populations, the more similar they are genetically. Recall from Chapter 3 that in most organisms, including humans, geographic distance limits the amount of gene flow. We expect that the closer two populations are geographically, the more gene flow between them, and the smaller the genetic distance. The farther apart two populations are geographically, the less gene flow between them, and therefore the greater the genetic distance. The isolation by distance model predicts that genetic distance will increase geometrically as geographic distance increases.

Figure 13.11 shows the fit of the isolation by distance model to the genetic distances between the 42 populations shown in Figure 13.10. Each dot in Figure 13.11 represents the average genetic distance for pairs of populations separated by a given interval of geographic distance, such as 0–499 kilometers, 500–999 kilometers, and so forth. The solid line is the expected fit for the isolation by distance model. The correspondence between observed

isolation by distance A model that predicts that the genetic distance between populations will increase as the geographic distance between them increases.

FIGURE 13.11

Isolation by distance in human populations. The genetic distances between all 42 populations in Figure 13.10 were computed and then averaged within different groups depending on the geographic distance between them. Geographic distances were computed from the longitude and latitude of each population with some restrictions based on the known paths of migration in the past. Each dot represents the average genetic distance for all pairs of populations within a given geographic distance group. The solid line represents the expected fit of the isolation by distance model. (Adapted from Relethford 2003.)

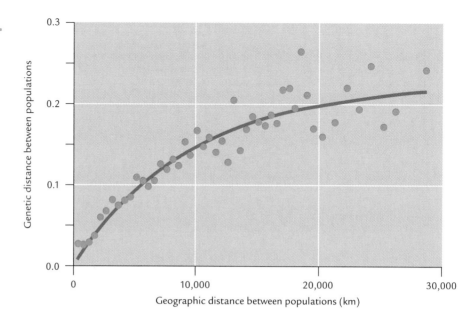

and expected genetic distances is very high, as there is only a small amount of scatter in the plot. This shows that the overall pattern of genetic relationships among human populations around the world is to a large extent a function of geography. The isolation by distance model has been found to fit global variation in a variety of traits, including blood group markers, DNA markers, and cranial measures (Relethford 2004b).

Instead of a view of humanity as geographically dispersed separate races, Figure 13.11 shows that average differences between human populations are smooth and gradual over geographic space. Of course, geographic distance is not the only factor that explains human genetic variation. Although the *average* genetic distances fit the isolation by distance model, the genetic similarity between any given pair of populations is often also affected by unique aspects of population history. Nor does isolation by distance explain variation at all loci to the same extent. By chance, some genes have been affected by genetic drift to a greater extent than others. In addition, some genes are clearly affected by natural selection in ways that cause their patterns of variation to deviate from the expected pattern of isolation by distance. To see the influence of factors such as population history and natural selection, it is necessary to move beyond average global analyses. The next two chapters do this by considering a number of case studies of genetics and population history (Chapter 14) and natural selection in human populations (Chapter 15).

Summary

Many methods exist for assessing biological variation within and between human populations. A number of biochemical traits, such as red blood cell polymorphisms, provide a means of assessing genetics at the level of the molecular structure of blood types and blood proteins and enzymes. Other measures of genetic variation focus specifically on the underlying genetic code by directly examining differences in DNA sequences. A number of physical traits, such as anthropometrics and skin color, provide data on phenotypic variation, which reflects both underlying genetic differences and environmental and developmental influences.

Throughout much of history, human biological variation has been discussed in terms of race and racial classification, with an emphasis on identifying discrete groups of human populations that differ widely in genetics. In the past, race was used as a crude means by which to describe patterns of human variation. A major problem in using race as a concept is that distinct "races" take on a reality of their own in people's minds. The race concept has limited use in analyses of biological variation, particularly for widespread species such as human beings, because it uses arbitrary classifications of predominantly continuous traits.

Studies of genetic variation in the human species do not produce results consistent with the race concept. Instead, we find evidence of geographic differences between human groups, but with no clear boundaries between them. Genetic variation is greatest within local human populations, such that for many traits only 10 percent of the total genetic variation is found between major geographic groups. The pattern of genetic distances between human populations is strongly related to geography and its effect on gene flow.

Supplemental Readings

Brace, C. L. 2005. *"Race" Is a Four-Letter Word: The Genesis of the Concept.* New York: Oxford University Press. A detailed discussion of the history of the biological race concept.

Cavalli-Sforza, L. L. 2000. *Genes, Peoples, and Languages.* New York: North Point Press. A short, readable introduction to genetic variation in the human species.

Cavalli-Sforza, L. L., P. Meonozzi, and A. Piazza. 1994. *The History and Geography of Human Genes.* Princeton, NJ: Princeton University Press. Similar in focus to the above book, but with much greater, and exceptional, detail.

Mielke, J. H., L. W. Konigsberg, and J. H. Relethford. 2006. *Human Biological Variation.* New York: Oxford University Press. An intermediate-level text that covers different measures of human variation and their evolutionary interpretation.

VIRTUAL EXPLORATIONS

Visit our textbook-specific online learning center Web site at
www. mhhe.com/relethford7 to access the exercises that follows.

1. **Dermatoglyphics**   **http://www.handanalysis.net/library/derm
   _easter3.htm.**   Read the "Fingerprints on the Easter Islands" article
   on the IIHA (International Institute of Hand Analysis) Web site. The
   article discusses both dermatoglyphics (measurement of palm and
   fingerprints) and issues of race and human variation

   ■ The construction of the huge monoliths on Easter Island remains a
     mystery since Captain Cook first discovered them in the early nine-
     teenth century. How was dermatoglyphics used to find a solution?
   ■ Comparative fingerprint data was used in the study. From which
     population were fingerprints compared to the Easter Islanders'?
   ■ What were the "scientific" interpretations concerning racial supe-
     riority?
   ■ What were the results?

2. **The Biological Race Concept**   **http://serendip.brynmawr.edu/
   biology/ b103/f00/web2/ramon2.html.**   Read Gloria Ramon's
   essay "Race: Social Concept, Biological Idea." In it, she traces the
   concept of race, the attributes once thought to identify race, and the
   validity of "race" in the twenty-first century.

   ■ In 1758, Swedish botanist Carolus Linnaeus established the con-
     cept of race, referring to human "varieties" as part of his classifi-
     cation system. What were the races he identified?
   ■ On what basis were differences attributed?
   ■ How many races did European scientists later identify?
   ■ What was the scientific justification?
   ■ Biological anthropologists use three criteria for determining vari-
     ation in animal species. What are the three?
   ■ How has the concept of race changed today?

3. **A SNP Off the Old Block**   **http://www.sciencemag.org/products/
   sequel.dtl.**   Read Peter Gwynne and Guy Paga's article "Technologies
   in Genomic Research: The Sequel." The article discusses technologies
   originally developed for the Human Genome Project and how in the
   twenty-first century they will help revolutionize such diverse fields

as agriculture, medicine, and crime-fighting. Scroll down to the sub-head "A SNP Off the Old Block." This section discusses single nucleotide polymorphisms, or SNPs. Continue reading through the sections "Dawn of Personalized Medicine" and "Attack on the Killer Pathogens."

- As a DNA base pair, why are SNPs useful?
- How do SNPs play an important role as disease markers?
- What do SNPs tell us about how truly unique we are as individuals? How will this help in treating disease?
- How will this information become useful against microbial pathogens?

A Polynesian mother and child. Ancestors of Polynesians spread across the Pacific Ocean several thousand years ago, populating islands from New Zealand, to Hawaii, to Easter Island. Studies of genetic variation in today's Polynesians provide us with evidence about their history and the relative amounts of ancestry from Southeast Asia and Melanesia.

Genetics, History, and Ancestry

W here do you come from? This question is common among people with an interest in genealogy. How would you go about researching your own family tree? You would probably begin with oral histories provided by your relatives and with written family records. Generally, this information is easy to get for at least two generations—back to your grandparents—but not always. As you search further into the past, you may have to dig through written vital records of births, marriages, and deaths, as well as other written sources, such as diaries, wills, and tax listings. In most cases, oral and written records are limited to a few generations. In rare cases, very well-documented genealogies may have written records for a few hundred years. Within certain limits, genetic data can provide additional information on ancestry, for both individuals and entire groups. The use of genetic data to reconstruct population history is well known in anthropology, and the use of newly discovered genetic markers as tools to reconstruct individual ancestry has increased rapidly in recent years (Brown 2002).

It is important to understand both the promise and the limitations of using genetic data to reconstruct human history. Although genetics provides a link over the course of generations, it is not always possible to determine where particular genes or DNA sequences originated. Recombination shuffles genetic material each generation, which means that a particular DNA sequence passed from your mother to you might have come from either her mother or her father. The exceptions to this rule, as described in previous chapters, are mitochondrial DNA and Y-chromosome polymorphisms, which are inherited from a single parent, making them favorite tools for reconstructing ancestry.

This chapter provides a number of case studies that illustrate in a general way how genetic data can be used to reconstruct history. The first section describes the use of genetic data to look at the history of entire *populations,* focusing on the origin of genetic variation in different populations and their genetic relationship with other populations in the world. The second section deals with how genetic data can be used to examine the ancestry of *individuals.* The third section returns to the more general question of ancestry, examining the frequent differences between a person's genetic ancestry and his or her cultural identity.

THE GENETIC HISTORY OF POPULATIONS

Some questions about population history focus on the origin of populations. For example, where did a given population come from? Did it form as a splinter group from another population? Did it result from the movement of some group of initial colonizers or settlers? Did it form from the genetic merging of two or more groups? Other questions about population history focus on the relationship between historical events and genetic outcomes. For example, if a population was invaded from elsewhere, did the invaders introduce any genes, and if so, how much of an effect was there?

Human populations are constantly interacting with each other, and we are interested here in the genetic effects of such events. In general, we look at genetic relationships between populations in terms of common ancestry and gene flow, both of which are expected to result in populations being more similar genetically to each other. We assume that, for the most part, common ancestry and gene flow affect all genes and DNA sequences to the same extent (an exception is a possible difference between mitochondrial DNA and Y-chromosome polymorphisms because of differences in female and male gene flow). However, other evolutionary forces do not always have the same impact on all of our genomes. Genetic drift, for example, could make the allele frequencies in two closely related populations different by chance (or make two less-related populations appear more similar). Natural selection could also have this effect. As noted in the previous chapter, it is for these reasons that we try to use averages based on a large number of traits and to limit analysis to traits that appear to have little or no relationship to natural selection.

The Origin of Native Americans

One example of population origins and history is the case of Native American populations. Europeans became aware of the existence of the New World (the Americas) and Native Americans following the initial exploration of Christopher Columbus in 1492, when he attempted to circumnavigate the earth to find an alternate route from Europe to Asia. Indeed, when Columbus arrived in the New World, he thought he had succeeded in reaching the "Indies," the term then used for Asia. Consequently, the native peoples found in the New World became known as "Indians." A number of people contemplated exactly where these people had originated. For those who interpreted the natural world from a strict biblical perspective, Native Americans were seen as one of the lost tribes of Israel (Crawford 1998).

As discussed previously, humans first evolved in Africa, later spreading throughout the Old World (Africa, Asia, Europe, and Australia), and later still into the New World. All human fossils found in the New World are modern; no earlier species of humans lived here. In the late sixteenth century, some argued that Asia was the place of origin for Native Americans, and the dominant view since then has been that Asians moved into the Americas across the Bering Land Bridge (Figure 14.1). During periods of glaciation, the sea levels fell, exposing a stretch of land connecting Asia and North America

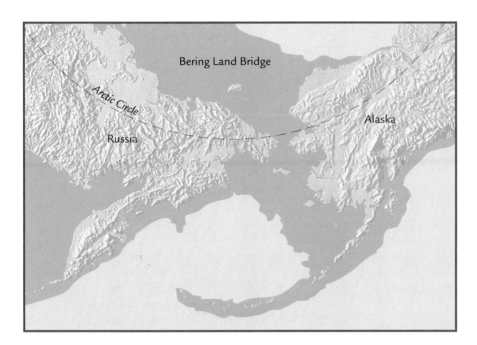

FIGURE 14.1

The Bering Land Bridge. Today Siberia and Alaska are separated by water. During the "Ice Ages," water was trapped in glaciers, producing a drop in the sea level that exposed the land known as the Bering Land Bridge. This "bridge" connecting Asia and North America was actually 2,100 km (1,300 miles) wide!

that was almost 2,100 km (roughly 1,300 miles) wide. This "land bridge" did not appear or disappear suddenly but developed slowly over thousands of years as sea levels dropped. Under this model, groups of humans following game herds moved across this region and eventually down into North, Central, and South America. In recent years, some archaeologists have suggested that humans may have used boats to migrate to the New World (Nemecek 2000). Either way, the archaeological record shows a connection between Asia and the New World.

Archaeologists continue to debate when this event happened. For many years, it was thought that humans moved into the New World roughly 12,000 years ago. These dates were consistent with the dates of sites containing the first examples of the Clovis stone tool culture, which dates back to 11,500 years ago. Over time, archaeologists have found evidence of a number of more ancient pre-Clovis sites, perhaps dating back as far as 15,000 years ago (Nemecek 2000; Marshall 2001). Depending on confirmation of the most ancient dates, and allowing for different estimates of the speed at which the New World was settled, a range of initial entry from 15,000 to 20,000 years ago seems reasonable.

The Genetic Evidence for an Asian Origin   A number of physical traits, such as the presence of shovel-shaped incisors, tend to support a genetic connection between Asians and Native Americans. These traits tend to be more common in both groups and are found at lower frequencies in other populations. The best evidence, however, comes from analysis of genetic markers and DNA analysis. These studies have consistently found that Native Americans are more similar to populations in Asia, particularly Northeast Asia, than to other human populations.

FIGURE 14.2

The genetic distance between Native Americans and those in other geographic regions, based on an analysis of 120 allele frequencies for red and white blood cell polymorphisms. The lower the genetic distance, the greater the genetic similarity. Northeast Asian populations are the most similar genetically to Native Americans. (Data from Cavalli-Sforza et al. 1994.)

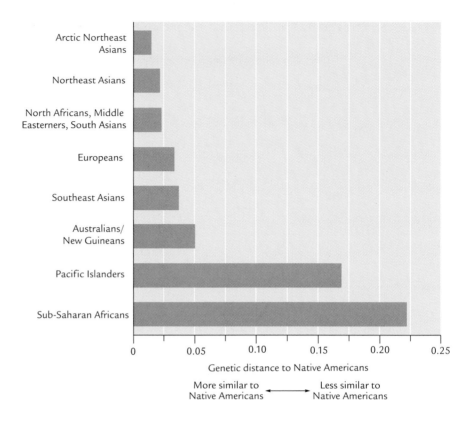

An example of the closer genetic link to Asia is presented in Figure 14.2, which shows the average genetic distances from Native Americans to populations in eight other geographic regions based on 120 allele frequencies (Cavalli-Sforza et al. 1994). Not only are Native Americans more similar genetically to Asians than to other geographic groups, but the closest relationship is to Northeast Asians, which is consistent with archaeological evidence that the first migrants to the New World came from Northeast Asia.

Even greater insight into genetic relationships with Native American populations has been provided through the analysis of mitochondrial DNA haplogroups. Recall from the previous chapter that a haplotype is a combination of DNA sequences that is inherited as a single unit. Geneticists can examine different haplotypes and determine how they are related evolutionarily by finding groups of haplotypes that share common mutations; these related haplotypes are known as **haplogroups.** Relethford (2003) looks at the difference between haplotypes and haplogroups using an analogy to the make and model of automobiles. Different manufacturers produce different models of cars, but these different models often have some common equipment, such as similar radios or climate controls. In this example, the different models of automobiles (Bronco or Mustang) are analogous to haplotypes, and the different makes (Chevy or Ford) are analogous to haplogroups.

Mitochondrial DNA from Native Americans (both living and from ancient skeletal material) belongs to one of five different haplogroups, labeled

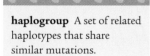

haplogroup A set of related haplotypes that share similar mutations.

A, B, C, D, and X (Schurr 2000). Four of these haplogroups (A, B, C, D) are found in Northeast Asian populations and are absent or rare in other parts of the world (Schurr 2000; Derenko et al. 2001). The fifth haplogroup, X, is found in both Northeast Asian populations and parts of Europe, the latter likely suggesting migration between Asia and Europe. Collectively, the mitochondrial DNA haplogroup distributions support the connection between Asia and North America, confirming that Native Americans are the descendants of migrants from Northeast Asia.

How Many Migrations?   Although virtually everyone agrees with an Asian origin of Native Americans, there remains considerable debate over the number of major migration events. Did humans move into the New World only once, or were there two, three, or more separate migration events, perhaps each from a different region of Asia? New methods of molecular analysis of DNA markers have potential for answering this question. Schurr (2000) notes that specific mutations in the mitochondrial DNA haplogroups of Native Americans are found in different parts of Asia, such as Siberia and East Asia, suggesting at least two different sources for migrants to the New World. Analysis of Y-chromosome polymorphisms also supports the idea of at least two major migrations. Two Y-chromosome haplotypes, labeled 1C and 1F, are found at high frequencies among Native Americans. Both of these are also found in Asia, but their geographic distribution in Asia is different, again suggesting two separate migration events out of Asia (Karafet et al. 1999).

The Origin of Polynesians

The three major cultural and geographic regions in the Pacific Islands—Micronesia, Melanesia, and Polynesia—were named for particular features. *Micronesia* means "small islands," and this region is made up of more than 2,000 small-sized islands. *Melanesia* means "dark islands," so named because of the dark skin color of the native populations. *Polynesia* means "many islands," and indeed it covers a wide area in the Pacific Ocean roughly forming a triangle bounded by New Zealand, Easter Island, and Hawaii (Figure 14.3).

Although humans have inhabited Melanesia for at least 35,000 years, Micronesia and Polynesia were settled more recently. Polynesia was first settled near New Guinea roughly 3,500 years ago, and by 1,600 years ago, Polynesians had made it to Easter Island and the Hawaiian Islands. The interesting aspect of Polynesian expansion is that they traveled very long distances over water using canoes, making their story a fascinating example of human cultural adaptability. Of course, the canoes used by Polynesians are a specific sort known as double-outriggers (Figure 14.4), which cannot easily be capsized (Diamond 1999). In addition, the Polynesians possessed keen navigation abilities.

Where Did They Come From?   The origin of the Polynesians lies in what is referred to as the Austronesian expansion, a movement of farmers who spoke languages classified as *Austronesian* out of Asia into the Pacific Islands.

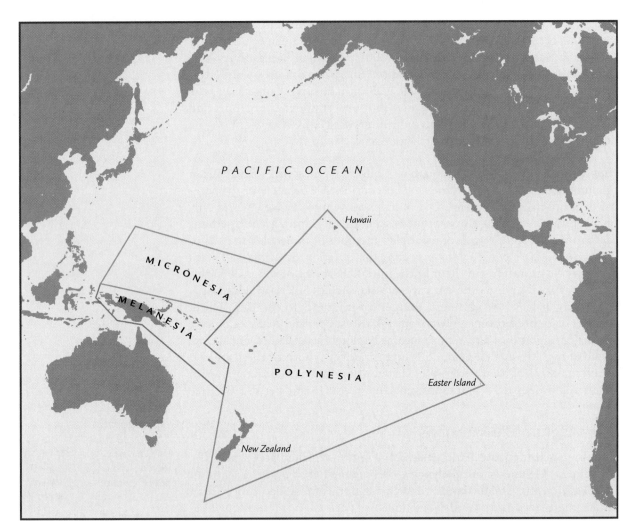

FIGURE 14.3

Locations of Micronesia, Melanesia, and Polynesia in the Pacific Ocean. (Based on Lum et al. 1998.)

Archaeological and linguistic evidence suggests Taiwan or south coastal China as a likely origin for this expansion. An alternate explanation was championed by Norwegian explorer Thor Heyerdahl, who suggested that the Polynesians came from South America. Today genetic evidence shows quite clearly that Polynesians are more closely related to Southeast Asians than to East Asians or to Native Americans. Figure 14.5 shows a genetic distance map for a number of Pacific Island, Southeast Asian, East Asian, and Native American populations based on red and white blood cell polymorphisms. This map shows clearly that Polynesians are most similar to Southeast Asians and other Pacific Islanders, and not that close to Native Americans, thus ruling out a South American origin. Although this map shows close genetic similarity between Polynesians and Southeast Asians, they are also similar to Melanesians and Micronesians. The general similarity of Polynesians, Southeast Asians, and Melanesians is harder to interpret from this analysis, and debate continues over the role of Melanesia in Polynesian origins.

FIGURE 14.4

Polynesians today still use the outrigger canoes used by their ancestors. Outriggers have supporting structures attached perpendicular to the side of the canoe, which provide additional buoyancy and reduce the chances of capsizing.

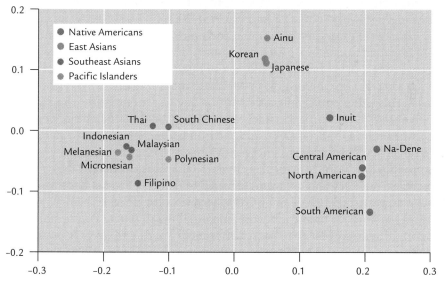

FIGURE 14.5

This genetic distance map shows the genetic relationship between human populations in the Pacific Islands, Southeast Asia, East Asia, and the New World based on 120 allele frequencies for red and white blood cell polymorphisms. This map was constructed using a method known as *principal coordinates analysis*. The scales correspond to positions in genetic space and are dependent on the method used to construct the map. Polynesians are genetically most similar to populations in Southeast Asia and elsewhere in the Pacific Islands, and more genetically different from populations in East Asia or the New World. (Data from Cavalli-Sforza et al. 1994.)

"Express Train" or "Slow Boat"? Looking at the Pacific Islands map (see Figure 14.3), it is clear that any movement of seafarers out of Southeast Asia into Polynesia would pass by New Guinea and the rest of Melanesia, an area that had been occupied by humans long before the expansion of the Polynesians. Consequently, in an expansion out of Southeast Asia, it is possible that these migrants interacted with human populations in Melanesia. If so, then there was an opportunity for Polynesians to genetically mix with Melanesians. There has been considerable debate over whether this happened, and if so, then how much?

Jared Diamond (1988) has proposed the "express train" model of Polynesian origins. He suggests that the movement of Polynesian ancestors out of Asia was very rapid, analogous to an express train, such that they had little if any genetic contact with Melanesians. In this model, Polynesians are exclusively of Southeast Asian origin. Others have suggested that Diamond's model is too extreme and that the expansion was not so fast as to preclude any genetic mixing along the way. The most recent version of this hypothesis is the "slow boat" model proposed by Kayser and colleagues (2000).

DNA analysis has been used in recent years to examine these hypotheses, with the key question being whether we can detect any evidence of past gene flow from Melanesian populations. Studies of mitochondrial DNA haplotypes found at high frequencies in Polynesians show a definite geographic gradient out of Southeast Asia that is consistent with the express train model (Redd et al. 1995; Sykes et al. 1995). The evidence from Y-chromosome DNA gives a different picture. In one study (Kayser et al. 2000), a Y-chromosome haplotype was found at very high frequency (82 percent) in a Polynesian sample. This haplotype is also present, although at lower frequency, in some Melanesian populations, but it is completely absent in Southeast Asian populations. This finding suggests Melanesian gene flow. Another study of different Y-chromosome haplotypes did not find this pattern but instead found a connection with Southeast Asia (Su et al. 2000).

When we examine *all* of the mitochondrial DNA and Y-chromosome DNA evidence, the most likely explanation for Polynesian origins is the slow boat model because it combines an initial origin out of Southeast Asia with *some* genetic mixing with Melanesians along the way. Differences between studies could reflect deviations due to genetic drift. The study of Polynesian DNA is particularly interesting because of the differences between mitochondrial DNA and Y-chromosome DNA; the former shows stronger evidence of Asian ancestry while the latter suggests some genetic contribution from Melanesia. Given that mitochondrial DNA detects maternal ancestry and Y-chromosome DNA detects paternal ancestry, some have suggested that there might have been sex differences in gene flow, with more Melanesian men than women contributing to the Polynesian gene pool. Others suggest that these differences are due to greater male gene flow *after* the initial settlement of Polynesia (Lum et al. 1998; Underhill et al. 2001). It is also possible that greater male gene flow occurred both during and after the initial expansion. In any case, the genetic history of the Polynesians is more complex than a single movement of people into the Pacific Ocean.

The Population History of Ireland

From the perspective of genetic variation, the population history of Ireland is fascinating because of the numerous possibilities for gene flow in Ireland's past. ("Ireland" refers here to the entire island, which is currently made up of

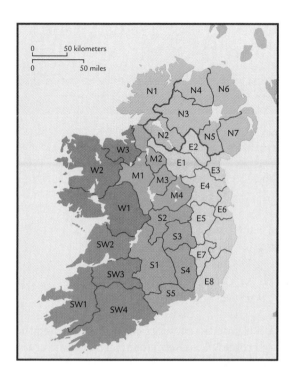

FIGURE 14.6

Geographic map of Irish counties used in the genetic distance analysis. The labels correspond to six regions: W = west coast, SW = southwest, M = midlands, N = north, E = east, S = south. This map can be compared with the genetic distance map in Figure 14.7. One county in the east is not labeled because data were not available for that county. (Adapted from Relethford and Crawford 1995.)

two countries—the Republic of Ireland and Northern Ireland.) Through the years, Ireland has seen many different invasions and settlements from England, Scotland, Wales, and Scandinavia. What was the genetic impact of these different sources of gene flow?

Relethford and Crawford (1995) investigated the patterns of biological variation among Irish populations using 10 anthropometric measures of the head and face. With appropriate methods, anthropometric data can be used to estimate genetic distances (Relethford et al. 1997). Data originally collected in the 1930s on more than 7,000 adult Irish men were used to look at genetic distances between 31 Irish counties (political units). Figure 14.6 shows the geographic location of these counties, and Figure 14.7 shows the genetic distance map. For easy comparison of the two figures, counties have been grouped into six major geographic units (west coast, southwest, midlands, northern, eastern, and southern).

The major pattern shown in the genetic distance map in Figure 14.7 is the distinctiveness of the four midland counties (M1–M4), which are dissimilar from all remaining counties. Looking at the geographic location of these four counties in Figure 14.6, we see that they are right in the middle of the island, posing an interesting question: What accounts for the distinctiveness of the midlands? We would expect the midland counties to be genetically similar to all other counties because they are right in the middle of all possible migration routes from one part of Ireland to another. This is clearly not the case. To solve this puzzle, we must look elsewhere.

Genetic Impact of the Viking Invasion   One possibility is gene flow from the Viking invasion and settlement. Irish history reveals that the Vikings first came

FIGURE 14.7

Genetic distance map of 31 Irish counties based on head and facial measurements of adult Irish males. This map was constructed using a method known as *principal coordinates analysis*. The scales correspond to positions in genetic space and are dependent on the method used to construct the map. The labels are the same as in Figure 14.6. The midland counties (M1–M4) are clearly the most distinct. There is also some correlation with longitude along the horizontal axis; counties in the western part of Ireland plot near the top, and those in the eastern part of Ireland plot near the bottom. (Adapted from Relethford and Crawford 1995.)

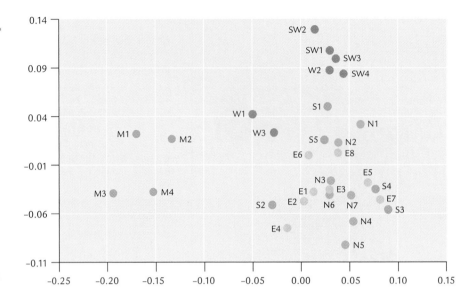

into contact with Ireland in A.D. 794, and that contact continued through the early thirteenth century. Although some Viking settlements were on the coast, substantial numbers of Vikings moved into the Irish midlands, which are accessible by river from the Atlantic Ocean. At least one of these incursions involved as many as 12,000 men, which would be expected to have a noticeable genetic impact. Relethford and Crawford (1995) suggest that the distinctiveness of the Irish midlands reflects this Viking influence and that Viking settlements along the Irish coast had less genetic impact because the genetic makeup of later migrants from England and Wales overrode any Viking influence.

Genetic Impact of Gene Flow from England and Wales   The genetic distance map in Figure 14.7 shows another interesting pattern. Separation of counties along the vertical dimension of the plot corresponds strongly to longitude. Populations at the top of the genetic distance map are in the west and southwest of Ireland, whereas populations toward the bottom are in the northern and eastern part of Ireland. Thus, genetic similarity follows a west-to-east gradient, a pattern also seen in a number of studies of Irish blood groups and other genetic polymorphisms (e.g., Tills et al. 1977; North et al. 2000). This gradient most likely reflects differences in past immigration into Ireland. Historically, we know that much immigration from England and Wales began in the early 1600s, and these immigrants settled predominantly in the north, east, and southeast of Ireland.

Comparative Analysis of Genetic Distance   If the two historical hypotheses described above are correct, we can make two predictions regarding the genetic similarity of the regions of Ireland with other European populations. First, if the Vikings had a disproportionate effect on the Irish midlands, then the midlands should be the most similar in all of Ireland to Norway and Denmark, the populations from which the Vikings came. Second, if the

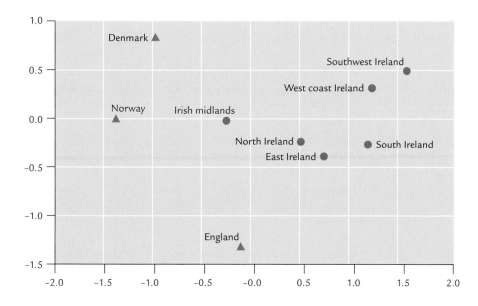

FIGURE 14.8

Genetic distance map comparing six regions of Ireland with data from Norway, Denmark, and England. The genetic distances were based on head and facial measures. This map was constructed using a method known as *principal coordinates analysis*. The scales correspond to positions in genetic space and are dependent on the method used to construct the map. The Irish midlands is closest to Norway and Denmark, whose populations represent the source of Viking invaders to Ireland, thus supporting the hypothesis of Viking gene flow. The closer proximity of the northern and eastern regions to England supports the hypothesis that English immigration occurred primarily in these parts of Ireland, and less so in the west. (Adapted from Relethford and Crawford 1995.)

west–east gradient is due to differential immigration from England and Wales, the eastern counties of Ireland should be the most similar to those populations. Relethford and Crawford (1995) used their Irish data along with comparative data from England, Norway, and Denmark (data from Wales were not available) to derive a comparative genetic distance map, shown in Figure 14.8. This map confirms the two hypotheses. Within Ireland, the midlands is the most similar to Norway and Denmark, and the northern and eastern regions of Ireland are the most similar to England. Although there is no association of geography and genetic distance among Irish counties, the observed patterns of genetic distance make sense in terms of the history of invasion and settlement.

THE GENETIC HISTORY OF INDIVIDUALS

In addition to reconstructing the history of entire populations, genetic analysis can be used to answer questions about the specific history of individuals. What is a particular person's identity and ancestry? Such analyses have forensic and historical applications as you will see in the following sections.

Was Anna Anderson the Missing Grand Duchess Anastasia?

The monarchy of Russia was overthrown during the Russian Revolution of 1917. The Czar, Nicholas II, and his family were sent into exile, and in 1918, they were assassinated. For many years, the fate of the bodies was unknown. Eventually, some skeletal remains were found and identified as members of the royal family. However, these remains did not include the Czar's son and one of his daughters, and it was not clear which of the daughters was missing. In 1920 a woman claiming amnesia appeared in a Berlin hospital after a suicide attempt. Hospital workers noted that she bore a resemblance to Nicholas's youngest daughter, Anastasia. The woman later took the name Anna Anderson, and she eventually married and settled in the United States, where she died in 1984. Her claim of identity was hotly contested until mitochondrial DNA evidence settled the case once and for all (Melton 2003).

Because of its maternal mode of inheritance, mitochondrial DNA can be used to examine shared ancestry through the maternal line. Anna Anderson's mitochondrial DNA was extracted from two sources after her death and cremation. One sample came from intestinal tissue that had been collected during a biopsy before she died. The other sample came from some locks of hair that had apparently been saved by her husband. To test the claim that Anna Anderson was really Anastasia, a known sample of Anastasia's mitochondrial DNA was needed, but none was available. This seeming obstacle was overcome by obtaining a sample from someone who shared maternal ancestry with Anastasia. In this case, a sample was obtained from Prince Phillip, Duke of Edinburgh, who shared maternal ancestry with Anastasia. Phillip's mother's mother's mother was Princess Alice, a daughter of Queen Victoria. Princess Alice was also Anastasia's mother's mother, making Phillip a great-nephew of Anastasia. Phillip's mitochondrial DNA would be the same as Anastasia's and could be used to test the claim of Anna Anderson.

Anna Anderson's mitochondrial DNA was found *not* to be the same as that of Prince Phillip (and, by extension, of Anastasia). Six different sites in the mitochondrial DNA sequence range showed a difference (Table 14.1). Interestingly, these data have also been used to test the claim put forth in the 1920s that Anna Anderson was actually Franzisca Schanzkowska, a Polish factory worker who had disappeared at about the same time that Anderson first surfaced. The mitochondrial DNA of a maternal relative of Schanzkowska is identical to that of Anna Anderson, which supports (although does not prove)

| | | Intestinal Tissue | |
Mitochondrial DNA Position	Blood Sample from Prince Phillip	from Anna Anderson	Hair Sample from Anna Anderson
16111	T	C	C
16126	T	C	C
16266	C	T	T
16294	C	T	T
16304	T	C	C
16357	C	T	T

TABLE 14.1 Mitochondrial DNA Differences between Prince Phillip, a Maternal Relative of Anastasia, and Anna Anderson

Source: Data from Melton (2003).

the claim that Anderson was this missing Polish woman who had developed amnesia (Melton 2003).

Who Was Eston Hemings's Father?

A long-standing historical debate concerns the paternity of two of the five children born to Sally Hemings, an enslaved African American woman who was born in 1773 and died in 1835. She and her family were slaves on the Jefferson plantation, and she accompanied Thomas Jefferson and his daughter to France when Jefferson served as ambassador there. Some have claimed that Jefferson, third president of the United States, was the father of Hemings's first child, Thomas Woodson, and her fifth child, Eston Hemings. The last names of the children offer no clue as to ancestry because it was common practice for slaves to be given the last name of their subsequent owner. The claim of Jefferson being Eston's father has been argued strongly by some who note the fact that Eston bore a strong physical resemblance to Jefferson. Others have argued that Eston's father might have been not Jefferson but one of Jefferson's relatives, perhaps one of his nephews, Peter or Samuel Carr.

Paternal ancestry can be investigated using Y-chromosome DNA because it is inherited through the father's line. Although DNA is not available from the actual people involved, it is available from living male descendants of Thomas Jefferson, his nephews (whose mother was a Jefferson but whose father was not, thus having different Y-chromosome DNA), Thomas Woodson, and Eston Hemings. Thomas Jefferson did not have any surviving sons, and thus has no surviving male relatives. However, there are living male descendants of Jefferson's paternal uncle, Field Jefferson, who would have the same Y-chromosome DNA as Thomas Jefferson.

Foster and colleagues (1998) examined a number of Y-chromosome haplotypes and found that those of Thomas Woodson's male descendants did *not* match those of the Jefferson or Carr lines. Nor did Eston Hemings's male descendants have the same haplotypes as found in the Carr descendants. However, the male descendants of Eston Hemings *did* have the same Y-chromosome haplotypes as the male descendants of Field Jefferson.

Although this might seem to be proof that Thomas Jefferson was Eston Hemings's father, the situation is more complicated. What these analyses show is that Eston Hemings was fathered by someone who had the same Y-chromosome haplotypes as Thomas Jefferson. Although this means that Jefferson *could* have been the father, there are other possibilities, including Thomas Jefferson's brother Randolph or any of Randolph's five sons (Abbey 1999). In truth, the father could be any male in the Jefferson line, including any slave children fathered by Jefferson's father or grandfather who subsequently fathered children with Sally Hemings (Davis 1999). The Y-chromosome evidence can show only that it was a male in the Jefferson line, but not which male. Some historians continue to argue that Thomas Jefferson was the father based on other evidence, and this will continue to be debated. The genetic evidence has not answered the question conclusively other than to show that Thomas Jefferson *could* have been Eston Hemings's father.

What Is the Genetic Legacy of Genghis Khan?

This last example looks at how genetic variation might reflect the dispropor-tionate genetic influence of a single male, and how historical data can then be used to identify this male. Tatiana Zerjal and colleagues (2003) conducted a survey of more than 30 Y-chromosome markers on over 2,000 men in Asia. Most of the males had unique Y-chromosome haplotypes, and few were found among males from different populations. The major exception was a Y-chromosome lineage consisting of a group of closely related Y-chromosome haplotypes that was found in roughly 8 percent of all the Asian males surveyed. This pattern was found in 16 populations across Asia, with the highest frequency in Mongolia, which suggests that it originated there. Zerjal and colleagues suggest that this pattern resulted from a form of social selec-tion, whereby some males had more sons than other males.

DNA data can be used to estimate when the most recent common an-cestor of a sample of individuals lived; for mitochondrial DNA, this method provides a date for the most recent common female ancestors, and for Y-chromosome DNA, the method provides a date for the most recent male an-cestor. Zerjal and colleagues applied this method to the Y-chromosome pat-tern they discovered and found that all males possessing this chromosome pattern had a recent common male ancestor who lived roughly 700–1,300 years ago. This date, combined with data on the geographic distribution of the Y-chromosome, suggests that this male may have been Genghis Khan.

Genghis Khan (1162–1227) was an infamous Mongol conqueror who founded the Mongol Empire and lived during the period estimated from the genetic data. During his rule, his empire covered much of Asia, and he and his close male relatives are said to have fathered many children. In addition, his armies often slaughtered populations that they conquered. Both of these factors would lead to a rapid spread of his Y chromosome (also carried by his male relatives). The geographic distribution of this chromosome in Asia today matches the known distribution of Genghis Khan's empire with one exception, the Hazara of Pakistan, who live outside the geographic limits of his empire. However, genealogical evidence suggests that the Hazara are de-scended from the male descendants of Genghis Khan, so this exception also fits the genetic and historical evidence. Furthermore, other populations in Pakistan without a genealogical connection with Genghis Khan do not pos-sess this Y-chromosome variant.

Taken together, the genetic, geographic, and historical evidence suggests that Genghis Khan may have left a major genetic legacy due to his conquests and murders. If confirmed, this study provides an interesting example of so-cial selection. Another possible example of social selection comes from Ireland, where about 20 percent of the men living in the northwest possess a unique Y-chromosome haplogroup that appears to be associated with the dominance of a historic dynasty (the *Uí Néill*) of medieval Ireland (Moore et al. 2006). This study, along with the Genghis Khan example, shows how the patrilineal inheritance of the Y chromosome allows us to illustrate dispro-portionate patterns of mating in the past.

Our Common Ancestry

As noted several times in this text, the number of your ancestors doubles each generation in the past. One generation ago, you have two ancestors—your parents. Your parents each had two parents (your grandparents), making four ancestors two generations in the past. As we go back further in time, the number of genealogical ancestors increases geometrically—8, 16, 32, 64, and so on. To be mathematically precise, the number of ancestors that you had n generations in the past is 2^n. This means that 20 generations ago (roughly 500 years), you had over a million ancestors ($= 1,048,576$). If we go back 40 generations (roughly 1,000 years), you had almost 1,100 billion ancestors ($= 1,099,511,627,776$). This is impossible because this is many more people than were alive at that time (or today)! Because you cannot have more ancestors than there were people, how do we explain this seeming paradox?

The doubling of ancestors each generation refers to the *maximum* number of *separate* ancestors. In reality, many ancestors are not separate ancestors. For example, if someone's great-great-grandmother's parents on their mother's side were also their great-great-grandfather's parents on their father's side, they would then have 30 ancestors five generations ago rather than 32 (and their parents would be distant cousins).

Because this happens to everyone, this means that as we go further back into the past, the more likely it is that any two people are bound to have overlapping ancestors at some point. This means that *all* people have overlapping ancestors some time in the past. How far back in time did this ancestor live? Although mathematical predictions have been made based on probability theory, they often required unrealistic assumptions to get the mathematics

to work. Rohde and colleagues (2004) addressed this question in a different way by using a computer to model more realistically factors such as mate choice, migration patterns, and population growth (see also Hein 2004). They found that a common ancestor of all of humanity would have lived only several thousand years ago. Their simulations also found that there was likely a point only about 5,000 years ago when each person then living would have either left no descendants or been an ancestor of every person in the world today. Thus, all humans alive today had the same set of ancestors 5,000 years ago! We are, genealogically speaking, all cousins.

It is important to remember that Rohde and colleagues' study dealt with *genealogical* ancestry, which is not the same as *genetic* ancestry in this context. For one thing, we are not equally related to all of the common ancestors. For example, if your recent ancestry is from sub-Saharan Africa, then your genetic ancestry will likely derive more from your African genealogical ancestors than from elsewhere, because the African ancestors will be represented more frequently in your family tree than the ancestors from elsewhere. Another point to keep in mind is that you do not receive genetic ancestry equally from your own set of ancestors. If you have 32 great-great-great-grandparents, this does not mean that each one of them contributed $\frac{1}{32}$ of your nuclear DNA. Because of recombination and probability, most of the set of common ancestors 5,000 years ago would have contributed nothing genetically to any living person. Wiuf and Hein (1997) have shown that only a small fraction of an ancestral population will have actually contributed DNA to any one of us. Genealogical ancestry and genetic ancestry are different concepts.

GENETIC ANCESTRY AND CULTURAL IDENTITY

When we look at genetic data in a genealogical context, we are looking at genetic ancestry. If we broaden our outlook to include one's "roots," we are also considering cultural ancestry. The disparity between biology and culture is nowhere greater than when we consider the specific difference between a person's genetic ancestry and his or her cultural identity, a statement of group membership. What do you call yourself? Are the groups you identify with based on biological features, cultural characteristics, or both? If cultural, are these characteristics based on national origin of ancestors (and which ones), language, religion, or some combination of these and other characteristics?

Although many people have a clear idea of who they are in cultural terms and often describe group membership in terms of race, the correlation between such groupings and biological reality is not always that clear. Consider, for example, someone who has one parent identified as white and one parent identified as black. Is this person white, black, or other? In many cases, the person might self-identify as black, which is a statement of cultural identity based on the skin color and other physical characteristics of *one* parent. But it would be inaccurate to describe this person's genetic ancestry as solely black because that person also has a white parent (Marks 1994). The situation becomes even more complex when considering more distant relatives and the ubiquitous mixing of humans around the world. The further back in time we go, the more complicated our ancestry becomes.

Genetic Ancestry of African Americans

The genetics of African Americans provides an example of the potential confusion between genetic ancestry and cultural identity. Between the early 1600s and the early 1800s, an estimated 380,000–570,000 Africans, primarily from West and West-Central Africa, were brought to the United States as part of the slave trade. Over time, there has been gene flow from Europeans into the African American gene pool, mostly from European men who fathered children with enslaved African women (Charkaborty 1986; Parra et al. 1998). As a result, allele frequencies in African Americans tend to be between those of Europeans and Africans but remain closer to Africa.

Analysis of allele frequency differences between Africans, Europeans, and African Americans allows us to estimate the overall proportion of African and European ancestry in different African American populations. Figure 14.9

FIGURE 14.9

Estimates of European ancestry in African American populations in the United States based on DNA markers. (Data from Parra et al. 1998, 2001.)

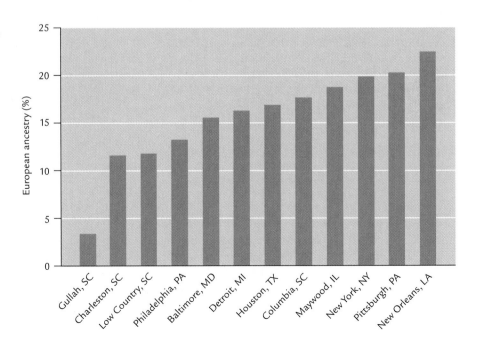

reports the results of one study using DNA markers; the estimated amount of European ancestry varies from 4 percent in parts of South Carolina to 23 percent in New Orleans. These numbers represent *average* patterns of ancestry of the different populations, and the amount of European ancestry of individuals within each group varies. For example, the average amount of European ancestry in the African American population in Columbia, South Carolina, is 18 percent, but researchers have found that the amount of European ancestry for any given *individual* in that population varies from less than 10 percent to more than 50 percent (Parra et al. 2001).

Differences have also been found when comparing maternal and paternal ancestry. Parra and colleagues (1998, 2001) have used mitochondrial DNA to estimate maternal European ancestry in African Americans and Y-chromosome polymorphisms to estimate paternal European ancestry. In each of their samples, the amount of European ancestry was greater on the father's side than on the mother's side (Figure 14.10). This means that it was more common for European men to father children with African American women than for European women to have the children of African American men, which is consistent with the history of slavery in the United States. Male slaveholders often fathered children with enslaved African American women.

These studies illustrate the confusion between genetic ancestry and cultural identity. All of the individuals in these studies classified themselves culturally as African American even though some had a large proportion of European ancestry. Further, these studies show that African Americans are

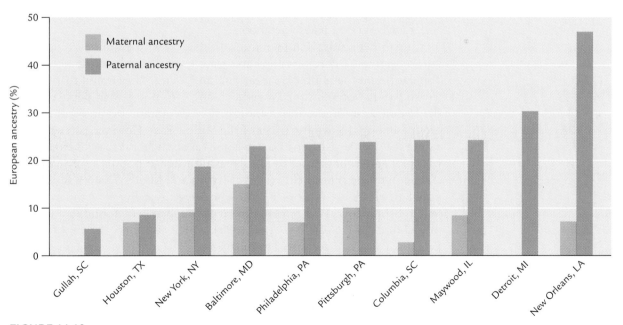

FIGURE 14.10

Estimate of European maternal and paternal ancestry in African American populations in the United States. Maternal ancestry is estimated from mitochondrial DNA, and paternal ancestry from Y-chromosome DNA. (Data from Parra et al. 1998, 2001.)

genetically diverse in their ancestral makeup and cannot be treated as a single homogeneous biological population, which is sometimes done in studies of health and disease. In addition, individuals with a mixed genetic ancestry often use a single grouping for cultural identity despite genetic differences.

What Does It Mean to Be Jewish?

Despite references throughout history to the "Jewish race," being a Jew is a matter of cultural identity. The Jewish religion and culture originated in the Middle East more than 4,000 years ago. Roughly 2,500 years ago, the Diaspora began when the Jews were exiled to Babylonia following the destruction of the Jerusalem Temple in Palestine. This initial exile was followed by others as Jews moved into Europe, North Africa, and elsewhere. Further dispersal occurred about 500 years ago when the Sephardic Jews of the Iberian Peninsula and North Africa became isolated from the Ashkenazic Jews of Europe.

A number of genetic studies have investigated Jewish communities in different parts of the world, attempting to determine to what extent they have remained genetically isolated or been involved in gene flow from their non-Jewish neighbors. The most comprehensive studies to date suggest somewhat mixed results. Livshits and colleagues (1991) examined the genetic distance based on red and white blood cell polymorphisms between 12 Jewish populations and 12 non-Jewish populations from the same locations in Europe, North Africa, and the Middle East. They found that there was an average tendency for the Jewish populations to cluster together, suggesting a common origin and subsequent isolation, but there was also some effect of gene flow from non-Jewish neighbors.

In another study, Hammer and colleagues (2000) examined genetic distances based on Y-chromosome haplotypes from 7 Jewish and 16 non-Jewish populations in the Middle East, Europe, and Africa. They found that 6 of the Jewish populations clustered together along with non-Jewish populations in the Middle East (Figure 14.11), indicative of a common origin of all of these groups among the Semitic tribes of the Middle East. However, there are indications of non-Jewish gene flow in some cases, such as the Ashkenazic Jews who plot somewhat closer to non-Jewish European populations. A notable exception to the general clustering of Jewish and Middle Eastern non-Jewish populations are the Ethiopian Jews, who are genetically very similar to non-Jewish Ethiopians. This genetic similarity has also been found in studies of mitochondrial DNA (Ritte et al. 1993), which supports the view that the Ethiopian Jews had converted to Judaism.

The results of these and other studies show that the myth of a "Jewish race" is just that—a myth. Although many Jewish populations are genetically similar to each other to some extent, Jews are not a distinct biological population. In addition, some non-Jewish populations of the Middle East are genetically similar to Jewish populations, but this does not make them Jewish.

Being Jewish is a condition not of genetic ancestry but of cultural identity. There are two traditional ways in which individuals can be considered Jewish: Their mother was Jewish, or they converted to Judaism (some practitioners of the Reform branch of Judaism also consider children of a Jewish

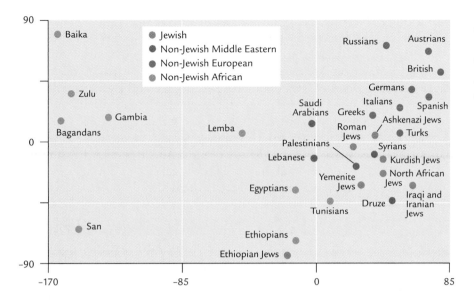

FIGURE 14.11

Genetic distance map of Jewish and non-Jewish populations based on Y-chromosome haplotypes. This map was constructed using a method known as *multidimensional scaling.* The scales correspond to positions in genetic space and are dependent on the method used to construct the map. Most Jewish populations cluster together along with Middle Eastern non-Jewish populations, except for Ethiopian Jews, who cluster with non-Jewish Ethiopians. (Adapted with permission from Hammer et al. 2000. Jewish and Middle Eastern non-Jewish populations share a common pool of Y-chromosome biallelic haplotypes. *Proceedings of the National Academy of Sciences, USA* 97:6769–6774. Copyright © 2000 National Academy of Sciences, U.S.A.)

father to be Jewish, but this is not accepted by all Jews). Conversion is a cultural phenomenon and not a matter of genetic ancestry. There is some genetic connection for the criterion of one's mother being Jewish, but even here, the situation is likely to be complicated if the woman had converted. Note that one cannot be "half-Jewish." The cultural identity is present or absent; either you meet the criteria or you don't. Membership in a cultural group is often complex and does not always have a relationship with genetic ancestry.

The difference between genetic ancestry and cultural identity in Jews can be illustrated by considering the Lemba, also known as the "black Jews," of Southern Africa. This group has an oral tradition of Jewish ancestry stemming from an influx of Jewish male traders more than 2,000 years ago. The Lemba practice some traditions associated with Judaism, such as certain food taboos and circumcision, but these cultural traits are also practiced by some other African and Middle Eastern societies. Note in Figure 14.11 that the Lemba are genetically more similar to Jewish populations than to other sub-Saharan African populations, which is consistent with their oral history. Furthermore, some Lemba men possess a Y-chromosome haplotype found most often in Jewish populations (Thomas et al. 2000). Although this evidence suggests that the Lemba are genetically related to Jewish populations, this does not make them Jewish, because they cannot show matrilineal descent (through the mother's line) or evidence of conversion.

Summary

The case studies presented in this chapter illustrate how data on genetic variation between populations can be used to examine a number of questions concerning population history and individual ancestry. Studies of the genetic history of populations attempt to answer questions about the origin of a population and its interactions with other populations, including invasion, colonization, and settlement. Genetic studies of Native Americans show a clear origin in Northeast Asia, although it is not yet clear how many migrations were involved in the peopling of the New World. Studies of Polynesian genetic history show that this group originated in Southeast Asia but experienced gene flow from Melanesia during and after their expansion into the Pacific Ocean. Studies of Irish population history reveal the genetic influence of several major movements of people into Ireland, notably the Viking invasions and the later settlement from England and Wales.

Genetic data can also be used to examine questions of ancestry for individuals, such as the question of the identity of Anna Anderson and the paternity for Eston Hemings. Both population and individual genetic studies reveal the problems in equating genetic ancestry with cultural identity.

Supplemental Readings

Jobling, M. A., M. E. Hurles, and C. Tyler-Smith. 2004. *Human Evolutionary Genetics: Origins, Peoples and Disease.* New York: Garland Science. A comprehensive survey of human population genetics, with a number of chapters on population history.

Olsen, S. 2002. *Mapping Human History: Discovering the Past through Our Genes.* Boston: Houghton Mifflin.

Relethford, J. H. 2003. *Reflections of Our Past: How Human History Is Revealed in Our Genes.* Boulder, CO: Westview Press. Two books, written for a general audience, that show how genetic data can provide information on history and ancestry, covering most of the examples in this chapter and others.

VIRTUAL EXPLORATIONS

Visit our textbook-specific online learning center Web site at **www. mhhe.com/relethford7** to access the exercises that follow.

1. **Paleoamerican Origins: New Evidence**   **http://www.si.edu/ resource/Faq/nmnh/origin.htm**. Read the Smithsonian Institution story "Paleoamerican Origins." The long-standing "land bridge" theory suggesting that the first Americans entered Alaska from Siberia along an ice-free corridor 11,500 years ago is called into question. Sometimes referred to as the "Clovis hypothesis," it has remained popular since first proposed by a Jesuit priest in 1589. New evidence from a site in Chile suggests an earlier entry. Archaeological, genetic, and linguistic evidence is presented to indicate a possible coastal migration.

   - Why do you think the land bridge theory has enjoyed such long-standing popularity?
   - What evidence has the Monte Verde site in south central Chile yielded?
   - How might these first Americans have traveled as far south as Chile? What would have been the motivating factors?
   - What other evidence is offered that might indicate an Old World connection? From what parts of the Old World?

- Mitochondrial DNA (mtDNA) may offer new insights into connections between American Indians and an Asian or Siberian connection. What does the evidence indicate concerning migrating founding groups?
- How many mtDNA lineages are suggested?
- Why is it important to consider the diversity of American Indian languages when discussing migration theory?

2. **Kennewick Man-News and Information** http://archaeology .about.com/od/kennewickman/Kennewick_Man_and_the_New _World_Entrada.htm. Read this article by K. Kris Hirst at about.com. Choose some chapters relating to Kennewick Man that interest you. Parts II and III in particular deal with the assignment of geographic origin (or "race") to Kennewick Man. Read about the skeleton and the political controversy surrounding its identification.

- Why is this find so important? Why has it been the subject of so much controversy?
- Why is it so difficult to assign a single individual to a racial or geographic category?
- Will DNA studies be done on the Kennewick Man in the future?
- What do you think should be done with the Kennewick Man remains?

3. **The Blood of the Vikings** http://www.orkneyjar.com/history/ vikingorkney/genetics.htm. Orkney is a string of approximately 20 inhabited islands located roughly 10 miles off the coast of Caithness in northeast mainland Scotland. The article "The Blood of the Vikings—Orkney's Genetic Heritage" discusses recent controversial genetic evidence linking early Norse arrivals to the takeover of the islands. Male DNA evidence was used in a study conducted in 2000–2001 which indicated an exclusive Scandinavian influence.

- Why did the study involve only males?
- DNA analysis focused exclusively on the Y chromosome. Was there a particular reason for using Y-chromosome evidence?
- What other sampling besides Orkney males was used?

Follow the article down to the link about family groups: http:// www.nature.com/hdy/journal/v95/n2/abs/6800661a.html. The abstract of another article from *Heredity* involved female as well as male participants.

- What evidence besides Y-chromosome evidence was used in the 2005 follow-up study? Why do you think this was necessary?
- How does this new material add to the information already known concerning the original habitation of other Northern European countries?

A child sleeping under a mosquito net. Malaria, an infectious disease spread by a particular species of mosquito, is common in parts of the world. Mosquito nets represent a form of cultural adaptation to help reduce the incidence of malaria. In some human populations, natural selection has led to an increase in the sickle cell hemoglobin allele, which helps protect against one form of malaria if the person inherits a single copy of the allele.

Natural Selection in Human Populations

T he previous chapter focused on the analysis of *neutral* traits (those presumably not affected by natural selection) because the objective was to reconstruct patterns of population relationship and ancestry, and genes or traits that are affected by natural selection can distort such patterns. This chapter presents several case studies of natural selection, focusing on the evolutionary history of specific traits as opposed to populations.

NATURAL SELECTION AND DISEASE

Natural selection operates to change allele frequencies through variations in the survival and reproduction opportunities of individuals with different genotypes. For example, if some individuals are more likely to acquire and die from a disease because of their genetic makeup, then allele frequencies can change rapidly as individuals who are more genetically susceptible to the disease are selected out of the gene pool. This section provides several examples of how natural selection is (or might be) linked to differential disease susceptibility.

Hemoglobin, Sickle Cell, and Malaria

Perhaps the best-known example of natural selection operating on a discrete genetic trait is the relationship of hemoglobin variants to malaria. One of the proteins in red blood cells is hemoglobin, which functions to transport oxygen to body tissues (see Chapter 2). The normal structure of the beta chain of hemoglobin is coded for by an allele usually called hemoglobin *A.* In many human populations, the *A* allele is the only one present, and as a result everyone has the *AA,* or normal adult hemoglobin, genotype.

Hemoglobin Variants   Many hemoglobin variants are produced by the mutation of an *A* allele to another form. The most widely studied mutations include hemoglobin *S, C,* and *E.* The *S* allele is also known as the sickle cell allele. A person who has two *S* alleles (genotype *SS*) has **sickle cell anemia,** a condition whereby the structure of the red blood cells is altered and oxygen

sickle cell anemia A genetic disease that occurs in a person homozygous for the sickle cell allele, which alters the structure of red blood cells.

FIGURE 15.1

Sickle cell anemia. The blood cell on the lower left is twisted and deformed compared to the round, normal red blood cells.

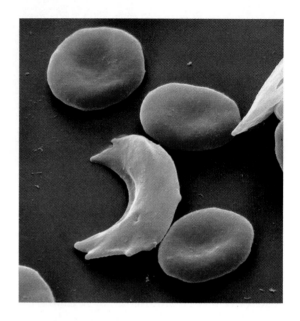

transport is severely impaired (Figure 15.1). Untreated, few people with sickle cell anemia survive to adulthood.

If the *S* allele is harmful in homozygotes, we expect natural selection to eliminate *S* alleles from the population in such a way that the frequency of *S* should be relatively low. Mutation introduces the *S* allele, but natural selection eliminates it. Indeed, in many parts of the world, the frequency of *S* is extremely low, fitting the model of mutation balanced by selection. In a number of populations, however, the frequency of *S* is much higher—often between 5 and 20 percent. Such high frequencies seem paradoxical given the harmful effect of the *S* allele in the homozygous genotype. Why does *S* reach such high frequencies? Genetic drift might seem likely, except for the definite association of geography and higher frequencies of *S*. That is, higher frequencies of *S* occur only in certain environments. But genetic drift is random and is influenced by population size, not environment. If genetic drift were responsible for the high frequencies of *S*, we would expect to see high frequencies in isolated groups in many different environments.

infectious disease A disease caused by the introduction of an organic foreign substance into the body.

noninfectious disease A disease caused by factors other than the introduction of an organic foreign substance into the body.

Distribution of the Sickle Cell Allele and Malaria   The distribution of the sickle cell allele is related to the prevalence of a certain form of malaria. Malaria is an **infectious disease**—that is, a disease caused by the introduction into the body of an organic foreign substance, such as a virus or parasite. (A disease that is not caused by an organic foreign substance is a **noninfectious disease.**) Malaria is caused by a parasite that enters an organism's body, and four different species of the malarial parasite can affect humans. Malaria remains one of the major infectious diseases in the world today. There are an estimated 300 million to 500 million cases of malaria each year and between 1 million and 3 million deaths (Sachs and Malaney 2002).

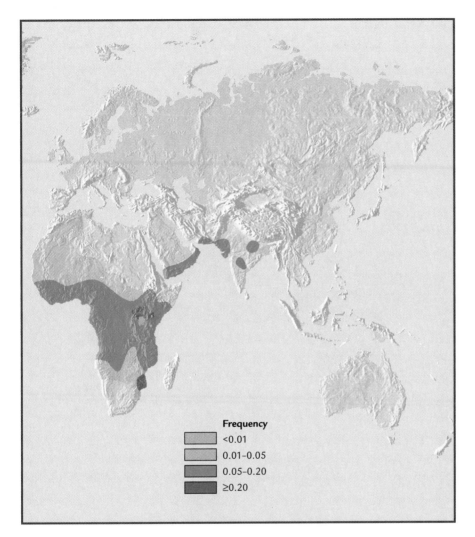

FIGURE 15.2

Distribution of the sickle cell allele in the Old World. Compare high-frequency areas with the high-frequency areas of malaria in Figure 15.3.

Frequency

	<0.01
	0.01–0.05
	0.05–0.20
	≥0.20

The Old World shows a striking correspondence between higher frequencies of the *S* allele (Figure 15.2) and the prevalence of malaria caused by the parasite *Plasmodium falciparum* (Figure 15.3). This parasite is spread through the bites of certain species of mosquitoes. Except through blood transfusions, humans cannot give malaria to one another directly. Those areas with frequent cases of malaria, such as Central Africa, also have the highest frequencies of the sickle cell allele. The falciparum form of malaria, which is the most serious, is often fatal.

The strong geographic correspondence suggests that sickle cell anemia and malaria are both related to the high frequencies of the *S* allele. Further experimental work has confirmed this hypothesis. Because the *S* allele affects the structure of the red blood cells, it makes the blood an inhospitable place for the malaria parasite.

FIGURE 15.3

Regions where falciparum malaria is common (shown in green).

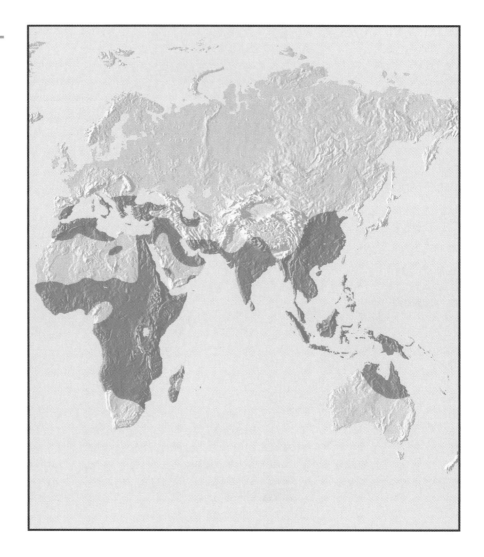

The Evolution of the S Allele   In a malarial environment, people who are heterozygous (genotype *AS*) actually have an advantage. The presence of one *S* allele does not give the person sickle cell anemia, but it does change the blood cells sufficiently so that the malaria parasite does not have as serious an effect. Overall, the heterozygote has the greatest fitness in a malarial environment. As discussed in Chapter 3, this is a case of balancing selection, in which selection occurs for the heterozygote (*AS*) and against both homozygotes (*AA* from malaria and *SS* from sickle cell anemia).

In addition to greater survival of the heterozygote in malarial environments, it has also been suggested that women with genotype *AS* have greater fertility. If so, then is selection for the heterozygote in environments with malaria a function of differential mortality, differential fertility, or both? Some studies have found no effect of hemoglobin genotype on fertility (e.g., Madrigal 1989), whereas others have found that women with the *AS* genotype had a higher number of live births (Hoff et al. 2001), suggesting that there might be selection related to fertility in some populations.

If the effects of sickle cell anemia and malaria were equal, then we would expect the frequencies of the normal allele (A) and the sickle cell allele (S) ultimately to reach equal frequencies. The two diseases, however, are not equal in their effects. Sickle cell anemia is much worse. The balance between these two diseases is such that the maximum fitness of an entire population occurs when the frequency of S is somewhere between 10 and 20 percent (Figure 15.4).

For example, a study of one African population suggests that for every 100 people with AS who survive to adulthood, 88 people with AA and only 14 of those with SS survive (Bodmer and Cavalli-Sforza 1976). Clearly, the relationship among hemoglobin, sickle cell anemia, and malaria represents a very strong case of natural selection. Instead of a difference in survival between genotypes of only several percent, the differences are quite striking. Such differences can lead to major changes in allele frequencies in a very short time. To illustrate the rapidity of such change, Figure 15.5 shows a hypothetical example of changes in the frequency of the sickle cell allele. In this example, the initial frequency of S from mutation was set equal to a reasonable estimate of 0.00001. The fitness values mentioned earlier were used to examine the kind of change in the frequency of S that could take place. Because the initial allele frequency is low, there is little change for the first 40 generations or so. (Of course, if the initial allele frequency were higher, the rate of change would be greater; a higher initial frequency could occur due to genetic drift or the initial occurrence of the mutation in a small population.) As the frequency of S increases, change takes place more rapidly because there are more people with the AS genotype to be selected for. After 100 generations, there is little change in the frequency of the S allele because it has reached an equilibrium based on the balance between the effects of sickle cell anemia and malaria. In this example, the sickle cell allele would reach an equilibrium frequency of 0.122. Of course, this simple illustration does not take other evolutionary forces into account, but it does show how quickly allele frequencies can change under strong natural selection.

The sickle cell example clearly shows the importance of the specific environment on the process of natural selection. In a nonmalarial environment, the AS genotype has no advantage in terms of differential survival, and the AA genotype has the greatest evolutionary fitness. In such cases, the frequency of the S allele is very low, approaching zero. In a malarial environment, however, the situation is different and the heterozygote has the advantage. Clearly, we cannot label the S allele as intrinsically "good" or "bad"; it depends on circumstances.

The example of sickle cell also shows that evolution has a price. The equilibrium is one in which the fitness for the entire population is at a maximum. The cost of the adaptation, however, is an increased proportion of individuals with sickle cell anemia, because the frequency of S has increased. People with the heterozygous genotype AS have the greatest fitness, but they also carry the S allele. When two people with the AS genotype mate, they have

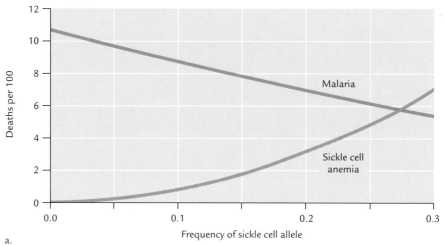

a.

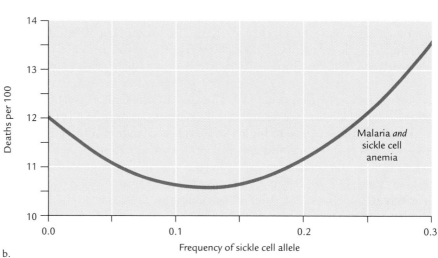

b.

FIGURE 15.4

Illustration of balancing selection for the hemoglobin *S* allele. Selection was modeled using these estimates of fitness from Bodmer and Cavalli-Sforza (1976): 88 percent of individuals with the genotype *AA* survive, but 12 percent die due to malaria; 14 percent of individuals with the genotype *SS* survive, but 86 percent die due to sickle cell anemia; everyone with genotype *AS* survives. Figure 15.4a shows the expected number of deaths due to malaria and sickle cell anemia for every 100 people in the population. As the frequency of *S* increases, the number of deaths due to malaria declines because more people now have the genotype *AS* and fewer people have the genotype *AA*. At the same time, however, the number of deaths due to sickle cell anemia increases because there are more people with genotype *SS* in the population. The result is a trade-off. Figure 15.4b shows what happens when we consider the *total* number of deaths due to malaria *and* sickle cell anemia. The total number of deaths declines at first because of increased resistance to malaria. The total number of deaths reaches a minimum point for a frequency of 0.122 for the *S* allele. If *S* were to increase further, the increased number of sickle cell anemia deaths would offset the decrease in malaria deaths. Natural selection will lead to an optimal balance corresponding to the minimum number of total deaths.

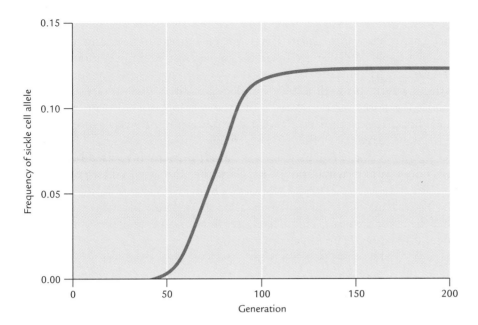

FIGURE 15.5

Reconstruction of past changes in sickle cell allele frequency in malarial Africa. This simulation assumes an initial allele frequency of 0.00001 caused by mutation. Relative fitness values are assumed constant over time: *AA* = 88%, *AS* = 100%, *SS* = 14%. The first 40 generations would show little change because the initial allele frequency was so low. After 40 generations, the allele frequency would increase rapidly, reaching an equilibrium after roughly 100 generations.

a 25 percent chance of having a child with sickle cell anemia (in the previous example, 1.5 percent of all children in a population are expected to have the *SS* genotype). This is not advantageous from the perspective of the individual with the disease. From the perspective of the entire population, however, it is the most adaptive outcome. Every benefit in evolution is likely to carry a price.

The Duffy Blood Group

Malaria has also been implicated in the evolution of another biochemical trait, the Duffy blood group. There are three alleles for the Duffy blood group: *FY*A, FY*B,* and *FY*O.* The *FY*O* allele, also known as the Duffy negative allele, is recessive. Individuals with two copies of the Duffy negative allele are completely resistant to a form of malaria caused by the parasite *Plasmodium vivax* (the previous example of a sickle cell allele dealt with a different parasite, *Plasmodium falciparum*). The vivax parasite enters red blood cells by clinging to Duffy A or Duffy B molecules, which are coded for by the *FY*A* and *FY*B* alleles. Because individuals with two Duffy negative alleles lack both of these molecules, the parasite cannot enter the red blood cells, and these people are resistant to vivax malaria.

The worldwide distribution of the Duffy negative allele is somewhat confusing, however. The highest frequencies are found in West and Central Africa, often reaching 100 percent, and the allele is virtually absent in most of Europe and Asia. In areas where the Duffy negative allele is high, vivax malaria is absent. At first glance, we might expect higher frequencies in areas where vivax malaria was common, under the assumption that individuals with two Duffy negative alleles would be selected for, thus increasing the frequency of the allele. Instead, we see a negative correlation between the incidence of vivax malaria and the frequency of the Duffy negative allele.

Livingstone (1984) suggested two scenarios to account for the distribution of vivax malaria and the Duffy negative allele. The first is that some populations wound up with a high frequency of the Duffy negative allele by chance (because of genetic drift), and so vivax malaria could not spread in these populations, thus resulting in the pattern we see today—populations with high frequencies of Duffy negative and no vivax malaria. The second possibility is that the Duffy negative allele initially increased because of selection to vivax malaria, and vivax malaria then died out in these populations once the frequency of Duffy negative was high enough to limit the spread of the disease. Analysis of molecular variation in the Duffy blood group suggests that the latter scenario is more likely, representing a case of recent and rapid natural selection (Hamblin et al. 2002).

The ABO Blood Group

Recall from Chapters 2 and 13 that the ABO blood group has three alleles—*A, B,* and *O*—where *A* and *B* are codominant and *O* is recessive. There are four possible phenotypes—A, B, O, and AB—and ABO blood types can be identified by the reaction of blood to certain antibodies. This antigen–antibody reaction also has significance for natural selection because each ABO blood type has both antigens and antibodies associated with it (Table 15.1). People with blood type A have the anti-B antibody, people with blood type B have the anti-A antibody, people with blood type O have both antibodies, and people with blood type AB have neither. These antibodies are present in your red blood cells your entire life.

The fact that different ABO blood groups have different antibodies has implications for disease resistance and natural selection. If you have blood type A, and hence anti-B antibodies, your immune system will be better able to fight off infection from microorganisms that are biochemically similar to type B molecules. For example, the microorganism that causes venereal syphilis is biochemically similar to A molecules. This means that people with blood type B or O will have greater resistance to venereal syphilis because they have the anti-A antibodies. People with blood type A or AB will not have this resistance because they lack the anti-A antibodies.

TABLE 15.1   ABO Blood Group Phenotypes and Antibodies

Genotypes	Phenotypes	Antigens	Antibodies
AA	A	A	Anti-B
AO			
BB	B	B	Anti-A
BO			
AB	AB	A, B	None
OO	O	None	Anti-A, anti-B

ABO Blood Types and Infectious Disease   Associations have been found between a number of infectious diseases and the ABO phenotypes. Many of these diseases have been serious in the past or continue to be so, thus providing an opportunity for natural selection. The likely nature of this selection is complicated by the fact that each ABO blood type has associations with different diseases; no single phenotype is resistant to all infectious diseases. For example, blood type A seems to be more susceptible to smallpox, type B more susceptible to infantile diarrhea, and type O more susceptible to bubonic plague. Thus, it appears that ABO allele frequencies are subject to a variety of types of selection. The influence of selection on ABO allele frequencies may vary from population to population depending on the history of infectious disease in that population. For example, India has a history of smallpox and bubonic plague epidemics, and also has a high frequency of the *B* allele. This may be due, in part, to selection against people with blood type A because of smallpox and people with blood type O because of plague (Mielke et al. 2006).

ABO Blood Types and Noninfectious Disease   ABO blood types also appear to be related to noninfectious diseases. Some hospital studies have suggested that people with blood type O have a greater chance of getting duodenal and stomach ulcers (this might be related to antibodies; some ulcers are actually infectious in nature, being caused by bacteria). People with blood type A have a greater chance of getting certain types of cancer. The differences between phenotypes appear strong, but we do not understand the reasons for these associations. In any case, it is unclear what evolutionary importance these associations have. Most of the noninfectious diseases have severe effects late in life, and therefore should not be subject to natural selection, because they usually occur after an individual's reproductive life is over. Some people, however, do acquire these diseases early enough in life that at least the possibility exists that natural selection could be operating through differential survival to noninfectious disease. Natural selection for the ABO gene is obviously complex and most likely reflects a number of factors.

The *CCR5* Gene

The *CCR5* gene is located on chromosome 3 and codes for a chemical receptor. A mutant allele, known as *CCR5-Δ32*, is characterized by a deletion of 32 base pairs. This allele has been found in moderate frequencies (0.03–0.14) in Europeans but is absent in Africans, East Asians, and Native Americans. The mutation has been linked to resistance to HIV (human immunodeficiency virus), the virus that causes AIDS. Individuals homozygous for the *CCR5-Δ32* allele are almost completely resistant to HIV-1 infection.

At first glance, this association might suggest selection for the allele due to HIV infection. However, the allele is found at low frequencies in some populations and not at all in others, and does not account for much of the difference in risk of AIDS between individuals or populations (Bamshad et al. 2002).

More important, it is unlikely that differences in HIV resistance led to variation in allele frequencies because AIDS has not been around long enough to have had any evolutionary impact. Instead, it appears that there was selection for the *CCR5-Δ32* allele for resistance to *some other* infectious disease in the past, and the HIV resistance seen today is a by-product of that previous selection. In other words, the *CCR5-Δ32* allele arose as a mutation and was then selected for because of its impact on the susceptibility to an infectious disease in Europeans, resulting in an increase in the frequency of the allele in Europe. Once established, this allele now provides resistance to HIV infection.

What might this earlier selection involve? Bubonic plague in the fourteenth century (the "Black Death") had initially been suggested as a possibility, but the finding of the *CCR5-Δ32* allele in Bronze Age skeletons in Germany dating back 2,900 years shows that the allele has been around much longer (Hummel et al. 2005). A strong case has been made for selection due to resistance to smallpox (Galvani and Slatkin 2003), a disease that caused many deaths until a vaccine became widespread in the nineteenth century. It is also possible that another infectious disease might have been involved. Whatever the actual cause(s), the *CCR5-Δ32* allele provides an excellent example of how past selection can affect future selection. As often happens in evolution, a trait that evolves by selection for one reason can be adaptive for some other reason later in time.

NATURAL SELECTION AND SKIN COLOR

Human skin color is a complex trait. It has a strong genetic component (Williams-Blangero and Blangero 1992) and is also affected by the environment, particularly the amount of direct sunlight.

The Biology of Skin Color

One pigment, melanin, is responsible for the majority of variation in lightness and darkness in skin color. Melanin is a brown pigment secreted by cells in the bottom layer of the skin. Much of the variation in skin color appears to be due to three genes: the *MC1R* gene, which regulates production of melanin, and the *OCA2* and *OCA4* genes, which affect proteins that influence skin color (Jobling et al. 2004).

Another pigment affecting skin color is hemoglobin, which gives oxygenated blood cells their red color. Light-skinned people have little melanin near the surface of the skin, and so the red color shows through. Because of this effect, "white" people are actually "pink."

Skin color is also affected to a certain extent by sex and age. In general, males are darker than females, probably because of differential effects of sex hormones on melanin production. Age also produces variation. The skin darkens somewhat during adolescence, particularly in females.

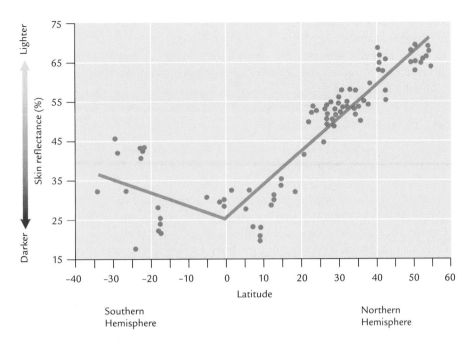

FIGURE 15.6

Geographic distribution of human skin color for 102 male Old World samples. Circles indicate the mean skin reflectance measured at a wavelength of 685 nanometers plotted against latitude. Negative values of latitude correspond to the Southern Hemisphere (below the equator), and positive values of latitude correspond to the Northern Hemisphere (above the equator). The solid line indicates the best-fitting curve relating skin color and latitude. Closer analysis shows that skin color is darker in the Southern Hemisphere than in the Northern Hemisphere at equivalent distance from the equator. (Adapted from Relethford 1997.)

The Distribution of Skin Color

As mentioned in Chapter 13, human skin color is measured by the percentage of light reflected off the skin at a given wavelength of light. Figure 15.6 shows the worldwide distribution of human skin color based on data from 102 male samples from the Old World. Skin color is darkest at the equator and tends to be lighter with the increasing distance from the equator, north or south. Closer investigation shows that there is also a hemispheric difference—skin color tends to be darker in the Southern Hemisphere (below the equator) than in the Northern Hemisphere, even at equivalent latitudes (Relethford 1997). The distribution of skin color and latitude corresponds to the amount of ultraviolet radiation received at the earth's surface. Because of the way sunlight strikes the earth, ultraviolet radiation is strongest at the equator and diminishes in strength as we move away from the equator. Further, ultraviolet radiation tends to be greater in the Southern Hemisphere than in the Northern Hemisphere due to a number of astronomical and meteorological factors (McKenzie and Elwood 1990; Relethford 1997). Jablonski and Chaplin (2000) have confirmed that human skin color is correlated with ultraviolet radiation; populations living in areas with high levels of ultraviolet radiation tend to be darker than those living in areas with less ultraviolet radiation.

The distribution of human skin color in the world today suggests past evolutionary events relating to natural selection. Current thinking suggests that dark skin evolved among our early ancestors in Africa as a means of protection against the damaging effects of ultraviolet radiation, most likely relating to the loss of hair and increase in sweat gland density that we suspect took place as our ancestors became increasingly adapted to the hot climate in Africa. Later, as some humans began moving out of Africa, lighter skin color evolved farther away from the equator. This scenario poses two questions: (1) What were the selective effects of ultraviolet radiation leading to dark skin near the equator? and (2) Why did light skin evolve in regions with less ultraviolet radiation?

The Evolution of Dark Skin

Ultraviolet radiation can have several harmful effects. Loomis (1967) suggested that dark skin protects from overproduction of vitamin D. As noted earlier, the major source of vitamin D throughout human history has been the sun, which stimulates vitamin D synthesis. Too much vitamin D, Loomis argued, would be harmful, and darker individuals would be at less risk for vitamin toxicity. However, Holick and colleagues (1981) have shown that vitamin D synthesis reaches a maximum level during continued exposure to ultraviolet radiation and does not reach toxic levels, thus rejecting Loomis's hypothesis.

Several hypotheses have focused on damage to the skin. In sufficient amounts, ultraviolet radiation can lead to skin cancer. The greater the intensity of ultraviolet radiation, the greater the risk for skin cancer at any given level of pigmentation. Among the European American populations of the United States, skin cancer rates are much higher in Texas than in Massachusetts (Damon 1977). Dark-skinned individuals have lower rates of skin cancer because the heavy concentration of melanin near the surface of the skin blocks some of the ultraviolet radiation. Some have suggested that dark skin evolved in human populations near the equator to protect against skin cancer (Robins 1991). Others have rejected skin cancer as a significant factor in the evolution of human skin color because it tends to affect primarily individuals past their reproductive years (Jablonski and Chaplin 2000). If someone dies from skin cancer after reproducing, his or her death does not affect the process of natural selection.

Sunburn has also been suggested as a potential factor in natural selection. Severe sunburn can lead to infection and can interfere with the body's ability to sweat effectively. Dark skin could protect from these effects and thus be selected for in areas of high ultraviolet radiation (Robins 1991), although the exact magnitude of this selection is not clear.

Jablonski and Chaplin (2000) argue that the potential selective effects of skin cancer and sunburn are minimal and that the most significant factor leading to darker skin in equatorial populations was the damaging effect of ultraviolet radiation on folate levels in the body. Folic acid, a necessary nutrient, is converted into folate in the body. Ultraviolet radiation can destroy folate, leading to several serious consequences. Folate deficiency has been linked to disorders in developing fetuses, including an increase in neural tube defects, which reduces survivability. Folate levels also affect reproductive capabilities; folate deficiency can disrupt the production of sperm and lead to male infertility. Jablonski and Chaplin suggest that photodestruction of folate has serious consequences for both mortality and fertility and that dark skin evolved for protection in areas with high levels of ultraviolet radiation.

The Evolution of Light Skin

As some humans moved farther from equatorial regions, they lived in areas with lower levels of ultraviolet radiation, and consequently, the risks from ultraviolet radiation decreased. Lighter-skinned individuals would be at less risk from folate deficiency (as well as sunburn and skin cancer if they are indeed selective factors). This does not explain *why* light skin evolved farther from the equator, however, only that it *could* evolve. To construct a complete model for the evolution of human skin color variation, we need to have one or more reasons *why* light skin would have been adaptive farther from the equator. In the absence of such reasons, we would not expect a strong correlation with latitude. Factors that explain the evolution of dark skin near the equator do not explain light skin farther from the equator.

The most widely accepted model for the evolution of light skin focuses on the synthesis of vitamin D. As noted earlier, the major source of vitamin D throughout human history and prehistory has been the sun because ultraviolet radiation stimulates vitamin D synthesis. Today, we may receive vitamin D through vitamin supplements or through the injection of vitamin D into our milk. Both of these dietary modifications are recent human inventions, however. Formerly, humans had to obtain their vitamin D through diet or through stimulation of chemical compounds by ultraviolet radiation. Some foods, such as fish oils, are high in vitamin D but are not found in all environments. For most human populations in the past, the major source of vitamin D was the sun.

Vitamin D deficiency can cause a number of problems relating to poor bone development and maintenance, including diseases such as rickets, which leads to deformed bones. Such health hazards can affect fertility as well as mortality. One frequent consequence of childhood rickets is the deformation of a woman's pelvis, an effect that can hinder or prevent successful childbirth. In one U.S. study, only 2 percent of European American women had such pelvic deformities as compared to 15 percent of African American women (Molnar 1998). This difference presumably relates to skin color; darker women are unable to absorb enough vitamin D for healthy bone growth.

Vitamin D deficiency can be linked to the evolution of light skin. As discussed previously, dark skin protects against the harmful effects of ultraviolet radiation in populations near the equator, where ultraviolet radiation is the most intense. As human populations moved away from the equator, these risks declined and the risk for vitamin D deficiency increased because darker skin blocked too much ultraviolet radiation. Natural selection thus produced a change toward lighter skin color that would be adaptive in such environments.

Temperature has also been suggested as a factor in the evolution of light skin. Because temperature is roughly correlated with latitude, some have suggested that the correlation between human skin color and latitude is actually a reflection of a link between skin color and cold adaptation. Reviewing a wide range of data, Post and colleagues (1975) noted that in cold climates

FIGURE 15.7

Schematic diagram of the relationship between latitude, ultraviolet radiation, and the relative risks of folate deficiency and vitamin D deficiency. Near the equator, dark skin is selected for to block the photodestruction of folate due to high levels of ultraviolet radiation. Farther away from the equator, this risk decreases and the risk for vitamin D deficiency increases, facilitating the evolution of lighter skin color to allow sufficient vitamin D synthesis.

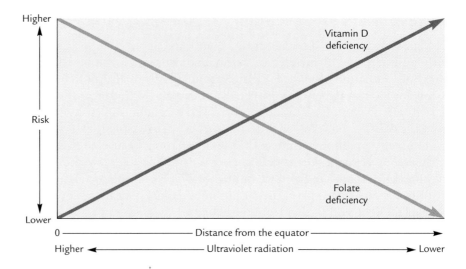

dark-skinned individuals are at greater risk for frostbite than are light-skinned individuals. Data reporting this difference are available for soldiers during the first and second World Wars and the Korean War. During the Korean War, African American soldiers were more than four times as likely to get frostbite as European American soldiers. Closer analysis of the data shows that this difference persists even after controlling for other sociological and health factors. These observations suggest that in the colder northern climates darker skin is more prone to cold injury than is lighter skin, a hypothesis supported by laboratory experiments on piebald guinea pigs (having both light and dark skin). Cold injury could be induced more frequently and more severely in the darker patches of skin. Beall and Steegmann (2000) question the cold-injury hypothesis, noting that the higher rates of frostbite among African and African American soldiers reflect differences in vascular responses to cold, and not skin color. They also note that the guinea pig data are not useful because the temperatures involved in the lab experiments are not typical of those experienced during human evolution and are therefore not relevant.

There has been considerable debate over causal factors in the evolution of human skin color and their relative importance. As noted by Jablonski and Chaplin (2000), current evidence suggests that the primary reason for the evolution of human skin color is the balance between the need for darker skin to protect against photodestruction of folate and the need for lighter skin to facilitate vitamin D synthesis. At any given latitude, the optimal skin color reflects the balance between these risks. Near the equator, the primary risk is folate deficiency, leading to darker skin for protection. As we go farther from the equator, this risk decreases and the risk for vitamin D deficiency increases, thus leading to lighter and lighter skin color farther and farther from the equator (Figure 15.7). It is possible that other factors, such as protection against sunburn near the equator, also contribute to the observed correspondence between skin color and latitude.

NATURAL SELECTION AND CULTURE CHANGE

Natural selection acts on individuals in a specific environment. In humans, the interaction with the environment is often strongly affected by cultural practices and culture change. The general issue of the interaction between human biology and culture change is discussed further in Chapter 17. Here, we look at two examples of how culture change has affected natural selection in human populations.

Horticulture and the Sickle Cell Allele in Africa

Sickle cell anemia provides an excellent example of the interaction of biology and culture. Livingstone (1958) and others have taken information on the distribution and ecology of the malaria parasite and the mosquito that transmits it, along with information on the prehistory and history of certain regions in Africa, and presented a hypothesis about changes in the frequency of the sickle cell allele. Several thousand years ago, the African environment was not conducive to the spread of malaria. Large areas of the continent were covered in dense forests, and the mosquito that spreads malaria thrives best in ample sunlight and pools of stagnant water. Neither condition then existed in the African forests, where extensive foliage prevented much sunlight from reaching the forest floor. In addition, the forest environment was highly absorbent, so water did not tend to accumulate in pools. In other words, the environment was not conducive to large populations of mosquitoes. Consequently, the malaria parasite did not have a hospitable environment either. This situation changed several thousand years ago when prehistoric African populations brought horticulture to the area. **Horticulture** is a form of farming employing only hand tools and no animal labor or irrigation. As the land was cleared for crops, the entire ecology shifted. Without the many trees, it was easier for sunlight to reach the land surface. Continued use of the land changed the soil chemistry, allowing pools of water to accumulate. Both changes led to an environment ideal for the growth and spread of mosquito populations, and therefore the spread of the malaria parasite. The growth of the human population also provided more hosts for the mosquitoes to feed on, thus increasing the spread of malaria.

horticulture A form of farming in which only simple hand tools are used.

Before the development of horticulture in Africa, the frequency of the sickle cell allele was probably low, as it is in nonmalarial environments today. When the incidence of malaria increased, it became evolutionarily advantageous to have the heterozygote *AS* genotype because those who had it would have greater resistance to malaria without suffering the effects of sickle cell anemia. As shown earlier, this change could have taken place in a short period of time, roughly 100 generations, because of the large differences in fitness among hemoglobin genotypes. The initial introduction of the sickle cell allele, *S,* through mutation or gene flow was followed by a rapid change, reaching an equilibrium point in which the fitness of the entire human population was at a maximum.

Are Humans Still Experiencing Natural Selection?

When we compare ourselves with the African apes, we see many traits that have been selected for during the course of human evolution, including habitual bipedalism, an enlarged brain relative to body size, and development of vocal anatomy for language. We have also changed culturally, including the origins of agriculture and civilization. Over the past 12,000 years, our species' cultural evolution has been very rapid, particularly relative to the much slower pace of biological change (see Chapter 17). As we increasingly adapt to new challenges culturally, does this mean that the biological process of natural selection no longer operates in human populations? Some scientists have argued that there is now little selection pressure operating in human populations because of our technology and medical advances, but others disagree and note that selection still operates on the human genome (Balter 2005).

Some of the examples given in this chapter should convince you that much of natural selection in human populations has been recent. Changes in sickle cell allele frequency in malarial environments (as well as other genetic adaptations to malaria) are likely to be relatively recent in human evolution because only with the development of agriculture, which led to larger population sizes, have epidemic diseases been widespread among humanity (see Chapter 17 for further discussion). The evolution of the lactase persistence allele described in this chapter is another example; its spread dates back only as far as the origin of dairy farming in human populations, which is a recent event in evolutionary time. In both cases, culture change has altered the trajectory of genetic change in human evolution. Given our species' proclivity for culture change and its effect on us, there is no reason to expect

natural selection to stop. New diseases, such as AIDS and Ebola virus, continue to emerge and will affect differences in survival and reproduction.

Indeed, new research in molecular genetics suggests that there are many examples of recent and ongoing natural selection in human populations. Our ability to sequence our genome has helped in our search for DNA sequences affected by natural selection. There are a number of statistical tests for selection. These tests examine the frequency of different SNPs and DNA haplotypes, and compare observed patterns of genetic diversity with those expected under a balance between mutation and genetic drift; any differences from the expected numbers are potential clues to natural selection (Sabeti et al. 2006; Voight et al. 2006).

A good example of current natural selection that has been detected using new molecular data is the discovery of a chromosomal inversion (where a section of DNA is reversed) on chromosome 17 that is 900 base pairs in length. One variant of this inversion, named the H2 haplotype, is found in 20 percent of Europeans but is rare or absent elsewhere in the world. Statistical analysis suggests that this haplotype has been under selection in European populations. An examination of a sample of women in Iceland showed that those women who carry the H2 haplotype have slightly more (3.5 percent) children on average, although the reason why is not yet clear (Stefansson et al. 2005). Regardless of the mechanism, the H2 haplotype example, along with the examples of malarial-related genes and lactase persistence discussed in this chapter, show that natural selection is still occurring in the human species (Balter 2005).

This scenario shows that human cultural adaptations (horticulture) can affect the ecology of other organisms (the mosquito and malaria parasite), which can then cause genetic change in the human population (an increase in the frequency of the sickle cell allele). This sequence of events is summarized in Figure 15.8.

Of course, we cannot observe these events directly because they occurred in the past. Nonetheless, all available evidence supports this hypothesis. We know the physiological differences between different hemoglobin types. We also know that low frequencies of the S allele occur in nonmalarial environments and higher frequencies occur where there is malaria. Archaeological evidence shows when and where the spread of horticulture took place in Africa. From studies of modern-day agriculture, we also know that malaria spreads quickly following the clearing of land. Taking all this information

Initial forest with few
mosquitoes and little malaria

Humans arrive with
horticulture

Forest ecology changes

Land is cleared

Stagnant pools of
water develop

Mosquito population increases

Malaria increases

Increased selection for
AS heterozygotes

Frequency of the sickle cell
allele increases

A balance is reached
between selection against
A and *S* alleles

FIGURE 15.8

Sequence of cultural and
environmental changes
leading to changes in the
frequency of the sickle cell
allele in malarial Africa.

together, the scenario for changes in the frequency of the sickle cell allele in Africa seems most reasonable.

The study of human history provides another example of the evolution of the sickle cell allele. In African American populations, the frequency of the *S* allele ranges from 0.02 to 0.06, which is higher than the frequency in European Americans (essentially zero) but less than that in malarial regions of Africa (Workman et al. 1963). The biological history of African Americans explains part of this difference; as noted in Chapter 14, some degree of European gene flow has taken place. This gene flow would have the effect of reducing the frequency of *S* in African Americans. Extensive calculations have shown, however, that gene flow is not the only factor involved. Researchers found that if gene flow alone were operating, the frequency of *S* in African Americans should be higher than it actually is. Another reason that the frequencies of the sickle cell allele are lower in African Americans than in West Africans is that natural selection has been operating to remove *S* from the population. In general, malaria has not been epidemic in the United States. The enslaved people brought to the United States came from areas in Africa with high frequencies of malaria and the sickle cell allele. When they arrived in the United States, there was no longer the same evolutionary advantage for high frequencies of *S* because there was less malaria. As a result, the frequency of *S* has been reduced through natural selection, along with European admixture.

Sickle cell anemia is a health problem among modern African Americans. During the 1960s, there was a tendency to label sickle cell anemia a "black disease." The reason for higher levels of sickle cell anemia among African

Americans has nothing to do with skin color but rather is the result of their ancestors coming from a malarial environment with high frequencies of the *S* allele. Sickle cell anemia is not confined to dark-skinned populations in Africa. High frequencies of *S* are also found in malarial environments in parts of Europe, India, and South Asia.

Lactase Persistence and Lactose Intolerance

As mammals, human infants receive nourishment from mothers' milk. Infants produce an enzyme, lactase, which allows milk sugar to be digested. In most human populations, lactase production stops by around 5 years of age. Lactase production is related to a gene on chromosome 2 that has two alleles (Mielke et al. 2006). The *LCT*R* allele causes lactase to stop being produced after several years of age. The *LCT*P* allele is dominant and causes lactase to be produced throughout life, a condition known as **lactase persistence.** Individuals with the recessive homozygote (*LCT*R/LCT*R*) will not produce lactase later in life and have difficulty digesting milk, a condition known as **lactose intolerance,** which can lead to diarrhea, cramps, and other digestive problems (Beall and Steegmann 2000).

Table 15.2 lists the frequency of lactose intolerance in a number of human populations. In general, the frequency of lactose intolerance is high in most African and Asian populations and tends to be lower in European populations. A noticeable exception to this rule is the Fulani in Africa, who

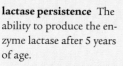

lactase persistence The ability to produce the enzyme lactase after 5 years of age.

lactose intolerance A condition characterized by diarrhea, cramps, and other intestinal problems resulting from the ingestion of milk.

TABLE 15.2	Frequencies of Lactose Intolerance in Some Human Populations	
Population		*Percentage of Lactose Intolerance*
African ancestry	African Americans	70–77
	Ibos	99
	Bantus	90
	Fulani	22
	Yoruba	99
	Baganda	94
Asian ancestry	Asian Americans	95–100
	Thais	97–100
	Eskimos	72–88
	Native Americans	58–67
European ancestry	European Americans	2–19
	Finns	18
	Swiss	12
	Swedes	4

Sources: Lerner and Libby (1976:327); Molnar (1998:133).

have a much lower prevalence (22 percent) of lactose intolerance than the rest of Africa. A number of analyses have found that the frequency of lactose intolerance is lowest in populations that have a history of dairy farming (Holden and Mace 1997; Leonard 2000).

According to this model, the original condition in our ancestors was the cessation of lactase production early in childhood. A dominant allele conferring lactase persistence arose and was selected for in human populations that relied extensively on dairy farming for survival. In situations in which milk provided a critical addition to the diet, individuals who were lactase persistent had an evolutionary advantage because of increased dietary resources, and they passed the allele on to the next generation. The variation in allele frequencies thus corresponds to the specific cultural history of populations. This variation is clearest in Africa, where populations such as the Ibo and Bantus—known agricultural populations that did not practice dairy farming—typically have high rates of lactose intolerance. The Fulani, however, are nomadic cattle herders who rely extensively on milk in their diet. The rise of the lactase persistence allele in some human populations provides a good example of recent and rapid selection. Molecular analysis suggests that this selection may have taken place within the past 5,000–10,000 years, which is consistent with the estimated date of origin for dairy farming (Bersaglieri et al. 2004).

There may be a relationship between lactase persistence, dairy farming, and latitude. Calcium is needed for proper bone growth, and vitamin D facilitates the absorption of calcium. Prior to the introduction of vitamin D into food products, the major source of vitamin D was the sun, as ultraviolet radiation is needed for the synthesis of vitamin D. Ultraviolet radiation is strongest at the equator and less strong farther north or south of the equator. Populations living farther from the equator would thus be at increased risk for inadequate vitamin D production and would therefore have problems with calcium absorption and bone growth. In such environments, the ability to digest lactose throughout one's life would be an advantage because lactose increases calcium absorption (Allen and Cheer 1996; Beall and Steegmann 2000). Although the frequency of lactose intolerance does correlate to some extent with latitude, the relationship is far from perfect, as illustrated by the Fulani case. Perhaps specific dietary requirements relating to calcium absorption influenced selection for lactase persistence in some populations, whereas the general need for improved nutrition was a factor in others.

Studies of lactase persistence illustrate that we need to consider biological variation and evolutionary change when making policy decisions. In the United States, which has a large dairy economy, milk is regarded as an essential part of a "normal" diet. We think of milk as intrinsically good and in the past have sent milk to people in less developed nations in the belief that what was good for us must be good for them. It soon became clear, however, that many of these people were lactose intolerant and that milk was not good for them. Health and dietary policies must always consider biological and cultural diversity.

Summary

Perhaps the best-documented example of natural selection in human populations is the relationship between hemoglobin alleles and two selective forces: sickle cell anemia and malaria. In environments where malaria is common, selection has led to an increase in the sickle cell allele because the heterozygotes are the most fit—they show greater resistance to malaria but do not suffer from the adverse effects of sickle cell anemia. Studies of blood groups and other genetic markers also suggest a role for natural selection in human variation.

Skin color is another example of a trait that shows a strong environmental correlation, in this case with latitude. This distribution, combined with other evidence, suggests that dark skin is selected for near the equator primarily to protect against the harmful effects of excess ultraviolet radiation (photodestruction of folate). Light skin may have evolved farther from the equator to facilitate sufficient vitamin D synthesis.

Natural selection in human populations is often affected by culture change. In the case of the evolution of the sickle cell allele in Africa, the introduction of horticulture by humans altered the physical environment, making it a more hospitable environment for the reproduction of mosquitoes that transmit malaria. As a consequence, higher frequencies of the sickle cell allele were selected for. The distribution of lactase persistence in human populations also shows the impact of culture change; higher frequencies are found in populations that have a long history of dairy farming.

Supplemental Readings

Jablonski, N. G., and G. Chaplin. 2000. The evolution of human skin coloration. *Journal of Human Evolution* 39:57–106. A long article that provides the best current review and synthesis regarding the evolution of human skin color.

Stinson, S., B. Bogin, R. Huss-Ashmore, and D. O'Rourke. 2000. *Human Biology: An Evolutionary and Biocultural Perspective.* New York: John Wiley. A comprehensive volume consisting of review chapters on a variety of topics relating to human population biology. Many chapters include valuable summaries of topics considered here, including population history, genetic polymorphisms, lactase persistence, and skin color.

VIRTUAL EXPLORATIONS

Visit our textbook-specific online learning center Web site at **www.mhhe.com/relethford7** to access the exercises that follow.

1. **Human Blood**   **http://anthro.palomar.edu/blood/default.htm**. Read the "Human Blood" tutorials from the Palomar College tutorial Web site. Review the genetics of ABO and RH blood types.

   - What is your blood type?
   - What is the blood type of each of your parents? Does the pattern in your case follow simple rules of inheritance? If not, is it possible that the H antigen plays a role? If so, how?

- Which blood type can cause a problem in fetuses? Rh⁻ or RH⁺?
- Why can it be a problem for the baby? Is it also a problem for the mother?

Take the practice quiz for each section. Spend more time reading and testing yourself on the areas about which you are unsure.

2. **Why Skin Comes in Colors**   http://www.calacademy.org/calwild/2000winter/stories/horizons.html. Read "Why Skin Comes in Colors" by Blake Edgar.

- What does the research of Jablonski and Chaplin tell us about the role of UV radiation in natural selection on skin color?
- Does melanin in skin function mainly to protect against sunburn?
- How does skin color relate to reproductive success?

Observe the map of UV radiation and skin color across the world.

- Is there a correlation?
- What part of the world do your ancestors come from? Does your skin tone accord with the skin color zone for that area? If not, why might that be?

3. **ABO Blood Types and Infectious Disease**   http://www.findarticles.com/p/articles/mi_m0GVK/is_5_5/ai_n6276065. Coccidioidomycosis, or "Valley fever," is a mild, flu-like infection that progresses into a more serious form in a small percentage of those infected. The article "Disease Influence of Host Genetics on the Severity of Coccidioidomycosis" is based on a study which sought to discover how genetics (specifically HLA class II alleles & haplotypes and ABO phenotypes) affects the onset of severity.

- Which segments of the Kern County, California, population were selected for the study?
- In which region in the United States is "Valley fever" endemic?
- What conditions contribute to incidence of this disease?
- How does blood type predispose the respective populations?
- What is the "host gene" that caused this disposition?
- Which group in the Kern County population is most susceptible?

4. **Evolutionary Population Genetics: Were the Vikings Immune to HIV?**   http://www.nature.com/hdy/journal/v96/n4/full/6800806a.html. This February 2006 article appeared in the journal *Heredity*. It discusses the genetic bases of disease resistance and suggests that AIDS spread rapidly over great distances but in a very selective area. Human resistance to the disease is also explained via a chance mutation.

- Where did the initial resistance likely occur?
- What is the name of the evolutionary biologist who originally suggested this model?
- How do Vikings play a role in this theory?

Sherpas in Nepal returning from a trip to Mount Everest. The Sherpa are an example of a population that has adapted, both biologically and culturally, to the stresses of living at high altitudes.

Human Adaptation

As discussed in Chapter 1, adaptation is the successful interaction of a population with its environment. Thus far, adaptation has been discussed in terms of genetic adaptation—that is, natural selection. In this chapter, we examine a broader perspective. Central to the study of adaptation is the concept of **stress,** broadly defined as any factor that interferes with the normal limits of operation of an organism. Organisms maintain these limits through an ability known as **homeostasis.** As ways of dealing with the stresses that alter your body's functioning, adaptations restore homeostasis. For example, within normal limits, your body maintains a relatively constant body temperature. When you stand outside in a cold wind, you may shiver. This is your body's way of adapting to cold stress. You might also choose to put on a jacket.

As human beings, we can adapt both biologically and culturally. It is important to note, however, that our biocultural nature can work against us. In adapting to stresses culturally, we can introduce other stresses as a result of our behavior. Pollution, for example, is a consequence of cultural change that has had a negative impact on our physical environment in numerous ways.

Key to the interaction between human biology and culture, human adaptation operates on a number of levels—physiologic, developmental, genetic, and cultural—all of which are interrelated, for better or for worse. Thus, countering a biological stress such as disease with the cultural adaptation of medicine can lower the death rate for human populations but can also increase population size, which in turn can lead to further stresses, such as food shortages and environmental degradation.

Besides genetic and cultural adaptation, humans are capable of three other forms of adaptation that are physiologic in nature: acclimation, acclimatization, and developmental acclimatization. **Acclimation** refers to short-term changes that occur very quickly after exposure to a stress, such as sweating when you are hot. **Acclimatization** refers to physiologic changes that take longer, from days to months, such as an increase in red blood cell production after moving to a high-altitude environment. When a change occurs during the physical growth of any organism, it is known as

CHAPTER OUTLINE

- Climate and Human Adaptation
- SPECIAL TOPIC: Cranial Plasticity—Did Boas Get It Right?
- High-Altitude Adaptation
- Nutritional Adaptation

stress Any factor that interferes with the normal limits of operation of an organism.

homeostasis In a physiologic sense, the maintenance of normal limits of body functioning.

acclimation Short-term physiologic responses to a stress, usually within minutes or hours.

acclimatization Long-term physiologic responses to a stress, usually taking from days to months.

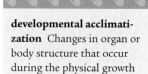

developmental acclimatization Changes in organ or body structure that occur during the physical growth of any organism.

plasticity The ability of an organism to respond physiologically or developmentally to environmental stress.

developmental acclimatization. An example (covered later in the chapter) is the increase in chest size that occurs when a person grows up in high altitudes. The ability of organisms to respond physiologically or developmentally to environmental stresses is often referred to as **plasticity.**

CLIMATE AND HUMAN ADAPTATION

Though originally tropical primates, we humans have managed to expand into virtually every environment on our planet. Such expansion has been possible largely because of multiple adaptations to the range of temperatures around the world.

Physiologic Responses to Temperature Stress

As warm-blooded creatures, humans have the ability to maintain a constant body temperature. This homeostatic quality works well only under certain limits.

Cold Stress   When you are cold, your body is losing heat too rapidly. One response is to increase heat production temporarily through shivering, which also increases your metabolic rate. This response is not very efficient and is costly in terms of energy. A more efficient physiologic response to cold stress is minimization of heat loss through alternate constriction and dilation of blood vessels. **Vasoconstriction,** the narrowing of blood vessels, reduces blood flow and heat loss. **Vasodilation,** the opening of the blood vessels, serves to increase blood flow and heat loss. These responses are examples of acclimation to cold stress.

vasoconstriction The narrowing of blood vessels, which reduces blood flow and heat loss.

vasodilation The opening of blood vessels, which increases blood flow and heat loss.

When a person is first subjected to cold stress, vasoconstriction acts to minimize the loss of heat from the body to the extremities (i.e., the hands, feet, and face). As a result, skin temperature drops. This response becomes dangerous, however, if it continues too long. Should this start to happen, vasodilation begins, causing blood and heat to flow from the interior of the body to the extremities. The increased blood flow prevents damage to the extremities, but now the body is losing heat again! Neither vasoconstriction nor vasodilation by itself provides an effective physiologic response to cold stress. *Both* must operate, back and forth, to maintain a balance between heat loss and damage to the extremities.

An interesting phenomenon occurs after initial exposure to cold stress. The cycles of alternating vasoconstriction and vasodilation, accompanied by alternating cycles of cold and warm skin temperatures, begin to level out, becoming more frequent and less extreme. Skin temperature changes more quickly, but the increases and decreases are not as great. This pattern, called the *Lewis hunting phenomenon,* demonstrates how effective the body's ability is to adapt. The smaller and more frequent cycles are more efficient (Figure 16.1).

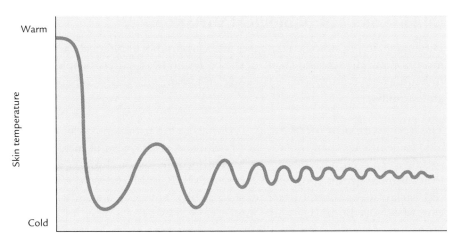

FIGURE 16.1

The Lewis hunting phenomenon. Initial exposure of a finger into ice water produces a decrease in skin temperature, caused by vasoconstriction. After a while, this response gives way to vasodilation, which causes skin temperature to increase. The cycles continue over time but become more frequent and less extreme, thus providing more efficient adaptation. (Modified after Frisancho 1993:85.)

Heat Stress   When experiencing heat stress, your body is not removing heat quickly enough. There are four ways in which heat is lost from the body, three of which can also increase heat (Frisancho 1993). *Radiation* is heat flow from objects in the form of electromagnetic radiation. The body removes heat through radiation but also picks up heat radiated by other objects. *Convection* refers to the removal or gain of heat through air molecules. Heat flows from a warm object to a cooler object. *Conduction* is heat exchange through physical contact with another object, such as the ground or clothes. Conduction generally accounts for a very small proportion of heat exchange. *Evaporation* is the loss of heat through the conversion of water to vapor. In the process of sweat evaporation, heat energy is consumed. Evaporation is the only one of these four mechanisms that results in heat loss without heat gain.

The amount of heat loss through these mechanisms varies according to both temperature and humidity. As the temperature increases, the only way your body can cope is to increase the amount of evaporation (your body can't amplify any of the other three mechanisms). As a result, evaporation is the most effective mechanism for heat removal in excessively hot temperatures. At comfortable temperatures, most heat is lost through radiation, and evaporation accounts for only 23 percent of the total lost. At hot temperatures (35°C = 95°F), evaporation accounts for 90 percent. Vasodilation is also important in heat loss. The opening of the blood vessels moves internal heat to the outside skin. The heat can then be transferred to the environment through radiation, convection, and evaporation.

Evaporation has its drawbacks. The removal of too much water from the body can be harmful and even fatal. The efficiency of evaporation is also affected by humidity. In humid environments, evaporation is less efficient, making heat loss more difficult under hot and humid conditions than under hot and dry conditions.

Climate and Morphological Variation

Differences in physiologic responses and certain morphological variations—most notably, the size and shape of the body and head—affect people's ability to handle temperature stress. Nose size and shape are related to temperature and humidity.

The Bergmann and Allen Rules   Human populations in colder climates tend to be heavier than those in hotter climates. This does not mean that all people in cold climates are heavy and all people in hot climates are light. Every human group contains a variety of small and large people. Some of this variation is caused by factors such as diet. However, a strong relationship of *average* body size and temperature does exist among indigenous human populations (Roberts 1978).

A nineteenth-century English zoologist, Carl Bergmann, noted the relationship between body size and temperature in a number of mammal species. Bergmann explained his findings in terms of mammalian physiology and principles of heat loss. **Bergmann's rule** states that if two mammals have similar shapes but different sizes, the smaller animal will lose heat more rapidly and will therefore be better adapted to warmer climates, where the ability to lose heat is advantageous. Larger mammals lose heat more slowly and are therefore better adapted to colder climates.

The reason for these relationships is that heat production is a function of the total volume of a mammal, whereas heat loss is a function of total surface area. Consider two hypothetical mammals whose body shape is that of a cube. Imagine that one cube is 2 cm long and the other is 4 cm long in each dimension (Figure 16.2). As a measure of heat production, we can compute

Bergmann's rule States that among mammals of similar shape, the larger mammal loses heat less rapidly than the smaller mammal, and that among mammals of similar size, the mammal with a linear shape will lose heat more rapidly than the mammal with a nonlinear shape.

FIGURE 16.2

Geometric representation of Bergmann's rule relating body size and heat loss. The larger cube has a larger volume (heat production) and a larger surface area (heat loss). The larger cube also has a smaller surface area/volume ratio, however, indicating that it would lose heat less rapidly and therefore be adaptive in colder climates.

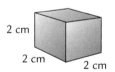

Surface area = 24 cm^2
Volume = 8 cm^3
Surface area/volume = 3

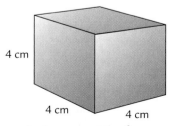

Surface area = 96 cm^2
Volume = 64 cm^3
Surface area/volume = 1.5

the volume of each cube (volume = length × width × height). The volume of the 2-cm cube is 8 cm^3, and that of the 4-cm cube is 64 cm^3. The larger cube can produce more heat because of its greater volume. The greater the volume of a mammal, the greater the heat produced.

As a measure of heat loss, we can compute the surface area of each cube. The surface area of each side is length times width. There are six sides to a cube, so we multiply our result by 6. The surface area of the 2-cm cube is 24 cm^2, and that of the 4-cm cube is 96 cm^2. With the greater surface area, the larger cube seems to produce more heat and to lose it at a greater rate. The relevant factor in heat loss in mammals, however, is the ratio of surface area to volume—that is, the rate of heat loss relative to the amount of surface area. The surface area/volume ratio is 24/8 = 3 for the smaller cube and 96/64 = 1.5 for the larger cube. Therefore, the larger cube loses heat at a slower rate relative to heat production. In cold climates, the larger cube would be at an advantage because it loses heat less quickly. In hot climates, the reverse would be true; hot climates would favor the smaller cube, with its quicker rate of heat loss.

Another aspect of Bergmann's rule involves the shape of an object and its relationship to heat production and loss. Figure 16.3 shows two objects with the same volume but different shapes. The first object is a 4-cm cube with a volume of 64 cm^3, a surface area of 96 cm^2, and a surface area/volume ratio of 1.5. The second object is a rectangular block 2 cm wide, 4 cm deep, and 8 cm high. The volume of this block is also 64 cm^3. The surface area is 112 cm^2, and the surface area/volume ratio is 112/64 = 1.75. Even though both objects produce the same amount of heat as measured by their volumes, the rectangular block loses heat more quickly. Linear objects such as the block would be at an advantage in hot climates, whereas less linear objects such as the cube would be at an advantage in cold climates. Accordingly, Bergmann's rule predicts that mammals in hot climates will have linear body shapes and mammals in cold climates will have less linear body shapes. Another zoologist, J. Allen, applied these principles to body limbs and other appendages. **Allen's rule** predicts that mammals in cold climates will have shorter, bulkier limbs, whereas mammals in hot climates will have longer, narrower ones.

Body Size and Shape Do the Bergmann and Allen rules hold for human body size and shape? Figure 16.4 shows a Masai cattle herder from Africa and an Inuit (Eskimo) man. Note the thinness and length of the Masai's body and limbs compared to those of the Inuit. These physiques do in fact conform to Bergmann's and Allen's predictions. Analysis of data from many human populations has found the rules to be accurate in describing the *average* trends among populations in the world today and in the past (Ruff 1994). Again, don't forget that extensive variation exists within populations. Also, some populations are exceptions to the general rule. African pygmies, for example, are short and have short limbs, yet they live in a hot climate. The pygmy's short size appears to be due to a hormonal deficiency (Shea and Gomez 1988).

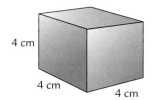

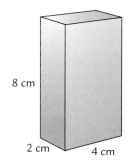

Surface area = 96 cm^2
Volume = 64 cm^3
Surface area/volume = 1.5

Surface area = 112 cm^2
Volume = 64 cm^3
Surface area/volume = 1.75

FIGURE 16.3

Geometric representation of Bergmann's rule relating body shape and heat loss. The cube has a lower surface area/volume ratio than the rectangular block and would therefore lose heat less rapidly.

Allen's rule States that mammals in cold climates tend to have short, bulky limbs, allowing less loss of body heat, whereas mammals in hot climates tend to have long, slender limbs, allowing greater loss of body heat.

FIGURE 16.4

An Inuit (*left*) and a Masai cattle herder (*right*) illustrate the relationship between body size, body shape, and climate predicted by the Bergmann and Allen rules. The shorter and stockier build of the Inuit is better adapted for a cold climate, and the taller and thinner body of the Masai herder is better adapted for a hot climate.

The Bergmann and Allen rules apply to adult human body size and shape. Are these average patterns the result of natural selection (i.e., genetic adaptation) or changes in size and shape during the growth process (i.e., developmental acclimatization)? Do infants born elsewhere who move into an environment attain the same adult size and shape as native-born infants? If so, this suggests a direct influence of the environment on growth. If not, then the growth pattern leading to a certain adult size and shape may be genetic in nature and determined by natural selection. If the growth pattern is entirely genetic, then we can expect to see the same ultimate size and shape regardless of environment. That is, an infant born in a cold climate but raised in a hot climate will still show the characteristic size and shape of humans born in cold climates. Of course, if *both* environmental and genetic factors are responsible for adult size and shape, then the expected pattern is more complex. Unraveling the potential genetic and climatic effects is a difficult process because other contributing influences, such as nutrition, also vary with climate.

The evidence to date suggests that both genetic and environmental factors influence the relationship among climate, growth, body size, and body shape. When children grow up in a climate different from that of their ancestors, they tend to grow in ways the indigenous children do (Malina 1975; Roberts 1978). Changes in nutritional patterns also have an effect. Katzmarzyk and Leonard (1998) examined the relationship between body size and shape and average annual temperature using data collected from 1953 to 1996, and compared their results with previous studies. They found that although the

Cranial Plasticity—Did Boas Get It Right?

The famous American anthropologist Franz Boas collected anthropometric measures on thousands of European immigrants to the United States and their children between 1908 and 1910 (Boas 1912). He used some of these data to examine the potential role of cranial plasticity: changes in the shape of the head resulting from growing up in a new environment, a form of developmental acclimatization. At that time, cranial shape was often considered an innate "racial" trait that was inherited, with little environmental influence. Boas compared the cephalic index of children born in the United States with that from children born in Europe in seven different ethnic groups of immigrants. He found differences in the cranial shape of U.S.- and foreign-born children, a study that soon became a classic example of plasticity that occurs during one's growth and development.

Debate over Boas's study and its implications recently arose when two independent sets of researchers reanalyzed Boas's original data and came to two different conclusions. Sparks and Jantz (2002) argued that Boas's data showed only minimal evidence for cranial plasticity, whereas Gravlee and colleagues (2003b) argued that Boas had gotten it right and that the data did show evidence of cranial plasticity. Although some of the media portrayed this as a major debate, careful reading of these papers, as well as subsequent comments (Gravlee et al. 2003a; Sparks and Jantz 2003), suggests that there is an element of truth to both groups' claims—it depends on the specific questions being asked (Relethford 2004a).

The accompanying figure shows some basic information from Gravlee and colleagues' (2003b) analysis of cephalic index in the Boas data. This graph compares the average cephalic index in the U.S.- and foreign-born samples of immigrant children for seven different ethnic groups. These averages represent the mean cranial shape in each group after statistical adjustment for each subject's age. There is no statistical difference between the U.S.- and foreign-born samples of children born to Hungarians, Poles, or Scots, but there is a significant difference for the remaining four ethnic groups. This difference demonstrates that there is evidence of cranial plasticity and that Boas was right. However, the claims of Sparks and Jantz are also reflected. The actual changes in cephalic index, even though statistically significant, are relatively minor. Further, even though the relative rankings

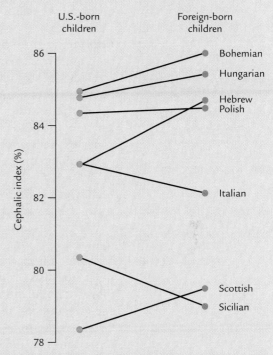

Comparison of average cephalic index in U.S.- and foreign-born children of immigrants to the United States for seven ethnic groups. (Data from Gravlee et al. 2003b.)

of cephalic index are different in the U.S.- and foreign-born samples, the overall distinction in cranial shape between Scots and Sicilians and all other groups is the same for both the U.S.- and foreign-born samples. Thus, the overall pattern of relationship between ethnic groups is obscured somewhat by developmental plasticity, but it is not erased.

The take-home lesson from these studies is that Boas was correct in refuting earlier statements regarding the innate and purely genetic nature of cranial shape in humans; cranial shape can change as a result of growing up in a different environment. However, rejection of a purely genetic argument does not mean that a purely environmental argument is correct. As with all complex traits, variation in cranial shape reflects *both* genetic and environmental influences.

445

more recent data still showed the patterns expected from the Bergmann and Allen rules, this relationship was not as strong as in previous decades, suggesting that other factors, such as changes in nutrition and health care, have obscured the relationship between climate and morphology to some extent.

Cranial Size and Shape   The size and shape of the human head has long been of interest to anthropologists. In past times, the shape of the head was the focus of studies of racial classification. In the nineteenth century, the Swedish anatomist Anders Retzius developed a measure of cranial shape called the **cephalic index.** This index is derived from two measurements: the total length of the head and its maximum width. To compute the index, you simply divide the width of the head by the length of the head and multiply the result by 100. For example, if a person has a head length of 182 mm and a head width of 158 mm, the cephalic index is $(158/182) \times 100 = 86.8$. That is, the person's head width is almost 87 percent of head length. Among human populations today, the cephalic index ranges from roughly 70 percent to 90 percent.

At first, cranial shape was felt to be a measurement capable of determining racial groupings. For example, African skulls were found to have lower cephalic indices than European skulls. Further study showed *rough* agreement but also produced many examples of overlap and similar values in different populations. For example, both Germans and Koreans have average cephalic indices of about 83 percent. Likewise, both African pygmies and Greenland Eskimos have average cephalic indices of approximately 77 percent (Harrison et al. 1988). These values do not correspond to any racial classification; they represent *averages* for each population. There is also considerable variation *within* each population.

As more data were obtained and compared geographically, a different pattern emerged—a correspondence was found to exist between cranial shape and climate. Beals (1972) examined the cephalic index and climate around the world. He found a direct relationship: Populations in colder climates tend to have wider skulls relative to length than those in hot climates (Figure 16.5). In particular, he found the average cephalic index for populations that experienced winter frost to be higher than for those in tropical environments.

This correspondence makes sense in terms of the Bergmann and Allen rules. The shape of the upper part of the skull is related to heat loss. Rounded heads (those with a high cephalic index) lose heat slowly and therefore are at an advantage in cold climates. Narrow heads lose heat more quickly and are therefore at an advantage in hot climates. It appears that as human populations moved into colder climates, natural selection led to a change in the relative proportions of the skull. Beals and colleagues (1983) have extended this analysis to fossil human crania over the past 1.5 million years and found similar results.

Nasal Size and Shape   The shape of the nasal opening in the skull is another morphological variation that has a strong relationship to climate. The **nasal index** is the width of the nasal opening divided by the height of the nasal opening, multiplied by 100. Typical values of the nasal index range from roughly

cephalic index A measure of cranial shape defined as the total length of the skull divided by the maximum width of the skull.

nasal index A measure of the shape of the nasal opening, defined as the width of the nasal opening divided by the height.

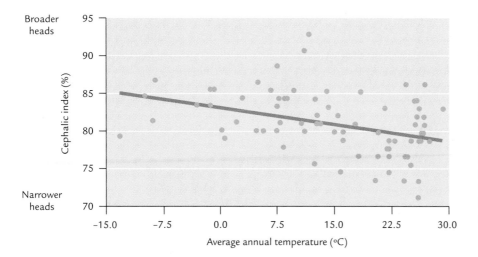

FIGURE 16.5

Relationship between cranial shape (cephalic index) and average annual temperature across the world. The solid line indicates the best-fitting linear equation. The cephalic index is greater (broader head) in colder climates because a round shape has a lower surface area/volume ratio, which minimizes heat loss. (Data from Kenneth Beals, unpublished.)

64 percent to 104 percent (Molnar 1998). Stereotypic racial views associate wide noses (large nasal indices) with African peoples. Although it is true that some African populations have very wide noses, others have long, narrow noses.

Numerous studies have found positive associations between the average nasal index of populations and average temperature. Populations in cold climates tend to have narrow noses; those in hot climates tend to have wide noses. Relationships have also been found between average nasal index and average humidity. Populations in dry climates tend to have narrow noses; those in humid climates tend to have wide noses (Franciscus and Long 1991). The mucous membranes of the nose serve to warm and moisten incoming air. High, narrow noses can warm air to a greater extent than low, wide noses and therefore may be more adaptive in cold climates. High, narrow noses also have a greater internal surface area with which to moisten air and are thus more adaptive in dry climates.

Cultural Adaptations

In Western societies, we tend to take cultural adaptations to temperature stress for granted. Housing, insulated clothing, heaters, air conditioners, and other technologies are all around us. How do people in other cultures adapt to excessive cold or heat?

Cold Stress   The Inuit, or Eskimo people, of the Arctic have realized effective cultural adaptations to cold stress, most notably in their clothing and shelter. It is not enough just to wear a lot of clothes to stay warm; if you work hard, you tend to overheat. The Inuit wear layered clothing, trapping air between layers to act as an insulator. Outer layers can be removed if a person overheats. Also, the Inuit design their clothing with multiple flaps that can be opened to prevent buildup of sweat while working.

While out hunting or fishing, the Inuit frequently construct temporary snow shelters, or igloos, that provide quite efficient protection from the cold.

FIGURE 16.6

Forms of human shelter such as this igloo (*top*) and this Pueblo house (*bottom*) reflect adaptation to a wide range of climatic conditions.

The ice is an excellent insulator, and its reflective surface helps retain heat (Figure 16.6). More permanent shelters also provide ample protection from the cold. Inuit houses have an underground entry, which is curved to reduce incoming wind. Inside, the main living area lies at a higher level than the fireplace; this architectural feature serves to increase heat and minimize drafts (Moran 1982).

Not all cold-weather housing is as effective as the types constructed by the Inuit. Among the Quechua Indians of the Peruvian highlands, the temperature inside temporary houses is often not much warmer than it is outside. However, these shelters do provide protection against rain and to some extent the cold. The bedding used by the Quechua is their most effective protection against heat loss (Frisancho 1993).

Heat Stress   Human populations live in environments that are dry and hot (i.e., deserts) and that are humid and hot (i.e., tropical rain forests). Moran (1982) has summarized some basic principles of clothing and shelter that are used in desert environments, where the objectives are fourfold: to reduce heat production, to reduce heat gain from radiation and from conduction, and to increase evaporation. Clothing is important because it protects from both solar radiation and hot winds. Typical desert clothing is light and loose, thus allowing circulation of air to increase evaporation. The air between the clothing and the body also provides excellent insulation.

Shelters are frequently built compactly to minimize the surface area exposed to the sun. Light colors on the outside help reflect heat. Doors and windows are kept closed during the day to keep the interior cool. Building materials are also adaptive. Adobe, for example, is efficient in absorbing heat during the day and radiating it at night (see Figure 16.6); nighttime temperatures may drop precipitously in desert environments.

Heat stress in tropical environments is often a problem because the extreme humidity greatly reduces the efficiency of evaporation through sweating. Cultural adaptations to tropical environments are similar throughout the world. Clothing is minimal, helping to increase the potential for evaporation. In some cultures, shelters are built in an open design, without walls, to augment cooling during the day; in others, shelters are built closed to increase warmth at night. The combination of high heat and high humidity obviously affects daily routines. Generally, people start work early in the day, taking long midday breaks to keep from overheating.

In sum, humans have adapted to a number of environments that produce temperature stress. They have managed to adapt to extremes of hot and cold through physiologic changes, long-term genetic adaptations, and adaptive behaviors, particularly those manifested in clothing and shelter technology and in the pace of daily life.

HIGH-ALTITUDE ADAPTATION

Some human populations have lived for long periods of time at elevations of over 2,500 m, or roughly 8,200 ft.

High-Altitude Stresses

High-altitude environments produce several stresses, including oxygen starvation, extreme cold, and sometimes poor nutrition. Studies of high-altitude populations have provided insight into how humans cope with multiple stresses.

Hypoxia   Oxygen starvation, or **hypoxia,** is more common at high altitudes because of the relationship of barometric pressure and altitude. Although the percentage of oxygen in the atmosphere is relatively constant up to almost 70 miles above the earth, barometric pressure decreases quickly with altitude

hypoxia Oxygen starvation, which occurs frequently at high altitudes.

FIGURE 16.7

The relationship between barometric pressure and altitude. Barometric pressure decreases as altitude increases, causing a decrease in the percentage of arterial oxygen saturation (see Figure 16.8). (Data from Frisancho 1993:223.)

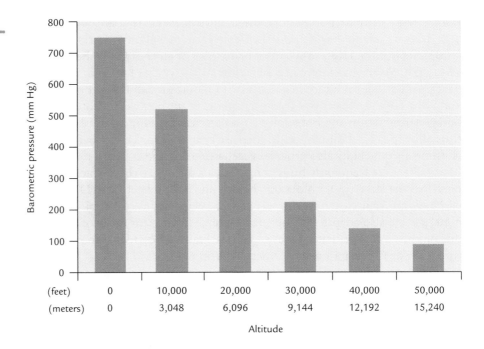

(Figure 16.7). Because air is less compressed at high altitudes, its oxygen content is less concentrated, and less oxygen is thus available to the hemoglobin in the blood. The percentage of arterial oxygen saturation decreases rapidly with altitude (Figure 16.8). For persons at rest, hypoxia generally occurs above 3,000 m; for active persons, it can occur as low as 2,000 m (Frisancho 1993).

FIGURE 16.8

The relationship between arterial oxygen saturation and altitude. (Data from Frisancho 1993:223.)

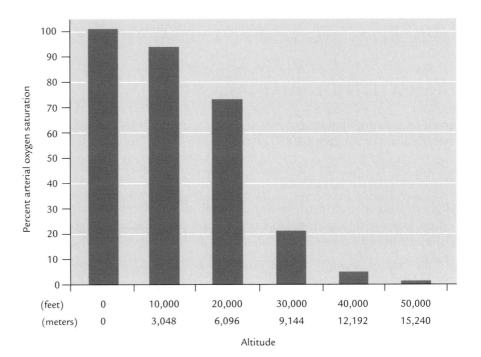

Other Stresses   Because the air is thinner at high altitudes, the concentration of ultraviolet radiation is greater, and the air itself offers less protection against it. The thinner air also causes considerable heat loss from the atmosphere, resulting in cold stress. In many high-altitude environments, conditions are also extremely dry because of high winds and low humidity. In addition, hypoxia affects plants and animals; for lack of oxygen, trees cannot grow above 4,000 m. The limited availability of plants and animals means that nutritional stress is likely in many high-altitude environments.

Numerous studies have compared the physiology and morphology of high-altitude and low-altitude populations. Early research tended to attribute any differences to the effects of hypoxia on the human body. More recent studies have shown that other stresses of high altitude are significant factors as well (Frisancho 1990). When dealing with human adaptation, we do best to consider the effect and interaction of *multiple* stresses.

Physiologic Responses to Hypoxia

People who live at low altitudes experience several physiologic changes when they enter a high-altitude environment. Some of these happen immediately; others occur over several months to a year. Such physiologic responses help to maintain sufficient oxygen levels. Respiration increases initially but returns to normal after a few days. Red blood cell production increases for roughly 3 months. The weight of the right ventricle of the heart is greater than the weight of the left ventricle in individuals who have grown up at high altitudes. Other changes include possible hyperventilation, higher hemoglobin concentration in the blood, loss of appetite, and weight loss. Memory and sensory abilities may be affected, and hypoxia may influence hormone levels. These changes are not all necessarily adaptive, and some (such as weight loss) can be harmful.

The physiologic differences between high-altitude and low-altitude natives are primarily acquired during the growth process. Studies of children who were born at low altitudes but moved into high altitudes during childhood clearly substantiate this phenomenon. In terms of aerobic capacity, for example, the younger the age of migration, the higher the aerobic capacity (Frisancho 1993). In other words, the longer a child lives in a high-altitude environment, the greater the developmental response to that environment. Age at migration has no effect on the aerobic capacity of adults, however, further indicating that most physiologic changes are the result of developmental acclimatization.

Physical Growth in High-Altitude Populations

Studies conducted by Paul Baker and colleagues of high-altitude and low-altitude Indian populations in Peru found two peculiarities in growth. Chest dimensions and lung volume were greater at all ages in the high-altitude group (Figure 16.9), and high-altitude populations were also shorter at most ages than low-altitude populations (Figure 16.10) (Frisancho and Baker 1970).

FIGURE 16.9

Chest circumference for
high-altitude and low-altitude
Peruvian Indian populations.
At all ages, the high-altitude
population has the greatest
chest circumference. (Courtesy
A. R. Frisancho.)

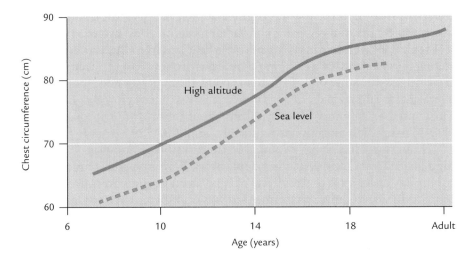

The shorter stature is related to delayed maturation, whereas the increase in
chest size is due to growth acceleration during childhood.

Initially, the researchers interpreted both patterns of physical growth as
direct developmental responses to hypoxia and cold stress at high altitude.
Larger chests and larger lung volumes relative to body size would be better
able to provide sufficient oxygen levels. More energy devoted to the growth
of oxygen transport systems, however, would leave less energy available for
growth in other organ systems, especially the skeletal and muscle systems.
Compounded by cold stress at high altitudes, this energy deficit would lead
to an increase in basal metabolic rates and further reduction in energy available for body growth. As discussed later, this view is now being questioned.

Studies in high-altitude environments around the world have shown a similar pattern of growth in chest dimensions, although the extent of growth varies.
Migrants to high-altitude populations also show an increase in chest dimensions, particularly among those who migrate at an early age. Increased growth
of oxygen transport systems appears to be a developmental response to hypoxia.

FIGURE 16.10

Stature for high-altitude and
low-altitude Peruvian Indian
populations. At most ages, the
low-altitude population is
taller. (Courtesy A. R. Frisancho.)

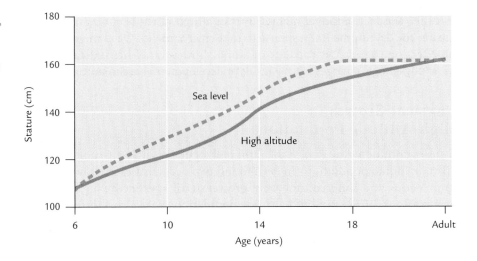

Are the developmental changes in chest and lung growth in high-altitude populations genetic in nature? Were they shaped by natural selection? Most research to date assigns a relatively minor role to genetic factors. One study examined high-altitude and low-altitude populations of European ancestry in Bolivia (Greksa 1990). Because these groups do not have a long history of residence at high altitude, they would not possess any genetic predisposition for high-altitude adaptations. The study showed that there was an increased capacity of the oxygen transport system in these populations at high altitude even though they were not of high-altitude ancestry. The observed changes were instead direct effects of a chronic hypoxic stress. Weitz and colleagues (2000) did not find any such effect in low-altitude Han Chinese who had migrated to a high-altitude environment, however, suggesting that there might be genetic differences between populations that underlie their differential response to hypoxia. It appears that chest dimensions and lung size are affected by both developmental and genetic factors that interact differently in different human populations (Greksa 1996).

The delayed maturation and small stature of the Peruvians have not been found in all studies of growth in high-altitude populations. As a result, some researchers have questioned the initial premise that hypoxia and cold stress have necessarily led to these characteristics, suggesting instead that other causal factors might be at work. A study undertaken in Peru has in fact shown that nutrition is a major influence on stature (Leonard et al. 1990). Though high altitude may play a role in nutritional stress in the Peruvian highlands, income levels and access to land are of greater consequence. Also, other high-altitude populations, such as those found in Ethiopia, have a higher standard of living and do not show the growth deficits observed in Peru. Thus, it appears that although increased chest growth is a functional adaptation to hypoxia, the smaller body size is not necessarily related to high altitude. These results amply illustrate the complexity in assessing the relative value of stresses in any given environment.

NUTRITIONAL ADAPTATION

The previous examples of human adaptation have focused on adaptive responses to the stresses imposed by the physical environment—specifically, temperature and high-altitude stress. This section examines adaptation to nutritional needs and differences in the availability of food resources.

Basic Nutritional Needs

Proper nutrition is needed for body maintenance, growth, and the energy needs of daily activity. Ingested nutrients provide the energy for these. During infancy, childhood, and adolescence, a greater proportion of nutrient energy goes into physical growth. Too little energy can result in a reduction in overall size and speed of maturation. Too much nutrient energy can result in accumulation of fat and acceleration of maturation. Inadequate amounts of certain critical nutrients can also affect basic biological processes, such as insufficiency in vitamin A or C, both of which can increase susceptibility to certain diseases.

Ingested energy (measured in calories) comes from carbohydrates, proteins, and fats. Dietary proteins are also necessary for certain metabolic functions. Proteins provide amino acids, of which 20 are needed by the body for synthesis and repair of body tissues. Although the body synthesizes some amino acids, adult humans require 8 amino acids available only through diet (children need 9). Without adequate sources of protein in the diet, lack of these amino acids can lead to growth retardation, illness, and death. The major sources of proteins in Western human populations are animal products, including meat, eggs, fish, and milk. Plants provide proteins, but they are lacking in one or more amino acids and must be eaten in combination with other plants to ensure adequate nutrition.

Dietary requirements in the United states are referred to as Dietary Reference Intakes (DRIs) and are published by the Institute of Medicine of the National Academies (www.iom.edu). Energy needs (caloric intake) varies by sex, height, weight, and average level of activity, with larger and more active individuals having greater energy needs. Energy needs decline with age. Protein needs are generally higher in men than women, unless the woman is pregnant or nursing, in which case her protein needs are, on average, over 25 percent higher than a man, and over 50 percent higher than a woman who is not pregnant or nursing (www.iom.edu/File.aspx?ID=21372).

Our bodies also require other nutrients, such as fatty acids, vitamins, and minerals. A diet lacking in one or more of these nutrients can lead to medical problems. A lack of iodine, for example, can lead to thyroid problems, and a lack of vitamin C can lead to the disease scurvy.

Variation in Human Diet

Human nutritional needs have been shaped by evolution. In a general sense, the nutritional needs of humans are similar to those of other omnivorous primate species. Our physiology reflects the general primate adaptation to a diet comprised of large amounts of fruit and vegetation, such as our shared inability to synthesize vitamin C, forcing us to acquire it from our diet (Leonard 2000). Humans, however, have a considerably more diverse diet, reflecting the broad range of environments we have adapted to and the diversity in cultural adaptations developed to acquire food.

As is discussed elsewhere, the primary means of acquiring food throughout most of human evolution has been hunting and gathering. This way of life began close to 2 million years ago and was the only way humans obtained food until about 12,000 years ago, when an increasing number of human populations became reliant on agriculture. As discussed further in Chapter 17, this shift in subsistence has had a noticeable biological impact on our health as we frequently eat a diet quite unlike that which we adapted to in the past.

Hunting and Gathering   It is important for us to understand the diet of hunting and gathering societies because most of our biological evolution took place in this type of environment. Hunting and gathering populations do not all have the same type of diet; their specific patterns of resource utilization are shaped by their specific environments. For example, you cannot fish if there are no fish around, and you will have fewer plant foods in colder environments. Early studies of living hunter-gatherer societies such as the San of South Africa suggested that the bulk of their caloric intake came from gathering activities rather than animal proteins (Lee 1968). It is now recognized that this is not the case. In a review of data from hunting-gathering societies, Cordain et al. (2000) found that 73 percent of these societies obtained more than half of their energy needs from animal foods (hunting and/or fishing) and only 14 percent obtained more than half of their energy needs from gathered plant foods. They also found that while there is not a single hunting and gathering population that was primarily dependent on gathering, one out of five populations were almost entirely dependent on animal foods. Relative to contemporary Westernized societies, hunting-gathering societies have diets that are much higher in proteins, lower in carbohydrates, and as high, or higher, in fats (although the type of fat is different from that typically found in Western diets).

Agriculture There is also variation among agricultural populations, dependent largely on available resources and the level of technology. Some populations practice simple horticulture, such as slash-and-burn agriculture; other populations rely on intensive agriculture. The specific food crop(s) exploited depends on the environment; rice is a main crop in Southeast Asia, wheat in Europe, and corn in the Americas.

Different ways of processing food can improve its quality. Leonard (2000) discusses one example—corn among Native American populations. Corn (maize) has advantages and disadvantages; it is high in protein but lacks two amino acids (lysine and tryptophan) and niacin. Many Native American populations use alkali substances, such as ash or lime, when cooking corn, which act to increase amino acid and niacin concentrations. Comparative research has shown that the more a society relies on corn, the more it uses such methods.

Malnutrition

We tend to equate the term **malnutrition** with a diet deficient in calories, proteins, or other nutrients, but it literally means "bad nutrition." Malnutrition often does refer to having too little food (quantity and/or quality), but it can also refer to having too much. If you ingest more calories than are needed for growth, body maintenance, or physical activity, the excess is deposited as fat in your body. Obesity can lead to medical problems such as high blood pressure, heart disease, and diabetes. Obesity is a growing problem in industrialized nations such as the United States.

Throughout much of the world, however, the major nutritional problem is the lack of food, or at least the lack of a balanced diet. Poor nutrition acts to slow down the growth process, leading to small adult body size. In one sense,

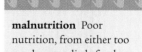

malnutrition Poor nutrition, from either too much or too little food or from the improper balance of nutrients.

this change in growth is adaptive, because a smaller adult will require fewer nutrients. By focusing on this relationship, however, we ignore the problem that the slowing of growth is an indication of potential harm. Severe undernutrition, especially in infancy and childhood, can have serious effects. Not only is physical growth stunted but mental retardation also may result, and susceptibility to infectious disease increases. Severe undernutrition is common in much of the Third World, compounded by problems of poverty, overpopulation, inadequate sewage disposal, contaminated water, and economic and political conflicts.

A number of nutritional problems, collectively known as **protein-calorie malnutrition,** result from an inadequate amount of proteins and/or calories in the diet. Protein-calorie malnutrition is the most serious nutritional problem on the planet. Its various forms have different physical symptoms, but all stem from the basic problems of an inadequate diet and have the same ultimate effects, ranging from growth retardation to death.

The most severe types of protein-calorie malnutrition are **kwashiorkor** (a severe deficiency in proteins but not calories) and **marasmus** (severe deficiencies in *both* proteins and calories). Kwashiorkor occurs most often in infants and young children who are weaned from their mother's breast onto a diet lacking in proteins. The infant suffers growth retardation, muscle wasting, and lowered resistance to disease. One of the symptoms of kwashiorkor is the swelling of the body due to water retention (Figure 16.11). Marasmus is also most prevalent during infancy and similarly leads to growth retardation, muscle wasting, and death. A child suffering from marasmus typically looks emaciated (Figure 16.12).

Although the physical appearance of children with kwashiorkor and marasmus differs, both suffer from an inadequate diet. Population pressure and poverty certainly play a major role in much of protein-calorie malnutrition, but they are not the only factors. Some researchers, such as anthropologist Katherine Dettwyler, have argued that cultural beliefs regarding nutrition are at least as important. Such beliefs include stressing quantity over quality, postponing the age at which children eat solid foods, and following other practices that compromise proper nutrition. Thus, the elimination of protein-calorie malnutrition will require more than an attack on population growth and the reduction of poverty and disease; it will also require nutritional education (Dettwyler 1994). Dettwyler's work also shows us the folly of assuming that all cultural behaviors are necessarily adaptive.

protein-calorie malnutrition A group of nutritional diseases resulting from inadequate amounts of proteins and/or calories.

kwashiorkor An extreme form of protein-calorie malnutrition resulting from a severe deficiency in proteins but not calories.

marasmus An extreme form of protein-calorie malnutrition resulting from severe deficiencies in both proteins and calories.

FIGURE 16.11

A child with kwashiorkor in Mali, West Africa.

FIGURE 16.12

A child with marasmus, a severe protein and calorie deficiency.

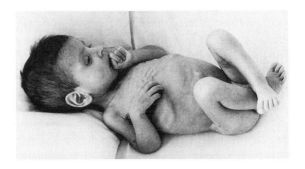

The devastating impact of malnutrition should not be underestimated. Worldwide, 26 percent of children under the age of 5 are classified as moderately or severely undernourished (this is 160 *million* people). And more than 5.5 million children under the age of 5 die each year for reasons linked to malnutrition (UNICEF 2005).

Biological Costs of Modernization and Dietary Change

Increasingly, formerly "traditional" societies have undergone economic and technological development. Compared to rates of change in historical and prehistoric times, modernization in many parts of the world today is occurring almost instantaneously. Such rapid modernization has produced many new biological stresses due to rapid population growth, economic and political change, increased use of natural resources, and increased levels of pollution, to name but a few. With these rapid changes, populations face new stresses. One of these changes is the impact of modernization on traditional diets.

Modernization and Obesity There is a tendency for populations undergoing modernization to show increased height and weight. Weight gain, in particular, has often been quite dramatic in recently modernized populations, resulting in part from dietary changes and a more sedentary lifestyle. These populations show high rates of obesity, which in turn predisposes them to serious health problems (Figure 16.13).

A number of studies of the biological impact of modernization have been conducted in Samoa, a Polynesian island group in the southern Pacific Ocean.

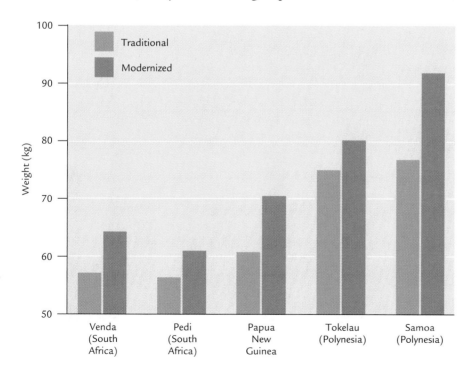

FIGURE 16.13

Comparison of average weight (in kilograms) for adult males in traditional and modernized groups within various populations. In each case, adult males in modernized groups weigh more. (Data from Harrison et al. 1988:536.)

Samoa had been relatively homogeneous in both genetics and lifestyle until the beginning of the twentieth century, at which time dramatic socioeconomic development took place. At present, Samoa is divided into two groups: Western Samoa, characterized by traditional diet and lifestyle, and American Samoa, characterized by a shift to modern employment patterns and diet. Bindon and Baker (1985) found that adult males and females from modernized islands weighed more and had greater amounts of subcutaneous fat. They concluded that modernization has led to a rapid increase in the frequency of obesity. In the traditional sample, for example, 14 percent of adult males older than 45 years of age were obese, whereas 25 percent were obese on one modernized island and 41 percent on another. This study illustrates how quickly some aspects of human biology can change in response to a changing environment—and the dramatic cost of modernization in much of the world.

Modernization and Blood Pressure   Blood pressure provides a measure of health. Excessive blood pressure, or hypertension, is a serious condition, both in itself and as a risk factor for other diseases. Blood pressure is measured using two readings: *systolic* blood pressure, measured during ventricular contractions, and *diastolic* blood pressure, measured during ventricular relaxation. Blood pressure tends to be higher in modernized societies and increases with age in these populations (Little and Baker 1988). In traditional societies, blood pressure tends to be lower and does not increase with age. Changes in blood pressure patterns in modernized societies reflect a number of factors, including changes in diet, lifestyle, physical activity, and overall level of stress.

Figure 16.14 presents the results of a study of modernization and blood pressure conducted by Lewis (1990) in the Gilbert Islands of the Republic of

FIGURE 16.14

Effects of modernization on adult male diastolic blood pressure (mm hg) in the Gilbert Islands. From 1960 to 1978, the area underwent modernization. Note that the average blood pressures in 1978 are higher than in 1960 and that they show an increase with age. These observations are common findings in studies of modernization and blood pressure. (Data from Lewis 1990:146.)

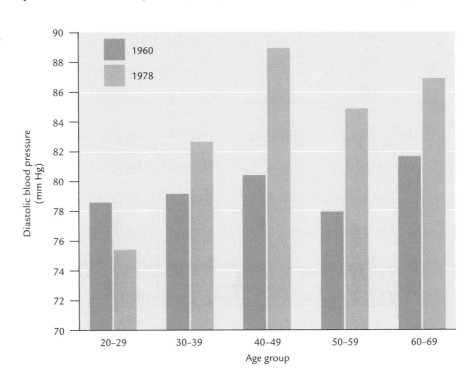

Kiribati in the central Pacific Ocean. Measurements collected during two time periods were compared: the first in 1960, when the islands had a more traditional economy, and the second in 1978, by which point the islands had undergone extensive modernization. There is a clear increase in blood pressure over time; blood pressure is higher in the 1978 sample than in the 1960 sample for all but one age group. There is also a noticeable increase in blood pressure with age in the 1978 sample, characteristic of a modernized population, but there is no apparent age-related pattern in the 1960 traditional sample. Culture change significantly affects human biology, and there is a biological cost to modernization.

Summary

Studies of adaptation focus on the many ways in which organisms respond to environmental stresses. Human adaptation is particularly interesting because humans not only adapt both biologically and culturally but also must deal with stresses from their physical and cultural environments. Biological adaptation includes physiologic responses and genetic adaptation (natural selection). Cultural adaptation includes aspects of technology, economics, and social structure. In any study of human adaptation, we must look at multiple stresses and multiple adaptive (or nonadaptive) mechanisms.

Many studies of human adaptation have focused on cold and heat stress. Though as mammals humans have the capacity for maintenance of body temperature, they must still cope with extremes in temperature. Physiologic responses of the human body to temperature stress include changes in peripheral blood flow and evaporation. Studies have shown that general relationships exist worldwide between body size and shape and temperature. These observed trends agree with the predictions of the Bergmann and Allen rules. In hot climates, small body size and linear body shape maximize heat loss. In cold climates, large body size and less linear body shape minimize heat loss. Cranial studies show that worldwide the shape of the skull also varies predictably, according to the principles of differential heat loss and the Bergmann and Allen rules. Although some of these biological features are the result of genetic adaptation, studies of children have revealed that response to temperature stress can affect growth. Cultural adaptations, especially those involving clothing, shelter, and physical activity, are also important in climatic adaptation.

Millions of people around the world live at high altitudes. The major stresses of a high-altitude population are hypoxia (oxygen shortage) and cold stress. Many physiologic changes have been documented in high-altitude peoples, including short-term physiologic responses and long-term increases in the size of the lungs and other components of the oxygen transport system. These changes are caused by hypoxic stress during the growth period, and their degree of change is related to the time spent living at high altitudes: the longer one has lived there as a child, the more adapted one is. Early studies of high-altitude populations also noted small body size that, along with delayed maturation, could be due to insufficient energy levels for body growth because of hypoxia and cold stress. More recent studies have shown that this is not always the case because some high-altitude groups do not show this growth deficit. Instead, variation in diet appears to be the key factor.

Humans have adapted culturally to basic nutritional demands in a variety of ways. For millions of years, human ancestors utilized different methods of hunting and gathering to feed themselves, and about 12,000 years ago, humans adopted agriculture as their primary means of subsistence. Although humans have a number of ways of adapting to their nutritional needs, there are some basic biological limits to adaptation, and an increasing number of children are malnourished. Modernization has altered traditional diets as well as other aspects of lifestyle, resulting in an increased biological cost in many cases.

Supplemental Readings

Frisancho, A. R. 1993. *Human Adaptation and Accommodation.* Ann Arbor: University of Michigan Press. A thorough review of adaptation studies, focusing on physiologic adaptation.

Moran, E. F. 1982. *Human Adaptability: An Introduction to Ecological Anthropology.* Boulder, Colo.: Westview Press. A general text that provides another review of human adaptation but focuses more on cultural adaptations.

Stinson, S., B. Bogin, R. Huss-Ashmore, and D. O'Rourke. 2000. *Human Biology: An Evolutionary and Biocultural Perspective.* New York: John Wiley. A comprehensive volume consisting of review chapters on a variety of topics relating to human population biology. Several chapters deal with climatic, high-altitude, nutritional, and infectious disease adaptation.

VIRTUAL EXPLORATIONS

Visit our textbook-specific online learning center Web site at **www. mhhe.com/relethford7** to access the exercises that follow.

1. **Human Adaptability**   http://www.as.ua.edu/ant/bindon/ant 475/. Dr. Jim Bindon's Human Adaptability Web site provides his University of Alabama Anthropology students with a selection of interesting articles on human adaptability. All of these articles will open as Adobe (.PDF) files. You can either save them to your hard drive or read them online. (Please abide by the terms stipulated by JSTOR.)

   Read the Paul T. Baker article, "The Adaptive Limits of Human Populations" (*Man,* 19 (1984): 1–14 at **http://www.as.ua.edu/ant/ bindon/ant475/Readings/r1.pdf**. Baker argues in broad outline that all hominin populations that came after *Homo erectus* adapted to environmental and cultural stress. However, the adaptive process of the past created implications for life in the modern world, and with it, further stresses. Andean Amerindians and Samoan examples are given.
   ■ Baker defines *adaptation* as "simply any biological or cultural trait which aids the biological functioning of a population in a given environment." In what ways does he speculate that this happened? Did all hominin populations solve their survival and reproductive problems in similar fashion?

- *Stresses* are defined as "those natural or cultural environmental forces which potentially reduce the population's ability to function in a given situation." Besides climate and food, what, according to Baker, were some of the stresses hominin populations dealt with?
- Does it now seem likely that morphological differences within *Homo erectus* groups could be attributed to the diversity of environmental change?
- Baker assumes that most *Homo erectus* forms "contributed to the genetic and cultural repertoire of *Homo sapiens*." What was the end result, and what evidence (cultural or otherwise) indicates that this was happening among succeeding hominin populations?
- In spite of evidence indicating technological and cultural variation, Baker feels that with adaptation, these changes also produced *biological* stress. What are some possible stresses he identifies?
- What effect did water vapor variation and ultraviolet radiation have? Infectious disease and alterations in potential food sources?

Return to Dr. Bindon's home page. Scroll down to the "Bergmann's Rule and the Thrifty Genotype" link. This 1997 *American Journal of Physical Anthropology* article was co-authored by Drs. Bindon and Baker. Read the article at **http://www.as.ua.edu/ant/bindon/ant475/Readings/r7.pdf**.

- How is "Bergmann's Rule" defined?
- In what ways has modernization affected the Bergmann formula?
- In what geographic region were population samples drawn for the longitudinal study referenced in the article?
- What is the "thrifty genotypes" hypothesis, and what genetic condition does it specifically address? Which specific populations does the hypothesis reference?
- How is genetic predisposition to NIDDM (non-insulin-dependent diabetes mellitus) explained by this hypothesis?
- Why did modernization among the target population require modification of the "thrifty genotypes" model?

2. **Darwinian Gastronomy** **http://www.pbs.org/wgbh/evolution/library/10/4/1_104_02.html**. Read "Darwinian Gastronomy" on the PBS Evolution Web site. Click on the Larger Image link under the photo. Read the two recipes from Norway and India.
   - What are some of the striking differences in the ingredients?
   - How would these dishes affect the body differently?
   - What do scientists believe are the adaptational reasons for eating spicy foods?
   - What happens when humans in northern climates eat spicy foods? What happens when people in hot climates eat bland foods?
   - Is natural selection operating on people today in terms of the food they eat?

Chinese farmers working in rice paddies. The transition to agriculture began in the human species 12,000 years ago. This major cultural event has led to many changes in human biology, including shifts in rates of disease, death, and fertility.

Human Biology and Culture Change

H uman evolution has been increasingly driven by cultural changes in our species' recent history. Although we continue to evolve biologically, these changes are much slower than changes in human cultural adaptation. During the past 12,000 years, we have changed from being hunters and gatherers to being agriculturalists; an increasing portion of humanity lives in or near large urban centers; and our population has exploded from 5-10 million people to more than 6.5 billion. In many ways, we live in a world very unlike that of our ancestors.

These cultural changes have happened much faster than biological change. As a result, biologically, we are still hunters and gatherers to some extent, but we live in conditions that are often quite different from those under which our ancestors evolved. We live in larger groups, eat different foods, and structure our societies in different ways. The disparity between rates of cultural change and biological evolution has had serious consequences for our biology. An example of this type of change was described briefly in the section on nutritional adaptation in the previous chapter, which noted the biomedical impact of a changing diet and lifestyle on Samoan populations. This example is only one of many that show how rapid cultural changes have affected our biology—not always to our benefit. This chapter considers the impact of culture change on human biology by focusing on some major cultural changes in human evolution over the past 12,000 years.

THE BIOLOGICAL IMPACT OF AGRICULTURE

A major shift in human adaptation was the transition from hunting and gathering to agriculture. Human populations began relying increasingly on agriculture starting 12,000 years ago. Although a small proportion of human populations today still rely on hunting and gathering, most are agricultural. The reasons for this change are still widely debated, and there was probably no single overriding cause. Feder (2000) notes that there is a general pattern in the archaeological record showing that human populations became more **sedentary** (settled in one place) *before* agriculture developed. Human

sedentary Settled in one place throughout most or all of the year.

463

FIGURE 17.1

Osteoarthritis. The head of the femur is deformed.

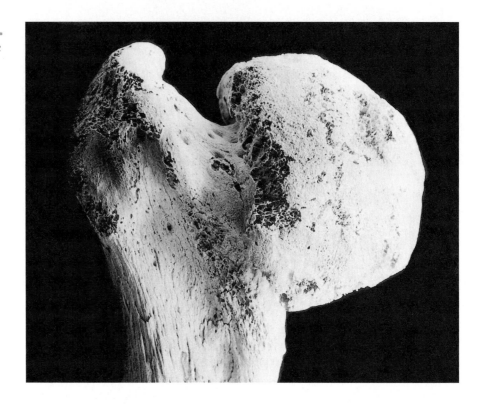

paleopathology The study of disease in prehistoric populations based on analysis of skeletal remains and archaeological evidence.

populations might have been able to settle down because of increased efficiency at hunting and gathering and/or changes in the environment resulting from the warming climate near the end of the Pleistocene. Some archaeologists suggest that the shift to a sedentary life led to population growth, which in turn led to the need for more food resources. Under such conditions, sedentary populations would shift their methods of acquiring food and adopt a variety of agricultural strategies to increase the food supply, such as weeding, protecting plant resources, and clearing forests. Over time, human populations became more reliant on such methods, and the domestication of plants and animals became their primary means of feeding themselves.

The study of the biological impact of the transition to agriculture relies extensively on the field of **paleopathology,** the study of disease in prehistoric populations. The primary evidence is from skeletal remains, which provide a variety of information on health and disease, including age at death, cause of death, nutritional status, growth patterns, and trauma (Cohen 1989; Larsen 2000). Diseases such as osteoarthritis may affect bones directly (Figure 17.1). Other diseases, such as syphilis and tuberculosis, may leave indications of their effects on the skeletal system (Figure 17.2). Physical trauma due to injury or violence often leaves detectable fractures. Signs of healing or infection tell us the long-term effects of such trauma (Figure 17.3). X-ray and chemical analysis can provide us with information about nutrition and growth patterns. Collectively, these methods and others provide us with a view of the health of prehistoric populations.

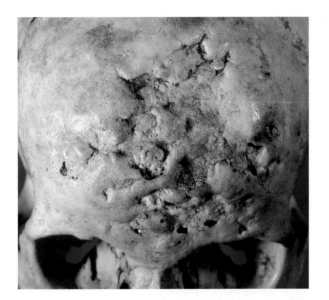

FIGURE 17.2

Skull showing signs of treponemal infection. The marks on the top of the skull are typical of a long-term syphilitic infection.

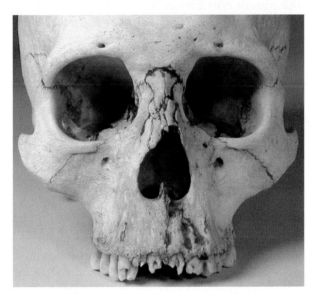

FIGURE 17.3

Nasal fracture.

Population Growth

The shift to agriculture led to many changes in human populations. A major change was the increase in population size, which in turn led to a greater reliance on agriculture, and ultimately to further population growth. The relationship between population size and agriculture is clear when considering the maximum size, or **carrying capacity,** of human populations. Hunting and gathering populations tend to be small, usually no more than a few dozen people, because there would not be enough food for more. Agriculture can support much larger populations.

carrying capacity The maximum population size capable of being supported in a given environment.

natural increase The number of births minus the number of deaths.

life expectancy at birth A measure of the average length of life for a newborn child.

life table A compilation of the age distribution of a population that provides an estimate of the probability that an individual will die by a certain age, used to compute life expectancy.

Why did agricultural populations become larger? Population growth results from the net effects of fertility, mortality, and migration. Births increase the population size, and deaths decrease the population size. Migration can either increase or decrease the population size, depending on whether more people move into a population or leave it. Ignoring migration for the moment, the change in population size because of **natural increase** is the number of births minus the number of deaths. If the number of births exceeds the number of deaths, then the population grows. If the number of births is less than the number of deaths, then the population declines.

The fact that the human species grew in numbers following the rise of agriculture suggests that this growth was due to an increase in fertility (more births per year), a decrease in mortality (fewer deaths per year), or both. There does not appear to have been a reduction in overall mortality, as assessed by estimates of the **life expectancy at birth,** a measure of the average length of life for a newborn child. Life expectancy at birth is derived by looking at a population's **life table,** which is the age distribution of members of a population that is used to compute the probability that someone will die by a certain age based on the current distribution of the age at death. Life tables are routinely used in demographic research (and by the insurance industry) and can be compiled for prehistoric populations by estimating from skeletal remains the age at death.

Hunting and gathering populations typically have a low life expectancy at birth—roughly 20–40 years (Cohen 1989). Keep in mind that the life expectancy at birth is an *average* length of life. The value of 20–40 years does *not* mean that everyone lives only 20–40 years total. Some live much longer, and others do not live this long. This average provides a crude index of overall health in a population. Skeletal evidence suggests that, in general, agricultural populations did not improve on this figure; in fact, in some cases, mortality rates actually increased and life expectancy at birth declined somewhat following the transition to agriculture. For example, analysis of skeletal remains from Dickson Mound, a prehistoric Native American site in Illinois, shows that life expectancy at birth was 26 years at a time when the people at Dickson Mound were exclusively hunter-gatherers but decreased to 19 years following the transition to agriculture (Cohen 1989). Such studies focus on *overall* mortality, however, and there is evidence for a reduction in *childhood* mortality during the transition to agriculture, which could contribute to population growth without having much impact on overall life expectancy (Pennington 1996; Sellen 2001).

The population growth that accompanied the agricultural revolution is often attributed to an increase in fertility. The traditional explanation is that the shift to a sedentary life and diet resulted in improved ovarian function and shorter intervals of breast-feeding. Studies of living hunter-gatherers have shown that breast-feeding has a contraceptive effect. When a woman nurses her child, hormonal changes take place that reduce the probability of ovulation (Wood 1994). Among some contemporary hunting-gathering populations, the women breast-feed for several years, contributing to a long interval between births—44 months on average among the !Kung of the Kalahari Desert in Africa (Potts 1988). The shift to agriculture resulted in foods being available to infants, which allowed for earlier weaning, and hence shorter intervals between children, leading to an increase in population size. In addition, there would be less need to carry dependent children. In nomadic populations, the need to carry children limits the number of dependent children; it is not easy to care for another child until the earlier children can walk on their own. The sedentary nature of agricultural populations may have allowed short birth intervals (Livi-Bacci 1997).

Disease

A popular myth is that life improved across the board when humans developed agriculture. Clearly, this is not the case. The transition to agriculture resulted in major shifts in the leading causes of disease and death, including an increase in infectious diseases and nutritional diseases, leading Jared Diamond (1992b) to consider agriculture a "mixed blessing."

Disease in Hunting-Gathering Populations   Before considering the effect of the transition to agriculture on disease, it is necessary to review briefly general patterns of health and disease in hunting-gathering populations. Information on health and disease in hunting-gathering populations has been obtained by studying the few remaining hunting-gathering societies and from studying prehistoric hunter-gatherers using the methods of paleopathology.

The two most common types of infectious disease in hunting-gathering populations are those due to parasites and those due to **zoonoses,** diseases that are transmitted from other animals to humans. Parasitic diseases may reflect the long-term evolutionary adaptation of different parasites to human beings. Among hunting-gathering societies, these parasites include lice and pinworms. The zoonoses are introduced through insect bites, animal wounds, and ingestion of contaminated meat. These diseases include sleeping sickness, tetanus, and schistosomiasis, among others (Armelagos and Dewey 1970). The prevalence of various parasitic and zoonotic diseases varies among different hunting-gathering environments. The disease microorganisms found in arctic or temperate environments are generally not found in tropical environments.

The spread of infectious diseases is often classified as being either epidemic or endemic. An **epidemic** pattern is one in which new cases of a disease spread quickly. A typical epidemic starts with a few new cases of a disease, increases geometrically (exponentially) in a short period of time as more people are infected, and then declines rapidly as the number of susceptible individuals declines. An **endemic** pattern shows a low but constant rate; a few cases are always present but no major spread occurs. In general, hunting-gathering populations do not experience epidemics because of two ecological factors associated with a hunting-gathering way of life: small population size and a nomadic lifestyle (Figure 17.4). Hunter-gatherers live in small groups of roughly 25–50 people that interact occasionally with other small groups in their region. Under such conditions, infectious diseases tend not to spread rapidly. There are simply not enough people to become infected to keep the

zoonose A disease transmitted directly to humans from other animals.

epidemic A pattern of disease rate when new cases of a disease spread rapidly through a population.

endemic A pattern of disease rate when new cases of a disease occur at a relatively constant but low rate over time.

FIGURE 17.4

!Kung women gathering vegetables. The small size and nomadic nature of hunting-gathering populations mean that infectious disease is endemic, not epidemic.

disease going at high rates. Without enough people to infect, the disease microorganisms die off. This does not apply to chronic infectious diseases, whose microorganisms can stay alive long enough to infect people coming into the group. Certain diseases caused by parasitic worms fall into this category. In such cases, the prevalence of infectious diseases does not increase rapidly. Although infectious diseases are the leading cause of death in some hunting-gathering populations (Howell 2000), the rate is *endemic*, not epidemic. The difference has to do with whether the deaths are concentrated in a short interval of time (epidemic) or not (endemic).

The noninfectious diseases common in industrial societies, such as heart disease, cancer, diabetes, and high blood pressure, are rare in hunting-gathering societies. Part of the reason for these low rates may be the diet and lifestyle of hunter-gatherers, but it is also because fewer individuals are likely to live long enough to develop these diseases. The nutrition of hunting-gathering populations is varied and provides a well-balanced diet low in fat and high in fiber. In fact, some researchers have suggested that people in Western society should emulate this diet to improve their health (Eaton et al. 1988). A major nutritional problem in hunting-gathering societies is the scarcity of food during hard times, such as droughts. The rate of malnutrition and starvation in most hunting-gathering groups is usually very low (Dunn 1968).

Apart from endemic infectious disease, what else accounts for the major causes of death in hunting-gathering societies? Injury deaths are one factor. In most environments, death can result from hunting injuries and burns. Depending on the specific environment, death can result from drowning, cold exposure, or heat stress. In some hunting-gathering populations, injuries are the leading cause of death (Dunn 1968). For females, an additional factor is death during childbirth.

FIGURE 17.5

Farmers planting rice. The larger size and sedentary nature of agricultural populations contribute to epidemics of infectious disease.

Infectious Disease in Agricultural Populations   The pattern of disease is different in agricultural populations. Agriculture allows larger population size and requires a sedentary life. The increased size and lack of mobility have certain implications for the spread of disease (Figure 17.5). Large populations with many susceptible individuals allow for rapid spread of short-lived microorganisms. Such conditions exist in agricultural populations because of increased population size and the increased probability of coming into contact with someone who has the disease. As a result, agricultural populations have often experienced epidemics of diseases such as smallpox, measles, and mumps. The size of a population needed to sustain an epidemic varies according to the disease. Some infectious diseases, such as measles, require very large populations for rapid spread.

A sedentary lifestyle increases the spread of infectious disease in other ways. Large populations living continuously in the same area accumulate sewage. Poor sanitation and contamination of the water supply increase the chance for epidemics.

Agricultural practices also cause ecological changes, making certain infectious diseases more likely. The introduction of domesticated animals adds to waste accumulation and provides the opportunity for further exposure to diseases carried by animals. Cultivation of the land can also increase the probability of contact with insects carrying disease microorganisms. For example, standing pools of water are created when forests are cleared for agriculture, creating an opportunity for an increase in the mosquito population that transmits malaria.

The use of feces for fertilization can also have an impact on rates of infectious disease. In addition to potential contamination from handling these waste products, the food grown in these fertilizers can become contaminated. This problem was so acute in South Korea that steps had to be taken to reduce the use of feces as fertilizer (Cockburn 1971). In addition, irrigation can lead to an increase in the spread of infectious disease. One of the major problems in tropical agricultural societies is the increased snail population that lives in irrigation canals and carries schistosomiasis. Irrigation can pass infectious microorganisms from one population to the next.

Nutritional Disease in Agricultural Populations   Although agriculture provides populations with the ability to feed more people, this way of life does not guarantee an improvement in nutritional quality. Extensive investment in a single food crop, such as rice or corn, may provide too limited a diet, and certain nutritional deficiency diseases can result. For example, populations relying extensively on corn as a prime food source may show an increase in pellagra (a disease caused by a deficiency in niacin) as well as protein deficiency. Dependency on highly polished (white) rice is often associated with protein and vitamin deficiencies (McElroy and Townsend 1989).

Perhaps the greatest problem associated with reliance on a single crop is that if that crop fails, starvation can result. The population has become so dependent on a major crop that if a drought or plague wipes it out, not enough food is left to feed the people. An example of this is the Great Famine in Ireland between 1846 and 1851. The population of Ireland had grown rapidly since the introduction of the potato in the early 1700s, which provided a nutritious food that was easy to grow. Marriage in Ireland was linked to land inheritance; owning land was often a prerequisite for marriage, and only one son tended to inherit. However, the introduction of the potato provided more efficient use of the land, which allowed families to subdivide their property and give more sons the opportunity to start a family. The population of Ireland grew rapidly, but this resulted in a precarious ecology. The potato crop was often destroyed by blight, and during the Great Famine, there were five continuous years of blight with no relief (Connell 1950). Roughly 1.5 million people died and another million left the country (Woodham-Smith 1962), starting a pattern of population decline that continued into the

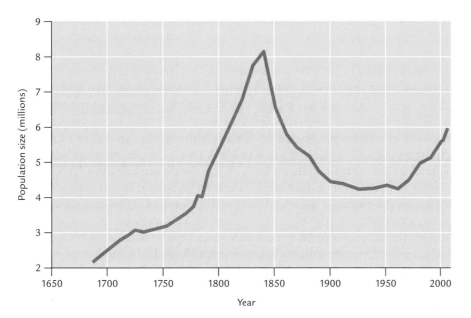

FIGURE 17.6

Population growth in Ireland, 1687–2006. Data from the two currently separate nations, the Republic of Ireland and Northern Ireland, have been pooled. (Data for 1687–1971 from Vaughan and Fitzpatrick 1978; for 1981–2006, from the Central Statistics Office, Ireland, www.cso.ie/, and the Northern Ireland Statistics and Research Agency, www.nisra.gov.uk/; 2006 is a projected figure for Northern Ireland based on 2004 data.)

twentieth century (Figure 17.6). The rapid increase in recent years is in part due to a high immigration rate (Population Reference Bureau 2006).

An agricultural diet can also lead to dental problems. The increased amount of starches in an agriculturalist's diet, combined with an increase in dirt and grit in the food, can lead to an increase in dental wear and cavities. Such changes are readily apparent in many studies of paleopathology (Cohen 1989; Larsen 2000).

THE BIOLOGICAL IMPACT OF CIVILIZATION

Following the origin and spread of agriculture in different parts of the world, a number of human populations began to develop urban centers and civilization as much as 6,000 years ago. As defined by archaeologists, a **civilization** is a large, state-level society that has a number of specific characteristics including large population size, high population density, urbanization, social stratification, food and labor surpluses, monumental architecture, and a system of record keeping (Feder 2000).

civilization A large, state-level society characterized by large population size, high population density, urbanization, social stratification, food and labor surpluses, monumental architecture, and record keeping.

Urbanization and Disease

Preindustrial cities date back several thousand years. Such cities often developed as market or administrative centers for a region, and their increased population size and density provided many opportunities for epidemics of infectious disease. In addition, a number of early cities had inadequate sewage disposal and contaminated water, both major factors increasing the spread of epidemics. To feed large numbers of people, food had to be brought in from the surrounding countryside and stored inside the city. In Europe during the Middle Ages, grain was often stored inside the house. Rats and other vermin had easy access to these foods and their populations increased, furthering the spread of disease. In preindustrial cities located in arid regions, grain was stored in ceramic containers, which limited the access of vermin.

Perhaps the best-known example of an epidemic disease in preindustrial cities is the bubonic plague in Europe during the fourteenth century. Bubonic plague, also known as the Black Death, is caused by a bacterium spread by fleas among field rodents. With the development of large urban areas and the corresponding large indoor rat populations, the disease spread to rats in the cities. As the rats died, the fleas jumped off them to find a new host, which was frequently a human being. The spread of bubonic plague during this time was **pandemic,** a widespread epidemic affecting large continental areas. Up to 20 million Europeans may have died from bubonic plague between 1346 and 1352 (McEvedy 1988). A major factor in the spread of plague was trade; rats would board ships sailing across the Mediterranean Sea and disembark at distant ports, infecting more rats and, ultimately, the human population. The ecological changes accompanying the development of urbanization in Europe provided an opportunity for the rapid spread of fleas and rats, and therefore the disease. Bubonic plague is still around today, including in the American Southwest, although treatment with antibiotics has kept the incidence of death close to zero.

Industrialization, which began more than 250 years ago, accelerated population growth in urban areas. Technological changes provided more efficient methods of agriculture and the means to support more people than in previous eras. Increased urbanization was accompanied initially by further spread of infectious diseases, compounded by problems in waste disposal. By the end of the nineteenth century, however, some populations had begun a transition wherein the rate of infectious disease declined and the rate of noninfectious disease increased. This shift in disease patterns was accompanied by a reduction in mortality, especially infant mortality, and an increase in life expectancy. In evolutionary terms, all of these changes are very recent.

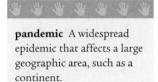

pandemic A widespread epidemic that affects a large geographic area, such as a continent.

Culture Contact

One consequence of expanding civilizations was an increase in long-distance contact with other societies through exploration, colonization, trade, and conquest. With the rise of European exploration in the 1500s, many previously separate human populations met one another. In addition to the vast cultural, economic, and political problems resulting from such contact, infectious diseases could now spread into populations that had no prior immune experience. The results were generally devastating.

The epidemiologic effects of culture contact have been documented for a number of populations, particularly Native Americans and Pacific Islanders. Many infectious diseases, such as smallpox, measles, and mumps, were introduced into the New World at this time, leading to massive loss of life in many populations (McNeill 1977; Cohen 1989). The actual impact of infectious disease varied across populations—some were hit much harder than others, and at different times (Larsen 1994). The overall impact was a severe reduction in population size across the Americas (Crawford 1998).

The flow of disease seems to have been primarily in one direction, from the Old World to the New World. The reason for this might have to do with the fact that there were fewer domesticated animals in the New World. These animals are often the initial source of diseases that infect humans (Diamond 1992a). One possible exception to this one-way flow of human disease is treponemal diseases, including venereal syphilis. Venereal syphilis (spread by sexual contact) increased rapidly in Europe after 1500, a date that coincides with the initial contact between New World and Old World populations. Following European settlement in the Americas, it was also noted that many Native Americans had syphilis. Did the disease evolve in Europe and then spread to the Americas? Or did it first appear in the New World and then spread to Europe? Or did it evolve independently in both the New World and the Old World? Evidence from paleopathology has shown that cases of treponemal disease occurred in the New World before European contact, suggesting a New World origin for venereal syphilis (Baker and Armelagos 1988). Recent research, however, has detected venereal syphilis in two English skeletons *before* European contact (von Hunnius et al. 2006), providing support for the hypothesis that syphilis evolved in *both* the New World and the Old World, prior to contact.

RECENT CHANGES

The past hundred years has seen dramatic shifts in our species. Industrialization and economic development have spread throughout much (but not all) of the world, resulting in major biological impacts on disease, mortality, fertility, and population growth. The exact changes experienced by a society are in part a reflection of its economic status. Demographers routinely classify nations into two groups: more developed countries (MDCs) and less developed countries (LDCs). Over much of the past century, the MDCs have seen a reduction in death rates and birth rates, a shift from infectious disease to noninfectious disease as the leading causes of death, a slowing (and in some cases a reversal) of population growth, and an aging population. The LDCs have seen some reduction in mortality and fertility, although infectious disease still dominates and birth rates remain high in parts of the world. Population growth continues at a high rate in many LDCs.

The Epidemiologic Transition

In the MDCs, life expectancy at birth has increased more than 50 percent, and the leading causes of death have shifted from infectious to noninfectious diseases. The increase in life expectancy and the shift from infectious to noninfectious diseases as the primary cause of death are a feature of the

FIGURE 17.7

Life expectancy at birth in the United States, 1900–2004. Life expectancy at birth increased over time, with the major exception of 1918, the year of an influenza pandemic. (Data for 1900–2003 from Arias 2006; for 2004, from Miniño et al. 2006.)

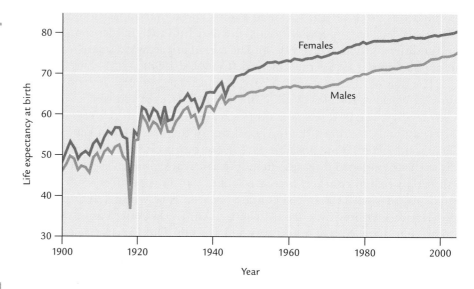

epidemiologic transition
The increase in life expectancy and the shift from infectious to noninfectious disease as the primary cause of death.

epidemiologic transition that has been observed in the MDCs and that is under way, to varying degrees, in the LDCs.

The Nature of the Epidemiologic Transition   According to the model developed by Omran (1977), a pretransition population has high death rates, particularly because of epidemics of childhood infectious disease. As public health, sanitation, and medical technologies improve, epidemics become less frequent and less intense. The overall death rate declines, and life expectancy at birth increases. Following the transition, the leading causes of death are primarily noninfectious rather than infectious diseases.

A major characteristic of the epidemiologic transition is the increase in life expectancy at birth. In the United States in 1900, life expectancy at birth was 47.3 years (Arias 2006), but by 2004, it had risen to 77.9 years (Miniño et al. 2006). Figure 17.7 shows life expectancy at birth for males and females in the United States from 1900 to 2004. Except for a major dip in 1918 (the year of a worldwide influenza pandemic), life expectancy at birth has continued to rise since 1900. Females tend to live longer, as reflected in their higher life expectancies; in 2004, the life expectancy of a newborn girl in the United States was 80.4 years, compared with 75.2 years for a newborn boy (Miniño et al. 2006).

The increase in life expectancy is not limited to the more developed societies. Other groups undergoing modernization and the epidemiologic transition have also shown an increase, such as the residents of the modernizing population of American Samoa. From 1950 to 1980, life expectancy at birth increased 10 years for males and 18 years for females (Crews 1989).

A controversial topic today is the extent to which life expectancy can be expected to increase in developed societies. Based on statistical analysis of death rates, Olshansky and colleagues (1990, 2001) argue that even with major reductions in chronic disease, life expectancy at birth will not increase

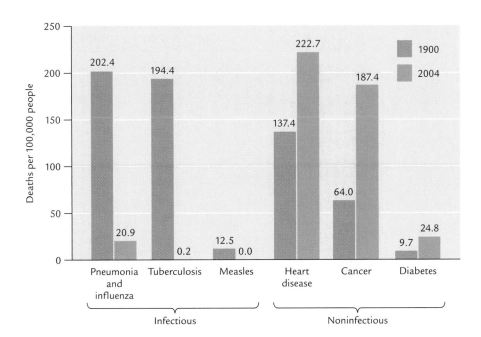

FIGURE 17.8

Death rates (per 100,000 people) for selected infectious and noninfectious diseases in the United States, 1900 and 2004. Note the decrease in infectious disease and the increase in noninfectious disease. (Data for 1900 from Centers for Disease Control and Prevention, www.cdc.gov/nchs/data/statab/lead1900_98.pdf, and Molnar 1998 for measles and diabetes; for 2004, from Miniño et al. 2006.)

past 85 years of age because the decline in mortality rates will slow down. Others, however, suggest that mortality rates will continue to decline and that life expectancy at birth could reach as high as 90 years of age in some developed nations by the year 2050 (Tuljapurkar et al. 2000).

The increase in life expectancy is related to a dramatic decline in deaths due to infectious diseases. Infants and young children are at greater risk for such diseases, and a large number of deaths in this age group lowers the average length of life in a population. As infectious disease death rates decline, the average length of life increases. A consequence of people living longer is that the death rate from degenerative noninfectious diseases, such as cancer and heart disease, begins to rise. Thus, there was a shift from infectious to noninfectious diseases as the primary causes of death. In the United States in 1900, the top three causes of death were all infectious diseases: pneumonia/influenza, tuberculosis, and diarrheal diseases. In 2004, the top three causes of death were all degenerative diseases: heart disease, cancer, and stroke (Miniño et al. 2006).

Figure 17.8 illustrates this dramatic shift by comparing the mortality rate (deaths per 100,000 people) for selected diseases in the United States in 1900 and in 2004. Note the tremendous decline in infectious disease mortality and the increase in noninfectious diseases. As we continue to live longer, we are more likely to die from a degenerative noninfectious disease. The major health problems today are quite different from what they were only several generations in the past, when infectious diseases were the primary cause of death. Figure 17.9 shows the 10 leading causes of death in the United States in 2004. Heart disease and cancer are the two major causes of death, accounting for 50 percent of all deaths. Only two of the top 10 causes of death are due to infectious disease: pneumonia/influenza and septicemia (blood poisoning). Heart disease, cancer,

FIGURE 17.9

The 10 leading causes of
death in the United States,
2004. (Data from Miniño et al.
2006.)

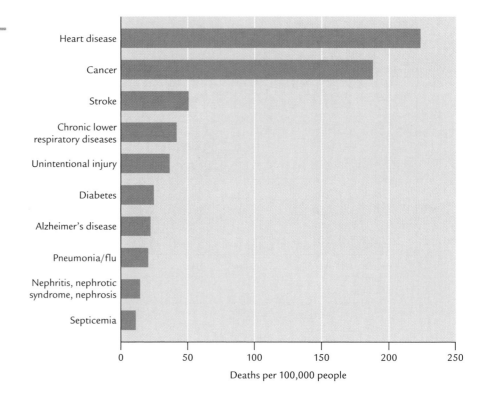

Deaths per 100,000 people

and stroke are likely to remain the major causes of death in the near future, but the other leading causes may change rapidly, primarily due to new technologies and aggressive public health measures.

It is important to remember that these figures for the United States are also typical of other nations that have undergone the epidemiologic transition, but not typical of the entire world. Infectious disease remains a leading cause of death in many human populations, particularly among the LDCs. Figure 17.10 shows the leading causes of death worldwide, illustrating that infectious disease is still a leading cause of death in the human species. HIV infection, which has dropped in the United States, remains high elsewhere in the world and is the sixth-leading cause of death in our species. The magnitude of infectious disease is even more apparent when considering the leading causes of death in the LDCs. For example, Figure 17.11 shows that the leading cause of death in Africa is HIV/AIDS, accounting for more than 20 percent of all deaths in Africa, compared with less than 1 percent of all deaths in the United States (World Health Organization 2004; Miniño et al. 2006). Population differences in disease and death are due to differences in the level of economic development and public health measures, and different populations are at different points in the epidemiologic transition.

Causes of the Epidemiologic Transition   What has caused these rapid changes in disease rates and life expectancy? Cultural changes in industrial societies have often resulted in major improvements in health care, public

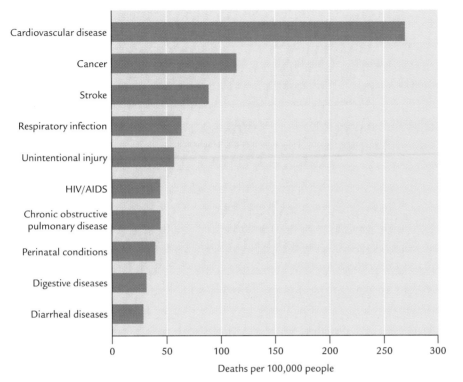

FIGURE 17.10

The 10 leading causes of death in the world, 2002. (Data from World Health Organization 2004.)

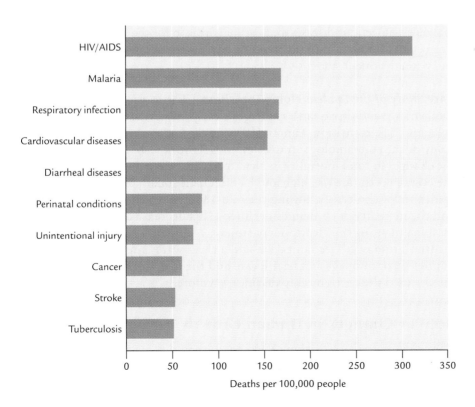

FIGURE 17.11

The 10 leading causes of death in Africa, 2002. (Data from World Health Organization 2004.)

FIGURE 17.12

Changes in the death rate in New York City during the nineteenth and twentieth centuries. (*Source:* Omran 1977:12. Courtesy Population Reference Bureau, Inc., Washington, D.C.)

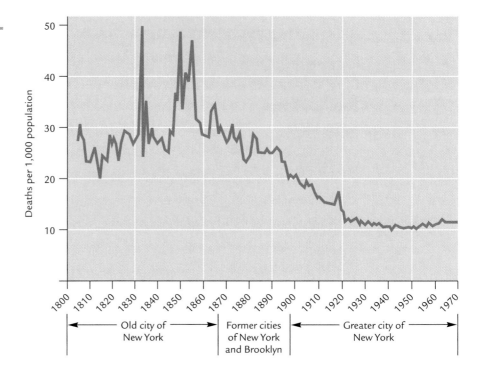

sanitation, and water quality. These factors aid in reducing the spread and effect of infectious diseases, particularly in infancy. Advances in medical technology, such as antibiotics and vaccination, have continued to help reduce the death rate due to infectious diseases, but the main reason for the initial decline was a cleaner environment brought about by civil engineering—particularly sewers and water treatment systems.

Case Study of the Epidemiologic Transition   The relationship between cultural change and disease rates emerges clearly in specific case studies of the epidemiologic transition. Omran (1977) looked at overall death rates in his study of the epidemiologic transition in New York City. Figure 17.12 shows the changes in total mortality in New York City over time. Before the 1860s, the overall death rate was high and had frequent spikes, primarily because of epidemics of cholera. Following the mid-1860s, both the overall death rate and the intensity of epidemics declined. This decrease corresponds to the establishment of the Health Department. After the 1920s, the continued incorporation of better sanitation and a clean water supply, along with an improvement in drugs and health care and the introduction of pasteurized milk, caused the death rates to decline even more.

Secular Changes in Human Growth

The epidemiologic transition affects more than disease and death rates; its effects have also been observed in studies of child growth. Since the turn of the twentieth century, many industrialized nations have shown several secular

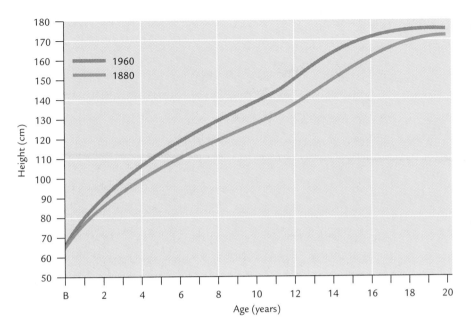

FIGURE 17.13

Secular change in European American males in North America. At all ages, the males living in 1960 have greater height than those who lived in 1880. (*Source:* Adapted from *Growth and Development* by Robert M. Malina, © 1975, publisher Burgess Publishing Company. Used by permission.)

changes in child growth. A **secular change** is simply a change in the pattern of growth across generations.

Types of Secular Change Three basic secular changes have been observed over the past century: an increase in height, an increase in weight, and a decrease in the age of sexual maturation. Children in many industrialized nations are taller and heavier today than children the same age were a century or so ago. Figure 17.13 shows the average distance curve for height of North American males of European ancestry in 1880 and 1960. There is no noticeable difference in body length at birth. Note, however, that at all postnatal ages the 1960 males are consistently taller than the 1880 males. This difference is most noticeable during adolescence. Comparison of distance curves for weight shows the same pattern.

Another secular change is a decrease in the age of maturation. This is most apparent in a specific measure of human development—the **age at menarche,** the age at which a female experiences her first menstrual period. Figure 17.14 plots the average age at menarche for the United States and several Western European nations over time. The general trend is one of earlier biological maturation.

Causes of Secular Change The basic secular changes observed in industrialized nations during the past century reflect environmental change. These changes came too fast and were too pervasive to be due to genetic change; rather, environmental changes have enabled more people to reach their genetic potential for growth. These trends, however, should not be projected indefinitely into the future. Some data suggest that the secular changes in height, weight, and age at menarche have slowed down or stopped in some countries

secular change A change in the average pattern of growth of development in a population over several generations.

age at menarche The age at which a female experiences her first menstrual period.

FIGURE 17.14

Secular change in age at menarche (the age of a female's first menstrual period) in the United States and several Western European countries. (*Source:* Adapted from *Growth and Development* by Robert M. Malina, © 1975, publisher Burgess Publishing Company. Used by permission.)

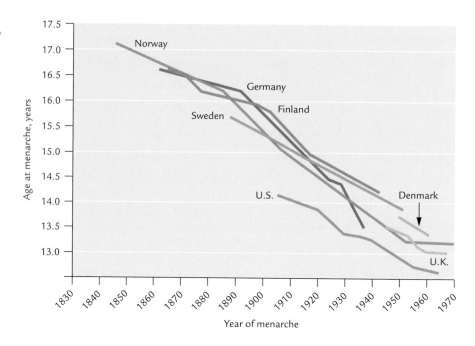

(Eveleth and Tanner 1990). Future environmental improvements could enable more and more children to reach their genetic potential for growth, but we should not expect average heights of 8 ft or more in another hundred years!

Many environmental factors have been suggested as being responsible for these secular changes, including improved nutrition, reduction of childhood infectious disease, improved availability of health care, improved standard of living, and reduction of family size. Many of these factors are interrelated, making precise identification of causes difficult. Malina (1979) has noted that improved nutrition is often cited as a primary cause of the observed secular changes. Though nutritional intake has improved for many people, especially during infancy, Malina does not think it is solely responsible for secular changes and argues that one of the most important factors was an improvement in health conditions resulting in the reduction in childhood infectious diseases. Thus, the epidemiologic transition appears to be related to secular changes in human growth as well.

The Reemergence of Infectious Disease

The success in reducing infectious disease in developed nations during the first half of the twentieth century gave rise to an overly optimistic view that *all* infectious diseases would be eliminated by the year 2000. Smallpox, once a killer of millions, had been eliminated by 1977, and polio and tuberculosis were close behind. This view is now known to be incorrect; despite our efforts, new infectious diseases are emerging, and old ones are coming back in new forms (Garrett 1994). A dramatic example occurred in May 1995 with the outbreak of a frequently fatal disease, Ebola, in the Democratic Republic of the Congo (then known as Zaire) in Africa. Although the Ebola virus was discovered only in 1976, previous epidemics had killed hundreds of people in Zaire and Uganda (Cowley et al. 1995).

Emergent Infectious Disease   This outbreak was not an isolated event. There are many other examples of **emergent infectious diseases,** newly evolved diseases that have appeared only in the past few decades, including Legionnaire's disease, Korean hemorrhagic fever, Hantavirus, and HIV (Armelagos et al. 1996).

The emergence of new diseases shows the evolution of microorganisms, a process often exacerbated by environmental changes brought about by human populations. New environments are created by rapid deforestation and conversion of land for cultivation and industrialization. Conversion of remote and isolated habitats provides the opportunity for previously rare microorganisms to encounter the human species. Continued pollution can increase the mutation rate of microorganisms in addition to interfering with ecosystems. New forms of quick travel, such as jet planes, and international commerce increase the amount of contact between human groups, enabling diseases to spread quickly and to new populations, many of which have no prior immune experience. New technologies often lend themselves to the emergence of infectious diseases by creating new microenvironments conducive to bacterial spread. Air conditioning, for example, has been implicated in the origin and spread of Legionnaire's disease. Cultural and environmental changes have provided new opportunities for the evolution of microorganisms (Garrett 1994; Levins et al. 1994).

Reemergent Infectious Disease   An additional problem is **reemergent infectious diseases,** which are infectious diseases that have evolved resistance to antibiotics. Tuberculosis, for example, is a respiratory disease that had been treated very successfully with antibiotics in the last half of the twentieth century, but tuberculosis rates began to increase in the 1980s and 1990s. Figure 17.15 shows tuberculosis rates in New York, a state hard hit by an increase in tuberculosis in the early 1990s. This increase was due to a number

emergent infectious disease A newly identified infectious disease that has recently evolved.

reemergent infectious disease Infectious disease that had previously been reduced but that increases in frequency when microorganisms evolve resistance to antibiotics.

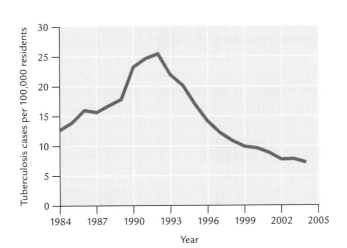

FIGURE 17.15

Tuberculosis rates in New York State, 1984–2004. (Data from New York Department of Health, www.health.state.ny.us/nysdoh/epi/mainrpt.htm.)

of factors, including the outbreak of antibiotic-resistant strains of the bacterium. Aggressive public health measures have reversed this trend, but it remains a problem for many residents and illustrates the danger of bacteria evolving resistance to antibiotics.

Antibiotic resistance illustrates the principle of natural selection applied to disease-causing microorganisms. Sometimes a mutant form of bacteria exists that is resistant to a specific antibiotic. Although most bacteria are killed, the mutant form will multiply and become more common in successive generations of bacteria. Because bacteria have short life spans, an antibiotic-resistant form of bacteria can spread very quickly. The problem of reemergence of infectious diseases is linked to indiscriminate use of antibiotics for treating illness in humans and the increasing use of antibiotics in animal feed (Armelagos et al. 1996). As these practices have increased, so have antibiotic-resistant forms of bacteria. This problem has required development of new antibiotics, which in turn leads to new forms of antibiotic resistance.

The problems of emergent and reemergent infectious diseases show us that infectious disease is not gone, and is unlikely ever to be gone. We will always have to deal with infectious disease, but the nature of this threat will change over time as the microorganisms continue to evolve and as we continue to change our environment. The ongoing struggle against infectious disease will require increased funding, global coordination, and a holistic approach to cultural, environmental, and technological factors affecting the spread of infectious disease (Binder et al. 1999).

Demographic Change

The reduction in death rates and the increase in life expectancy in much of the world have obvious implications for population growth. The natural increase of our species reflects the difference between the rate of births and deaths. If death rates drop but birth rates remain the same, a population will grow in size. This is what happened to our species during the twentieth century, when the world population more than tripled in size from less than 2 billion to 6.5 billion and counting (Figure 17.16).

The Demographic Transition   What led to such high rates of population growth in our species and to the variability in growth rates among nations today? As death rates dropped, there was a lag before birth rates also declined, resulting in a time of significant population growth. Observations of these demographic patterns in a number of European countries led to the development of **demographic transition theory.** The utility of this model to explain and predict demographic shifts in all human populations has been questioned (e.g., Cohen 1995), but it does provide a convenient summary of some basic demographic trends.

Demographic transition theory states that as a population becomes more economically developed, a reduction in death rates will take place first, followed by a reduction in fertility rates. Three stages are usually identified in this model (Swedlund and Armelagos 1976). Stage 1 populations are those

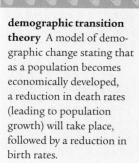

demographic transition theory A model of demographic change stating that as a population becomes economically developed, a reduction in death rates (leading to population growth) will take place, followed by a reduction in birth rates.

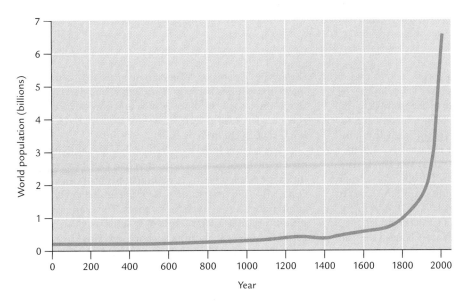

FIGURE 17.16

World population growth over the past 2,000 years. Rapid growth began after the eighteenth century. (Data for 1–1940 from Weeks 2005; for 1950–2005, from U.S. Census Bureau, www.census.gov/ipc/www/worldpop.html, database revision of April 26, 2005; for 2006, from Population Reference Bureau 2006.)

of undeveloped areas with high mortality and high fertility rates. Because the high number of births is balanced by the high number of deaths, the overall population size remains more or less stable. In stage 2, the transitional stage, demographic and economic factors are changing rapidly, and there is high fertility but lowered mortality. The transition to lowered mortality, especially in childhood, is a consequence of improvements in public health and medical technology. Because fertility rates remain high, there are more births than deaths, and the population grows quickly in size. Stage 3 populations have completed the transition with a reduction in fertility rates. Because of technological, social, economic, and education changes, people in the MDCs have more of a desire and opportunity to control family size, and the birth rate declines. Because the rates of both births and deaths are low, such populations tend to show little growth (ignoring migration).

The demographic transition model does describe the experience seen in some of the MDCs today, but it has a number of problems. Although it serves as a rough description of the types of changes that tend to take place as populations become more economically developed, there is considerable variation in the timing of these events, with some populations having less of a lag between falling death rates and falling birth rates than others. The model is less accurate in predicting the timing of fertility declines, and the assumption that economic development must occur before a decline in mortality rate does not fit all cases (Cohen 1995). There are also cases of the basic trends reversing, such as in the United States in the twentieth century, when fertility rates declined at first and then increased rapidly for a short time following World War II before falling again (see Special Topic box).

World Population Growth   In mid-2006, the world numbered over 6.5 billion people and had a rate of natural increase of 1.2 percent per year. At this rate, the world's population will double in 58 years. The MDCs, with roughly 19

The Baby Boom

A classic example of how changing social and economic factors affect population growth is the "Baby Boom" in the United States. At the beginning of the twentieth century, fertility rates in the United States had begun to decline, as expected under a demographic transition. In 1909, the fertility rate (the number of births per 1,000 women of reproductive age, 15–44 years) was 127. By the end of World War II, this number had declined to 85 per 1,000. As shown in the accompanying graph, the fertility rate *increased* dramatically after World War II, peaking at 123 in 1957, after which there was a subsequent decline.

This temporary increase in fertility is labeled the Baby Boom, a term for the generation of children born between 1946 and 1964, a period of high fertility relative to prewar years. Several social and economic factors account for the Baby Boom. It was not simply that men returning from the war made up for lost time with their wives. Such an effect often accompanies the end of a war, but the Baby Boom lasted much longer. The economic growth of the United States continued following World War II. As economic growth increases, so does the demand for labor. This demand is often met by new immigrants in a population. In the United States, however, restrictive laws had reduced the number of immigrants. The pool of available labor was also reduced by the fact that there had been fewer births during the 1920s and 1930s, perhaps in part due to the Great Depression. Thus, fewer men were available to meet the increased demand. Women tended to be locked out of many occupations because of sex bias. Though it is true that women took the place of men in the workforce during the war, afterward the preference for women to remain at home raising children prevailed.

The relative lack of available labor meant that young men returning from the war often had excellent opportunities for employment. A good income meant that men could afford to marry and raise families earlier than they could under different circumstances. The economic conditions prevailing after World War II meant that a couple could have several children without lowering their standard of living (Weeks 2005). People married earlier, and the spacing between births was shorter than in previous times, both of which contributed to an increase in the birth rate. Of course, not everyone married or had larger families or even shared in economic growth. On average, however, these changes were sufficient to affect the birth rate, and therefore the rate of population growth.

After 1958, the fertility rate in the United States began to decline. By the mid-1960s, the Baby Boom was over. From this point on, changing economic conditions and greater educational and economic opportunities contributed to delayed marriage and childbirth, as well as the desire for smaller families. By the mid-1980s, the fertility rate had dropped to 65 per 1,000, and the average number of children per couple was less than replacement

percent of the world's population, have low birth and death rates. Estimates in mid-2006 show a very low annual rate of natural increase of 0.1 percent in the MDCs, and their total population is expected to increase by only 4 percent by the year 2050. The LDCs, with 81 percent of the world's population, have a rate of natural increase of 1.5 percent per year, and their total population size is expected to increase by 50 percent by the year 2050 (Population Reference Bureau 2006).

There is variation in growth rates around the world. For example, China (an LDC) has a rate of natural increase of 0.6 percent per year, whereas sub-Saharan Africa has a rate of 2.4 percent per year. This rapid growth is due in large part to high fertility; the average woman in sub-Saharan Africa will have 5.5 children during her lifetime (Population Reference Bureau 2006). Some countries in Europe have negative growth rates and are actually losing population due to continued low fertility rates (Lutz et al. 2003).

There are two critical and interrelated questions regarding the growth of the human species: (1) What will global population size be in the immediate

Changes in fertility rate in the United States, 1909–2005. The fertility rate is the number of births per 1,000 women of reproductive age (15–44 years). From the start of the twentieth century, the fertility rate declined until the end of World War II, at which point it increased rapidly to give rise to the Baby Boom, and then declined afterward. (Data for 1901–1980 from the Centers for Disease Control and Prevention, www.cdc.gov/nchs/data/statab/t1x0197.pdf; for 1981–2003, from Martin et al. 2005; for 2004–2005, from Munson and Sutton 2006.)

(i.e., fewer than 2 children per couple). Of course, the United States continues to grow in part because so many women were born during the Baby Boom (and in part due to immigration). Even if the average number of children born per woman is less than 2, the sheer number of women will continue to lead to population growth in the short term. In fact, the total number of births in the United States rose starting in 1977 and peaked in 1990 (Gabriel 1995). This short burst of births is often referred to as the "Baby Boomlet," brought about by the fact that so many of the original Baby Boomers were now in their childbearing years. Thus, the Baby Boom continues to affect fertility levels and population growth a generation later.

future? and (2) How many people can the planet support? Estimates of future population size are difficult to make because the factors underlying population growth continue to change. If rates were constant, prediction of future numbers would be a simple mathematical exercise. For example, given a world population of 6.5 billion and assuming that the rate of growth observed in mid-2005 remains the same (1.2 percent per year), the expected size of the human species would be 11.1 billion in the year 2050 and 20.2 billion in the year 2100. This estimate would be inaccurate, however, because it assumes that the rate of growth will remain constant and that rates of the underlying components of growth (mortality and fertility) will remain constant. This is not the case; analysis of recent global demographic trends shows that the global rate of population growth is slowing (Lutz et al. 1997). Indeed, the lesson from studies of the epidemiologic and demographic transitions is that such rates have *not* stayed the same in recent times. According to current midrange estimates, based on trends in fertility reduction and other factors, the world's population will be somewhat more than 9 billion by the year 2050 (U.S. Census Bureau 2004; Population Reference Bureau 2006).

FIGURE 17.17

The age–sex structure of Chad in 2000, drawn to the same scale as Figures 17.18 and 17.19 for comparison. (Data from U.S. Census Bureau International Database, www.census.gov/ipc/www/idbpyr.html, database revision of April 26, 2005.)

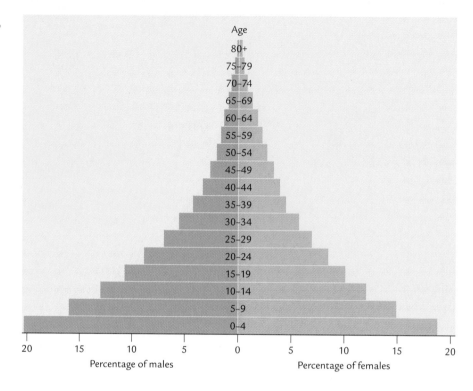

The question of global carrying capacity (the number of people that the earth can support) is also complex. An answer must take into account a number of variables that are difficult at best to estimate, including future economic, political, and technological changes. In addition, we also need to consider these factors in relationship to a desired standard of living; the actual number would be higher if we assume a level of bare subsistence, which is not desirable, as compared with a higher standard of living (Bouvier and Bertrand 1999). Cohen (1995) reviewed the history of answers to the question of global carrying capacity and found a wide range. Most estimates range from 4 billion to 16 billion, although some were as low as 1 billion. Cohen concludes that the range of likely values is dependent primarily on food and water supply.

Implications of Changing Age Structure   The demographic transition of decreasing mortality and fertility rates affects not only the size of human populations but also their composition. A major effect of a transition is on the age structure of a population. Most demographic studies look at the number of males and females in different age groups in a population—the **age-sex structure** of a population. A device known as a **population pyramid** is the best way to describe a population's age-sex structure at a particular point in time. The population pyramid is a graph showing the percentage of both sexes at different age groups, normally at five-year intervals (e.g., 0–4 years of age, 5–9 years of age, and so forth).

The population pyramid looks different in less developed and more developed countries. Figure 17.17 shows the population pyramid (age structure)

age-sex structure The number of males and females in different age groups of a population.

population pyramid A diagram of the age-sex structure of a population.

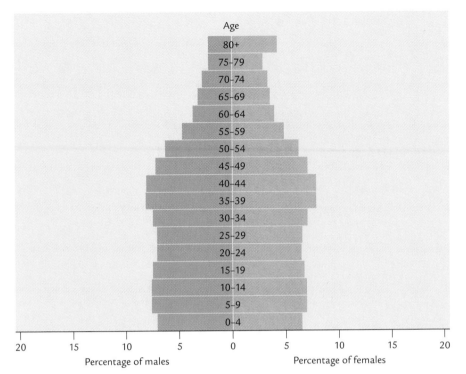

Age

FIGURE 17.18

The age-sex structure of the United States in 2000, drawn to the same scale as Figures 17.17 and 17.19 for comparison. (Data from U.S. Census Bureau International Database, www.census.gov/ipc/www/idbpyr .html, database revision of April 26, 2005.)

Percentage of males   Percentage of females

of Chad, an LDC in Africa. The bottom axis of the graph shows the percentage of males on the left and the percentage of females on the right. The vertical axis represents different age groups, from 0–4 years of age at the bottom to 80+ years of age at the top. The population pyramid has a true pyramid shape, broad on the bottom and tapering to a small point at the top. Note that the largest segment of society is infants and young children, which is characteristic of a population with high fertility rates. Because the majority of the population in Chad are infants and children, with fewer elderly people, the median age is 16 years (i.e., half the population is younger than 16 and half is older than 16). Only 3 percent of the population are 65 years of age or older.

By contrast, Figure 17.18 shows the age-sex structure of the United States in 2000 as an example of an MDC with lower fertility rates. The graph looks more like a rectangle than a pyramid. Fewer births mean a decreasing base, which carries over to the next age group over time. The median age of the United States in 2000 was 35 years, with 12 percent of the population age 65 or older. Note the greater proportion of females than males among the elderly, a reflection of the greater longevity of women. The graph also shows a noticeable bulge corresponding to people in their mid-30s to late 40s. This is the Baby Boom generation discussed in this chapter's Special Topic box. A rise in the birth rate in the United States occurred between 1946 and 1964, and by the year 2000, these babies were between 36 and 54 years of age. As this generation continues to age, this bulge will move upward on the population pyramid. Figure 17.19 shows the projected age-sex structure for the United States in the year 2050. The lower birth rates will continue to make

FIGURE 17.19

The projected age-sex structure of the United States in 2025, drawn to the same scale as Figures 17.17 and 17.18 for comparison. (Data from U.S. Census Bureau International Database, www.census.gov/ipc/www/idbpyr .html, database revision of April 26, 2005.)

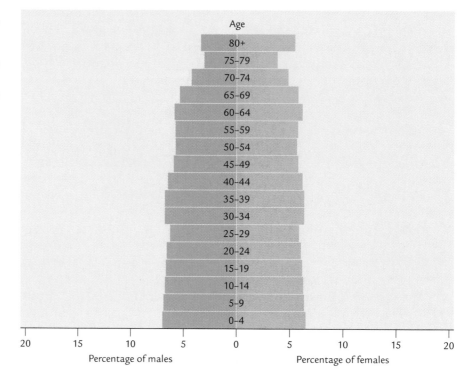

the shape of the graph even more rectangular in appearance. Median age in the year 2050 is projected to be 39 years, with an estimated 21 percent of the population age 65 or older.

We can expect many cultural changes to accompany such a shift to an older population. Many of these shifts are apparent today in the United States. For example, if we assume current average ages for retirement, there will be fewer people of working age in the future. Such a shift might be seen as having both advantages and disadvantages. A smaller labor pool might mean better economic opportunities for working-age people. On the other hand, we may also expect greater taxation to help provide for the well-being of the retired portion of the population.

Many questions are being asked by those concerned with social and economic shifts. For example, how well will our Social Security system function when more people are drawing from it? What changes need to be made in the insurance industries? How can we provide adequate health and other care to an aging population?

Economic shifts can also be examined. Perhaps one of the best examples of the effects of changing age structure is in our system of higher education. During the 1960s and early 1970s, as more and more Baby Boomers reached college age, the demand for colleges and universities increased. This demand was accompanied by an increased desire for a college education, in part because of a changing economy and the value of a college degree in terms of earning potential. As college enrollments increased, more schools were built, and more faculty and staff were hired. By the mid-1970s, the effects of the

Baby Boom were over, and enrollments began to diminish at many institutions. How, then, can we afford to maintain our colleges? Increases in tuition and taxes are remedies, but they are generally not popular. Should schools be closed? If so, what happens to the local economies, which are often highly dependent on these schools? What about the future? If we cut back on programs now, will we need to start them up again in a few years?

These questions have no easy answers. Awareness of the problems and their connections to a variety of economic, social, and political factors is a step in the right direction. Today's world is marked by high level of rapid change. A society's successful integration of demographic change requires analysis of current trends and, above all, a basic acknowledgment that, for good or ill, these changes are indeed taking place.

Summary

The evolution of the human species continues to the present day. Although biological change continues in human populations, the rate of such change is most often exceeded by the rapid rate of cultural change. Over the past 12,000 years, the human species has moved from hunting and gathering to agriculture to feed itself, and the total size of the human species has increased roughly a thousandfold. These rapid cultural changes have influenced aspects of human biology by affecting our patterns of health, physical growth, nutrition, mortality, and fertility, among other things. The transition to agriculture represented a major change in human adaptation, and the domestication of plants and animals provided the opportunity to maintain much larger populations, which in turn allowed for the development of complex state-level societies. Larger sedentary populations led to many epidemics of infectious disease. Although more food could be produced, many people in early agricultural societies suffered from nutritional stress. Overall, life expectancy did not increase with the origins of agriculture.

The subsequent rise of state-level societies with large urban populations was accompanied by further epidemics and nutritional problems. Exploration, trade, and conquest led to contact between cultures that had been isolated previously, resulting in catastrophic epidemics and social upheaval. By the end of the nineteenth century, modernization had begun the epidemiologic transition, whereby improvements in public health and civil engineering, later supplemented by improvements in medical science, led to a reduction in deaths from infectious diseases and a dramatic increase in life expectancy at birth.

As people lived longer on average, the death rate due to noninfectious degenerative diseases increased. In the more developed countries, children mature faster and grow larger because of changes in disease and diet. Recent decades have seen a resurgence in infectious diseases, in part due to the evolution of new diseases and in part due to the reemergence of diseases as microorganisms evolve resistance to antibiotics. The world's population tripled in size during the twentieth century as death rates declined. Many populations have since seen a reduction in fertility rates, such that the rate of population growth has declined somewhat. Even given this trend, most projections suggest a global population of roughly 9 billion by the middle of the twenty-first century. Another consequence of recent demographic change is the changing age structure of the more developed countries. As birth rates decline, populations become older on average. All of these demographic changes are interrelated with many contemporary social, economic, and political problems.

Supplemental Readings

Cohen, J. E. 1995. *How Many People Can the Earth Support?* New York: W. W. Norton. A comprehensive discussion of the demographic history of the human species, population projection, and global carrying capacity.

Howell, N. 2000. *Demography of the Dobe !Kung,* 2d ed. New York: Aldine de Gruyter. An extensive description of the demography of a hunting-gathering society focusing on mortality and fertility.

Larsen, C. S. 2000. *Skeletons in Our Closet: Revealing Our Past through Bioarchaeology.* Princeton, N.J.: Princeton University Press. A detailed survey of the field of paleopathology and what it can tell us about disease and life in prehistoric times, focusing on the transition to agriculture and on culture contact among prehistoric Native Americans.

Weeks, J. R. 2005. *Population: An Introduction to Concepts and Issues,* 9th ed. Belmont, Calif.: Wadsworth. A comprehensive review of the field of demography.

VIRTUAL EXPLORATIONS

Visit our textbook-specific online learning center Web site at **www.mhhe.com/relethford7** to access the exercises that follow.

1. **Indian/Non-Indian Life Expectancy: The Future of Health Care in Canada** http://www.findarticles.com/p/articles/mi_qa4014/ is_200301/ai_n9344253. In an article originally appearing in *Inroads* in 2003, John Richards discusses the Canadian government Health Department's First Nations and Inuit Health Branch and the programs it administers for First Nations and Inuit Canadians. During the "Red Power" period in the late 1960s, the Canadian government proposed and then tabled a plan to end the legal distinction between Indians and other Canadians.

   - Richards states that "communal features of culture are more important to Aboriginals than analogous cultural features are to non-Aboriginal Canadians." What does that statement mean to you?
   - Anthropological ideas, according to Richards, have served as a mixed blessing to First Nations and Inuit people in Canada, helping not only to define these Indigenous people, but also to point out the need for self-government and highlight their lack of power for self-determination in terms of treaty rights.

- As traditional hunter-gatherers, how have Indigenous people in Canada been effected by twentieth-century economic and social change?
- Does this concur with the discussion of hunting and gathering populations in your text?
- How has this rapid change impacted Indigenous people in Canada in terms of life expectancy? How did the gap between Indigenous and non-Indigenous peoples change in the second half of the twentieth-century?

Now go to the **Romanow Commission Report on the Future of Health Care in Canada:** http://www.hc-sc.gc.ca/english/pdf/romanow/pdfs/HCC_Chapter_10.pdf. The link discusses the Commission's 2003 Section Report specifically covering First Nations and Inuit people: "A New Approach to Aboriginal Health Care."

- Does the report give any indication that the unique health issues facing Indigenous people in Canada are being addressed?
- What specific objectives are recommended by the Commission?
- How does the non-Aboriginal community view the situation?
- What contrast do the several tables show concerning life expectancy?

2. **The Epidemiologic Transition** http://www.pitt.edu~/super1/lecture/lec0022/index.htm. Follow the slides from the University of Pittsburgh on "The Epidemiologic Transition." Click the start button and then use the arrows in the upper left to advance.

- How do mortality rates, population growth, and life expectancy change over the epidemiologic transition?
- How is disease related to socioeconomic status (SES)?
- What will be the most common fatal diseases in the future?
- Where does our current society lie in the epidemiologic transition?
- How do you explain the different rates for different socioeconomic groups?

3. **Why Menopause? Why Women's Reproductive Life Span Has a Limit, Whereas Men's Doesn't** http://calbears.findarticles.com/p/articles/mi_m1134/is_n6_v107/ai_21031845. Read this review of the original 1998 *Natural History* article by Craig Parker. In it, Parker considers a possible evolutionary advantage of female menopause. This is sometimes referred to as the "Grandmother Theory."

- What are some of the possibilities considered for the evolutionary advantages of menopause?
- Why do certain genetic traits that inflict damage persist in the general population?
- Most of us are somewhat familiar with the "risky childbirth" hypothesis. Is there a genetic explanation for this?
- List the shortcomings of the adaptive hypotheses of menopause.

- Anthropologists Kristen Hawkes and Nick Blurton-Jones have an explanation that may account for the selective advantage of menopause in hunter-gatherer societies. What is it?
- Is there a counter-argument for this hypothesis?

4. **Around the Indus in 90 Slides**   http://www.harappa.com/indus/ indus0.html. Go to "Around the Indus in 90 Slides" by Jonathan Kenoyer from the Harappa Web site, which is dedicated to the ancient cities of Harappa and Mohenjo-Daro (around 2600 B.C.) in Pakistan. Click on "Experience the Slide Show." Follow the slides, paying particular attention to the sewage and sanitation features of Harappa and Mohenjo-Daro.

- This is one of the earliest urban cities in the world. How did the inhabitants handle sewage and public health?
- Did these cities have effective tools to combat new, dangerous infectious diseases?
- How would the sanitation facilities of these cities compare to those of modern industrialized cities?
- How would you estimate the health of the inhabitants of Harappa and Mohenjo-Daro? What evidence would you need to test your hypothesis about the health of an early urban community?

THE FUTURE
OF OUR SPECIES

This book has focused on human biological variation and evolution, past and present. What about the future? Can biological anthropology, or indeed any science, make predictions about the future of our species? What directions might our biological and cultural evolution take?

One thing is certain—we continue to evolve both biologically and culturally, and will do so in the future. Human evolution is increasingly complex because of our biocultural nature. Much of our adaptive nature is culturally based. We can adapt to a situation more quickly through cultural evolution than through biological evolution. Theoretically, we can also direct our cultural evolution. We can focus our efforts on solutions to specific problems, such as finding a vaccine for AIDS or developing ways to further reduce dental decay. Biological evolution, however, has no inherent direction. Natural selection works on existing variation, not on what we might desire or need.

Our success with cultural adaptations should not lead us to conclude that we do not continue to evolve biologically. Regardless of our triumphs in the field of medicine, many incurable diseases still carry on the process of natural selection. Biological variation still takes place in potential and realized fertility. As many as a third to half of all human conceptions fail to produce live births. We still live in a world in which up to 50 percent of the children have an inadequate diet. Even if all inhabitants of the world were raised to an adequate standard of living tomorrow, we would still be subject to natural selection and biological evolution. The fact that we are cultural organisms does not detract from the fact that we are also biological organisms. Scholars in various fields throughout history have argued about whether humans and human behavior should be studied biologically, as products of nature, or culturally, as products of nurture. Both sides were wrong. Humans must be studied as *both* biological and cultural organisms.

Given that we will continue to evolve, *how* will we evolve? This question cannot be answered. Evolution has many random elements that cannot be predicted. Also, the biocultural nature of humans makes prediction even harder. The incredible rate of cultural and technological change in the past century was not predicted. What kinds of cultural evolution are possible in the next hundred years? We may be able to forecast some short-term changes, but we know nothing about the cultural capabilities of our species hundreds or thousands of years in the future.

Another problem is that our own viewpoint can influence our predictions. An optimistic view might focus on the success of past cultural adaptations and the rate of acquisition of knowledge, and then develop a scenario including increased standard of living for all, cheap energy sources, and an elevated life expectancy. A pessimistic view might consider all the horrors of the past and present, and project a grim future. A pessimist might envisage widespread famine, overcrowding, pollution, disease, and warfare. Most likely, any possible future will be neither pie-in-the-sky nor doom-and-despair, but rather a combination of positive and negative changes. If the study of evolution tells us one thing, it is that every change has potential costs and benefits. We need to temper our optimism and pessimism with a sense of balance.

In any consideration of the future, we must acknowledge change as basic to life. Many people find it tempting to suggest that we would be better off living a "simpler" life. Others argue that we should stop trying to deal with our problems and let nature take its course or that we should trust in the acts of God. This is unacceptable—indeed, our understanding of human evolution argues for the reverse. Our adaptive pattern has been one of learning and problem solving. More than that, this is our primate heritage. Our biology has allowed us to develop the basic mammalian patterns of learned behavior to a high degree. We have the capability for rational thought, for reason, and for learning. Even if many of our cultural inventions have led to suffering and pain, our *potential* for good is immense. In any case, we must continue along the path of learning and intelligence; it is our very nature. Good or bad, the capabilities of the human mind and spirit may be infinite.

MATHEMATICAL POPULATION GENETICS

Population genetics was discussed in Chapter 3 with a minimum of mathematical formulae. This appendix is intended for those wishing to obtain an elementary understanding of the mathematical basis of population genetics. Additional sources, such as Hartl and Clark (1997), are recommended for further information.

The formulae presented here are limited to a simple genetic case—a single locus with two possible alleles, A and a. Following convention, p is used to denote the frequency of the A allele, and q is used to denote the frequency of the a allele. Because there are only two alleles, $p + q = 1$. For this simple case, there are three genotypes: AA, Aa, and aa.

HARDY-WEINBERG EQUILIBRIUM

The Hardy-Weinberg equilibrium model, discussed briefly in Chapter 3, states that (1) under random mating, the expected genotype frequencies are $AA = p^2$, $Aa = 2pq$, and $aa = q^2$, and (2) under certain conditions, the allele frequencies p and q will remain constant from one generation to the next.

There are a number of ways to demonstrate the first conclusion of the Hardy-Weinberg model. Perhaps the simplest proof rests on the fact that p and q represent probabilities. If the frequency of the A allele is p, then the probability of drawing an A allele from the entire gene pool is equal to p. To obtain the AA genotype in the next generation, it is necessary to have an A allele from both parents. Assuming that the allele frequencies are the same in both sexes, the probability of getting an A allele from one parent is p and the probability of getting an A allele from the other parent is also p. The probability of *both* these events happening is the product of these probabilities, or

$p \times p = p^2$. The same method can be used to determine the probability of getting the *aa* genotype ($q \times q = q^2$).

Getting an *Aa* genotype in the next generation requires one parent contributing the *A* allele (probability $= p$) and the other parent contributing the *a* allele (probability $= q$). The joint probability is $p \times q = pq$. It is also possible, however, that the order may be reversed. The first parent could contribute the *a* allele, and the second parent the *A* allele. The joint probability of this happening is also equal to pq. The overall probability of having the *Aa* genotype is therefore $pq + pq = 2pq$.

The reasoning behind the Hardy-Weinberg model is summarized as follows:

	Allele from Parent		
Genotype of Child	*1*	*2*	*Probability*
AA	*A*	*A*	$p \times p = p^2$
Aa	*A*	*a*	$p \times q = pq$
		or	
	a	*A*	$q \times p = pq$
aa	*a*	*a*	$q \times q = q^2$

$$pq + pq = 2pq$$

Also note that the sum of genotype frequencies ($p^2 + 2pq + q^2$) is equal to 1.

The second part of the Hardy-Weinberg model states that in the absence of evolutionary forces the allele frequencies will remain the same from one generation to the next. This can be easily demonstrated by using the genotype frequencies in a given generation to predict the allele frequencies in the next generations. Allele frequencies are easily derived from genotype frequencies. In the present example, the frequency of allele *A* is computed as the frequency of genotype *AA* plus *half* the frequency of genotype *Aa* (we only wish to count the *A* alleles that make up half the total number of alleles in heterozygotes). The frequency of the *A* allele in the next generation, designated p', is therefore equal to

$$p' = \text{frequency of } AA + \left(\text{frequency of } \frac{Aa}{2} \right)$$

which is equal to

$$p' = p^2 + \frac{2pq}{2}$$

The 2s cancel out, giving

$$p' = p^2 + pq$$

Factoring p from the equation gives

$$p' = p(p + q)$$

Now, because the quantity ($p + q$) is equal to 1 by definition, the equation becomes

$$p' = p$$

The fact that the allele frequency in the next generation (p') is equal to the initial allele frequency (p) shows that given certain assumptions there will be no change in the allele frequency over time. Therefore, when we *do* see a change in allele frequency over time, we know that one of the assumptions of the Hardy-Weinberg model has been violated. Because the model assumes no evolution has taken place, the fact that the model does not fit means that this assumption is incorrect and, therefore, that a change in allele frequency (evolution) has taken place.

INBREEDING

Inbreeding does not change allele frequencies, but it does change genotype frequencies. The genotype frequencies predicted by Hardy-Weinberg require the assumptions that mating is random and there is no inbreeding. The inbreeding coefficient, F, is a measure of the probability that a homozygous genotype is the result of common ancestry of the parents. For example, the inbreeding coefficient for offspring born to first cousins is $F = 0.0625$. This value indicates the *additional* probability of the child having a homozygous genotype because the parents were first cousins. Inbreeding coefficients are most often computed from genealogical data, although with certain assumptions they may also be estimated from frequencies of last names and from allele frequencies (in certain cases).

At the population level, there is also a probability of having a homozygous genotype due to random mating (p^2 or q^2, depending on the genotype). Inbreeding increases this probability. Under inbreeding, the genotype frequencies are

AA: $p^2 + pqF$

Aa: $2pq (1 - F)$

aa: $q^2 + pqF$

Thus, inbreeding increases the frequency of homozygotes (*AA* and *aa*) and decreases the frequency of heterozygotes. As an example, consider a population where $p = 0.5$ and $q = 0.5$. Under random mating ($F = 0$), the genotype frequencies are $AA = 0.25$, $Aa = 0.50$, and $aa = 0.25$. If the population had an inbreeding coefficient of $F = 0.05$, these frequencies would be $AA = 0.2625$, $Aa = 0.4750$, and $aa = 0.2625$.

It is easy to see why inbreeding does not change allele frequencies. Given the genotype frequencies expected under inbreeding, we can compute the frequency of the *A* allele in the next generation as

$$p' = \text{frequency of } AA + \left(\text{frequency of } \frac{Aa}{2} \right)$$

Substituting the formulae for *AA* and *Aa* given earlier, this equation becomes

$$p' = p^2 + pqF + \frac{2pq(1 - F)}{2}$$

The 2s in the equation cancel out. When the remaining terms are multiplied out, the equation becomes

$$p' = p^2 + pqF + pq - pqF$$

After subtracting pqF from pqF, the equation then becomes

$$p' = p^2 + pq$$

Factoring the p in the equation gives

$$p' + p(p + q)$$

Because $p + q = 1$, the allele frequency in the next generation is

$$p' = p$$

Thus, the allele frequency does not change from one generation to the next under inbreeding.

MUTATION

Mutation involves the change from one allele into another. For the simple case given here, let us assume that allele a is the mutant form. The mutation rate, usually denoted as u, is the proportion of A alleles that mutates into a alleles in a single generation. The value u therefore represents the probability of any A allele mutating into the a allele. Models also exist to deal with backward mutation (a into A), but these are not presented here because the rate of back mutations is usually very low.

How can mutation change the allele frequency in a population over time? To answer that, assume that mutation is the only force acting to change allele frequencies. The frequency of allele a in the next generation (q') depends on the current frequency of a alleles (q), the frequency of A alleles that have not mutated ($p = 1 - q$), and the rate of mutation (u). The frequency of the a allele in the next generation, q', is therefore equal to

$$q' = q + u(1 - q)$$

The first part of this equation represents the initial frequency of a alleles (q), and the second part represents the expected increase in a alleles due to mutation of A alleles.

As an example, assume that the initial allele frequencies are $p = 1.0$ and $q = 0.0$ and that the mutation rate is $u = 0.0001$. The allele frequencies in the next generation are

$$q' = 0 + 0.0001(1 - 0)$$
$$= 0.0001$$
$$p' = 1 - q' = 0.9999$$

If we carry this to an additional generation, the allele frequencies in the second generation (q' and p') are

$$q'' = 0.0001 + 0.0001(1 - 0.0001)$$
$$= 0.0001 + 0.00009999$$
$$= 0.00019999$$
$$p'' = 1 - q'' = 0.9980001$$

Continued mutation, in the absence of any other evolutionary forces, will lead to an increase in q and a decrease in p. For example, after 50 generations of mutation the allele frequencies in the example here are $p = 0.99501223$ and $q = 0.00498777$.

The mutation model presented here is simplified and does not take into consideration back mutation, changes in mutation rates over time, or any of the other evolutionary forces. It does, however, illustrate how mutation will lead to a cumulative increase in the frequency of the mutant allele. These examples also show that such increases are relatively low, even over many generations. Of course, evolution is not caused only by mutation. Other evolutionary forces act to increase, or decrease, the allele frequencies.

NATURAL SELECTION

Natural selection is modeled mathematically by assigning a fitness value to each genotype. Fitness is defined as the probability that an individual will survive to reproductive age. The actual proportion of individuals surviving is known as *absolute fitness*. Mathematically, the effects of natural selection are easier to model if relative fitness is used; here, the absolute fitness values are converted such that the largest relative fitness equals 1.

As an example, consider absolute fitness values of $AA = 0.8$, $Aa = 0.8$, and $aa = 0.4$. These numbers mean that 80 percent of those with the AA genotype survived, 80 percent of those with the Aa genotype survived, and 40 percent of those with the aa genotype survived. Because the largest absolute fitness is 0.8, relative fitness values are obtained by dividing each fitness by 0.8. Thus, the relative fitness values are $AA = 1.0$, $Aa = 1.0$, and $aa = 0.5$. The genotype aa has a fitness value of 0.5 relative to the most fit genotypes (AA and Aa). As another example, consider the following absolute fitness values: $AA = 0.7$, $Aa = 0.9$, and $aa = 0.3$. The relative fitness values are $AA = 0.7/0.9 = 0.778$, $Aa = 0.9/0.9 = 1.0$, and $aa = 0.3/0.9 = 0.333$.

The symbol w is used to designate relative fitness. Here w_{AA} is the relative fitness of genotype AA, w_{Aa} is the relative fitness of genotype Aa, and w_{aa} is the relative fitness of genotype aa. The effect of natural selection can now be determined by looking at the genotype frequencies before and after selection. The genotype frequencies before selection are obtained from the Hardy-Weinberg model: $AA = p^2$, $Aa = 2pq$, and $aa = q^2$. The genotype frequencies after selection are obtained by multiplying the genotype frequencies before selection by the respective relative fitness values. After selection, the genotype frequencies are therefore

$$AA = w_{AA}p^2$$
$$Aa = 2w_{Aa}pq$$
$$aa = w_{aa}q^2$$

The frequency of the A allele after selection is then computed by adding the frequency of genotype AA to half the frequency of genotype Aa and dividing this figure by the sum of all genotype frequencies after selection. That is,

$$p' = (w_{AA}p^2 + (2w_{Aa}pq/2)) / (w_{AA}p^2 + 2w_{Aa}pq + w_{aa}q^2)$$
$$= (w_{AA}p^2 + w_{Aa}pq) / (w_{AA}p^2 + 2w_{Aa}pq + w_{aa}q^2)$$

As an example, consider a population with initial allele frequencies of $p = 0.8$ and $q = 0.2$. Assume relative fitness values for each genotype as $AA = 1.0$, $Aa = 1.0$, and $aa = 0.5$. In this example, there is partial selection against the homozygous genotype aa. Logically, we expect that such selection will lead to a reduction in the frequency of the a allele and an increase in the frequency of the A allele.

Using Hardy-Weinberg, the expected genotype frequencies before selection are

$$AA: p^2 = (0.8)^2 = 0.64$$
$$Aa: 2pq = 2(0.8)(0.2) = 0.32$$
$$aa: q^2 = (0.2)^2 = 0.04$$

Using the relative fitness values, the relative proportion of each genotype after selection is

$$AA: w_{AA}p^2 = (1)(0.8)^2 = 0.64$$
$$Aa: 2w_{Aa}pq = 2(1)(0.8)(0.2) = 0.32$$
$$aa: w_{aa}q^2 = (0.5)(0.2)^2 = 0.02$$

The frequency of the A allele after selection is computed as

$$p' = (0.64 + (0.32/2)) / (0.64 + 0.32 + 0.02)$$
$$= (0.64 + 0.16) / (0.64 + 0.32 + 0.02)$$
$$= 0.8 / 0.98$$
$$= 0.8163$$

Also, the frequency of the a allele after selection is

$$q' = 1 - p' = 0.1837$$

The entire process can be repeated for additional generations. To extend the analysis another generation, use the new values of $p = 0.8163$ and $q = 0.1837$. After an additional generation of selection, the allele frequencies will be

$p = 0.8303$ and $q = 0.1697$. If you continue this process, the frequency of A keeps increasing and the frequency of a keeps decreasing.

Some forms of natural selection can be represented using simplified formulae. For example, complete selection against recessive homozygotes involves relative fitness values of $AA = 1.0$, $Aa = 1.0$, and $aa = 0.0$. Given these values, the frequency of the A allele after one generation of selection is

$$p' = (w_{AA}p^2 + w_{Aa}pq) / (w_{AA}p^2 + 2w_{Aa}pq + w_{aa}q^2)$$
$$= ((1)p^2 + (1)pq) / ((1)p^2 + 2(1)pq + (0)q^2)$$
$$= (p^2 + pq) / (p^2 + 2pq)$$
$$= (p(p + q)) / (p(p + q + q))$$
$$= (p + q) / (p + q + q)$$
$$= 1 / (1 + q)$$
$$= 1 / (1 + (1 - p))$$
$$= 1 / (2 - p)$$

which is a much easier formula to work with. Other forms of natural selection also have simplified formulae and are listed in the reference given at the beginning of this appendix.

As an example, assume initial frequencies of $p = 0.5$ and $q = 0.5$. The frequency of the A allele in the next five generations of natural selection would be 0.6667, 0.7500, 0.8000, 0.8333, and 0.8571.

GENETIC DRIFT

The process of genetic drift is random. As a result, we cannot predict the exact allele frequencies resulting from a generation of genetic drift. We can, however, describe the probability of obtaining a given allele frequency caused by genetic drift. For example, assume a population of six people (and hence 12 alleles at each locus) with initial allele frequencies of $p = 0.5$ and $q = 0.5$. A generation of genetic drift could result in the frequency of the A allele ranging from $0/12 = 0.0$ to $12/12 = 1.0$. Other possible allele frequency values are $1/12 = 0.083$, $2/12 = 0.167$, $3/12 = 0.250$, $4/12 = 0.333$, $5/12 = 0.417$, $6/12 = 0.500$, $7/12 = 0.583$, $8/12 = 0.667$, $9/12 = 0.750$, $10/12 = 0.833$, and $11/12 = 0.917$.

The frequency of the A allele depends on how many A alleles are represented in the next generation (which can range from 0 to 12). Because genetic drift is a random process, we cannot tell how many A alleles will be represented in the next generation. We can, however, compute the probability of each of these events occurring. We would expect, for example, that getting 6 A alleles is more likely than getting 12 A alleles (just as we would expect it to be more likely that we get 6 heads than 12 heads or 1 head if we flipped a coin 12 times). The exact formula used is a bit complex and is not presented here (see Hartl 1988:70). Using this formula, the probability of getting 6 A alleles in the next generation (and an allele frequency of $6/12 = 0.5$) is 0.223. Therefore, the probability of getting *some* change in the allele frequency (some number *other* than 6 *A* alleles) is $1 - 0.223 = 0.777$. Mathematical investigation also shows that smaller populations are more likely to experience genetic drift than larger populations.

GENE FLOW

The process of gene flow is best described mathematically by considering allele frequencies in two populations, 1 and 2. The allele frequencies of population 1 are denoted p_1 and q_1, and the allele frequencies of population 2 are denoted p_2 and q_2. What happens when gene flow takes place between these two populations? Assume that populations 1 and 2 mix together at rate *m*. The term *m* is a measure of the proportion of migrants moving from one population into the other. For simplicity, further assume that the rate of migration from population 1 into population 2 is the same as the rate of migration from population 2 into population 1.

The frequency of the *A* allele in population 1 after one generation of gene flow is then expressed as

$$(1 - m)p_1 + mp_2$$

The first part of the right-hand side of the equation shows the contribution to allele frequency from the proportion of individuals who stayed in population $1(1 - m)$. The second part of the right-hand side of the equation shows the contribution to allele frequency caused by the proportion of individuals migrating from population 2 (*m*). Likewise, the frequency of allele *A* in population 2 after one generation of gene flow is

$$mp_1 + (1 - m)p_2$$

As an example, assume that initial allele frequencies in population 1 are $p_1 = 0.7$ and $q_1 = 0.3$, and that initial allele frequencies in population 2 are $p_2 = 0.2$ and $q_2 = 0.8$. Further assume a rate of gene flow of $m = 0.3$. After one generation of gene flow, the frequencies of the *A* allele are

$$(1 - 0.3)(0.7) + (0.3)(0.2) = 0.49 + 0.06 = 0.55$$

for population 1, and

$$(0.3)(0.7) + (1 - 0.3)(0.2) = 0.21 + 0.14 = 0.35$$

for population 2. Thus, the frequency of the *A* allele has made populations 1 and 2 more similar as a result of gene flow. An additional generation of gene flow at the same rate would result in allele frequencies of

$$(1 - 0.3)(0.55) + (0.3)(0.35) = 0.385 + 0.105 = 0.49$$

for population 1, and

$$(0.3)(0.55) + (1 - 0.3)(0.35) = 0.165 + 0.245 = 0.41$$

for population 2. The two populations continue to become more similar genetically. Another generation of gene flow would result in allele frequencies of 0.466 for population 1 and 0.434 for population 2. After only a few more generations of gene flow, the allele frequencies of the two populations would be essentially equal.

Summary

The formulae presented here represent a simplified view of mathematical population genetics. Each model ignores the effects of other evolutionary forces, although they can easily be extended to consider simultaneous effects. These models also deal only with a simple situation of one locus with two alleles. More complicated analyses require more sophisticated mathematical methods that are best performed on a computer. Nonetheless, these formulae do demonstrate the basic nuts and bolts of population genetics theory.

COMPARATIVE PRIMATE SKELETAL ANATOMY

This appendix provides a general background in comparative primate anatomy by showing the skeletons of three primates—a modern human, an ape (gorilla), and an Old World monkey (baboon). In addition to noting the differences between these species, you should also note the similarities, particularly in terms of the homology of the skeletons (see Chapter 4 for a review of the principle of homology).

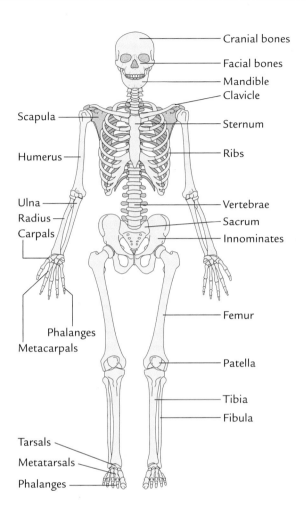

Cranial bones
Facial bones
Mandible
Clavicle
Scapula
Sternum
Humerus
Ribs
Ulna
Radius
Vertebrae
Carpals
Sacrum
Innominates
Phalanges
Metacarpals
Femur
Patella
Tibia
Fibula
Tarsals
Metatarsals
Phalanges

FIGURE 1

The human skeleton is made up of 206 bones on average (not all of which are shown here). Of these, 29 bones are found in the crania, 27 are found in each hand, and 26 are found in each foot. Note the homology between the human skeleton and the skeleton of the gorilla (Figure 2) and the baboon (Figure 3). Also note differences in certain anatomical structures, such as the pelvis, that reflect human bipedalism (discussed in Chapter 7).

FIGURE 2

Skeleton of a gorilla, one of the African apes (discussed in Chapter 6) shown in the typical knuckle-walking mode of locomotion. Note the longer arms and shorter legs when compared with the human (Figure 1) and the baboon (Figure 3).

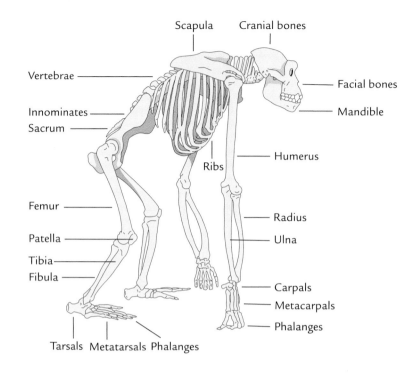

FIGURE 3

Skeleton of a baboon, an Old World monkey, shown in the typical quadrupedal mode of locomotion. Note the similar length of the arms and legs, particularly when compared with the human (Figure 1) and the gorilla (Figure 2).

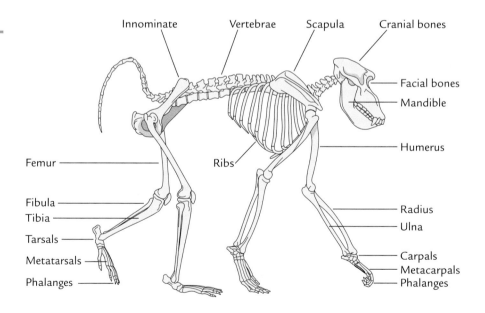

CONVERSION FACTORS

Conversion Factors for Common Measures Used in the Text		
To Convert	*Into*	*Multiply By*
Centimeters	Inches	0.3937
Cubic centimeters	Cubic inches	0.06102
Cubic inches	Cubic centimeters	16.39
Feet	Meters	0.3048
Grams	Ounces	0.03527
Inches	Centimeters	2.54
Inches	Millimeters	25.4
Kilograms	Pounds	2.205
Kilometers	Miles	0.6214
Kilometers	Yards	1,094.0
Meters	Feet	3.281
Meters	Yards	1.094
Miles	Kilometers	1.609
Millimeters	Inches	0.03937
Ounces	Grams	28.349527
Pounds	Kilograms	0.4536
Yards	Kilometers	9.144×10^{-4}
Yards	Meters	0.9144

Temperature conversion:
From Celsius to Fahrenheit: $(C° \times 1.8) + 32$
From Fahrenheit to Celsius: $(F° - 32) / 1.8$
Source: Frisancho (1993).

acclimation   Short-term physiologic responses to a stress, usually occurring within minutes or hours.

acclimatization   Long-term physiologic responses to a stress, usually taking from days to months.

Acheulian tradition   The stone tool culture that appears first with *Homo erectus* and is characterized by the development of hand axes and other bifacial tools.

adaptation   The process of successful interaction between a population and an environment. Cultural or biological traits that offer an advantage in a given environment are adaptations.

adaptive radiation   The formation of many new species following the availability of new environments or the development of a new adaptation.

affiliative   Friendly behaviors that promote social bonds.

African replacement model   The hypothesis that modern humans evolved as a new species in Africa 200,000 years ago and then spread throughout the Old World, replacing preexisting human populations.

age at menarche   The age at which a human female experiences her first menstrual period.

age-sex structure   The number of males and females in different age groups of a population.

agonistic   Unfriendly social relationships.

allele   The alternative form of a gene or DNA sequence that occurs at a given locus. Some loci have only one allele, some have two, and some have many alternative forms. Alleles occur in pairs, one on each chromosome.

Allen's rule   States that mammals in cold climates tend to have shorter and bulkier limbs, allowing less loss of body heat, whereas mammals in hot climates tend to have long, slender limbs, allowing greater loss of body heat.

allometry   The study of the change in proportion of various body parts as a consequence of their growth at different rates.

alloparent   An individual that cares for an infant but is not a biological parent.

***Alu* insertions**   A sequence of DNA repeated at different locations on different chromosomes.

anagenesis   The transformation of a single species over time.

anatomically modern humans   The modern form of the human species, which dates back 200,000 years.

Anthropoidea (anthropoids)   The suborder of primates consisting of monkeys, apes, and humans.

anthropology   The science that investigates human biological and cultural variation and evolution.

anthropometrics   Measurements of the human body, skull, and face.

antibody   A substance that reacts to other substances invading the body (antigens).

antigen   A substance invading the body that stimulates the production of antibodies.

arboreal   Living in trees.

archaeology   The subfield of anthropology that focuses on cultural variations in prehistorical and historical populations by analyzing the culture's remains.

Archean eon   The second geologic eon, dating from 3800 to 2500 Ma, characterized by the appearance of the first single-celled organisms.

Ardipithecus kadabba   An early primitive hominin with very apelike teeth from Africa dating between 5.8 million and 5.2 million years ago.

Ardipithecus ramidus   An early primitive hominid species from Africa dating between 5.8 million and 4.4 million years ago.

argon-argon dating   A variation of potassium-argon dating that can be applied to very small samples of volcanic rock.

assimilation model   The hypothesis that modern human anatomy arose first in Africa as a change within a species, and then spread through gene flow to populations outside of Africa. The gene pool of the non-African archaic populations was thus assimilated into an expanding population of modern humans out of Africa.

assortative mating   Mating between phenotypically similar or dissimilar individuals—for example, between two people with the same hair color.

Australopithecus   A genus of fossil hominin that lived between 4.2 million and 1 million years ago and is characterized by bipedal locomotion, small brain size, large face, and large teeth.

Australopithecus aethiopicus   The oldest robust australopith, dating to 2.5 million years ago in East Africa. It combines derived features seen in other robust australopiths with primitive features seen in *A. afarensis*.

Australopithecus afarensis   A primitive hominin found in East Africa, dating between 3.7 million and 3.0 million years ago. The teeth and postcranial skeleton show a number of primitive and apelike features.

Australopithecus africanus   An early hominin, dating between 3.3 million and 2.3 million years ago and found in South Africa. It is not as massive as the robust forms and may be an ancestor of the genus *Homo*.

Australopithecus anamensis   A hominin species that lived in East Africa between 4.2 million and 3.9 million years ago. It was a biped but had many primitive, apelike features of the skull and teeth.

Australopithecus boisei   A very robust species of robust australopith, dating between 2.4 million and 1.4 million years ago and found in East Africa.

Australopithecus garhi   An early hominin, dating to 2.5 million years ago in East Africa. It differs from other australopiths in having large front and back teeth, although the back teeth are not specialized to the same extent as found in the robust australopiths.

Australopithecus robustus   A species of robust australopith, dating between roughly 2 million and 1.4 million years ago and found in South Africa.

balancing selection   Selection for the heterozygote and against the homozygotes (the heterozygote is most fit). Allele frequencies move toward an equilibrium defined by the fitness values of the two homozygotes.

base   Chemical units (adenine, thymine, guanine, cytosine) that make up part of the DNA molecule and specify genetic instructions.

behavioral ecology   The study of behavior that focuses on the adaptive value of behavior from an ecological and evolutionary perspective.

Bergmann's rule   States that (1) among mammals of similar shape, the larger mammal loses heat less rapidly than the smaller mammal and that (2) among mammals of similar size, the mammal with a linear shape will lose heat more rapidly than the mammal with a nonlinear shape.

biface   A stone tool with both sides worked, producing greater symmetry and efficiency.

bilateral symmetry   Symmetry in which the right and left sides of the body are approximately mirror images, a characteristic of vertebrates.

binocular stereoscopic vision   Overlapping fields of vision (binocular), with both sides of the brain receiving images from both eyes (stereoscopic), thereby providing depth perception.

biocultural approach   A method of studying humans that looks at the interaction between biology and culture in evolutionary adaptation.

biological anthropology   The subfield of anthropology that focuses on the biological evolution of humans and human ancestors, the relationship of humans to other organisms, and patterns of biological variation within and among human populations. Also referred to as *physical anthropology*.

biological race   A group of populations sharing certain biological traits that distinguish them from other groups of populations. In practice, the biological concept of race has been difficult to apply to human populations.

biological species concept   A definition of species that focuses on reproductive capabilities, where by organisms from different populations are considered to be in the same species if they naturally interbreed and produce fertile offspring.

biostratigraphy   A relative dating method in which sites can be assigned an approximate age based on the similarity of animal remains to those from other dated sites.

bipedal   Moving about on two legs. Unlike the movement of other bipedal animals such as kangaroos, human bipedalism is further characterized by a striding motion.

blade   A stone tool characteristic of the Upper Paleolithic, defined as being at least twice as long as it is wide. Blade tools were made using an efficient and precise method.

B.P.   Before Present (1950), the internationally accepted form of designating past dates.

brachiation   A method of movement that uses the arms to swing from branch to branch. Gibbons are brachiators.

breeding population   A group of organisms that tend to choose mates from within the group.

brow ridges   The large ridges of bone above the eye orbits, very noticeable in *Homo erectus*.

burin   A stone tool with a sharp edge that is used to cut and engrave bone.

canine   One of four types of teeth found in mammals. The canine teeth are located in the front of the jaw behind the incisors. Mammals normally use these teeth for puncturing and defense. Unlike most mammals, humans have small canine teeth that function like incisors.

carbon-14 dating   A chronometric dating method based on the half-life of carbon-14 that can be applied to organic remains such as charcoal dating back over the past 50,000 years or so.

Carpolestes simpsoni   A species of primate-like mammal that had some derived primate traits, such as a grasping foot and an opposable big toe. This species is intermediate in many respects between primitive primate-like mammals and true primates.

carrying capacity   The maximum population size capable of being supported in a given environment.

Cenozoic era   The third and most recent geologic era of the Phanerozoic eon, dating to the last 65.5 Ma. Primate and human evolution occurred during the Cenozoic era.

cephalic index   A measure of cranial shape defined as the total length of a skull divided by the maximum width of the skull.

cerebrum   The area of the forebrain that consists of the outermost layer of brain cells. The cerebrum is associated with memory, learning, and intelligence.

Chordata   A vertebrate phylum consisting of organisms that possess a notochord at some period during their life.

chromosome   A long strand of DNA sequences.

chronometric dating   A method of dating fossils or sites that provides an estimate of the specific date (subject to probabilistic limits).

chronospecies   Labels given to different points in the evolutionary lineage of a single species over time. As a species changes over time, the different stages are labeled as chronospecies to recognize the biological changes that have taken place.

civilization   A large, state-level society characterized by large population size, high population density, urbanization, social stratification, food and labor surpluses, monumental architecture, and record keeping.

cladistics   A school of thought that stresses evolutionary relationships between organisms based on derived homologous traits.

cladogenesis   The formation of one or more new species from another over time.

codominant   Both alleles affect the phenotype of a heterozygous genotype, and neither is dominant over the other.

comparative approach   Comparing human populations to determine common and unique behaviors or biological traits.

continental drift   The movement of continental land masses on top of a partially molten layer of the earth's mantle. Because of continental drift, the relative location of the continents has changed over time.

convergent evolution   Independent evolution of a trait in rather distinct evolutionary lines. The development of flight in birds and certain insects is an example of convergent evolution.

cranial capacity   A measurement of the interior volume of the brain case measured in cubic centimeters (cc) and used as an approximate estimate of brain size.

crossing over   The exchange of DNA between chromosomes during meiosis.

cultural anthropology   The subfield of anthropology that focuses on variations in cultural behaviors among human populations.

culture   Behavior that is shared, learned, and socially transmitted.

cusp   A raised area on the chewing surface of a tooth.

demographic transition theory   A model of demographic change stating that as a population becomes economically developed, a reduction in death rates (leading to population growth) will take place, followed by a reduction in birth rates.

dendrochronology   A chronometric dating method based on the fact that trees in dry climates tend to accumulate one growth ring per year. The width of the rings varies according to climate, and a sample can be compared with a master chart of tree rings over the past 10,000 years.

dental formula   A shorthand method of describing the number of each type of tooth in half of one jaw of a mammal. The dental formula consists of four numbers: I-C-PM-M, where I is the number of incisors, C is the number of canines, PM is the number of premolars, and M is the number of molars. When a mammal has a different number of teeth in the upper and lower jaws, two dental formulae are used.

derived trait   A trait that has changed from an ancestral state. The large human brain is a derived trait relative to the common ancestor of humans and apes.

dermatoglyphics   Measurements of finger and palm prints, including type classification and ridge counts.

developmental acclimatization   Changes in organ or body structure that occur during the physical growth of any organism.

diastema   A gap next to the canine teeth that allows space for the canine on the opposing jaw.

directional selection   Selection against one extreme in a continuous trait and/or selection for the other extreme.

distance curve   A measure of size over time, for example, a person's height at different ages.

diurnal   Active during the day.

DNA (deoxyribonucleic acid)   The molecule that provides the genetic code for biological structures and the means to translate this code.

dominance hierarchy   The ranking system within a society that indicates which individuals are dominant in social behaviors.

dominant allele   An allele that masks the effect of the other allele (which is recessive) in a heterozygous genotype.

Dryopithecus   A genus of fossil ape that lived in Europe during the Middle and Late Miocene. This form and the related form *Ouranopithecus* have cranial traits that suggest one may have been an ancestor of African apes and humans.

electron spin resonance (ESR)   A chronometric dating method that estimates dates from observation of radioactive atoms trapped in the calcite crystals present in a number of materials, such as bones and shells. This method is useful for dating sites back to roughly 1 million years.

electrophoresis   A laboratory method that uses electric current to separate proteins, allowing genotypes to be determined.

embryo   The stage of human prenatal life lasting from roughly two to eight weeks following conception, characterized by structural development.

emergent infectious disease   A newly identified infectious disease that has recently evolved.

endemic   A pattern of disease rate when new cases of a disease occur at a relatively constant but low rate over time.

endocast   A cast of the interior of the brain case used in the analysis of brain size and structure.

Eocene epoch   The second epoch of the Cenozoic era, dating between 55.8 million and 33.9 million years ago. The first true primates, primitive prosimians, appeared during the Eocene.

eon   The major subdivision of geologic time.

epidemic   A pattern of disease rate when new cases of a disease spread rapidly through a population.

epidemiologic transition   The increase in life expectancy and the shift from infectious to noninfectious disease as the primary cause of death.

epoch   Subdivision of a geologic period.

era   Subdivision of a geologic eon.

estrus   A time during the month when females are sexually receptive.

Eurasia   The combined land masses of Europe and Asia.

evolution   The transformation of species of organic life over long periods of time. Anthropologists study both the cultural and biological evolution of the human species.

evolutionary forces   Four mechanisms that can cause changes in allele frequencies from one generation to the next: mutation, natural selection, genetic drift, and gene flow.

evolutionary systematics   A school of thought that stresses the overall similarity of all (primitive and derived) homologous traits in classification.

exon   A section of DNA that codes for the amino acids that make up proteins. It is contrasted with an intron.

experimental archaeology   A field of archaeology that involves the study of the manufacture and use of tools in order to learn how they were made and used by people in the past.

fetus   The stage of human prenatal growth from roughly eight weeks following conception until birth, characterized by further development and rapid growth.

fission-fusion   A primate society where the population splits into smaller subgroups at times (fission) and then later reunited (fusion). The process is affected by distribution of food resources.

fission-track dating   A chronometric dating method based on the number of tracks made across volcanic rock as uranium decays into lead.

fitness   An organism's probability of survival and reproduction. Fitness is generally measured in terms of the different genotypes for a given locus.

fluorine dating   A relative dating method based on the accumulation of fluorine in a bone that tells if two bones from a site are of the same age.

foramen magnum   The large opening at the base of the skull where the spinal cord enters. This opening is located more toward the center of the skull in hominins, who are bipeds, so that the skull sits atop the spine.

founder effect   A type of genetic drift caused by the formation of a new population by a small number of individuals. The small size of the sample can cause marked deviations in allele frequencies from the original population.

gene   A DNA sequence that codes for a functional polypeptide or RNA product.

gene flow   A mechanism for evolutionary change resulting from the movement of genes from one population to another. Gene flow introduces new genes into a population and also acts to make populations more similar genetically to one another.

generalized structure   A biological structure adapted to a wide range of conditions and used in very general ways. For example, the grasping hands of humans are generalized structures allowing climbing, food gathering, toolmaking, and a variety of other functions.

genetic distance   An average measure of relatedness between populations based on a number of traits. Genetic distances are used to understand the effects of genetic drift and gene flow, which should affect all loci to the same extent.

genetic distance map   A picture that shows the genetic relationships between populations, based on genetic distance measures.

genetic drift   A mechanism for evolutionary change resulting from the random fluctuations of gene frequencies from one generation to the next, or from any form of random sampling of a larger gene pool.

genome   The total DNA sequence of an organism.

genotype   The genetic endowment of an individual from the two alleles present at a given locus.

genus   Groups of species with similar adaptations.

gradualism   A model of macroevolutionary change whereby evolutionary changes occur at a slow, steady rate over time.

grooming   The handling and cleaning of another individual's fur. In primates, grooming serves as a form of communication that soothes and provides reassurance.

Hadean eon   The first geologic eon, dating from 4600 to 3800 Ma, which occurred before the oldest fossil evidence of life.

half-life   The average length of time it takes for half of a radioactive substance to decay into another form.

haplogroup   A set of related haplotypes that share similar mutations.

Haplorhini (haplorhines)   One of two suborders of primates suggested to replace the prosimian/anthropoid suborders (the other is the strepsirhines). Haplorhines are primates without a moist nose (tarsiers, monkeys, apes, and humans).

haplotype   A combination of genes or DNA sequences that are inherited as a single unit.

Hardy-Weinberg equilibrium   A mathematical statement whereby in the absence of nonrandom mating and evolutionary forces, genotype and allele frequencies will remain the same from one generation to the next.

hemoglobin   The molecule in blood cells that transports oxygen.

heritability   The proportion of total variance in a trait due to genetic variation. This measure is not always the same; the actual value depends on the degree of environmental variation in any population.

heterodontic   Having different types of teeth. Mammals have four different types of teeth: incisors, canines, premolars, and molars.

heterozygous   The two alleles at a given locus are different.

HLA (human leukocyte antigen) system   A diverse genetic system consisting of linked loci on chromosome 6 that control autoimmune response.

holistic   Refers to the viewpoint that all aspects of existence are interrelated and important in understanding human variation and evolution.

homeobox gene   A group of regulatory genes that encode a sequence of 60 amino acids that regulate embryonic development. Homeobox genes subdivide from head to tail a developing embryo into different regions, which then form limbs and other structures. These genes are similar in many organisms, such as insects, mice, and humans.

homeostasis   In a physiologic sense, the maintenance of normal limits of body functioning.

homeotherm   An organism capable of maintaining a constant body temperature under most circumstances. Mammals are homeotherms.

home range   The size of the geographic area that is normally occupied and used by a social group.

hominid   A family (Hominidae) within the hominoids. In recent years, this family has been defined as including humans and the great apes (orangutan, gorilla, chimpanzee, and bonobo). Some scientists still use a more traditional definition that refers only to humans and their humanlike ancestors.

hominin   Humans and their ancestors since the time of divergence from the common ancestor of humans, chimpanzees, and bonobos.

hominoid   A superfamily of anthropoids consisting of apes and humans. Hominoids have a shoulder structure adapted for climbing and hanging, lack a tail, are generally larger than monkeys, and have the largest brain to body size ratio among primates.

Homo   A genus of hominids characterized by large brain size and dependence on culture as a means of adaptation.

homodontic   All teeth are the same.

Homo erectus   A species of the genus *Homo* that arose 1.8 million years ago in Africa and then spread to parts of Asia and Europe.

Homo ergaster   A species suggested by some anthropologists consisting of the early African specimens of *Homo erectus*.

Homo floresiensis   The species name given to a very small hominin that lived in Indonesia in recent times, and is suggested by some to be a dwarf species of *Homo erectus*.

Homo habilis   A species of early *Homo* from Africa that lived between 2 million (or earlier) and 1.6 million years ago, with a brain size roughly half that of modern humans and a primitive postcranial skeleton.

Homo heidelbergensis   A species of archaic human, with a brain size close to that of modern humans but a larger, less modern face, that lived in Africa, Europe, and Asia between 800,000 and 200,000 years ago.

Homo rudolfensis   A species of early *Homo* from Africa that lived between 2.4 million and 1.6 million years ago, with a brain size somewhat larger than *Homo habilis* but with larger back teeth and a broader face.

Homo sapiens   Modern humans.

homology   Similarity due to descent from a common ancestor.

homoplasy   Similarity due to independent evolution.

Homo rudolfensis   A species of early *Homo* from Africa roughly 2 million years ago, with a brain size somewhat larger than *Homo habilis*.

homozygous   Both alleles at a given locus are identical.

horticulture   A form of farming in which only simple hand tools are used.

hypothesis   An explanation of observed facts. To be scientific, a hypothesis must be testable.

hypoxia   Oxygen starvation, which occurs frequently at high altitudes.

inbreeding   Mating between biologically related individuals.

incisor   One of four types of teeth found in mammals. The incisors are the chisel-shaped front teeth used for cutting, slicing, and gnawing food.

infanticide   The killing of infants.

infectious disease   A disease caused by the introduction of an organic foreign substance into the body. Such substances include viruses and parasites.

insectivore   An order of mammals adapted to insect eating.

intelligent design creationism   The idea that the biological world was created by an intelligent entity and did not arise from natural processes.

intron   A section of DNA that does not code for the amino acids that make up proteins. It is contrasted with an exon.

island dwarfism   The process by which natural selection favors smaller body size on an island with limited resources, leading to dwarfed species.

isolation by distance   A model predicting that the genetic distance between populations will increase as the geographic distance between them increases.

Kenyanthropus platyops   A species of early hominid in East Africa, dating to 3.5 million years ago. This species combines a number of primitive features (small brain, jutting face) and derived features (small molars, flat face). Its evolutionary status is unclear.

kin selection   The concept that altruistic behavior can be selected for if it increases the probability of survival of close relatives.

knuckle walking   A form of movement used by chimpanzees and gorillas that is characterized by all four limbs touching the ground, with the weight of the arms resting on the knuckles of the hands.

kwashiorkor   An extreme form of protein-calorie malnutrition resulting from a severe deficiency in proteins but not calories.

lactase persistence   The ability to produce the enzyme lactase after age 5.

lactose intolerance   A condition characterized by diarrhea, cramps, and other intestinal problems resulting from the ingestion of milk.

lemur   A prosimian found today on the island of Madagascar. Lemurs include both nocturnal and diurnal species.

Levallois technique   A method of making stone tools in which a stone core is prepared in such a way that finished tools can be removed from it by a final blow. Also known as the *prepared-core method*.

life expectancy at birth   A measure of the average length of life for a newborn child.

life history theory   The study of how characteristics of an organism's life cycle affect reproduction, focusing on tradeoffs between energy expended for numbers and fitness of offspring.

life table   A compilation of the age distribution of a population that provides an estimate of the probability that an individual will die by a certain age, used to compute life expectancy.

linguistic anthropology   The subfield of anthropology that focuses on the nature of human language, the relationship of language to culture, and the languages of nonliterate peoples.

linkage   Alleles on the same chromosome are inherited together.

locus   The specific location of a gene or DNA sequence on a chromosome.

loris   A nocturnal prosimian found today in Asia and Africa.

Lower Paleolithic   A general term used to refer collectively to the stone tool technologies of *Homo habilis/Homo rudolfensis* and *Homo erectus.*

macroevolution   Long-term evolutionary change. The study of macroevolution focuses on biological evolution over many generations and on the origin of higher taxonomic categories, such as species.

major genes   Genes that have the primary effect on the phenotypic distribution of a complex trait. Additional variation can be due to smaller effects from other loci and/or environmental influences.

malnutrition   Poor nutrition, from either too much or too little food, or from the improper balance of nutrients.

marasmus   An extreme form of protein-calorie malnutrition resulting from severe deficiencies in both proteins and calories.

mass extinction   Many species becoming extinct at about the same time.

meiosis   The creation of sex cells by replication of chromosomes followed by cell division. Each sex cell contains 50 percent of an individual's chromosomes (one from each pair).

Mendelian genetics   The branch of genetics concerned with patterns and processes of inheritance. This field was named after Gregor Mendel, the first scientist to work out many of these principles.

Mendel's Law of Independent Assortment   A law stating that the segregation of any pair of chromosomes does not affect the probability of segregation for other pairs of chromosomes.

Mendel's Law of Segregation   A law stating that sex cells contain one of each pair of alleles.

menopause   The permanent cessation of menstrual cycles.

Mesozoic era   The second geologic era of the Phanerozoic eon, dating from 251 to 65.5 Ma, when the dinosaurs were dominant and when mammals and birds appeared.

messenger RNA   The form of RNA that transports the genetic instructions from the DNA molecule to the site of protein synthesis.

microevolution   Short-term evolutionary change. The study of microevolution focuses on changes in allele frequencies from one generation to the next.

microsatellite DNA   Repeated short sequences of DNA; the number of repeats is highly variable.

Middle Paleolithic   A general term used to refer collectively to the stone tool technologies of *Homo heidelbergensis* and the Neandertals.

Middle Pleistocene   A geologic stage of the Pleistocene epoch that lasted from 781,000 to 126,000 years ago.

Miocene epoch   The fourth epoch of the Cenozoic era, dating between 23.0 million and 5.3 million years ago. Several adaptive radiations of hominoids occurred during the Miocene, and the oldest known possible hominins appeared during the Late Miocene.

mitochondrial DNA   A small amount of DNA that is located in the mitochondria of cells. Mitochondrial DNA is inherited only through the mother.

mitosis   The process of replication of chromosomes in body cells. Each cell produces two identical copies.

molar   One of four types of teeth found in mammals. The molars are back teeth used for crushing and grinding food.

molecular dating   The application of methods of genetic analysis to estimate the sequence and timing of divergent evolutionary lines.

monogamy   An exclusive sexual bond between an adult male and an adult female for a long period of time.

monosomy   A condition in which one chromosome rather than a pair is present in body cells.

Morotopithecus   A genus of fossil ape that lived in Africa 20 million years ago and whose postcranial anatomy was similar in a number of ways to that of living apes.

morphology   The physical structure of organisms.

Mousterian tradition   The prepared-core stone tool technology of the Neandertals.

multimale/multifemale group   The most common type of social group in nonhuman primates; it consists of several adult males, several adult females, and their immature offspring.

multiregional evolution model   The hypothesis that modern humans evolved throughout the Old World as a single species after the first dispersal of *Homo erectus* out of Africa. According to this view, the transition from *Homo erectus* to archaic humans to modern *Homo sapiens* occurred within a single evolutionary line throughout the Old World.

mutation   A mechanism for evolutionary change resulting from a random change in the genetic code; the ultimate source of all genetic variation. Mutations must occur in sex cells to cause evolutionary change.

nasal index   A measure of the shape of the nasal opening, defined as the width of the nasal opening divided by the height.

natural increase   The number of births minus the number of deaths.

natural selection   A mechanism for evolutionary change favoring the survival and reproduction of some organisms over others because of their biological characteristics.

Neandertals   A population of humans that lived in Europe and the Middle East between about 130,000 and 28,000 years ago. Debate continues about whether they are a subspecies of *Homo sapiens* or a separate species and to what extent they contributed to the ancestry of humans today.

nocturnal   Active during the night.

noninfectious disease   A disease caused by factors other than the introduction of an organic foreign substance into the body.

nonrandom mating   Patterns of mate choice that influence the distributions of genotype and phenotype frequencies. Nonrandom mating does not lead to changes in allele frequencies.

notochord   A flexible internal rod that runs along the back of an animal. Animals possessing a notochord at some period in their life are known as *chordates*.

nuclear DNA   The DNA that is contained in the nucleus of the cell.

occipital bun   The protruding rear region of the skull, a feature commonly found in Neandertals.

odontometrics   Measurements of the size of teeth.

Oldowan tradition   The oldest known stone tool culture.

Oligocene epoch   The third epoch of the Cenozoic era, dating between 33.9 million and 23.0 million years ago. Anthropoids underwent an adaptive radiation during the Oligocene.

one-female/multimale group   A social structure in which the primary social group consists of a single adult female, several adult males, and their immature offspring.

one-male/multifemale group   A social structure in which the primary social group consists of a single adult male, several adult females, and their immature offspring.

one-male/one-female group   A social structure in which the primary social group consists of a single adult male, a single adult female, and their immature offspring.

Orrorin tugenensis   An early primitive, possibly hominid, species from Africa, dating to the late Miocene (6 Ma).

orthogenesis   A discredited idea that evolution would continue in a given direction because of some vaguely defined "force."

outgroup   A group used for comparison in cladistic analyses to determine whether the ancestral state of a trait is primitive or derived.

paleoanthropology   The study of primate and human evolution.

Paleocene epoch   The first epoch of the Cenozoic era, dating between 65.5 million and 55.8 million years ago. The primate-like mammals appeared during the Paleocene.

paleoecology   The study of ancient environments.

paleomagnetic reversal   A method of dating sites based on the fact that the earth's magnetic field has shifted back and forth from the north to the south in the past at irregular intervals.

paleopathology   The study of disease in prehistoric populations based on analysis of skeletal remains and archaeological evidence.

paleospecies   Species identified from fossil remains based on their physical similarities and differences relative to other species.

Paleozoic era   The first era of the Phanerozoic eon, dating from 542 to 299 Ma, when the first vertebrates appeared.

palynology   The study of fossil pollen. Palynology allows prehistoric plant species to be identified.

pandemic   A widespread epidemic that affects a large geographic area, such as a continent.

parallel evolution   Independent evolution of a trait in closely related species. One example might be the parallel development of large back teeth in several hominid species.

parental investment   Parental behaviors that increase the probability that offspring will survive.

period   Subdivision of a geologic era.

Phanerozoic eon   The fourth geologic eon, covering the last 542 million years.

phenotype   The observable appearance of a given genotype in the organism. The phenotype is determined by the relationship of the two alleles at a given locus, the number of loci, and often environmental influences as well.

placenta   An organ that develops inside a pregnant placental mammal that provides the fetus with oxygen and food, and helps filter out harmful substances.

plasticity   The ability of an organism to respond physiologically or developmentally to environmental stress.

pleiotropy   A single allele that has multiple effects on an organism.

Pleistocene epoch   The sixth epoch of the Cenozoic era, dating from 1.8 million to 10,000 years ago.

Pliocene epoch   The fifth epoch of the Cenozoic era, dating from 5.3 million to 1.8 million years ago.

polyandry   In humans, a form of marriage in which a wife has several husbands. In more general terms, it refers to an adult female having several mates.

polygamy   A sexual bond between an adult male and an adult female in which either individual may have more than one mate at the same time.

polygenic   A complex genetic trait affected by two or more loci.

polygyny   In humans, a form of marriage in which a husband has several wives. In more general terms, it refers to an adult male having several mates.

polymorphism   A discrete genetic trait in which there are at least two alleles at a locus having frequencies greater than 0.01.

population pyramid   A diagram of the age-sex structure of a population.

postcranial   Referring to that part of the skeleton below the skull.

postnatal   The period of life from birth until death.

postorbital bar   The bony ring that separates the eye orbit from the back of the skull. The postorbital bar is a primate characteristic.

postorbital constriction   The narrowness of the skull behind the eye orbits, a characteristic of early hominins and *Homo erectus*.

potassium-argon dating   A chronometric dating method based on the half-life of radioactive potassium (which decays into argon gas) that can be used to date volcanic rock older than 100,000 years.

Precambrian   A term that is used informally to refer to earth's history before the Cambrian period of the Paleozoic era. Precambrian time includes the Hadean, Archean, and Proterozoic eons, and lasted from 4.6 billion to 542 million years ago.

prehensile   Capable of grasping. Primates have prehensile hands and feet, and some primates (certain New World monkeys) have prehensile tails.

premolar   One of four types of teeth found in mammals. The premolars are back teeth used for crushing and grinding food.

prenatal   The period of life from conception until birth.

prepared-core method   An efficient method of stone tool manufacture in which a stone core is prepared and then finished tools are removed from it.

primates   The order of mammals that has a complex of characteristics related to an initial adaptation to life in the trees, including binocular stereoscopic vision and grasping hands. The primates include prosimians, monkeys, apes, and humans.

primitive trait   A trait that has not changed from an ancestral state. The five digits of the human hand and foot are primitive traits inherited from earlier vertebrate ancestors.

Proconsul   A genus of fossil hominoid that lived in Africa between 21 million and 14 million years ago. Though classified as apes, this genus also shows a number of monkey characteristics. It most probably represents one of the first forms to evolve following the divergence of the monkey and ape lines.

Prosimii (prosimians)   The suborder of primates that are biologically primitive compared to anthropoids.

protein-calorie malnutrition   A group of nutritional diseases resulting from inadequate amounts of protein and/or calories. Protein-calorie malnutrition is a severe problem in less developed countries today.

Proterozoic eon   The third geologic eon, dating from 2500 to 542 Ma, characterized by the appearance of the first simple multicelled organisms.

punctuated equilibrium   A model of macroevolutionary change in which long periods of little evolutionary change (stasis) are followed by relatively short periods of rapid evolutionary change.

quadrupedal   A form of movement in which all four limbs are of equal size and make contact with the ground, and the spine is roughly parallel to the ground. Monkeys are typical quadrupedal primates.

race   As applied to humans, a vague term that has multiple meanings, both cultural and biological, referring to group membership.

recessive allele   An allele whose effect is masked by the other allele (which is dominant) in a heterozygous genotype.

reciprocal altruism The concept that altruistic behaviors will be directed toward nonkin if they increase the probability that the recipient will reciprocate at some future time.

recombination The production of new combinations of DNA sequences caused by exchanges of DNA during meiosis.

reemergent infectious disease Infectious disease that had previously been reduced but that increases in frequency when microorganisms evolve resistance to antibiotics.

regional continuity The appearance of similar traits within a geographic region that remain over a long period of time.

regulatory gene Gene that codes for the regulation of biological processes such as growth and development.

relative dating Comparative method of dating fossils and sites that provides an estimate of the older find but not a specific date.

reproductive isolation The genetic isolation of populations that may render them incapable of producing fertile offspring.

restriction fragment length polymorphism (RFLP) A genetic trait defined in terms of the length of DNA fragments produced when certain enzymes cut the DNA sequence.

RNA (ribonucleic acid) The molecule that functions to carry out the instructions for protein synthesis specified by the DNA molecule.

robust australopiths Species of *Australopithecus* that had very large back teeth, cheekbones, and faces, among other anatomical adaptations to heavy chewing. They lived in Africa between 2.5 million and 1.4 million years ago. Three species are generally recognized: *A. aethiopicus, A. robustus,* and *A. boisei.* Some anthropologists suggest that they be given their own genus name—*Paranthropus.*

sagittal crest A ridge of bone running down the center of the top of the skull that serves to anchor chewing muscles.

Sahelanthropus tchadensis An early possible hominid species from Africa dating between 6 million and 7 million years ago that has a number of hominid dental traits and may have been bipedal.

savanna An environment consisting of open grasslands in which food resources tend to be spread out over large areas.

secular change A change in the average pattern of growth or development in a population over several generations.

sedentary Settled in one place throughout most or all of the year.

semispecies Two or more populations that are partially reproductively isolated but are not yet completely separate species.

sexual dimorphism The average difference in body size between adult males and adult females. Primate species with sexual dimorphism in body size are characterized by adult males being, on average, larger than adult females.

sickle cell allele An allele of the hemoglobin locus. Individuals homozygous for this allele have sickle cell anemia.

sickle cell anemia A genetic disease that occurs in a person homozygous for the sickle cell allele, which alters the structure of red blood cells.

single-nucleotide polymorphisms (SNPs) Specific positions in a DNA sequence that differ at one base. For example, the DNA sequences CCTGAA and CCCGAA differ in the third position—one sequence has the base T and the other the base C.

Sivapithecus A genus of fossil ape that lived in Asia between 14 million and 7 million years ago, possibly an ancestor to modern orangutans.

soft hammer technique A method of removing flakes from a stone core by striking it with a softer material, such as bone, antler, or wood.

specialized structure A biological structure adapted to a narrow range of conditions and used in very specific ways. For example, the hooves of horses are specialized structures allowing movement over flat terrain.

speciation The origin of a new species.

species A group of populations whose members can interbreed naturally and produce fertile offspring.

stabilizing selection Selection against extreme values, large or small, in a continuous trait.

stable isotope analysis Analysis of the ratio of stable (nonradioactive) isotopes of elements, such as carbon, that provides information about ancient diet.

strategy A behavior that has been favored by natural selection and increases an individual's fitness.

stratigraphy A relative dating method based on the fact that older remains are found deeper in the earth (under the right conditions). This method makes use of the fact that a cumulative buildup of the earth's surface takes place over time.

Strepsirhini (strepsirhines) One of two suborders of primates suggested to replace the prosimian/anthropoid suborders (the other is the haplorhines). Strepsirhines are primates that have a moist nose (lemurs and lorises).

stress   Any factor that interferes with the normal limits of operation of an organism.

subspecies   Groupings within a species that are quite physically distinct from one another but capable of fertile interbreeding. When used, subspecies are often listed as a third name in a taxonomic classification, such *Homo sapiens sapiens*, the subspecies to which all living humans belong.

suspensory climbing   The ability to raise the arms above the head and hang on branches and to climb in this position. Hominoids are suspensory climbers.

taphonomy   The study of what happens to plants and animals after they die. Taphonomy helps in determining reasons for the distribution and condition of fossils.

tarsier   A nocturnal prosimian found today in Indonesia. Unlike other prosimians, tarsiers lack a moist nose.

taxonomy   The science of describing and classifying organisms.

terrestrial   Living on the ground.

territory   A home range that is actively defended.

theistic evolution   The belief that God operates through the natural process of evolution.

theory   A set of hypotheses that have been tested repeatedly and that have not been rejected. This term is sometimes used in a different sense in social science literature.

therapsids   An early group of mammal-like reptiles and the ancestors of later mammals.

thermoluminescence   A chronometric dating method that uses the fact that certain heated objects accumulate trapped electrons over time, which allows the date when the object was initially heated to be determined.

transfer RNA   A free-floating molecule that is attracted to a strand of messenger RNA, resulting in the synthesis of a protein chain.

trephination   Surgery involving the removal of a section of bone from the skull.

trisomy   A condition in which three chromosomes rather than a pair occur. Down syndrome is caused by trisomy by the addition of an extra chromosome to the 21st chromosome pair.

uniformitarianism   The observation that the geologic processes that operate in the world today also operated in the past.

Upper Paleolithic   A general term used to collectively refer to the stone tool technologies of anatomically modern *Homo sapiens*.

variation   The differences that exist among individuals or populations. Anthropologists study both cultural and biological variation.

vasoconstriction   The narrowing of blood vessels, which reduces blood flow and heat loss.

vasodilation   The opening of blood vessels, which increases blood flow and heat loss.

velocity curve   A measure of the rates of change in growth over time.

Vertebrata   A subphylum of the phylum Chordata, defined by the presence of an internal, segmented spinal column and bilateral symmetry.

zoonose   A disease transmitted directly to humans from other animals.

zygomatic arch   The cheekbone, formed by the connection of the zygomatic and temporal bones on the side of the skull.

zygote   A fertilized egg.

Abbey, D. M. 1999. The Thomas Jefferson paternity case. *Nature* 397:32.

Aiello, L. L., and R. Dunbar. 1993. Neocortex size, group size, and the evolution of language. *Current Anthropology* 34:184–193.

Aiello, L. C., and P. Wheeler. 1995. The expensive-tissue hypothesis: The brain and the digestive system in human and primate evolution. *Current Anthropology* 36:199–221.

Alemseged, Z., F. Spoor, W. H. Kimbel, R. Bobe, D.Geraads, D. Reed, and J. G. Wynn. 2006. A juvenile early hominin skeleton from Dikika, Ethiopia. *Nature* 443:296–301.

Allen, J. S., and S. M. Cheer. 1996. The non-thrifty genotype. *Current Anthropology* 37:831–842.

Altmann, J., S. C. Alberts, S. A. Haines, J. Dubach, P. Muruthi, T. Coote, E. Geffen, D. J. Cheesman, R. S. Mututua, S. N. Saiyalel, R. K. Wayne, R. C. Lacy, and M. W. Bruford. 1996. Behavior predicts genetic structure in a wild primate group. *Proceedings of the National Academy of Sciences, USA* 93:5797–5801.

Ambrose, S. H. 2001. Paleolithic technology and human evolution. *Science* 291:1748–1753.

Anderson, C. M. 1992. Male investment under changing conditions among Chacma baboons at Suikerbosrand. *American Journal of Physical Anthropology* 87:479–496.

Anderson, R. N. 1999. United States life tables, 1997. *National vital statistics report* 47(28). Hyattsville, Md.: National Center for Health Statistics.

Arensberg, B., L. A. Schepartz, A. M. Tillier, B. Vandermeersch, and Y. Rak. 1990. A reappraisal of the anatomical basis for speech in Middle Paleolithic hominids. *American Journal of Physical Anthropology* 83:137–146.

Arias, E. 2006. United States life tables, 2003. *National Vital Statistics Reports* 54(14). Hyattsville, Md. National Center for Health Statistics.

Armelagos, G. J., K. C. Barnes, and J. Lin. 1996. Disease in human evolution: The re-emergence of infectious disease in the third epidemiologic transition. *AnthroNotes, National Museum of Natural History Bulletin for Teachers* 18(3) (Fall 1996). Washington: Smithsonian Institution.

Armelagos, G. J., and J. R. Dewey. 1970. Evolutionary response to human infectious diseases. *BioScience* 157:638–644.

Armstrong, E. 1983. Relative brain size and metabolism in mammals. *Science* 220:1302–1304.

Asfaw, B., T. White, O. Lovejoy, B. Latimer, S. Simpson, and G. Suwa. 1999. *Australopithecus garhi:* A new species of early hominid from Ethiopia. *Science* 284:629–635.

Ash, M. M., and S. J. Nelson. 2003. *Wheeler's Dental Anatomy, Physiology, and Occlusion,* 8th ed. Philadelphia: Saunders.

Baba, H., F. Aziz, Y. Kaifu, G. Suwa, R. T. Kono, and T. Jacob. 2003. *Homo erectus* calvarium from the Pleistocene of Java. *Science* 299:1384–1385.

Backwell, L. R., and F. d'Errico. 2001. Evidence of termite foraging by Swartkrans early hominids. *Proceedings of the National Academy of Sciences, USA* 98:1358–1363.

Baker, B. J., and G. J. Armelagos. 1988. The origin and antiquity of syphilis: Paleopathological diagnosis and interpretation. *Current Anthropology* 29:703–737.

Balter, M. 2005. Are humans still evolving? *Science* 309:234–237.

Bamshad, M. J., S. Mummidi, E. Gonzalez, S. S. Ahuja, D. M. Dunn, W. S. Watkins, S. Wooding, A. C. Stone, L. B. Jorde, R. B. Weiss, and S. K. Ahuja. 2002. A strong signature of balancing selection in the 5′ *cis*-regulatory region of *CCR5*. *Proceedings of the National Academy of Sciences, USA* 99:10539–10544.

Bamshad, M. J., S. Wooding, W. S. Watkins, C. T. Ostler, M. A. Batzer, and L. B. Jorde. 2003. Human population genetic structure and inference of group membership. *American Journal of Human Genetics* 72:578–589.

Bar-Yosef, O. 1994. The contributions of Southwest Asia to the study of the origin of modern humans. In *Origins of Anatomically Modern Humans,* eds. M. H. Nitecki and D.V. Nitecki, pp. 23–66. New York: Plenum Press.

Barbujani, G., A. Magagni, E. Minch, and L. L. Cavalli-Sforza. 1997. An apportionment of human DNA diversity. *Proceedings of the National Academy of Sciences, USA* 94:4516–4519.

Bartlett, T. Q. 2007. The Hylobatidae: Small apes of Asia. In *Primates in Perspective,* eds. C. J. Campbell, A. Fuentes, K. C. MacKinnon, M. Panger, and S. K. Bearder, pp. 274–289. New York: Oxford University Press.

Bass, W. M. *Human Osteology: A Laboratory and Field Manual,* 4th ed. Columbia: Missouri Archaeological Society.

Beall, C. M., J. Blangero, S. Williams-Blangero, and M. C. Goldstein. 1994. Major gene for percent of oxygen saturation of arterial hemoglobin in Tibetan highlanders. *American Journal of Physical Anthropology* 95:271–276.

Beall, C. M., and A. T. Steegmann Jr. 2000. Human adaptation to climate: Temperature, ultraviolet radiation, and altitude. In *Human Biology: An Evolutionary and Biocultural Perspective,* eds. S. Stinson, B. Bogin, R. Huss-Ashmore, and D. O'Rourke, pp. 163–224. New York: John Wiley.

Beals, K. L. 1972. Head form and climatic stress. *American Journal of Physical Anthropology* 37:85–92.

Beals, K. L., C. L. Smith, and S. M. Dodd. 1983. Climate and the evolution of brachycephalization. *American Journal of Physical Anthropology* 62:425–437.

Beard, C. 2004. *The Hunt for the Dawn Monkey: Unearthing the Origins of Monkeys, Apes, and Humans.* Berkeley: University of California Press.

Becker, L., R. J. Poreda, A. G. Hunt, T. E. Bunch, and M. Rampino. 2001. Impact event at the Permian-Triassic boundary: Evidence from extraterrestrial noble gases in fullerenes. *Science* 291:1530–1533.

Begun, D. R. 2003. Planet of the apes. *Scientific American* 289(2):75–83.

Bermúdez de Castro, J. M., M. Martinón-Torres, E. Carbonell, S. Sarmiento, A. Rosas, J. van der Made, and M. Lozano. 2004. The Atapuerca sites and their contributions to the knowledge of human evolution in Europe. *Evolutionary Anthropology* 13:25–41.

Bersaglieri, T., P. C. Sabeti, N. Patterson, T. Vanderploeg, S. F. Schaffner, J. A. Drake, M. Rhodes, D. E. Reich, and J. N. Hirschhorn. 2004. Genetic signatures of strong recent positive selection at the lactase gene. *American Journal of Human Genetics* 74:1111–1120.

Binder, S., A. M. Levitt, J. J. Sacks, and J. M. Hughes. 1999. Emerging infectious diseases: Public health issues for the 21st century. *Science* 284:1311–1313.

Bindon, J. R., and P. T. Baker. 1985. Modernization, migration and obesity among Samoan adults. *Annals of Human Biology* 12:67–76.

Bittles, A. H., W. M. Mason, J. Greene, and N. A. Rao. 1991. Reproductive behavior and health in consanguineous marriages. *Science* 252:789–794.

Bloch, J. I., and D. M. Boyer. 2002. Grasping primate origins. *Science* 298:1606–1610.

———. 2003. Response to comment on "Grasping primate origins." *Science* 300:741c.

Blumenschine, R. J., C. R. Peters, F. T. Masao, R. J. Clarke, A. L. Deino, R. L. Hay, C. C. Swisher, I. G. Stanistreet, G. M. Ashley, L. J. McHenry, N. E. Sikes, N. J. van der Merwe, J. C. Tactikos, A. E. Cushing, D. M. Deocampo, J. K. Njau, and J. I. Ebert. 2003. Late Pliocene *Homo* and hominid land use from western Olduvai Gorge, Tanzania. *Science* 299:1217–1221.

Boas, F. 1912. *Changes in the Bodily Form of Descendants of Immigrants.* New York: Columbia University Press.

Boaz, N. T., and R. L. Ciochon. 2004. *Dragon Bone Hill: An Ice-Age Saga of* Homo erectus. New York: Oxford University Press.

Bodmer, W. F., and L. L. Cavalli-Sforza. 1976. *Genetics, Evolution, and Man.* San Francisco: W. H. Freeman.

Bogin, B. A. 1995. Growth and development: Recent evolutionary and biocultural research. In *Biological Anthropology: The State of the Science,* eds. N. T. Boaz and L. D. Wolfe, pp. 49–70. Bend, Ore.: International Institute for Human Evolutionary Research.

———. 1999. *Patterns of Human Growth,* 2d ed. Cambridge: Cambridge University Press.

———. 2001. *The Growth of Humanity.* New York: John Wiley.

Borries, C., K. Launhardt, C. Epplen, J. T. Epplen, and P. Winkler. 1999. DNA analyses support the hypothesis that infanticide is adaptive in langur monkeys. *Proceedings of the Royal Society of London B* 266:901–904.

Bouchard, T. J., D. T. Lykken, M. McGue, N. L. Segal, and A. Tellegen. 1990. Sources of human psychological differences: The Minnesota study of twins reared apart. *Science* 250:223–228.

Bouvier, L. F., and J. T. Bertrand. 1999. *World Population: Challenges for the 21st Century.* Santa Ana, Calif.: Seven Locks Press.

Bowler, J. M., H. Johnston, J. M. Olley, J. R. Prescott, R. G. Roberts, W. Shawcross, and N. A. Spooner. 2003. New ages for human occupation and climatic change at Lake Mungo, Australia. *Nature* 421:837–840.

Brace, C. L., K. R. Rosenberg, and K. D. Hunt. 1987. Gradual change in human tooth size in the Late Pleistocene and Post-Pleistocene. *Evolution* 41:705–720.

Bramble, D. M., and D. E. Lieberman. 2004. Endurance running and the evolution of *Homo. Nature* 432:345–352.

Bramblett, C. A. 1976. *Patterns of Primate Behavior.* Palo Alto, Calif.: Mayfield.

———. 1994. *Patterns of Primate Behavior,* 2d ed. Prospect Heights, Ill.: Waveland Press.

Bräuer, G. 2001. The KNM-ER 3884 hominid and the emergence of modern anatomy in Africa. In *Humanity from African Naissance to Coming Millennia,* eds. P. V. Tobias, M. A. Raath, J. Moggi-Cecchi, and G. A. Doyle, pp. 191–197. Firenze, Italy: Firenze University Press; and Johannesburg, South Africa: Witwatersrand University Press.

Breuer, T., M. Ndoundou-Hockemba, and V. Fishlock. 2005. First observation of tool use in gorillas. *PLoS Biology* 3(11):e380.

Brooks, A. S., D. M. Helgren, J. S. Cramer, A. Franklin, W. Hornyak, J. M. Keating, R. G. Klein, W. J. Rink, H. Schwarcz, J. N. L. Smith, K. Stewart, N. E. Todd, J. Verniers, and J. E. Yellen. 1995. Dating and context of three Middle Stone Age sites with bone points in the Upper Semliki Valley, Zaire. *Science* 268:548–553.

Brown, B., F. H. Brown, and A. Walker. 2001. New hominids from the Lake Turkana Basin, Kenya. *Journal of Human Evolution* 41:29–44.

Brown, F. H. 2000. Potassium-argon dating. In *Encyclopedia of Human Evolution and Prehistory*, 2d ed., eds. E. Delson, I. Tattersall, J. A. Van Couvering, and A. S. Brooks, pp. 582–584. London: Routledge.

Brown, F., J. Harris, R. Leakey, and A. Walker. 1985. Early *Homo erectus* skeleton from west Lake Turkana, Kenya. *Nature* 316:788–792.

Brown, K. 2002. Tangled roots? Genetics meets genealogy. *Science* 295:1634–1635.

Brown, P., T. Sutikna, M. J. Morwood, R. P. Soejono, Jatmiko, E. Wahyu Saptomo, and Rokus Awe Due. 2004. A new small-bodied hominin from the Late Pleistocene of Flores, Indonesia. *Nature* 431:1055–1061.

Brown, R. A., and G. J. Armelagos. 2001. Apportionment of racial diversity: A review. *Evolutionary Anthropology* 10:34–40.

Brues, A. M. 1977. *People and Races*. New York: Macmillan.

Brumfiel, G. 2005. Who has designs on your students' minds? *Nature* 434:1062–1065.

Brunet, M. 2002. *Sahelanthropus* or "*Sahelpithecus*"? *Nature* 419:582.

Brunet, M., F. Guy, D. Pilbeam, D. E. Lieberman, A. Likius, H. T. Mackaye, M. S. Ponce de León, C. P. E. Zollikofer, and P. Vignaud. 2005. New material of the earliest hominid from the Upper Miocene of Chad. *Nature* 434:752–755.

Brunet, M., F. Guy, D. Pilbeam, H. T. Mackaye, A. Likius, D. Ahounta, A. Beauvilain, C. Blondel, H. Bocherens, J. R. Boisserie, L. De Bonis, Y. Coppens, J. Dejax, C. Denys, P. Duringer, V. Eisenmann, G. Fanone, P. Fronty, D. Geraads, T. Lehmann, F. Lihoreau, A. Louchart, A. Mahamat, G. Merceron, G. Mouchelin, O. Otero, P. P. Campomanes, M. Ponce de Leon, J-C. Rage, M. Sapanet, M. Schuster, J. Sudre, P. Tassy, X. Valentin, P. Vignaud, L. Virlot, A. Zazzo, and C. Zollikofer. 2002. A new hominid from the Upper Miocene of Chad, Central Africa. *Nature* 418:145–151.

Buss, D. M. 1985. Human mate selection. *American Scientist* 73:47–51.

Cabana, T., P. Jolicoeur, and J. Michaud. 1993. Prenatal and postnatal growth and allometry of stature, head circumference, and brain weight in Québec children. *American Journal of Human Biology* 5:93–99.

Calcagno, J. M., and K. R. Gibson. 1988. Human dental reduction: Natural selection or the probable mutation effect. *American Journal of Physical Anthropology* 77:505–517.

Campbell, B. G. 1985. *Human Evolution,* 3d ed. New York: Aldine.

Campbell, C. J. 2007. Primate sexuality and reproduction. In *Primates in Perspective*, eds. C. J. Campbell, A. Fuentes, K. C. MacKinnon, M. Panger, and S. K. Bearder, pp. 423–437. New York: Oxford University Press.

Cann, R. L., M. Stoneking, and A. C. Wilson. 1987. Mitochondrial DNA and human evolution. *Nature* 325:31–36.

Carpenter, C. R. 1965. The howlers of Barro Colorado Island. In *Primate Behavior: Field Studies of Monkeys and Apes*, ed. I. DeVore, pp. 250–291. New York: Holt, Rinehart and Winston.

Carroll, S. B., S. D. Weatherbee, and J. A. Langeland. 1995. Homeotic genes and the regulation and evolution of insect wing number. *Nature* 375:58–61.

Cartmill, M. 1974. Rethinking primate origins. *Science* 184:436–443.

Caspi, A., K. Sugden, T. E. Moffitt, A. Taylor, I. W. Craig, H. Harrington, J. McClay, J. Mill, J. Martin, A. Braithwaite, and R. Poulton. 2003. Influence of life stress on depression: Moderation by a polymorphism in the 5-HTT gene. *Science* 301:386–389.

Cavalli-Sforza, L. L., and W. F. Bodmer. 1971. *The Genetics of Human Populations*. San Francisco: W. H. Freeman.

Cavalli-Sforza, L. L., P. Menozzi, and A. Piazza. 1994. *The History and Geography of Human Genes*. Princeton, N.J.: Princeton University Press.

Chaimanee, Y., D. Jolly, M. Benammi, P. Tafforeau, D. Duzer, I. Moussa, and J.-J. Jaeger. 2003. A Middle Miocene hominoid from Thailand and orangutan origins. *Nature* 422:61–65.

Chakraborty, R. 1986. Gene admixture in human populations: Models and predictions. *Yearbook of Physical Anthropology* 29:1–43.

Chapman, C. A., and C. A. Peres. 2001. Primate conservation in the new millennium: The role of scientists. *Evolutionary Anthropology* 10:16–33.

Chen, F.-C., and W.-H. Li. 2001. Genomic divergences between humans and other hominoids and the effective population size of the common ancestor of humans and chimpanzees. *American Journal of Human Genetics* 68:444–456.

Chimpanzee Sequencing and Analysis Consortium. 2005. Initial sequence of the chimpanzee genome and comparison with the human genome. *Nature* 437:69–87.

Ciochon, R. L., and R. A. Nisbett. 1998. *The Primate Anthology: Essays on Primate Behavior, Ecology, and Conservation from Natural History*. Upper Saddle River, N.J.: Prentice-Hall.

Ciochon, R., J. Olsen, and J. James. 1990. *Other Origins: The Search for the Giant Ape in Human Prehistory*. New York: Bantam Books.

Clarke, R. J. 1999. Discovery of complete arm and hand of the 3.3-million-year-old *Australopithecus* skeleton from Sterkfontein. *South African Journal of Science* 95:477–480.

Cockburn, T. A. 1971. Infectious diseases in ancient populations. *Current Anthropology* 12:45–62.

Cohen, J. E. 1995. *How Many People Can the Earth Support?* New York: W. W. Norton.

Cohen, M. N. 1989. *Health and the Rise of Civilization*. New Haven, Conn.: Yale University Press.

Collins, F. S., E. D. Green, A. E. Guttmacher, and M. S. Guyer. 2003. A vision for the future of genomics research. *Nature* 422:835–847.

Comuzzie, A. G., J. E. Hixson, L. Almasy, B. D. Mitchell, M. C. Mahaney, T. D. Dyer, M. P. Stern, J. W. MacCluer, and J. Blangero. 1997. A major quantitative trait locus determining serum leptin levels and fat mass is located on human chromosome 2. *Nature Genetics* 15:273–276.

Connell, K. H. 1950. *The Population of Ireland 1750–1845.* Oxford: Clarendon Press.

Conroy, G. C. 2005. *Reconstructing Human Origins,* 2d ed. New York: W. W. Norton.

Conroy, G. C., G. W. Weber, H. Seidler, P. V. Tobias, A. Kane, and B. Brunsden. 1998. Endocranial capacity in an early hominid cranium from Sterkfontein, South Africa. *Science* 280:1730–1731.

Cook, L. M. 2000. Changing views on melanic moths. *Biological Journal of the Linnean Society* 69:431–441.

Cook, L. M., R. L. H. Dennis, and G. S. Mani. 1999. Melanic morph frequency in the peppered moth in the Manchester area. *Proceedings of the Royal Society of London B* 266:293–297.

Cordain, L., J. B. Miller, S. B. Eaton, N. Mann, S. H. A. Holt, and J. D. Speth. 2000. Plant-animal subsistence ratios and macronutrient energy estimations in worldwide hunter-gatherer diets. *American Journal of Clinical Nutrition* 71:682–692.

Covert, H. H. 1997. The early primate adaptive radiations and new evidence about anthropoid origins. In *Biological Anthropology: The State of the Science,* 2d ed., eds. N. T. Boaz and L. D. Wolfe, pp. 1–23. Bend, Ore.: International Institute for Human Evolutionary Research.

Cowley, G., J. Contreras, A. Rogers, J. Lach, C. Dickey, and S. Raghavan. 1995. Outbreak of fear. *Newsweek,* May 22.

Crawford, M. H. 1998. *The Origins of Native Americans: Evidence from Anthropological Genetics.* Cambridge: Cambridge University Press.

Crews, D. E. 1989. Cause-specific mortality, life expectancy, and debilitation in aging Polynesians. *American Journal of Human Biology* 1:347–353.

Crockett, C. M., and J. F. Eisenberg. 1987. Howlers: Variations in group size and demography. In *Primate Societies,* eds. B. B. Smuts, D. L. Cheney, R. M. Seyfarth, R. W. Wrangham, and T. T. Struhsaker, pp. 54–68. Chicago: University of Chicago Press.

Crook, J. H., and J. S. Gartlan. 1966. Evolution of primate societies. *Nature* 210:1200–1203.

Daeschler, E. B., N. H. Shubin, and F. A. Jenkins, Jr. 2006. A Devonian tetrapod-like fish and the evolution of the tetrapod body plan. *Nature* 440:757–763.

Dalton, R. 2006. Decoding our cousins. *Nature* 442:238–240.

Damon, A. 1977. *Human Biology and Ecology.* New York: W. W. Norton.

Dart, R. A. 1925. *Australopithecus africanus:* The man-ape of South Africa. *Nature* 115:195–199.

Davis, G. 1999. The Thomas Jefferson paternity case. *Nature* 397:32.

Dawkins, R. 1987. *The Blind Watchmaker: Why the Evidence of Evolution Reveals a Universe without Design.* New York: W. W. Norton.

Day, M. H. 1986. Bipedalism: Pressures, origins and modes. In *Major Topics in Primate and Human Evolution,* eds. B. Wood, L. Martin, and P. Andrews, pp. 188–202. Cambridge: Cambridge University Press.

de Heinzelin, J., D. Clark, T. White, W. Hart, P. Renne, G. WoldeGabriel, Y. Beyene, and E. Vrba. 1999. Environment and behavior of 2.5-million-year-old Bouri hominids. *Science* 284:625–629.

Denham, W. W. 1971. Energy relations and some basic properties of primate social organization. *American Anthropologist* 73:77–95.

Dennis, C. 2005. Branching out. *Nature* 437:17–19.

Derenko, M. V., T. Grzybowski, B. A. Malyarchuk, J. Czarny, D. Miścicka-Śliwka, and I. A. Zakharov. 2001. The presence of mitochondrial haplogroup X in Altaians from south Siberia. *American Journal of Human Genetics* 69:237–241.

De Robertis, E. M., G. Oliver, and C. V. E. Wright. 1990. Homeobox genes and the vertebrate body plan. *Scientific American* 263(1):46–52.

Dettwyler, K. A. 1991. Can paleopathology provide evidence for "compassion"? *American Journal of Physical Anthropology* 84:375–384.

———. 1994. *Dancing Skeletons: Life and Death in West Africa.* Prospect Heights, Ill.: Waveland Press.

Devlin, B., M. Daniels, and K. Roeder. 1997. The heritability of IQ. *Nature* 388:468–471.

DeVore, I. 1963. A comparison of the ecology and behavior of monkeys and apes. In *Classification and Human Evolution,* ed. S. L. Washburn, pp. 301–309. Chicago: Aldine.

de Waal, F. B. M. 1995. Bonobo sex and society. *Scientific American* 272(3):82–88.

———. 1999. Cultural primatology comes of age. *Nature* 399:635–636.

Di Fiore, A., and C. J. Campbell. 2007. The atelines: Variation in ecology, behavior, and social organization. In *Primates in Perspective,* eds. C. J. Campbell, A. Fuentes, K. C. MacKinnon, M. Panger, and S. K. Bearder, pp. 155–185. New York: Oxford University Press.

Diamond, J. 1988. Express train to Polynesia. *Nature* 336:307–308.

———. 1992a. The arrow of disease. *Discover* 13 (October):64–73.

———. 1992b. *The Third Chimpanzee: The Evolution and Future of the Human Animal.* New York: HarperCollins.

———. 1999. *Guns, Germs, and Steel: The Fate of Human Societies.* New York: W. W. Norton.

Dickson, J. H., K. Oeggl, and L. L. Handley. 2003. The Iceman reconsidered. *Scientific American* 288(5):70–79.

Díez, J. C., Y. Fernández-Salvo, J. Rosell, and I. Cáceres. 1999. Zooarchaeology and taphonomy of Aurora Stratum (Gran Dolina, Sierra de Atapuerca, Spain). *Journal of Human Evolution* 37:623–652.

Dohlinow, P. 1999. Play: A critical process in the developmental system. In *The Nonhuman Primates*, eds. P. Dohlinow and A. Fuentes, pp. 231–236. Mountain View, Calif.: Mayfield.

Doran, D. M., and A. McNeilage. 1998. Gorilla ecology and behavior. *Evolutionary Anthropology* 6:120–131.

Duarte, C., J. Maurício, P. B. Pettitt, P. Souto, E. Trinkaus, H. van der Plicht, and J. Zilháo. 1999. The early Upper Paleolithic human skeleton from the Abrigo do Lagar Velho (Portugal) and modern human emergence in Iberia. *Proceedings of the National Academy of Sciences, USA* 96:7604–7609.

Dunn, F. L. 1968. Epidemiological factors: Health and disease among hunter-gatherers. In *Man the Hunter,* eds. R. B. Lee and I. DeVore, pp. 221–228. Chicago: Aldine.

Eaton, G. G. 1976. The social order of Japanese macaques. *Scientific American* 235(4):96–106.

Eaton, S. B., M. Shostak, and M. Konner. 1988. Stone agers in the fast lane: Chronic degenerative diseases in evolutionary perspective. *American Journal of Medicine* 84:739–749.

Eldredge, N., and S. J. Gould. 1972. Punctuated equilibria: An alternative to phyletic gradualism. In *Models in Paleobiology,* ed. T. J. M. Schopf, pp. 82–115. San Francisco: Freeman, Cooper.

Enard, W., M. Przeworski, S. E. Fisher, C. S. L. Lal, V. Wiebe, T. Kitano, A. P. Monaco, and S. Pääbo. 2002. Molecular evolution of *FOXP2,* a gene involved in speech and language. *Nature* 418:869–872.

Ereshefsky, M., ed. 1992. *The Units of Evolution: Essays on the Nature of Species.* Cambridge, Mass.: MIT Press.

Erlich, H. A., D. Gelfand, and J. J. Sninsky. 1991. Recent advances in the polymerase chain reaction. *Science* 252:1643–1651.

Eswaran, V. 2002. A diffusion wave out of Africa. *Current Anthropology* 43:749–774.

Eudey, A. A. 1999. Asian primate conservation—My perspective. In *The Nonhuman Primates,* eds. P. Dohlinow and A. Fuentes, pp. 151–158. Mountain View, Calif.: Mayfield.

Eveleth, P. B., and J. M. Tanner. 1990. *Worldwide Variation in Human Growth,* 2d ed. Cambridge: Cambridge University Press.

Falk, D. 1983. Cerebral cortices of East African early hominids. *Science* 221:1072–1074.

———. 2000. *Primate Diversity.* New York: W. W. Norton.

———2004. *Braindance,* rev. and exp. ed. Gainesville: University Press of Florida.

Falk, D., C. Hildebolt, K. Smith, M. J. Morwood, T. Sutikna, P. Brown, Jatmiko, E. Wayhu Saptomo, B. Brunsden, and F. Prior. 2005. The brain of LB1, *Homo floresiensis. Science* 308:242–245.

Falk, D., J. C. Redmond Jr., J. Guyer, G. C. Conroy, W. Recheis, G. W. Weber, and H. Seidler. 2000. Early hominid brain evolution: A new look at old endocases. *Journal of Human Evolution* 38:695–717.

Feder, K. L. 2000. *The Past in Perspective: An Introduction to Human Prehistory.* Mountain View, Calif.: Mayfield.

———. 2002. *Frauds, Myths, and Mysteries: Science and Pseudoscience in Archaeology,* 4th ed. New York: McGraw-Hill.

Fedigan, L. M. 1983. Dominance and reproductive success in primates. *Yearbook of Physical Anthropology* 26:91–129.

Fedigan, L. M., and M. S. M. Pavelka. 2007. Reproductive cessation in female primates: Comparisons of Japanese macaques and humans. In *Primates in Perspective,* eds. C. J. Campbell, A. Fuentes, K. C. MacKinnon, M. Panger, and S. K. Bearder, pp. 437–447. New York: Oxford University Press.

Fedigan, L. M., and S. C. Strum. 1999. A brief history of primate studies: National traditions, disciplinary origins, and stages in North American field research. In *The Nonhuman Primates,* eds. P. Dolhinow and A. Fuentes, pp. 258–269. Mountain View, Calif.: Mayfield.

Feldman, M. W., R. C. Lewontin, and M.-C. King. 2003. A *genetic* melting-pot. *Nature* 424:374.

Finlayson, C., F. G. Pacheo, J. Rodriguez-Vidal, D. A. Fa, J. G. López, A. S. Pérez, G. Finlayson, E. Allue, J. B. Preysler, I. Cáceres, J. S. Carrión, Y. F. Jalvo, C. P. Gleed-Owen, F. J. J. Espejo, P. López, J. A. L. Sáez, J. A. R. Cantal, A. S. Marco, F. G. Guzman, K. Brown, N. Fuentes, C. A.Valarino, A. Villalpando, C. B. Stringer, F. M. Ruiz, and T. Sakamoto. 2006. Late survival of Neanderthals at the southernmost extreme of Europe. *Nature*, advanced online publication doi:10.1038/nature05195.

Fisher, H. 1992. *Anatomy of Love: A Natural History of Mating, Marriage, and Why We Stray.* New York: Ballantine Books.

Fleagle, J. G. 1995. The origin and radiation of anthropoid primates. In *Biological Anthropology: The State of the Science,* eds. N. T. Boaz and L. D. Wolfe, pp. 1–21. Bend, Ore.: International Institute for Human Evolutionary Research.

———. 1999. *Primate Adaptation and Evolution,* 2d ed. San Diego: Academic Press.

Fleagle, J. G., D. T. Rasmussen, S. Yirga, T. M. Brown, and F. E. Grine. 1991. New hominid fossils from Fejej, Southern Ethiopia. *Journal of Human Evolution* 21:145–152.

Flynn, J. J., A. R. Wyss, R. Charrier, and C. C. Swisher. 1995. An early Miocene anthropoid skull from the Chilean Andes. *Nature* 373:603–607.

Flynn, J. R. 1980. *Race, IQ and Jensen.* London: Routledge.

Fossey, D. 1983. *Gorillas in the Mist.* Boston: Houghton Mifflin.

Foster, E. A., M. A. Jobling, P. G. Taylor, P. Donnelly, P. de Knijff, R. Mieremet, T. Zerjal, and C. Tyler-Smith. 1998. Jefferson fathered slave's last child. *Nature* 396:27–28.

Fouts, R., and S. T. Mills. 1997. *Next of Kin: What Chimpanzees Have Taught Me about Who We Are.* New York: William Morrow.

Franciscus, R. G., and J. C. Long. 1991. Variation in human nasal height and breadth. *American Journal of Physical Anthropology* 85:419–427.

Frayer, D. W. 1984. Biological and cultural change in the European Late Pleistocene and Early Holocene. In *The Origins of Modern Humans: A World Survey of the Fossil Evidence,* eds. F. H. Smith and F. Spencer, pp. 211–250. New York: Alan R. Liss.

Frisancho, A. R. 1990. Introduction: Comparative high-altitude adaptation. *American Journal of Human Biology* 2:599–601.

———. 1993. *Human Adaptation and Accommodation.* Ann Arbor: University of Michigan Press.

Frisancho, A. R., and P. T. Baker. 1970. Altitude and growth: A study of the patterns of physical growth of a high altitude Peruvian Quechua population. *American Journal of Physical Anthropology* 32:279–292.

Fruth, B., G. Hohmann, and W. C. McGrew. 1999. The *Pan* species. In *The Nonhuman Primates,* eds. P. Dohlinow and A. Fuentes, pp. 64–72. Mountain View, Calif.: Mayfield.

Fuentes, A. 1999. Variable social organization: What can looking at primate groups tell us about the evolution of plasticity in primate societies? In *The Nonhuman Primates,* eds. P. Dohlinow and A. Fuentes, pp. 183–188. Mountain View, Calif.: Mayfield.

———. 2000. Hylobatid communities: Changing views on pair bonding and social organization in hominoids. *Yearbook of Physical Anthropology* 43:33–60.

Futuyma, D. J. 1983. *Science on Trial: The Case for Evolution.* New York: Pantheon Books.

———. 1986. *Evolutionary Biology,* 2d ed. Sunderland, Mass.: Sinauer.

Gabriel, T. 1995. A generation's heritage: After the boom, a boomlet. *New York Times,* February 12.

Gabunia, L., A. Vekua, D. Lordkipanidze, C. C. Swisher III, R. Ferring, A. Justus, M. Nioradze, M. Tvalchrelidze, S. C. Antón, G. Bosinski, O. Jöris, M. A. de Lumley, G. Majsuradze, and A. Mouskhelishvili. 2000. Earliest Pleistocene hominid cranial remains from Dmanisi, Republic of Georgia: Taxonomy, geological setting, and age. *Science* 288:1019–1025.

Gagneux, P., C. Wills, U. Gerloff, D. Tautz, P. A. Morin, C. Boesch, B. Fruth, G. Hohmann, O. A. Ryder, and D. S. Woodruff. 1999. Mitochondrial sequences show diverse evolutionary histories of African hominoids. *Proceedings of the National Academy of Science, USA* 96:5077–5082.

Galdikas, B. M. F., and J. W. Wood. 1990. Birth spacing patterns in humans and apes. *American Journal of Physical Anthropology* 83:185–191.

Galik, K., B. Senut, M. Pickford, D. Gommery, J. Treil, A. J. Kuperavage, and R. B. Eckhardt. 2004. External and internal morphology of the BAR 1002'00 *Orrorin tugenensis* femur. *Science* 305:1450–1453.

Galvani, A. P., and M. Slatkin. 2003. Evaluating plague and smallpox as historical selective pressures for the *CCR5-Δ32* HIV-resistant allele. *Proceedings of the National Academy of Sciences, USA* 100:15276–15279.

Garrett, L. 1994. *The Coming Plague: Newly Emerging Diseases in a World Out of Balance.* New York: Farrar, Straus and Giroux.

Gee, H. 1996. Box of bones "clinches" identity of Piltdown palaeontology hoaxer. *Nature* 381:261–262.

Gibbons, A. 2006. *The First Human: The Race to Discover Our Earliest Ancestors.* New York: Doubleday.

Gibbs, S., M. Collard, and B. Wood. 2000. Soft-tissue characters in higher primate phylogenetics. *Proceedings of the National Academy of Sciences, USA* 97:11130–11132.

Gill, G. W. 1998. The beauty of race and races. Reprinted in *Taking Sides: Clashing Views on Controversial Issues in Anthropology,* eds. K. M. Endicott and R. Welsch, pp. 45–50. Guilford, Conn.: McGraw-Hill.

Gingerich, P. D. 1986. *Plesiadapis* and the delineation of the order Primates. In *Major Topics in Primate and Human Evolution,* eds. B. Wood, L. Martin, and P. Andrews, pp. 32–46. Cambridge: Cambridge University Press.

Gingerich, P. D., B. H. Smith, and E. L. Simons. 1990. Hind limbs of Eocene *Basilosaurus:* Evidence of feet in whales. *Science* 249:154–157.

Glass, H. B. 1953. The genetics of the Dunkers. *Scientific American* 189(2): 76–81.

Goodall, J. 1986. *The Chimpanzees of Gombe: Patterns of Behavior.* Cambridge, Mass.: Harvard University Press.

Goren-Inbar, N., N. Alperson, M. E. Kislev, O. Simchoni, Y. Melamed, A. Ben-Nun, and E. Werker. 2004. Evidence of hominin control of fire at Gesher Benot Ya'aqov, Israel. *Science* 304:725–727.

Gould, S. J. 1981. *The Mismeasure of Man.* New York: W. W. Norton.

———. 1983. *Hen's Teeth and Horse's Toes.* New York: W. W. Norton.

———. 1991. *Bully for Brontosaurus.* New York: W. W. Norton.

———. 1999. Non-overlapping magisterial. *Skeptical Inquirer* 23(4):55–61.

Gould, S. J., and N. Eldredge. 1977. Punctuated equilibria: The tempo and mode of evolution reconsidered. *Paleobiology* 3:115–151.

Gould, S. J., and R. C. Lewontin. 1979. The spandrels of San Marco and the Panglossian paradigm: A critique of the adaptationist programme. *Proceedings of the Royal Society of London* (Series B), 205:581–598.

Gradstein, F. M., J. G. Ogg, and A. G. Smith, eds. 2005. *A Geologic Time Scale 2004.* Cambridge: Cambridge University Press.

Grant, P. R. 1991. Natural selection and Darwin's finches. *Scientific American* 265(4):82–87.

Grant, V. 1985. *The Evolutionary Process: A Critical Review of Evolutionary Theory.* New York: Columbia University Press.

Graves, L. L., Jr. 2001. *The Emperor's New Clothes: Biological Theories of Race at the Millennium.* New Brunswick, N.J.: Rutgers University Press.

Gravlee, C. C., H. R. Bernard, and W. R. Leonard. 2003a. Boas's *Changes in Bodily Form:* The immigrant study, cranial plasticity, and Boas's physical anthropology. *American Anthropologist* 105:326–332.

———. 2003b. Heredity, environment, and cranial form: A reanalysis of Boas's immigrant data. *American Anthropologist* 105:125–138.

Green R. E., J. Krause, S. E. Ptak, A. W. Briggs, M. T. Ronan, J. F. Simons, L. Du, M. Egholm, J. N. Rothberg, M. Paunovic, and S. Pääbo. 2006. Analysis of one million base pairs of Neanderthal DNA. *Nature* 444:330–336.

Greksa, L. P. 1990. Developmental responses to high-altitude hypoxia in Bolivian children of European ancestry: A test of the developmental adaptation hypothesis. *American Journal of Human Biology* 2:603–612.

———. 1996. Evidence for a genetic basis to the enhanced total lung capacity of Andean highlanders. *Human Biology* 68:119–129.

Gross, P. R., U. Goodenough, S. Haack, L. S. Lerner, M. Schwartz, and R. Schwartz. 2005. *The State of State Science Standards*. Washington, D.C.: Thomas B. Fordham Institute. Available online at www.edexcellence.net.

Grün, R. 1993. Electron spin resonance dating in paleoanthropology. *Evolutionary Anthropology* 2:172–181.

Grün, R., N. J. Shackleton, and H. J. Deacon. 1990. Electron-spin-resonance dating of tooth enamel from Klasies River Mouth. *Current Anthropology* 31:427–432.

Grün, R., C. B. Stringer, and H. P. Schwartz. 1991. ESR dating of teeth from Garrod's Tabun cave collection. *Journal of Human Evolution* 20:231–248.

Grün, R., and A. Thorne. 1997. Dating the Ngandong humans. *Science* 276:1575.

Hagelberg, E. 1994. Ancient DNA studies. *Evolutionary Anthropology* 2:199–207.

Haile-Selassie, Y. 2001. Late Miocene hominids from the Middle Awash, Ethiopia. *Nature* 412:178–181.

Haile-Selassie, Y., G. Suwa, and T. D. White. 2004. Late Miocene teeth from Middle Awash, Ethiopia, and early hominid dental evolution. *Science* 303:1503–1505.

Hamblin, M. T., E. E. Thompson, and A. Di Rienzo. 2002. Complex signatures of natural selection at the Duffy blood group locus. *American Journal of Human Genetics* 70:369–383.

Hamer, D. H., S. Hu, V. L. Magnuson, N. Hu, and A. M. L. Pattatucci. 1993. A linkage between DNA markers on the X chromosome and male sexual orientation. *Science* 261:321–327.

Hammer, M. F., A. J. Redd, E. T. Wood, M. R. Bonner, H. Jarjanazi, T. Karafet, S. Santachiara-Benerecetti, A. Oppenheim, M. A. Jobling, T. Jenkins, H. Orstrer, and B. Bonné-Tamir. 2000. Jewish and Middle Eastern non-Jewish populations share a common pool of Y-chromosome biallelic haplotypes. *Proceedings of the National Academy of Sciences, USA* 97:6769–6774.

Harcourt, A. H., P. H. Harvey, S. G. Larson, and R. V. Short. 1981. Testis weight, body weight, and breeding system in primates. *Nature* 293:55–57.

Harding, R. M., S. M. Fullerton, R. C. Griffiths, J. Bond, M. J. Cox, J. A. Schneider, D. S. Moulin, and J. B. Clegg. 1997. Archaic African *and* Asian lineages in the genetic ancestry of modern humans. *American Journal of Human Genetics* 60:772–789.

Harlow, H. F. 1959. Love in infant monkeys. *Scientific American* 200(6):68–74.

Harlow, H. F., and M. K. Harlow. 1962. Social deprivation in monkeys. *Scientific American* 207(5):136–146.

Harpending, H., and T. Jenkins. 1973. Genetic distance among Southern African populations. In *Methods and Theories of Anthropological Genetics*, eds. M. H. Crawford and P. L. Workman, pp. 177–199. Albuquerque: University of New Mexico Press.

Harris, E. E., and J. Hey. 1999. X chromosome evidence for ancient human histories. *Proceedings of the National Academy of Sciences, USA* 96:3320–3324.

Harris, M. 1987. *Cultural Anthropology,* 2d ed. New York: Harper and Row.

Harrison, G. A., J. M. Tanner, D. R. Pilbeam, and P. T. Baker. 1988. *Human Biology: An Introduction to Human Evolution, Variation, Growth, and Adaptability,* 3d ed. Oxford: Oxford University Press.

Hartl, D. L. 1988. *A Primer of Population Genetics,* 2d ed. Sunderland, Mass.: Sinauer.

Hartl, D. L., and A. G. Clark. 1997. *Principles of Population Genetics,* 3d ed. Sunderland, Mass.: Sinauer.

Harvey, P. H., R. D. Martin, and T. H. Clutton-Brock. 1987. Life histories in comparative perspective. In *Primate Societies*, eds. B. B. Smuts, D. L. Cheney, R. M. Seyfarth, R. W. Wrangham, and T. T. Struhsaker, pp. 181–196. Chicago: University of Chicago Press.

Harvey, P. H., and M. D. Pagel. 1991. *The Comparative Method in Evolutionary Biology*. Oxford: Oxford University Press.

Hawks, J., S. Oh, K. Hunley, S. Dobson, G. Cabana, P. Dayalu, and M. H. Wolpoff. 2000. An Australasian test of the recent African origin model using the WLH-50 calvarium. *Journal of Human Evolution* 39:1–22.

Hein, J. 2004. Pedigrees for all humanity. *Nature* 431:518–519.

Henneberg, M. 1988. Decrease of human skull size in the Holocene. *Human Biology* 60:395–405.

Henshilwood, C. S., F. d'Errico, R. Yates, Z. Jacobs, C. Tribolo, G. A. T. Duller, N. Mercier, J. C. Sealy, H. Valladas, I. Watts, and A. G. Wintle. 2002. Emergence of modern human behavior: Middle Stone Age engravings from South Africa. *Science* 295:1278–1280.

Hill, K. 1993. Life history theory and evolutionary anthropology. *Evolutionary Anthropology* 2:78–88.

Hoff, H., I. Thorneycroft, F. Wilson, and M. Williams-Murphy. 2001. Protection afforded by sickle-cell trait (Hb AS): What happens when malarial selection pressures are alleviated? *Human Biology* 73:583–586.

Holden, C. 2003. Getting the short end of the allele. *Science* 301:291–293.

_____. 2006. An evolutionary squeeze on brain size. *Science* 312:1867.

Holden, C., and R. Mace. 1997. Phylogenetic analysis of the evolution of lactose digestion in adults. *Human Biology* 69:605–628.

Holick, M. F., J. A. MacLaughlin, and S. H. Doppelt. 1981. Regulation of cutaneous previtamin D$_3$ photosynthesis in man: Skin pigment is not an essential regulator. *Science* 211:590–593.

Holloway, R. L. 1985. The poor brain of *Homo sapiens neanderthalensis:* See what you please. In *Ancestors: The Hard Evidence,* ed. E. Delson, pp. 319–324. New York: Alan R. Liss.

Horai, S., K. Hayasaka, R. Kondo, K. Tsugane, and N. Takahata. 1995. Recent African origin of modern humans revealed by complete sequences of hominoid mitochondrial DNAs. *Proceedings of the National Academy of Sciences, USA* 92:532–536.

Hou, Y., R. Potts, B. Yuan, Z. Gou, A. Deino, W. Wang, J. Clark, G. Xie, and W. Huang. 2000. Mid-Pleistocene Acheulian-like stone technology of the Bose Basin, South China. *Science* 287:1622–1626.

Houle, A. 1999. The origin of the Platyrrhines: An evaluation of the Antarctic scenario and the floating island model. *American Journal of Physical Anthropology* 109:541–559.

Howell, N. 2000. *Demography of the Dobe !Kung,* 2d ed. New York: Aldine de Gruyter.

Howells, W. W. 1989. *Skull Shapes and the Map: Craniometric Analyses in the Dispersion of Modern* Homo. Papers of the Peabody Museum, vol. 79. Cambridge, Mass.: Harvard University.

Hrdy, S. B. 1977. *The Langurs of Abu.* Cambridge, Mass.: Harvard University Press.

Hu, S., A. M. L. Pattatucci, C. Patterson, L. Li, D. W. Fulker, S. S. Cherny, L. Kruglyak, and D. H. Hamer. 1995. Linkage between sexual orientation and chromosome Xq28 in males but not in females. *Nature Genetics* 11:248–256.

Hummel, S., D. Schmidt, B. Kremeyer, B. Herrmann, and M. Oppermann. 2005. Detection of the *CCR5-Δ32* HIV resistant gene in Bronze Age skeletons. *Genes and Immunology* 6:371–374.

Hunt, K. D. 1996. The postural feeding hypothesis: An ecological model for the evolution of bipedalism. *South African Journal of Science* 92:77–90.

International HapMap Consortium. 2005. A haplotype map of the human genome. *Nature* 437:1299–1320.

International Human Genome Sequencing Consortium. 2001. Initial sequencing and analysis of the human genome. *Nature* 409:860–921.

Jablonski, N. G., and G. Chaplin. 2000. The evolution of human skin coloration. *Journal of Human Evolution* 39:57–106.

Jobling, M. A., M. E. Hurles, and C. Tyler-Smith. 2004. *Human Evolutionary Genetics: Origins, Peoples and Disease.* New York: Garland Science.

Johanson, D. C., and M. A. Edey. 1981. *Lucy: The Beginnings of Humankind.* New York: Simon and Schuster.

Johanson, D. C., F. T. Masau, G. G. Eck, T. D. White, R. C. Walter, W. H. Kimbel, B. Asfaw, P. Manega, P. Ndessokia, and G. Suwa. 1987. New partial skeleton of *Homo habilis* from Olduvai Gorge, Tanzania. *Nature* 327:205–209.

Johanson, D. C., and T. D. White. 1979. A systematic assessment of early African hominids. *Science* 203:321–330.

Johanson, D. C., T. D. White, and Y. Coppens. 1978. A new species of the genus *Australopithecus* (Primates: Hominidae) from the Pliocene of Eastern Africa. *Kirtlandia* 28:1–14.

Jolly, A. 1972. *The Evolution of Primate Behavior.* New York: Macmillan.

———. 1985. *The Evolution of Primate Behavior,* 2d ed. New York: Macmillan.

Jolly, C. J. 2007. Baboons, mandrills, and mangabeys: Afro-Papionin socioecology in a phylogenetic perspective. In *Primates in Perspective,* eds. C. J. Campbell, A. Fuentes, K. C. MacKinnon, M. Panger, and S. K. Bearder, pp. 240–251. New York: Oxford University Press.

Jones, T., C. L. Ehardt, T. M. Butynski, T. R. B. Davenport, N. E. Mpunga, S. J. Machaga, and D. W. De Luca. 2005. The highland mangabey *Lophocebus kipunji:* A new species of African monkey. *Science* 308:1161–1164.

Jorde, L. B., A. R. Rogers, M. Bamshad, W. S. Watkins, P. Krakowiak, S. Sung, J. Kere, and H. C. Harpending. 1997. Microsatellite diversity and the demographic history of modern humans. *Proceedings of the National Academy of Sciences, USA* 94:3100–3103.

Karafet, T. M., S. L. Zegura, O. Posukh, A. Bergen, J. Long, D. Goldman, W. Klitz, S. Harihara, P. de Knijff, V. Wiebe, R. C. Griffiths, A. R. Templeton, and M. F. Hammer. 1999. Ancestral Asian source(s) of New World Y-chromosome founder haplotypes. *American Journal of Human Genetics* 64:817–831.

Karn, M. N., and L. S. Penrose. 1951. Birth weight and gestation time in relation to maternal age, parity, and infant survival. *Annals of Eugenics* 15:206–233.

Katzmarzyk, P. T., and W. R. Leonard. 1998. Climatic influences on human body size and proportions: Ecological adaptations and secular trends. *American Journal of Physical Anthropology* 106:483–503.

Kayser, M., S. Brauer, G. Weiss, P. A. Underhill, L. Roewer, W. Schiefenhövel, and M. Stoneking. 2000. Melanesian origin of Polynesian Y chromosomes. *Current Biology* 10:1237–1246.

Kennedy, K. A. R. 1976. *Human Variation in Space and Time.* Dubuque, Iowa: Wm. C. Brown.

Kimbel, W. H., D. C. Johanson, and Y. Rak. 1994. The first skull and other new discoveries of *Australopithecus afarensis* at Hadar, Ethiopia. *Nature* 368:449–451.

Kimbel, W. H., C. A. Lockwood, C. V. Ward, M. G. Leakey, Y. Rak, and D. C. Johanson. 2006. Was *Australopithecus anamensis* ancestral to *A. afarensis*? A case of anagenesis in the hominin fossil record. *Journal of Human Evolution* 51:134–152.